CANADA
1922-1939

JOHN HERD THOMPSON
with ALLEN SEAGER

CANADA
1922-1939

Decades of Discord

The Canadian Centenary Series

McClelland and Stewart

Canadian Cataloguing in Publication Data
Thompson, John Herd, 1946-
Canada 1922-1939

(The Canadian centenary series ; 15)
Includes bibliographical references and index.
ISBN 0-7710-8564-8.

1. Canada – History – 1918-1939.   2. Canada –
Politics and government – 1921-1930.   3. Canada –
Politics and government – 1930-1935.
I. Seager, Allen.   II. Title.   III. Series.

FC580.T52 1985   971.062   C84-099762-0
F1034.T52 1985

McClelland and Stewart Limited
The Canadian Publishers
25 Hollinger Road
Toronto, Ontario
M4B 3G2

Front jacket photograph: Demonstration of
strikers' families, Stratford, 1933.

Printed and bound in Canada by John Deyell Co.

To the memory of our parents,
who lived these decades of discord.

THE
CANADIAN
CENTENARY
SERIES

A History of Canada

Ramsay Cook, EXECUTIVE EDITOR

VOLUMES STARRED ARE PUBLISHED
†ALSO AVAILABLE IN PAPERBACK

CONTENTS

Canada 1922-1939

For material in the illustration sections of this book, acknowledgement is made to the following sources:

The Public Archives of Canada for Demonstration of strikers' families, Stratford (jacket); A Census Branch clerk working with a tabulator-calculator machine; Ukrainian Orchestra and Dramatic Society; Unloading supplies for a mining camp, Mud Lake, Quebec; Children playing in front of the Noranda smelter; A Model A Ford rolled off the assembly line every three minutes; The Atlantic fishing industry remained troubled throughout the inter-war period; Governor General Lord Byng was a soldier, not a politician; G. Howard Ferguson, Mackenzie King, and L.-A. Taschereau; Most women workers performed boring, repetitive, poorly paid tasks; Technical-vocational programs were rigidly segregated by sex; Lawren Harris; A New Brunswick Farmers' Co-op; The Canadian Authors' Association played on national feeling to sell its members' books; Teams like the Saskatoon Sheiks found professional hockey's new era too rich for their blood; Private charity for the homeless single unemployed; J.S. Woodsworth expounds the "distinctly Canadian socialism" of the CCF; Mitchell Hepburn; Maurice Duplessis; A visit to Germany in 1937 convinced Mackenzie King that Hitler had only peaceful intentions; The Canadian Blood Transfusion Service in Spain; Stuffed uncomfortably into their court dress, Ernest Lapointe and Mackenzie King welcome King George VI and Queen Elizabeth.

The Glenbow-Alberta Institute for A cartoonist's view of a bootlegger and his client; A new service industry sprang up around the automobile; "Amos and Andy" was a more powerful radio drawing card than Canadian programs; Nelson Eddy and Jeanette MacDonald in *Rose Marie*; A drought-stricken prairie family moves north to find a new farm; The unemployed organized to protest their treatment; William Aberhart.

The Manitoba Archives for The Manitoba Paper Company; E.N. Rhodes introduces new leader R.B. Bennett at the Conservative National Convention; Mounties escort a strike-breaker past a jeering picket line.

The Globe and Mail for CPR President Sir Edward Beatty heartily detested Sir Henry Thornton, his CNR counterpart.

Le Soleil for Vicious cartoons depicted a satanic Arthur Meighen.

Saskatchewan Archives Board for The On-to-Ottawa trekkers.

Metropolitan Toronto Library for The theme of the 1935 Liberal campaign was national unity.

The Canadian Centenary Series

Half a century has elapsed since *Canada and Its Provinces,* the first large-scale co-operative history of Canada, was published. During that time, new historical materials have been made available in archives and libraries; new research has been carried out, and its results published; new interpretations have been advanced and tested. In these same years Canada itself has greatly grown and changed. These facts, together with the centenary of Confederation, justify the publication of a new co-operative history of Canada.

The form chosen for this enterprise was that of a series of volumes. The series was planned by the editors, but each volume will be designed and executed by a single author. The general theme of the work is the development of those regional communities which have for the past century made up the Canadian nation; and the series will be composed of a number of volumes sufficiently large to permit adequate treatment of all the phases of the theme in the light of modern knowledge.

The Centenary History, then, was planned as a series to have a certain common character and to follow a common method but to be written by individual authors, specialists in their fields. As a whole, it will be a work of specialized knowledge, the great advantage of scholarly co-operation, and at the same time each volume will have the unity and distinctive character of individual authorship. It was agreed that a general narrative treatment was necessary and that each author should deal in a balanced way with economic, political, and social history. The result, it is hoped, will be an interpretative, varied, and comprehensive account, at once useful to the student and interesting to the general reader.

The difficulties of organizing and executing such a series are apparent: the overlapping of separate narratives, the risk of omissions, the imposition of divisions which are relevant to some themes but not to others. Not so apparent, but quite as troublesome, are the problems of scale, perspective, and scope, problems which perplex the writer of a one-volume history and are magnified in a series. It is by deliberate choice that certain parts of the history are told twice, in different volumes from different points of view, in the belief that the benefits gained outweigh the unavoidable disadvantages.

W.L. MORTON,
Executive Editor.
D.G. CREIGHTON,
Advisory Editor.

Executive Editor's Preface

W.L. Morton and D.G. Creighton, two of Canada's most distinguished historians, together conceived the Canadian Centenary Series, divided the work, recruited the authors, and presided over the publication of fifteen volumes. Regrettably, neither lived to see the final four books through the press. That responsibility has fallen to me. I intend to carry it through according to the letter and the spirit of the introductory statement written by the first editors, which will continue to appear in each volume. The series remains theirs, an appropriate reminder of the seminal contributions that they made to the understanding of Canada's past. Having served my apprenticeship as a historian with each of them, in different ways, it is a signal privilege for me to be able to oversee the completion of this fine series of Canadian historical volumes.

The present volume, *Decades of Discord,* fits perfectly into the general contours of the series. Its author, one of a new generation of Canadian historians, has taken the years assigned to him, re-assessed often familiar events, and added a number of new dimensions to our comprehension of these troubled years. All of this is presented in a vigorous style that would have delighted W.L. Morton and D.G. Creighton as much as it does their successor.

RAMSAY COOK

Decades of Discord

Manuscripts are never really finished; they are only reluctantly allowed to leave the author's hands. It has taken almost thirty years to produce this book, longer than it took Canadians to live the years that it describes. I am the third senior author. When the Centenary Series was conceived in the 1950s, my most important concern was making the Little League baseball team in Sturgeon Creek, Manitoba. Professor W.L. Morton conscripted me to write Volume 15 in 1977, when it was already a decade overdue at McClelland and Stewart. After five years of solitary struggle, I enlisted my friend Allen Seager to join me in the final assault on the mountain of books, articles, theses, and manuscript collections that had to be conquered if the original purpose of the series – "an interpretive, varied, and comprehensive account" – was to be fulfilled.

Not everyone, of course, will be satisfied that in our words and concepts we have achieved this or that such a goal is attainable. Goldwin Smith long ago insisted that writing a comprehensive history of Canada was impossible because of "the difficulty of running the histories of several provinces abreast and imparting anything like unity to the whole." Modern reviewers have echoed Margaret Prang's complaint that previous books in the series have displayed an "overall centralist and nationalist bias." Allen and I have tried to steer a middle course between Smith's Scylla and the Charybdis of Professor Prang. We accepted J.M.S. Careless's advice that the "limited identities" of class, region, ethnicity, and gender are essential to understanding the complexity of Canada, and our notes reflect the importance attached to these subjects by historians in recent years. But with the generation of historians who initiated the Centenary Series we share the conviction that there is a national experience that can transcend these boundaries. There is perhaps more national and provincial political history in *Canada 1922-1939* than is currently fashionable, not because we believe history should be depicted in terms of large events and "great" personalities, but because these political struggles had importance for ordinary Canadians, the real subjects of this book.

Dozens of colleagues provided us with insight and information. Most generous were those who read sections of the manuscript about which they are expert: Bernard L. Vigod, Ernest R. Forbes, Richard Allen, Alan Artibise, Peter Baskerville, Paul Davenport, Clarence Karr, Alec Lane, Jo LaPierre, Martin Petter, Allan Smith, Veronica Strong-Boag, Maria Tippett, Mary Vipond, and William Watson. David Frank and Ernest R. Forbes searched for illustrations, James Struthers shared his knowledge of unemployment statistics, and Brian McKillop created the alliterative subtitle. Roger North and Sandra Steiman worked as research assistants; other students asked penetrating questions and hundreds more endured chapters in lecture halls at McGill and Simon Fraser. McGill's Faculty of Graduate Studies and Research in part paid our remarkably efficient typist, Maureen MacLean-Gamble. Maureen uncomplainingly incorporated into the manuscript the changes suggested by our gentle but exacting editor, Janet Craig. Janet's comprehensive card files made our notes more consistent and the task of indexing much easier.

After the death of W.L. Morton in 1980, Roger Graham served as my unofficial senior editor, continuing the kindness that began on the day he became my graduate supervisor. In February, 1983, Ramsay Cook became the new Executive Editor of the Centenary Series. Allen and I quickly discovered the intellect, tolerance, and understanding that have earned Ramsay the respect and affection of the Canadian historical community.

The most special appreciation goes to Katrin and Anne Thompson, who accepted patiently the evenings and weekends without companion and parent. Katrin also made active contributions without number at all stages of the project. My final words of gratitude must be for her alone.

JOHN HERD THOMPSON

CHAPTER 1

Canada Counts Noses

I

On the morning of Wednesday, June 1, 1921, Canadians awoke to find their country in the hands of a uniformless army twelve thousand strong. Equipped with indelible pencils and bundles of blue printed forms, the enumerators of the Sixth Decennial Census were mercenaries paid a bounty of five cents a head for every Canadian captured for the national inventory. In remote Northern areas Mounted Policemen, Hudson's Bay Company factors, and missionaries joined their ranks to see that no man, woman, child, or farm animal was overlooked. "This census," Dominion Statistician R.H. Coats proudly told reporters, "is the largest peacetime operation ever organized by the Canadian government . . . nothing less than a great periodical stocktaking of the people and their affairs." No previous census, he boasted, had "supplied the public of Canada with results of equal volume or analysis." To ensure accuracy each enumerator was ordered to complete his questionnaires through personal interviews. Those reluctant to respond were warned that the enumerators had almost "inquisitorial power . . . a refusal to answer legitimate questions would constitute an offence against the state" punishable by three months' imprisonment.[1]

This attention to detail meant that the collection of the data took three weeks and that June was giving way to July when results from the 241 Census Districts began to arrive at the Dominion Bureau of Statistics. Throughout the hot and humid Ottawa summer, Coats and his staff of 350 auditors, coders, machine operators, and clerks turned to their new Hollerith sorters and tabulators to make sense of the ocean of information that flooded their offices. Beginning in August, press releases and then Census Bulletins presented the intermediate results of the count like a national adventure serial, each new episode

1

whetting the public appetite for another until the story was complete. The climax came on February 24, 1922, when full-column newspaper headlines announced that there had been exactly 8,888,483 Canadians as of the previous June 1.

The anticipation with which Canadians awaited the returns of the census demonstrates that population figures were not simply tables of statistics but a matter of profound importance, a progress report on their national development in the century that was to belong to Canada. The global figure of 8.8 million was considerably smaller than many had predicted and immediately became the subject of anxious analysis. From Toronto, the young *Canadian Forum* predicted solemnly that "in Canada the Golden Age is ended." The Province of Quebec was sufficiently disappointed by the 2.3 million people credited to it by the census to enact legislation to provide for its own provincial count, and la Chambre de Commerce de Montréal accused the Dominion Bureau of Statistics of failing to enumerate 100,000 Montrealers. The Dominion Statistician defended the accuracy of his figures. Since enumerators were paid only for those they reported, underenumeration was unlikely; in Regina four enumerators were prosecuted for padding the lists with fictitious names. To reassure those disturbed by the failure to reach nine or ten million, Coats pointed out that although the population growth of the previous decade had been less than that of the 1901-11 period, the absolute increase of 1,581,840 was nonetheless a substantial 22 per cent. This was the second largest decennial increase in Canada's history and a rate of growth exceeded only by Australia; more important, it was in percentage terms considerably better than the growth of the United States during the same years. "Roughly speaking," wrote Coats in a paraphrase of the late Sir Wilfrid Laurier, "Canadian progress in the twentieth century is duplicating that of the United States in the nineteenth." Had it not been for the Great War with its casualties, its effect on immigration, and the pandemic of influenza that followed it, he concluded, "the Canadian population in 1921 would be well over 9 million." This was what Canadians wanted to believe. Considerable national uneasiness was assuaged by this explanation and even the "boosters" of the Western provinces, who expected populations to double each decade, were inclined to accept it. "Canada would be disappointed in the census returns," rationalized the Calgary *Herald*, "were it not that the last decade has been decidedly unfavourable for large increase in population. In the circumstances, the showing the Dominion has made is not unsatisfactory."[2]

This expression of qualified optimism from Alberta, however, was tempered by the bitter despair with which the returns were greeted in the Atlantic Provinces. Population figures by province showed clearly that the shift of the balance within Canada already evident in 1911 had continued. Internal migration, immigration, and emigration to the United States had combined to produce above-average population growth in the West, moderate growth in Central Canada, and near-stagnation in the Maritimes. British Columbia and the Prairie Provinces now domiciled twenty-nine of every hundred Canadians, Nova Scotia, New Brunswick, and Prince Edward Island only eleven, whereas twenty years earlier the figures had been reversed. Prince Edward Island actually reported an absolute loss of people in 1921, and her sister Maritime Provinces demonstrated only modest increases, which did not reflect their surplus of births over deaths. More than 90,000 people had left the Maritimes since 1911, half of them for the West and most of the remainder for the "Boston States." Proud Nova Scotia underwent the further humiliation of falling from Canada's third largest to seventh largest province in a single decade. The national centre of gravity, despite the West's gains, still rested firmly in Ontario and Quebec. Although their dominant position had been slightly eroded, their populations of 2.9 and 2.3 million respectively meant that 60 per cent of the Canadian people resided in the two central provinces. Ontario had sent many of her sons and daughters to populate the West, and French Canadians continued to leave Quebec for New England; but as Canada's most urban provinces they benefited from migration from rural areas to cities, and these same cities attracted immigrants, particularly those from Britain.

Perhaps the most significant trend noted by the sixth census was the continuing urbanization of the Canadian people, evident in each census since 1881. The new figures had an increased psychological importance, however, for they revealed that, using the rather generous definition of an urban area as "any incorporated city, town, or village," more Canadians lived in the city than in the country by a tiny margin. Absolute rural population had continued to grow because of the expansion of agriculture on the Prairies, but cities, particularly the larger ones, had mushroomed. For the first time Canada had two cities, Montreal and Toronto, with more than 500,000 inhabitants. More Canadians lived in these two cities than in the Maritime Provinces, and if its new streetcar suburbs were included, "Greater" Montreal had a population in excess of 700,000 – more than that of six of the nine provinces. Winnipeg, Vancouver, Hamilton, and Ottawa occupied the next rungs on the urban ladder, each with 100,000 or more citizens. Obscured behind the "national" average of fifty-one townsmen to forty-nine country dwellers was the fact that this rural-urban ratio did not exist in any single province. Ontario and Quebec ex-

ceeded the national average with rates of urbanization above 55 per
cent while British Columbia most nearly approximated it with 47 per
cent of her population so classified. The Maritime and Prairie regions
had a pronounced majority of rural residents, in both cases almost 65
per cent of their populations, and even including Winnipeg the province of Manitoba still had six of every ten of its people living outside
urban areas. Nor should all urban areas, even in the central provinces,
be equated with the largest cities in terms of attitudes and behaviour.
Barrie, Ontario, which proudly reported some seven thousand
residents to the enumerators, still turned off its electric lights each
evening, blinking them at 10:55 P.M. to warn residents, then returning
those still awake to the thin light of kerosene lamps five minutes later.[3]

II

If Canadian society was more or less equally divided between city and
country, another of its fundamental divisions remained askew. In
every province except Quebec there were more men than women,
and of every 1,000 Canadians 515 were males, a rate of "masculinity"
exceeded only in the Argentine Republic. This imbalance was neither
new nor surprising. It had existed since the first Canadian census of
1851 and was a result of the preponderance of men among incoming
immigrants. In fact, the Dominion Statistician observed with approval,
Canada was only half as "masculine" as in 1911 and because of wartime casualties the number of men and women in the marriageable
years between twenty-five and thirty-four was now much closer to ap-
proximate equality.

In terms of its age structure as well Canada was coming to resemble
more closely a "normal" longer-established society – Coats choose
Sweden as his example. Immigration had raised the average age of
Canadians because most immigrants were already past adolescence,
but the shutting off of immigration meant a downward movement of
the median age – the age at which there were as many Canadians
younger as there were older – to slightly less than twenty-four years.
When distributed among age groups, out of every thousand Canadians
435 were under twenty years, 159 in their twenties, 146 in their thirties, 110 in their forties, 73 in their fifties, and an equal number over
the age of sixty years. This last figure was an increase from the 1911
census and represented in part the slightly longer life span brought
about by the tentative beginnings of public health schemes to combat
a number of formerly epidemic diseases. Distribution of the population by age varied widely from region to region. The older provinces

had older populations – the Maritimes had the largest percentage of their residents in the later years of life. The Western provinces, on the other hand, had almost half of their populations in the active years of adulthood between the ages of twenty-one and forty-five.

In all regions of Canada the cornerstone of Canadian society was the family. The 1921 returns showed that more Canadians were married, in both absolute and proportional terms, than at any previous time. The marriage rate fluctuated from year to year, increasing in good times and falling back with the economy, but overall more than 56 per cent of men and 60 per cent of women above the age of fifteen were married. More significantly, between the ages of thirty-five and fifty, 80 per cent of both sexes were married. Widows and widowers, involuntarily single, accounted for much of the remainder, but about a tenth of the Canadian population remained unmarried throughout their lives. Only an infinitesimal proportion – less than one tenth of 1 per cent – had ever resorted to divorce to break up a conjugal relationship. The Province of Manitoba recorded the first absolute decree of divorce in its history in 1919. The lowest divorce rate in the Western world was widely cited as evidence of the happiness of Canadian families, but it was also mute testimony to the restrictiveness of divorce laws and the social strictures that surrounded matrimony as an institution. The figures for single men, Coats admitted, undoubtedly included married men who had simply deserted their wives and families and moved on to another city or province.[4]

Because the collection of vital statistics was a subject of dominion-provincial controversy, the schedule of questions for the census did not permit the DBS to calculate accurately fertility rates – the number of children born to Canadian women during their childbearing years – nor did it permit an overall calculation of family size, since it counted only children who lived at home with their parents. Seven out of ten families reported children at home, ranging from a high of 75 per cent among Quebec families to a low of 60 per cent in British Columbia. More than half of the families with children had three or more, while 12 per cent reported six or more children. Family size, observed Coats, seemed to be influenced by the obvious variables of ethnicity and religion and the less obvious one of urbanization, for city families reported fewer children than their rural counterparts. Quebec's crude birth rate of 37.6 live births per thousand was described as "the highest rate of natural increase of any civilized country," but within the city of Toronto the rate was observed to fluctuate from 12.3 per thousand in Rosedale, "the fashionable quarter where dwell the magnates of finance and commerce," to 43 per thousand in East Toronto, "largely inhabited by foreign-born immigrants."[5]

III

No part of the census aroused as much interest as the returns that outlined the ethnic composition of the population, although the term "ethnic" appeared infrequently in the five volumes of the 1921 census. Instead, the words "race" or "racial origin" were employed to categorize Canadians into the two major and the innumerable minor cultural subdivisions. Ten questions on nativity, citizenship, race, language, and religion were grouped together as Numbers 15 to 25 on the schedule used to enumerate the population. The organization of the table that set out the responses to the question "Place of Birth" was an excellent indicator of contemporary Canadian attitudes to ethnicity. The information was displayed in four columns: "Canadian Born," "British Born," "Born in the United States," and – the *real* foreigners – "Born in Other Foreign Countries." It revealed that a smaller percentage of the population, 77.7 per cent, had been born in Canada than at any previous census year, but in case native-born Canadians became alarmed by this statistic, the Census Bulletin observed with alacrity that those born in Britain made up half the remainder, and that the natives of foreign countries other than the United States made up a smaller percentage of the population than they had in 1911. Furthermore, the foreign born were fulfilling the formal legal requirements of citizenship in ever-increasing numbers, and almost 60 per cent of them had become Canadians by naturalization.

To the census-takers, however, naturalization could make an immigrant a Canadian citizen without making him a "Canadian." The most controversial question on the population schedule was Number 21, which demanded a respondent's "racial or tribal *origin*." Enumerators were instructed that "Canadian" was an unacceptable answer, no matter how far into the past an individual traced his or her roots on this side of the Atlantic. To those who argued, like the Toronto *Globe*, that such questions retarded the development of a national consciousness and who demanded "an end to this farce," the Dominion Statistician replied that "notwithstanding the desirability of racial assimilation . . . racial origin is especially important in a 'new' country like Canada" since the statistics obtained were vital to "the student of ethnology, criminology, and the social and biometric sciences in particular." There was a more obvious political reason, however, which Georges Pelletier of *Le Devoir* made clear in an editorial. "Millions of French Canadians," he wrote in answer to the *Globe*, wanted to be counted that way in the census for precisely the reason that many English Canadians wanted the distinction abolished, "to remind their fellow-citizens of other languages and races of their origin." To *l'Ac-*

tion française, "in a country where numbers play such an important part in determining the supremacy of one group over another," the census was a "battle communiqué. . . . Does the census taker record a retreat in our positions?"[6]

The answers to Question 21 showed that French Canadians had declined very slightly to 27.9 per cent of the national population, despite the substantial numerical increase produced by their high birth rate. Those of British Isles ancestry – English, Irish, Scottish, or Welsh – were a clear majority, 55.4 per cent of all Canadians, a slight increase from the previous census largely attributable to immigration from Britain. Together the "two great racial stocks" made up almost five sixths of the Canadian population. The remainder was scattered among twenty-two different "races" or lumped into the category "various and unspecified." No single group apart from the British and French came to more than 3.3 per cent, but considered together these groups demonstrated that "The Race Question in Canada," as sociologist André Siegfried had christened the French-English dichotomy in 1906, was no longer as clear cut as it had once been. Persons of German background formed the largest single group of those whose origins were neither British nor French – thirty-three of every thousand Canadians. To their numbers should be added many of the "Dutch," who had mysteriously doubled since 1911 to 1.3 per cent of the population in response to the anti-German sentiments generated by the Great War. "Ukranians," recognized as such for the first time despite the misspelling of *Ukrainian* throughout the *Sixth Census*, accounted for another 1.3 per cent, and would have been more numerous had not many been reported as "Austrians" or "Russians" according to which empire dominated that part of Ukraine in which they or their parents had been born. The imprecise term "Scandinavian" gathered together the 1.9 per cent of the population that traced itself to Norway, Sweden, Denmark, or Iceland. No other European group made up as much as 1 per cent of the Canadian people save the "Hebrews," who were not defined by their country of origin but given simultaneous status as a race and as a religion.

For those English and French Canadians who saw these "New Canadians" as a national problem, the *Sixth Census* contained the further disturbing news that Canada's "Asiatic population" had increased from 0.44 to 0.75 per cent in ten years, and added the warning that "over 800 Japanese and Chinese children were born in Canada in 1921." The Black population, however, had decreased to 0.21 per cent, and white Canadians were assured that immigration policies would continue to be designed to maintain Canada as a "White Man's Country." One final minority, 110,000 Native Indians, made up 1.2

per cent of the Canadian people, a percentage that had declined steadily since 1871. Their minuscule absolute increase – there had been
105,000 Indians in 1911 – reflected the despair, disease, and social disintegration to which the rest of Canada had abandoned them.

The diversity revealed by the question of "racial or tribal origin" is
less apparent when the results of questions about languages spoken
and mother tongue, defined as "language of customary speech," are
considered. The responses demonstrated clearly that except in
Quebec English was overwhelmingly the everyday language of affairs
in Canada. Almost 85 per cent of Canada's residents could speak
English, and 59 per cent spoke English only. Even in Quebec, more of
those whose mother tongue was French spoke English than the
reverse; two thirds of the English-speaking population of Quebec reported itself unable to speak French. Almost all of the 13 per cent of
the Canadian population who spoke only French resided in Quebec or
in the northern counties of New Brunswick. The French-Canadian
communities of Ontario and the Prairie Provinces had not been assim-
ilated, but the assault on French-Catholic educational rights and the
pressure of economic necessity were forcing them to learn to speak
English. It was English Canada that was the model for newcomers. Virtually all immigrants who reported a second language other than their
mother tongue spoke English rather than French. Over 175,000 of
those who gave their racial origin as German, Dutch, or Scandinavian
reported English as their mother tongue.

Inextricably connected with race and language in the eyes of Canadians was religion, and the importance of religious affiliation in Canadian life in 1921 is illustrated by the fact that only 22,000 of 8.8 million
respondents asked to be enumerated in the category "no religion."
The remainder were arranged according to some sixty-four religions
and a general category called "various sects." This apparent diversity
of belief was tempered by two considerations: first that 97.6 per cent
of Canadians belonged to "some Christian denomination or sect,"
leaving only 125,000 Jews, 40,000 "Eastern religions," and 7,000
"Pagans" outside the Christian pale, and second that eight of ten of
the Christian majority were either Roman Catholic, Presbyterian,
Anglican, or Methodist. The churches took their relative standing very
seriously, and church members and church leaders scanned the census
bulletin on religion to see how their denomination was performing in
the competition for Canadian souls. The 1921 returns gave the
Anglican Church the greatest cause for joy. British immigration had
added heavily to its numbers and placed it in a virtual tie with the
Presbyterian Church with 16 per cent of the Canadian population.
Methodists had the greatest cause for alarm. Once the largest Protes-

tant denomination, they had slipped to third place, adding weight to the arguments of those Methodists who called for a fusion of the major Protestant groups. The Roman Catholic Church remained the largest single Christian denomination, claiming the allegiance of 40 per cent of Canada's Christians. To the relief of the 100,000 members of the Orange Lodge, however, this Catholic predominance was not nation-wide. Two million of Canada's 3.3 million Catholics lived in Quebec; every other province had a Protestant majority. In Ontario, Roman Catholics were less numerous than Anglicans or Presbyterians or Methodists, and in each Western province one or another of the Prot-estant denominations outnumbered them.

IV

The Census of 1921 provided only the most rudimentary statistics with which to evaluate the educational level of the Canadian people. Education was of course a provincial responsibility, and the Dominion Bureau of Statistics was at the time of the census compilation engaged in a conference with provincial authorities to arrange for a uniform na-tional system of reporting educational statistics. Thus the census schedule made no attempt to measure scholastic attainment but simply asked the respondent if he could read and write and if he had attended a school during the previous nine months. The definition of literacy as being able to read or write *any* language, not necessarily English or French, was a very imprecise one. R.H. Coats admitted that people who could be thus described as literate might be unable "to read the current news correctly or intelligently" or to write more than their names, and further that many would not confess to being unable to read or write. Thus the statistical conclusion that 5.49 per cent of the non-aboriginal population of Canada was illiterate understated those who were functionally illiterate. A large proportion of the illiterates, however, was confined to the older age groups in the population and to those who were foreign born. Younger people born in Canada – with the exception of those born in Quebec – showed a much higher rate of literacy.[7]

This was the result of the fact that more Canadian children were receiving at least a rudimentary primary education. Statistics con-tained in the 1921 census show that school attendance among Cana-dians between the ages of five and nineteen years increased from 53 per cent in 1911 to 61 per cent in 1921. This was a truly remarkable in-crease in a short period and reflected the new importance an increas-ingly urban society placed on education, an importance which all provinces save Quebec had sanctioned with legislation. Ontario, for example, had extended the compulsory school attendance age to sixteen and eighteen in some cases. The Prairie Provinces, anxious to use the public school to assimilate the children of immigrants, had also extended the school leaving age and introduced methods of enforcing the new laws. With British Columbia, these four provinces had the highest percentage of their school-age populations actually in school. Farther east, Prince Edward Island and Nova Scotia, which had had high rates of school attendance in 1911, continued to have them, while Quebec and New Brunswick had rates considerably below the national averages. New Brunswick's children were permitted to leave school on the twelfth birthday, while Quebec had no compulsory school attendance legislation whatsoever. In Canada's second largest province education remained the responsibility of the Roman Catholic and Protestant Committees for Public Instruction; in fact, no provincial department of education would exist in Quebec to parallel the educational administrations of the other provinces until 1964.

The good news that more of Canada's young people were now attending school had to be qualified; a majority never left the primary grades. Despite the removal of tuition fees for secondary education in most provinces, few students got beyond elementary school and only a tiny minority went on to study at one of Canada's twenty-three universities or forty-four colleges, or at a French Catholic *collège classique*. Actual enrolment in post-secondary institutions was less than 50,000 in 1921, and it did not even occur to the framers of the questions for the census schedules to ask adult Canadians if they had attended a college or university.[8]

V

The final questions of the Sixth Census were designed to obtain a profile of the Canadian workforce and thus indirectly of the Canadian economy. The census was unlike its predecessors in that it did not include a census of industries; this investigation was being carried out through extensive ongoing research by the Dominion Bureau of Statistics and was eliminated from the questionnaires provided to enumerators. Canadian industry had become so complex that enumerators employed on a temporary basis were simply unable to deal with it. It was difficult enough for an enumerator to obtain answers to Question 19, which asked a respondent to "state definitely what you work at," for as Coats pointed out, "the complexity of present day industrial organizations makes it difficult, sometimes impossible, to determine whether a worker or group of workers belongs to one or another of a variety of occupations." The data collected, however, did provide a picture of the distribution of Canadian workers by industry.[9]

For men in the labour force, the picture in its overall dimensions was essentially similar to that of 1911. Despite a tiny decline, farmers and farm labourers still made up the largest percentage of working men, thirty-eight of every hundred. Agriculture was the largest employer of men in every province except British Columbia, and the Dominion Statistician reassured those who worried about the decline of rural Canada that farming was still Canada's "basic industry." This much-repeated platitude overlooked one significant statistic: almost all of the absolute expansion of agriculture between 1911 and 1921 had taken place in Western Canada. While farmers had increased as a percentage of the working male population in the four Western provinces, in every other province they had declined.

Next in significance to agriculture as an employer of men was manufacturing, with twelve of every hundred gainfully employed, a figure almost identical to that of 1911 despite the industrial expansion induced by the war. Trade and merchandising came third with nine per hundred, edging out construction, which was mired in a post-war recession. Transportation continued to be a critical sector of the Canadian economy, employing seven of each hundred workers – more than in any other country that kept similar statistics. Other occupations trailed far behind: the professions at 2.9 per cent of employed males, domestic service at 2.7 per cent, mining at 1.9 per cent, logging at 1.5 per cent, and fishing and hunting at 1.1 per cent. The percentage of employees of all three levels of government remained identical with that of 1911 – 3.1. In 1921 working in the private sector of the economy was only slightly less common than professing Christianity!

For working women, however, the pattern of employment had changed substantially in a decade. Women were entering the paid labour force in increasing numbers – there were 183 women workers for every 1,000 males in 1921 as compared to only 155 in 1911 – and the 16 per cent of females over the age of ten who held jobs were doing different kinds of work. In 1911 40 per cent had been domestic servants, performing household tasks in someone else's home, while another 27 per cent had been factory workers in light industry. The new returns showed both a percentage and an absolute decline in these two groups as women found new occupations open to them. The number of women office workers tripled to 90,000 in a decade, to the point that the typical clerk was no longer Charles Dickens's Bob Cratchit but Tillie the Toiler of the newspaper comic page. Women in professional service had doubled, although the increase was made up of school teachers and nurses rather than doctors or lawyers. Women in "transportation" became 3 per cent of the female work force because of the employment of 13,000 women as telephone operators. These new jobs – even when combined with the suffrage in federal elections and in the eight English-speaking provinces – did not give women complete equality with men, or demonstrate that women sought it. Most Canadian men and women still believed that woman's "proper sphere" was the home, even though statistics demonstrated that this image no longer corresponded to reality. The largest group of working women were single and below the age of thirty and expected one day to marry and attend to the duties of a home. Married women entered the labour market not to seek careers but because they were forced by economic necessity after being widowed or deserted. [10]

Some working-class families were unable to survive without both adults – and in some cases the children – making a contribution to family income. More than 12,000 children under the age of fifteen were permanently employed outside agriculture in 1921, and the DBS issued a special census bulletin dealing exclusively with this continuing problem. Child labour was a symptom of family poverty, and the *Sixth Census* made only a rudimentary study of this through an examination of the incomes of Canadians. Restricting its inquiries to the fifteen cities of over 30,000 population, the DBS attempted to gather and analyse data on the annual earnings of male heads of families, and thus to determine if the standard of living of the Canadian wage earner had improved since 1911 by providing figures that could be compared to the Department of Labour's Cost of Living Index. The results showed that in most occupations and in most cities, workers were earning substantially more dollar income than they had ten years earlier. Based on prevailing rates, a forty-four-hour week and a forty-week year, a carpenter in Halifax made $1,042 as compared to $550 in 1911, his counterpart in Toronto $1,188 as compared to $666, and a third carpenter in Vancouver $1,116 as compared to $915. A 60-percent increase in the cost of living, however, meant that these higher incomes were less impressive in real terms. In fact, since the 1921 census was taken in the midst of the post-war recession, "a much greater degree of unemployment" meant that many workers did not work enough hours to receive the hypothetical salaries calculated in the census tables. [11]

One other generalization emerged from the wage tables. Wage increases were unevenly divided by region, and the regional differences within the Canadian economy were also underlined by the statistics of occupations, which showed very different patterns of employment in the Maritimes, Quebec, and Ontario, the Prairie Provinces, and British Columbia. No better measure of the success of the National Policy in encouraging specialized regional economies can be found. British Columbia's dependence on primary extractive industries meant that, with fewer than one tenth of the nation's workers, the province had one third of its loggers and one fifth of its miners. In Manitoba, Saskatchewan, and Alberta seven of every ten workers were directly engaged in agriculture, and most of the remainder were dependent upon transporting agricultural products or supplying the wants of the farm community. Ontario and Quebec had 60 per cent of the working population but four fifths of the jobs in secondary manufacturing. The Maritimes, with the exception of Prince Edward Island, had a better-developed industrial base than the Prairies, but the slow pace of industrialization was underlined by the larger percentage of the workforce in fishing and the smaller percentage in transportation and construction jobs.

In his introduction to the occupational statistics included in the 1922 *Canada Year Book*, R.H. Coats cautiously suggested the significance of the "widely differing occupational distribution of the population." From these differences, he concluded, "arise many of the divergences of interest which are reflected in Canadian social and political life." This was a careful civil servant's way of alluding to the general election of December 1921. Like the census returns, the election results demonstrated that there was not one but several Canadas, each determined to shape the nation in its own image and to guide it in different directions.[12]

CHAPTER 2

Liberal Opportunism and Progressive Frustration

I

The federal general election of December 6, 1921, completed the work of the Great War in destroying the Canadian two-party system. For half a century the Liberal and Conservative parties had had the hustings virtually to themselves, despite the momentous changes that had transformed the country. Industrialization, western expansion, and massive immigration had exacerbated the regional and national diversities inherent in Confederation, but the Tories and the Grits – *les bleus et les rouges* in Quebec – battled for control of the amorphous world of Canadian politics, still identifying themselves in the political slang of the 1850s. After each of the twelve federal elections between 1867 and 1911 either the Liberals or the Conservatives had enjoyed a clear-cut majority in the House of Commons; in every election but one the winning party had also received a majority of the popular vote. The election of the Union government to enforce conscription in 1917 had disrupted the usual patterns of political partisanship, but the traditions of majority government and of two contending parties were continued. The election of 1921 defied both these traditions; for the first time the Canadian electorate failed to produce a simple, unambiguous decision.

The three months' campaign that led up to election day saw only one of the three national party leaders give the voters a precise statement of what he and his followers represented. Prime Minister Arthur Meighen, who had inherited the battered Union government from Sir Robert Borden in July, 1920, returned to the first principles of Canadian Conservatism by making the central theme of his campaign the protective tariff. The economic nationalism of the tariff had saved the Macdonald government in 1891 and given the Borden Conservatives an unexpected victory in 1911, and Meighen hoped the old magic could work once more. Although he made no attempt to hide from the wartime record of the Union government, even defending conscription in his speeches in Quebec, Meighen insisted to audiences in every province that the alternatives were the Conservative party and the National Policy tariff or the "absorption of Canadian industries and with them Canadian manhood and womanhood in the ever-expanding system of the United States." Unfortunately for Meighen, only one of his adversaries was prepared to do battle on his chosen ground. The Progressive party's Farmers' Platform, drafted by the Canadian Council of Agriculture, described the protective tariff as "the most wasteful and costly method ever designed for raising national revenue," blamed it for "building up a privileged class at the expense of the masses," and accused it of being the "chief corrupting influence in our national life." If Progressive leader Thomas Crerar had any misgivings about playing the free trade foil to Meighen's patriotic defence of protectionism, his platform left him little choice, for it committed him to demand "an immediate and substantial all-round reduction of the customs tariff."[1]

Liberal leader Mackenzie King supposedly also was committed to "substantial reductions" in the tariff by the Liberal platform drafted at the 1919 convention that had chosen him as leader. But King knew that the members of his party were divided on the issue, and he was determined not to allow the Liberals to be pinned down to any concrete position on trade policy. Commitment to reciprocity with the United States had defeated his mentor, Sir Wilfrid Laurier, twice, and Mackenzie King had no thought of making himself a sacrifice on the altar of free trade. He was convinced that the Conservatives were sufficiently unpopular that no dramatic effort on his part would be required to persuade the voters to turn them out of office; using the talent for obfuscation that was to serve him well throughout his career, King promised a "tariff for the consumer and producer" that would also "take care of the needs of all the industries," while carefully avoiding defining what that might mean. Individual Liberal candidates tailored their campaigns to their ridings, interpreting their leader's position in whatever way was best suited to local conditions. While Meighen assailed Crerar as a "wrecker" and the Progressive leader replied in kind, King piously informed his brother Max that he had "gone through the campaign without saying one unkind or harsh expression that I am aware of." This wasn't strictly correct, for he had denounced Meighen as a "usurper, autocrat, subverter of the constitution and [a] puppet," but to a remarkable extent he had evaded committing himself to anything. The Conservative Montreal *Gazette* described King's campaign as "misrepresentation, confusion and evasion which stands without parallel in Canadian history"; the Liberal Toronto *Globe* was understandably less harsh. Mackenzie King's "remarkable campaign," it concluded, "contributed more than anything else to the party's success."[2]

For the Liberal party was obviously the winner of the 1921 election, even though it polled only 40.7 per cent of the popular vote and its 116 seats left it short of an absolute majority in the Commons. Equally obviously the "National Liberal and Conservative Party," as the Tories had christened themselves to perpetuate an illusion of the non-partisan unity of wartime, was the loser. As the party that had taken Canada through her most difficult decade, the Conservatives had expected losses, but they were stunned by the vehemence of the voters' rebuke. No previous government had ever been so resoundingly rejected. Only fifty Conservative candidates were able to win their constituencies; Prime Minister Meighen and half of his cabinet colleagues were defeated. The new third factor in the national political equation, the Progressive party, should have been happy with the results. The sixty-four Progressives elected would be the second-largest group in the House and would presumably hold a balance of power. The Progressives' achievement had not matched their expectations, however, and the party's disappointingly small popular vote – 23 per cent as compared to the Conservatives' 30 per cent – dampened the enthusiasm of those who had looked for a more dramatic breakthrough. Progressive supporters blamed "the moneyed interests," who had abandoned the Tories for the Liberals to prevent a radical party from gaining office (see Table Ia).[3]

The division of seats exaggerated Conservative weakness and Progressive strength, but the electoral map revealed an uncertain Canada. The wartime election of 1917 had split the country along lines of race; that of 1921 exposed the further divisions of region. No party could truly claim to be the national choice. The Liberals had representatives from eight of the nine provinces, but 90 of their 116 members sat for ridings east of the Ottawa River. More than half of the Liberal caucus was from Quebec, which had avenged itself for conscription by returning Liberals in every last one of its sixty-five seats. The Conservatives had been shut out in six provinces, but won seven of British Columbia's thirteen seats, five in the English-speaking counties of New Brunswick, and – because of Meighen's emphasis on the protective tariff – thirty-seven seats in Ontario. Progressive strength had a similar narrow regional base. Prairie voters chose Progressives to fill thirty-nine of their forty-three seats, but only twenty-four of the forty members confidently expected from rural Ontario were actually elected. Beyond those four provinces, the Progressive penetration was confined to a lone New Brunswick constituency and two narrow victories in British Columbia. In Quebec even the blessing of Henri Bourassa and *Le Devoir* was unable to earn the Progressives a single seat or more than 4 per cent of the popular vote.[4]

The regional and ethnic diversity made evident by the election results obscured another division in Canadian society, class cleavage. The wave of industrial unrest that swept the nation in 1919 – 3.4 million workdays were lost through strikes – reverberated through the political structure for the next two years. Local and provincial Labour parties, loose coalitions of socialists and trade union leaders, sprang up to challenge the Liberals and Conservatives; by 1920 Labour legislators had been elected in Nova Scotia, Ontario, Manitoba, Alberta, and British Columbia. Labour, socialist, or working-man candidates appeared on the ballot in over thirty federal constituencies in 1921, among them W.A. Pritchard and R.B. Russell, both jailed for sedition in the aftermath of the Winnipeg General Strike. Four Labour nominees won election – in Timiskaming, Kootenay West, Calgary East, and Winnipeg Centre. In another handful of ridings they made respectable showings. J.B. McLachlan, the popular Nova Scotia miners' leader, won 35 per cent of the vote in Cape Breton South. Labourism had no support in Quebec, however, and returns from the industrial heartland of southern Ontario were disappointing. There most workers rejected class politics in favour of the protectionist program of the Tories. Of the four Labour M.P.s elected, only the two from the Prairies – J.S. Woodsworth of Winnipeg and William Irvine of Calgary – retained enough of their independence to leave a mark on parliament. In a curious manner, their presence in the Commons accentuated the sectional cleavages that their ideology of working-class unity rejected.[5]

Editorial reaction to the election returns was as narrowly regionalized as the election itself. *La Presse* of Montreal felt pride that Quebec would "again take her rightful place in government"; the *Orange Sentinel* warned English-Canadian Protestants that "French Canada is on top now with a vengence." It was left for more thoughtful journals to consider the election's implications from a less biased national perspective. "The Union of the regions is but partially accomplished," wrote Professor W.A. Mackintosh in *Queen's Quarterly*. "The sectionalism apparent in the election results is no mere surface phenomenon but rooted deeply in the fundamental facts of geology, topography, climate and the resulting industrial conditions." The *Canadian Forum* reached a similar conclusion about "the tendency shown in this election to develop regional blocs. . . . No federation," it argued, "can prosper or even exist permanently if they are allowed to fester." What Canada needed was a "man who can restore and foster a spirit of unity between city and country, between Ontario and Quebec on the one hand and Ontario and the West on the other. . . ." Such a man, prophesied the *Forum*, "is the man of destiny."[6]

II

Prime Minister-elect William Lyon Mackenzie King would have agreed with this description of his task as the creation of a "spirit of unity." He would also have savoured the phrase "man of destiny." While still a teenager he had confided to his diary, ". . . surely I have some great work to accomplish before I die"; since that time he had devoted most of his energy to making certain that destiny would not have an opportunity to overlook him. Born in 1874 in Berlin, Ontario, King was the first child of John King, an undistinguished lawyer, and Isobel Grace Mackenzie, youngest daughter of William Lyon Mackenzie, the rebel of 1837. His sense that he was marked for future greatness was fuelled by his mother, who reminded him constantly that the blood of his grandfather was "coursing through [his] veins." King's pre-prime ministerial career was markedly dissimilar to that traditional for Canadian politicians. Perhaps because his father never earned enough as a lawyer to escape genteel poverty, he rejected the law for the new fields of political economy and sociology, earning five degrees from three universities, the last a Ph.D. from Harvard in the field of industrial sociology.[7]

In 1900 he was able to use his father's friendship with Sir William Mulock, Laurier's Postmaster General, to land a job as editor of a new government publication, the *Labour Gazette*. Shrewd and industrious, young "Rex" King demonstrated a good general intelligence and a capacity for very hard work that quickly won him promotion to the post of deputy minister in the newly created Department of Labour. This position enabled King to cultivate further his growing reputation as a "progressive" who could understand and deal with the tensions industrial capitalism had created within Canadian society. King's proudest achievement while a civil servant was the Industrial Disputes Investigation Act (1907), which created a voluntary conciliation process that could be invoked in labour disputes to seek a solution before a strike occurred. King was most unhappy when his special child became popularly known as the Lemieux Act after its official sponsor, his minister, Rodolphe Lemieux. Craving a place on centre stage, in 1908 the young bureaucrat moved to active politics. Elected Liberal member for Waterloo North, he entered the cabinet as Minister of Labour the next year.[8]

But King's careful plans received a rude jolt when both he and his party were defeated in the reciprocity election of 1911. He landed on his feet in the United States, however, obtaining the position of Director of Industrial Relations for the Rockefeller Foundation. King's new job temporarily interrupted his political career in Canada, but it created important continental connections and paid him handsomely to evolve and propagate his doctrine of industrial harmony through conciliation, with government serving as an "impartial umpire" between labour and capital. Although his pious phrases were occasionally inaudible beneath the rattle of the machine guns that formed the essence of John D. Rockefeller's industrial relations policy, King's Rockefeller years also gave him time to write the book that completed his credentials as an "expert" in his chosen field. *Industry and Humanity*, published in 1918, both summarized King's career to that time and pointed the way to his future. It was pompous, long-winded, full of platitudes, and very short on practical suggestions. John D. junior dismissed it at once as "too philosophical and somewhat long," and dismissed King along with it. When one penetrates the platitudes, however, the book does represent a departure from orthodox Liberal thinking of the era. However ambiguous his specific proposals, King was prepared to concede the state a much larger role in national economic life than were most members of his party and at least professed to believe that "wherever, in social or industrial relations, the claims of Industry and Humanity are opposed, those of Industry must make way. . . ."[9]

Fortunately for King's political ambitions, *Industry and Humanity* became – in Grattan O'Leary's words – the "book which more Canadians have failed to read than almost any other." Very few of the delegates to the Liberal leadership convention in August 1919 were prepared to wade through more than four hundred pages of his turgid prose to discover that they disagreed with his conclusions. King inherited the mantle of Laurier not for his progressive ideas but because he was one of the few prominent English-speaking Liberals who had not deserted the old man for the banners of Union government and conscription in 1917. He had even made a half-hearted attempt to save an Ontario seat from the Unionist tide, and two years later he collected his political debts. Solid support from the Quebec delegation made possible his narrow third-ballot selection. Twenty-eight months later the election of 1921 made him Canada's tenth prime minister.[10]

With only two years as party leader behind him before taking office – Laurier had had nine, Borden ten – the new prime minister was not yet well known to the public. At forty-seven he was the second-youngest first minister ever; only his opponent, Arthur Meighen, had been younger. Even so, King was touching the limit at which he could be considered an "eligible" bachelor. His sedentary life-style had thickened the middle and doubled the chin of an already short, unattractive body, and his artless hair style did little to conceal a rapidly widening part. It was an age, however, in which the public did not demand that its leaders *look* like leaders. With radio at the crystal set and earphone stage, it scarcely mattered that King did not *sound* like a leader either. One parliamentary reporter, complaining of "the decline of oratory in parliament," described a King speech as "conspicuously deficient in structure, in logical sequence and in power of exposition." King made up for this deficiency, as he did for all his deficiencies, with hard work. Throughout his parliamentary career he sat up with his secretary after the House had adjourned, perfecting his speeches so that the published version would read better than what he had actually said in the Commons. He applied this same diligence to the formation of his first government. [11]

Since the concession of responsible government in the 1840s, both Liberal and Conservative cabinets had been delicately crafted to reflect a careful balance of regional, religious, and linguistic groups. The outcome of the election of 1921, however, meant that choosing a group of ministers that could represent or mediate national divisions was a difficult undertaking. With the Liberal party overrepresented in Quebec and the Maritimes, weak in Ontario, and almost non-existent in the West, King had to do the best job he could with the limited material at hand. His initial plan was to obtain both Western representation and a parliamentary majority at one stroke by convincing two or three of the former Liberals prominent in the Progressive party to enter his cabinet. Negotiations with Progressive leader T.A. Crerar and with Herbert Greenfield and E.C. Drury, premiers of farmer governments in Alberta and Ontario, ended unsuccessfully. Each of the three was tempted, but the loud cries of outrage from the Progressive grassroots at the hint of any such compromise convinced the would-be ministers that accepting a cabinet post meant losing any control they had over their followers. J.J. Morrison, secretary of the United Farmers of Ontario, warned Crerar that any deal with the Liberals "would be a retrograde and a bad political move. Our men here would regard it as traitorous." [12]

Although King was disappointed that his overtures had miscarried, there were others in the Liberal party who firmly opposed any attempt to come to terms with the farmers. The financial, transportation, and industrial magnates of Montreal, though scarcely liberal by any definition of the term, had broken with the Conservative party because of its "most demented form of Socialism," the nationalization of the Canadian Northern, the Grand Trunk, and Grand Trunk Pacific railways. This group of "Montreal Tycoons," once denounced by Mackenzie King as a "privileged coterie of wealthy and influential men" who were "the real though invisible Government" of Canada, had helped make possible his election. Now they demanded a national government that would operate on "sound business principles," the big businessman's code words for a protective tariff, a sound currency, and no government interference in the economy unless specifically requested. The men who ran the Canadian Pacific Railway and the Bank of Montreal did not, of course, enter politics on their own. Their spokesman was Sir Lomer Gouin, fifteen years the Premier of Quebec and now the new federal member for Laurier-Outremont. As "amiably dispassionate as a bank manager," the stout and jowly Gouin had run Quebec like a corporation with himself as chairman of the board of directors. He had absolutely nothing in common with such nationalist firebrands as Henri Bourassa and for this reason had the friendship and the complete confidence of the English-Canadian men of affairs he so closely resembled intellectually.[13]

Mackenzie King knew that Gouin's friends could turn on him as savagely and suddenly as they had on Arthur Meighen. Rumours had already floated about of an attempted coup d'état that would substitute Gouin for the "Boy Leader" – the *Montreal Star*'s derisive nickname for King – at the head of the Liberal party and of the government. For this and other reasons, King's personal preference for *chef* among the Quebec Liberals at Ottawa was Ernest Lapointe, member for Quebec East. The architect of King's leadership campaign in Quebec, Lapointe represented the rural and agrarian opinion of the province and was more willing to accommodate the low-tariff Progressives. But Gouin's insistence that he would accept only the prestigious ministry of Justice spoiled the plan to establish Lapointe as the leading French-Canadian in the cabinet; instead, he was relegated to Marine and Fisheries. The creation of King's first government was thus to be characterized by the same sort of politically prudent compromise that became the hallmark of his twenty-three years as prime minister.[14]

The new administration that was King's New Year's gift to Canada for 1922 was designed with an eye to regional symmetry; ministerial competence had been a consideration, but as usual in Canadian cabinet making it had placed a distant second. Quebec and Ontario were each to have six ministers, Nova Scotia two, and all other provinces but Manitoba, despite their small Liberal contingents, one each. The important ministry of Finance went to seventy-three-year-old W.S. Fielding, who had held the same position in all Liberal cabinets since 1896. Despite his wartime defection to the conscriptionist cause, Fielding had almost defeated King for the party leadership in 1919; two years later he no longer seemed a threat, and the presence of the old Nova Scotian lion would both reassure nervous protectionist businessmen and demonstrate that intraparty wounds were closing over. The other economic departments went to Quebec ministers. Jacques Bureau, a close associate of Lapointe, took charge of Customs and Excise, and James A. Robb, the requisite cabinet spokesman for the English Protestant minority, became Minister of Trade and Commerce. In addition to Gouin and Lapointe, Quebec was also represented by Senator Raoul Dandurand as Minister without Portfolio and by Henri-S. Béland with authority for the small and new departments of Soldiers' Civil Re-establishment and Health.

Never before had Quebec had six members of a cabinet. To avoid giving offence, Nova Scotia had to be bribed with a second portfolio and Ontario provided with positions equal in number, if not in prestige, to those of Quebec. D.D. Mackenzie, a cantankerous old warhorse who had served as acting leader after Laurier's death, became Solicitor General to satisfy the Maritimers. Choosing five others of cabinet quality to accompany himself as Ontario representatives proved more difficult for King. With only twenty members from whom to choose, the chosen were not particularly distinguished. George Graham and Charles Murphy, two Laurier veterans whom King disliked, were appointed to Militia and Defence and the Post Office, departments with good patronage potential for aging party hacks. Murphy not only represented Ontario but was useful as the essential Irish Roman Catholic member of cabinet. The one important department given an Ontarian, Railways and Canals, went to political newcomer W.C. Kennedy, a utility company president and one of the few businessmen the Liberals had been able to elect outside Quebec. To demonstrate his concern for the working class, King chose as his Minister of Labour James Murdock, a former vice-president of the Brotherhood of Railway Trainmen, one of those "legitimate and responsible trade unions" that King encouraged as preferable to the militant industrial unions with their "latent possibilities of evil." Toronto's workers had rejected Murdock at the polls, but King found him a more bourgeois constituency he was able to carry at a by-election. The Ontario slate was completed with T.A. Low, given no department but assigned the important task of resurrecting the Liberal party electorally in that province.[15]

Prince Edward Island's contribution to King's plurality did not go unrewarded. John E. Sinclair, a genial fox farmer who was not considered capable of managing a department, joined the cabinet as

Minister without Portfolio. New Brunswick, however, had "not played fair"; its electors had had the temerity to elect Tories in five of its eleven seats and were thus denied the second place afforded loyal Nova Scotia. A.B. Copp, a Sackville lawyer who kept his convictions to himself to avoid making enemies, saw his silence rewarded with the Secretaryship of State. With only five Liberal members elected west of Ontario, choosing ministers from British Columbia and the Prairie Provinces was both difficult and very simple. King rejected his corporal's guard from the Pacific province and borrowed Dr. J.H. King, provincial minister of Public Works, to perform the same task in Ottawa. Similarly Charles Stewart, the recently defeated Liberal premier of Alberta, came from outside parliament to become Minister of the Interior. Finding a British Columbia riding for Dr. King was easy enough, but Stewart had to be parachuted into a by-election for a Quebec riding, since the voters of Alberta showed no inclination to elect him. The other portfolio regarded as "western," Agriculture, went to W.R. Motherwell, the only Liberal to win a seat in Saskatchewan. As an experienced administrator and a practical farmer, Motherwell was also the only new minister particularly qualified for his job.[16]

The weakness of the cabinet contrasted sharply with the "cabinet of all the talents" assembled by Wilfrid Laurier to inaugurate the previous period of Liberal rule. Only J.H. King, Motherwell, Stewart, Robb, Lapointe, and Dandurand were still ministers after the next election. Kennedy died after just a year in office; Fielding and Gouin, once men of stature, proved spent bullets in the King cabinet. The remaining nine made unremarkable contributions and with one exception soon found oblivion in the Senate or on the bench. That exception was Jacques Bureau, who in 1926 achieved national notoriety for running a scandalously corrupt Customs Department in a country not easily shocked in such matters. Still, Mackenzie King's first cabinet achieved one of his important personal objectives in that its very weakness solidified his own not-too-secure position as party leader. King was careful throughout that supreme authority remained his own. His acceptance of Gouin as Justice Minister was a vacillation, but he refused to bow to direct pressure from banking interests to appoint Walter Mitchell, former Quebec provincial treasurer, to his cabinet. To allow flexibility should he find prominent Progressives ready to be co-opted into his government, King made the unusual request of written promises from five of his older ministers that they would resign should he so request.[17]

There was another reason, however, why the meagre talent of his ministers did not disturb Mackenzie King's self-satisfaction. Just a year earlier, a most unremarkable Republican senator named Warren G.

Harding had become President of the United States by promising Americans "not heroics but healing, not nostrums but normalcy." Mackenzie King knew America well enough to comprehend the appeal of Harding's message. Canadians too were tired of war and post-war turbulence. A return to the pre-war style of limited, inactive government would suit the capabilities and interests of the Liberal party, and such a strategy was not at odds with his character. If this course of action was inconsistent with his book *Industry and Humanity* and with the resolution on "Labour and Industry" in the Liberal platform of 1919, the printed word would have to give way. An unusually perspicacious observer of the Canadian political scene had commented on this trait while King was still Opposition Leader. "Men are often greater," wrote "Domino" in *The Masques of Ottawa*, "in what they say than in what they are able to do."[18]

III

The Fourteenth Parliament was not summoned to Ottawa until March 8, 1922, but the limited legislative program outlined in the Speech from the Throne read by Governor General Lord Byng contained nothing to suggest that the King government had spent its first ten weeks in office charting new directions for the country. In response to war the Canadian government, like those of all the combatant nations, had intervened in social and economic life to an unprecedented degree, and the recession and social unrest of 1919 and 1920 had forced the Union government to continue and to expand its interventionism. The nationalization of the three railways was the most striking evidence of this new direction for government, but it was also visible in the creation of regulatory boards to control food and fuel and to market wheat and in programs with such diverse objectives as the development of technical education and the control of venereal disease. This expansion of the Canadian state was undertaken for pragmatic reasons, not on principle, and it was designed to assure the survival of the largely *laissez-faire* economy of pre-war Canada, not to end it. Nonetheless, "in the attempt to preserve that way of life the government . . . had changed it almost beyond recognition." Because of this, and because of unfavourable public and business reaction to the apparent ineffectiveness of such agencies as the Board of Commerce, the Union government had by 1920 grown tired of interventionism and begun a withdrawal from the marketplace, allowing its regulatory experiments to wither and die. Their Liberal successors at the helm were vague about announcing a precise course for Canada, but their actions indicated that under their control the ship of state would drift backwards in search of the more tranquil seas of the pre-war period.[19]

This desire for a diminished government role was reflected in W.S. Fielding's budget. Unlike Unionist Finance Minister Sir Henry Drayton, whose 1920 and 1921 budgets had attempted to deal with the problem of recession, Fielding possessed no inkling that federal spending and taxation could be used to influence the nation's economic future. A balanced budget was the only target the ancient Minister of Finance thought worth aiming for; he did not consider what effect such a budget might have on the lingering recession. To achieve balance Fielding reduced government expenditures by almost a quarter, from $605 million to $466 million, and doubled the federal sales tax. Despite Liberal campaign promises of "freer" trade, the tariff reductions were minor. What the budget demonstrated, said Fielding in his introduction, was the King government's determination to avoid "any interference of a serious character with the business of the country"[20] (see Table II).

The proposals that followed the budget confirmed this. In response to pressure from organized farmers to re-create the monopolistic marketing board used to market the wheat crop between 1917 and 1919, the government found a way to give the impression of activity when its intention was to do nothing. First the wheat board question was referred to a committee, then to legal advisers who suggested that without specific provincial acquiescence, such a board was illegal in peacetime. Alberta and Saskatchewan were eager to co-operate, and a Canada Wheat Board Act was drafted, debated, and approved by parliament. But the new board was very different from the original. The federal government accepted virtually no responsibility for its operation, refusing to grant the necessary control of railway transportation that had made the original board effective; the burdens of operation were shunted on to the provinces that had agreed to participate. The long delays in committee meant that it was impossible to implement a new board for the 1922 crop, and the provincial governments were unable to find a grain-trading expert prepared to run such an emasculated agency. Government wheat marketing was thus still-born, to the relief of its parliamentary sponsor, Trade and Commerce Minister James Robb, a member of the private grain trade the board was meant to replace.[21]

Railway nationalization was one act of the Union government that could not be undone, however much the Canadian Pacific Railway, the Montreal business community, and its political representatives Sir Lomer Gouin and Rodolphe Lemieux might wish to undo it. The King government hired Sir Henry Thornton, an American railwayman with a British knighthood, to manage the national system, and groped half-heartedly towards a transportation policy that would merge the government roads into an efficient transcontinental system. Unionist acceptance of partial federal responsibility for unemployment was more vulnerable than their railway policy, however, and King and his ministers quickly dissociated themselves from it. The post-war recession, which still dogged the Canadian economy in 1922, had created large numbers of jobless workers. As much to prevent social unrest as from humanity the Meighen government in 1920 began to pay one third of the cost of unemployment relief, a charge normally left to municipalities. In addition, the Employment Service of Canada, established in 1918, co-ordinated a national system of employment offices and provided research and statistical information on the problems of Canadians without work. The Department of Labour had gone so far as to prepare a proposal for a system of unemployment insurance, similar to that enacted in Great Britain in 1911.[22]

The Meighen government never did implement the plan, but in both *Industry and Humanity* and the Liberal platform of 1919, King and his party had promised precisely such national responses to unemployment. Privately King expressed the opinion that unemployment insurance was constitutionally within federal power. "The will," he wrote to the widow of a former Liberal M.P., "is all that is necessary to the finding of the way." In public, however, King cited the BNA Act as an insurmountable obstacle to action, and Canadian workers waited another two decades for unemployment insurance. Worse still for Canadians without work, King used the same constitutional pretext to end federal contributions to municipal relief, despite levels of unemployment estimated to be between 11 and 15 per cent in the winters of 1922-23 and 1923-24. The Employment Service of Canada was one of the victims of Fielding's budget cutting; its placement operations were reduced in scope and its research and statistical work discontinued altogether. By 1927 the Canadian government did not even know how many Canadians were unemployed, let alone what to do with them. A report prepared for the government of Manitoba described Canada's response to the problem of unemployment as "totally inadequate" and warned that "it is a question that must be dealt with sooner or later . . . as in other countries," but the federal government refused to listen. This refusal cost ordinary Canadians dearly during the massive unemployment of the 1930s.[23]

Reviewing the meagre fruits of the parliamentary session, the *Canadian Forum* observed that the new government was "liberal by name and conservative by inclination" and that "singularly little has been accomplished." The editor of the *Canadian Annual Review* disagreed with this evaluation. "The leadership of the Rt. Hon. W.L. Mackenzie King," wrote J. Castell Hopkins, "was not an easy position. . . . With a fluctuating and doubtful support in the Commons, [for King to have] come through without serious mistake or misadventure, was in itself an evidence of administrative skill and political wisdom." King's biographers have echoed this conclusion. One should not, however, exaggerate the skill with which King comported himself between 1922 and 1925, his first chance at the prime ministership. True, he faced a Senate stuffed with Tory appointees who might have blocked some of his promised reforms. But he presented them with no reforms to block, nor did he reform the Senate itself. From the day his first session began, it became obvious that an unexpected defeat in parliament was extremely unlikely.[24]

King's careful cabinet construction had minimized the possibility of defections from Liberal ranks. Sir Lomer Gouin never established himself as a formidable rival to King and diminished in influence until he retired from active politics in 1924. After a decade in the wilderness, most Liberals were not interested in depriving themselves of power and its attendant patronage by internecine warfare over a political principle. The only Liberal back-bencher to challenge party unity was A.R. McMaster, a committed free trader who represented Brome, Quebec; when McMaster challenged the government, his only allies were the Progressive and Labour members. A McMaster motion to require cabinet ministers to divest themselves of company directorships – an idea King had supported while in opposition – was soundly defeated, the Conservatives voting with the King government. The McMaster resolution provided a further demonstration that King's minority position was less vulnerable than it appeared. In combination the other parties outnumbered the government, but the Conservative, Progressive, and Labour members had no common ground from which to launch a co-ordinated attack.[25]

The Progressives made King's task of placating them easier by flatly refusing to become the official opposition. This decision was initially taken by T.A. Crerar and was one of the few decisions he made that was accepted unquestioningly by the Progressive back-benchers. Crerar's explanation was that "our fellows are all inexperienced [and] will not be able to make much of a showing for a year or two," but he was also anxious not to close the door that might lead him and those Progressives of like mind into a reconstructed Liberal party committed to free trade. Some of his followers shared this reason for avoiding the duties of the Opposition; others argued that the very institution of an opposition was "ridiculous," "immoral," and "unintelligent," part of the old way of doing things that the farmers had gone into politics to destroy.[26]

Whatever its motivation, the Progressive abdication was an opportunity for the shattered Conservatives that Arthur Meighen was quick to exploit. Despite their crushing electoral defeat, few Conservatives had thought seriously of replacing Meighen as their leader; a willing back-bencher stepped aside to open an Ontario constituency for him which he won easily in a by-election in January 1922. An expert parliamentarian and an effective debater, Meighen in his performance as Opposition Leader by default justified his party's faith in him. Intellectually brilliant, confident to the point of arrogance, Meighen suffered fools neither gladly nor at all. He considered his opponent to be one of these, and a pompous ass besides, and heaped scorn on the "guesswork government," describing King's cautious attempts to avoid offending significant interest groups as "impotency . . . helplessness . . . drift, sterility and inefficiency." But although Meighen's trenchant speeches scored debating points and earned him the lifelong hatred of his Liberal counterpart, the division of forces in the Commons left him with no real chance to defeat the King government before the life of the Fourteenth Parliament expired. Any Liberal measure the Tories attacked obtained Progressive support, and the Conservatives found themselves voting with the government to defeat motions like McMaster's resolution on ministerial conflict of interest. Meighen's performance did not pass unnoticed, and it restored the morale and the credibility of the Conservative party in all provinces but Quebec. But by demonstrating that the Conservatives and not the Progressives were the real alternative government, Meighen frightened the less radical and less resolute farmer members into overt support of Mackenzie King. Late in 1922 two Ontario Progressives crossed the floor to join the Liberals, providing King with a reliable, if narrow, working majority.[27]

IV

These defections from the Progressive caucus demonstrated the difficulty the farmers' movement was experiencing in its attempt to become an effective political force. Barely a year after its dramatic national electoral breakthrough, it was becoming clear that the rural revolt that had begun with the election of a United Farmer government in Ontario in October, 1919, had reached its apogee in December, 1921, and was now crashing back to earth. The two-year interval had been a period of almost uninterrupted success: a provincial victory for the United Farmers of Alberta, a near-victory in Manitoba, strong showings in Nova Scotia and New Brunswick, and federal by-election triumphs in Alberta, Saskatchewan, Ontario, and New Brunswick. In 1922, however, there was to be only one more achievement to celebrate, the election of a farmers' government in Manitoba in July. For the organized farmers the remainder of the decade brought only the division, defeat, and eventual dissolution of their movement.

The ineffectiveness of the Progressive party in parliament was both a cause and a symptom of the decline in the party's political fortunes. The 1922 session, with its unsatisfactory wheat-marketing legislation, reactionary budget, and minuscule tariff reductions, was to be typical of the failure of the Progressives to achieve their most basic objectives; subsequent sessions produced few accomplishments that could be used to justify re-election. The Progressives lost their parliamentary battles because the sixty-four-member caucus was never forged into an effective instrument within the Commons. Beginning with their unwillingness to accept the responsibility of opposition, the Progressives refused to conform to the accepted techniques of parliament. Although they met in caucus, appointed a party "whip," and outwardly assumed the traditional structure of a party, many Progressives rejected on principle the concept of party discipline. William Irvine, Member for Calgary East, put the case against partyism very clearly in his book *The Farmers in Politics*. The farmers' movement could not win by adopting the same methods it had entered parliament to eradicate. "If the path which leads to party government be taken," he maintained, "little of value will be obtained and the whole democratic fight will have to be fought over again." Members of parliament had no right to allow themselves to be dictated to by any party, concluded the Member for Battle River, Alberta, Henry Spencer; instead, they were "individually answerable to the people who elected them."[28]

Such convictions also led to the rejection, for all practical purposes, of another characteristic of political parties, allegiance to a common leader. "We follow principles rather than leaders" was the way J.J. Morrison liked to put it. This distrust of authority had a practical as well as a philosophical side. The Progressive leaders – "leading Progressives" might be a better term – shared neither the commitment nor the enthusiasm of the back-benchers and the rank and file for independent political action. The decision of the farm movement to enter politics had not been taken by its leadership; instead, it had been *forced* on the leaders by the membership. Unable to stop the "demand for action," officials of farm organizations decided "to guide the movement along sane and rational lines rather than oppose it." Several important farm leaders had been active Liberals. To these men a "sane and rational line" for the Progressive party would have been support for and eventual fusion with a Liberal party purged of its high-tariff wing and rededicated to free trade. T.A. Crerar, Ontario Premier E.C. Drury, and party "whip" J.F. Johnston were not Progressives but "crypto-Liberals" who hoped for Progressive-Liberal co-operation which "would in a few years ripen into fusion."[29]

The unseemly haste of these crypto-Liberals to bring about this fusion produced a wariness among those whom they hoped to lead. This distrust destroyed any authority Crerar hoped to exert and resulted in rejection of his plan to harness the enthusiasm of the agrarian movement to a more conventional party organization. In previous provincial electoral campaigns, farmer candidates had simply borrowed a ready-made political organization from the United Farmers groups. On the national level co-ordination had been provided by the Canadian Council of Agriculture, a federation composed of provincial bodies. Crerar, backed by Premier Drury, proposed that the Progressive party create its own central organization and that it begin a process of "broadening out" to attract followers outside the rural community.

Both proposals drew an immediate hostile reaction from those who had opposed Progressive participation in the Liberal cabinet. The leading spokesmen for the opposition were both influential officers in the farm movement, J.J. Morrison of Ontario and Henry Wise Wood, president of the United Farmers of Alberta. A national organization, they said, would violate the principle of local autonomy; Progressive M.P.s were to be loyal to their constituents, not to a central organization beyond their control. "Broadening out" was even more obnoxious, since it ran counter to Wood's ill-defined but often-expressed theory of "group government," in which each "group" in society was expected to organize as farmers had, and to elect parliamentary representatives who would "cooperate with other groups to secure justice" in a national government. If the farmer group "broadened out" as Crerar suggested, how could such a system function? Instead, they would be simply "building another party machine on the model of the old." Although no clear explanation of how "group government" would function in practice nor even a definition of the "groups" to be represented was ever provided by Wood, Morrison, or their followers, the influence of the theory combined with well-founded suspicions that Crerar and Drury were thinly disguised Liberals to check any plans to reorganize the Progressive party on a broader base. The acrimonious debate over this question seriously damaged the party, particularly in Ontario, where the battle between

Morrison and Drury left both sides with tarnished reputations. Frustrated at the party's unwillingness to behave as he wanted it to, T.A. Crerar resigned as national Progressive leader in November 1922.[30]

Crerar's successor, Robert Forke, was chosen, significantly, as chairman rather than leader of the Progressives, and his attempts at leadership were more conciliatory and less brusque and insensitive. But although he was not as obvious about it, Forke shared Crerar's conviction that the essential purpose of the agrarian revolt was to reform Canadian Liberalism. Because of this, he was no more successful than Crerar in creating a unified party either inside or outside parliament. It quickly became obvious that a significant group of Progressives did not see themselves as "Liberals in a hurry" and were determined to remain true to their conception of the movement's founding principles. Open rupture came in July 1924, when fourteen Progressives rejected the caucus's decision to support the moderate tariff reductions of the King budget; after this, even the pretence of common action was abandoned.

This dissident "Ginger Group," as the rebels were dubbed by journalists, made their defection official. In an open letter to Forke they announced that to preserve "the virility and independence of the political movement of the organized farmers of Canada," they would no longer participate in caucus meetings. The Progressive party, concluded Arthur Darby of the Canadian Council of Agriculture, had become "a queer proposition, lacking leadership, policy and organization . . . without any unity of purpose." Robert Forke, sneered one of his alleged followers, "does not control one Progressive vote other than his own, and he is not always sure about that." The divisions within the parliamentary caucus reflected divisions of purpose within the farm movement itself, divisions that the early political successes and the rhetoric of agrarian unity could no longer obscure. In British Columbia, Quebec, and the Maritimes, Progressivism had established only shallow, insubstantial roots. The two mainstays of agrarian strength, Ontario and the Prairie West, could not always work harmoniously together, and within the Prairies themselves there were philosophical differences that eventually destroyed the federal Progressive party, although farmer provincial governments survived longer in Manitoba and Alberta.[31]

The failure of Progressivism in British Columbia is not difficult to explain; what is remarkable is that farmers' candidates were elected at all. Progressive candidates received 15 per cent of the popular vote and won two seats in 1921; the census of that same year revealed that only 12 per cent of the province's labour force were farmers. This group was subdivided into fruit growers, stock raisers, and dairy producers, all of whom faced different problems. The United Farmers of British Columbia, founded in 1918, never enrolled more than three thousand members and never became as important as organizations like the B.C. Fruit Growers' Association. UFBC conventions refused to endorse the policy of direct political action. In keeping with the Pacific West's "spirit of Conservative insularity," the UFBC never joined the Canadian Council of Agriculture either. Farmers in British Columbia refused to follow the lead of Ontario and the Prairies for the excellent reason that they profoundly disagreed with free trade, the official policy of the CCA. British Columbia agriculture was based not on an export market but on fruit and vegetable production for Canadian domestic consumption; a tariff on imported fruit was critical to their industry. Small wonder the pleas of both Crerar and Wood drew only polite applause at UFBC conventions! The best representatives of British Columbia's interests, countered a provincial farm leader, were men "who would not blindly follow the prairie farmers." Neither British Columbia Progressive survived the general election of 1925, nor was any farmers' candidate elected to the provincial legislature.[32]

Agrarian protest seemed at first to be on a sounder foundation in Nova Scotia and New Brunswick. Agriculture was an important part of the Maritime economy and farmers and their families the largest group in the provincial populations. Inspired by the Ontario victory, United Farmer organizations appeared in both provinces and affiliated with the CCA. In Nova Scotia a hastily created Farmer-Labour party contested the provincial election of July 1920. Six farmers and five labour members became the Opposition to the governing Liberals, reducing provincial Tories to a pair of seats. Three months later the United Farmers of New Brunswick elected six of its candidates, although without concluding an alliance with labour and without unseating the Conservative opposition. When this was combined with a successful federal by-election in the constituency of Victoria-Carleton, future Progressive growth appeared certain.[33]

Like their counterparts in British Columbia, however, Maritime farmers had reservations about a Prairie-dominated Progressive party. The provincial advances proved an exception rather than a portent, for the diversified agricultural economy of the Atlantic provinces prevented the sort of unified opinion on the tariff question that contributed to Progressive support elsewhere. Only one federal Progressive was ever to sit for a Maritime constituency. T.W. Caldwell, president of the UFNB, represented the heart of New Brunswick's potato-exporting area. His constituents sold their crops in an export market and bought fertilizer in a protected domestic market; thus their attitude to the tariff was identical to that of Western wheat growers. In mixed farming districts or in the apple orchards of the Annapolis Valley, however, Progressive candidates lost their deposits. Economic differences aside, Maritime farmers and their leaders resented their lack of influence in both the Canadian Council of Agriculture and the National Progressive party. When the United Farmers of New Brunswick or of Nova Scotia complained about trade or transportation policies, the Progressive response was not to compromise and reshape them better to suit Maritime needs but to send Prairie Progressives east on "a kind of missionary movement to convince Maritimers that what was desired by the West was good for everyone." With the Progressive party viewed as a spokesman for Prairie regional interests, it was the Conservatives who were able to reap the political harvest of Maritime discontent in the mid-twenties, in Ottawa and in the provincial capitals. By 1925, not one Maritime farmer representative was left in the House of Commons or in the New Brunswick or Nova Scotia legislatures, and the membership of the United Farmers had almost vanished.[34]

The Maritimes toyed with the agrarian revolt before rejecting it as the solution to their problems. In Quebec the political side of the farm movement never really got started. Agriculture's problems and the dramatic growth of the UFO prompted the creation of two organizations: les Fermiers unis de Québec and the Union des cultivateurs. Two weeks before the election of 1921, the two organizations merged to enter politics and draft a manifesto considerably less radical than the "Farmers Platform" that formed the basis of the Progressive campaign in the English-speaking provinces. The convention emphatically rejected a motion to declare T.A. Crerar the leader of its candidates; "we are the followers of no leader," said FUQ president A.H. Clement. It is interesting to speculate about the new possibilities for disunity a half-dozen Quebec members would have presented to the Progressives' fractious federal caucus, but the poorly financed and badly organized Quebec campaign was a disaster. The Liberals had no intention of allowing organized farmers to poach in their electoral preserve and made the contradictory accusations that the FUQ candidates were "bolsheviks eager for the class struggle" and "a diversion organized by Meighen to steal votes from the Liberal party." Without journalistic resources to challenge such calumnies, the twenty-one candidates polled only 19 per cent of the vote in their ridings, less than 4 per cent overall. The results convinced the farm association to withdraw from active politics. Premier Taschereau expressed his satisfaction at this decision; Quebec farmers, he told the press, "have refused to follow the agitators and exploiters and have put them in their place."[35]

Weak in the Maritimes and British Columbia, almost non-existent in

Quebec, the Progressive party had no prospect of becoming a national force. The defeat of the Drury government in Ontario in July 1923 left agrarian political protest with only Prairie regionalism for its base. There were many reasons for the defeat, for the Farmer-Labour government had managed to alienate farmers, workers, and most other significant interest groups in Ontario. Attorney General W.E. Raney's determined enforcement of prohibition had angered urban "wets" without satisfying rural "drys"; the lukewarm enforcement of Regulation 17 against the teaching of French by Education Minister R.H. Grant brought the government the wrath of the Orange Lodge without winning it any new friends among Franco-Ontarians. Drury, committed to "broadening out" and aware of his responsibility to govern *all* Ontario, had refused to accept the dictation of the UFO. The United Farmers took their revenge in 1923 by remaining aloof from the campaign, contributing neither the money nor the organizational support that had been critical in 1919.[36]

The parliamentary alliance with labour also hurt the Drury government at the polls. Both workers and farmers saw few common interests between themselves, a discovery that was not unique to Ontario. In the House of Commons the hopes of J.S. Woodsworth and William Irvine for farmer-labour unity quickly dimmed; by 1925 they saw "no bright hopes in the Progressive party so far as labour is concerned." In Nova Scotia the Farmer-Labour opposition broke into "warring cabals" separated by a "virtually unbridgeable chasm." "Labour and farmer elements," the Halifax *Morning Chronicle* explained with some satisfaction, "are as incapable of mixing as sugar and salt. . . . The farmer's a capitalist, and Organized Labour's at war with all capitalists."[37]

The collapse of the Drury government revealed something deeper about rural protest in Ontario, however, and underlined a fundamental difference between Ontario Progressives and those of the Prairies. The UFO had entered politics as the representatives of a rural community that was in retreat before the advance of an urban, industrial society, "a class whose back was pushed to the wall and which was fighting back out of desperation." The most important issue to this class was rural depopulation and the resulting decay of rural social institutions. J.J. Morrison described the demographic decline of agricultural Ontario as "one of the great tragedies of the Anglo-Saxon race." Compared to this question, "tariffs . . . transportation and all other subjects dwindle[d] into insignificance." In Manitoba, Saskatchewan, and Alberta, farmers were unchallenged as the dominant occupational group. On the Prairies the Progressive movement was a way in which an almost monolithic wheat economy still in the process of expansion could unite regional pride and anger and focus it against central Canada's banks, factories, and railways.[38]

But even within the Prairie West, the agrarian movement had internal contradictions. If regionalism served as a lowest common denominator, the Crerar resignation and the emergence of the Ginger Group demonstrated that except for agreement that the "big vested interests" hiding behind the protective tariff were the common enemy, no co-ordinated plan of attack existed. In *The Progressive Party in Canada*, W.L. Morton uses geographic labels to delineate two tendencies within Prairie Progressivism. A moderate "Manitoba" wing, characterized by Crerar and Forke, spoke through George F. Chipman's *Grain Growers' Guide* and J.W. Dafoe's Manitoba *Free Press*. In fundamental agreement with free market capitalism, these men were *laissez-faire* liberals who simply sought to remove the unfair obstacles that national transportation and tariff policies placed in the path of agriculture. Just as they would accept economic orthodoxy, once it could be "reformed," their political goals were also limited. A revitalized low-tariff Liberal party met their specification; if this were impossible, a realignment of parties based on attitudes to the tariff was their alternative solution. "Alberta" Progressives differed in that they rejected entirely the party system and embraced in general terms the group government ideas of Henry Wise Wood. Their economic philosophy also contrasted with that of the Manitobans in that they accepted as necessary and desirable the continuation and expansion of state intervention in the market economy that had begun during wartime. The classic example of Progressive cleavage on this principle came over the compulsory, government-operated wheat board, which most Albertans favoured and most Manitobans opposed, but there was also disagreement about state regulation of banks and other financial institutions.[39]

The inconsistency with describing this division in terms of provincial boundaries is that "Albertan" Progressives were not confined to Alberta nor "Manitoban" Progressives to Manitoba, as Morton himself carefully pointed out. Wood and Crerar disagreed publicly over the theory of group government, yet both men were united in opposition to government intervention into marketing of grain. The similarity between the men who headed the farmers' governments in Alberta and Manitoba is striking. Herbert Greenfield (1921-25) and John Brownlee (1925-34) of Alberta and John Bracken of Manitoba could scarcely be characterized as agrarian radicals in their approach to the role of the state in economic life. "The time has come," announced Greenfield after the UFA's election, "when people must learn there is a limit to paternalism. We have overstepped that limit . . . in recent years and our people have learned to lean unduly on the government." Bracken adhered to the same principle; the first act of both the UFM and the UFA governments was to slash expenditures and dismiss civil servants to balance provincial budgets.[40]

The Alberta-Manitoba division within Progressivism could also be described as one of economic class as much as provincial geography. Most often it was the wealthier, well-established English-Canadian farmers who agreed with C.W. Petersen, editor of the Calgary-based *Farm and Ranch Review*, that "under a system of free enterprise, the efficient generally reap their due reward." The role of the state was to "check abuses" like the protective tariff and monopolistic transportation rates "to afford each citizen a fair opportunity to receive his just reward." To a small farmer struggling to survive – "actual dirt farmer" was how they liked to describe themselves – such a philosophy was cold comfort. These men demanded more than the Progressive leadership was interested in obtaining. "We have in the past erred . . . on the side of conservatism," wrote a disillusioned farmer to the Saskatchewan Grain Growers' Association. "I believe we must resort to more radical measures to really accomplish anything."[41]

Others shared his disappointment with the traditional farm organizations and with the whole political experiment. Membership in the SGGA and the United Farmers of Manitoba and Alberta had soared between 1918 and 1921; by 1924 the number of members declined by half. In Saskatchewan a "grass root organization which would go out and fight for the farmers" appeared to speak for the disaffected and made a special appeal to the operators of small- and medium-sized farms and to immigrant farmers of the northern part of the province. Dismissing direct political action as a failure, the Farmers' Union of Canada, Saskatchewan Section, renounced politics for economic action along the lines used by militant industrial unions. When attempts in 1922 to force the creation of a government wheat board came to nothing, FUC directors L.P. McNamee and Louis C. Brouillette initiated the campaign that created a farmer-owned marketing agency, the Saskatchewan Wheat Pool. By 1924 similar pools existed in Manitoba and Alberta, and an interprovincial Central Selling Agency under the direction of A.J. MacPhail was handling the marketing of half the Western wheat crop.[42]

The success of the Western wheat pools exemplified the farm movements' substitution of practical economic remedies like co-operatism for illusory political solutions to the problems of rural Canada. Building livestock pools, dairy pools, egg and poultry pools absorbed the energies that had gone into political organization, and improved prices for farm products in the mid-twenties seemed to prove that co-operation was a better idea than challenging Liberals or Tories. This development was by no means confined to Manitoba, Saskatchewan, and Alberta. In Quebec the Union catholique des cultivateurs, formed in 1924, was encouraged by its leaders and the provincial Department of Agriculture to concentrate on "the social and economic organization of farmers" rather than on awakening their political consciousness. In Nova Scotia a decentralized system of local co-operatives appeared to "redirect the frustration and animosity of disenchanted Nova Scotians" as the Farmer-Labour party vanished from provincial politics. [43]

Divided by region, class, and ideology, Canada's first significant third party had died as quickly as it had come to life for reasons as complex as those that had given it birth. Crushed in Nova Scotia, New Brunswick, and Ontario, farmers' governments soldiered on in Manitoba and Alberta, proving themselves no more radical than the Liberal government of their sister province, Saskatchewan. The national Progressive party, with renewal of the Crow's Nest Pass rates on grain its only concrete achievement, was reduced to twenty-four M.P.s in 1925 and twenty in 1926, all but two from the Prairie Provinces. The irresistible political force of 1921 was "now gasping and wriggling like a fish stranded on the beach before the receding tide." For Progressivism, said William Irvine, the "flood time has passed and the ebb has set in." [44]

CHAPTER 3

The Empire, America, and the League

I

Caught between the need to maintain his solid base in Quebec and his desire to recapture the Liberals among the Progressives, Mackenzie King sought an issue that could serve to unite the two groups. He found it in their similar isolationist attitudes toward Canada's external relationships, in particular that with Great Britain. Organized farmers and French Canadians alike rejected active membership in the Empire and the notion of a common imperial foreign policy, which they feared might lead Canada without her consent into another European war. Respecting this sentiment made good political sense for King. It fitted in well with the resolution on "Canadian Autonomy" contained in the Liberal platform, was popular with most of his party, and corresponded nicely to his personal opinions on the subject. Although King had expressed his views cautiously while in opposition, others who shared them were more outspoken. Michael Clark, an Alberta Liberal who had become a Progressive, exploded during a 1921 Commons debate on whether Canada should demand an "adequate voice" in shaping imperial foreign policy. "We have certainly had our fill of foreign policy for the last seven years," he thundered. Rather than considering ways to "multiply and complicate the obligations of this country," he suggested, "we can well afford to rest for a while from artificial Empire building."[1]

"Artificial Empire building" was Clark's reference to Sir Robert Borden's attempt to reconcile increased Canadian international autonomy with continued membership in the British Empire. At the Imperial Prime Ministers' Conference of 1917, Borden had moved Resolution IX, which had asserted that as "autonomous nations" the dominions had the "right . . . to an adequate voice in foreign policy," and proposed that "effective arrangements for continuous consultation in all important matters of common Imperial concern" be established at the end of the war. Borden's participation in the 1919 Paris Peace Conference as a member of a British Empire delegation was the first experiment with such "cooperative unified diplomacy." Arthur Meighen accepted Borden's concept, although he was more interested in practical results than in the constitutional form by which they might be obtained. At the Imperial Conference in June 1921, Meighen suggested "regular and . . . continuous conferences" between the dominions and Britain for "determining and clarifying the governing principles of our relations with foreign countries . . . and advancing common interests thereupon." But when the conference got down to specific questions, there was very little agreement on what these "common interests" might be. Meighen pressed for the non-renewal of Britain's Pacific alliance with Japan, arguing that the alliance could damage relations with the United States, with dangerous results for Canada. Prime Ministers W.M. Hughes of Australia and W.F. Massey of New Zealand loudly protested that renewal was essential to their countries' security. In part because of Meighen's persistence, Britain began negotiations that eventually replaced her bilateral treaty with Japan with a four-power Pacific agreement, which included the United States and France.[2]

The 1921 Imperial Conference thus sent contradictory messages. Meighen's apparent success on the Japanese alliance seemed to show that a dominion could play a role in shaping an imperial decision, but the confrontation with Hughes and Massey over the issue revealed that there was no consensus among Britain and the dominions upon which to construct a common foreign policy. Nor were any concrete proposals for "continuous consultation" ever discussed. Borden still believed that it was possible for "all the British self-governing nations" to speak with one voice. "The precise method . . . has not yet been fully determined," he admitted, and there were "difficulties of undoubted gravity," but the problems were "not incapable of solution." A second and final experiment at co-operative imperial diplomacy was made at the conference to limit naval armament that met in Washington in November 1921. Borden himself was appointed as the Canadian member of a unified British Empire delegation. Before the deliberations of the conference had concluded, however, the Meighen government that had appointed him was defeated. Any chance of the realization of Borden's dream of Canada as a senior partner in "a new and greater Imperial Commonwealth" ended when Mackenzie King took over.[3]

II

King saw Canada's external relationships as a domestic problem, for in any international emergency the country could be suddenly and profoundly divided as it had been in 1917. But despite the appeal of anti-imperialism in French Canada, the imperial connection could not be ignored. Over half the population was of British descent, more than a million born in the British Isles, and most of these people had a profound attachment to the Empire and its symbols. Edward, Prince of Wales, had drawn wildly cheering crowds to every royal whistle-stop during his visit to Canada in 1919. To complicate Canada's French-English ambivalence, a growing number of Canadians who belonged to neither group had very definite opinions about international affairs. In April 1922, for example, 10,000 Ukrainian Canadians paraded in Winnipeg to demand that the King government support the creation of an independent Ukraine; in July the Zionist Federation of Canada met in Ottawa to lobby for increased trade with Palestine to help build a Jewish state. A sensitive politician like King respected these constraints on the shaping of external policy, and he made the internal unity of Canada his primary external affairs objective. This was a formula for both domestic peace and political longevity, and King adhered to it with remarkable consistency throughout his prime ministership.[4]

King also had personal attitudes and convictions that contributed to the philosophy that was to dominate Canadian external policy for three decades and to make them the "Age of Mackenzie King." First, because he considered himself Sir Wilfrid Laurier's protégé and desired to emulate his mentor, King consciously followed Laurier's policy of "passive resistance to involvement in British Councils," which had been the dominant motif of Canada's relationship with the Empire until Laurier had been defeated by Borden in 1911. Second, King had a strong distaste for war and a dislike of the military and all things connected with it. True to his view of industrial relations, King felt that international conflict should be resolved by conciliation and compromise. Finally, King recognized that Canada was a North American nation as well as a member of the British Empire–Commonwealth. He understood the importance of the United States to Canada, worked hard to maintain good relations with America, and, in dozens of nauseatingly platitudinous speeches, extolled the century of peace between the two countries as an example that war-torn Europe could follow to its advantage.[5]

King was not, however, a continentalist eager to launch Canada out of a British orbit into an American one. He felt that Canadian society was superior to and distinct from that of the Republic and that the British inheritance was the most important reason for this. During his first month in office, King bent the immigration laws in the case of an American Black who had entered Canada illegally to escape a lynching. King advised the minister responsible "to use his discretion to prevent . . . return to the U.S. – Let the British flag stand for a refuge against lawlessness." King had no desire to sever the British connection. Although he sometimes sought his opinion, King was always careful to define the difference between himself and a radical autonomist like J.S. Ewart, author of *The Independence Papers*, who advocated that Canada become a republic. Ewart, he confided to his diary after a dinner discussion, was "too extreme. Is for separation. I am not, I believe in the Br[itish] Empire as a 'Co-operative Commonwealth!' "[6]

To put his imprimatur on policy making, Mackenzie King served as his own Minister of External Affairs as had Laurier, Borden, and Meighen before him. He set to work at once on reconstructing the tiny department to suit his inclinations, for as far as he was concerned External Affairs was "a Tory hive" that could not be expected to sympathize with him or his policies. The under-secretary, Sir Joseph Pope, was old, sick, and soon to retire. The only serious threat to King's having his own way was Loring Christie, the departmental legal adviser, who had played a critical part in the formation and articulation of the Borden version of the Commonwealth. Had the Conservatives remained in office, Christie might have assumed the under-secretaryship, but King distrusted him from the beginning and ignored him until he resigned in May 1923. King's choice as Pope's replacement was Dr. O.D. Skelton, Professor of Political and Economic Science at Queen's University and the author of a eulogistic two-volume biography of Laurier. Although he shared many of King's attitudes, Skelton was a more convinced autonomist than King, in general disliked and distrusted Britain, and was suspicious of the motives of those in the British Colonial and Foreign offices with whom he had to deal. Skelton remained under-secretary from July 1924 until his death in 1941, and became King's closest (in fact his only close) adviser. He did not formulate King's external policy, but he did serve as "the keeper of King's conscience . . . keeping him up to the mark" if ever his resolution to resist imperial advances seemed to weaken.[7]

To a remarkable degree, however, Canada's external policy between the two world wars was Mackenzie King's personal creation. None of his cabinet colleagues save Ernest Lapointe had any particular interest or expertise in the area, and external affairs were rarely debated in parliament. Although his favourite response to British requests for Canadian participation in imperial adventures was "parliament will decide," King continued his predecessors' tradition of giving it few decisions to make. Between 1920 and 1925 the Commons was in session for 548 days; fewer than 14 were devoted to discussions of *all* aspects of external affairs. [8]

III

On his second day in the Commons as prime minister, Mackenzie King gave notice of the direction his imperial policy would take. Arthur Meighen intended to report on the Imperial Conference of the previous June and asked King to consult the British government as to which documents might be quoted and which, for reasons of security, should be kept confidential. King misconstrued this request as residual colonialism on Meighen's part. "Equality of status among countries of the Empire is a reality," he replied indignantly; "I do not propose to return to colonial status so far as this country is concerned by asking permission to quote from this report." King watched the Progressives and his own back-benchers to gauge their reaction, and what he saw reassured him; his assertion had "pleased our boys immensely," he recorded that night in his diary. [9]

The "boys" were also pleased with Liberal defence policy. Military expenditures were reduced by more than 25 per cent, and the administration of the Navy, Army, and Air Force unified under a new Department of National Defence. What he hoped to create, said Minister of Militia George Graham, was "a well-organized, snappy defence force that will be a credit to Canada without being too expensive." The latter objective was more readily served by Liberal policy than the former. The meagre defence budget proposed by the government was cut still further by the House, not by the Conservative opposition but by Liberals acting with the support of Progressive and Labour members. When they had finished, Canada was spending $1.46 per capita for its "snappy defence force," a fifth of what was spent by the United States. All three services were affected by the cuts, but the Royal Canadian Navy was most severely damaged. Most of its ships were sold, and it was reduced to a reserve nucleus, upon which a navy could presumably be constructed if war made one necessary. The British Admiralty, still hopeful for a truly imperial navy, expressed its disappointment. The RCN, an Admiralty memorandum concluded, "can be of no real assistance in the naval defence of the Empire." That, Britain was soon to learn, was precisely what King intended. [10]

The first lesson was not long in coming. The Chanak Crisis of

September 1922 was the most important single event in Mackenzie King's career. It demonstrated the effectiveness of the techniques of passive resistance and delay as responses to difficult situations, confirmed his distrust of the British government, helped to cement his isolationist Progressive-Quebec alliance, and for good measure fatally wounded Arthur Meighen. Chanak was a place almost no Canadian could have found on a map, just as Sarajevo had been in 1914. Located on the Asian side of the narrow route that links the Mediterranean to the Black Sea, Chanak was defended by a British garrison posted there under the terms of the 1920 Treaty of Sèvres to prevent Turkey from closing the passageway, vital to British interests in the region. The treaty had been forced on the Sultan of Turkey by the Allies, and when the sultan was pushed aside by the revolutionary nationalist government of Mustapha Kemal, its terms were immediately repudiated. By August 1922, the garrison at Chanak found itself facing a Turkish army 80,000 strong and waited with its back to the Dardanelles for the onslaught it was certain would come. The Lloyd George government decided a dramatic show of force was the only possible response. Colonial Secretary Winston Churchill was instructed by the British cabinet to attempt to rally the dominions around the imperial standard. Not all of the many historians of the Chanak affair agree on Churchill's motives, but all are unanimous that the way in which he sought a commitment from the dominions was "a grave violation of the principle . . . that the foreign policy of the Empire must be made in concert." Churchill cabled them at once, without even consulting his own Dominions Department officials, to invite them "to associate themselves with [British] action" and ask "whether they desire to be represented by a contingent." Shortly afterward, before the first cable to Canada had even been decoded and its contents conveyed to Mackenzie King, Churchill issued a statement to the press explaining the British decisions and revealing that an invitation to send troops had gone to Ottawa and the other dominion capitals. This statement, transmitted to Canada by the international wire services, blared in large headlines across Canadian newspapers before the Prime Minister or his cabinet had been officially *informed*, let alone consulted, on the question. "British Lion Calls Cubs to Face the Beast of Asia" was how the Toronto *Globe* featured the dispatch; "Motherland Musters Resources of Empire to Face Turk Menace," echoed the rival Toronto *Star*. On Saturday, September 16, when the story broke, King received his first news of the British invitation when a *Star* reporter demanded to know how his government intended to answer![11]

Nothing the British government could have done or said at this point would have soothed King's justifiable outrage, but subsequent communications from Churchill and Lloyd George exacerbated rather than calmed the situation. The Chanak incident had exposed the glaring inadequacies of the idea of continuous consultation to create a common imperial foreign policy. No mechanisms for consultation existed, and no information on the situation in Turkey had been sent to Canada, although had it been sent it must be doubted that King would have paid much attention to it. Like Laurier, King knew that participation in decision making implied responsibility for carrying out the decisions, something he was anxious to avoid. But British behaviour had clearly gone "well beyond the established forms of inter-imperial diplomacy" in an attempt to influence and inflame public opinion in the dominions and consequently their governments in favour of contributing a contingent. King leapt to the conclusion that Churchill had tried to bully Canada into action without giving the Canadian government time for consideration; the British invitation, he instantly decided, was "drafted designedly to play the imperial game, to test out centralization vs. autonomy as regards to European wars." [12]

King weighed the likely responses of Canadians to the British appeal and decided that after the initial English-Canadian enthusiasm was given a few days to cool, most Canadians would be "against participation in this european [sic] war." The Progressives, he felt certain, would be "opposed almost to a man," and he toyed with the notion of using the incident to bring T.A. Crerar into his cabinet. "No contingent will go without parliament being summoned," he determined. Fortunately for his plan, parliament was not in session, and he did not call its members to Ottawa. The cabinet was not unanimous in support of King's non-response of "parliament will decide," but since both W.S. Fielding, the strongest supporter of sending a contingent, and Ernest Lapointe, the strongest opponent, were in Geneva representing Canada at the League of Nations Assembly, King's decisions quickly became Canada's policy. By September 19, completely forgetting that the beleaguered Chanak garrison still sat beneath the muzzles of Turkish guns, he had convinced himself that the whole incident had been "not unfortunate . . . the best that could have come up" for both domestic and international reasons. [13]

His conclusion was borne out the next day, for Arthur Meighen chose to make a public statement on the crisis in the Near East. Had Meighen been in office, he too surely would have been appalled by the high-handed, insensitive treatment of dominion autonomy, but Meighen knew neither the circumstances nor the exact content of the communications between London and Ottawa. Thus he interpreted King's response to the situation at Chanak as "a selfish, halting exhibition of procrastination and impotency," and in a speech to a Conservative businessmen's club in Toronto he made plain his dissatisfaction. King was acting as if "Great Britain were not our good partner and friend but our chief antagonist"; Britain had not asked for troops, but "merely sought a declaration of solidarity. . . . When Britain's message came then Canada should have said 'Ready, aye ready; we stand by you.' " Meighen's declaration expressed the feelings of many English Canadians, and his Toronto audience stood to roar out its approval. To French Canadians, however, his bold declaration simply reopened the wounds of conscription – with grave political consequences in Quebec for Meighen and his party. The Chanak Crisis exaggerated the differences between Meighen and King with regard to Canada's role in the Empire. Meighen was no supine colonial, ready to follow British leadership blindly over the precipice of war; even his much-quoted "Ready, aye ready" had been deliberately taken from a speech by Sir Wilfrid Laurier on Canada's entry into the World War. His ill-considered statement was used thereafter to label him as a "jingo-Tory-militarist" ready without question to abandon Canada's interests and her young men to British imperialism.[14]

King's policy had little if any effect on the resolution of the Near Eastern crisis. The attack on Chanak never came, and the control of the straits was eventually resolved without war. Had the garrison been overrun and had a general conflict ensued, King might have been unable to continue his policy of no commitments; because there was no need for military action, King avoided a domestic crisis and saw the wisdom of his strategy confirmed. This was not enough justification for him, however. He insisted, without evidence, on giving his policy designed for domestic tranquillity the credit for achieving international peace as well. Canada's attitude, he later told parliament, "had a very wholesome and restraining effect at a very critical moment." To his diary he was less restrained in his self-praise. "I have been able," he wrote, "to render the cause of peace in the world a lasting service." The battle of telegrams over Chanak had so poisoned Anglo-Canadian relations that, for practical purposes, any attempt at creating a common imperial foreign policy was dead. The dominions were not invited to the Lausanne Conference to participate in the making of a new peace with Turkey, either as individuals or as part of a British Empire delegation. Lord Curzon, the British Foreign Secretary, did not want his hands tied by a group of dominion politicians untrained in the intricacies of diplomacy, and Mackenzie King and his colleagues were privately delighted not to be summoned to Switzerland. King "had expected an invitation and was dreading the refusal it might be necessary to send"; now he could demonstrate Britain's unwillingness to consult Canada without again revealing his own reluctance to be consulted.[15]

The Imperial Conference of October and November 1923 permitted King no such happy luxury of equivocation. The conference was his first, and he prepared for it with characteristic attention to detail. Steamship reservations were made for the large Canadian delegation; King ignored imperialist critics like the editor of the Shelburne, Nova Scotia, *Gazette*, who suggested that he travel on a tiny Royal Canadian Navy trawler since this "would speak more eloquently for Canada's share in Empire solidarity" than anything he could say at the conference itself. The Prime Minister headed the Canadian delegation, accompanied by the Ministers of Justice and National Defence, Sir Lomer Gouin and George P. Graham. Nine senior civil servants went along to take part in specialized discussions, and two additional appointments were made to the delegation at King's specific request. J.W. Dafoe, editor of the Manitoba *Free Press*, was invited to London to ensure Canadian newspapers received a steady flow of dispatches sympathetic to the Liberal position on the Empire, and O.D. Skelton was hired as a special assistant to prepare memoranda and to advise King during the conference. Skelton's background papers provided King with the historical justification he wanted to help him to resist the attempts at imperial centralization he was certain would come in London. The Borden-Meighen version of a consultative, co-operative Empire, argued Skelton, had been an aberration, "a direct reversal of the whole of Dominion development in the past half century." King's task at the conference "was to see that the effects of this aberration were removed."[16]

The conference went on for more than six weeks, but King never wavered in his determination to challenge any statement that hinted, however vaguely, at a centralized Empire. In every address he made, King repeated the same general arguments at tiresome length. There would be no co-ordination of naval or air defence; Canada would decide her own defence policies and the other dominions should do the same. Canada would make no advance commitments to support British external policies; there would be no "blank cheque" given to Britain "to be filled in at a moment's notice without reference to a particular situation that might arise." Not only would there be no "continuous consultation" established, but the Imperial Conference could not be regarded as an "Imperial Cabinet" for such purposes. "We have no right," said King on several occasions, "to regard ourselves as a Cabinet shaping policy for the British Empire." The Empire was not "one and indivisible," as Australia's new prime minister, Stanley Bruce, liked to claim, but "very distinctly divisible . . . geographically, racially, politically and in a thousand ways. . . ." Each of those divisions had to decide for itself what its attitude and contribution to any international crisis should be. This did not mean that Canada would *refuse* to support Britain. King expressed his certainty that "if a great and clear call of duty comes," as it had in 1914, "Canada will respond": on "lesser issues" like Chanak, however, Britain had best not count on bellicose resolutions or expeditionary forces from her senior dominion as long as his government was in power. King summed up his position in one of those infuriating, ambiguous statements for which he had a special gift. "Our attitude is not one of unconditional isolation," he said, "nor is it one of unconditional intervention."[17]

King was quietly seconded by the delegates of the Irish Free State; otherwise he stood alone. The most vehement opposition he encountered came from Bruce of Australia and W.F. Massey of New Zealand. Geography gave them a much greater sensitivity to questions of naval security and made them outspoken believers in a co-ordinated approach to imperial defence. The attitude of the British government was equivocal. Foreign Secretary Lord Curzon, the senior British representative, made stirring speeches about imperial unity and the military contribution the colonies could make to British power and world influence, but he was not in the least interested in making Canada, Australia, New Zealand, South Africa, and the Irish Free State overseas partners in the running of his Foreign Office. The consultative machinery demanded in Borden's Resolution IX was to Curzon an unwanted complication; Mackenzie King's version of the Empire meant that no unwanted dominion noses would be poked into Foreign Office business. Curzon locked horns verbally with King in discussion and described him in private as "obstinate, tiresome and stupid," but "in practical terms," concludes Philip Wigley, "they were far closer to each other than they ever realized, with neither wanting essentially to restrict his freedom of action." The decentralized British Empire that emerged from the Imperial Conference of 1923 was satisfactory to both of them. The final report committed the member-nations to virtually nothing. The section on defence was cautious and imprecise, and a special section on treaty making supported one of King's constitutional contentions, that treaties concerning only one dominion did not need to be approved and signed by Britain as representative of the Empire. At King's specific request the report concluded with the statement that all "views . . . recorded above are necessarily subject to the action of the Governments and Parliaments of the various portions of the Empire."[18]

The Imperial Conference of 1923 was the most significant step in the transformation of the British Empire into a looser commonwealth, not for what it did but "by virtue of the things it declined to do."

Afterwards the notion of a common imperial foreign policy was never again on the agenda. Borden's vision of Canada's role in the Empire, writes John Holmes, was "unsound but imaginative," while King's was "sound but unimaginative"; Borden's vision died in 1923 "not because it was ignoble or reactionary, but because it was quite impractical." Mackenzie King never understood that the British government, the Foreign Office in particular, had been cool toward the idea of consultation with the dominions all along. King was convinced that the British intention was to centralize the Empire and that the 1923 conference was "one of the great personal triumphs of his career," in which he "beat off the attack [of the British government] almost single handed." The ease and the completeness of his victory, however, suggest that "Mackenzie King was slaying imperial paper tigers."[19]

The Locarno Treaty of 1925 illustrates the separation of the foreign policies of Britain and the dominions. Under its provisions, Britain guaranteed to maintain militarily the boundaries of France, Belgium, and Germany. Canada was kept informed of the negotiations but neither asked for nor was offered an opportunity to participate in them. King made no attempt to influence the British government or to advise it of Canada's opinion. British Foreign Secretary Austen Chamberlain had inserted into the Treaty of Guarantee a clause that specifically exempted any dominion from obligation "unless the government of such dominion . . . signifies its acceptance thereof." Canada's response was to thank British statesmen for their "unceasing striving for peace and reconciliation" but to refuse politely any support for the Locarno guarantees. As further proof that a common imperial foreign policy was a dead issue, there was no partisan division within parliament over Locarno. The Conservatives made no attempt to assert a Canadian right to participation or consultation, nor did they suggest that Canada make a contribution in the event Britain had to enforce her guarantee. Conservative and Liberal conceptions of Canadian autonomy, it seemed, had become almost identical.[20]

The Imperial Conference that met in the autumn of 1926 began the process of giving legal form to the *de facto* decentralization that had already taken place. Mackenzie King no longer led the autonomists. One of the Irish delegates commented privately that King had " 'disimproved' since 1923 – gone fat and American and self-complacent. The onus of the 'status push' " now fell on the Irish Free State and on South Africa. South African prime minister J.B.M. Hertzog went so far as to threaten secession if the "independent national status" of his country were not officially recognized. King was nervous about the term "independent," for it violated his concept of the Commonwealth and threatened to have political repercussions among English Canadians who felt attached to the Empire. He found himself cast as the "umpire of the conference," mediating between South Africa and the Irish Free State, who really wanted its dissolution, and Australia and New Zealand, who worried that decentralization had already gone too far. The prime ministers met in a committee chaired by Lord Balfour, in which King is credited with persuading Hertzog that "autonomous" was as good a word as "independent." That was the word used in the famous Balfour Report, which defined Britain and the dominions as "autonomous Communities within the British Empire, equal in status, in no way subordinate to one another in any aspect of their domestic or external affairs, though united by a common allegiance to the Crown, and freely associated as members of the British Commonwealth of Nations." Britain agreed that the dominions had the right to establish their own diplomatic representation abroad, and to the removal of "anomalies": the British power to disallow or reserve dominion legislation and to regulate dominion shipping, the appeal of dominion cases to the Privy Council, and the dual role of the governor general as the representative of both the monarch and the British government.[21]

Over the next five years these things were largely accomplished. Between 1927 and 1929 Canada established legations in three foreign capitals: Washington, Paris, and Tokyo. In 1928 Britain appointed a High Commissioner to Ottawa, so that the governor general could serve exclusively as head of state. The following year Ernest Lapointe negotiated for Canada at the Conference on the Operation of Dominion Legislation, at which Britain renounced the powers of disallowance and reservation and promised to amend the Merchant Shipping Act and the Colonial Laws Validity Act. With the exception of amendments to the British North America Act and appeals to the Judicial Committee of the Privy Council – matters that Canada's political leaders *chose* to leave in British hands – the Statute of Westminster in 1931 completed the development of Canada's autonomous dominion status.[22]

IV

Canada's relationship with the United States was as important as that with Britain, in practical if not in sentimental terms. During the nineteenth century Anglo-American hostility had made war between Canada and the United States a constant threat, but by the 1920s such a war was usually described as "unthinkable." Soldiers on both sides of the border still thought about it: Canada's Defence Plan No. 1 called for the use of "flying columns" to capture "key invasion bases" such as Seattle and Minneapolis in order to stall an American drive northward until the British Army arrived; the U.S. Army's Strategic Plan Red hypothesized a conquest of Canada, after which the "territory gained . . . will become states and territories of the Union [and] the Dominion government will be abolished." Not even the soldiers, however, took these plans very seriously. The biggest post-war problem Canada faced with the United States was persuading America that she was a mature nation, an independent actor on the international stage. Canadian-American relations had always been conducted through the British Embassy in Washington, a system that functioned well enough to satisfy all three parties until the Great War made Anglo-American relations so complicated and time consuming that Canadians began to complain that their interests were no longer being adequately represented. After considerable negotiation among Ottawa, Washington, and London, the Borden government announced in 1920 that a separate Canadian minister would be appointed. In keeping with the Borden notion of imperial unity, the new minister would serve in the additional capacity of second-in-command of the British Embassy and "also speak as a representative of the Empire though primarily as a Canadian." Such an appointment was not made before the Conservatives were defeated.[23]

Mackenzie King was critical of the ambivalent position of the Canadian representative outlined in the Conservative proposal. Better, he suggested, to "let British diplomatists manage British affairs and let us manage our own affairs." Because of this it was expected that King would act quickly to establish separate Canadian representation in Washington. Instead, because public opinion and his cabinet were divided on the matter, he waited five years to do so. But he did want the American government to notice Canada and to begin to accept her new status. For this reason, Mackenzie King's first venture in diplomacy was a personal trip to Washington in July 1922. There were several problems in need of resolution: difficulties in enforcing Prohibition, destructive American economic nationalism as expressed in the Fordney-McCumber tariff, and illegal water diversions from Lake Michigan by the municipal government of Chicago. None of these thorny subjects was on King's agenda. The ostensible purpose for the journey was to revise the Anglo-American Rush-Bagot agreement of 1817, which limited naval armament on the Great Lakes, in the light of twentieth-century changes in naval technology. Such a revision was "as unobjectionable as motherhood," and Americans were puzzled as to why King had chosen to request it. The *New York Times* pointed out that "there has been no suggestion formally from this [Harding]

Administration that modification was considered necessary." No new agreement ever came about from the visit, but it was the visit itself that interested King. He was able to drop in on Secretary of State Charles Evans Hughes, to chat with President Harding, and to issue a statement to the press that Canadian-American friendship was "an object lesson to the continents of Europe and Asia of New World methods in the maintenance of international peace." The trip was also an example of what would become King's favourite technique for conducting Canadian-American relations; during his twenty-three years as prime minister he was to make twenty-four such visits for "summit diplomacy" with Presidents Coolidge, Roosevelt, and Truman.[24]

The real and symbolic significance that King attached to the United States in Canada's external policy was demonstrated again in March 1923 when he chose Washington as the place to establish a historic precedent, the signing of a treaty between a dominion and a foreign state without the co-signature of a representative of the British government. Canada had been negotiating her own commercial agreements with other countries since 1907, but the treaty had always been signed by the British ambassador to the country concerned. The notion of ending this practice was not original to King but had been considered in 1919 by Sir John Douglas Hazen, who had concluded two fisheries treaties with the United States as the representative of the Union government. Fish were also the subject four years later when Mackenzie King and Ernest Lapointe resolved to remove the "badge of 'colonialism.' " Over the objections of the British ambassador, but with the acquiesence of the British government, the Pacific Halibut Fisheries Treaty was signed for the United States by Charles Evans Hughes and for Canada by Minister of Marine and Fisheries Lapointe only. The procedure used on the occasion was subsequently endorsed by an Imperial Conference and became standard practice for all dominions. For Canada the Halibut Treaty, despite its mundane subject, had the additional significance of "securing from the United States . . . recognition of its international status." Hughes is alleged to have said: ". . . this may turn out to be a very significant day in the history of relations between Canada and the United States." Only the passage of time has made this apparent, for it was not recognized as such then. The discussion of the treaty in the American Senate contained no hint of recognition of Canada and described it as a "convention between the United States and Great Britain," and in Canada both autonomist and imperialist newspapers ignored it editorially. The most extensive news coverage was received in the Maritimes and in British Columbia, where readers were interested more by the piscatorial implications than the constitutional precedent.[25]

In February 1927 Washington was chosen for a second milestone in Canada's development as an international person when Vincent Massey was appointed Minister to the United States, the first direct Canadian representative in any foreign capital. Massey was to represent only Canada; the complicated formula in which the Canadian minister would also run the British Embassy in the absence of the ambassador was forgotten. The opening of a legation was controversial. The Conservatives criticized it as "separation . . . the end of our connection with the Empire," and Massey received a threat on his life from an imperialist who blamed him for "a parting of the ways too serious to contemplate." To placate such sentiment, the terms "Minister" and "Legation" were used instead of "Ambassador" and "Embassy." Massey was chosen in part for his ostentatious anglophilia – he and his wife, Alice, went to England to purchase all the furnishings for the new Canadian Legation House. He worked closely with British Ambassador Sir Esme Howard, creating in practice the sort of co-operation that Borden had once envisaged.[26]

Americans, Massey discovered, were mystified by the workings of the Commonwealth and remarkably ignorant about their northern neighbour. At the formal presentation of his credentials he was asked by President Coolidge if Toronto was anywhere near Lake Ontario! Coolidge had initially dismissed the establishment of a United States legation in Ottawa, arguing that there would be nothing for it to do. Massey's arrival in Washington, however, forced the appointment of William Phillips as the first American minister to Canada in July 1927. Phillips was a career diplomat who brought experience and prestige to his post until he left it in 1929; his successors, party faithful with "no discernible qualifications for the position," were a better indication of how lightly the White House took the new legation in Ottawa. The Canadian-American relationship, it seemed, was much more important to Canada than to the United States. Governor General Lord Willingdon made a state visit to Washington in November 1927, and in keeping with the Balfour Report, he was "received with the honours accorded by custom to a sovereign." Ottawa was eager for a reciprocal visit from a president, but neither Calvin Coolidge nor Herbert Hoover was sufficiently interested to find the time to come.[27]

The existence of the two legations, however, made it possible for the Canadian government to remind the United States gently that Canada was no longer a British colony to be dealt with through London. When an over-zealous American Coast Guard captain chased and sank the Canadian rum-running ship *I'm Alone*, the American government at first contacted the British embassy before being firmly redirected to the Canadian legation. In 1928 when American Secretary of State F.B. Kellogg and French Foreign Minister Aristide Briand invited all nations to join America and France in renouncing war as a means to settle international disputes, the American State Department assumed that Britain would act on behalf of the dominions. Mackenzie King was determined that he himself would go to Paris to sign the Kellogg-Briand Pact for Canada as a means of advertising dominion autonomy to the world and – because no machinery was to be set up to enforce the agreement – to endorse a worthy ideal without any practical cost. Hints were relayed to the State Department through the American legation, and soon King was able to report in his diary "the presentation by the U.S. Minister in person to me at my office of the invitation of the U.S. to Canada to become a party to the multi-lateral peace pact." It was, he noted with justifiable satisfaction, "the high water mark of achievement and recognition thus far of Canadian nationality."[28]

Looking backward through King's long prime ministership one sees Canada grow more distant from Great Britain and closer to the United States: diplomatically, economically, and culturally. Historians like W.L. Morton, who disapprove of this change, argue that King caused it, that his nationalism was a negative, destructive force that eroded the British connection and led Canada down the fork in the road that ended in Americanization, "the present condition of Canada in which the country is so irradiated by the American presence that it sickens and threatens to dissolve in cancerous slime." Whatever attitude one takes to the decline of the British and the increase of the American influence in Canadian life, Mackenzie King has received both more credit and more blame than he deserves. While it is true that he advocated a close and cordial Canadian-American relationship, so did virtually every other Canadian who expressed an opinion on the subject. Canadians saw no need to make a choice between the British Empire and the United States, for they saw "no genuine conflict between imperial ties and friendship with the Americans."[29]

Canadian-American friendship, far from weakening the Empire, was seen as a medium through which Britain and America could be induced to co-operate. This notion of Canada as the "linchpin" in Anglo-American amity was not new. Borden had spoken of it before 1914, and Loring Christie had written that Canada was "destined to be . . . mediator between the two great branches of the English-speaking world." Unity of action by "the three great democracies, Great Britain, Canada, and the United States," would save civilization from the "animalism and savagery and crime [of] the Oriental group, the Slav-German group and the Latin-American group." Mackenzie King rejected the militaristic implications of such statements but accepted the general premise. He believed that Canadian-American friendship would save the world through the shining example of peace that it offered. King never tired of delivering addresses about the "century of peace" in North America and the "unfortified line running between two great countries," conveniently forgetting how many Anglo-American quarrels had come within a hair's breadth of war.[30]

V

The invaluable lesson Canadian-American harmony offered to the world was repeated in Mackenzie King's address to the League of Nations Assembly in Geneva in 1928. This platitude was not unique to King but had been the essence of the speeches to the assembly of every Canadian delegation, Conservative as well as Liberal, since the League's founding at the end of the war. Delegates from the fifty member-states had grown so accustomed to hearing about the "three thousand miles of undefended frontier" that such self-righteous moralizing was known colloquially as "the Canadian speech." This conviction that North America offered the solutions and Europe caused the problems had been passionately voiced by Newton Rowell at the first assembly in 1920: "It was European statesmen, European policies and European ambitions that drenched the world in blood. . . . Fifty thousand Canadian soldiers under the soil of France and Flanders is what Canada has paid for European statesmanship."[31]

Fear of becoming embroiled in another European war conditioned Canadian governments to caution about the League of Nations. They were especially nervous about Article X of the League Covenant, which required member-states "to respect and preserve as against external aggression the territorial integrity and existing political independence of all members." This promise of collective security obviously might call for economic or military action by League members to sanction an aggressor, and neither Canada nor the United States was prepared to take such action. America took what seemed the most reasonable course and refused to accept the Covenant and join the League. Canada's position was more complicated. A seat in the League assembly was a tangible sign of the more independent status Canada sought; J.W. Dafoe described it as "a simply invaluable argument at the disposal of those who urge the opinion that the Dominions have obtained sovereign power." The Canadian solution was to join the League and to try to convince the membership to delete Article X from the Covenant. At the assemblies of 1920 and 1921, delegates appointed by the Meighen government proposed motions to this effect, arguing that the United States might be persuaded to enter the League if Article X were erased. Both motions received very little support.[32]

The delegates sent to Geneva by the King government in 1922 were given the same strategic objective but were instructed to change their tactics. First Delegate W.S. Fielding tried, not to strike Article X, but to amend it to give a country the right to opt out of the enforcement of collective security if it so decided. This tack was only slightly more successful; Persia accused Canada of trying to turn the League into "a charitable and public health organization," and the amendment fell far short of the unanimous approval it required to pass. Undaunted, the Canadians returned in 1923 to seek an "interpretation" of Article X that would reflect Canada's desires. As Senator J.P.B. Casgrain observed sarcastically, "whenever lawyers desire to insert an interpretation clause, the purpose is to make the document say something other than what people read in it." This was precisely the Canadian intention. The interpretation as finally worded was not as all-encompassing as Canada desired, but it contained in slightly different words the familiar "parliament will decide" formula King so frequently utilized. The interpretation came within one vote of unanimity. Although technically a defeat for Canada, in practical effect she had at last won her case. If collective security as described in Article X was not destroyed, it was seriously undermined.[33]

Those nations that supported Article X tried to reinvigorate it with the Protocol for the Pacific Settlement of International Disputes, presented to the assembly in 1924. This "Geneva Protocol," as it was called, provided for compulsory arbitration to settle disputes. Any state that went to war instead of to arbitration was to be dealt with by economic or military sanctions. Canadian delegate Senator Raoul Dandurand supported the first part of the proposal but opposed the second. Canada and the United States had used arbitration to preserve "a hundred years of peace" in North America, but Canadians were not willing to go to war to persuade European countries to do likewise. Collective security, Dandurand observed, was like fire insurance. Canada should not be called upon to pay the heavy premium of military sanctions because she faced little risk to her property. "We live," he continued, "in a fire-proof house, far from inflammable materials." The protocol was passed by the League assembly, but the King government refused to adhere to it and was supported in its action by the opposition parties. Canadian rejection alone did not seal the fate of the protocol – Britain's abrupt shift from support to opposition did that – but in the frustration of all attempts to establish an effective system of collective security within the League, Canada played a role out of proportion to her international significance. As Senator

W.A. Griesbach, a lonely defender of Article X, later described it, "of all the members of the League Canada was the first to . . . have torpedoed the organization, or, to use another metaphor, to have robbed it of any teeth that it had."[34]

After 1925, with the threat that Canada might be dragooned into military or economic sanctions safely passed, Canadians took a more active role in League affairs. In his note rejecting the Geneva Protocol, Mackenzie King had promised "whole-hearted support to the League of Nations and particularly to its work of conciliation, cooperation, and publicity"; anything, in other words, that had no potential military or economic cost. In 1925 Dandurand was chosen President of the Assembly, and in 1927 Canada ran for and was elected to a three-year term on the League council. Canadians were prominent in the League's International Labour Organization and in the forefront of League attempts to halt white slavery and the international drug traffic.[35]

These were the only League programs that most Canadians were prepared to accept. Few spokesmen appeared during the 1920s to argue the case for an activist League with an effective system of collective security. A League of Nations Society attempted to educate Canadians about the League's purposes, but even within the society's ranks there was disagreement about what those purposes should be. Sir Robert Borden, its first president, found that most people regarded goings on at Geneva with "indifference" or with "an extraordinarily apathetic attitude." There was, however, vocal criticism of the League from both autonomists and imperialists. The autonomists, men like J.S. Ewart and O.D. Skelton, rejected a powerful world organization with the same skittish colonialism with which they fended off the British Empire. Imperialists like J.B. Maclean and J.S. Willison rejected the League as useless "uplift"; to them the only way Canada could assure her security in the "lions' jungle" of international politics was to help make Britain strong enough to "knock the block off any nation that talks war." Most cynical of all about the League was the business newspaper the *Financial Post*. "It is only the Borden–[Sir George] Foster–Rowell idealists and the Toronto *Star* communists who have any use for it in Canada," commented the *Post*'s editor. An unstable Europe was in Canada's interest, a business opportunity not to be overlooked: "We should positively avoid involvement in European . . . political complications; sell them all we can, but be sure of our payments. . . . In the more distant view, will not these unsettlements in Europe mean more agricultural and industrial settlers and more European capital in Canada?"[36]

VI

As he prepared to go to Paris to sign the Kellogg-Briand Pact, Mackenzie King listed with pride the accomplishments of the 1920s: autonomy within the Empire, representation in Tokyo, Paris, and Washington, a seat in the League of Nations and a place on the council. "I am convinced," he wrote in his diary, "the period of my administration will live in this particular as an epoch in the history of Canada that was formative and memorable." There was "a new Canada emerging" on the international stage. Despite these worthy achievements, however, Canada had done little with this "new station" in the world but proclaim it. Canadian external relations had a new form but very little substance, apart from a determination to avoid any and all international commitments. Canadian editors often contrasted Canadian and American external policies, criticizing the United States for failing to "take more responsibility in world affairs." A young history professor at the University of Saskatchewan, an exponent of the principle of collective security, pointed out the hypocrisy of such self-satisfaction. "No candid observer of the Canadian scene," protested Frank Underhill, "can escape the conclusion that the chief desire of our people and our leaders since 1919 has been to escape responsibilities. . . . We talk of national autonomy when we really mean national isolation. We prate of our desire for a place in the world, but when we say peace we really again mean isolation. . . . Our attitude to the world is exactly that of our American cousins."[37]

CHAPTER 4

An End to Idealism

I

The collapse of international idealism evident in the attitude of Canadians toward the League of Nations mirrored a similar decline in enthusiasm for projects of social reform within Canada. The *Canadian Forum* observed sadly that just as Canadians "remain unmoved by troubles that threaten the peace of the world, [they] maintain a cold detachment towards questions of social justice." This "cold detachment" signalled the end of an era. For three decades the quest for social justice had been a constant intellectual current, but in the 1920s what had been a torrent slowed to a trickle.[1]

Though such secular ideas as socialism had gained a small audience, the ideological infrastructure of an "Age of Reform" between 1890 and 1920 was religious. Protestant churches in Britain, the United States, and Canada were all influenced to some degree by the Social Gospel. More a tendency than a specific dogma, the Social Gospel attempted to apply the principles of Christianity to the problems of industrial capitalism. Although the roots of the Social Gospel lay deep within Christianity, the visible misery produced by rapid industrialization, urbanization, and immigration accounted for its spreading influence. Congregations raised their voices against "those dark Satanic mills," and vowed, in the Canadian adaptation of Blake's famous hymn, "not to cease from mental fight/Till we have built Jerusalem/within our broad and bounteous land." The Social Gospel had a Roman Catholic counterpart, which drew its inspiration from Pope Leo XIII's encyclical *Rerum Novarum*. The influence of this social Catholicism is clear in the thought of French-Canadian intellectuals like Henri Bourassa, Olivar Asselin, and Father Joseph-Papin Archambault. Language and denomination were strong barriers to common action, however, and according to Richard Allen, "the two movements ran on parallel but largely unconnected lines."[2]

58

The Social Gospel turned the emphasis of Christianity from the spiritual to the temporal and from the individual to the collectivity. Jesus, the new theology argued, was concerned with more than men's souls. He had also been "the greatest social reformer the world has ever seen." To a Social Gospeller it was not enough that the church promise, in the mocking phrase of an irreverent labour song, "pie in the sky when you die" to the working man. It had the responsibility of providing him and his family with a better life here on earth. The Social Gospel placed a religious seal of approval on social and economic reforms. Ministers and active church members became the most important source for the leadership of movements dedicated to a variety of causes ranging from the abolition of "drink" to urban sanitation. As Rev. C.W. Gordon, Canada's best-known Presbyterian, put it, in the "New State" built on Social Gospel principles, "community interest will be the prime consideration . . . no man or corporation, however big, shall spoil the good of the community." Democratic government would make sure they did not. A willingness to use the state as a vehicle for reform marked another departure from individualism, and by 1920 an impressive proportion of the reform programme had been enacted by the federal government, the provinces, and the municipalities.[3]

In the early 1920s the Social Gospel went into retreat, and the reform impulse it had helped to generate began to wane. Mackenzie King recognized the new mood. His own prescription for a society that would "substitute faith for fear," *Industry and Humanity*, was now out of temper with the times, and it gathered dust even on his own bookshelf. It was a commonplace to blame the end of idealism on the searing experience of the Great War. Fought – so reformers had argued – to make the world "safe for democracy" and Canada "a home fit for heroes" to which to return, the war ended with both objectives far from view. Reformers who "talked about the war to end war" and who "earnestly believed they were fighting the last great battle" found it difficult to maintain their enthusiasm when neither prophecy proved correct. Less dramatic and more specific reasons for the decline of the Social Gospel suggest themselves, however. The rapid demise of the Progressive party both resulted from and contributed to this decline in Canada. Most of the Progressive leaders – Wood, Irvine, Drury, E.A. Partridge – professed religious inspiration and were active in Social Gospel causes. The fragmentation and defeat of the federal and Ontario Progressives thus represented a broader failure of hopes to reform society as well.[4]

The Social Gospel also lost influence in religious circles themselves. Those individuals who remained dedicated to reform causes complained of an "appalling amount of apathy" when canvassing church members for financial or even moral support. Canadian Christians, it seemed, were "weary of well-doing." In French Canada, where social Catholicism had never been a dominant influence, social reform lagged behind concern about other problems. In December 1923 Cardinal Bégin issued a pastoral letter warning against "lascivious modern dances such as the 'Tango,' the 'Fox-Trot,' the 'Turkey-Trot' [as well as] the 'Polka,' the 'Waltz,' and others, which are commonly danced lasciviously now." The enduring faith of ordinary Catholics in tried-and-true methods of salvation was revealed in the amazing popularity of Montreal's beloved Brother André, né Alfred Bessette. Regardless of language, race, or social station, Catholics were drawn to André's increasingly famous shrine on the slope of Mount Royal, the Oratoire Saint-Joseph, dedicated to the patron saint of the artisans. Its construction began in 1916 and, funded mainly by small donations, continued apace through the twenties. Here, alleged miracles of healing were performed through direct intercession on behalf of individuals by Brother André; he received thirty thousand letters a year from people too sick to be cured by the men of science, or too poor to afford to have them try.[5]

Among Protestants the Anglicans, last to be converted to social activism, were the first to fall away; the Church of England reasserted the paramountcy of individual over social salvation, and refused its support for such reform causes as unemployment insurance. There was a renewed emphasis on liturgy, which a frustrated reformer described as "obviously sincere and deeply felt, but so utterly inadequate" as a response to the problems of post-war Canada. The attention of Anglican bishops was distracted by peripheral issues, like the obscure controversy over the precise status of the "colonial clergy" within the mother Church of England. The subject dominated the 1930 Lambeth Conference, the international conclave of the episcopacy. Denied the recognition of the status they felt they deserved, some Canadian bishops vowed never to attend another conference until they were placed on an "equal footing" with the English bishops.[6]

In the other Protestant churches the Social Gospel and the liberal theology that underlay it came under vigorous attack. Baptist ministers and educators backed away from social issues to avoid antagonizing resurgent fundamentalists. Within the Presbyterian Church, projects like the settlement houses engendered a "smouldering conflict" between traditionalists and Social Gospellers. Even Methodism, backbone of activist Christianity, turned on its radicals. Few went as far as millionaire Methodist Sir Joseph Flavelle, who criticized Social Gospel notions for their "pernicious and mischievous" influence on the working class, but many middle-class Methodists shared his perception that they had had something to do with such disturbing events as the Winnipeg General Strike. Focus of much of their ire was Rev. Salem Bland, whose *The New Christianity* (1920) was an enthusiastic exposition of the Social Gospel. Bland was already well known for his ties with the labour movement, and his suggestion that "Plutocratic or Capitalist Christianity" be replaced by "Labour Christianity" was badly received by some prestigious members of his Toronto congregation; a group of them lobbied for his dismissal. The book's first printing sold out quickly, but there was never a second. By the mid-twenties, complained a disillusioned reformer, "books of the Social Gospel [were] largely set aside in favour of manuals of devotion."[7]

II

The union of the Presbyterian, Methodist, and Congregationalist churches in 1925 was expected to advance the Social Gospel cause by concentrating its forces within the new United Church of Canada. Interdenominational co-operation to pursue social reforms had helped to create a climate in which fusion was possible, and Social Gospellers had consistently advocated union, for economical as well as ecumenical reasons. In Western Canada, where the churches functioned against a backdrop of scattered homesteads and isolated resource towns, union was the only means by which Protestant communions were financially and spiritually viable. Over a thousand union congregations, most of them in the West, already existed when the final negotiations for organic union began in 1921; because union had worked at the grassroots, it was assumed that it would be easily accomplished at the top. Instead, its consummation became an enervating struggle that absorbed much of the enthusiasm that had previously been poured into reform causes.[8]

One Presbyterian in three refused to accept the majority decision to enter the United Church. Their objections were so diverse as to defy any simple categorization. Some anti-unionists rejected the whole notion on theological grounds, while others protested its form, arguing that a federative union would work better than fusion. A theme repeated by the anti-unionists, however, was the fear that the new church would be preoccupied with reform politics rather than religion and "would move steadily to the left into a thinner and thinner liberalism." The anti-unionists were also motivated by sentiment, tradition, and the feeling of many Presbyterians that they were socially superior to the Methodists; objections to the union were stronger among more prosperous congregations. The anti-unionists battled the enabling legislation introduced in parliament and the nine provincial houses to create the new church and obtained the right for non-concurring Presbyterian congregations to remain outside the union. The confrontation released "a flood of bitterness, rancour and recrimination," which was followed by several years of most un-Christian legal haggling over Presbyterian property. It was an unedifying spectacle which augured poorly for the building of the new Jerusalem in Canada.[9]

Methodists attempted to reconcile their Presbyterian partners to the United Church through compromises. One of these was the new church's stand on social issues, which was more in keeping with the passive Presbyterian than the militant Methodist position. Methodist Social Gospeller S.D. Chown stood aside so that Presbyterian George Pidgeon, who was "essentially a conservative," could become the first moderator, and during the first years of the union, the United Church sought to avoid the divisive controversies an activist approach to social questions might arouse. Thus the anticipated rededication to Social Gospel principles never happened. Instead, the opposite occurred, as the United Church's treatment of the Social Service Council illustrates. A national federation of religious and lay groups, the council at the peak of its influence in 1919 had representation from all provinces, and its journal, *Social Welfare*, had a circulation of six thousand. Ten years later the council was decimated, "facing a lingering death." The biggest problem was financial, for the United Church reduced its subsidy to less than half of the amount formerly contributed by the Presbyterians and Methodists.[10]

The demise of the Social Service Council was a sign that its functions were passing from religious to secular hands. Out of the Social Gospel concern for the victims of urbanization and industrialization had been born the profession of social work. The new professionals wanted careers, not sainthood, and rejected the "tendencies to moralism" of the council, with its ministerial leadership and religious heritage. In June 1925, when the American National Conference of Social Work held its convention in Toronto, Canada's "scientific" social workers used the occasion to create a "Canada-wide secular organization of social workers and agencies," the Canadian Association of Social Workers. The National Conference of Social Workers quickly supplanted the Social Service Council; the 1928 convention of the former had 710 delegates, while only 32 attended the national meeting of the council. More significantly, the bureaucratic approach replaced the more dramatic crusades of Social Gospel-inspired reformers; ameliorating the problems of an urban industrial society was now "a technical matter entrusted to those who claimed professional expertise."[11]

III

Nothing symbolizes the turning away from the path of the Social Gospel to a new society better than the fate of the Gospel's most fervently and universally sought reform: prohibition of the sale of alcoholic beverages. The transformation of the nineteenth-century temperance movement, with the individual drinker as its target, into an attempt to use the power of the state to deny liquor to the working class and immigrants who lived in the new industrial city typifies the style of the Social Gospel and suggests its limitations. To those who believed in prohibition, alcohol and the "liquor traffic" of barrooms, breweries, and distilleries were the cause of the problems they wished to confront, rather than their symptoms. Aided by the enthusiasm of wartime, prohibitionists succeeded in convincing a majority of English Canadians that they were correct. Every province except Quebec went "dry" between 1915 and 1917, most of them after referenda had confirmed that prohibition was the public desire, and in 1918 the federal government used its emergency powers to extend prohibition to Quebec and to ban the interprovincial transportation of liquor. To enthusiastic reformers, the booze-free millennium had arrived. Disgruntled "wets" did not share their joy, but both supporters and opponents of prohibition expected it to endure. "There is no return," concluded Stephen Leacock with regret. "The door of the beer cellar is locked and the key is thrown away."[12]

Leacock's misery was short-lived. Quebec, his home province, had endured prohibition only as a federally imposed war measure and dispensed with it as rapidly as possible once peace returned. Prohibitionists were not surprised by this; it simply confirmed many English Protestant prejudices. The real shock came from British Columbia. In October 1920, a referendum majority of almost two to one ended prohibition and approved the sale of liquor in government-operated stores. The implications of the British Columbia decision frightened reformers. They explained it by pointing to the high percentage of Anglicans and urban residents, but still they were forced to admit that the peak of wartime prohibition sentiment had passed. Equally frightening was the thought that the Pacific province could now become a source of liquor for bootleggers and of inspiration for those who would undo the great reform. To help contain the contagion, the federal government provided the constitutional means for prohibition provinces to block interprovincial commerce in alcohol. Since the federal legislation required referenda to put it into operation, prohibitionists gathered forces for another campaign. In 1920 and 1921 the electorates of the other provinces quarantined Quebec and British Columbia, theoretically completing the process of prohibition. "Dry" majorities, however, were much smaller than those of 1915 and 1916, for the counter-attack of the "wets" had already begun.

The argument used most effectively against prohibition was a simple one. It had, its detractors claimed, "no more effect in prohibiting liquor than a similar mandate against the housefly." There was certainly plenty of evidence that provincial temperance acts were not completely successful in eradicating alcohol, for they banned its sale rather than its manufacture or consumption. Liquor could still be legally used for scientific, sacramental, or medical purposes. The prescription of whisky or brandy as "medicine" multiplied spectacularly under prohibition as the "tortures of transition" were eased by physicians and pharmacists. One Manitoba doctor found 5,800 patients in need of such treatment in a single month in 1920! The drugstore avenue to alcohol was relatively easily regulated. A more serious leak in the prohibition dam was the moonshiner, who manufactured liquor outside the law, and the ubiquitous bootlegger, who sold the illicit hootch or diverted legitimately distilled liquor into illegal channels. In both trades profits were steady, fines small, and the chance of avoiding arrest excellent. The Alberta Provincial Police estimated, for example, that no more than one tenth of the operators of unlicensed stills were actually prosecuted. [13]

Antiprohibitionists maintained that this meant that the temperance acts were impossible to enforce; defenders of the new legislation, probably closer to the truth, countered that law enforcement agencies were not trying hard enough. The most spectacular case of official corruption occurred in pre-repeal British Columbia, where Prohibition Commissioner W.C. Findlay was found guilty of importing seven hundred cases of whisky. In every province similar incidents cast long shadows on lawmen's reputations but rarely cost them their jobs. It was common knowledge, according to the Calgary *Herald*, that Alberta Provincial Policemen "wink, drink and don't enforce the Act." In Nova Scotia, where special temperance inspectors were appointed to enforce prohibition, a symbiotic relationship developed between the hunters and their quarry. Veterans explained to young officers that "without bootleggers, we wouldn't have jobs," and warned them not to "scare the trade too much" lest they "kill the goose that lays the golden eggs." The inspectors maintained a delicate balance, using occasional well-publicized raids to demonstrate their vigilance without seriously inconveniencing the bootleggers. [14]

When temperance acts were vigorously enforced, the rare shootout that took place provided the opponents of prohibition with a new complaint, that prohibition was responsible for an increase in violent crime in Canada. Two cases in particular attracted national attention.

In November 1920, Ontario Special Inspector J.O.L. Spracklin shot and killed Beverly "Babe" Trumble, the proprietor of the hotel against which Spracklin was leading a raid. Spracklin was an Essex County Methodist minister who had been made an inspector at his own request. He was acquitted of a charge of manslaughter, but the national publicity given the case did the cause no good. Two years later in Coleman, Alberta, Florence Lessandro pumped a bullet into the back of Constable Steve Lawson as the policeman wrestled over a revolver with her companion, bootlegger Emilio "Mr. Pick" Picariello. Since Picariello was a Sicilian immigrant who had made himself "emperor" of the Crow's Nest Pass liquor trade and Lessandro was a pretty twenty-two-year-old, the murder and their trial made lurid headlines until their double execution in May 1923. Lending further credence to wet claims of a wave of prohibition-related crimes of violence were newspaper reports of the difficulties authorities were having in drying up the United States with the Volstead Act. Canada, according to the *Ladies Home Journal*, was "one of the headwaters of the Niagara of booze" that was drowning prohibition in the republic. Provincial governments lacked the constitutional power to prevent their citizens from selling liquor to Americans for export, and the term "rum-runner" joined "bootlegger" and "moonshiner" in the vocabulary of Canadians whose slang was up to date. "The rum-running industry," complained the Winnipeg *Tribune*, "has attracted to the Canadian border criminals of a desperate type, and has led to a reign of lawlessness and criminality." As proof, the paper pointed to a series of bank robberies in small Western towns in 1922 and 1923. It was all the fault of prohibition, wrote an angry reader; as a cure for a sick society, prohibition was "ten times worse than the disease." [15]

Both prohibitionists and historians have correctly dismissed these attacks as inaccurate. Statistics illustrate the success of the prohibition experiment: dry provinces recorded decreases in drunkenness and crime compared to the pre-war period. As James H. Gray comments sarcastically, "in Western Canada nobody even punched anybody else in the nose." Although liquor certainly was available during prohibition, he continues, "the comparison would be between a chain-store supermarket-type booze economy" before prohibition and "a booze economy reduced to push cart status" after it was introduced. But in pointing to statistics both the prohibitionists and the historians missed the point. Canadians measured the success of prohibition not against what it achieved but against what had been promised from it. Judged this way it was a disappointment; from this disappointment came the impetus to end the "noble experiment." [16]

In Manitoba, Saskatchewan, Alberta, and Ontario, antiprohibitionists mounted an aggressive campaign through groups called Moderation Leagues patterned after the victorious repeal association in British Columbia. Wet sentiment in the Maritimes, on the other hand, never solidified into any formal organization. Whatever structural form opposition to prohibition took, the opponents and their rhetoric were remarkably consistent from province to province. Antiprohibition spokesmen were never openly connected with the liquor industry. Brewers, distillers, and hotel-keepers remained in the background, providing surreptitious financial support. The executives of the Moderation Leagues were solid, upstanding citizens who loudly defended "true temperance" as resolutely as they denounced prohibition. Many of them were former army officers. The Great War Veterans' Association, anxious to serve liquor in its clubrooms, provided an enthusiastic supply of wet campaign workers. [17]

The attack on prohibition used as its central theme the accusation that it simply hadn't worked, but a number of ancillary arguments were also applied strategically to appeal to particular audiences. Those with a strong sentimental attachment to the Empire were told that prohibition was "un-British," an unwanted import from the United States backed by "a vast *continental* propaganda." Americans might be so weak as to need to legislate temperance, but Canadians were British, and thus "know how to be moderate. . . . Red-blooded Britishers are not afraid of temptation." With more justice, prohibition was also criticized as a law designed by middle-class English-Canadian Protestants to extend their social control over Roman Catholics, immigrants, and the urban working class. "The leaders of the Prohibition League," wrote the editor of a German Catholic newspaper, "are in the main men filled with a virulent hatred for the Roman Catholic Church and all that belongs to it . . . who have striven to destroy our separate school system . . . who class all Catholics as 'foreigners' [and] who vaunt the superiority of the Anglo-Saxon." When Rev. William Ivens, Independent Labour party member of the Manitoba legislature, tried to defend prohibition before a working-class audience, he was greeted with yawns and jeers. But J. Kensington Downes of the Manitoba Moderation League brought Winnipeg workers to their feet when he shouted that "the city should not be subject to the dictates of any one-horse town in the country." [18]

The opponents of prohibition did not advocate a return to the unregulated saloon. They proposed, in the words of the Ontario Moderation League, "a sane, moderate compromise": government control and sale of liquor. The idea of putting provincial governments in the booze business had an almost magic appeal for taxpayer and legislator alike, for it promised a source of new revenue and a solution to the prohibition question at one stroke. Balance sheets from Quebec and British Columbia showed that millions in profits could be realized almost painlessly. As a further incentive for government sale, the end of prohibition seemed to have provided a remarkable stimulus to the tourist trade in both wet provinces. In Montreal, said an antiprohibition propaganda pamphlet, "money from the pockets of dry America" had created a boom. Hotels were "jammed beyond the overflow point" with American conventioners attracted by safe, legal liquor. The example was not lost on other cities. Winnipeg, mused Mayor Ralph Webb, could be advertised in the United States as "the City of snowballs and highballs" if Manitoba were wet and America still dry.[19]

The momentum of the wet campaign gathered most rapidly in the provinces where prohibition had originally been the strongest. In 1922 and 1923, Prairie Moderationists used the same techniques that the reform movement had originated ten years earlier, presenting petitions with thousands of signatures demanding that prohibition be submitted to a test of popular opinion. The Farmers' governments of Manitoba and Alberta, despite their intimate connections with the temperance movement, were firmly committed to majoritarian democracy. In referenda in Manitoba and Alberta in 1923 prohibition was rejected by substantial majorities. Rural English-Canadian voters remained faithful to the cause, but in Winnipeg, Brandon, Calgary, and Edmonton two out of every three ballots were cast for government sale. In districts like North Winnipeg, with large immigrant and working-class populations, wets made up almost 80 per cent of the electorate. Saskatchewan waited until 1924, but the result of its referendum was identical; government sale was approved by 40,000 votes.

Each provincial rebuke for prohibition lent strength to its opponents in Ontario, which became the symbolic fortress of Canadian prohibitionists. Ontario's new Conservative government did not share the enthusiasm of its UFO predecessor for the Ontario Temperance Act, but Premier Howard Ferguson was a practical enough politician to recognize that unambiguous support for government sale, however tempting, might wreck his party. "Foxie Fergie" chose to let the public speak in a plebiscite. With a remarkable reversal of form, the dry machine in Ontario pulled itself together for one final campaign and convinced 51.5 per cent of the voters that prohibition was worth preserving. The victory was a hollow one. Despite prohibitionist claims that the wet vote had been "largely made up by Jews, Foreigners and Roman Catholics," it was obvious that many Ontarians who had wanted to try prohibition in 1919 had changed their minds. The urban vote was heavily wet; every ward in Toronto voted against prohibition. As a concession to this sentiment, 4.4 per cent beer – popularly dubbed Fergie's Foam – was put on sale in 1925 to the applause of the Toronto Trades and Labour Council, among others. Premier Ferguson planned his next step carefully. In October 1926, almost exactly two years after the plebiscite, he announced his belief in a system of government control and called an election on the issue. The election results confirmed Ferguson's bold course. His government was returned, its majority undiminished and its share of the popular vote the largest in Ontario history.[20]

Defeated in Ontario, prohibition was for all practical purposes dead. Canadian prohibitionists muttered ineffectually when the Conservative government of Premier J.B.M. Baxter introduced government sale to New Brunswick with neither a plebiscite nor an election. Two years later, promised that revenues from liquor would finance provincial participation in the new old age pension scheme, Nova Scotians joined New Brunswickers in the alcohol business. Demonstrating their fierce individuality, only Prince Edward Islanders were to remain unpersuaded of the merits of such a step. In July 1929, they sustained prohibition in a plebiscite and rejected government sale.[21]

The end of the prohibition era in Canada, as the Moderation Leagues had promised, brought a situation vastly different from both the pre-war liquor trade and the alcoholic explosion that accompanied repeal of the Eighteenth Amendment in the United States in 1933. Ontario provides a good example, for the Ontario Liquor Control Board administered an act somewhat more restrictive than those in Quebec and the Western provinces, but less severe than those in force in the Maritimes. Liquor could be sold only in government stores, which had severely limited hours of operation. A purchaser had to buy a permit, sign his name and address before receiving his order, and go directly home with his brown paper bag before opening the bottle concealed therein. Ontario permitted no public consumption of liquor in hotels or restaurants, with or without meals. In provinces like Manitoba and Alberta that permitted the sale of beer by the glass, the system was scarcely more liberal. The beer parlour was not allowed to serve food, to provide entertainment, or even to have windows, lest the innocent be tempted inside. Beer parlours served men only. Legislation provided for separate parlours for women, but none were ever established. What evolved were "crude, bleak ill-ventilated rooms" designed for the "mass transfer of beer from kegs to customers." The new system of government control reduced bootlegging but did not eliminate it. The restricted hours and venues of government sale meant that there was still a field open for the enterprising, and rum-running to the United States continued until 1934. Rum-runners in fact had an easier time of it, since one of the things the provincial governments spent their new revenues on was improved highway systems! By 1930, provinces had become so dependent on this new source of income that "to cut it off would mean plunging into financial chaos." Nor did most Canadians *want* to get out of the liquor business; by and large they were happy that Canada had found a compromise, and the zeal of the social reformers seemed an anachronism.[22]

IV

Prohibition was the most spectacular failure among the middle-class attempts to smooth Canada's transition to industrial capitalism, but it was not the only social reform panacea that failed to produce the results expected. Women's suffrage, the single most important political improvement sought by the progressive reformers, was equally a disappointment to them. Women had been well represented in reform ranks, as individuals and through women's organizations like the Woman's Christian Temperance Union that were dedicated to Social Gospel-inspired causes. Although some Canadian feminists like Laura Hughes of Toronto or Carrie Derick of Montreal based their claim for the vote on the argument that natural justice demanded equality for both sexes, the most common rationale advanced for women's suffrage was one of expediency, not principle. Once women had the franchise, male and female reformers alike were certain their programs would ride into the statute books on the shoulders of a phalanx of female voters.

This dominant ideology of the mainstream of Canadian suffragists has been described as "maternal feminism" by historians of the movement. Unlike the theorists of the second Canadian women's movement, which appeared a half-century later, maternal feminists did not believe that women were or should be equal to men other than in a strictly legal sense. Quite the contrary. Because they "possessed unique biological qualities" required for their role as mothers, women were *superior* to men when it came to making decisions about the moral and social well-being of Canada. This superiority depended, however, on woman's remaining within her "proper sphere" as a mother and homemaker. Despite, or perhaps because of, the increasing number of women who were entering the labour market, the preservation of home and family were the central preoccupations of maternal feminists. The reforms urged on society by "aroused motherhood" – better public health, elimination of child labour and regulation of women's work, prohibition – were intended to protect the

family, and the franchise was needed to secure and maintain the reforms. Nellie McClung, Canada's most famous maternal feminist, put
the case succinctly. "When the hand that rocks the cradle rules the
world," she wrote in 1916, "it will be a safer, cleaner world for the oc-
cupant of the cradle."[23]

The first steps toward women's suffrage were taken during the
Great War in the Prairie Provinces, Ontario, and British Columbia. Partial federal enfranchisement was granted by the Union government to
help it win the 1917 election, and in July 1920 the Dominion Elections
Act was amended to give all women the right both to vote and to
become candidates in national elections. When Prince Edward Island
conceded women's suffrage in 1922, women in every province save
Quebec had the provincial franchise as well. Nellie McClung was one
of the first women to win elected office. A letter from a friend applauding McClung's election as a Liberal member of the Alberta
legislature in 1921 captures the vision feminist social reformers had of
the future. "You are to have a part in working out perhaps the most interesting experiment politically which Canada has ever seen," wrote
Margaret McWilliams. "It ought to be a time of great achievement in
those things for which women care." The fears of male opponents of
women's suffrage were as dark as the hopes of suffragists were rosy.
"The place of women in this world," said J.J. Denis during the
parliamentary debate on federal enfranchisement, "is not amid the
strife of the political arena, but in her home." Henri Bourassa voiced
the concern of many French-Canadian men when he predicted gravely
that the vote for women would reduce the birth rate, undermine
parental authority, and eventually destroy the family as an institution.[24]

Neither feminist hopes nor Bourassa's fears were to be realized.
Women's votes did not stir up a whirlwind of new reform legislation,
and they did not save prohibition. Two provinces, British Columbia
and Alberta, passed a Sex Disqualification Removal Act that established complete legal equality, but of the thirty planks in the
"Women's Platform" issued by the National Council of Women in
1920 only one, mothers' allowances for women with children and
without means of support, had been effectively enacted by 1930. As
Veronica Strong-Boag has pointed out, mothers' allowances were an
"ironic fulfillment of the feminists' maternalist ideology," for the
allowances simply transferred the women who received them "from
dependence upon one man to dependence upon a male-dominated
state." And the Canadian state remained male-dominated, for the
Canadian woman did not use her new political weapon to capture it.[25]

The federal election of 1921, the first in which all women twenty-one years old and older were eligible voters, established a pattern that would be repeated at all three levels of government. Instead of voting *en bloc*, as feminists had urged and politicians had feared, women divided their votes among Conservative, Liberal, Progressive, and Labour candidates in almost the same proportions as men did. Rather than voting according to sex, women voted as members of a class, region, or ethnic group. "Principles or prejudices, interests or appeals affect the two sexes in about the same proportions," concluded a Montreal *Gazette* editorialist. Male politicians drew the same lesson from the results. During the 1921 campaign, women had found "someone speaking at them or about them every other minute," in an attempt to solicit their votes. Appeals for women's support varied from promises to enact planks of the Women's Platform to the clumsy sexism of a Conservative candidate in Alberta, who passed out hand mirrors with the backs inscribed, "The lady on the other side is requested to vote for A.L. Smith, Calgary East." But once the hand that rocked the cradle had demonstrated that it marked the ballot no differently from hands that pushed pens, swung picks, or pitched hay, politicians realized that the suffragist threat of a massive women's vote was much less serious than they had feared. Just like the working-class males enfranchised during the nineteenth century, the new female voters could be accommodated within the traditional parties.[26]

The candidates among whom voters had to choose changed very little after women were added to the electorate. There is no evidence that political parties felt "compelled to choose pure, honest men with clean records as candidates" as suffragists had imagined; what is clear is that parties overwhelmingly continued to choose candidates who were men. Female candidates were few in number and a successful woman candidate so rare as to be cause for national comment. Few feminists sought active political careers. Only five women ran in the federal election in 1921 and only one won her constituency, a success rate of 20 per cent that has never been surpassed. A trend that has persisted became evident in this first election: the parties chose women candidates as sacrificial lambs in seats they had no hope of winning. Only one woman was nominated by the major parties; Elizabeth Keeley carried the Liberal standard in Toronto East, so safely Tory that it had not elected a Liberal since 1874. Although defeated, Keeley saved her deposit. Three other unsuccessful female candidates, two Labour and one Progressive, did not.[27]

The only woman elected in December 1921 was Agnes Macphail, a thirty-one-year-old teacher elected as a Progressive for the rural Ontario riding of Grey South East. Macphail had not been directly associated with the suffrage movement, nor did she share its maternal ideology. "I do not want to be the angel of any home," she told reporters, "[I want] absolute equality. After that is secured then men and women can take turns being angels." Isolated from the old maternal-minded activists by her convictions and from her political colleagues by her gender, Macphail was miserable in her first years in Ottawa. She lost twelve pounds during the first session in the Commons, eating in greasy spoons to avoid the stares in the parliamentary dining room. Macphail fought back against her sense of alienation and was re-elected four times, but she remained the only woman in the House until 1935, when Mrs. George Black became the Conservative member for the Yukon. Mrs. Black's election, far from a symbolic triumph for Canadian women, demonstrated the degree to which the women's movement had declined. Like Agnes Macphail, she rejected maternal feminism, but unlike her she did so from the opposite perspective. Martha Black made no secret of the fact that she had "never been an ardent suffragist." A woman's role in society was "not administering artificial respiration to a dying world, nor working perspiringly in a forward movement," but "child-bearing and child-rearing." She had run for office only because her husband, Speaker of the House George Black, had been too ill to defend his seat. Elected in what she described as a "sob-sister" campaign, Martha Black referred to herself as a "political pinch-hitter . . . [a] substitute for the real thing, keeping the seat warm for George." "I know he would make a more desirable member," was her comment as she stepped aside in 1940 to allow her husband to resume his place in parliament.[28]

This female political vacuum was not confined to Ottawa. Only nine women sat in provincial legislatures before 1940, all of them in the four Western provinces. Seven of them were elected in the initial enthusiasm that followed the granting of suffrage; no *new* woman candidate was elected between 1922 and 1933. Two women became cabinet ministers, Mary Ellen Smith in the Liberal government of British Columbia and Irene Parlby in the UFA government of Alberta, but neither was given the responsibility of a portfolio. Continued male dominance of electoral politics led to suffragist demands that women be injected into public office by appointment. Alberta, as was its custom, led the way, naming Emily Murphy and Alice Jamieson as police magistrates, and British Columbia made Helen Gregory MacGill a judge of the juvenile court, a position consistent with maternal feminism. The real objective, however, was not the bench but the Senate, and it was the campaign for women senators that initiated the celebrated Persons Case. Demands that a woman be appointed to the Senate were rejected by both the Meighen and the King governments, which argued that the constitutionality of such an appointment was unclear because the BNA Act did not specify if "persons" qualified to become senators included both sexes or referred only to men. In 1927 Judge Emily Murphy and four other Alberta women – Irene Parlby, Henrietta Muir Edwards, Louise McKinney, and Nellie McClung – used little-known Section 60 of the Supreme Court Act to demand an interpretation. The Canadian Court was unanimous. In April 1928, all five judges ruled that women in Canada were not "persons" as described in law. An appeal to the highest authority, the Judicial Committee of the British Privy Council, reversed this decision. In October 1929 their Lordships ruled that "the exclusion of women from all public offices is a relic of days more barbarous than ours," and that women were "persons" and prospective senators.[29]

Women activists were thrilled by the outcome of the case, for it seemed to portend a revitalization of their movement. But the Judicial Committee's decision was a moral victory, not a practical one. Prime Minister King's choice as the first woman in the red chamber was a calculated insult to the suffragists who had launched the legal odyssey. Emily Murphy was rejected because King thought her "a little too masculine and possibly a bit too sensational," and as an additional handicap she was a Conservative. Mrs. Norman Wilson, called to the Senate in February 1930, was a wealthy Ottawa matron who had played no role in the suffrage struggle. Her qualifications for the job were those of the men who already held it. The daughter and wife of former Liberal M.P.s, Cairine Wilson had made certain that the National Federation of Liberal Women, over which she presided, indulged in no feminist excesses that might embarrass the King government, particularly in its base in antisuffrage Quebec. Mrs. Wilson, King explained to his diary, was the ideal choice because she "speaks English and French and is in a position to help the party and will. Was a close friend of Lady Laurier [and] is a lady." Feminists, even maternal ones we must assume, were not "ladies" in King's eyes, and the angry disappointment they expressed at the Wilson selection probably confirmed the Prime Minister's opinion of them. The new senator received more coverage on the fashion pages than in the political columns. Her biggest political decision was what to wear to the opening of parliament, and her choice of a powder blue lace gown, blue satin shoes, and an orchid bouquet won the approval of fashion editors dismayed by Agnes Macphail, whose simple navy dress they had made a national joke. As Senator Wilson was sworn in, however, the train of her gown became tangled with the sword of Senator Raoul Dandurand as he offered his arm to escort her. This comic-opera touch provided only amusement for suffragists; it brought no consolation.[30]

"Is Woman Suffrage a Fizzle?" Anne Anderson Perry asked the

readers of *Maclean's Magazine*. Reviewing the meagre achievements of "ten full years of citizenship," she concluded that "dressed up with the vote [women] have found nowhere to go." Perry offered several explanations. Canadian women lacked universally recognized leaders, she argued, and were confused between the "old ideals of a shrinking dependent Femininity and the more modern concept of woman as an independent entity with a destiny of her own." Younger women were less willing to espouse the causes of the maternal feminists. Complaining that the majority of its members were "looking down the valley over the crest of the fifties," the Woman's Christian Temperance Union issued "A Call to Young Women," but did not attract a response; its membership and that of many women's groups plummeted during the 1920s.[31]

Like the society it had wanted to reform, the Canadian women's movement was divided by region, race, and class. The National Council of Women, bourgeois and urban-based, was almost like "the ladies' auxiliary of the class that controlled Canada" and had little contact with rural or working-class women. Its Ontario base meant that the NCWC did not provide unity even for middle-class women. The "Famous Five" who launched the Persons Case, for example, felt that "Eastern women" regarded them as "coal-heavers and plough-pushers from Alberta," and were bitter at the lack of Ontario support for their efforts. Unlike the Westerners, maintained Anne Anderson Perry, Ontario and Quebec women "go round and round in circles in our manifold organizations, passing much the same hardy perennial crop of resolutions as in pre-voting days."[32]

For Quebec women the 1920s *were* pre-voting days, for they were denied even the limited victories of their counterparts in English Canada and did not receive the provincial franchise until 1940. Despite similarities of class background and ideology, French-speaking feminists in Quebec never co-operated closely with English-speaking women in Quebec or in the wider Canadian movement. Religion as much as language was the source of this division, for the Catholic Church in Quebec worked first to obstruct and then to control the course of French-Canadian women's organizations. The most important of these, the Fédération Nationale Saint-Jean-Baptiste, was constrained directly by the hierarchy of the church and indirectly by its doctrines on the role of women in society. The professions of nursing and teaching were fertile recruiting grounds for feminists in English Canada, but in Quebec these jobs were filled by nuns who might sympathize but were forbidden to form links with the suffrage movement. When a Catholic laywoman, Marie Gérin-Lajoie, accepted the presidency of a Provincial Franchise Committee formed in 1921 to co-ordinate the activities of English- and French-speaking suffragists, church pressure forced her resignation after less than a year. Like those of the NCWC and the WCTU, the maternal feminists of the FNS-J-B declined in number and influence during the 1920s. The maternal side of its work was taken up by organizations even more directly under church influence; suffrage was left to secular groups like Thérèse Casgrain's League for Women's Rights.[33]

V

In Quebec as in the rest of Canada, the women's movement had been unable to realize the new and better society it had envisaged. As Ramsay Cook has pointed out, "the very extent of the suffragists' claims ensured that the movement would ultimately be judged a failure." His remark could be extended to Social Gospel-inspired reform in general, for reformers had overestimated the potential of their movement to effect far-reaching social change, just as they underestimated the power of the vested interests they challenged. During the post-war conservative counter-attack, defenders of the status quo replaced the words "reform" and "reformer" with the derisive terms "uplift" and "uplifter." Ontario Premier Howard Ferguson mocked reform pretensions. "Doesn't a lot of this uplift stuff that's talked about nowadays make you tired?" Ferguson is alleged to have asked rhetorically of Ontarians. His massive electoral majorities suggested that he and hardboiled politicians like him had their fingers on the public pulse.[34]

Reformers like Nellie McClung recognized that they had fallen short of their goals. "There are still a few rivers to cross," she concluded sadly in a letter to a friend. In the 1920s, Canadians showed little sign that they wanted to wade in.[35]

CHAPTER 5

The New Economic Era

I

Historians sometimes explain the loss of interest in social reform in the early twenties as a result of buoyant economic conditions, but the reaction against reform actually began while the economy touched the depths of a serious recession. By whatever yardstick one chooses, the early twenties were difficult and uncertain. Canada's gross national product declined by 20.1 per cent in 1921 and shrank again in 1922. The economic nationalism of the Republicans in power in Washington, expressed in emergency tariff increases in 1921 and in the Fordney-McCumber Tariff Act of 1922, had severe effects for the United States' northern neighbour. Exports, the lifeblood of the Canadian economy, decreased in value from $1,239 million in 1920 to $740 million two years later. Farmers suffered most severely, as farm prices collapsed and farm incomes along with them. There were twice as many business failures in 1921 as in the previous year, and in 1922 and 1923 new records were established for commercial bankruptcies. Even banks were not immune. La Banque Nationale and the Dominion Bank required emergency loans to remain open, the Bank of Hamilton was absorbed by the Commerce to avoid collapse, and in August 1923 the seventy branches of the Home Bank locked their doors in Canada's most celebrated bank failure. Layoffs and unemployment loaded the burden of hard times onto the shoulders of the working class, as the total income earned by Canadian workers was reduced by one fifth between 1920 and 1922. In the working-class suburb of South Vancouver, the medical officer of health reported that half of all children registered in the schools showed symptoms of malnutrition during the winter of 1921-22.[1]

The policies of the King government did not improve the situation. Finance Minister Fielding's budgetary parsimony was a reflection of the commonly accepted notion that governments could do nothing to stimulate recovery and should do little to relieve distress. "There is no economic panacea, no short cut to prosperity and sound finance," said an editorial in the *Journal of the Canadian Bankers' Association* entitled "Back to Economic Sanity." Big businessmen nodded wisely in agreement. The recession crushing farmers, workers, and small entrepreneurs was the working-out of the immutable economic laws of nature, the inevitable result of "many unhealthy factors in the prosperity of recent years." Those in distress should have been better prepared, wrote Sir Joseph Flavelle to a friend. "No one need spend undue sympathy [on] agriculturalists, businessmen and labour. . . . The old fashioned discipline incident to suffering," he concluded, "will do good on the whole rather than harm."[2]

The suffering lasted much longer than anticipated. A modest recovery began in some sectors in 1923, but it was not until the autumn of 1924 that Canada's economic health was largely regained. In an article in the September 1924 issue of the *Canadian Magazine*, journalist Archibald Blue commented on an increase in international trade and improved prices for agricultural products and minerals, which had given "the business interests of this country . . . a new hope. . . . It is well that this new promise has appeared at this time, for the past four years have been a trying time indeed. . . . During the early months of the present year the way was dark and the outlook gloomy, but overnight as it were the clouds were lifted and the rosy dawn of prosperity is beckoning on the eastern horizon." As if convinced by his own rhetoric, Blue claimed to see ahead "a new era of prosperity for Canada, which in degree and extent may be without parallel." This bold forecast was journalistic puffery, a reflection of the relentless boosterism characteristic of his magazine; Blue was probably as surprised as any of his readers when his prediction turned out to be remarkably accurate.[3]

II

Like all previous Canadian booms, the rapid economic growth between 1924 and 1929 had as its foundation the exploitation of natural resources. The development of the West had fuelled Canadian expansion for the first two decades of the century; in the early 1920s editorialists counselled Canadians that "we must face north . . . for economic salvation, it is imperative that . . . we take possession of our northern heritage." Pulp and paper production, mining and the generation of hydroelectric power were the three new staple industries based on this heritage whose growth rang in the "rosy dawn of prosperity.'' The paper industry, in particular the manufacture of newsprint, was the most important part of this resource trinity. Many statistics testify to the suddenness with which pulp and paper became one of Canada's leading industries. At the inter-war peak in 1929, over 33,000 workers were directly employed and 180,000 partially dependent on its success. Total annual production of newsprint had increased to 2,725 million tons from 805 million tons in 1921. There were 108 mills scattered across six provinces. Quebec had about half of the national production, Ontario a third, and British Columbia a tenth, but there were also mills in New Brunswick, Nova Scotia, and Manitoba. Production capacity is the most revealing measure of rapid expansion, and the most important in understanding the industry's development. In 1920 Canadian paper mills could make 2,783 tons of newsprint each day; in 1930 they were able to manufacture 10,690 tons (see Table V).[4]

The new monarch of the Canadian woods was crowned by foreign rather than domestic demand; almost 90 per cent of the newsprint produced was exported, three quarters to the United States. The per capita consumption of paper by Americans tripled between 1900 and 1925. The circulation of newspapers increased faster than population growth as universal public education created a new class of readers. Americans read sixty-one million newspapers in 1919; ten years later they read ninety-three million. Newspapers themselves doubled in thickness, their pages filled with advertisements aimed at the huge readership. The 1920s witnessed the birth of an American institution: the Sunday newspaper. Viewed through the avaricious eyes of the *Pulp and Paper Magazine of Canada*, the Sunday paper was ''a heterogeneous mass of illustrated pages, fashion plates, automobile supplements, book reviews, magazine sections, *etc.*, aggregating as many as 150 or 160 pages.'' The weekend edition of the *Chicago Tribune* required 50,000 tons of newsprint a year, ''all for the benefit of Canadian manufacturers of newsprint.''[5]

Expansion of the paper industry took place in Canada, rather than in the United States, for a number of reasons. Ontario, Quebec, and New Brunswick were close to the heavily populated cities of the northeastern states responsible for 70 per cent of all American newsprint consumption and could reach those markets by rail or water transportation. Canadian pulpwood was abundant, easily accessible, and particularly suitable for newsprint manufacture. Water needed in processing was in good supply and electric power was available cheaply from existing power companies or could be water generated. Northern settlement programs in Quebec and Ontario had created a labour force of pulp cutters and unskilled workers, and the provincial political climates for pulp and paper development were excellent. The governments of Ontario, Quebec, British Columbia, and New Brunswick, anxious to ensure industrial development, refused to allow the export of pulpwood cut on Crown land so that American mills could not simply import unprocessed pulpwood to make newsprint in the United States. The Magna Carta of the Canadian pulp and paper industry was the Underwood Tariff Act, passed by the U.S. Congress in 1913, which eliminated the import duty on newsprint. Once granted this privilege, American publishers used the power of their newspapers to protect it; Congress never dared to reimpose the duty.[6]

Unlike timber cutting or sawmilling, the pulp and paper industry required a heavy capital investment and thus a more permanent commitment on the part of both the capitalists and the provincial governments with whom they negotiated. Except in Nova Scotia and New Brunswick, where much of the public domain had already passed into private hands, the industry relied on wood cut on Crown land to feed its mills. Pulp and paper companies demanded to be provided with a security of tenure never needed or sought by lumber companies, and provincial politicians obliged them with "pulpwood concessions," twenty-one-year leases with options of renewal for another twenty years. These concessions were by law open for public bids, but as a commentator on forestry policy observed, "for some reason or other the right company has never failed to make the successful tender." Governments also established regulations designed to protect the forests from destruction. Some of the requirements for conservation and fire protection were neither strictly enforced by the governments nor fully respected by the forest industry, but the sheer size of their investments made better corporate citizens of the paper companies and tempered the "old lumbering psychology which viewed the forest . . . as wealth to be grabbed as quickly and as crudely as possible."[7]

What happened in the paper industry – and in other resource industries – was that businessmen and provincial politicians became partners in development. The relationship between politicians and developers was intimate; it bordered in many cases on what might today be considered scandalous. Sir Lomer Gouin became a director of the Laurentide Paper Company the moment he left the premiership of Quebec and continued to act in this capacity while Minister of Justice. "Sir Lomer [has] become definitely identified with Canada's great pulp and paper industry in a direct and personal way," reported *Pulp and Paper Magazine* proudly. "Both may be truly congratulated." Louis-Alexandre Taschereau, his successor as premier, served with pulp and paper company directors on the boards of banks and insurance companies, and his son's legal firm represented paper companies in their dealings with his government. "[I] . . . have given special personal attention to our forestry industries," Premier Howard Ferguson of Ontario told a paper company executive, "and I have sought to lend what assistance I might." Such co-operation was not restricted to Liberals and Tories. The United Farmers government of Ontario behaved no differently from the Conservatives with regard to pulpwood concessions, and Premier Bracken of Manitoba promised a pulp and paper entrepreneur that his government would do "anything within its jurisdiction . . . consistent with its responsibilities to the people" to encourage construction of a mill in his province. No provincial premier saw any conflict between public interest and private profit. Howard Ferguson expressed this attitude succinctly. "We are just as deeply interested in the success of your Company as its shareholders," he told the legal adviser of the Spruce Falls Pulp and Paper Company. "In fact, we are in a way the largest shareholders. . . . You need not be nervous about anything occurring that will embarrass or retard your development." Small wonder that Arthur Lower observed of the forest industries' frenetic development in the 1920s that it seemed as if "the persons who determine the forest policy . . . are the same persons as head the various lumber and pulpwood companies."[8]

Because of poor judgement and short-sighted optimism displayed by both paper companies and provincial governments, Canada's capacity to produce newsprint began by 1927 to outstrip American ability to absorb it. Every province wanted its share of the new industry, and unco-ordinated provincial development policies were helped along by financial promoters who professed to believe that there was no limit to potential demand. After 1930 this excess capacity was to have catastrophic effects for both the industry and the Canadian economy, but between 1926 and 1929 it created an instability that led to concentration within the industry through a round of mergers. By 1930 the "Big Three" – International Paper, Abitibi Power and Paper, and Canada Power and Paper – controlled 55 per cent of paper-making capacity, and the "Little Three" – Backus-Brooks, St. Lawrence Paper, and Price Brothers – a further 26 per cent. In addition, over a third of the pulp and paper industry was owned and controlled by American capital. After the stagnation of the early twenties, however, Canadians were untroubled about either oligopoly or foreign ownership; instead, the industry became a source of national pride. As a *Maclean's* article pointed out, in newsprint production ". . . the Dominion dominates the earth. Canada rubbed an Aladdin lantern of pulp and paper, and now – *behold*!"[9]

The simultaneous expansion of the mining industry had a slightly less spectacular impact on the economy but an even greater impact on the national imagination. Canada has the most extensive exposure of Precambrian rock in the world, almost two million square miles of it; during the 1920s, in Harold Innis's words, "the Precambrian Shield became a phrase to conjure with." Once a barrier to national development, the Shield was now a "new North pulsing with wealth." By opening "her northern treasure box," said an advertisement for an investment firm that specialized in mining stocks, Canada would pass "through the portals of a great mining era – *perhaps the greatest any country in the world has ever known.* The nation with mines is the nation that has the whip-hand of industry." When one reviews the statistical dimensions of the mining boom of the 1920s it is easy to understand this excitement and difficult to avoid succumbing to the superlatives of the stock promoters. In Ontario and British Columbia, Canada's traditional mining provinces, production at existing mines increased and new sites were developed. Quebec and Manitoba were newcomers to the mineral rush, as major new mining and smelting complexes were developed at Rouyn-Noranda and Flin Flon. Although it was the search for precious metals that opened most new areas, base metals were usually present in the ores. Between 1921 and 1929 production of silver doubled and that of gold tripled, but nickel, lead, and zinc production quadrupled and copper production was seven times greater in 1929 than in the recession year of 1921. The total value of these six non-ferrous minerals rose without interruption from $41 million in 1921 to $150 million at the end of the decade, and the number of employees involved in producing them increased from 10,000 to 23,000 (see Table VI).[10]

This remarkably rapid expansion came about because of a conjuncture of increased demand and improved prospecting, smelting, and refining techniques. As with newsprint, demand for base metals came primarily from the United States; the automobile, electrical, and radio industries were heavy consumers. Nickel use was increased by Canada's decision in 1922 to adopt nickel coinage. The discovery and exploitation of mineral resources was greatly simplified by the airplane, described by a veteran prospector as "the greatest single aid to the extension of our mining areas that we have ever had." Other developments such as selective flotation and electrolytic refining made extraction of metals cheaper and more efficient. In gold refining, the adoption of the rod mill lowered the cost of crushing ore, and the vacuum filter increased the percentage of gold that could be recovered.[11]

The reality of Canadian mining was at odds with its romantic image. Discoveries were made, not by the "solitary prospector who made his way upward in the world through sheer wit and pluck without assistance from any quarter," but by the "geophysical prospecting" of

mining engineers using "electric, magnetic, gravity and seismic in-
struments . . . developed chiefly by Americans." A writer who followed the "Trail of Twenty-Six" into the gold fields at Red Lake, Ontario, arrived by air to find "a weary, unromantic business" at the
McIntyre Mine: ". . . it would be impossible to conceive anything less
like the traditional gold camp of the oft-told tales of Dawson days.
Here were no gambling hells; not one saloon; no dance halls with their
cracked pianos and their predatory, gold-toothed damsels." The Hollinger Mine in Timmins set the standard for modern mining operations.
The second-largest gold mine in the world, it was "an industrial spectacle, adapting every advance of engineering to the job." Three thousand men worked in three shifts to "set up a new production record
one day to tear it down the next." "Hollinger gold is not mined,"
wrote another awestruck journalist, "it is manufactured." [12]

Although an individual mining venture was often financed by selling
stock directly to the public, the creation of a large-scale mining-
smelting enterprise required large amounts of capital, much of which
was imported from the United States. Hudson Bay Mining and
Smelting, which opened the copper and gold deposits at Flin Flon, was
controlled by the H.P. Whitney Company of New York. Noranda
Mines named its Quebec mine after Ed Horne, the Canadian prospector who had made the initial strike, but the mining, smelting, and
concentrating operation was developed by two American engineers
backed by a syndicate that included a Rockefeller, a Du Pont, and a
former president of United States Steel. By 1930, almost 40 per cent of
mineral production in Canada was in the hands of American-
controlled or American-affiliated companies. [13]

Mining companies, domestic or foreign, were welcomed by provincial governments with the same enthusiasm shown to pulp and paper
producers. The provinces moved with alacrity to create the necessary
infrastructure of railways and power plants and then rediscovered
laissez-faire when it came to regulating the mining industry or taxing
its profits. "You will not find us slow to help you," Quebec's Minister
of Mines, J.-E. Perrault, assured the Noranda company. "I'll come
north to study your needs and find out how the provincial government can assist you." "We look to see an even more rapid [mining]
development in this province than has taken place in Ontario," said
John Bracken to a convention of the Canadian Institute of Mining and
Metallurgy assembled in Winnipeg. Pandering to the industry's out-of-
date self-image as the last preserve of rugged individualism, Bracken
drew applause as he proclaimed it Manitoba's "privilege to be of as
much assistance as we can to the pioneer prospector and investor, in

all the activities that go with the development of this great mineral industry."[14]

The assistance universally required by the extractive industries was long-term guaranteed access to cheap hydroelectric power. Electricity generated by Canadian rivers provided a partial solution to the problem of a lack of strategically located sources of high-quality coal. A staple industry in itself, hydroelectricity also – in John H. Dales's words – "pointed the way to a more mature, more diversified economy," for it could serve as power to run industrial machines and as a source of the energy needed for smelting certain ores. In addition to its indispensability to pulp and paper and mineral refining, abundant hydroelectricity brought the Aluminum Company of America to the Saguenay River in Quebec in 1924 and led to an expansion of the chemical industry. Almost four times as much electricity was generated in 1930 as in 1921, and every intervening year registered an increase (see Table VII). The capacity of hydraulic turbine installations was 1.8 million horsepower in 1921 and 5.1 million in 1930. Despite the massive capital costs, economies of scale and better technology of distribution meant that the unit cost of power to residential and industrial consumers actually decreased; Canadians could boast that they enjoyed the cheapest power in the world and that only Norway exceeded Canada in per capita generating capacity. Power visionaries maintained that "the mighty possibilities which power holds for the future of this land" had scarcely been touched. Tens of millions of horsepower were waiting in mighty rivers, and once these were tapped, maintained journalist Grattan O'Leary, six million new jobs would be created and the population of Canada would leap to forty million.[15]

O'Leary's prediction was only slightly more incredible than the actions of the power companies, which built for the future on the assumption that the increases in demand of the 1920s would continue at the same rate perpetually. Total capital invested in fixed assets in the power industry increased from $448 million in 1920 to $1.1 billion in 1930. In the electric industry, public ownership coexisted with private enterprise; Ontario, Manitoba, and New Brunswick experimented with public power, and the Ontario Hydro-Electric Power Commission eventually so dominated supply and distribution as to become a virtual public monopoly. As H.V. Nelles has demonstrated, however, Ontario Hydro can scarcely be considered a socialized industry. Created at the demand of businessmen anxious for inexpensive power, it was "managed in such a way as to debase the concept of *public* ownership. . . ." Hydro's aggressive behaviour during the rapid

expansion of the 1920s did not differ greatly from that of Southern
Canada Power, Shawinigan Power, or Montreal Light, Heat and
Power, the three corporate giants that dominated the electrical industry in Quebec. Ontario Hydro's chairman, Sir Adam Beck, treated
his supposed legislative masters with disdain and regarded any suggestion that he be accountable in detail for the millions he spent as unwar-
ranted political interference. After Beck's death in 1925, Hydro continued to act as a power unto itself. Ten new generating stations were
added to its northern network, and the Queenston-Chippewa station,
already the world's largest, was increased in size. Demand seemed so
insatiable that Ontario Hydro signed long-term contracts to purchase
additional power from three private utilities in Quebec. Like its best
customers, the paper mills, the Canadian hydroelectric industry was
creating a generating capacity far in excess of anything the economy
could absorb. Tighter political control would have made little difference; in Victoria, Regina, Winnipeg, Toronto, Quebec City, and
Fredericton, provincial politicians urged power companies to still
greater efforts. [16]

The unco-ordinated exploitation of Canada's resources is sometimes
blamed on the allocation of resources to provincial control by the
British North America Act. But the attitude of the federal government,
Liberal or Conservative, to resource development did not differ
significantly from that of the provinces. Had natural resources been a
national responsibility, the identity of the capitalists who were granted
the development rights might have changed; precious little else would
have. In the Prairie Provinces the federal government retained legal
control of resources throughout the 1920s; in practice it administered

them jointly with the provinces between 1922 and the assumption of
complete provincial control in 1930. John Bracken's biographer
argues that, for Manitoba at least, Mackenzie King and the federal
Department of the Interior were less able stewards of the public interest than the provincial administration. It was the dominion-owned
Canadian National Railways that provided the heavily subsidized rail
connections between Hudson Bay Mining and Smelting in Flin Flon
and the outside world. When Alberta's farmers' government introduced a mineral tax act in 1923 that proposed to tax private holders of
mineral rights within the province, the federal government disallowed
the act after protests from the Canadian Pacific and the Hudson's Bay
Company. Had the federal government been able to assert a claim to
the generating rights on navigable rivers, as it tried to do, the St.
Lawrence and the Ottawa would have been developed by private
companies that intended to export much of the electricity generated
to the United States. Given the attitudes that prevailed in Ottawa,

federal rather than provincial control of the new staple industries would not have resulted in any comprehensive national strategy for their development. When federal-provincial disagreements occurred over resource development they were founded on petty questions of the division of the spoils; neither level of government disagreed with the principle of rapid development for private profit.[17]

III

Pulp and paper manufacturing and smelting are classic Canadian primary manufacturing industries. Their inputs are raw materials and their outputs are industrial materials that are sold in export markets, rather than being processed further at home. Important in terms of the value of their production, these industries are capital rather than labour intensive; they create relatively few jobs despite the large sums invested in them. The precentage of the labour force engaged in manufacturing increased only slightly between 1921 and 1931, despite the success of the new primary manufacturing industries (see Tables XIa/XIb). Secondary manufacturing industries, which are more labour intensive and involve a higher degree of processing because they produce a finished product rather than an industrial material, recovered slowly from the 1921-24 recession. The total number of workers in factories and the gross value of their production did not return to 1920 levels until 1927. The textile, garment, electrical, chemical, rubber, and leather industrial groups grew modestly thereafter, but the tobacco and food processing industries failed to regain the production levels of 1920 until the 1940s. Meat packing provides an example of a once-prosperous food-processing industry in crisis. Export markets in Britain were lost to Danish competition, and despite reductions in staff and the sale of assets, all but one Canadian packing house lost money steadily after 1920. The result in 1927 was a merger, as four smaller firms became one large one, Canada Packers Limited. Such corporate concentration to create bigger and bigger companies was characteristic of the period. In 1930, 3 per cent of Canadian firms accounted for 62 per cent of total output, and 26 per cent of the workforce in manufacturing was employed by firms with more than five hundred employees as compared to only 20 per cent in 1922.[18]

The only secondary manufacturing industry to match the spectacular growth of pulp and paper and mining was the automotive industry. After the United States, Canada was "the most motorized country on the globe"; the number of cars, trucks, buses, and motorcycles registered increased in every year of the twenties, from 408,000 in 1920 to a peak of 1,235,000 in 1930. Automotive production grew rapidly to keep pace and, after a slump in 1921, went on to set records during the rest of the decade. The auto industry went from eighth to fourth place among Canadian manufacturing industries: total capital invested increased from $40 million to $98 million (see Table VIII).[19]

Sales of automobiles would have been even greater had there not been a 35-per-cent *ad valorem* Canadian protective tariff on imported passenger cars. But the tariff did what it was intended to do, encouraging American auto makers to establish branch plants in Canada. W.P. Shillington of Studebaker bluntly explained the decision of his company and its competitors to manufacture cars in Canada. "We are in Walkerville [Ontario] purely because of the tariff," he told the Canadian Tariff Commission. "If it were not for the present tariff on the completed automobile," he continued, "it would simply be a case of there being no advantage in being over here." Studebaker, Packard, Willys-Overland, and the small American manufacturers only *assembled* cars in Canada; Ford, General Motors, and Chrysler established factories that actually built automobiles. This enabled them to take advantage of the preferential duties allowed by Canada's membership in the Empire-Commonwealth to export cars to other British countries. For this reason the auto industry was unusual among Canadian manufacturing industries in that almost one third of its products were sold outside the domestic market.[20]

As a "miniature replica" of the American auto industry, Canadian automobile production followed the trend of the 1920s toward concentration in a small number of large corporations. Small firms died or were absorbed into large ones, until by 1930 three of every four cars made in Canada were Ford, GM, or Chrysler products. Among the small firms that vanished were all the independent Canadian auto makers. The McLaughlin Motor Car Company of Oshawa, most successful among Canada's auto pioneers, was completely merged with General Motors in November 1918 and its product renamed the McLaughlin-Buick. The Parker Motor Company of Montreal collapsed in 1923, and the Gray-Dort Motor Company of Chatham, Ontario, which in its eight-year life had turned out 23,000 units of a car Canadians nicknamed "the rolling bathtub," followed Parker in 1924. There had at one time been as many as seventy companies manufacturing, assembling, or selling automobiles in Canada; by 1926 there were only fourteen.

The fate of Brooks Steam Motors of Stratford, Ontario, the last remaining wholly independent Canadian auto manufacturer, is illustrative of the problems that doomed an indigenous auto industry. The choice of steam power when better internal combustion engines were being developed annually might seem to make Brooks atypical, but that was just the sort of decision favoured by Canada's auto makers. Brooks was like some already vanished Canadian manufacturers in that it aimed its Steamer at a small luxury market at a time when the most profitable models were those that could be mass produced and priced inexpensively. In 1925 a Model T Ford cost $595 and a Chevrolet $625; the Brooks Steamer cost $3,600. On the Ford assembly line in Walkerville a new car was finished every three minutes; Brooks Steamers were completed at the rate of one a day. In 1926, a year in which almost 160,000 passenger cars were sold in Canada, the Brooks Motor Company was unable to sell all of the 360 it produced. By year's end it was out of business.[21]

The collapse of small manufacturers was not unique to Canada. Hundreds of small American companies also failed to survive. "Automotive amalgamation," said Bill Gray of Gray-Dort Motors just before it suspended operations, was "a logical outcome" of the development of the industry, but ". . . this in Canada is particularly true, where the problems of distribution are so severe on account of the tremendous distance over which a product must be scattered to meet the market of a small population. . . . That is why the successful companies of Canada have found it necessary to affiliate themselves with American interests, because with our small and limited outputs it is impossible to carry the tremendous burden of engineering expenses. [This] is simply a problem which we must face until we have more population."[22]

The impact of the automobile on Canadian society extended far beyond the presence of the industry itself. By 1929, 13,000 workers, almost all of them in Ontario, were employed building motor vehicles, but thousands more were employed supplying primary materials for auto makers, manufacturing tires and spare parts, or repairing and servicing automobiles. It was possible to conclude, without exaggeration, that "the motor vehicle industry is so bound up in the social, commercial and industrial life of the country that there is scarcely an industry that does not benefit directly or indirectly."[23]

The new motorists also wanted good all-weather roads, and formed lobby groups to demand that governments build them. In 1920 Canada had over 300,000 miles of highways and roads, but only 49,000 were surfaced and fewer than 1,000 of these were paved. "Many of these highways," complained S.L. Squire, president of the Canadian Good Roads Association, "are little better than trails." Nor was there anything approaching a trans-Canada highway. When Percy Gomery of the Vancouver Auto Club attempted a "Motor Scamper Across Canada" from Montreal to Vancouver, half of his trip had to be made through the United States. The Canada Highways Act of 1919 provided the provinces with $20 million of dominion money and the provinces quadrupled their own expenditures, so that by 1930 they could boast of 80,000 miles of surfaced roads, 9,200 of which were concrete or blacktop. The goal of a national highway system remained a distant vision, however. The best roads, like Manitoba's Lord Selkirk Highway from Winnipeg to Emerson, which opened to traffic in 1925, ran north and south to connect with American roads. Highway building improved transportation within regions and between provinces and neighbouring states, but it did little to facilitate interregional intercourse within Canada.[24]

A few grumpy taxpayers complained that these new highways would "benefit mostly bootleggers, pleasure tourists and thirsty Americans," but attracting visitors from the United States was one of the justifications for spending money on road construction. With improved roads "revenue from across the line will increase tremendously," argued the Calgary *Herald* in an editorial entitled "Good Highways Bring New Money." One small-town editor was even more plain spoken. He admitted to having little love for Americans as a people but was prepared to overlook his opinions because "they are great spenders, those American folk." The tourist invasion took place as anticipated; by 1929 tourism contributed $309 million to the Canadian economy, three times more than it had in 1920. An estimated 94 per cent of this came from the pockets of Americans, most of whom crossed the border in automobiles. "The tourist traffic," said the Brantford *Expositor*, "has become one of the most lucrative industries in Canada." Looking after the needs of tourists was one reason why the personal service sector of the labour force, which had been growing steadily smaller until 1921, increased rapidly during the next ten years. Between 1921 and 1931, the precentage of the labour force employed in the service sector in general increased from 36 per cent to 40 per cent (see Tables XIa/XIb).[25]

IV

Just as American travellers found Canada a congenial place to visit, so also did American capital. Canadian development has always been financed in part by foreign investment, and the rate of flow of imported capital has fluctuated from period to period. In relative terms, Canada was actually somewhat less reliant on foreign investment in the inter-war period than she had been before 1914, but during the 1920s foreign capital was extremely important in absolute terms in the four industries that grew dramatically: pulp and paper, mining and smelting, hydroelectricity, and automobile manufacturing. What was most significant about foreign investment in the twenties was that both its source and its nature changed. Great Britain was displaced by the United States as Canada's principal creditor sometime in 1922, as American investment exceeded British for the first time; the American advantage continued to widen thereafter (see Table IX). New British investment in Canada ceased because the costs of the Great War left little capital for export. American business faced no such impediments and had no fears about Canada as a source of supply for raw materials, as a market for American products, or as a place to carry out monopolistic activities that would have been illegal in the United States because of anti-trust laws. Canada scarcely seemed alien to American capitalists used to dealing with Latin America: ". . . governments were stable and friendly . . . people, institutions, values, and customs were similar . . . risks [were] minimal." Food processors like Swift, Borden, Kellogg, and Kraft even found that "tastes seemed similar to those in the United States."[26]

American investment in Canada differed from British in that a greater proportion of it was *direct* investment ("subsidiaries and branch plants controlled by externally-based parent corporations") than *portfolio* investment ("the import of foreign capital by the sale of bonds or debentures or non-controlling equity stock.") The *Journal of the Canadian Bankers' Association* explained the difference to its readers with a concrete example: ". . . the capital for Canadian railways has come chiefly from England, and the lenders remained at home; the capital for mining . . . has come largely from the United States, and the investors have often come with it in person to see it put into the ground." British capital had rarely been used to establish branch plants; American capital owned 466 of them in 1918 and established 641 more in the next twelve years. British portfolio investments in the form of bonds or common stock could expire or be patriated; American direct investments remained and grew larger from the profits earned in Canada. The expansion of the American-owned automobile industry, wrote O.J. McDiarmid in 1940, had been in part "financed by earnings [in Canada] reinvested under the supervision of the American concerns, and not by actual imports of capital." Thus foreign control could increase even if the international flow of investment slackened. As of 1930, one fifth of the "book value" of Canadian industry and more than two fifths of mining, smelting, and petroleum was controlled by American firms.[27]

Economists and economic historians have suggested that heavy reliance on foreign investment has had several negative effects on the development of the Canadian economy. The American companies that came to Canada in search of raw materials usually intended to do very little processing in Canada; such investment created "truncated export industries" and "frustrate[d] the attempt to stimulate a larger secondary manufacturing industry." Quebec's experience with asbestos mining companies demonstrates this. During the 1920s demand greatly increased for the "wonder rock" for automobile brake linings and in the high-voltage electrical industry in addition to its previous uses in making fire-retardant construction materials. Only a negligible amount of raw asbestos was transformed into these items in Canada; with the exception of the fibre absorbed by one plant that used asbestos to manufacture shingles, as much as 90 per cent of the rest of the asbestos mined was exported to the United States. The Taschereau government threatened an embargo on exports of unprocessed asbestos, but it was unsuccessful in bluffing the mining companies into manufacturing in Canada. Most asbestos mines were located not on Crown land but on private property ceded to the mining companies in the nineteenth century; an embargo on exports would have been constitutionally difficult. Raw asbestos entered the United States free of duty, but there was a 25-per-cent *ad valorem* tariff on imported asbestos products, and the American government was unprepared to lower or remove it. When the Quebec government proposed a "manufacturing clause," the mining companies threatened to transfer their operations to newly developed deposits in Rhodesia, leaving the Quebec asbestos industry to "fold up and die with scarcely an audible groan." Not surprisingly, the provincial government retreated, and things went on as before.[28]

As a resource-exporting economy provided much less employment than an economy with a well-developed secondary manufacturing sector, Canadians were forced to move to the United States to seek jobs. United States immigration restrictions did not subject Canadians to quotas, and between 1921 and 1931 there was a steady southward migration amounting to almost a million people. Quebec and the Maritimes suffered the most; in 1925 the Halifax *Citizen* complained with only slight exaggeration that "there are more Nova Scotians in Massachusetts than there are in Nova Scotia." The exodus was not composed entirely of the unskilled. Because the most advanced sectors of the Canadian economy were dominated by branch plants, industrial research was done in the American laboratories of the parent corporations; thus Canada lost a substantial percentage of the "trained brains" who graduated each year from her universities. "Can We Stem the Exodus?" asked *Maclean's* in a series published in 1927. The magazine reported that between 1919 and 1926, 11 per cent of University of Toronto graduates, 15 per cent of Western Ontario graduates, and 36 per cent of Acadia graduates had moved to the United States. In medicine and engineering the figures were substantially higher. Interviewing the emigrants revealed that most preferred Canada; eight out of ten had migrated for "economic reasons" or for "better opportunities." Their typical comment about their Canadian experiences was that research in Canada was "a dead failure." A University of Toronto mechanical engineer had worked in a machine shop in Canada; in Detroit he landed a well-paid design position in the auto industry. Significantly, however, the *Maclean's* articles made no connection between the engineer's dilemma and Canada's branch-plant auto industry. On the contrary, Canadians thought greater imports of foreign capital would solve the problem rather than make it worse. "Import dollars and keep our children," argued Quebec's Premier Taschereau. "I prefer to import American dollars than to export Canadians to the United States." Taschereau's smashing election victories and those of other premiers who followed similar development programs leave no doubt that a majority of Canadians accepted this analysis. [29]

Serious, reasoned criticism of the American economic penetration of Canada was seldom heard. Such an old Tory as J.W. Flavelle grumbled about "the absence of guts" of Canadian businessmen in the face of the American challenge and wished that he could "put the clock back thirty years" so that he could "share in an effort to organize Canadian capital to have a more important participating interest," but he would have been horrified by and opposed to any attempt by the provincial or federal governments to intervene in the market to deal with the situation. At the opposite end of the political spectrum, A.A. Heaps, Labour Member of Parliament for Winnipeg North, lamented Canadians' roles as "hewers of wood and drawers of water to American capitalists," but his views were not necessarily representative of the social democratic left or of the labour movement. The most persistent critique of American foreign investment came from French-Canadian nationalists, but their concern was a reflection of a more general fear about the effects of urbanization and industrialization upon Quebec society, and their own uneasiness about their consequent loss of status and influence. The nationalist message was confused and often self-contradictory; it offered no serious alternative path to development, but instead preached the return to agriculture as the salvation of French Canada. [30]

Thus though there was a general public awareness of American foreign investment, there was little alarm about it. The bogy of annexation, which had been so effectively exploited by the Tories in the elections of 1891 and 1911, no longer seemed to frighten anyone. "The [American] flag," concluded the Regina *Leader*, "does not follow cash." The owners of the branch plants, far from advocating continental economic unity, became the most vociferous defenders of the protective tariff; that, after all, was why they had come to Canada in the first place. Canada in the 1920s raised no barriers to continued American investment; Canadians expressed less concern about United States investment than any other country in which American corporations did business. Stopping over in Vancouver in 1923 after a trip to Alaska, American President Warren G. Harding praised Canada's co-operativeness. Speaking from the bandstand in Stanley Park, he told Canadians: "We think the same thoughts, live the same lives and cherish the same aspirations. . . . A further evidence of our increasing inter-dependence appears in the shifting of capital. Since the Armistice . . . approximately $2,500,000,000 has found its way from the United States into Canada for investment. That is a huge sum of money and I have no doubt it is employed safely for us and helpfully for you. . . ." Few of his 40,000 listeners, or those who read the next day of the first visit to Canada by an American president while in office, would have found anything to object to in his remarks.[31]

V

As Canada entered the new economic era of the 1920s, industries that had been dominant in the past declined in relative importance. The industries that had defined the National Policy years of westward expansion – railways, iron and steel, coal, and agriculture – were weak economic sectors despite the general prosperity. The success of the automobile came at the expense of the passenger train. In 1929, private cars accounted for six of every ten passenger miles travelled in Canada, and railway passenger revenue had declined by one fifth since 1920. Automobile and truck competition for passengers and freight had serious repercussions for railways everywhere, but the new competition hit Canadian railways at a stage in their histories at which they were particularly vulnerable. Canada had just concluded a long orgy of railway building that had resulted in 41,000 miles of track, a ratio of rails to residents much greater than that of any other country in the world. The Canadian Pacific system was over 13,000 miles and the "crazy patchwork structure" of the Canadian National more than 22,000. The two transcontinentals provided a spinal cord of steel for a nation that was otherwise invertebrate, but – to extend the physiological analogy – who needed two backbones? The most prudent course for the Canadian Pacific and the Canadian National would have been retrenchment and co-operation to secure the greatest possible use of existing mileage and equipment. There was Western opposition to such a course, however, and neither company chose to attempt it. Instead they embarked on a trial of strength from which both emerged gravely wounded.[32]

The decision to do battle rather than co-operate was as much the result of the personalities of the two railway entrepreneurs involved as of the broader economic and political considerations. Sir Henry Thornton, who assumed the presidency of the CNR in December 1922, and Sir Edward Beatty, his counterpart at Canadian Pacific, were men of polar opposite personalities who heartily detested one another. The twice-married Thornton was an immense man: handsome, affable, and athletic, with a taste for fine wines, good food, and all-night parties. A year after his arrival in Canada he had made himself one of the best-known and most popular men in the country, both with the public and with CNR's 90,000 workers. He hated to be beaten at anything; Thornton once had a maintenance crew cut down a tree on the company's Jasper Park golf course to give him a clear shot to the green to win an important match. The bachelor Beatty was a small stocky man who spent his private hours out of the public eye, fishing and playing poker with cronies. Also fiercely competitive, he consciously patterned his dress and his posture after Admiral Beatty, the hero of Jutland, wearing double-breasted suits, tilting his hat down over his right eye, and thrusting his jaw forward to project a suitably pugnacious image. Beatty resented both Thornton's popularity and the need to share the role of Canada's most important railwayman. Each railway had its head office in Montreal, and the two rivals lived opposite each other at prestigious addresses on Pine Avenue on the slope of Mount Royal. Soon after Thornton's arrival, a rumour passed through the clubs of the city's business élite that Beatty had described the new CNR president as a "showman" rather than a railway executive. "Beatty says I am a showman," Thornton is alleged to have answered – "I'll show him a three-ring circus."[33]

The centre ring in which the two knights and their companies jousted was branch line construction; the side rings were the hotel and steamship businesses that each railway also operated. Thornton's Canadian National was under the greatest compulsion to expand. As a public corporation, it was subject to political pressure to complete the rail network that had been originally planned for the Prairie Provinces. The Canadian Pacific was determined not to be excluded from any new areas, particularly those in the North, where the possibility existed for profitable investments for its mining subsidiary, Cominco. The result was the construction of extensive and expensive duplicate branch lines, which operated in the red. CNR's decision to enter the shipping field is understandable in terms of an attempt to provide more passengers and freight for the railway by integration with ocean transportation, but the hotel and resort war that took place in the later twenties cannot be explained by rational projections of expected profits. Canadian Pacific built the Hotel Saskatchewan in Regina, spent $4.7 million to refurbish the Chateau Frontenac in Quebec City and another $16.5 million to make Toronto's Royal York the biggest – and the most expensive – hotel in the British Empire. Canadian National built the Hotel Charlottetown, the Nova Scotian in Halifax, the Bessborough in Saskatoon and poured $6 million into the Chateau Laurier in Ottawa. Each railway raced to build resort hotels; CNR's Jasper Park Lodge was designed to outdo the CPR's Banff Springs, but a $6-million facelift restored the latter to supremacy in the Rockies. Unable to reach agreement with Canadian Pacific on a union station for Montreal, the CNR began work in 1928 on its own brand-new facility.[34]

Because of branch line, hotel, and steamship expansion, the two railways were unable to use the relatively prosperous years between 1925 and 1928 to consolidate their positions. Instead, their madcap expansion incurred a larger debt burden. Between 1923 and 1931 the annual fixed cost of the CNR's debt increased by $22.3 million and that of the CPR by $8 million. A royal commission investigation in 1933 spoke of a "red thread of extravagance . . . running through [the CNR's] administrative practices" during this period, but the excesses were not the government railway's alone. As Sir Edward Beatty admitted to the same commission, that paragon of private enterprise the Canadian Pacific had been equally guilty of "building branch lines and providing facilities in advance of necessities and . . . which traffic returns did not justify." The mistakes of judgement were remarkably consistent with the Canadian tradition of building railways to nowhere as an act of faith in the national future; in that sense the 1920s can be seen as the final binge of a railway bender that had begun in the Laurier era.[35]

When viewed alongside the investment in railways during the first twenty years of the century, the railway investment of the 1921-25 and 1926-30 quinquennia is in fact rather modest whether measured absolutely or comparatively. Between 1911 and 1915 it was $682 million, 26.5 per cent of all construction investment; between 1926 and 1930 it was $583 million and only 12.5 per cent of all construction investment. This relative decline of the railways was a severe blow to two industries that had traditionally depended upon them, steel making and coal mining. The coal crisis was general throughout the industrialized world, as electricity and petroleum emerged as energy sources. "The day of King Coal seems passing," observed the *Journal of the Canadian Bankers' Association* as coal prices began to dip in late 1920. Production levels of 1920 were gradually restored, but the annual value of coal mined did not equal that of 1920 until after the Second World War. American coal operators were also in difficulty, and because their mines were closer to Canada's industrial heartland in Ontario and Quebec than were the coalfields of Nova Scotia, Saskatchewan, Alberta, or British Columbia, they were able to increase their share from 50 per cent to 60 per cent of the Canadian coal market during the 1920s.[36]

Competition from imports and a decline in demand from the railways for its products created a similar situation for primary iron and steel. With reduced orders for rails and steel to build rolling stock and without the artificial demands of war, the industry did not share in the manufacturing expansion of the 1920s. Only one of Canada's three large steel producers, the Steel Company of Canada in Hamilton, was in good condition; both British Empire Steel and Coal in Nova Scotia and Algoma Steel at Sault Ste Marie tottered from crisis to crisis throughout the decade. The reasons for these difficulties were simple. For all her mineral wealth, Canada lacked accessible deposits of high-grade iron ore; iron mining in Canada ceased in 1923 and was not revived until 1940. Iron and steel makers were forced to import the raw material to feed their furnaces, and rising ore costs and declining steel prices caught the industry in a squeeze. New demands for steel came from such consumer industries as the auto manufacturers, who wanted sheet steel rather than semi-finished steel and rails. Algoma and Besco were ill equipped to meet these new demands, and their locations made it difficult and expensive to supply themselves with ore and to reach new customers located in south-central Ontario. Stelco, blessed with technological superiority and its location in Hamilton, increased its share of the market for steel, but foreign manufacturers snatched up some of the opportunities lost by Besco and Algoma. Canada's tariff schedules did not keep abreast of the changes in steel technology, with the result that manufacturers had diminished protection against American and European competition for the newer types of steel. Steel imports more than doubled in the 1920s; 57 per cent of the rolled steel used to build automobiles, washing machines, and other consumer durables was imported between 1926 and 1929.[37]

A fourth weak sector during the 1920s was agriculture. Although farmers and farm labourers remained the largest single group within the Canadian male labour force, agriculture declined considerably as a factor in national production. Prices of grain, livestock, meat, eggs, and dairy products fell farther than those of other commodities in the recession of 1921; they recovered slowly and incompletely as

American tariffs and competition from Argentina, Australia, New Zealand, and Denmark for the British and European markets kept prices down. "In the last three years," wrote economist C.R. Fay at harvest time in 1924, "if the average Canadian farmer had charged against his product a wage at the rate of that paid to unskilled town labour, he would have been put out of business." A price depression was more serious for the farmer of the 1920s than it had been for his father or grandfather, for he was bound up inextricably in a commercial economy. The Great War had brought high prices and expanded markets which encouraged borrowing to invest in land or machinery; even in rural Quebec, *l'Action française* pointed out, "the farmer is no longer the isolated individual of former days [but] is in almost daily contact with merchants or manufacturers' representatives." Financial obligations made it impossible to retreat into subsistence to wait out hard times. The crisis of the early twenties, continued *l'Action française*, was thus destroying "not only our mediocre farmers, but also . . . devoted young agriculturalists anxious to farm progressively. These newcomers, having bought at high prices, find themselves forced today to abandon the career of their choice." A series of extraordinarily high yields of grain between 1925 and 1928 revived the agriculture of the Prairie Provinces despite low wheat prices, but the aggregate increases in national farm income served only to disguise temporarily the problems of agriculture. In the Maritimes, Quebec, and Ontario the number of occupied farms declined between the censuses of 1921 and 1931 and the number of farms operated by tenants rather than owners increased by half over the same period.[38]

VI

"How're you gonna keep 'em down on the farm," asked the most popular song of 1919, "after they've seen Paree?" Groucho Marx understood the problems of rural North America better than did the song writer. "How're you gonna keep 'em down on the farm," he quipped, "after they've seen the *farm*?" During the 1920s Canadians began to accept the fact that they were no longer a rural, agricultural people and that the development of large cities was natural, inevitable and even desirable. Although leaders of farm organizations and French-Canadian nationalists continued to warn against the evils of the city, their glorification of country life was dismissed as "a threadbare platitude . . . a habit – a mere figure of speech." C.W. Petersen, editor of the *Farm and Ranch Review*, admitted sadly that the farm was "generations behind the town in conditions of life . . . [and] the younger generation positively declines to put up with the present economic handicaps and isolation of rural life." No longer was the farmer held up universally as the ideal Canadian; far from a superior being, said Winnipeg's Mayor Ralph Webb, "the average farmer is not much more than the average sewer digger in the city." Canadians need not fear urbanization, wrote S.A. Cudmore of the Dominion Bureau of Statistics, for "the history of civilization is very largely the history of cities . . . where the most original minds of a country are able to meet and exchange ideas."[39]

By 1922 the process of urbanization had been under way in Canada for half a century. Almost half the population was urban by the generous definition of the 1921 *Census*, and an "urban network" of cities and towns had become established. The astounding rate of urban growth that had transformed Canada between 1901 and 1921 moderated in the twenties, but urban population nevertheless increased by 31 per cent between 1921 and 1931, very considerable growth in real terms. Large metropolitan areas experienced the greatest population growth; in 1931 two Canadians in seven lived in or around Montreal, Toronto, Vancouver, Winnipeg, Quebec, Ottawa, or Hamilton (see Table Xa). Urban growth was not evenly distributed across Canada's five regions. Maritime cities failed to keep their own natural increases and Prairie cities, which had gone from buffalo to board of trade almost overnight in the years before the war, expanded slowly after it. Ontario registered steady growth upon an already large urban population base, while in British Columbia and Quebec the pace of urbanization actually speeded up. The result was an interregional urbanization gap, which became wider between 1921 and 1931. Ontario, Quebec, and British Columbia had 60 per cent or more of their populations living in urban areas, while in the Maritime and Prairie provinces ruralites predominated by greater margins (see Table Xb).[40]

The Canadian "urban hierarchy" – the relative importance of her cities as measured by their size and functions – was also generally established by 1922. Montreal and Toronto had become "primate cities," national metropolitan centres many times larger than other cities in Central Canada with "the whole economy shared as a hinterland between them." The decline of Kingston, Saint John, and Halifax, which had been important nineteenth-century centres, was clear, as the newer communities of Winnipeg and Vancouver became Canada's third- and fourth-largest cities. As the older urban places had learned, however, the importance of any individual city was more transitory than the process of urbanization itself. Both Montreal and Winnipeg had their metropolitan dominance eroded during the inter-war period, and each lost ground to its competitors. Although Montreal remained

the national transportation centre, Toronto received a greater share of
the benefits of northern development. The mineral wealth of northwestern Quebec became part of its hinterland rather than Montreal's,
and as American investment capital replaced British, Toronto replaced
Montreal as the funnel through which it was poured into Canada.
Southern Ontario attracted the largest share of new branch plant manufacturing, in particular the automobile industry.[41]

Montreal had only lost ground; it had not yet been defeated in its
struggle to maintain national economic leadership. It was Winnipeg,
the fabulous Western city that had epitomized the urban explosion of
the first decade of the century, that suffered the more serious shock to
its regional dominance. A series of political and technological changes
doomed its ambition to become the "Chicago of the North" and condemned it to "slow growth and relative decline after 1920." The
opening of the Panama Canal and the decision of the Board of Railway
Commissioners to strike down Winnipeg's preferential freight rate
structures made it more economical to bypass Winnipeg with bulk
shipments and to import and export through Vancouver. Manufacturers sold directly to the larger stores, ignoring Winnipeg wholesalers.
The wheat pools undermined the once mighty Winnipeg Grain Exchange, and meat packers diversified into other Western cities. The
legacy of class antagonism left by the General Strike of 1919 drew a
"red circle" around the city and warned foreign and domestic capitalists that its working class was "unreliable." Vancouver extended its influence eastward in direct proportion to Winnipeg's retreat; symbolic
of this penetration across the Rockies was the expansion of Woodward's, a large Vancouver department store, into Edmonton in 1928.
By 1931, Vancouver had knocked Winnipeg from third place in the
national urban hierarchy.[42]

Winnipeg's large garment industry and its functions as an administrative centre allowed it to remain the pre-eminent urban centre
of the Prairie Provinces even if its national status was diminished.
Many of Canada's smaller towns, in all five regions, stagnated or re-
gressed because of changes in the patterns of wholesaling and retailing
that undermined their positions as trading centres. In the 1921 *Census*,
369 towns reported populations between one and five thousand; 101
of them actually lost population during the 1920s, while another 44
grew by less than 5 per cent. Aggressive mail-order houses enabled
"Toronto to invade Main Street"; their catalogues provided rural
Canadians with a "total shopping service" that no country store or
small-town merchant could hope to match. The local board of trade
boosters vainly tried "Trade at Home" campaigns, and local editors
denounced "Bob" Simpson and "Tim" Eaton for destroying the liveli-

hood of their communities but with no apparent result. The automobile and improved provincial road networks also crippled the small towns' trade. Travelling salesmen became more mobile and dangerous competition, and formerly captive customers drove farther afield in search of better-quality goods and bargain prices. The number of merchants in Copper Cliff, Ontario, declined from thirty-seven to twenty between 1903 and 1931, as its residents motored to larger stores in the city of Sudbury. [43]

As familiarity with city life increased, the sense that urbanization was a national crisis began to dissipate. Since the 1880s, the city had been the target of a reform movement that had tried to plan a more attractive urban environment, to control the behaviour of the working class in order to improve its physical and moral welfare, and to restructure municipal government. Middle-class in its membership, essentially conservative in many of its objectives, and often undemocratic in its methods, the municipal reform movement had accomplished some of its goals by 1920. The inadequate sanitation that had inflated infant mortality rates had been replaced with modern sewage systems, and – although urban death rates still exceeded those in rural areas – rudimentary public health arrangements had reduced the ravages of epidemic disease. Much remained to be done. The *Census* of 1931 reported "over-crowded slum areas" in the larger cities, and in Montreal in particular, as Terry Copp has shown, "the conditions of life for the working-class population had improved only very slightly." Yet during the twenties the urban reform movement disintegrated. The recession between 1921 and 1923 doomed the schemes of architects and engineers for a "city beautiful." Civic governments dismissed town planning as an "artistic fad" beyond municipal means and turned to more modest proposals such as zoning by-laws instead of the more comprehensive schemes of the planners. The King government cut off federal aid to urban housing and dismantled the Town Planning Branch of the Department of the Interior. Canadians, complained an urbanist in 1926, seemed "incapable of cooperating for the public good. . . . Civic development in Canada is a riot of stupid selfishness." [44]

One reason for this was that the class that had been most anxious to reform the city had continued to move away from it. Suburbanization was not new, but it went on much more rapidly in the post-war period. Between 1921 and 1931, areas adjacent to major cities grew two and a half times faster than the cities they surrounded. While Montreal's population increased by a third, that of Verdun, Outremont, Westmount, and St. Lambert doubled; Toronto itself registered a modest growth of 21 per cent, but the suburbs of Mimico, New To-

ronto, and Forest Hill increased by 198 per cent. The automobile and
to a lesser extent the motor bus were what made the new suburbs possible. They provided cheap, efficient transportation and allowed an individual to live five or ten miles away from his job, so that suburbs
could be developed without waiting for the costly street-railway ex-
tensions that had once been critical to the success of a development. It
was the automobile that, paradoxically, became the chief beneficiary
of the skills of the town planners; city engineers "never spoke of
streets as places of interaction of local residents; rather their function
was to bear the vehicular traffic of the public at large."[45]

The *Census* of 1931 explained the implications for urban reform of
the flight to the suburbs: suburbanization had "defects from the broad
point of view of social welfare, since people of certain classes may
withdraw themselves from the problems of the social unit of which
they are a part." The exodus from the central city was not composed
exclusively of the middle class, for there were working-class suburbs
as well: South Vancouver, Winnipeg's Brooklands and Transcona,
Montreal's Verdun. But the suburbs were homogeneous in terms of
class and ethnicity to a far greater degree than the cities had been, so
that bourgeois suburbanites never encountered "people like that" in
their new neighbourhoods. John Weaver's study of the Hamilton
suburb of Westdale demonstrates that residential segregation was consciously sought. To keep out blue-collar workers and their families,
the developers required contractors to sign a covenant promising to
adhere to a minimum value for dwellings that was beyond the means
of working-class purchasers. A second part of the covenant required
that "none of the lands . . . shall be used, occupied by or let or sold to
Negroes, Asiatics, Bulgarians, Austrians, Russians, Serbs, Rumanians,
Turks, [or] Armenians, whether British or not, or foreign-born Italians,
Greeks or Jews." To further insulate the residents, "patterns of segregation [were] supported by the location of parks, business districts
and school property." The developers' attempts to create an exclusive
suburb were successful; the *Census* of 1931 revealed that while
"Hamilton was a lunch-bucket city, Westdale was a white collar suburb."[46]

In the suburbs ownership of a detached house on a separate lot was
overwhelmingly the rule, but in the city itself home ownership declined. In urban areas in 1921, 46 per cent of heads of families owned
the homes they lived in, but by 1931 this had declined to 43 per cent.
The decline was more rapid in larger cities, which had a greater
percentage of tenants than the national average. Many of the tenants
lived in apartment blocks, which were an insignificant fraction of urban construction in 1922 but made up a quarter of it by 1928. The in-

crease in apartment dwellers was another sign of growing acceptance of city life, and further evidence was provided by the emergence of a new style of municipal politics.[47]

Perhaps because they correctly sensed that the municipal reformers were motivated more by self-interest than by humanitarianism, urban working-class electorates rejected reform leadership and turned to a different breed of civic politician, best exemplified by Montreal's mayors Médéric Martin and Camillien Houde, Louis D. Taylor of Vancouver, and Ralph Webb of Winnipeg. Usually of humble origins – Taylor barely met the property qualification – the new mayors were colourful and flamboyant, attracting national attention to themselves and their cities with circus antics and outrageous statements. They won office on their personal reputations, shattering the Canadian tradition of faceless businessmen as the prudent first magistrates of large cities, and they also put an end to the practice of passing the mayoralty from one member of the business élite to another at short and regular intervals. Martin was re-elected four times, Houde and Webb eight, and Taylor eleven. They won because they expressed the arrogant urban ethos of a pavement-bred generation, scorning the moral reform of cities as a plot by rural bluenoses. Houde and Martin presided over the most wide-open city in North America, Webb instructed Winnipeg police to ignore Manitoba's liquor laws, and Taylor told Vancouver's finest to "concentrate on murders and hold-up men" and to leave "disorderly houses and gambling joints" alone. Taylor was narrowly defeated in a "purity campaign" in 1928 by businessman W.H. Malkin and a group called the Christian Vigilance League, but two years later he was back in office with a large majority. Vancouverites, he told the press, didn't want a "Sunday school town." But despite the new mayors' working-class support, the change-over in urban politics was more symbolic than real; as far as actual power was concerned, Montreal, Vancouver, and Winnipeg were like other Canadian cities, run by and for their business communities. L.D. Taylor's bright red necktie was not meant to announce his political convictions, and Webb and Houde sat in their provincial legislatures as members of the Conservative party.[48]

Next to suburban development, the most significant change in the pattern of Canadian urbanization during the twenties was the rapid expansion of an urban frontier in the middle north to service the new staple industries. Resource exploitation gave birth to new settlements and caused existing villages to mushroom into towns and towns into cities. Pulp and paper doubled the population of Dalhousie, New Brunswick, from 1,958 to 3,974 and quadrupled that of Kapuskasing, Ontario, from 900 to 4,000; gold mining caused Timmins to balloon from 3,843 to 14,200. Between 1919 and 1939, fifty-six new communities were created by the resource extractive industries. To avoid the dislocation which would accompany uncontrolled growth, large companies sometimes established their own "company towns" to insulate their workers from liquor and vice. In Quebec, Rouyn and its sister city, Noranda, serve to demonstrate the two directions that urbanization on a resource frontier could follow. During its explosion from a few dozen to five thousand residents, Rouyn was a rough, brawling, wide-open town, with "naked women careering through the streets in broad daylight" and "two houses out of every three . . . occupied by bootleggers." Noranda, in contrast, was "a model industrial community" planned by the mining company whose name it bore; in some respects it resembled a big-city suburb more than a mining camp, with churches, a hospital, service clubs, and a golf course "laid out by a high-priced specialist, brought from afar to produce a layout designed to satisfy the meticulous taste of the golfer who takes his recreation seriously." Not all company towns equalled Noranda, but given a choice, workers with wives and families almost invariably chose a house in the company townsite over the squalid shanties that appeared on its fringes; demand for company housing was usually greater than supply. [49]

Whether they were company owned or simply company dominated, however, life was not idyllic in the single-industry towns. The residents, complained a Labour M.P., "hardly dare call their souls their own." The corporate presence in municipal life and institutions was as pervasive as the acrid fumes from the smelter or the mill that filled the air. Streets were named after unknown company directors. Local government was in the hands of managers and senior employees, and the mayoralty and council posts were often filled by acclamation. Medical care was provided by doctors who worked for the company, police protection by the company's security department; even the churches were company built. Resource communities had rigid and highly visible class structures in which a family's position depended on the breadwinner's position in the company's hierarchy. Executives were assigned large houses with desirable locations on "Snob Hill," white-collar workers and skilled employees came next in line, and labourers rented "monotonously standardized frame cottages" on "immigrants' row." Single workers lived in dormitories or company-owned "residential clubs." Bootleggers and prostitutes were not the only unwelcome visitors in a company town; workers were also "protected" from trade unions by the well-co-ordinated system of paternalistic social control or, if necessary, by the forcible eviction of organizers. But industrial disputes could and did take place and were sometimes "more than just a protest against working conditions," being instead manifestations of "discontent within the townsite towards the single-enterprise nature of the community."[50]

Towns that lived by resource extraction could also die by it, for they were dependent communities at the mercy of unstable international markets for staple products. As Timmins and Kirkland Lake entered their golden ages, Cobalt and Haileybury, the mining boom towns of an earlier era, withered. The distant boards of directors of giant resource companies could close a mine, a mill, or a smelter with little sensitivity to the fact that they closed a town along with it; for some of the Cinderella cities of the 1920s the clock was to strike midnight during the economic crisis of the following decade.[51]

VII

It was not apparent to Canadians as they rode "on the tide of prosperity," but the problems of single-enterprise resource communities were those of the Canadian economy in microcosm. Post-war Canada had become increasingly specialized in the production of a small number of exports; the prices of those exports were determined by international demand over which the Canadian producers had no control. The appearance of diversification presented by the growth of primary manufacturing and the automobile factories was deceptive; the seemingly sophisticated modern urban industrial society rested on a foundation that could be easily shaken by a sudden change in the international economic climate. "If anything," concludes A.E. Safarian, "the Canadian economy became more susceptible in the twenties to any collapse in world export demand."[52]

Nor did the new economic era solve the problem of Canada's internal regional divisions. The new resources enhanced the power and prestige of the provincial governments that administered them, and constitutional and ideological barriers stood in the path of any federal attempts to assert national economic leadership. Urbanization made the everyday lives of Canadians in different regions more similar, but it also reinforced regional identities, for large metropolitan centres provided a base for provincial power structures and fought to maintain or extend their dominance over their hinterlands. The final flaw in the economic growth of the 1920s was its uneven distribution. Ontario, Quebec, and British Columbia enjoyed a proportionately greater share than the Prairies or the Maritimes, strengthening the conviction of the less successful regions that the cards of Confederation were stacked against them.[53]

CHAPTER 6

Patching Up the Old Political Order

I

The Prairie demand for a new deal within Confederation was louder, but it was the Maritime Provinces that had the greater reason to protest the hand they had been dealt. Nova Scotia, New Brunswick, and Prince Edward Island had long complained about national economic policies that favoured Central Canada. Before 1918, however, both Nova Scotia and New Brunswick had been able to share in some of the growth of industrial capitalism that had accompanied westward expansion. Although the mercantile economy based on shipping and shipbuilding declined rapidly after 1870, the Maritime Provinces were not economically stagnant after they became part of Canada. Nova Scotia and New Brunswick underwent significant industrialization; between 1880 and 1910 the per capita value of Maritime manufacturing more than doubled. Nova Scotia's iron and steel industry, using Maritime coal and ore imported from Newfoundland, grew dramatically after 1900. Two large and diversified corporations, Dominion Iron and Steel and Nova Scotia Steel and Coal, produced basic steel and finished products ranging from railway cars to barbed-wire fencing. Light industry also flourished as other Maritime factories shipped shoes, textiles, and furniture to markets in Western Canada and were efficient enough to compete successfully for this hinterland with the factories of Quebec and Ontario.[1]

In the years that followed the Great War, this Maritime manufacturing economy was shattered. Between 1917, the peak of wartime prosperity, and 1921, manufacturing employment and value of production decreased by 40 per cent, and the lost industrial strength was never regained. During the 1920s the Maritimes' share of Canadian manufacturing was cut almost in half; twenty industrial towns in the region showed absolute losses of population during the decade. The post-war recession complicated the economic collapse in the Maritimes but did not cause it; the severe and permanent downturn was the sum of broader changes in the Canadian economy and political decisions of the federal government that deprived the Atlantic provinces of special economic arrangements enabling them to get a fair return on their membership in the Canadian confederation. Industrialization in Nova Scotia and New Brunswick was based on their monopoly of the only coalfields east of Saskatchewan. Maritime coal heated the furnaces and turned the wheels of the region's factories and was also exported to coal-less Quebec. The dethroning of King Coal by oil and particularly by electricity was a critical blow. The growth of hydroelectric generating capacity in Central Canada was a double disaster, for it stole customers for Maritime coal and provided manufacturers in Ontario and Quebec with a competitive advantage in energy costs. No similar power development took place in Atlantic Canada. Some analysts blamed "the solid conservatism . . . of the provinces down by the sea" for retarding hydro expansion, but shortages of public and private capital and the lack of large rivers to provide potential generating sites were the real barriers to development.[2]

Changes in national tariff and transportation policies were equally important in the decline of coal and of the Maritime economy in general. The regional coal and steel industry depended on tariff protection against American competition. Pressure from politically stronger regions gradually eroded the original National Policy tariff structure to the point at which it became cheaper for Quebec manufacturers to import their coal from the United States. Dominion Iron and Steel and Nova Scotia Steel and Coal were also affected by the *de facto* reductions in steel tariffs. These changes took place over a twenty-year period, and their effects were mitigated by the increased demand during the World War. Most devastating of all to the Maritimes' industrial base were the sudden increases in the region's railway freight rates in 1920. Until 1918, the Atlantic provinces enjoyed a low and flexible rate structure which was the envy of Ontario, Quebec, and Western Canada. Goods shipped west from the Maritimes travelled at rates from 20 to 50 per cent lower than goods hauled similar distances in other parts of the country, but higher rates were applied to freight moving east into the Maritimes. The lower westbound schedule provided Maritime manufacturers, despite their location, a chance to compete on an equal footing in the Prairies and British Columbia; the higher eastbound schedule shielded their local market from outside competition. This low and flexible rate structure came through the courtesy of the federal government-owned Intercolonial Railway, which connected Halifax with Montreal. The Intercolonial's rate schedule reduced the railway's income from each ton of freight but so stimulated the Maritime economy that the increased *volume* of the trade permitted the railway to break even. Other railways, including the Canadian Pacific, were forced to match the Intercolonial or lose the region's business.[3]

Maritimers regarded their freight rate advantages as their right, as compensation for the disadvantages the creation of Canada had meant for the Atlantic partners in Confederation. Central and Western Canadians, the former conveniently forgetting the subsidy extended to Ontario and Quebec for canals on the St. Lawrence, to say nothing of the protective tariff, denounced the Intercolonial and its rates as special privileges that discriminated against the rest of the country. The other regions had the political power to get their way; the Maritime Members of Parliament were too few to defend their interpretation of the bargain they thought their provinces had made a half-century earlier. When Western and Central Canada decided to alter national sleeping arrangements, it was the Maritimes who were pushed out of the economic bed. The East-West differential was eliminated, and in 1918 the Intercolonial was stripped of its independence and the first steps taken towards its eventual integration into the Canadian National system. As a second step, the freight rate structure upon which Maritime industrialization had been predicated was methodically demolished. After 1920, rates were established on the advice of the federal Board of Railway Commissioners, who operated on the seemingly unimpeachable principle that the cost of shipping a ton of freight a mile should be the same everywhere in Canada. Determined to put this principle into practice, the board subjected Maritimers to four years of successive rate increases; between 1918 and 1922, these increases totalled 111 per cent. "The effect on the Maritime producer," concludes Ernest R. Forbes, "was almost as if he had been suddenly thrust a thousand miles out into the Atlantic." More than just the rate advantages was lost. The Intercolonial's head office in Moncton was closed and its functions were moved first to Toronto and then to Montreal; ". . . with the absorption of the Intercolonial into the Canadian National Railways, a major agency for independent regional development was extinguished and the metropolitan domination of the Maritime economy firmly consolidated."[4]

Most Maritime secondary industry was controlled not by local capitalists but by entrepreneurs based in Montreal or Toronto. Their response to the economic crisis of the early 1920s was to shutter their factories and relocate in Quebec or Ontario rather than stay and weather the storm. In 1921, for example, both Canadian Car and Foundry of Amherst, Nova Scotia, and the Maritime Nail Company of

Saint John transferred their operations to Montreal. During the four years that followed the two provinces lost almost 10,000 skilled jobs in industries related to iron and steel. Symbolic of the problems that besieged the Maritime economy was the spectacular rise and fall of the British Empire Steel and Coal Corporation. Formed in March 1920 by a merger of Nova Scotia Steel and Coal and Dominion Iron and Steel, Besco was the plaything of Montreal financier Roy Wolvin, a man who quickly became "the most powerful, respected, feared and hated individual in Nova Scotia." The new corporate giant did not solve the problems of the industry through integration; instead, it made them worse. The costs of acquiring the older companies saddled Besco with annual obligations of $8 million, which had to be met before it could show a profit. To permit his corporation to survive, Wolvin tried to squeeze the necessary profit margin out of the employees. The workers fought back against pay cuts, and in the end neither capital nor labour won the struggle. In 1926 Disco, the iron and steel subsidiary, was forced into receivership, and in 1928 Wolvin himself was edged out in a reorganization of the ramshackle Besco empire.[5]

While the manufacturing sector was being "hammered down to rock bottom," other sectors of the Maritime economy were unable to compensate. The Atlantic provinces had neither the metallic ores nor the hydroelectricity that stimulated mining and smelting development elsewhere. Modest growth of the pulp and paper industry was offset by decline in lumbering; in 1924 a once-prosperous Nova Scotia saw-milling centre was described as looking like "an abandoned town in the war area." Tourism brought some investment and created a few new jobs, but the Maritimes were hundreds of miles away from the large cities where Canadian and American tourists originated. Agriculture was handicapped by the Fordney-McCumber tariff, which kept Nova Scotia apples and P.E.I. and New Brunswick potatoes off American dinner tables; because new United States regulations for the sale of fresh fish acted as a non-tariff barrier to the fishing industry, the "larders" of Maritime fishermen "went as empty as Mother Hubbard's cupboard of doggerel reknown." About the only exports America accepted freely from Maritimers were their sons and daughters, as over 100,000 of them emigrated to the "Boston States" during the 1920s; the populations of Nova Scotia and Prince Edward Island were smaller in 1931 than in 1921, and New Brunswick's increased by barely 5 per cent despite a prodigious birth rate.[6]

Although Nova Scotia had a history of protest against the Canadian connection that dated back to 1867, the people of Nova Scotia, New Brunswick, and Prince Edward Island were slow to acquire a sense of regional solidarity. Their political cultures were characterized by an intense localism that retarded the emergence of a concept of provincial, let alone regional, cohesion. What finally created this solidarity was an external threat, the relative decline in the importance of the Atlantic provinces because of the more rapid growth of the rest of Canada. From forty-three Members of Parliament in 1882, Maritime representation in the House of Commons had by 1921 slipped to thirty-one. Since the size of the Commons had increased, the percentage drop was even larger. Resentment of the success of the West, which seemed to receive more favoured treatment in terms of federal subsidies, also contributed to a common Maritime frustration that transcended provincial boundaries. "It is time the east came out from behind the skirts of the west," said a 1919 article in the *Busy East of Canada*, a New Brunswick magazine devoted to promoting the Maritimes and to Maritime unity; "there is more to Canada than gigantic farms, more than great sweeps of prairie, more than Rocky Mountains and mushroom cities. . . . It is time for Maritime men . . . to realize that they are Canadians, and more than that, a special kind of Canadian – 'Maritimers' – . . . 'Self Determination for the Maritimes' – that is something which might be preached about. . . . The eastern provinces are waking from their dream."[7]

Post-war economic difficulties acted as midwife to the birth of a full-fledged regionalist movement, which rallied behind the slogan of "Maritime Rights." The movement had a broad base of support that cut across the dividing lines of class, ethnicity, and local identity, but its leadership was provided by businessmen and professionals, the traditional élite in Maritime communities. The structural framework was provided by local boards of trade grouped into a transprovincial Maritime Board of Trade, a moribund organization founded in 1895 that came back to life in the economic crisis of 1919. Three general demands were grouped under the heading "Maritime Rights": larger annual subsidies for the three provincial governments; a return to customary transportation policies with increased use of Halifax and Saint John as terminal ports for Canadian exports; and improved tariff protection for steel and coal. Most Maritime Rights advocates were protectionists, not free traders; "having been recently excluded from the benefits of the National Policy blanket, their immediate reaction was to try to get back under" rather than to "seek to wrest the blanket from others." These objectives were the antithesis of the program of the Progressive party, and the third-party tactic of Prairie protest was also rejected as unlikely to be successful; instead, regional discontent was expressed through the prevailing two-party system.[8]

The Liberal party was the first beneficiary of Maritime anger, as it had been the Borden and Meighen governments that were originally responsible for undermining the Intercolonial Railway. During the federal election campaign in 1921, Liberal candidates swore "to advocate and stand by Maritime rights first, last and all the time," a pledge that helped to return Liberals in all but six Maritime constituencies. Liberal performance in power, however, fell far short of the promises made when soliciting votes. The King government's policy toward the problems of Atlantic Canada did not differ visibly from that of the Union government. There can be no doubt of the Maritime Rights sincerity of Liberal back-benchers like Hance J. Logan, M.P. for Cumberland, Nova Scotia, but the need for party unity to maintain the government's narrow majority made it impossible for them to press their demands. When Maritime Liberal M.P.s met Mackenzie King to discuss the Intercolonial Railway issue in February 1922, he uncharacteristically lost his temper and "without tact . . . opened fire" upon their spokesmen, Logan and E.M. Macdonald, reminding them that "the Liberal party had not a majority in the house" and that "there was room for the farmers and the tories to combine" against it. Preoccupied with his plans to destabilize the Progressives, King never took this new Maritime assertiveness seriously, dismissing the "ugly and belligerent spirit" of the delegation as a front for the personal ambitions of Logan and Macdonald, "resentful at not having been taken into the cabinet." Despite warnings from Maritime Liberals that "our industries are decaying and the industrial picture of the future is indeed sad to contemplate," during the next four years King demonstrated, says Blair Neatby, "a complete disregard for the interests of the Atlantic provinces."[9]

Maritime Liberals paid the price of this shortsightedness, for their neglect of the region allowed the Conservative party to use Maritime Rights as an all-purpose elixir to restore itself to political health in New Brunswick, Nova Scotia, and Prince Edward Island. Tory fortunes in the Maritimes had hit bottom in 1921. Their dismal performance in the federal election was the last of a series of disasters that had begun with the defeat of the A.E. Arsenault government in Prince Edward Island in 1919 and continued with provincial pummellings in Nova Scotia and New Brunswick the next year. After the New Brunswick defeat in October 1920, there were only 20 Tories among the 121 members of Maritime legislatures. In Nova Scotia the party had been humiliated, reduced to three seats and replaced as the opposition by the Farmer-Labour group.

The Tories began to play the role of regional champions in July 1922, when an editorial in the Halifax *Herald*, owned by Conservative supporter W.H. Dennis, announced that it was "time for the people of the Maritimes to put shoulder to shoulder and fight for their rights."

The Liberals had made "frothy assurances and fulsome promises," but had failed to *"deliver the goods."* What the Maritimes needed was "action and practical rational results." As an attention-getting device, Conservative H.W. Corning rose in the Nova Scotia legislature to propose a provincial referendum "to ascertain whether or not the people were in favour of secession from Canada and the setting up of Nova Scotia as an independent, self-governing British Dominion." In Ottawa the handful of Maritime Tory M.P.s also took up the cry; J.B.M. Baxter of Saint John quickly made himself the recognized national spokesman for Atlantic Canada. The Conservatives became the self-appointed party of Maritime Rights with surprising ease and without any commitments from national leader Arthur Meighen; without promising a thing, Meighen still seemed more sympathetic to the region than King.[10]

The first Conservative success came in the P.E.I. election of July 1923, as Tories captured all but five provincial seats. The role of Maritime Rights in the campaign is difficult to assess precisely, but the issue was paramount in two December federal by-elections in Halifax and in Kent, New Brunswick. Both victories were gains for the Conservatives; Kent was a Liberal stronghold with an Acadian majority that had returned only one Tory since 1896. The remarkable result, Arthur Meighen was told, was less a vote for his party than "a crushing verdict of the Maritime Provinces in criticism of the non-recognition of this present [Liberal] government of Maritime Provinces rights." Despite the electoral evidence, Mackenzie King refused to believe that the region that had been second only to Quebec in its Liberal loyalties could slip so suddenly from his grasp. He attributed the by-election defeats to poor timing of the elections and to bad organization; he rebuffed delegations that attempted to present the Maritime case and ignored pleas that his indifference was alienating voters and party workers.[11]

But in 1925 Nova Scotia sent King a message that was impossible to ignore. Liberals had ruled in Halifax for forty-three consecutive years; at dissolution the Conservatives had held only three seats. In the June 25 provincial election, the positions were reversed, as the Tories won 61 per cent of the popular vote and forty out of forty-three constituencies. The Conservative renaissance was the result of a masterful and rapid reorganization. Party leader W.L. Hall was pushed aside for E.N. Rhodes, a former Speaker of the House of Commons, and a platform drafted in which the "promotion and maintenance of Nova Scotia rights" was a prominent plank. In a campaign partly financed by underwear baron Frank Stanfield, the electorate was served a mixture of nine parts raw regionalism delicately flavoured with one part of mildly reformist social welfare legislation. The Conservatives were particularly successful in seducing working-class and farm voters who had expressed their alienation in 1920 by supporting Farmer-Labour candidates. During the Cape Breton coal strikes, the Tories had castigated the Liberal government and Premier E.H. Armstrong for sending troops "to aid the British Empire Steel Corporation in its determined efforts to crush the workers in their demand for a square deal," and in 1925 they collected the return on their rhetorical investment. The class war in Cape Breton was easily distorted to fit into the Maritime Rights theme used by the Tories, who painted a black picture of a "foreign" corporation pushing Maritimers around. The ten Labour candidates' more coherent critique of capitalism could not compete with Conservative appeals to regional pride. Every Labourite was defeated, including five incumbents, and seven of them lost their deposits. Even in Cape Breton every seat went to the Tories.[12]

The Conservative upset in Nova Scotia, particularly its lopsided nature, came as "a complete surprise" to those outside the Maritimes. Canadians were "accustomed to discover political storms in the West," so that "ominous rumblings in the provinces down by the sea" ran so counter to the stereotype of the overcautious, phlegmatic Maritimes as to be almost incomprehensible. Another surprise was still to come, as six weeks later the Maritime Rights tornado roared through New Brunswick. Liberal Premier Peter Veniot tried without success to demonstrate that his opponents had no monopoly on New Brunswick patriotism. Led by J.B.M. Baxter, who had left federal politics to take over the provincial party, the Conservatives reduced the Veniot Liberals to a corporal's guard concentrated in the Acadian counties, where loyalty to an Acadian premier outweighed the appeal of regionalism.[13]

II

The landslide Conservative victories in Atlantic Canada came amid speculation about a federal election, for the Liberals were completing their fourth year in office. Most political commentators guessed that the cold wind from the Maritimes would mean a postponement until 1926. "The King Government," said the Calgary *Herald*, "has been shivering on the brink of an election; New Brunswick will intensify the shivers." The Prime Minister himself, however, still refused to believe that the Maritimes were an accurate barometer of national opinion. He received the news of Veniot's defeat just as he was about to dine with C.A. Dunning, the Liberal premier of Saskatchewan. "[It] dampened our ardour a bit at the table," he wrote in his diary, but "we agreed it was of local significance." King was determined to press ahead with his plans for an October election, despite Maritime Liberals' attempts to convince him that it would be nothing short of "Hari Kari [*sic*]." Even after the disaster in New Brunswick, he firmly believed that the Liberal party would not only win but obtain a comfortable majority to boot; how could it be otherwise, for "the party has a fine record to date. The Govt. stands four square and with a clean record and much accomplished despite hardships of a most exceptional kind."[14]

Mackenzie King was alone in this positive assessment of his government's record. Both historians and contemporary observers have agreed that it is impossible to point to a single conspicuous legislative achievement between 1922 and 1925. Liberal budgets blazed no new fiscal trails, and despite moans from manufacturers that the government was intent on "tariff butchering," the system of protection remained in place. The only difference between Conservative and Liberal tariff policies was that the Tories were openly and enthusiastically protectionist, while the Liberals saw an advantage to be gained by working both sides of the street. None of the projects outlined in the Liberal platform of 1919 had been realized; the "adequate system of insurance against unemployment, sickness [and] dependence in old age" seemed to have vanished altogether as an objective. The King government had steadily withdrawn from wartime and immediate post-war responsibilities and refused to assume new ones; between 1920 and 1925 the number of federal government employees was reduced from 47,000 to 39,000. Nor had promised electoral and governmental reforms been pressed any more vigorously. The "Important Debates of the 1923 Session," as described in the *Canadian Annual Review*, give an indication of the burning topics that occupied Canada's lawmakers. The most heated confrontations were over two private member's bills, one to abolish betting at race tracks (the gamblers won) and another to legalize the sale of margarine (butter turned back the challenge).[15]

This did not mean that there was nothing about the King government that could inspire admiration. "I have been very much surprised," admitted Labour M.P. William Irvine, "at the agility of their movements and their resources in finding excuses to get away from their own promises." King's was "the most inept, incapable, shuffling and procrastinating administration that we have known in federal politics for fifty years," fumed former prime minister Robert Borden, a man seldom given to narrow partisanship. Writing on "The Canadian Political Situation" in *Queen's Quarterly*, D.A. McArthur summarized these points of view in careful, academic prose: "The present ministry has not impressed itself on the public imagination.

Whether with justification or not there has been a widespread opinion that the government has not brought to the very urgent problems . . . the energy and initiative which the present situation demands. The last session of Parliament [1925] did not improve the position of the government in public esteem."[16]

However vocal his critics, Mackenzie King had one very good reason for self-satisfaction. There were no longer any threats to his leadership of the party, as both Lomer Gouin and W.S. Fielding had left his cabinet, the first voluntarily and the second because of a crippling stroke. King had no intention of allowing anyone of their stature to emerge; he recognized talent in his ministers and was quick to make use of it, but he made certain no rival became sufficiently popular to encourage regicide. King was, said the *Canadian Annual Review* in 1925, "in control of the situation . . . Master of His Party."[17]

Arthur Meighen, on the other hand, was never able to command the same sort of mastery over the Conservative party. Meighen was the first victim of that fractious tendency to devour leaders that has been designated the "Tory Syndrome." From almost the moment he assumed the party leadership, he was forced to expend a considerable part of his energy defending himself from attacks from within. He met these attacks head on, just as he confronted everything else. It has become a cliché to compare Meighen's personality with Mackenzie King's, as if their contrasting characters alone explain the course of Canadian politics in the twenties. This interpretation can be carried too far, but there is certainly much to contrast. Born in 1874 to Presbyterian families in small-town Ontario, educated at the University of Toronto – at that point any resemblance between the two men ends. At university King was a "big man on campus," active in student politics; Meighen was a reclusive mathematician. King went from Toronto to Harvard to Ottawa and entered politics at the top; Meighen went to Winnipeg and to Portage la Prairie to read and then to practise law. He accepted a federal nomination in 1908 when local Conservatives thought him a suitable sacrificial lamb in a Liberal bastion; he won, to his own and others' surprise. In the Commons the gaunt lawyer with the high forehead and the trouser cuffs that never quite reached his shoes had found his *métier*. In 1911 he became the youngest member of the Borden cabinet, and during the next nine years the self-confident Solicitor General was recognized as the *éminence grise* behind the Prime Minister, closely associated with the most controversial legislation of the Union government: conscription, wartime manipulation of the franchise, railway nationalization, and the suppression of the 1919 general strike in Winnipeg.[18]

Meighen was chosen to succeed Borden by the Conservative caucus rather than by an American-style convention of party delegates, and while his parliamentary skill was universally acknowledged, his popular appeal was uncertain. Those offended by the barrage of legislation he had unloosed could hardly be expected to be enthusiastic about him as prime minister, and Meighen never attempted to apologize for past actions. He had the unusual faculty in a politician of stating his convictions clearly, frankly, and concisely, even when circumstances might dictate equivocation or silence as politically more prudent courses. "I favoured conscription," he bluntly informed a Quebec audience during the 1921 election campaign. "I did it because I thought it right." In the House and on the hustings, Meighen was capable of caustic invective which infuriated his opponents. He lacked, says his biographer, Roger Graham, the technique of the soft answer that turneth away wrath. Tory elder statesmen expressed concern that this deficiency was hurting their party's image. Sir Joseph Flavelle admitted that Meighen made "a rather painful exhibit of King's duller mind and duller work in parliament," but feared that "the destructive character of his criticism . . . does not awaken enthusiasm." Sir Robert Borden worried that his protégé did "more harm than good by violent attack and bitter sarcasm."[19]

The contrasting political styles of Arthur Meighen and Mackenzie King did not determine the outcomes of their three electoral battles, but their profound dislike for one another gave each confrontation a uniquely personal flavour. During the autumn campaign of 1925, King's diary describes Meighen as "a frightful liar and a willful and knowing one" and as "mean, narrow and contemptible." Meighen's speeches ridiculed King's "time worn truisms, dusty platitudes and meaningless though prolific phraseology" and denounced his "dishonest campaign." The Liberal platform had as its themes the encouragement of immigration, Senate reform, transportation policy, and the inevitable tariff, but neither King nor his candidates presented any specific solutions to these problems; their request was for a decisive majority in order to deal with them. As he had in 1921, King remained deliberately vague, illustrating his own axiom that "any concrete scheme was target for an attack." Meighen, predictably, accused his opponent of "unprincipled political quackery" and dismissed the Liberal program as "an opaque mass of ill-founded and contradictory excuses." "What does he want a mandate to do?" Meighen asked his audiences. "He has not told us and he is not going to tell us." The Conservative leader was forthright about his own intentions and once again preached economic nationalism. "No single country in the world," he explained to his hearers, "requires a tariff so vitally as does this Dominion." Listening only to Meighen and King, the voters might have imagined they were caught in a time-warp, but the absence of Thomas Crerar enabled them to distinguish the election of 1925 from that of four years earlier. Progressive leader Robert Forke pretended that he had a national force behind him, but with only seventy-two candidates, forty-five of them in the Prairie Provinces, he was unable to conceal both the regionalization and the gradual disintegration of his party. Labour was weaker as well, with only twenty-three candidates nominated and no semblance of national co-ordination.[20]

The choice was between King and Meighen, and Meighen's task of convincing the electorate to embrace the man, the party, and the policies it had spurned in 1921 was immeasurably easier in 1925. There were four newly minted Conservative provincial governments to throw their machines into the fray on his behalf, and four fresh Tory premiers were available to join him on the platform in Ontario and in the Maritime provinces. King received less than enthusiastic assistance from Saskatchewan's Dunning and from "Honest John" Oliver of British Columbia and none at all from Farmer premiers Bracken of Manitoba and Greenfield of Alberta, who privately preferred King to Meighen but maintained a scrupulous public neutrality.[21]

The national campaigns of both parties stopped at the boundaries of Quebec. French-Canadian Liberals and Conservatives were left to design their own election strategies. Mackenzie King accepted the concept of a virtually autonomous Quebec wing with a French-speaking *chef* to lead it. King spoke no French and despite occasional guilty twinges made no attempt to learn. Although he did not have any special understanding of Quebec, he did understand its importance to his political survival; without a solid Quebec behind him he could kiss the prime ministership goodbye. King carefully chose Ernest Lapointe as his French-Canadian lieutenant and gave him a special place in cabinet and in party councils. When Sir Lomer Gouin retired, Lapointe became Minister of Justice and remained in this senior portfolio in all Liberal governments until his death in 1941. As C.G. "Chubby" Power remembered it, "Lapointe became so completely the representative of the Liberal Party in Quebec that for many years King counted little in the political life of the province. . . . It was to Lapointe that we looked for leadership, for generalship, and for anything relating to either policy or tactics in Quebec political life."[22]

Arthur Meighen was less enthusiastic about an autonomous Quebec Conservative party that would operate along such lines. There was no Quebec Tory who was an obvious candidate to lead it; Meighen preferred to assume rather than to delegate responsibility, and the idea of separate appeals to French and English Canada ran counter to his nature. As Opposition Leader he had worked to acquire competence in French, and although he never became *un parfait bilingue*, by 1925 he was able to prepare and deliver a speech with remarkable fluency in his second language. Meighen got no chance to use his new linguistic skills, however, for the party chose to try for instant credibility by appointing a Quebec *chef* who would campaign as if the Conservatives and their national leader did not exist. E.L. Patenaude, the designated Messiah, had served in the Borden government and resigned in 1917 over the issue of conscription. Patenaude accepted the economic positions taken by the Tory platform but added a special Quebec codicil on external affairs that Canada should not go to war unless the electorate was consulted on the question beforehand. Although he denied that he had formed a "parti québécois" and affirmed his support for "the tradition and principles" of the Conservative party, Patenaude also declared himself and the other Tory candidates in Quebec to be independent of the national party. *"I am in every way free,"* he said in his speeches and campaign literature; *"I am free from Mr. Meighen even as I am free from Mr. King."* With their new Quebec acquisition combined with their strength in the rest of the country the Conservatives sensed victory just ahead. J.B.M. Baxter was only one of many to invoke the image of Patenaude "acting as Cartier to Meighen's Macdonald." As Roger Graham points out, however, "it is not on record that the real Cartier had declared himself free from John A. Macdonald even as he was free from George Brown."[23]

Quebec Liberals had no intention of allowing Patenaude to dissociate himself from Arthur Meighen, for Meighen's connection with the Military Service Act was central to their campaign. They fought hard and dirty, with scant concern for truth and even less thought to the damage that resurrecting the racial animosities of wartime might do to the "national unity" Mackenzie King professed as his objective. Liberal editorials recited a litany of Meighen's crimes: "Conscription! Blood spilt! The blood of our sons! Spilt in far away countries on the other side of the ocean!" Vicious cartoons depicted a demonic Meighen driving soldiers to war with a whip or handing them over to the satanic, skeletal hands of "l'imperialisme." Ignoring the fact that not a single conscript had died in the Great War, Premier Taschereau described Meighen as "the man of conscription . . . who, with his conscription law, has filled the cemeteries of Flanders with 60,000 Canadians." Local Liberal organizers canvassed house to house, warning mothers that after a Meighen victory "the entrails of their sons would be scattered on the streets of Constantinople." Grattan O'Leary, Conservative candidate in Gaspé, was introduced at an open meeting as "the candidate of the Protestants and the Jews." When he rose to speak he found the front row of the hall packed with elderly ladies chanting rhythmically "conscription, conscription, conscription . . ." Mackenzie King did not personally contribute to this vilification of his opponent, but he made no attempt to halt or to moderate it. In his own speeches he "stress[ed] unity Fr[ench] and Eng[lish], Protestant and Catholic . . . using Lapointe and myself as examples." His support in Quebec, he convinced himself, came because "by standing by Laurier I have won the hearts of the French Canadians and they are a most lovable people."[24]

Despite the excellent prospects in Quebec, however, there was gloomy news from every other province save Saskatchewan. For reassurance King turned to a source of information not consulted by his colleagues. When his campaign train stopped in Kingston he paid his first visit to Mrs. L. Bleaney, a fortune teller/spiritualist. Mrs. Bleaney obliged King with a vision of "two sinister figures, one a man with high cheek bones, sunken a little beneath, thin and inclined to be tall. . . . They would like to destroy you . . . they would like to take away your power and position," she warned, "but they won't succeed." King had no trouble recognizing Arthur Meighen as the first sinister figure; the other, he decided, was Senator Gideon Robertson. Mrs. Bleaney then described the deceased members of King's immediate family: father, mother, brother Max and sister Bella, assured him they were beside him and that he "wd. certainly win the elections." King was enormously impressed; he pronounced the conversation "the most remarkable interview I have ever had." Mrs. Bleaney had acquired a customer who would return, for she had confirmed King's conviction that he was not fighting alone. He wrote in his diary that he felt "more and more a nearness to the great realities of existence, a belief in unseen influences directing it all." Confident that God would not back a loser, Mackenzie King predicted a Liberal majority of twenty-five seats.[25]

III

October 29, 1925, came as a rude shock. Narrow margins in some constituencies meant that it took several days before all returns could be declared final, but the outcome suggested that the electorate had failed to heed the "unseen influences." Only ninety-nine Liberals were elected, fifty-nine of them from Quebec. The Prime Minister lost in his own riding of North York, and eight other cabinet ministers suffered defeat. The Conservatives made an incredible recovery from the disaster of 1921. They more than doubled their representation from

49 to 116; in Ontario the Tories won 68 of 82 seats. The Progressives were decimated, reduced to twenty-four members, all but two from Manitoba, Saskatchewan, and Alberta. J.S. Woodsworth was returned to lead the "Labour group," but the group's other member was now A.A. Heaps from Winnipeg North, as William Irvine lost to a Conservative in Calgary East. The popular vote – 45.6 per cent Conservative, 39.9 per cent Liberal, 8.9 per cent Progressive – could have only one interpretation. "The meaning is unmistakeable," said the Toronto *Globe*, a paper usually squarely in the Liberal camp; "[it is] a severe vote of want of confidence in the administration." The election was unequivocally a Liberal disaster, but it was not an unconditional Tory victory. The problem for the Conservatives continued to be Quebec. Patenaude had almost doubled the party's popular vote to 33.7 per cent, but the party won only four seats, all in English-speaking areas. Despite the massive Canada-wide improvement in their electoral fortunes, the Conservatives were seven seats short of the 123 needed for majority control of the Commons (see Table Ib).[26]

Thus no one, Conservatives included, could deny that the Liberals had a right to meet parliament, submit a legislative program, and attempt to secure enough Progressive and Labour support to enact it. Mackenzie King, seatless and without a third of his cabinet, was constitutionally entitled to remain in office until parliament could meet and pass judgement on what was left of his government. He never seriously considered handing over power to Meighen, despite widespread editorial advice to the effect that "his wise course in the public interest and in consideration of his own prestige and dignity would be to resign." Here King's capacity for rationalization was helpful, for he quickly convinced himself that the electorate had not really rejected him. "There can be no doubt," ran the self-justification in his diary, "that money lies at the basis of our whole defeat – money from the big interests – seeking further protection – and lack of organization on our part." His own loss in North York was the result of Tory corruption and "reveal[ed] what money and whiskey can do" to subvert an election. The Liberal cabinet supported King's plan to cling to power as long as possible. A second election would almost certainly be required before long to resolve the near deadlock, and the Liberals intended to have the governmental advantage of control of the electoral machinery. Another session of parliament would give them a chance to shore up their sagging popularity with a legislative basket of pre-election goodies; it would also, as it turned out, provide the Conservatives with an opportunity to snatch defeat from the jaws of victory.[27]

Many Liberals had strong doubts about the quality of King's leadership after the electoral débâcle, but their finely honed instinct for survival guided their criticism into intraparty channels. The Conservatives, instead of consolidating their partial victory, were soon in the midst of another public round of internal friction and leader bashing. The source of their conflict was Meighen's announcement in an address in Hamilton that in the event of war, a Conservative government of which he was prime minister would call an election to obtain a mandate before sending Canadian soldiers overseas. The declaration was obviously intended to win support in Quebec, and was not made on the spur of the moment but after careful deliberation with senior Tories. Meighen also made his own sentiments clear: ". . . if danger threatened the Empire," he hoped that "this country would respond as it responded in 1914." His "Heresy at Hamilton," however, brought him denunciations from Tory imperialists without improving the Conservative position in Quebec. A good example of contrasting degrees of party fidelity is provided by J.W. Dafoe and M.E. Nichols, editors respectively of the Liberal Manitoba *Free Press* and the Conservative Winnipeg *Tribune*. Dafoe swallowed his distaste for King, and his paper supported every manoeuvre of the discredited government; Nichols's *Tribune* insisted on "sticking its spear into [Meighen] quite savagely." After the Hamilton speech an outspoken *Tribune* editorial accused Meighen of bringing about the "end of Canada's attachment to the British Empire."[28]

Tory disunity revived Liberal morale for the coming struggle in parliament. The direction in which Progressive support would move was uncertain, for election losses had reduced the Liberal-leaning wing of the party and made its less predictable Ginger Group correspondingly stronger. Progressive "leader" Robert Forke was ready as ever to simply merge his followers with the Liberals and become Minister of Agriculture as his reward, but the more radical Progressives suspected that King would "stall them off with promises but he will not come through." A straw vote in the Progressive caucus revealed that a slight majority accepted this argument and intended to support Meighen. To test the opinions of each leader, a shopping list of fourteen Progressive desires was submitted to both for their approval. Meighen was non-committal, referring them to the Conservative platform; Mackenzie King wrote each Progressive M.P. individually and promised his real answer would come in the Speech from the Throne which would open the parliamentary session on January 8, 1926. The brush with defeat had snapped the Liberals out of their legislative lethargy; things that had been impossible six months earlier now became priorities: a farm loan program, rapid completion of the Hudson Bay Railway, immediate transfer of Alberta's natural resources to provincial control. Tariff changes would be studied by a non-partisan tariff advisory board which would report at an unspecified future date. This was enough to buy the votes of nineteen of the Progressives, but the Liberals were still short of the magic number, so that the votes of J.S. Woodsworth and freshman Labour member A.A. Heaps were indispensable. Heaps and Woodsworth did not come cheap; in return for their support, King was forced to promise a system of old age pensions and amendments to anti-radical sections of the criminal code and the immigration laws. They knew the man they were dealing with well enough to demand that King put the bargain in writing, and to make absolutely certain it was kept Woodsworth read the letter into Hansard! In the first division of the session the Liberals, led by Ernest Lapointe in his seatless leader's involuntary absence, squeezed through with a margin of three.[29]

For the next six months King's plan succeeded. The session was one of the most acrimonious in Canadian parliamentary history, but the Liberals continued to win critical divisions, twice with majorities of one vote. King found a safe seat in Saskatchewan and marvelled at the ruthless efficiency with which the provincial Liberal machine prepared the ground for his by-election triumph. The name of his new constituency was also that of a popular style of overcoat, giving rise to the worst joke of 1926 as wags punned that the Prime Minister had "borrowed a Quebec fur coat to go west and now he has returned in the spacious folds of his Prince Albert." With King came Charles Dunning, the Western Lapointe he had sought since 1921, to become his Minister of Railways and Canals. The long economic recession had finally lifted, and as the April sun warmed winter-weary Canadians, Finance Minister James Robb introduced a "sunshine budget" which lowered postal rates and reduced income taxes for the quarter million whose incomes were high enough to pay them. There was also a genuine tariff bombshell. The rate on automobiles valued at less than $1,200 was to be lowered, knocking ninety dollars off the dealer price of a Ford or a Chevy. "The effect of the Budget on the Liberal Party," remarked a political commentator, "has been the same as when smelling salts are applied to the nose of a delicate lady who is on the verge of fainting. It has revived their drooping spirits, consolidated their *rapprochement* with the Progressives, and offered proof that the King ministry is a living, functioning administration – a point concerning which grave doubts were hitherto entertained." The Old Age Pension Bill passed without much opposition; the fact that a majority of crusty Conservative senators ultimately blocked it in the Upper House meant that the King Liberals won the praise of those who supported it without incurring the full wrath of Quebec's Premier Taschereau, who was opposed.[30]

Only one issue clouded the government's horizon. Exporting liquor illegally to the United States was one of Canada's leading growth industries in the 1920s; as the *Financial Post* pointed out, "rum-running has provided a tidy bit towards Canada's favorable balance of trade." There was, however, a serious economic side-effect. Like the other great staple trades so prominent in Canadian economic history – fish, fur, timber – rum-running needed a return cargo to fill the empty trucks and boats on the way home. The result was an escalation of smuggling of clothing, cigarettes, radios, and auto parts, a traffic which Minister of Customs Jacques Bureau estimated to be worth $50 million annually by 1925. Bureau was in a position to know. One of his senior civil servants, Joseph Bisaillon, chief preventive officer of the Montreal Customs district, was Canada's leading smuggler – "a protectionist by day and a free trader by night." Bureau had received gifts of confiscated liquor from Bisaillon, and his chauffeur had purchased a smuggled automobile. King was aware of the corruption. Diary entries in August, 1925, note that Bureau was "on another drunken spree," and that it was "outrageous and disgraceful the manner in which the customs dept. was being run. It is well-nigh a sink of iniquity." But an alcoholic, dishonest minister could not be dismissed without considering the political implications. Bureau had represented Trois-Rivières in the Commons since 1900 and was extremely popular with his Quebec colleagues and particularly close to Ernest Lapointe. King feared that "we w[oul]d be defeated in 3 Rivers in a by-election that w[oul]d mean a break in Quebec and a sign of disintegration getting in there." In September Bureau was appointed to the Senate, Georges Boivin appointed to replace him, and Joseph Bisaillon quietly fired.[31]

This proved to be neither a political nor a practical solution to problems of smuggling and of the complicity of the Customs Department. Manufacturers hurt by the illegal competition had formed the Commercial Protective Association to demand that it be stopped. Unsatisfied with the feeble response of the government, association president R.P. Sparks turned a bulging dossier on the Customs Department over to H.H. Stevens, Conservative member for Vancouver Centre. To silence Stevens temporarily, Boivin referred the question to a special committee, made Stevens a member, and waited. The committee's report revealed "an amazing series of . . . smuggling incidents" and produced "convincing evidence that for some years gangs of smugglers and crooks have enjoyed not merely the tacit connivance of a multitude of customs officials, but in many cases their active cooperation in making a wholesale mockery of the Customs laws." The treasury had been defrauded of hundreds of thousands of dollars in unpaid duty and uncollected fines. Boivin had not only failed to clean up the unsavoury mess, but had, as Ralph Allen has put it, "approached it like a man who has inherited a concession." Most damaging to the new minister was the revelation that he had arranged the release from jail of Moses Aziz, a convicted bootlegger and smuggler from Caraquet, New Brunswick. The Liberal M.P. for Gloucester had counted on the bootlegger as an election worker; "I need the help of all my friends," he indiscreetly wrote to Boivin. "Mr. Aziz is the highest help for us during this campaign, and we cannot do without his services."[32]

Frustrated in their previous attempts to defeat the government, the Conservatives now had the explosive evidence they needed. When the report was presented to parliament, H.H. Stevens moved an amendment that the committee be specifically instructed to censure not only Boivin but also the Prime Minister and the government itself. It quickly became clear that the amendment was likely to pass, bringing down the King government and tagging it with responsibility for the ugliest political scandal since the 1870s. The first Progressive to speak to the amendment reminded his colleagues that they were "the one hope of cleaning up our public life and bringing about a better condition of affairs in this Canada of ours"; failure to censure such flagrant corruption would break faith with all that their movement represented. J.S. Woodsworth, who hoped to extract further social legislation from King, held his nose and tried to save the government by moving a sub-amendment that took the sting out of Stevens's condemnation. After a long and impassioned debate before packed galleries, it failed to carry; when the House adjourned in exhaustion at 5:15 on the morning of Saturday, June 27, 1926, the success of the Stevens amendment and the defeat of the King government seemed certain to follow when it resumed sitting on Monday afternoon.[33]

IV

Neither event took place as expected. To avoid a Commons defeat and the censure of his government, Mackenzie King asked the Governor General to dissolve parliament so that he might "appeal to [the] higher court from which parliament derives its authority," the electorate. This course had the double advantage of dodging Stevens's bullet and leaving the Liberals in charge of the electoral machinery; the snag was that Governor General Byng refused to grant King a dissolution. Baron Julian Hedworth George Byng of Vimy was a soldier, not a politician or an imperial statesman. He had been a second choice when he was appointed in 1921; the qualification that won him the job despite his lack of experience was his year in command of the Canadian Corps in

France during the war. At his first official luncheon, Byng admitted that he expected to "make mistakes. I made some mistakes in France, but when I did the Canadians always pulled me out of the hole. That's what I'm counting on here." The new representative of the Crown was too modest; he became a very popular governor general with the public and he made very few mistakes. As Byng's five-year term of office drew to a close in April, 1926, Mackenzie King assured British Prime Minister Stanley Baldwin that "responsible government in Canada has never reached a more satisfactory stage of development than that enjoyed under Lord Byng. . . ." This opinion changed quickly during that weekend in June. By remaining in office after the 1925 election, King had violated Lord Byng's military ideal of honourable, dignified, and sportsmanlike behaviour; for King to demand another election without giving Meighen a chance to attempt to govern seemed to Byng "wrong and unfair, and not for the welfare of the people." He resolved in "the best interests of the country" not to permit it.[34]

This is the essence of what has been called the "Constitutional Crisis" of 1926 or more accurately the "King-Byng Affair," for there never was a "constitutional crisis" other than in the hyperbole of the subsequent election campaign. In his *Colony to Nation*, first published in 1946, Arthur Lower observed that "oceans of ink have been spilled to prove that Lord Byng (a) had, (b) did not have, the right to refuse dissolution to King." Since that was written several additional "oceans of ink" have flowed on the question, but the answer can be stated very simply: Byng's action was unquestionably a legal use of the prerogatives of his office. Eugene Forsey argues that it was not only Byng's right but even Byng's *duty* to refuse to dissolve parliament while a motion censuring the government was still before it. It was King's behaviour, not the Governor General's, that was constitutionally outrageous. King produced arguments to justify his position, but "he was trying to use the constitution as the Devil quotes Scripture, to serve his own ends." In his desperation even "the sacred principle of [Canadian] autonomy was overshadowed by the need for a dissolution," as he asked Byng to seek advice from L.S. Amery, Secretary of State for the Dominions in the *British* cabinet. On Monday, June 29, after Byng had rejected his request for the third time, Mackenzie King disregarded a third constitutional precedent; he handed the Governor General a letter of resignation from the prime ministership and refused to remain in office during the transitional period while Byng sought an alternative government. That afternoon he announced to a flabbergasted House of Commons that he was now but "a humble member" and that "at the present time there is no government."[35]

Arthur Meighen's decision to accept the Governor General's invitation to attempt to form a government turned out in retrospect to be a major political mistake. Several things persuaded him to accept office: the enthusiasm of the Conservative caucus, the desire to avoid leaving Lord Byng twisting in the wind without advisers, and his own feeling that he had won the election of 1925 and been cheated of his victory. After discussions with several Progressives, Meighen expected that his government would have a narrow but reliable parliamentary majority. There was only one technical obstacle in Meighen's path to power. At that time (and until 1931) any Member of Parliament who accepted a ministry had to give up his seat and be re-elected at a by-election. To conform to this requirement would have temporarily deprived the Conservatives of votes they needed in the Commons. To circumvent it, only Arthur Meighen himself formally accepted office (as prime minister) and vacated his seat; six of his senior colleagues were appointed Ministers without Portfolio and assigned *acting* responsibility for various departments, a manoeuvre that legally entitled them to remain in parliament.

To the Tories' surprise, the government of acting ministers lasted less than three days. It won three major divisions, one a motion of non-confidence in its economic policy. But when the Liberals attacked the "Shadow Government" of acting ministers as unconstitutional, it was unable to retain enough Progressive support to survive. A motion by James Robb that challenged the Conservatives' legal right to hold office was passed by a majority of one at 2 A.M., July 2. Without Meighen in parliament to lead it, his ministry had established two dubious records: it was the shortest-lived government in Canadian history and the first to be defeated by a vote in the House of Commons. Since there was no possibility of a government that could command a majority, Lord Byng accepted Meighen's advice and dissolved parliament.[36]

It is difficult, after their rejection of the King government only eleven months earlier, to explain the voters' decision to give the Liberals a majority government of 128 seats in the general election on September 14, 1926. The Conservatives had been certain of victory; instead they were reduced to ninety-one members (see Table Ic). The long campaign was a gruelling marathon for the party leaders, who crossed and re-crossed the country, living on railway trains. Apart from local experiments with radio broadcasts, direct contact was the mainstay of both campaigns. Meighen and King spoke several times a day, without the aid of modern sound systems. Only in larger cities did they have the luxury of a stage in an auditorium or a theatre; most of their speeches were given from station platforms or in armouries or skating rinks. Old-timers grumbled that Canadian politics had gone soft compared to the nineteenth century, when axe handles were routinely taken to rallies, but if the worst goon tactics had disappeared, overripe tomatoes and rotten eggs had not, and leather-lunged hecklers and pre-arranged disruptions of meetings were still the rule rather than the exception. A journalist's description of Arthur Meighen campaigning in Winnipeg on a blazing August day gives an idea of what the Canadian system of electioneering forced party leaders to endure: ". . . travel-tired, he is languid with fatigue, his throat is like a file; his voice is just a croak. . . . His face is red and moist with heat . . . his eyes are pits beneath his forehead. . . ." King put himself through the same agony; it was, said the Ottawa *Journal*, "a body and mind-killing pace."[37]

King in particular bore the torment willingly. Unlike 1925, this time he had an issue, or at least believed he had one, in the "constitutional crisis." " 'The God of our fathers hath chosen me,' " he wrote in his diary. "I see it all so clearly. . . . I go forward in the strength of God & His Might and Right to battle as my forefathers battled for the rights of the people and God's will on earth." In King's version of the events of June and July, Arthur Meighen had usurped power, threatening "constitutional liberty, freedom and right in all parts of the world." By refusing to accept King's advice, Lord Byng had stabbed at "the very heart of self-government of the Dominions." Only by voting Liberal could Canadians save "the principles of liberty and freedom embedded in the British constitution" from these perfidious attacks. John S. Ewart and Henri Bourassa, the best-known advocates of Canadian autonomy, helped Mackenzie King to get his argument across. A man's attitude on the constitutional question, said Ewart, was "an infallible test of his Canadianism"; Lord Byng, wrote Bourassa, had done "violence to the constitution" and allowed himself to be used by "shameless politicians." The Liberals also received the enthusiastic endorsement of the infant Communist Party of Canada, which promised to "help them with all their might . . . in their fight for complete independence from Downing Street."[38]

It is impossible to measure the importance of the King-Byng affair to the election in terms of seats won or lost. It was certainly less important to the Liberal gains than the reduction of postal rates and auto prices brought about by the Robb budget. Arthur Meighen stated flatly that "there [was] no constitutional issue," and John G. Diefenbaker, candidate against Mackenzie King in Prince Albert, described King's use of the "alleged constitutional crisis" as "so phoney it made Barnum look like an amateur." From the opposite perspective, J.H. King, former and future Liberal cabinet minister, claimed that "Meighen's usurpation of power and the means he adopted have caused a feeling of great unrest . . . [in] the man in the street." The answer lies somewhere between these extremes, but J.H. King's comment suggests that the importance of the constitutional issue was that it rallied the Liberal party to its newly inspired leader. It also provided some Progressives with the excuse they needed to return to the Liberal fold, put the Conservatives on the defensive, and served as a counterpoise to Conservative use of the Customs Scandal. By making the scandal a major element of their campaign, the Tories overplayed their hand. Even Conservative papers like the Calgary *Herald* complained that "Canada has heard enough . . . nothing that [the Conservative party] can say, no elaboration of nasty details, will further assist its candidates." Since the principal characters in the scandal were all French Canadians – Bureau, Bisaillon, Boivin – pursuing the culprits with such diligence made it seem like a Tory vendetta against Quebec. On August 7, Georges Boivin died of appendicitis while attending a Knights of Columbus convention in Philadelphia; the zeal of his tormentors, implied *Le Devoir*, had caused his premature passing. Mackenzie King made only brief appearances in Quebec during the campaign, but one of these was a well-publicized pilgrimage to Boivin's grave. It was all the Liberals needed.[39]

The Conservatives integrated their Quebec and national appeals in 1926. E.L. Patenaude had been made acting Minister of Justice in the Meighen cabinet and could hardly claim to be independent. The changes solved nothing. Meighen's Hamilton pledge had had absolutely no effect on his image among French Canadians. He and Patenaude toured rural Quebec together, talking crops as well as politics; the farmers were open and hospitable, but every conversation ended the same way: "I can't vote for you; I've got a seventeen-year-old son." There was a marginal improvement in the Conservative popular vote in Quebec, but Patenaude again failed to win a seat and the party was confined to the same four English-speaking ridings that it had won in 1925.[40]

In Nova Scotia, however, the Conservatives were still identified as the friends of Maritime Rights, and they strengthened the firm grip they had taken a year earlier. Liberal promises of a royal commission to investigate Maritime claims helped them win back three Acadian seats in New Brunswick and one seat in Prince Edward Island. This slight change was offset by British Columbia, where the Conservatives won twelve of fourteen seats, a gain of two from the Liberals. British Columbians, complained a disgruntled Liberal, were "provincial in the National aspect and out of touch with Canadian affairs"; the Tory candidates had convinced them that "McKenzie [*sic*] King is disloyal" and their sentimental attachment to the British Empire had done the rest.[41]

Ontario and Manitoba were the two provinces that lifted the Liberals to their majority, as they gained fifteen and ten seats respectively. Those Progressives who were sympathetic to the Liberals, frightened to death of a Tory government, came out of the closet; Forke appeared on the platform with King, and his wing of the Progressive party dealt openly with the Liberals. Twelve ran as hyphenated Liberal-Progressives, while in thirty-six other constituencies three-cornered fights were avoided by one party's agreeing not to nominate a candidate. In Winnipeg and Calgary the local Independent Labour parties, nervous about Meighen's attitude to trade unions and fearful that the Tories would kill the Old Age Pension Bill, made similar arrangements. H.B. Adshead in Calgary East and J.S. Woodsworth in Winnipeg North Centre were unopposed by official Liberal candidates, while Labour returned the favour in Calgary West and in two south Winnipeg constituencies. This strategy of concentrating forces behind a single candidate was devastating to the Conservatives. R.B. Bennett was the sole Tory to be elected between the Red River and the Rockies. In 1925 the Conservatives had won seven seats in Manitoba; they added to their popular vote in 1926, and yet all of their candidates were wiped out.[42]

Arthur Meighen was one of the Manitoba casualties; he lost Portage la Prairie by 428 votes. The narrow margin of his personal defeat reflected what had happened to his party nationally. Overall, its share of the popular vote declined by only 1.2 per cent and the absolute number of Conservative votes increased slightly over 1925. What made the end of Arthur Meighen's career as the "first swordsman of parliament" so bitter was, not that he lost, but that he had come so close to winning. Meighen's low esteem for his opponent rubbed salt into his wounds, and the suggestion of some Conservatives that those wounds were self-inflicted added pain to his humiliation. He moved out of the prime minister's office on September 25, 1926, and resigned the party leadership the next morning.[43]

Although another leader would reap the benefit of it, Arthur Meighen had restored his party as a national political force, just as Mackenzie King had done for the Liberals. It never occurred to either of the bitter enemies that they were also collaborators: partners in patching back together the Canadian pattern of party politics. They had diverted the regional discontent of the Maritimes and the West, the national consciousness of French Canada, and the latent consciousness of the working class into the deep, slowly moving channels of the traditional two-party system. In 1921 Labour candidates, Progressives, and assorted independents had attracted the votes of one Canadian in three; in the 1926 election only one voter in twelve chose these options. Once Meighen was gone, the personality conflict that had given a chimera of significance to the minor differences between the major parties vanished with him. When Hugh Guthrie, Meighen's temporary replacement, defined "the more outstanding principles of the Conservative party," he spoke in vague generalities about "speedy development of our natural resources . . . fair, equal and generous treatment of every section of Canada . . . [and] the building up of Canadian national spirit. . . ." Any one of these platitudinous pearls could have dropped from the lips of Mackenzie King without disturbing the sleep of a single listener. A veteran political journalist remarked that ". . . the line of cleavage between the parties is not so sharply drawn as it was fifty years ago. Men then talked about their 'political principles' and meant something by it, or fancied that they did. . . . It would be difficult in these peaceful days to identify anything in the nature of sharp-cut principle separating Grit from Tory. . . . It has really come to be largely a matter of ins and outs."[44]

V

One of Lord Byng's final duties before his return to Great Britain was to swear in Mackenzie King and his new government. Both men behaved with punctilious correctness, a charade that was much easier for the incoming prime minister than the outgoing governor general. One by one the seventeen ministers were introduced and took the oath, eight of them for the first time. Among the new faces were Minister of Labour Peter Heenan, a locomotive engineer elected as a Liberal-Labour candidate in northwestern Ontario, and J.L. Ralston, a Nova Scotian war hero who became Minister of National Defence. Lapointe and Robb were in their familiar portfolios of Justice and Finance, Motherwell in Agriculture, Dunning in Railways and Canals. Customs and Excise, which had caused all the trouble, was turned over to W.D. Euler, a tiresomely rectitudinous Ontarian. Lest anyone think this was a sign that King doubted the capacity of his French-Canadian colleagues, Fernand Rinfret became Secretary of State, Lucien Cannon Solicitor General, and P.J. Veniot – after an investigation of his honesty – Postmaster General. Robert Forke, all pretence of Progressivism behind him, became Minister of Immigration and Colonization; T.A. Crerar joined him in the cabinet in 1929, completing the reintegration of the "crypto-Liberal" Progressives. Alberta was represented in the cabinet by Minister of the Interior Charles Stewart and British Columbia by Health Minister J.H. King, so that every province had a place. Political analysts had speculated that the Canadian Liberals might be "doomed to follow the Liberal Party of England into the limbo of forgotten things"; now William Lyon Mackenzie King had brought it back to its pre-war state by reconstructing the Prairie-Quebec axis that had been the foundation of its power.[45]

Bankers and businessmen welcomed the new political stability. All economic indices were good and 1926 had "undoubtedly been the most satisfactory year for business since the setback of 1921." Canada had at last rediscovered "the pathway to continued prosperity" that had eluded her since the end of the war; she would remain upon it, said Sir John Aird, President of the Bank of Commerce, if the government would avoid "the tendency towards multiplying the activities of the State . . . that nullifies the work of constructive industry in increasing production." What Canada needed, according to Sir Herbert Holt of the Royal Bank, was "to follow the example set by the United States in the reduction of all taxes and in the cost of government." Holt was referring to the Republican administration of President Calvin Coolidge, every capitalist's idea of a model statesman, and the author of such profundities of the new economic era as "the business of America is business." Canadian politicians took such advice very seriously; one of the many common convictions of Liberal "ins" and Conservative "outs" was that they should balance the budget and then leave the rest to the "captains of industry." Total spending by the federal government declined from $476.3 million in 1921 to a low of $352.2 million in 1924 and rose more slowly than population growth to $405.3 million in 1929. Between 1921 and 1929 there was a 25-percent decrease in per capita federal spending, from $54.20 to $40.41 for each Canadian (see Table II).[46]

This was accomplished by cutting out programs established by the Union government and by not establishing new ones. The Department of Health, created in a flurry of federal activism in 1919, was allowed to deteriorate throughout the subsequent decade, suffering staff and program reductions. In 1928 the department was amalgamated with Soldiers' Civil Re-establishment as the Department of Pensions and National Health. The structure of the new name indicates the low priority the federal government assigned to health and welfare activities. The exception to the general federal retreat would seem to be the Old Age Pensions Act of 1927, but the act's origins and its limited scope suggest that it was not really an exception. The pension system introduced was scarcely the harbinger of the welfare state. It provided British subjects over the age of seventy and with twenty years' residence in Canada with $20 a month, if they could demonstrate in a means test that their annual income from all sources was less than $125. On the pensioner's death, the pension was to be repaid by the sale of any property remaining in the estate – with 5 per cent compound interest added. The plan was to be jointly financed by the federal and provincial governments, but although the four Western provinces joined with alacrity, Ontario dragged its feet until November 1929, and many elderly Canadians were left without pensions until the mid-thirties when the Maritime Provinces and Quebec at last signed agreements with Ottawa. Quebec's hesitation was philosophical; Nova Scotia, New Brunswick, and Prince Edward Island held back because their battered economies left their governments unable to pay their half-share of the costs.[47]

The federal government had investigated the complaints of the Maritime Rights movement as it had promised. During the politically turbulent summer of 1926, a commission headed by British jurist Sir Arthur Rae Duncan produced a catalogue of far-reaching recommendations as to how Ottawa could assist the prostrate regional economy back to its feet. The *Report of the Royal Commission on Maritime Claims* called for a 20-per-cent reduction in all rail rates, revitalization of Atlantic ports, aid to the steel and coal industries, and – its most controversial recommendation – increased federal subsidies to be based on provincial need rather than any historical justification. Those Maritimers who hailed the report as a "Maritime Magna Carta" were exaggerating its potential, but it was nonetheless "a real attempt to attack the basic problems of the region." Despite professions of support for the principles of the report, however, the federal government refused to implement them fully. Constrained by the horror of spending any of its budgetary surplus and by the fear that concessions to the Maritimes would alienate the politically more important Western provinces, King and his ministers vitiated the Duncan recommendations. Rail rates were reduced only on a limited scale, and although the railways were paid direct subventions to move Nova Scotia coal to market in Quebec, further aid to coal and to the steel industry was "deferred." Instead of the "substantive program for Maritime rehabilitation" proposed by the Duncan Commission, the King government had provided just enough reform for a "program of political pacification."[48]

The most remarkable federal abdication of responsibility was the so-called Railway Agreement of September 1925. This allowed the Canadian National and the Canadian Pacific to recruit immigrants in Europe and transport them to Canada without the immigrants passing through the normal channels of the Department of Immigration and Colonization. In theory the railways were agents of the government bound by policies established by federal legislation; in practice they made their own policies, ignoring the requirement that migrants from the "non-preferred" countries of southern and eastern Europe be admitted to

Canada only if guaranteed permanent employment as domestic servants or farm hands. The CNR and CPR established "colonization boards" which filled fictitious jobs or pretended that temporary harvest work was year-round employment. During the period the Railway Agreement was in effect, Canada received a higher proportion of her immigrants from those countries from which entry was supposedly restricted than from Britain, the United States, or the "preferred" countries of northern Europe, from which immigration was supposedly encouraged! The railway companies broke the law, not to aid those discriminated against by Canada's nativist immigration policies, but to ensure themselves of a steady supply of cheap foreign workers. Despite protests from churches, organized farmers, and trade unions in French and English Canada, and in the face of evidence that the railways had – in the words of Labour Minister Peter Heenan – "flagrantly violated both the letter and the spirit of the agreement," it was renewed by parliament in 1928 and remained in force until the soaring unemployment of 1930 forced its cancellation.[49]

VI

Dominion quiescence was both cause and effect of a shift in the federal-provincial balance of power. During the inter-war period, Canada's federal system became more truly federal as the provinces acquired an authority and prestige co-ordinate with rather than subordinate to the national government. The decentralization of Confederation coincided with Mackenzie King's prime ministership, but it cannot be attributed exclusively to his style of political leadership. As King liked to point out, had his government pressed ahead with the agenda of social legislation outlined in the Liberal platform of 1919, it would have been in all likelihood invalidated by the Judicial Committee of the Privy Council, the ultimate arbiter of Canadian constitutional questions.

Beginning in 1883 with the case of Hodge v. The Queen, the members of the Judicial Committee had made themselves "stepfathers of Confederation" with a series of decisions that reshaped the tightly knit fabric designed by its natural parents. Interpreting the British North America Act "in the same narrow, literal way that they would have interpreted a statute which required the carrying of lamps on bicycles," they chipped away at the importance of Section 91, which gave the federal government the power to legislate for the "peace, order and good government of Canada," and expanded that of a previously little-noticed phrase of Section 92 which gave the provinces sole

authority to legislate respecting "property and civil rights in the province." Until the 1920s, however, the central government remained
paramount, even if some of its dominance had been whittled away to
create a looser federation than that envisaged by Sir John A. Macdonald and his colleagues. The settlement of the West was a national
project for which the dominion was allotted almost unquestioned
authority, and the Great War provided the federal government with
the constitutional authority to intrude into areas that in peacetime
belonged to the provinces.[50]

When the war ended the Judicial Committee served notice that unchallenged federal eminence ended along with it. Two judgements
severely limited the scope of action of the federal government: *In re
Board of Commerce and Fair Prices Act* (1922) found that an attempt
to curb profiteering by controlling prices was *ultra vires*, while
Toronto Electric Commissioners v. *Snider* (1925) struck down the Industrial Disputes Investigation Act, in force since 1907. In his written
decisions, Viscount Haldane argued that "under normal circumstances" the federal government could not legally interfere "on such a
scale as the statutes in controversy involve, with the property and civil
rights of the inhabitants of the provinces." Only in time of an
"emergency putting the national life of Canada in unanticipated peril"
could the federal government deal with such subjects, and Haldane
made clear that "instances of this . . . are highly exceptional."[51]

These Privy Council decisions took more from the dominion than
they gave to the provinces, for their effect was not only to impose a
decentralized conception of federalism but to undermine the notion
that any level of government had the right to intervene in the economic and social affairs of the nation. The cases that established the
precedents were not brought to court by angry provinces trying to
drive Ottawa from their legislative bailiwicks but by private businessmen who cared nothing for the constitutional niceties of the situation.
The Board of Commerce case, for example, was launched by a group
of haberdashers who wanted to raise their prices above the ceiling imposed by the board. As J.R. Mallory has commented, "the plea of *ultra
vires* [became] the automatic litigious response to attempts by governments to regulate economic life." The federal government was the
target more often simply because it had introduced more regulatory
legislation; when provincial legislation offended private interests it
was similarly attacked and often similarly struck down. A British Columbia statute setting up a compulsory fruit marketing board was
ruled *ultra vires* for interfering with federal jurisdiction over interprovincial commerce, while federal boards were held to be an en-
croachment on property and civil rights. What the courts created was

not so much an exalted concept of provincial powers as "a no man's land in the constitution" in which no government could act.[52]

Of more significance than judicial review in aggrandizing the provinces was social and economic change. As the Rowell-Sirois Report was later to explain, the fact that the new resource extractive industries were under provincial control "gave the provincial governments an enhanced importance in the eyes of private enterprise." The rapid development of the automobile required new highway systems, and it was the provincial governments that let the contracts to construct them. Although the welfare state grew at a snail's pace compared to its progress in every other industrialized country save the United States, after the war the provinces assumed larger responsibilities for education, paid the new mothers' allowances, and in some cases participated in the old age pension scheme. As federal expenditure in these areas declined between 1921 and 1929, provincial expenditure almost doubled, from $91.4 million to $163.2 million. In 1921 the nine provinces spent an amount equal to 19.2 per cent of the federal budget; in 1929 that had increased to 40.3 per cent (see Table IV). Auto licences, gasoline taxes, and the profits from provincial liquor monopolies brought in the new revenue that made this possible, but provincial governments felt the need for still larger incomes commensurate with their responsibilities. All provinces had revenue increases between 1921 and 1929, but because the economic development of the 1920s was regionally uneven there was a considerable disparity among these increases nation wide. Ontario and Quebec led with increases of 150 per cent and 119 per cent respectively, while the average for the other seven provinces was a much more modest 65 per cent.[53]

The two provinces best able to afford constitutional upward mobility were the most aggressive in their insistence that the dominion government respect "provincial rights." Ontario-Quebec co-operation to press provincial claims on Ottawa had begun in the 1880s when Honoré Mercier and Oliver Mowat had occupied the premiers' chairs in Toronto and Quebec City, but the common front had fallen apart when Ontario restricted the educational rights of its French-speaking minority in 1912. The two men who resurrected the alliance during the 1920s were unlikely partners. Louis-Alexandre Taschereau, Premier of Quebec, was the scion of a distinguished seigneurial family whose Liberal roots reached back to the early nineteenth century; his father had been a member of the first Canadian Supreme Court, his uncle the first Canadian Cardinal of the Roman Catholic Church. Partner in a prestigious legal firm, he spoke flawless French and excellent English; reserved, cultured, dignified, Taschereau had an aloof, aristocratic manner. G. Howard Ferguson, his Ontario counterpart, was the son of a rural doctor who had been a Tory back-bencher under Sir John A. Combining politics with a small-town law practice, the garrulous, folksy Ferguson met his constituents in his regular chair in the back of the shoe repair shop in Kemptville. He shared with them membership in the Orange Lodge, with its attendant values and prejudices: British patriotism, anti-Catholicism, and francophobia. The physical appearances of Ferguson and Taschereau also heightened the impression that they were strange bedfellows; when the fleshy Ontarian Orangeman with the bulbous nose and the slightly built, fine-featured French-Canadian patrician posed together for the photographers, their resemblance to film comedians Laurel and Hardy was striking.[54]

Whatever their personal dissimilarities, Ferguson and Taschereau shared common economic and constitutional philosophies. Each believed that it was in the public interest that his government encourage private enterprise to exploit the natural wealth of his province as rapidly as possible: what was good for the timber tycoons and the mining magnates would eventually trickle down to the people of Ontario and Quebec. There was no cause for federal-provincial antagonism over most resource industries, but constitutional authority for the hydroelectric development of major waterways like the St. Lawrence was ambiguous because the BNA Act assigned jurisdiction over navigable rivers to the dominion. Electricity was critical to the plans for economic progress of both premiers. When the Meighen government issued a federal water-power lease to tap the Ottawa River in 1921, and the King government later insisted on the validity of such leases, Ferguson and Taschereau were forced to make common cause. Ferguson opened the way for a renewal of the Ontario-Quebec axis against the dominion by making an educational concession to Franco-Ontarians – the repeal of the notorious Regulation 17. The entente was proclaimed when Taschereau spoke at the ceremonies marking the 1927 centenary of the University of Toronto. While a beaming Ferguson presided over the platform, Taschereau gave the audience a constitutional history lesson: "Every Canadian must understand that sixty years ago we formed not a homogeneous country but a confederation of different provinces for certain purposes, with the distinct understanding that each of these provinces should retain certain things. . . . Traditions, creed, laws, national aspirations, language and a heritage were abandoned by none of the contracting parties. . . . To live and endure the spirit as well as the letter of the Confederation must be respected."[55]

This was Taschereau's version of the "compact theory" of Confederation, a theory that was a rigidly held dogma to both him and Ferguson. In this historically fuzzy interpretation, the agreement of 1867 is seen as a compact or treaty among sovereign and equal provinces, each of which retained all those powers not specifically given up in the BNA Act. Federal legislative competence, the compact theorists argued, was restricted to items enumerated in Section 91; any residual power in areas not specifically defined in the BNA Act belonged to the provinces. Any amendment to the original terms of Confederation could be made only with the consent of all the provinces, since they were the original parties to the compact. Neither Ferguson nor Taschereau felt he was demanding new provincial rights at Ottawa's expense. In their minds they were simply restoring the correct interpretation of the dominion-provincial relationship, perverted during the Great War, and defending themselves against further federal encroachments. In addition to the dispute over the control of revenues from water-power development, there had been a long-standing squabble over the right to regulate insurance companies and dissatisfaction with the new federal tendency to attach conditions to grants to the provinces for such projects as housing and highway construction and the old age pension. There was also the ultimate provincial nightmare: the fear that the federal government would impose unilaterally a procedure for amending the BNA Act.[56]

Such subjects formed the agenda of the Dominion-Provincial Conference of November 1927. There had been such gatherings in 1906 and in 1918 in addition to purely provincial conferences on five other occasions, but none of these meetings had attracted as much attention as this latest foray into federal-provincial diplomacy. The premiers arrived like foreign plenipotentiaries, with retinues of cabinet ministers and civil servants. New Brunswick's J.B.M. Baxter was trailed by five members of his government, three provincial bureaucrats and – a portent for such affairs in future – a university professor as a "special adviser." Mackenzie King called the conference to order with an uncharacteristically short speech in which he extolled the significance of such a "bringing-together" taking place during the Diamond Jubilee year of Confederation; then the doors were closed to the press and the order of business began.[57]

One old chestnut of federal-provincial acrimony didn't even enter the discussion. The dominion power to disallow provincial legislation had been used no fewer than ninety-six times between 1867 and 1920, but it had been invoked only three times thereafter, the last of these in 1924. By 1927 some went so far as to argue that the disallowance power had become obsolete and would never be used again. Another perpetual point at issue remained an active topic of debate, however.

The premiers made various suggestions as to how the federal government might provide them with the money to finance their new spending habits, suggestions that ranged from having the CNR absorb provincially owned railways and their deficits to federal surrender of the right to collect personal income tax. Every premier spoke against the principle of conditional grants; money granted to support such programs as the old age pension, which were clearly within provincial jurisdiction, should have no strings attached. It was up to the provinces to decide if such programs were to be enacted; as Premier Taschereau argued, the provincial governments knew what was best for Canadians because they "were more in contact with the people, educating them, building their roads and looking after their health." Only Taschereau, however, felt strongly enough about the principle to announce that Quebec would accept no conditional grants. The English-Canadian premiers complained but declared themselves willing to spend the tainted federal dollars. The decision to increase subsidies to the Maritime Provinces as proposed by the Duncan Commission was submitted to the conference for approval. On this issue, Ferguson and Taschereau were strategically magnanimous. After reminding the other premiers that increased subsidies meant higher federal taxes for Ontarians, Ferguson announced that he "did not intend . . . to cavil about small things."[58]

The *quid pro quo* for this generosity was that the premiers of Nova Scotia and New Brunswick, the other original members of Confederation, support Ferguson and Taschereau in their opposition to the formula to amend the BNA Act in Canada that was proposed by Justice Minister Ernest Lapointe. Lapointe argued in vain that it was a humiliation for Canada to have to petition the British parliament to amend the Canadian constitution and promised an amending procedure that would require unanimous provincial consent before changes touching on provincial rights or the rights of racial, linguistic, or religious minorities could be made. The premiers of the four Western provinces seemed prepared to endorse such a scheme, but Taschereau and Ferguson, backed by J.B.M. Baxter and E.N. Rhodes of Nova Scotia, refused to budge an inch. Taschereau again summarized their arguments: "Constitutional amending power in Canada would mean constant conflict with the provinces. . . . Men far removed from the battlefield are better qualified to pass an impartial judgment." Roughly translated, this meant that the premiers of the powerful provinces were perfectly content with recent decisions rendered by the Judicial Committee and saw no reason to change the rules of a game that they seemed to be winning. The questions of water-power rights and the regulation of insurance companies also proved impossible to solve by compromise. In the end it was agreed to submit them to the courts for a judicial interpretation.[59]

Prime Minister King adjourned the conference by thanking the participants "for the light they have thrown on the various problems." Every man in the conference "would go forth with a greater desire for the unity of the Dominion," he said in summation. King believed the conference had been a personal triumph. He had avoided opening the federal purse any wider than absolutely necessary, and all the premiers had gone home happy. The real winners, however, were Ferguson and Taschereau. The court decision on insurance company regulation went in their favour, and although the decision in the water-power case was less clear cut, the federal government backed away from the issue. The two premiers had blunted Lapointe's constitutional amendment initiative and had established a precedent – the right of the provinces to be consulted before the BNA Act could be amended. Further proof that a new constitutional era had begun was provided when the King government asked the approval of the other six provinces before granting new financial arrangements to Nova Scotia, New Brunswick, and Prince Edward Island.[60]

By the end of the 1920s the *status quo ante bellum* of Canadian political life had been restored to the extent that the two-party system was once again firmly in place in federal politics. The relationship between the two levels of government, however, had been substantially altered. But in the prosperous atmosphere of the later twenties, those who had the power to change things saw little wrong with the new decentralized Canadian federalism.

CHAPTER 7

Ordinary Canadians

I

What did the prosperity of the New Economic Era mean to ordinary Canadians? In 1929, only 143,600 citizens earned the $2,500 necessary to make themselves liable for federal income tax; this group, fewer than 5 per cent of all income earners, comprised little more than the upper middle class, unusually prosperous farmers, and the corporate élite. Sixteen hundred individuals in the top tax brackets took in more in salaries alone (dividends were non-taxable) than "the entire combined income of 105,504 workers in the protected textile industry!" The average wage in 1929 was $1,200. The Department of Labour's 1929 estimate of a budget to maintain an average Canadian family at a "minimum standard of health and decency" was $1,430. Grattan O'Leary put these disturbing figures into human perspective in the *Canadian Magazine*:

> . . . according to this budget, which certainly seems conservative, a Canadian worker with four of a family and working full time, would find himself $230 behind. . . . This assumes that . . . he would not have been laid off [or taken ill]. The idea of a vacation, of travel, or of having a radio, or of indulging the slightest luxury is not even considered. . . . Canadians are not able to do more than meet living expenses from month to month. . . . There is little chance, so far as the average family is concerned, for saving to take care of sickness, to pay for the costs of death. And this is the condition after five years of prosperity unequalled in our history.[1]

The first five years of the decade had been worse. Post-war deflation saw a drop in the government's crudely calculated index of the cost-of-living of 20 per cent between 1920 and 1924, and the business prosperity of 1924-29 was for the most part non-inflationary, which theoretically meant an increase in "real wages" for the working man. Merciless wage cutting in industry, however, played a large role in the deflationary and non-inflationary cycles, and widespread unemployment and underemployment diminished most of the implied gains for the urban worker. Workers benefited, on the whole, from the stabilization of the later twenties; they would have benefited more had it not been for the government's and the railways' immigration schemes. Studies of four Canadian cities – Halifax, Montreal, Winnipeg, and Vancouver – suggest slight evidence of any real improvement in the material condition of the working classes during the New Economic Era. The structured maldistribution of wealth and purchasing power that was to lead to the catastrophes of the 1930s was a constant factor in Canadian economic life.[2]

Movies and advertising inculcated expectations among consumers for such products as mechanical refrigerators, electric ranges, and automobiles. These new "necessities" were clearly beyond the financial reach of most Canadian families. Such modern devices as consumer credit, instalment buying, and mortgage lending to individuals had only just appeared. As cities grew, cheap urban land slowly disappeared, driving up the cost of housing. As the economic world grew more complex, the psychological burden on the working man also increased. "Years ago," said Tom Moore, president of the Trades and Labour Congress of Canada, "a man even though his pay was smaller could look forward to something. It was possible to save, and it didn't need a great deal to set up a home. . . . Now everything seems against the young fellow with domestic ideas."[3]

II

What did Tom Moore, head since 1918 of the country's major labour federation, propose to do about bettering the lot of the Canadian working man? Moore and his closest colleague, long-time TLC secretary-treasurer Paddy Draper, represented the conservative consensus in Canada's most influential labour organizations: the international craft unions, like Moore's International Brotherhood of Carpenters and Joiners and Draper's International Typographical Union. Most were affiliated with the even more reactionary American Federation of Labor, which had dominated the overall policies of the TLC since 1902. Jealously guarding their ancient jurisdictional pretensions and the principles of "safe and sane" business unionism, they were utterly unprepared to deal with the harsh realities of the post-war world.[4]

Canadian labour had seemed on the threshold of a brave new era in 1919. With 378,000 members, the unions had organized 18 per cent of the non-agricultural workforce and the percentage of union members in the blue-collar industrial workforce was much higher. Public sector and white-collar unions, though novel, were being created, and the dominion Civil Service Federation was exploring the possibilities of transforming itself from an association of employees into a real trade union. When the working class in the city of Winnipeg went out on a general strike to support the trade unions' demand for collective bargaining, sympathy strikes took place across the country, from Victoria to Amherst. Politicians feared that the radical spirit of labour's rank and file might "kick the government off Parliament Hill," but they were not the only ones who trembled at the thought. The TLC leadership disavowed the sympathy strikes and rubber-stamped the federal government's decisive intervention on the side of the employers in Winnipeg. The arrest of the strike leaders and the violent repression of their followers on Winnipeg's "Bloody Saturday" ended the great strike, but its memory hung like Banquo's ghost over the Canadian labour movement. In 1926, Minister of Labour Peter Heenan apologized to the workers of Canada for the state's repressive role. But Tom Moore remained unrepentant. Interviewed in 1925, Moore recalled the Winnipeg events as "semi-revolutionary madness" which, if repeated, would again have to be met with "the whole armed force of the state, if necessary."[5]

In the half-decade after 1919, union membership plummeted by over one third, bottoming out at 260,000 in 1924 (see Table XII). The post-war depression played a role, but the critical new feature was the employers' campaign for the open shop, a drive to eliminate unionism altogether that spilled over from the United States and was pursued with special vigour by the managers of American-owned branch plants. Unions, said the modern corporate manager, were a relic of an unenlightened past. The same line was mouthed by such prestigious organs of Canadian public opinion as *Saturday Night*, which indiscriminately lumped all unions and union leaders in a "most ingenious conspiracy to destroy the morale of the human race" and predicted in 1922 that organized labour was all but "doomed to destruction." Other popular writings decried the unions' "Karl Marx German theories . . . of class warfare," propaganda geared to a middle class that knew nothing and cared less about industrial relations. On a more sophisticated level, it was argued that "co-operation" rather than competition should somehow prevail at the heart of capitalist productive relations. The old adversarial relationship between labour and capital, the cause of such massive social and political confrontation in 1919, was to be replaced with a neo-paternalist relationship between employee and employer, institutionalized in the form of the plant-level industrial council. At International Harvester, Massey-Harris, Imperial Oil, Western Fuel Company, Swift's, Bell Telephone, and other firms such councils came into existence, and worker and management representatives came together to discuss matters of mutual interest. The system worked tolerably well in dealing with day-to-day grievances, but on major issues such as lay-offs or pay scales the councils' role was purely ceremonial; they were a place where company policies were announced, not formulated.[6]

The anti-union drive was dressed up in a great deal of rhetoric about "welfare capitalism." This usually involved the provision of services or facilities to employees called for by the most elementary justice or business sense, such as washrooms, first-aid stations, company nurses, and cafeterias. A handful of larger firms introduced what appeared to be more significant measures. The B.C. Electric Railway Company offered its employees low-interest mortgage loans and paid the premiums on a thousand-dollar insurance policy for those with five years of continuous service. Imperial Oil, taking a different tack, introduced a stock-purchase plan. Agricultural implement manufacturer Massey-Harris set aside thirteen acres of land for a workers' vegetable garden and gave employees with ten years of uninterrupted service a munificent one-week annual paid vacation. The Canadian railways had already pioneered in a key area of welfare capitalism: pension schemes for loyal workers with long years of service. The threat of withdrawal of such "carrots" hung over the heads of the workers. One piece of unfinished business left over from the Winnipeg General Strike was the plight of the railwaymen whose seniority rights and pensions had been cancelled as a result. Welfare capitalism was at bottom a coldly "calculated business policy" to produce "stability in the labour element" and increase a company's profits.[7]

The Edmonton *Journal* hailed the retreat of the unions in 1925 as a "peaceful revolution," but it was also forced by violent confrontation. The portrait of the "torpid twenties," when "labour virtually abandoned the fight against capital," has been overdrawn. The incidence of strikes and lockouts declined after 1919 and 1920, yet those had been years of unprecedented industrial unrest. Industrial warfare still simmered, finding statistical expression in an average of ninety-four strikes or lockouts recorded every year between 1921 and 1929 (see Table XII). The B.C. Shipping Federation crushed the International Longshoremen's Association in the West Coast ports in 1923 at the cost of crippling strikes fought between the dockers and armies of professional strike-breakers. The near destruction of the Lumber Workers' Industrial Union of Canada, which claimed 20,000 members in British Columbia and Ontario in 1920, was accomplished with the blacklist, brass knuckles, and worse. In 1928, lumber workers in northwestern Ontario served notice that their union was not dead by widespread strikes in the camps. In December 1929, Viljo Rosvall and John Voutilainen, two Finnish organizers for the LWIU, mysteriously disappeared near Onion Lake; their badly mutilated corpses were found when the ice melted the next spring. Five thousand workers marched in their honour in Port Arthur, an event made memorable by a solar eclipse. Said one of the eulogists: "God himself . . . is ashamed of this heinous crime, ashamed that the murderers remain free."[8]

The most dramatic events unfolded in the nation's coalfields. Mine operators in the West and the Maritimes were united in their determination to do away with the collective agreements negotiated by the miners during and immediately after the Great War. The tottering Besco was joined by the Western Canada Coal Operators' Association and its ally the CPR in demanding wage reductions of 35 to 50 per cent, and the moment the last vestiges of federal wartime regulation of wages in the coal industry lapsed at the end of 1921, the notices of wage reductions went up at a hundred pits in Nova Scotia, Alberta, and British Columbia. The Canadian members of the United Mine Workers of America were determined not to yield. "War is on, class war," announced J.B. McLachlan, secretary-treasurer of the UMW's eastern District 26. "There can be no harmonious relations between the slave and his master," seconded Phil Christophers, former president of western District 18 and newly elected member of the Alberta legislature.[9]

By August of 1922 there were 22,000 coal miners on strike across the country; in Nova Scotia the strikers refused to man the pumps and fans necessary to prevent flooding and explosions. Troops were rushed into the strike zone to preserve, in the words of Labour Minister James Murdock, "peace, order, and good government" – in fact, the property of Besco. Their presence had been formally requested by local magistrates whose request, the Prime Minister emphasized, was constitutionally binding. The federal government was officially "neutral" in the struggle, but not the polarized political authorities in Nova Scotia. The Armstrong Liberal government openly supported Besco, while mayors and councils in the coal towns backed the union. When the Defence Department tried to collect payment for its unwanted services from the town of Glace Bay, miner-mayor Dan Willie Morrison sent the reply: "Send the bill to BESCO." The crisis was resolved by negotiations; the miners agreed to small concessions in new contracts, but their militancy had apparently paid off.[10]

In July 1923 the battleground shifted to the steel industry, as Besco refused even to negotiate with the Amalgamated Association of Iron,

Steel and Tin Workers. Strikers blockaded the Sydney plant, and a wild mêlée ensued as mounted provincial police chased picketers through the streets, injuring innocent bystanders. Once more the armoured troop trains rumbled into industrial Cape Breton. To enforce a demand for withdrawal of the soldiers, the coal miners walked out of the pits, technically breaking their hard-won contract with Besco. The UMW leadership had underestimated the forces arrayed against them; McLachlan and district president "Red" Dan Livingston were arrested for seditious libel and spirited away to Halifax, where the Nova Scotia attorney general secured a two-year penitentiary term for McLachlan. John L. Lewis, the international president of the UMW, stepped in to end the illegal walkout, put District 26 under trusteeship, and banished McLachlan and Livingston from union office. Trades and Labour Congress president Tom Moore also washed his hands of them, further evidence to radical unionists that the TLC was a mere puppet of the American Federation of Labor. When AFL strong man Samuel Gompers died later that year, McLachlan was extended the courtesy of an invitation to the funeral. "Sorry, duties will not permit me to attend," he reportedly replied, "but I heartily approve of the event."[11]

Were the Nova Scotia miners, by virtue of reckless tactics and intemperate leadership, the authors of their own misfortunes? The experience of Alberta miners suggests that tactics made little difference. District 18 president William Sherman and his supporters were socialists who believed that the only solution to the coal crisis lay in the nationalization of mines and railways to "best balance the trade of the country, East and West," but they scrupulously respected their collective agreements. Even during the gruelling eight-month strike of 1924 they provided their employers with the essential services of unionized maintenance men. Their moderation brought no material aid from the TLC and only token relief from their international union. By October, desperate for a settlement, District 18 went back to work at a dollar-a-day reduction. That winter the Crow's Nest Pass Coal Company determined to finish off the UMW locals at Fernie, British Columbia. Breaking the contract, the company locked its miners out and forced them to accept a further pay cut and the introduction of an open shop. Other mine operators successfully copied this tactic, smashing District 18 into fragments.[12]

Not to be outdone by its Western counterparts, Besco sought the same result by shutting down its pits and cancelling credit at the company stores. After riots in New Waterford, these "pluck me" stores were burned to the ground all across Cape Breton. Canadian trade unionists finally awoke to the fact that the miners and their bosses were playing for high stakes and organized a belated relief operation for District 26. Nova Scotia's new Conservative administration arranged in August 1925 for the miners to accede to Besco's wage cuts in order to save their union shop. That was more than the United Farmer government had done for Alberta's miners. The UFA did, however, undertake an investigation of the background of the coal crisis, and the Report of the Alberta Coal Commission revealed a sorry tale of mismanagement and exploitation. The disastrous decline of the coalmining industry was not altered by crushing the miners. As Alberta commission member Frank Wheatley, president of the new Mine Workers' Union of Canada, predicted, "profits cannot permanently be secured, nor bankruptcy avoided, by crucifying the workers." [13]

III

In March, 1927, the Mine Workers joined fifteen independent Canadian unions in Montreal to form the All-Canadian Congress of Labour, a new central organization that they hoped would lead them out of the wreckage of the 1920s. The tattered remnants of the once mighty One Big Union were present at the creation, but most of the founders of the ACCL were unions that had been denied affiliation to or expelled from the Trades and Labour Congress, usually on the ground that their membership overlapped with the jurisdiction claimed by an AFL international union. More than half the delegates were from the Canadian Brotherhood of Railway Employees, a national union that had been excluded from the TLC in a classic instance of jurisdictional conflict in 1921. An AFL affiliate had laid claim to the railway clerks and freight handlers the CBRE had organized and represented since before the First World War. Tom Moore had no choice then but to oust the CBRE from the congress, but its members remained faithful to their union and rejected the international. CBRE president Aaron Mosher became the president of the All-Canadian Congress, while Frank Wheatley of the Mine Workers received a vice-presidency, reflecting the overall balance of forces. All the delegates pledged themselves to achieve "complete independence from United States control" over the trade unions, in their exaggerated view the root of all evil in the Canadian labour world. [14]

More than simply nationalist, the ACCL was also an alliance of the left. Mosher was a social democrat who steered the ACCL toward the goal of an ill-defined "co-operative commonwealth" – though no parliamentary socialist party then existed. The central plank in the left wing's platform was industrial unionism: the abolition of craft jurisdictions altogether. Within that context an alliance soon emerged between the ACCL forces and those commanded by the fledgling Communist party, whose members included such labour notables as J.B. McLachlan, "Red" Dan Livingston, "Big John" Stokaluk, Ukrainian-born vice-president of the Mine Workers' Union of Canada, and John "Moscow Jack" MacDonald, a veteran socialist and Toronto pattern-maker who was the founding secretary and leading spirit of the Communist party of Canada throughout the 1920s. All were colourful personalities whose popularity with the workers extended well beyond the ranks of the Communist party. When the red-led Lumber Workers sought and were granted affiliation to the ACCL, the outlines of the new coalition became clear. The *Canadian Congress Journal*, organ of the TLC, smeared its rival as the "All-Red Congress of Labour" and "all-Canadian rats inspired by Moscow." The ACCL's *Canadian Unionist* responded in kind, branding the TLC as "yellow," "alien," and "Yankee-dominated." This mud slinging, or, in the words of one disgruntled miner who read both newspapers, "vapouring," was the least edifying feature of the new situation. On balance, however, the founding of the ACCL suggested that the trade union movement was coming back to life.[15]

An ACCL striker named James Rafferty was bludgeoned to death by a security guard near Wayne, Alberta, on Christmas Day, 1928; the Wayne strike, said the *Canadian Unionist*, showed that "a national union possesses a fighting spirit and a stamina that are not to be trifled with . . . which bribery, cajolry, and threats, can do nothing to undermine." The movement needed members, however, not more martyrs. "What we want," declared president Mosher at the 1929 convention, "is a national union covering each industry in Canada, which will be fully organized and . . . strong enough to take a share in the control as well as the profits of industry." This meant that the ACCL would have to assault the major ramparts of the open shop, above all in auto and steel, where the rise of mass production on a non-union basis had led some observers to predict that these workers would never be organized. Technological innovation – not just troops and police – had severely undermined the Amalgamated Association of Iron, Steel, and Tin Workers in Canada by the mid-twenties, especially in Ontario. At the modernized Stelco plant in Hamilton, a workforce of 5,200 produced 25 per cent more steel in the period 1926-30 than a much more highly skilled labour force of 6,900 had turned out in the years 1916-20. The ACCL Communist forces made one foray into the steel-fabrication industry at Hamilton in 1928-29 with a strike at the National Steel Car plant, without tangible success.[16]

In the auto industry the record was more encouraging. John Kenneth Galbraith, critic of the "sombre social histories of the 1920s," which portray the "workingman as a helpless automaton on the assembly line," reminds us of the special context. The auto plants were not yet organized on anti-union lines, since unions had never existed in this sector. For rural Ontarians, moving into the auto plants was a liberating experience, and they saw at first no need to organize. The boys he knew, Galbraith recalls, "liked their work, were fascinated by their surroundings, debated ardently the merits of Fisher Body and Briggs . . . and were profound admirers of Henry Ford." Consciousness of being *workers* came slowly but by the end of the decade was finding expression in plant-level "Motor Workers' Unions," organized quite spontaneously on the shop floor, to fight grievances and wage cuts. It must have been a revelation to these farm boys to see the attention suddenly lavished upon them by General Motors, Peter Heenan, the Communist party, and other outsiders when three thousand auto workers struck at Oshawa in 1928. The ACCL parlayed the shop-floor organizations into an Ontario-wide Auto Workers' Industrial Union in 1928 and 1929. It collapsed under diverse pressures on the eve of the Great Depression, but the movement would reemerge as a powerful element in Canadian labour during the 1930s.[17]

The ACCL played a role in stimulating a general revival of Canadian labour activism in this period. Notwithstanding the many obstacles to unionization, overall membership increased slowly but steadily after 1925; 322,000 Canadians belonged to unions on the eve of the Depression. The ACCL had about 40,000 members compared to perhaps 190,000 in the TLC. A large number of Canadian union members belonged to non-affiliated bodies such as the railway running trades' brotherhoods. Another bloc was affiliated to the most nationalistic and in many ways the most remarkable of Canadian labour organizations: the Confédération des travailleurs catholiques du Canada, the "confessional" unions of Quebec, grouped together as the CTCC in 1921. The CTCC had in 1922 ninety locals in its several federations: textiles, pulp and paper, and so forth. In 1926 its effective membership was only 15,450, but it mustered at least 20,000 members in 1930. Other unionists, national or international, inside or outside Quebec, scarcely concealed their belief that the CTCC member-unions were but stalking horses for capital. Like other generalizations about labour in the 1920s, this perception was wrong headed. The CTCC held barely a quarter of the total Quebec union membership, Jacques Rouillard has shown, but accounted for a very respectable proportion of the large number of strikes and lockouts in the province between 1921 and 1930: 32 among 242.[18]

Catholic unionism, which first arose in Germany and other European countries during the nineteenth century, represented part of the encounter between the universal ideals of social harmony and social

Maurice Duplessis (hat in hand) was described by Lord Tweedsmuir as "a pious, alcoholic buccaneer."

A visit to Germany in 1937 convinced Mackenzie King that Hitler had only peaceful intentions.

Stuffed uncomfortably into their court dress, Ernest Lapointe and Mackenzie King
welcome King George VI and Queen Elizabeth.

The Canadian Blood Transfusion Service in Spain, 1937, Norman Bethune
second from right.

justice cherished by the church and the realities of industrial capitalism. Modern economic structures meant that workers needed unions, urged Abbé Philippe Desranleau in 1922. Instead of wasting the energies of the church in trying to block their formation, and thereby alienating the working class, the goal should be to "take possession of them to put them in order, to lecture to them and to change them for the better." The problem seemed pressing at the end of the Great War, which stimulated both class and national consciousness among French-Canadian workers. The conscription riots of 1918 were followed by a labour crisis in 1919. At the time of the Winnipeg General Strike, 26,000 Quebec workers were out on strike on their own account and "reds" like Albert Saint-Martin of Montreal's Parti ouvrière agitated in favour of joining the general strike. Catholic unionism responded with a contradictory program that promised to do away with the exploitation of labour while rejecting the "claim that capital, capitalists and employers are born enemies of labour." It attracted active and committed lay leaders like Alfred Charpentier, who had been converted to the teachings of social Catholicism in workers' study circles sponsored by the clergy during the war. Long a leader in the TLC building trades in Quebec, Charpentier brought some of their members into the CTCC's construction federation. The CTCC solved internal jurisdictional problems, if they arose, by means of a centralized and unitary structure borrowed from that of the old Chevaliers du Travail.[19]

Like the ACCL, the CTCC vehemently decried "foreign" – that is, American – influence in the labour movement, albeit with the appropriate linguistic accent and from a more conservative standpoint. "It is not in the interest of any country," read its official declaration, "that its labour movement be "controlled by strangers. Labour is too essential a factor in the life of a nation." In theory, CTCC jurisdiction included all Catholic workers in Canada, in practice, only French-Canadian workers in Quebec. In theory, again, the CTCC member-unions were to adhere to all the directives and teachings of the Catholic Church, the link cemented through the agency of the union chaplain, or *aumonier*. The chaplains answered to the bishops and were supposed to have veto power over the unions' most important activities, collective bargaining and strikes. Strikes were to be undertaken under only the most extreme circumstances, after all avenues of negotiation and conciliation had been exhausted, and only in a "just" cause. In practice, the CTCC became embroiled in dozens of controversial strikes, while the chaplains often became outspoken and even radical advocates of workers' rights in their respective communities.[20]

Two strikes in the twenties highlighted CTCC-led labour activism in

Canada. In 1926 the shoe manufacturers' association of Quebec City began a vicious campaign to destroy the CTCC unions in their factories. Even the intervention of Monsignor Alfred Langlois was insufficient to persuade the manufacturers to accept conciliation. After a violent four-month dispute in which the factory owners used scabs and police, the five thousand shoe workers were starved into submission and forced back into an open shop, the union leaders fired and blacklisted. The Quebec shoe strike convinced CTCC president Pierre Baulé that "open war" had been declared against his movement, and it marked the beginning of a more overtly militant orientation for the confederation. Its locals amassed such strike funds – formerly eschewed as temptations to idleness – as they could. CTCC conventions resolved in favour of old age pensions, family allowances, and health and unemployment insurance – social legislation which the church hierarchy did not support. The gap between CTCC practice and its corporatist theory was wide and growing wider while the distinctions between the CTCC and the "secular" unions were becoming more obscure. Yet there was no move towards unity with the other federations. The TLC, whose conventions favoured liberalized divorce legislation and state-controlled public education, was to the Catholic unionists godless as well as "American." The nationalist credentials of the All-Canadian Congress were cancelled out, in the eyes of the Catholic unionists, by its socialism.[21]

An earlier strike had put the CTCC briefly at the forefront of the movement for the rights of working women. The conflict at the E.B. Eddy matchworks at Hull in 1924, said Le Droit, was "a struggle which will go down in history," as the plant's mainly female workforce, with strong public support, faced down the managers and E.B. Eddy's board of directors, among them a "Mr. R.B. Bennett of Calgary." The workers had already endured dangerous working conditions, lay-offs, and wage cuts. They drew the line on two questions: management's demand that each worker sign a "yellow dog" contract, by which she pledged never to join the CTCC or any other union, and the attempt to replace female overseers with male foremen. That would at once block avenues of individual job mobility for the workers on the shop floor and, argued the union's chaplain, expose them to dangerous sexual harassment. "Shall the virtue of a young girl not be protected as well as her lungs?" he asked. "What can a weak girl do to protect herself against an influential and cunning foreman? . . . She has no choice," explained aumonier Philémon Bourassa to reporters. "It is dishonour or the door." The strikers won a compromise settlement after shutting down the factory for one month.[22]

IV

The matchworkers were one contingent of a growing army of working women in Canada, which numbered almost 700,000, or 17 per cent of the labour force, at the end of the 1920s, up two percentage points since 1921. Unionism was particularly weak in the sectors where they were to be found. A survey of Canadian unions having significant numbers of female members in 1929 reported a total membership of only 12,419 among nine different organizations. The largest of them was the Industrial Union of Needle Trades Workers of Canada, which had come into existence only in 1928. The CTCC, not counted in the survey, would have added a few thousand more. The low rate of unionization led some to conclude that unions took no interest in working women or were infused with sexist bias. There was, however, a sturdy group of women trade union organizers who also considered themselves to be feminists: Toronto's Mary McNab, Montreal's Becky Buhay, Vancouver's Helena Gutteridge. They were also people on the left, and as such their ideas were rejected by the mainstream labour movement. The case of the Federation of Women's Labour Leagues, founded in 1924, illustrates this. The WLL pledged to support not only women wage earners but also women in the home, a very radical notion for the time. As an example, J.B. McLachlan's daughter Eina organized miners' wives and daughters in Glace Bay, although they were not themselves workers. Perhaps not surprisingly, when the federation applied for membership in the Trades and Labour Congress, it was turned down with the argument that it did not represent real "producers." Tom Moore and his colleagues were sceptical of the WLL project of organizing working women, but they were even more suspicious of its left-wing orientation.[23]

Oblivious of these developments, bourgeois spokesmen drew a sanguine picture of women's emancipation. "This is a wonderful age for women," wrote Gertrude Pringle in an article entitled "Breaking into Business Today." "The bars are down. . . . Women today are free as air . . . to wrest from the workaday world at least some measure of their hopes and aspirations." Just as political equality had proved illusory, however, economic equality remained an elusive promise. A closer look at the patterns of female employment shows that over 95 per cent of the female labour force was hived into five of the twelve occupational categories as defined by the census: manufacturing, transportation and communication, trade and finance, personal service, and clerical (see Table XIb). More than 70 per cent of working women worked at jobs that were almost exclusively filled by women.

Female work in manufacturing meant the boring, repetitive tasks of garment, textile, or tobacco factories, canneries or fish plants. Communications was another way of saying telephone operators, a group which had once been significantly unionized but whose bargaining power had been entirely removed by technological change and the open-shop campaign. Trade and finance, less prestigious than the title suggests, described for the most part women employed as salespersons in department stores – the impersonalized "factories" of the retail industry – and those who held positions as clerks in banks and insurance firms. A little less than one fifth of the female wage-labour force was concentrated in the "clerical" sector proper. Their numbers had increased dramatically since before the war, a fact which Dominion Statistician R.H. Coats attributed to "the more general application of the typewriter and other machines, in the operation of which women have shown a marked ability." In fact, the office was becoming increasingly proletarianized. A clean-faced steno-typist, not the factory wage slave, was the stereotyped "working girl" of fiction, film, and comic strip. Certainly this work was considered infinitely preferably to most of the alternatives open to women.[24]

More than half of the total increase in the female labour force between 1921 and 1931 was in the service sector, including a substantial rise in the number of female domestics. These women, many of them recent immigrants recruited specifically for that purpose, rarely worked with large household staffs of the "Upstairs-Downstairs" variety. They scrubbed and cleaned in isolation from their fellow workers in the homes of the prosperous middle classes, many simply as day workers. Old "feudal conditions," as *Chatelaine* pointed out in 1928, had not changed: the servant's "life and time is not her own. . . . She is not an adult of free will." Domestic service was definitely work of last resort. Other service-sector jobs were more desirable: the rise of the hairdressing industry created six thousand new jobs in the 1920s. The number of waitresses doubled, as they were employed in preference to waiters in the new restaurant chains. Waitresses were subject to an arduous regimen of employer control, as suggested by the manager of Toronto's Honey Dew Shops. The "girls whom we hire," he instructed his junior manager, "must have good teeth and good appearance. . . . No stout or angular girls are wanted. We do not want girls with raucous, disagreeable voices, or those who habitually use the kind of slang likely to irritate the customer."[25]

Most of the rest of the female workforce was found not in business but in the "professions," which included a very large number of overworked and underpaid (in some cases unpaid) teachers and nurses and a very small number of physicians, lawyers, and professors. The participation of women in post-secondary education showed an encouraging increase, but the absolute numbers remained small. At the end of the decade women made up a quarter of the national post-secondary student body; as of 1925, just over five thousand were attending college or university, and 856 received degrees, mostly from Education and the other so-called "female faculties." In medical school a woman was a curiosity; in an engineering school she was unheard of. The true professions were male-dominated closed shops. At least one woman, however, gained a precarious toe-hold in a profession hitherto closed to women, the Christian ministry. In 1923 Lydia Gruchy graduated with honours in her theology program and found a posting in a small town in Saskatchewan. Her congregation seemed eminently satisfied with her work, but not the United Church of Canada, which refused her official ordination. She carried on without it, subject to the humiliation of having to bring in male ministers to serve communion or to perform marriages. The United Church did not consent to ordain her until 1936. As a comparative study of the status of women in Britain, the United States, and Canada concluded, there was "a strong Canadian prejudice against women in the professions."[26]

In 1931, the average male wage earner in Canada took home a depression-level $942, the average female a depressing $559. Feminist historians argue that systematic sex-discrimination was at work. Judge Helen Gregory MacGill, head of the Female Minimum Wage Board in British Columbia, explained the low economic standing of working women in terms of a dense web of "custom [and] prejudice, the women's timidity and lack of confidence, their poor bargaining ability, the difficulty in moving from place to place, their habit of not valuing their work, and their lack of initiative and opportunity to learn better work." The operative word, perhaps, was "opportunity." A woman in a bank stood not the "ghost of a chance" of ever becoming branch manager. Marjorie MacMurchy warned that even with a university degree, a Canadian woman ought not to consider herself "too-well equipped" to become a stenographer. In any case the average working woman's career in the labour market lasted only eight years, that of the working man thirty-nine years.[27]

V

Unquestionably many a woman tolerated her situation on the job out of the expectation that paid work was a transitory stage in her life cycle, which would end in marriage. That being the case, McGill sociologist Leonard Marsh theorized, social and economic mobility for

female workers depended less on their individual or collective efforts
at betterment and more on the choice of suitable mates. Manufacturers
played shamelessly upon the anxieties of women in this position,
using advertisements targeted to eligible females that stressed the
dangers of "halitosis" and "B.O.," or warned that without "regular
Lysol douches" Canadian womanhood would wilt on the vine of
romance. This dire prediction seldom happened. Three quarters of
Canadian women had entered into matrimony by age thirty-four, and
over 90 per cent eventually married at some time in their lives. Their
marriages rarely ended in divorce. Would-be opinion makers be-
moaned the increasing incidence of divorce, and *Chatelaine* blamed it
on "modern women's tendency to use prepared food and to serve
paper bag meals," but in 1931 there were fewer than eight thousand
divorced people in the entire country. Divorce was the privilege of the
rich; ordinary people simply separated, leaving no statistical trace to
be recorded.[28]

Once married, a woman usually left the wage-labour market. Some
occupations, teaching and the civil service being the most notorious,
compelled them to leave. The underlying ideology was endorsed in
1922 by the Calgary Business Girls' Club, which petitioned the government for a law "compelling married women to stay in their homes
where they belonged." Its strength made no such statute necessary.
All the institutions of the popular and the official culture promoted the
same message, and as Veronica Strong-Boag notes of the period, home-
making was "the female occupational job ghetto *par excellence*."[29]

Alongside the ritual affirmation of the traditional values of hearth
and home, however, could be seen the beginnings of significant
changes in the Canadian family and household. Industrial capitalism
had transferred the production of countless household commodities
outside the home. The homemaker was thus increasingly a consumer
rather than a producer of goods and, as such, more and more the object of the manipulation of symbols and ideas that were the stock-in-
trade of the advertising and "advice" industries. *Saturday Night* exhorted the middle-class Canadian housewife to "apply the same principles of management to her work that her husband does to his" and
outfit the home with the latest labour-saving machinery. The extent of
the introduction of these devices, however, should not be overestimated; because family incomes did not allow such purchases, most
rural and working-class women lacked the tools for what was called
"efficient" home management. They did without vacuum cleaners,
water-heaters, clothes-washing machines and the like. As late as 1948,
fewer than half of Canadian households had a gas or electric stove; the
rest stoked their kitchen fires with coal and wood. Fewer than a third

had a mechanical refrigerator; daily shopping was still the routine. In rural areas conditions were the most primitive. As of 1931, one in ten Canadian farms had electricity, while on the prairies, only one in fifty had running water.[30]

These were continuities; the most important single change for Canadian women was the diminishing size of the average Canadian family, which now contained three offspring instead of five or six. The falling birth rate, from 29.3 per thousand in 1921 to 23.5 in 1929 and 20.6 in 1939, became the subject of much public discussion. After tearing over a half-million sons from the hearths of the nation in 1914-18, the government not surprisingly sponsored a post-war celebration of maternalism, that "highest of all professions." But the project was a failure. Since deliberate family limitation was an obvious reason, birth control was stridently attacked as "race suicide" by prominent figures like Dr. Helen MacMurchy, director of the Dominion Division of Child Welfare. Dr. Elizabeth Bagshaw, whose pioneering birth control clinic in Hamilton offered services to married women only, was condemned as "blasphemous, degraded and depraved" from local pulpits. Section 207 of the Canadian Criminal Code actually prohibited the "advertising and selling of contraceptive drugs and devices." Authorities occasionally used the law to harass family planners; in 1936 Dorothea Palmer, of the Parents Information Bureau in Kitchener, was arrested under the statute while leaving the home of one of her clients.[31]

The reduced size of the family might seem to imply a lightening of the burden of motherhood, but not if one were to heed the advice of the new child-care experts led by Dr. Alan Brown of Toronto, the inventor of Pablum and author of the influential *The Normal Child: Its Care and Feeding* (1923). The book applied management principles to parenting, a theme taken up with alacrity by columnists, insurance companies, and bureaucrats. It laid out a regime regarding feeding, sleeping, bathing, airing, and the performance of bodily functions at stated times every day. If the schedule called for sleep, sleep it would be, and Baby was to be left alone regardless of any calls for attention. Excessive cuddling was taboo. *The Normal Child* inspired the publication of special pamphlets by the Child Welfare Division, printed in English and French and distributed to new mothers free of charge from coast to coast. One of these "little blue books" dealt with the all-important problem of toilet training, which was to start at six weeks. If an infant failed to produce a bowel movement "on schedule" Mother was instructed to insert a "soft rubber catheter" into its bottom to stimulate the action. At best this reflected a rational concern for public health; at worst, it was a potentially totalitarian foray into the field of human engineering. It is impossible to know how many Canadian mothers followed the state's regime, but it seems clear that "bringing up the kids," like so many other aspects of Canadian life, was becoming ever more complicated.[32]

VI

Of all the voices of ordinary Canadians, none were more muted than those of the children and youth – their unheeded cries in the nursery, murmerings in the classrooms, or suppressed laughter in the workshop. Very rarely protests were heard; here a one-day walkout by caddies at the Toronto Golf and Country Club, there a "strike" by working-class schoolchildren in small-town Alberta who refused to salute the Union Jack. For the most part, youth's experience can only be inferred from other sources. Neil Sutherland suggests that Canadian children born after 1921 "found that the world treated them more tenderly than it had their predecessors." This says more about the brutality routinely meted out to children in the nineteenth century than about any special enlightenment in the inter-war years. Laws to regulate child labour were still a controversial political issue, although most provinces attempted to protect young females with minimum-wage laws. The "future mothers of young Canadians" who packed shingles in a grimy sawmill on the Fraser River in 1929 received a special hearing from the British Columbia Female Wage Board. But in Manitoba in that same year, the provincial Employers' Association protested vigorously against the hint of a minimum-wage law for boys: "No greater calamity could befall the wage-earning boys of this province. It would deprive them of the most sacred safeguard which our Canadian constitution affords. Take from the boy *and his parents* [emphasis ours] the right to freely contract and sell his labour for the highest wage which his individual skill will command and the boy would be reduced to an automaton – a mere creature of the state."[33]

In 1931, considerably less than half (46 per cent) of the nation's sixteen-year-olds were still in school. The rest were at work – in the store, or the mine, or on the farm – or simply wandering the streets. Thousands of the most ambitious and intelligent young Canadians, potential leaders and innovators, especially from the immigrant communities, the working class, and rural areas, were cut adrift at age sixteen. Education was denied them for reasons beyond their control. Nevertheless, the average time spent in school per scholar increased from 6.58 years in 1911 to 8.55 years two decades later. The task of compiling accurate statistics on school attendance was formidable, and in Quebec the Provincial Association of Protestant Teachers noted fraud in the tabulations. Still, there was enough evidence for the conclusion in a 1931 Census Monograph that "now, more than ever, the years at school form an important part of a lifetime," and that "life was becoming progressively fuller, or more difficult," for Canadian youth.[34]

There were vocal critics of what was going on inside the schools. William Irvine quoted in parliament the words of an educator who described the system as "a vast Prussianized enterprise, quantitatively impressive, qualitatively moribund." The 1920s saw a flowering of the movement for "progressive" education in Canada, spearheaded by the Progressive Education Association, founded in 1919. It drew inspiration from the American movement of the same name, and the widely read writings of educator and philosopher John Dewey; "Dewey versus the traditionalists" became the debate in Canada, the United States, and Great Britain. Dewey had seen, long before this, the futility of traditional authoritarian-style pedagogy: rote learning backed up by the strap and cane. He favoured more creative, child-centred programs. "There must be provision for the child to *do* things," read a typical Dewey-inspired brief in New Brunswick. But Dewey's seemingly radical ideas were made acceptable to conservative educators, and to politicians, by their authors' added emphasis on the inculcation of new methods of enforcing social discipline. Progressive educators never resolved the inherent ambiguities. One scholar has complained that the movement in Canada was a façade for the uncritical acceptance of the business philosophy of "scientific management" at the sacrifice of real innovation structured on "sound educational principles."[35]

Society as a whole only reluctantly accepted changes in the schooling and upbringing of children, even when presented as a *fait accompli*. One of the most important was the spread of secondary education, implying the existence of a new, distinctive, and awkward stage of development – which came to be known as adolescence – between childhood and working adulthood. A superficial tempest in a teapot at the Ottawa Collegiate in 1927 illustrated the resistance to the trend. A great campaign was got up against the school as an alleged "cesspool of sin" and site of unsupervised dances. The Ontario government had to placate critics by appointing a royal commission to investigate; it found nothing extraordinary, beyond the normal caprice of human nature. In many communities, however, there were no high schools to worry about. The first "High School Canadien français," as distinct from the élitist *collèges classiques*, opened in Montreal in 1922.[36]

Canadian school reformers faced the challenge of first converting nine different provincial bureaucracies to their ideas, then selling them to the voters. Despite their best efforts, the proverbial one-room schoolhouse, a pedagogical charnelhouse in too many instances, remained the norm in rural Canada. Educational progressives found sympathetic audiences in the Farmer-Labour government of Ontario (1919-23) and the United Farmers government in Alberta (1921-35), whose leaders advocated a solution to the "rural problem" by consolidating schools and school districts and upgrading the professional standards of the teachers. Both projects involved sizeable investments of public funds. The non-parliamentary wing of the UFA successfully blocked reform initiatives in Alberta. In Ontario, the voters turfed the Farmer-Labourites out of office before they could accomplish anything. Fiscal restraint was the motto of conservatives everywhere; in British Columbia and in Alberta this led to walkouts or lockouts involving angry teachers facing salary cuts by local boards in 1921 and 1925.[37]

Some progress was made in the area of technical and vocational training, the schools' response to industrial capitalism. "Tech-voc" had a heavy class inclination, which its advocates did not try to hide. "A young life properly 'fitted into' the niche of industry to which it naturally belongs wears soon into an integral cog of industrial progress," wrote one British Columbia enthusiast. "Improperly 'fitted' it threatens and impedes industrial and social progress, and thereby the peace of mind and well-being of the whole national life." Could this have been an unconscious reference to men like W.A. Pritchard, British Columbia's foremost socialist, the son of an uneducated immigrant worker who eschewed that life, received an academic training, and thrilled the working class with his dazzling "Address to the Jury" at the Winnipeg Strike trials? Paradoxically, practical or manual training in schools, once denounced by unionists as a breeding ground "for rats or scabs," won increasing favour in the eyes of the trade union movement. The workers' leaders discarded the notion, common in the nineteenth century, of public education as a vehicle for social mobility. Instead, through vocational training they sought to make the system relevant to workers' lives, or at least those of their children. Pritchard's fellow defendants in the 1919 trials, R.B. Russell and R.J. Johns, made their mark in Winnipeg in the 1920s and 1930s as authorities in the field of technical education. While these efforts were real contributions, they reflected a saddening solidification of social cleavage. A liberal-minded critic told miners' leader Frank Wheatley that he "would hate to see any class of men raise their families to be miners." Wheatley responded indignantly; he had two sons, and they would certainly become miners.[38]

Where programs of practical education existed, they were rigidly segregated by sex. Boys learned woodworking or auto mechanics, girls clay modelling or "domestic science" – sewing and cooking. But the real mandate of the public school system was to do little more than pass on the tools of an elementary and uncritical literacy. By that yardstick it was successful. Excluding aboriginal peoples, there were only 300,000 illiterates counted in the census of 1931, 3.79 per cent as compared to 5.49 per cent in the post-war census. The critics were not silenced by such crude measures of progress. "Our education system," dissident intellectuals complained, "remains the most satisfactory means of producing the standardized 'Babbitt' type, the educational equivalent of the identical interchangeable parts which our mass industrial process turns out."[39]

CHAPTER 8

The Conundrum of Culture

I

To members of English Canada's intellectual community, the end of the Great War symbolized their country's coming of age. The only attribute of full-grown nationhood that post-war Canada appeared to them to lack was a culture that could reflect this new national status and demonstrate, to Canadians and the world, that Canada had left behind her unlettered adolescence and entered a more refined adulthood. "After 1919," wrote Arthur Lismer, "most creative people, whether in painting, writing or music, began to have a guilty feeling that Canada was as yet unwritten, unpainted, unsung. . . . In 1920 there was a job to be done." Led by Lismer and his colleagues in the Group of Seven, a small contingent of "creative people" committed themselves to the task of bringing into existence an indigenous cultural tradition. Their efforts had surprising success; when measured in terms of quantity, the outpouring of art, prose, and poetry during the twenties and thirties is astonishing. A rough measure is the special section the *Canadian Annual Review* began in 1922 to chronicle developments in "Canadian Art, Literature and Music"; by 1928-29 the section had doubled in length to forty pages. What was occurring, said publisher Hugh S. Eayrs, was a "Renaissance in Canadian Life." Although Eayrs overlooked the fact that a renaissance requires a previous classical age that can be reborn, something definitely was happening in the once-somnolent world of Canadian arts and letters.[1]

There were many components to the cultural conjuncture. Universities made their contribution by nurturing a native Canadian intelligentsia. Those who attended university were a tiny percentage of the population, but the 1920 enrolment of 21,869 students surpassed pre-war figures. The University of Toronto almost doubled in size in the two years after the war, and the incoming class of 1920 at the University of Alberta was more than twice as large as any previous group of freshmen. Growth continued throughout the inter-war period; there were 35,164 undergraduates in universities and colleges in 1939, and although most who went beyond the master's level still left for Britain or the United States, the number enrolled in Canadian graduate programs had quadrupled to 1,550 from 383 twenty years earlier. As they expanded, English-Canadian universities moved farther from their origins as church colleges and became more secular; theology programs shrank as the new students chose instead courses in history, literature, or political economy. Despite heavy teaching loads, faculty members encouraged the post-war cultural efflorescence by extending their responsibilities beyond the classroom. At the University of Saskatchewan, for example, historian Frank Underhill organized an extracurricular discussion group among his students with the objective of building "a higher type of Canadian national spirit." Such efforts were repaid. Citing a remarkable increase in library circulation as his evidence, librarian W.S. Wallace of the University of Toronto claimed that "among the undergraduates there has arisen since the Great War a new spirit . . . a thirst for knowledge . . . such as was unknown before." Campuses, particularly McGill and the University of Toronto, became intellectual gathering places and served as foci for young painters, poets, writers, and musicians.[2]

The universities created an urban middle class literate and leisured enough to serve as cultural consumers. This class expressed its support for the Canadian "renaissance" through voluntary organizations like the Association of Canadian Clubs, which claimed to have 115 branches in 1928. The Canadian Clubs' aim was to "foster patriotism by encouraging study of the institutions, history, arts and literature of Canada" through sponsorship of lecture tours, poetry readings, and art exhibitions. The Native Sons of Canada, a nationalist organization founded in 1921, sent speakers across the country to proselytize for "greater recognition of Canadian literature." Such capitalist patrons as Sir Edmund Walker of the Bank of Commerce, J.S. McLean of Canada Packers, and Vincent Massey and his agricultural implement millions helped create the cultural infrastructure of galleries and concert halls, in addition to aiding individual artists.[3]

Canadian culture also received the backing of periodicals. *Maclean's Magazine* pledged to print only Canadian non-fiction, to reduce fiction by foreign authors to a minimum, and to use "thoroughly Canadian spelling." The *Canadian Magazine* made "Canadian content rather than quality" its criterion, and editor Joseph Lister Rutledge set his target as an entire issue untainted by foreign authors or subject matter. An even less restrained chauvinism

animated *Canadian Bookman,* a monthly founded in 1919. Its aggressive cultural nationalism was reflected in shamelessly uncritical
reviews of Canadian books. The *Canadian Forum* was more
discriminating in its taste and judgement but no less determined to
help build a cultural identity. In the inaugural issue in 1920 the editors
promised that the *Forum* would "trace and value those developments
of arts and letters which are distinctively Canadian."[4]

Two academic quarterlies born at the same time also served the cultural cause. *Dalhousie Review* provided book reviews and essays
about art, literature, and contemporary affairs. The *Canadian Historical Review* was aimed not simply at professional historians, for there
weren't enough of them to support a journal, but at amateur historians
and the informed general reader. In an article entitled "The Growth of
Canadian National Feeling," published in the *Review*'s second issue,
its editor put the convictions of the cultural nationalists into historical
perspective. The evolution of "a national consciousness," maintained
W.S. Wallace, was "the central fact in Canadian history"; its evolution
had culminated with the Great War until "to-day . . . he would be a
bold man who would deny to Canada the existence of a national feeling."[5]

To capitalize on this sentiment Canadian publishing houses for the
first time began to print significant numbers of original Canadian titles
in addition to their bread-and-butter businesses of publishing school
texts and serving as "agency houses" for British and American publishers. Leader in this new direction was Lorne Pierce of the Ryerson
Press, a company originally founded to publish the books of the Methodist Church. Pierce published Canadian authors at an unprecedented
pace, toured the country to promote them, and sponsored a gold
medal to be awarded by the Royal Society to outstanding native
literary figures. Pierce's efforts were paralleled by the work of
Hugh S. Eayrs at Macmillan of Canada, Donald French, literary editor
at McClelland and Stewart, and by a new entry to the field, Graphic
Publishers. Located in Ottawa, away from the Toronto-based industry,
Graphic was founded in 1924 with the ambition of "producing and
marketing all-Canadian books by Canadian writers." It is arguable
whether the new policies of publishing houses were a cause or a result
of the *zeitgeist* of cultural nationalism. Public demand for Canadian
writers was sufficiently compelling to create a "Canadiana Revival,"
as McClelland and Stewart reprinted nineteenth-century books by
Susanna Moodie, T.C. Haliburton, and Catherine Parr Traill. Also re-
published were Bliss Carman and his cousin Charles G.D. Roberts,
who came back from the United States for lecture tours to enthusiastic
audiences. The two poets found a mood very different from that of the

country they had abandoned – or that had abandoned them – in the 1890s. "A new and mighty impulse is stirring the Canadian people at the present moment," Vancouver poet A.M. Stephen explained to the elderly Roberts; "even as the culture of Athens was superseded . . . so will the centres of culture move from the British Isles to the Dominions." Canadians were living, he concluded, "in the greatest epoch in the known history of man."[6]

Stephen's pretentious comment distills the essence of the cultural nationalism of the twenties. Canadian intellectuals escaped the disillusionment that in the wake of the war drowned their counterparts in Britain; few of them displayed the bitter cynicism that drove America's "lost generation" to refuge in Greenwich Village or into exile in Paris. The temper of mainstream Canadian poets, writers, and painters was buoyant, not bleak, and their work was used to celebrate their native land more often than to castigate it. Even the Depression of the 1930s did little to change this. This is not to say that they found nothing to be angry about. They condemned the influence of Britain and the United States, which they felt suffocated true Canadian forms of expression. Literary critic William Arthur Deacon defined his task as "protecting this germ civilization from too great dominance by the two sizeable and proximate English-speaking nations . . . to keep out English and American ideals, institutions and viewpoints." In *Highways of Canadian Literature* (1924), J.D. Logan argued for a distinct "Canadian literary creation, taste and judgment . . . based not on the work of British or American masters . . . but on that of Canadian masters." To replace the cultural heritage that it intended to slough off, the interwar generation chose the land itself, the Canadian environment, the "true north strong and free," which both distinguished Canada from the Old World and provided a familiar shared experience with which their Canadian audiences could identify.[7]

II

The artists who called themselves the Group of Seven – James E.H. MacDonald, Lawren Harris, A.Y. Jackson, Fred Varley, Frank Carmichael, Arthur Lismer, and Frank Johnston – best exemplify the postwar nationalist ethos of Canadian cultural life.* Except for Harris, the

---

* Johnston left the Group in 1924 and was replaced by A.J. Casson. Edwin Holgate and Lemoine Fitzgerald joined in 1931 and 1932 respectively. Tom Thomson, whose *West Wind* and *Jack Pine* define the movement's popular image, worked closely with the members but died in mysterious circumstances in 1917, before the Group was formed.

Group's members began their careers as commercial artists. Their col-loboration began before 1914 in the studios of a Toronto firm of graphic designers for whom they worked, as their mutual attempts to capture the Canadian Shield on canvas drew them together as friends and allies. Their formal association was delayed by the departure of Lismer, Johnston, Varley, and Jackson to serve as official war artists, an experience that sharpened an already acute national consciousness. In May 1920, the Group of Seven was officially launched with an ex-hibition at the Art Museum of Toronto. Their "vision concerning art in Canada" was clearly set out in the exhibition catalogue written by Lawren Harris: "An Art must grow and flower in the land before the country will be a real home for its people." The Group felt it had created a Canadian art movement that "sincerely interprets the spirit of a nation's growth" and was for all the people, not just a sophisti-cated élite. It threw down the gauntlet to "so-called Art lovers" who "refuse to recognize anything that does not come up to the commer-cialized, imported standard of the picture sale room"; the responsibil-ity of true Canadians was to "accept the production of artists native to the land whose work is more distinctive, original and vital, and of *greater value to the country*." Unlike the sombre Dutch pastoral scenes which some well-to-do Canadians "collected like cigarette cards," the Group of Seven's passionately intense landscapes of the Northern Ontario wilderness were brilliant mosaics of crashing col-ours: reds, greens, oranges, blues, and yellows. Their thickly textured brush strokes were crude and violent when compared to traditional techniques; their bold canvases seemed to their viewers to "vibrate," to become, "moving, living" things. Just as they had immodestly claimed, the Seven had evoked for Canadians the grandeur and the im-mensity of their harsh and lonely land. "Canadians were challenged," wrote A.Y. Jackson of that first exhibition, "to replace the Dutch cow with the northern bull moose."[8]

It was no contest: Canadians chose the moose. No artists before or since have captured public favour as completely as did the Group of Seven. The Group took its self-assigned mission of painting Canada very seriously, and during the remainder of the decade its members painted all five of her regions. It was their paintings of Northern On-tario, however, and those done by their late colleague, Tom Thom-son, that were accepted as symbolic representations of the Canadian character. Their pictures, concluded a *Maclean's* article, might "well be labelled Canada, for in their stark intensity they typify the spirit of a race." Their landscapes stirred emotions other than national pride. David Milne, a more talented but less heralded contemporary of the Group, could have been describing any member of the Group when he attributed Tom Thomson's popularity to his subjects, "ones that have pleasant associations for most of us, holidays, rest, recreation. Pleasant association, beautiful subjects, [therefore] good painting. . . . In Canada we like to have our heavens made to order and in our own image."[9]

Whatever the reason for their appeal, in creating Canadian myths the Group of Seven also encouraged some hardy myths about their movement. The first was their contention that their painting was unique and original. The Group of Seven were neither the first painters to marry art and nationalism nor the first to concentrate on the northern landscape. Quebec artists Maurice Cullen and Marc-Aurèle de Foy Suzor-Coté had done innovative work similar to that of the Group in the 1890s, and the Canadian Art Club (1907-15) had attempted to surround Canadian art with a patriotic aura a decade before the Group was conceived. As William Colgate has pointed out, the Group of Seven "marked the culmination of all the progressive and converging influences of painting in Canada." The Group's claim to have made a revolutionary departure from the traditions of western art is also unsupportable. Carmichael, Jackson, Lismer, Varley, and Harris had studied in Europe, and whether they were aware of it or not, the influence of French Post-Impressionism on their work is clearly evident. As an English critic observed of the Group's work, "the points of similarity [to Van Gogh and Cézanne] are more immediately noticed than the features which promise or already mark a divergence."[10]

The final Group of Seven myth is that their movement was harshly received by critics and had to struggle for survival against the hostility of a reactionary art establishment. Two Toronto *Star* critics used colourful language to express their distaste for the Group's landscape technique: H.F. Gadsby referred to them in 1913 as the "Hot Mush School," while Hector Charlesworth suggested in 1916 that J.E.H. MacDonald's *The Elements* and his *Rock and Maple* be renamed *Hungarian Goulash* and *Drunkard's Stomach*. By the early twenties, however, such condemnation was rare and easily outweighed by praise; the Group members magnified any criticism for its publicity value and cultivated an image as rebellious young men defending Canadian culture from unpatriotic philistines imbued with foreign values. "We encouraged it [opposition]," Lawren Harris later confessed. "We goaded the reactionary and cocksure writers of the press of that day to give full rein to their breezy diatribes." When Hector Charlesworth, writing for *Saturday Night*, obliged them by calling the Group "Paint Slingers" and their techniques a "rigid formula for ugliness," his comments were quoted in advertisements for the Group's next exhibition![11]

The Group of Seven, with its affluent and influential patrons, aroused the envy of other artists. A Toronto ophthalmologist financed their trips to Northern Ontario and rented them studios at nominal cost; the Canadian Manufacturers' Association praised them in its journal, *Industrial Canada*. Sir Edmund Walker, chairman of the Arts Advisory Council, and Eric Brown, director of the National Gallery, saw that the National Gallery bought many of their paintings and featured them prominently in the travelling exhibits that went to the United States and to small galleries across the country. As a result, the National Gallery and the Group were criticized for the alleged favouritism shown to one particular approach to art. The selection of the paintings for the British Empire Exhibition at Wembley in 1924 turned into an acrimonious confrontation between Eric Brown and the Royal Canadian Academy, which had become the spokesman for older artists outraged by the acquisition policies of the National Gallery. When the gallery trustees won the right to choose the jury that would assemble the Canadian exhibit, Brown helped make certain that a major part of it was Group of Seven landscapes. British reviewers were ecstatic. The art critic for the *Daily Chronicle* typified the torrent of praise when he called them "the most vital group of paintings produced since the war – indeed this century." The triumph at Wembley, concludes Ann Davis, was "a clear turning point in the history of Canadian art"; among the many paradoxes of the Group of Seven is that in spite of their ostentatious disdain for the Old World, it was international recognition in Britain that confirmed them as the dominant force in Canadian art. By the time they disbanded in 1931, their popular acceptance was so complete that Group members, in Douglas Cole's words, were "elevated to the status of Canadian cultural heroes and their work enshrined as national icons."[12]

The Group did, however, encourage other painters whose vision did not accord with their own. Winnipeg's Lemoine FitzGerald was invited to exhibit with them, and was even briefly a member. Emily Carr was lifted out of obscurity in part by the efforts of Lawren Harris, and her contacts with the Group inspired her to resume working in 1927. Young artists like Charles Comfort and Carl Schaefer studied with Group members yet were never confined by their mentors' patriotic preoccupation. But to a degree the Group of Seven's success precluded the acceptance of other approaches: David Milne's delicate watercolours, W.J. Phillips's perpetuations of the English romantic-realist tradition, and John Lyman's modernism. Founder of Montreal's Contemporary Art Society, Lyman was the most outspoken critic of the notion of art as Canadian consciousness-raising. "The real Canadian scene," he wrote in 1938, "is in the consciousness of Canadian painters, whatever the object of their thought.'' The ultimate irony of the Group of Seven's nationalist crusade was that their hegemony of public taste obscured the work of other talented artists, just as they had once claimed to be crowded out by "Dutch art.'' Their revolution against the art establishment had turned into an establishment of its own. [13]

III

No literary movement had the cohesion or achieved the fame of the Group of Seven, but cultural nationalism nevertheless served as a literary common denominator in the inter-war period. The Canadian Authors' Association, founded in 1921, used national feeling as a marketing device more effectively than its members used it as a theme or an inspiration for their work. Conceived initially as a guild to represent the interests of professional writers, the CAA found these in short supply and, as Madge Macbeth joked, accepted "practically anyone who professed an interest in literature and whose cheques would be honoured by a bank.'' At its largest, the CAA had eight hundred members affiliated with its ten local branches. Earnestly trying to be pan-Canadian, the association established a French-Canadian branch and rotated its central headquarters from Montreal to Toronto to Ottawa to Winnipeg. There was more show than substance to this, however, and the real base of the association was in Central Canada where writers, magazines, and publishing houses were concentrated. Its cultural goal was to use literature to articulate a national identity and to foster a sense of community within the country, but from its inception the CAA had a paramount commercial objective as well. "The first thing,'' wrote young member Paul Wallace "is to get our people to buy Canadian books as well as American books, and the next thing is to get them to buy the best.'' The CAA, however, never implemented phase two of its program; instead, it concentrated on pushing the work of its members without regard for quality, "persuading trusting housewives that literary kitsch was not kitsch if it was Made in Canada.'' The association's principal ploy was the annual Canadian Book Week, held in November to capitalize on the pre-Christmas demand for books as gifts. Association spokesmen like A.C. Garner assured the public that its hucksterism was "a National movement and . . . one of the mediums of creating a real National Spirit.'' All this promotion seems to have worked. There was, reported *Bookseller and Stationer* in 1923, "a wave of reading spreading across the country''; the CAA, wrote poet Charles Mair to a friend, "has mightily furthered Canadian Letters.'' [14]

The authors and poets who cashed in on this literary boom were by and large an undistinguished bunch. In painting, nationalism had been used to supplant the traditionalists; in literature, it was the traditionalists themselves who appropriated nationalism and turned it to their ends. Compared with the pre-war period, more Canadian novels, stories, non-fiction, and poems were written, published, and read between the wars, but they showed little change in content or style from late-Victorian romanticism. The most popular Canadian writers continued to be those who had been popular a decade before: novelists Ralph Connor (C.W. Gordon), Lucy Maude Montgomery, and Nellie McClung; humorist Stephen Leacock; poets Robert Service, Bliss Carman, and Charles G.D. Roberts. Younger writers who aspired to literary careers followed their paths; most Canadian novels written during the period are either historical romances or sentimental regional idylls filled with romantic local colour and complete with the requisite happy ending. Mazo de la Roche's *Jalna* (1927), the first of the sixteen novels of her "serialized soap opera," was the most widely read new addition to what Louis Dudek has called "the middle-class literature of appeasement," but there were several hundred other less memorable Canadian contributions to it. Short fiction was simply the novel in microcosm. As H. Napier Moore advised the CAA, *Maclean's* was not interested in "gloomy stories" but wanted "short stories of romance and adventure and love stories in a lighter vein." Canadian fiction was above all relentlessly moral and upright. The literary critic of the Toronto *Globe* attributed this to "the cleaner methods of our Canadian authors and the stricter censorship exercised by Canadian editors in choosing their material." The American novel, said the speaker to a London, Ontario, literary society, was "a tainted mass of sordid life, reeking with the filth and mire of a corrupt society. . . . The much-vaunted realism of modern fiction is usually vulgar and frequently immoral."[15]

The courageous few who attempted realistic fiction were abused by critics and ignored by readers. Jessie Sime's *Our Little Life* (1921), set in working-class Montreal, and Charles Yale Harrison's *Generals Die in Bed* (1930), a private soldier's view of the Great War, were virtually unnoticed. R.J.C. Stead's *Grain* (1926), the story of a farmer who resists community pressure to enlist, was much less popular than his more romantic early novels. Frederick Philip Grove's *Settlers of the Marsh* (1925) was banned from some public libraries because Grove's presentation of his characters' sexuality was considered obscene. The greatest shock to Canadian sensibilities was Martha Ostenso's *Wild Geese* (1925), whose teenage heroine runs naked through the bush and happily bears her lover's illegitimate child. Ostenso's own relationship with married novelist Douglas Durkin added to the scandal, and when *Wild Geese* won a $13,500 prize in the United States as "the best novel by an American author," it simply confirmed Canadian opinions about the depravity of Ostenso, her book, and American society. Unquestionably the best of the new Canadian novelists was Morley Callaghan, a Torontonian who spent a year in the American expatriate community in Paris. His *Strange Fugitive* (1928), although set in Toronto, was dismissed by B.K. Sandwell as "an American novel" because of its urban setting and because its central character was a bootlegger.[16]

The mainstream of Canadian poetry was even more resolutely romantic than that of prose. S.I. Hayakawa, a sarcastic University of Toronto graduate student, divided Canada's poets into four types: "Victorian, Neo-Victorian, Quasi-Victorian and Pseudo-Victorian." Hayakawa's complaint was not so much about Carman, Roberts, or Duncan Campbell Scott, acknowledged masters of their idiom, as about the legion of second-rate imitators whose work appeared in Canadian magazines and newspapers and was occasionally collected into chapbooks by Toronto publishers. *Vacation,* by CAA member Jean M. Douglas, provides a perfect example of this sort of verse:

> O when your work has lost its zest
> And you are tired or overspent
> Pack up your kit for trails of rest
> That make for gladness and content.
>
> Go far beyond the postman's call
> And in some gentle leaf-lulled way
> 'Midst song of bird and waterfall
> Make life a happy holiday.

Not all Canadian poets touched the bathetic depths of these saccharine stanzas, but most wrote in traditional ways about unexceptionable subjects using quaint and cumbersome language with slavish adherence to the convention of end-rhyme. The poems in Nathaniel Benson's misnamed anthology *Modern Canadian Poetry* (1930), were, in Peter Stevens's words, "generally imitative verse" which "made no significant attempt to relate poetry to life in Canada" but "existed in a romantic Arcadian Never-Neverland." Canadians, wrote Lionel Stevenson thankfully in his *Appraisals of Canadian Literature* (1926), need have no fear that their poets would succumb to the influence of modernists like T.S. Eliot or Edgar Lee Masters: ". . . for some time to come, Canadian literature will provide a refreshing haven of genuine romanticism to which the reader may retreat when he seeks an antidote to the intellectual tension imposed by . . . *The Wasteland* and *Spoon River*."[17]

In hindsight it is possible to see that Stevenson's prediction was being disproved even as he made it, for despite the prevailing critical hostility to modernist poetry, the twenties marked the beginning of Canadian modernism, as younger poets experimented with free verse, abandoned stilted, archaic language, and used dramatic imagery to describe contemporary subjects. *Newfoundland Verse* (1923) by E.J. Pratt, a Toronto English professor, marked the first significant Canadian departure from poetic traditionalism. Raymond Knister and W.W.E. Ross could also be considered important pioneers of the genre, as could the "Montreal Group" of Leo Kennedy, A.J.M. Smith, and Frank Scott, three McGill students who were the driving force behind two short-lived little magazines, the *McGill Fortnightly Review* (1926-27), and the *Canadian Mercury* (1928-29). All shared a common revulsion against heavy-handed literary nationalism, which Pratt described as the "Maple Leaf psychosis." They rejected the fawning reviews of the *Canadian Bookman* and the tendency "to abolish critical standards and be a booster" if the writer were a Canadian. The worst example of this boosterism was the Canadian Authors' Association. "That pillar of flim-flam," wrote Leo Kennedy, "is a stumbling block over which the aspiring young Canadian writer must first climb." The CAA, said A.J.M. Smith, should change its name to the "Journalists' Branch of the Canadian Manufacturers' Association and quit kidding the public every Christmas that it has a moral obligation to buy poor Canadian, rather than good foreign books."[18]

For all their contempt for the Canadian Authors' Association, however, the *avant garde* poets were very much a part of the cultural climate of their age. They were every bit as anxious as conservative CAA members to have a distinctive native Canadian literature, "reflecting," in the words of a *Canadian Mercury* editorial, "as modern Canadian painting has begun to do, a unique experience of nature and life." E.J. Pratt, W.W.E. Ross, Frank Scott, and A.J.M. Smith were all admirers of the Group of Seven, and their poetry often "described the same landscape – harsh, vital, northern – that the Group of Seven had helped to make dominant." The other modernists shared this enthusiasm for their country: ". . . the Dominion of Canada!" wrote Raymond Knister; "there are infinite spiritual possibilities in a land as huge and undeveloped as this." The modernists hoped for a Canadian literature that could earn international recognition when viewed from a more cosmopolitan critical perspective. They were more open to American and European influences such as Ezra Pound, T.S. Eliot, and Carl Sandburg than were most Canadian intellectuals, but they were not colonialists who bent their art to a metropolitan model. Instead, they adapted the modernist techniques to the Canadian environment, and with considerable poetic success. Cultural nationalism's modernist variant was summed up by W.W.E. Ross in the foreword to *Laconics* (1930), a collection of poems inspired by Northern Ontario:

> But it is hoped
> that they will seemingly contain
> something of
> what quality may mark us off
> from older Europe –
> something North American –
> and something of
> the sharper tang of Canada.[19]

The nationalist literary tide ebbed only slightly during the Depression of the 1930s. *Masses* (1932-34) and *New Frontier* (1936-37), magazines edited by members of the Communist party's Progressive Arts Club, published "socialist realist" short fiction that portrayed the plight of ordinary people. But the stories in the mass circulation magazines that ordinary people actually read continued to be escapist and romantic – served, complained Clyde Gilmour, "not with a grain of salt but with several spoonsful of powdered sugar." The thirties are sometimes assumed to be the cradle of critical realism in the Canadian novel, but with the exceptions of Callaghan's *Such Is My Beloved, They Shall Inherit the Earth,* and *More Joy in Heaven* (1934-37), most of the novels thought of as Depression classics were published long afterwards: W.O. Mitchell's *Who Has Seen the Wind* (1947), Hugh MacLennan's *The Watch That Ends the Night* (1959), and Hugh Garner's *Cabbagetown* (1951). The best-selling novels of the period were international successes like *Anthony Adverse* and *Gone With the Wind*, and Canadian authors who wanted to sell took note of this. Poets were more responsive to the economic crisis, and the thirties saw an increased use and acceptance of social themes and modernist techniques. Two major new poets, A.M. Klein and Dorothy Livesay, displayed both tendencies in their work, leading F.R. Scott to hope that "late Victorian God-and-Maple Tree romanticism" was dead. It proved a hardy perennial, however. When Ruth McKenzie surveyed "the stream of Canadian literature" in 1939, she found "no indication of a vigorous current threatening to sweep the stream out of its placid course."[20]

IV

In the performing arts the omnipresent nationalism of literature and painting was less in evidence. Music was an important part of the lives of all Canadians, and its place in the churches gave it a seal of approval denied other forms of expression. With recording technology still primitive and with radio in its infancy, every town of any conse-quence had church choirs or a musical club that gave concerts while larger centres provided a wider variety of musical activity. Each of the four Western provinces had annual competitive festivals. In Manitoba, for example, the festival sponsored by the Men's Musical Club of Win-nipeg brought instrumentalists, soloists, and choirs to the city for a single nervous performance before an adjudicator of a piece practised hundreds of times over in a country church or schoolroom.

Toronto was Canada's musical capital, however. The University of Toronto's Music Faculty opened in 1919 with affiliations to the To-ronto Conservatory of Music, and with Montreal, Toronto shared the distinction of a symphony orchestra. Each orchestra had a core of pro-fessionals who earned their livings as movie theatre musicians or music teachers, supplemented by enthusiastic amateurs. Montreal's dignity suffered somewhat because the TSO performed in Massey Hall while the Montreal Symphonic Concerts were sometimes held in the Forum, where the cold from the artificial rink made the musicians shiver and the brass sound sharp when it resumed after a rest in the score. Torontonians could also boast, again thanks to the Masseys, that their city was home to Canada's most celebrated musical ensemble, the Hart House String Quartet.[21]

The music performed by Canadian musicians was seldom the work of Canadian composers. Toronto *Star* music critic Augustus Bridle estimated in 1929 that Canada had about fifty serious composers, most of whom were unknown in their own country. "We get our popular songs from Tin Pan Alley, our futurist pieces from Europe and our classics from dead men," he lamented. "You can find folk in any of our largest cities who have bought Canadian pictures and an occa-sional Canadian book. . . . Once in a dog's age do you find any Cana-dian composer's latest piece on the piano." The composers' problem, admitted Bridle, was that "most of them do not write music that could be labelled Canadian . . . as the music dramas of Wagner are German." Canadian composers remained impervious to any suggestion that they emulate the Group of Seven and write music that would "describe a northern lake." The most serious attempt to steer music in nationalist directions was made by Marius Barbeau of the National Museum, who tried to induce prominent musicians to compose and perform works based on the folk music he was collecting for the museum. Assisted by John Murray Gibbon, a past president of the Canadian Authors' Association who was publicity director for the Canadian Pacific Rail-way, he obtained a three-thousand-dollar grant from the CPR for two festivals of such compositions at the Chateau Frontenac in 1927 and 1928. Barbeau's bribe persuaded Ernest MacMillan, Alfred Whitehead, and Claude Champagne to compose works based on folk music motifs; the Hart House String Quartet was brought to Quebec to perform MacMillan's *Six bergerettes du bas Canada*. But only Champagne was even partially converted to Barbeau's ideas; other composers and performers rejected or ignored them. When the festivals produced no nationalistic surge, Barbeau concluded sadly that although "it seemed at the time that Canadian music was coming into its own, perhaps we were too optimistic."[22]

Another aborted nationalist scheme to Canadianize the performing arts was the Trans-Canada Theatre Society, capitalized at $4 million in 1919 to "achieve the impossible: complete control of a professional theatre route entirely in Canada." Canada had never had an indigenous professional theatre. Since the 1890s the Canadian stage had been a series of profitable northern extensions of the American touring circuits controlled by the New York-based Theatrical Syndicate; only a handful of Canadian theatre owners had the financial resources to maintain "open door" houses that would book companies not sponsored by the syndicate. It was never a question of replacing American theatre with the work of Canadian playwrights; Trans-Canada intended to buy up a chain of theatres and inaugurate a series of coast-to-coast tours of British plays, maintaining an "open door" policy at other times. Even with the backing of Lord Shaughnessy, former president of the CPR, the society was an artistic and commercial disaster. The theatres it acquired were old and shabby, as were most of the British road companies willing to cross the Atlantic to appear in them. Moreover, competition from the movies was hurting the legitimate theatre. When Calgarians refused to turn out to see a TCTS production, the *Herald* explained that motion pictures had "made them impatient of anything except the best. . . . If the public cannot see stage productions of very high quality it goes off to the movies, content to see these at less expense." The society suspended operation in 1924, and professional theatre continued a steady decline. The more modern buildings, like Winnipeg's Walker, were converted into cinemas; Toronto's Victoria Street theatre suffered the ultimate humiliation of being razed to make way for a miniature golf course.[23]

The departure of foreign professionals did not mean that all of Canada's stages were bare. A Little Theatre movement flourished in the burgeoning cultural nationalism of the twenties until by 1930 there were an estimated eighteen hundred amateur theatre groups functioning, although only a hundred of them put on more than one production annually. Most of the plays performed were American, British, or

European, yet the amateur stage did provide an outlet for the work of the handful of talented Canadian playwrights, notably Merrill Denison and Gwen Pharis Ringwood. When the Depression completed the work of motion pictures in destroying the touring professional companies, amateur theatre entered its most dynamic decade. At the initiative of Governor General Lord Bessborough, the Dominion Drama Festival was inaugurated in 1933. Each spring thereafter, until halted by war in 1940, the winners of regional competitions performed their short plays before a distinguished – usually British – adjudicator to determine the best among them. To encourage Canadian playwrights, British actor Sir Barry Jackson donated a trophy to be awarded for the best performance of a Canadian play, although there were never more than a dozen to choose from. In terms of national participation, however, the success of the festival was spectacular: in the first year, 110 plays were entered, representing all nine provinces. There were separate sections for plays presented in English and in French, but a play in either language could and did win the top honour, the Bessborough Trophy. One of the adjudicators for the 1939 festival applauded Canadians for their remarkable achievement: they had created a "national theatre of their own," said George Skillan, "national in the true sense since it is run and developed by the people themselves."[24]

V

The Dominion Drama Festival was an anomaly in its ability to encompass both language groups, for the most obvious crack in the foundation of the temple of cultural nationalism was French Canada. The experience of the Great War, which to an English Canadian had been a unifying step toward national maturity, meant to his French-speaking compatriot the frustration and humiliation of conscription, and the memory of the Union government through which English Canada had imposed its will upon Quebec. One explanation of the impulse to find the Canadian identity in the forests of the Shield was that the landscape was a metaphor that ignored such fundamental differences and encompassed both founding peoples. A.Y. Jackson could paint Quebec, but French-Canadian characters all but disappeared from the work of English-Canadian poets and novelists. There was an unspoken understanding that the sympathetic and romantic portrait of a peasant society that had been drawn by William Henry Drummond or William Kirby was no longer entirely adequate, but there was no certainty about what should replace it. The only novel about French Canada that was widely read in English Canada was by a Frenchman: Louis

Hemon's *Maria Chapdelaine*, which appeared in translation in 1922. Although an excellent novel, it dealt with a rural Quebec that was fast disappearing; as Ramsay Cook has pointed out, "as sociology *Maria Chapdelaine* was already obsolete when it was originally published in 1913." Nor did a new understanding come from the English universities, where French Canada was ignored as a subject of scholarly inquiry; the scant attention devoted to French Canada in the three academic quarterlies both "reflected and contributed to the profound isolation of the English-Canadian intellectual community from the affairs of Quebec."[25]

That ignorance and incomprehension was reciprocated. French-Canadian intellectuals were very much aware of the English-speaking sea in which French Canada was an island, but they thought of English Canada and of English Canadians in one-dimensional stereotypes. The Anglo-Saxons, said a character in Abbé Groulx's pseudonymous novel *l'Appel de la race* (1922), had two consuming passions, "material gain and a sense of their racial superiority." Groulx's English-Canadian characters demonstrated these traits throughout the novel and confirmed them in its sequel, *Au cap Blomidon*. Because Groulx was the moving force of *l'Action française*, the extreme voice of French-Canadian Catholic nationalism, his work has sometimes been argued to be atypical. But the same sort of English characters appeared in the work of authors without such connections. In Jean-Charles Harvey's *Marcel Faure* (1922) the protagonist is a French-Canadian industrialist whose benevolent treatment of his employees is contrasted with that of his English competitors who exploit their workers. Faure's success infuriates these competitors, who plot to ruin him by persuading a large English-Canadian bank to call Faure's loan at a critical moment. Only the intercession of a French-Canadian bank foils the conspiracy and saves the business from English domination. Thus while English-Canadian intellectuals ignored or misunderstood French Canada, their French-speaking counterparts saw English Canada only through the narrow window of its dominant class as a soulless, materialistic monolith bent on French Canada's destruction.[26]

Yet despite the chasm that separated the French- and English-Canadian intelligentsias there were some remarkable similarities between their literary outputs. Both French-Canadian and English-Canadian literatures were self-conscious colonial segments of larger literatures whose vital centres were outside Canada in Paris and in London and New York. Both were preoccupied with romantic portraits of things past and pastoral and avoided realistic treatments of modern urban-industrial Canadian society; both were resolutely moral and moralistic; both were nationalistic. Their nationalisms were different in content and mutually exclusive in their objectives; the English-Canadian goal of building a "Canadian national spirit" was the antithesis of the French-Canadian resolve to survive as a French Catholic nation. But as Ronald Sutherland has argued, "there are many significant parallels" between the literatures of English and French Canada: "obviously we have twin solitudes."[27]

Poetry rather than prose was the more important form of literary expression, and in Quebec just as in English Canada the romantic poetry of the nineteenth century dominated. The *école littéraire de Montréal*, founded in 1890, continued to be the most important influence on French-Canadian poetry. Its surviving founder and major figure, Jean Charbonneau, led younger poets like Blanche Lamontagne, Eve Sénécal and Alice Lemieux into voluntary isolation from the modernist influences of European and American poetry as they celebrated the virtues of traditional rural life and of *"la campagne de chez nous."* Albert Ferland summarized their objective: to "create an art that is simple and proud, and worthy of an upright heart."[28]

Just as a small group of modernist poets rebelled against the traditional romanticism of English-Canadian verse, young Québécois poets challenged the "terroiriste" tradition. The avant garde journal *Le Nignog* introduced Jean-Aubert Loranger, the most remarkable of these new poets, and with Robert Choquette, Simone Routier, and Alfred Desrochers he helped to lay the foundations of modern French-Canadian poetry. The similarities between the technique and content of Choquette's *A travers les vents* (1925) or Desrochers's *l'Hymne au vent du nord* and the work of Montreal group poets Frank Scott and A.J.M. Smith are striking, yet despite their common struggle to liberate their literatures from the dead hand of romanticism, the young English and French poets of Montreal worked in isolation from each other, even as they shared the same city.[29]

French-Canadian novelists' preoccupations also mirrored those of their English-Canadian homologues. The historical romance was represented by Robert de Roquebrune's *Les Habits rouges* (1923), a story of the 1837 Rebellion, or by his *D'un océan à l'autre* (1924), a sentimentalized version of the destruction of the Métis. Many novels were idealizations of rural life in which the virtues of a pious peasantry were held up as models for contemporary Quebec. Groulx's two novels are the most explicit of these morality plays, but Damase Potvin's *l'Appel de la terre* (1919), Adélard Dugré's *La Campagne canadienne* (1925), and Harry Bernard's *La Terre vivant* (1925) express their themes clearly in their titles. Bernard, a young nationalist journalist who belonged to l'Action française, produced seven novels between 1924 and 1932 in which stalwart *habitants* and their wives, counselled by fatherly *curés*, reject the lure of the city for the more virtuous life of the country. Until the publication by Ringuet (Dr. Philippe Panneton) of *Trente arpentes* in 1938, the only realistic novel written about rural life in Quebec was *La Scouine* (1918) by Albert Laberge. Laberge's depiction of the hardship and misery of rural poverty has been seen by literary historians as a critical moment in the evolution of the French-Canadian novel, but when it first appeared it was rejected by critics and readers just as Frederick Philip Grove and Martha Ostenso were rejected. English- and French-speaking, concludes Ronald Sutherland, the Canadian reading public shared an unwillingness to "admit the existence of sordid realities by according these attention."[30]

VI

English- and French-Canadian intellectuals shared something more: a common fear that their struggle to define and proclaim a cultural identity might be of consuming uninterest to the great majority of Canadians. The mutual dilemma of the nationalist intelligentsias was how to protect the Canadian culture they were so diligently articulating from those cultural forces that seemed to be drawing Canada closer to the United States. For every active member of the Canadian Club, for example, two others attended the weekly luncheon of one of the many Canadian chapters of the four American "service" clubs. Rotary had been the first to come north, establishing a Winnipeg chapter in 1910. By 1928 it had eighty-five Canadian chapters, and during the twenties it was joined by the Lions, Kiwanis, and Gyro clubs, each of which expanded rapidly into all regions of Canada. Their administrative structures linked clubs in Canadian provinces with those in adjoining American states; a Gyro pamphlet proudly proclaimed that the club "recognizes no boundary between the United States of America and the Dominion of Canada." Every summer at binational conventions, Rotarians, Gyros, Lions, and Kiwanians met in happy celebration of the "invisible border" at which "no form of armed protection" was necessary and babbled clichéd nonsense about "the harmonious relationship that has always existed between the United States and Canada."[31]

More alarming to cultural nationalists than the vapid Babbittry of the service clubs was the northbound tidal wave of American mass culture: radio programs, professional spectator sports, magazines. The crest of the wave was the motion picture. The silent film had evolved into a much more attractive product than the early "flickers," and silent dramas like D.W. Griffith's *Birth of a Nation* (1915) had removed the movies' lower-class stigma and made them more or less respectable entertainment. They were also very inexpensive entertainment. A children's matinee cost a dime or less, and adults paid a quarter for the early show or thirty-five cents later in the evening; by 1929, 1,100 theatres were selling two million tickets a week. On Saturday night, when lodge halls, church basements, and rural schools joined the urban movie houses in showing movies, over a million Canadians sat in the dark in front of the screen. Almost all of the movies they watched were American-made products of a Los Angeles suburb that suddenly became the most famous town in North America.[32]

Although films made in Hollywood always predominated, Canada did have a short-lived domestic feature film industry of its own during the movies' pioneer era. The period between 1919 and 1923 has been described by Canadian cinema historians as the "fruitful years" when a number of companies used Canadian settings, casts, and crews to turn out films that compared favourably with prevailing international standards. Ernest G. Shipman produced and directed screenplays based on the novels of Ralph Connor and Alan Sullivan and an impressive commercial success called *Back to God's Country* (1919). Adanac Producing Company's *The Great Shadow* (1919), an anti-Bolshevik film that attempted to capitalize on the post-war Red Scare, was praised by *Saturday Night* as the equal of Griffith's *Intolerance*. Because of her sunshine and her spectacular scenery, wrote Toronto director Alan Dwan in *Maclean's* in 1920, "Canada has a movie future"; by 1930, however, Canada's movie future was already behind her.[33]

The rapid disappearance of the Canadian film industry can be explained more readily in economic than in artistic terms. There was certainly no lack of Canadian creative talent, for Canadian directors, performers, and technicians were overrepresented among the success stories of Hollywood's golden age. Directors Mack Sennett, Sidney Olcott, and Alan Dwan, producers Louis B. Mayer and Jack Warner, a number of important screen writers, art directors and photographers, and a host of performers made their contribution to American cinema; young Canadian movie fans could proudly repeat the name of the famous actor or actress who came from their town or province. Leading men Walter Huston and James Rennie learned their craft on the stage in Toronto, as did Gladys Smith – better known as "America's Sweetheart," Mary Pickford. Norma Shearer of Westmount, Quebec, won the Academy Award as best actress in 1929; her successor in 1930 was Marie Dressler of Cobourg, Ontario.* Film stars

---

* Some stars Canadians claimed as their own, like Rubie Keeler of Dartmouth, N.S., had gone to the United States as children, but Huston, Rennie, Pickford, Shearer, Dressler, and others like them left as mature talents seeking opportunities that did not exist in Canada.

and film makers moved south in such numbers that in 1934 *Maclean's* reported "a veritable army of Canadians" living in Hollywood. Canadian cinema was caught up in a vicious circle: because the best native talent went to the United States, Canada failed to develop a national focal point for a strong cinematic community; because Canada lacked a cinematic focal point, the best native talent moved away. Canadian movie companies were small and scattered across the country. Trenton, Ontario, shooting site for *The Great Shadow*, was the closest approximation to a "Hollywood of the North"; it is not difficult to understand why a small eastern Ontario town failed to hold a pool of movie people together after production was completed.[34]

The lack of a Canadian movie industry did not mean that no movies were made about Canada. As Lewis Selznick pointed out impatiently, "if Canadian stories are worthwhile making into films, American companies will be sent into Canada to make them." In 1922 and 1923, Hollywood made sixty-five pictures set in Canada, although only a tiny minority of them were actually filmed on location. Competition from the larger American studios was certainly a major factor contributing to the Canadian industry's decline. "However banal and escapist most Hollywood pictures might be," concludes C.C. Alexander, "the people who made motion pictures in America had learned their technical lessons well." American films were the state of the art; the American product dominated the screens of such cinematically advanced countries as Germany, Britain, and France; Hollywood became the *world* centre for motion picture production. It is hardly surprising that Canada should have succumbed so quickly and so totally. Giant and predatory Hollywood studios devoured independent Canadian producers like Ernest Shipman not because they were Canadian but because they were independent. Within the American industry itself, the "Big Five" – Paramount, MGM, Warner Brothers, Fox, and RKO – produced 90 per cent of all feature films by 1929.[35]

Canada was regarded as part of Hollywood's "domestic" box office, and the vertical integration of production, distribution, and exhibition that the major studios developed was routinely extended northward. To assure a market for their products, they assembled cinema chains that showed the films of one studio exclusively or required independently owned movie houses to agree to "block book" – to acquire a desirable movie meant a contractual obligation to show less attractive films produced by the same studio. This had the effect of killing off independent producers by making it impossible for them to get their films shown in downtown first-run theatres. Canada at first had several rival chains, but Famous Players, managed by Nathan L. Nathanson, bought out its principal competitor, Allen Theatres, to make Nathanson the unchallenged "Mussolini of Entertainment." He

was in turn eased out by Adolph Zukor of Paramount in what
Maclean's described as a "screen war which has resulted in virtual
domination of the Canadian motion picture field by a gigantic United
States Corporation." Famous Players owned fewer than three hundred
theatres, but it monopolized the "movie palaces" with the large
seating capacities and prime downtown locations. Taking Vancouver
as his example, R.J. Dawson of the Independent Theatres Association
pointed in 1932 to Famous Players' Orpheum, whose "weekly
receipts alone amount to more than combined weekly receipts of the
Vancouver Independent Theatres. . . . The cream of the photoplays
are controlled by and are shown at Famous Players theatres while independents are forced to show what product is rejected by them."[36]

The classic case used by cinema historians to illustrate the problems
of feature film production in this country is *Carry On, Sergeant*,
"Canadian cinema's most expensive flop. . . ." Made in Trenton by a
company called Canadian International Films, *Carry On, Sergeant* was
designed to exploit the resentment many Canadians felt at Hollywood
war movies that attributed the Allied victory in the Great War exclusively to the American army. The writer-director was the famous
British war cartoonist Bruce Bairnsfather, and the company attracted
investors, R.B. Bennett and Arthur Meighen among them, using
patriotism as much as profit as a lure. Everything that could go wrong
did. Bairnsfather had no movie experience; no one saw a completed
shooting script; actors and technical crew imported from the United
States and Britain sat idle on high salaries, driving the picture over
budget. *Carry On, Sergeant* opened in Toronto on the eve of Armistice Day, 1928, and vanished after a short run, despite houses
packed with the curious drawn to see a Canadian feature film. Famous
Players refused to continue to show the film in Toronto or to book it
elsewhere, claiming the decision was purely economic. A scene in
which the film's central figure walks upstairs with a prostitute in a
French cabaret shocked upright Torontonians, yet the film was not
considered a sufficiently realistic war drama to enable Canadian International to obtain distribution contracts outside Canada. It was also a
silent movie released in a city that had witnessed the Canadian
premiere of the talkies almost exactly one month before! Not one
penny was returned to the investors. "Raising funds for Canadian
feature film production after *Carry On, Sergeant*," says Peter Morris,
"was a practical impossibility."[37]

The *Carry On, Sergeant* fiasco increased the concern about the unchallenged influence of American movies. The Canadian bourgeoisie
applauded Mackenzie King for emulating the economic policies of
Calvin Coolidge but was profoundly disturbed to see young working-

class women use make-up like the "It girl," Clara Bow, to watch "young sheiks of the sidewalk . . . pattern their mannerisms after their celluloid heroes," or meet a teenager "who spots the Woolworth Building on sight" in a movie but "has to have a title to explain Westminster Abbey and the Tower of London." To protect "this pure, clear and starry-eyed land of innocence," all provincial governments censored movies. Although several attempts to establish a national censorship system came to nothing, provincial standards for cutting or banning films were essentially similar. The things "the Censor Saves Us From" were enumerated in an article by R. Laird Briscoe. "Foreign glorification carefully is pruned," as were scenes that demeaned clergymen or marriage, and the censors kept a watchful eye on "the revolver that every he-man seems to have on one hip." Briscoe particularly commended the decision by all provinces to prohibit a movie about an innocent girl gone wrong in which "her maudlin actions are portrayed in revolting detail . . . its effect on weak and degenerate minds might be dangerous to the highest degree." The censors also worried that by occasionally holding an authority figure up to ridicule, movies might do more to inspire social unrest "than all the Bolshevist agitators." They need not have been concerned; during the Depression of the 1930s, Hollywood's "dream factory" became one of the most important buttresses of the status quo.[38]

There were suggestions that Canada protect her youth from Hollywood with a quota requiring that a certain percentage of pictures shown in a theatre be filmed within the Empire. No such legislation was ever enacted, for like British theatrical companies, British films did not exist in sufficient quantity or quality to make it feasible. Quotas were vehemently opposed by theatre operators, who maintained that British movies were like "citrus fruits, and more specifically, the lemons." Even staunch imperialists like Lt.-Col. George Drew admitted that "the Hollywood production was on the average vastly superior to the British" and that "experience taught any but the blindest partisan that good British pictures were few and far between."[39]

To neutralize further the propaganda from Hollywood, the federal government, British Columbia, and Ontario produced their own films. The Canadian Government Motion Picture Bureau, the B.C. Educational and Patriotic Film Service, and the Ontario Motion Picture Bureau were modest operations typified by such blockbuster documentaries as *Niagara the Glorious, Pacific Coast Scenics*, and *Fishing Just for Fun*. John Grierson said of the work of the CGMPB, "if life in the Dominion is as these films represent . . . there are practically no industries, very little work and no working people." The Ontario and Canadian government bureaus made films that although "lifeless and dull" were at least technically competent, but the BCFS could not attain even that standard. A tongue-in-cheek review in the Vancouver *World* described one of its productions as "very good in every detail except photography, subtitles and editing." When civil service pictures were screened before Canadian audiences, they fidgeted or went for popcorn. Moviegoers "resent[ed] any substitute for pure amusement. They don't want to be educated or to line up at the box office as a service to their country." The cinematic experiments of Ontario and British Columbia were mercifully ended; the CGMPB survived to make a more substantial contribution after it was restructured as the National Film Board in 1939. Except for the NFB, however, there were no serious attempts to stimulate a native Canadian cinema.[40]

VII

Canada's cinematic quandary paralleled her puzzled response to another purveyor of post-war American popular culture, the radio. The first radio programs in Canada were transmitted by Montreal station XWA – later CFCF – only a month after KDKA Pittsburgh baptized the American airwaves with its broadcast of the returns of the 1920 presidential election. But subsequent development of the medium in the United States was much more rapid. During the next decade the fundamental decisions that would create the American broadcasting industry were taken; radio in America was to be a private enterprise supported financially by the sale of advertising time, with the government's role limited to regulation by the Federal Radio Commission. Ten years after KDKA's inaugural broadcast, there were 612 stations operating in the United States, and two private networks of affiliated stations had spread across America, the National Broadcasting Company and the Columbia Broadcasting System. In Canada both private entrepreneurs and governments moved more slowly. The federal government stood back from radio through ignorance of its potential and unwillingness to decide whether Canada should follow the private commercial model of the United States or make radio broadcasting a public non-commercial monopoly as was being done in Britain.

The legislative framework of the radio age in Canada was provided by the Radiotelegraph Act of 1913, administered by the Dominion Department of Marine and Fisheries. A transmitting licence cost a commercial applicant fifty dollars a year and an amateur applicant only ten dollars. Since the department had no criteria by which to refuse to grant a licence, just about any company or group that wanted to go on the air could and did get one: universities, churches, a distilling company, and the Canadian National Railways among them. The two largest groups of station owners, however, were newspapers and manufacturers of radio receivers. The former saw in radio a publicity gimmick that could be linked to the paper to boost circulation while the latter went into broadcasting with the very practical purpose of giving potential radio purchasers something to listen to. The number of licences issued, seventy by 1923, exaggerated the amount of broadcasting that was being done. Some licensees were never active, while others were "phantom" stations that had no transmission facilities of their own but used the equipment of larger stations. This was possible because the department allotted frequencies more parsimoniously than it handed out licences. [41]

By an agreement reached with the United States in 1924, Canada obtained the exclusive use of six frequencies and the partial use of another eleven of the ninety-five then in operation. Canadian broadcasters joined the Edmonton *Bulletin* in complaining that while "86 per cent of the impulse carrying power of the atmosphere" had been handed over to extol "the superior qualities of American soap, pills and jazz," they themselves had no choice but to share frequencies and thus to share air time as well. In Montreal, CFCF and CYAC, owned by radio manufacturers, CKAC, owned by *La Presse*, and the CNR's CNRM all made do with one frequency. No station could be on the air every day or for more than a few hours a day, so that episodic scheduling combined with static and interference to make things difficult for listeners. Ludicrous situations were possible. When the Edmonton *Journal's* station CJCA carried the Dempsey-Tunney fight of 1927, the available time expired before either of the boxers. CJCA continued to broadcast, but CFCY, the voice of the International Federation of Bible Students, was determined not to be cheated of its daily quota of religious broadcasting. Both stations broadcast simultaneously, creating an incomprehensible cacophony in the earphones and "sound reproducers" of their befuddled listeners' sets. [42]

Canadian stations had other problems. As their small transmitters had limited ranges, many parts of rural Canada received no service while in others interference from more powerful American transmitters drowned the domestic signal out. Despite these difficulties sales of radio sets were strong and the number of radio listeners in Canada increased steadily. Radio ownership required an annual one-dollar licence, and thus it is possible to get an accurate measure of radio's rapid rise in popularity; there were fewer than 10,000 sets in use in 1923 but 297,000 in 1929. Most were tuned to American stations, for there were so many more of them available. "Nine-tenths of the radio fans in the Dominion hear three or four times as many United States stations as Canadian," reported a journalist, and at northern RCMP detachments the Mounties got their daily bulletins over KDKA Pittsburgh. [43]

More than reception alone influenced the choice of an American station, for superiority in transmission power was accompanied by superiority in program production techniques. Canadian stations' offerings were usually news, lectures, or recorded music, while the American network stations featured comedy, drama, and live variety programs. Commercial stations in Canada soon decided that the best way to compete with stations south of the border was to obtain the right to broadcast these shows themselves. When CFRB Toronto became an affiliate of CBS, CKGW Toronto countered by joining the NBC network, and stations in other cities hurried to follow. "Amos and Andy," it was clear, was a more powerful drawing card than the CNR network's "Uncle Dick's Talks for Boys and Girls." By the end of the twenties it was estimated that 80 per cent of the programs listened to by Canadians were American. As one writer protested, "Canada's radio consciousness" was "throwing us all the more under United States influence." [44]

It was not concern about Americanization, however, that led the federal government to review its broadcasting policy in 1928; the motivation came from a more typically Canadian problem, a religious controversy. In addition to its station in Edmonton, the International Federation of Bible Students, sponsored by the Jehovah's Witnesses, operated stations in Vancouver, Saskatoon, and Toronto. Their programs were unpopular with the mainstream denominations, which described them as "unpatriotic and abusive of our churches." This was a complaint that no government could afford to ignore. The Jehovah's Witness licences were cancelled, but the affair resulted in a full-scale debate on broadcasting in the Commons in which long-neglected issues at last were aired. J.S. Woodsworth raised the most fundamental of these, the fear that through station ownership or program content Canadian airwaves would fall forever into the hands of "highly organized private commercial companies in the United States." This could only be prevented, he argued, by "a comprehensive national policy . . . leading to public ownership and control of this new industry." Minister of Marine P.J.A. Cardin wanted only to be rid of his department's biggest headache; his time-honoured solution was to refer the broadcasting question to a royal commission chaired by Sir John Aird, president of the Bank of Commerce. [45]

Aird and his fellow commissioners, Charles A. Bowman, editor of the Ottawa *Citizen*, and Dr. Augustin Frigon, Quebec's director of technical education, visited Europe and the United States and held public hearings across the country before submitting their final conclusions: broadcasting in Canada should be a public monopoly without private competitors and with very strictly limited commercial content. Because the chairman had been outspokenly unsympathetic to the general principle of public enterprise, the Aird Report was a surprise. The decision had been reached, said Bowman, because "the drift under private enterprise . . . would lead broadcasting on this continent into the same position as the motion picture industry has reached. . . ." It was a logical conclusion in the nationalist ambiance of the 1920s, and submissions before the royal commission suggested that it would have wide public support. But the Aird Report reached parliament at the worst possible moment. The gathering recession of 1929 made its proposal to spend millions to create the national system an unlikely extravagance, and the federal election of 1930 resulted in the defeat of the Liberal sponsors of the royal commission. The private broadcasters used their newspaper connections to attack Aird's proposal, and a campaign against nationalization initiated by *La Presse* rallied support from the CPR and the Canadian Manufacturers' Association. The radio question was to remain unanswered until a nationalist campaign for public radio found a way to spike these heavy cannons of Canadian capitalism.[46]

VIII

American radio broadcasts and movies were new, and although they provoked general unease among cultural nationalists their impact was difficult to assess and their presence challenged no established Canadian film or radio industry. "In the case of American periodicals," concluded a study by Professor Henry Angus of the University of British Columbia, "even more clearly than in that of motion pictures or radio, we find an Americanizing influence widely accepted by the Canadian people." American magazines had been sold in Canada since the 1890s, and after 1920 their circulation increased to fifty million by 1926. *Ladies Home Journal, Saturday Evening Post, Pictorial Review*, and *McCall's* were read by more Canadians than any single domestic magazine. The *Saturday Evening Post* without any exaggeration advertised itself as "Canada's leading magazine," much to the chagrin of *Maclean's*, the best seller among magazines actually produced in Canada.[47]

The Canadian National Newspaper and Periodicals Association, formed in 1919, and the Magazine Publishers' Association, founded in 1922, demanded government action. American magazines, the publishers' lobbyists contended, were a "menace to Canadian ideals and to the moral development of the youth of this country." It was impossible to sustain such a charge against the *Ladies Home Journal,* so the MPA concentrated its fire upon the "pulps," fiction magazines printed on newsprint with garish covers and names like *Black Mask, Dime Detective,* or *Spicy Adventure.* Although a later generation would acclaim the work of "pulp" authors Dashiel Hammett and Raymond Chandler among others, many Canadian parents agreed with the Toronto *Globe* that the "pulps" were the "off-scourings of the moral sewers of human life," a "putrid flood" of "undisguised filth." Canadian magazines, claimed the MPA, were not only cleaner reading but also a positive force; they provided hundreds of jobs to printers and engravers, encouraged Canadian writers and artists, and even helped solve the problem of national unity by "bringing together the diverse interests of our Dominion."[48]

What was needed, in the MPA's opinion, was government assistance to the magazine publishing industry in the form of reduced duties and taxes on paper and printing materials and a protective tariff to discourage American imports. The Canadian publishers' case had one major weakness. Despite large and increasing sales of magazines from the United States, Canada's periodicals prospered during the 1920s as never before. *Maclean's,* for example, went from monthly to semi-weekly publication in 1920 and earned its owner, Col. John B. Maclean, large enough profits to expand and diversify. He bought *Canadian Homes and Gardens* in 1925 and redesigned and expanded it, in 1927 launched *Mayfair,* and in 1928 followed with *Chatelaine,* a new magazine for women. Such success made the King government reluctant to act to protect an "infant" industry that was growing so quickly. In 1928 magazines were given some tax relief, but it was not until 1931, in completely changed economic circumstances, that the Bennett Conservative government gave the industry the tariff protection it demanded. This reduced the margin of American dominance but did not end it; "the people of this large and proud Dominion," concluded an exasperated editor, "have been content to accept their reading inspiration almost entirely from a foreign land."[49]

Unlike their magazines, the newspapers read by Canadians were owned and published in Canada, but as in the United States newspapers underwent a transformation in their content and in their corporate structure. The day when a young reporter like Hugh Graham, with a hundred dollars in his pocket, could found the Montreal *Star* had long since disappeared. A mass circulation daily like the *Star* required a huge staff and expensive presses and equipment to produce the features and special sections that attracted a large readership;

modernizing the Toronto *Star* in 1928-29 cost Joseph Atkinson almost $4 million, and since not all dailies could afford such heavy capital investment not all could survive. Although circulation increased from 1.6 million a day in 1921 to 2.1 million ten years later, the number of daily papers published in Canada declined from a peak of 138 in 1913 to just 100 in 1931. Some papers died outright: the Kitchener *Telegraph*, the Winnipeg *Telegram*, the Vancouver *World*. In other cities two dailies merged under a hyphenated name: the Saint John *Times-Globe*, the Kingston *Whig-Standard*, the Regina *Leader-Post*. Newspaper chains, pioneered in the United States by William Randolph Hearst and in Britain by Lord Northcliffe, appeared more slowly in Canada, but two groups controlled by the Sifton and Southam families were emerging.[50]

Owned by chains or not, Canadian dailies became more alike and lost some of the individuality and local identity that idiosyncratic editor-publishers had once given them. There was still the occasional anachronism, like W.G. Jaffray of the Toronto *Globe*, who refused to print ads for cigarettes, whisky, or ladies' undergarments, but newspapers had begun to earn their profits from advertising rather than from sales. To avoid alienating their advertisers and consumers of the advertisers' products, newspapers had to refrain from the partisan biases and scurrilous diatribes common to nineteenth-century newsheets. The result was fairer news coverage, but it also meant that newspapers became depersonalized until one was very much like another. This tendency to homogeneity was reinforced by the continued development of wire services. These used the new teletype machine to speed stories simultaneously to a network of subscribing newspapers, which often reprinted them with little editing or rewriting. Three such services were available to Canadian newspapers, the American services, Associated Press and United Press, and a national wire service, the Canadian Press. The CP was the basic source of most domestic news read by Canadians in all provinces, but the international news in Canadian papers – English or French language – was usually gathered by American correspondents and came from AP or UP wires. Most international news on the CP wire was based on AP dispatches, which the CP bought and passed to subscribers. Thus Canadian readers learned about British-American relations from stories written in the United States, and viewed their own delegates to the League of Nations through the eyes of American reporters in Geneva in stories that reflected America's attitude as an isolationist non-member.[51]

The similarity between Canadian and American newspapers was not confined to international news content, for Canadian newspapers emulated their opposite numbers in the United States by redesigning their form and supplementing their "hard" news with new features. Led by Montreal's *La Presse*, the Toronto *Star*, and the Vancouver *Sun*, Canadian dailies adopted larger photos, bolder type, and banner headlines to report sports, crime, and the marriages and divorces of movie stars. Columns on bridge, hobbies, auto repair, and personal advice appeared, distributed by American newspaper syndicates. Most popular of the new syndicated features were the "funnies," black-and-white comic strips in the weekday papers supplemented by a colour comic section on Saturday; circulation of the Toronto *Star Weekly* doubled when it acquired *Bringing Up Father, Barney Google, Mutt and Jeff*, and five other American strips in 1923. The audience for the comics was not restricted to children or to the semi-literate; millionaire businessman Sir Joseph Flavelle was a faithful follower of *Little Orphan Annie*, and industrial relations expert Mackenzie King was said never to miss his favourite strip, *Tillie the Toiler*.[52]

IX

The new direction of journalism was also evident on the sports pages, as a new kind of journalist called a sportswriter fabricated larger-than-life heroes out of Babe Ruth, Jack Dempsey, Bobby Jones, and Bill Tilden, and just as with the comic strips, America's sports heroes became Canada's also. America's national sport became the Canadian summer game at the same time. As S.F. Wise and Douglas Fisher note bitterly, "mesmerized by baseball's big league glamour, and spoon-fed by the American wire services, sports editors and reporters gave major coverage to baseball at the expense of lacrosse," with the result that both professional and senior amateur lacrosse became extinct in the inter-war years. For the participant the basic skills of baseball – or softball, its simpler version – were easier to master than those of lacrosse. It was as a spectator sport, however, that baseball was enjoyed by most Canadians.[53]

Every Canadian community had an amateur baseball team, and many cities and larger towns had franchises in minor professional leagues. "Organized baseball has been a good thing for the towns that have participated," wrote "Knotty" Lee, manager of the Brantford Red Sox of the Michigan-Ontario League. "Baseball, in fact, is one cure for Bolshevism." Baseball was also bicultural. "Your French Canadian citizen likes his *base pelotte*," concluded a Montreal journalist who reported in 1928 that "three or four thousand folks have howled themselves hoarse as a matter of habit every Sunday" at minor league ball games. Larger crowds followed the fortunes of the Montreal Royals and Toronto Maple Leafs, who played in the International League, one step below the majors. Toronto's 1926 victory over Louisville in the Little World Series occasioned an outpouring of local and national pride, pride accented because one Maple Leaf outfielder, Lionel Conacher, was actually a Canadian![54]

Yet every Canadian ball fan's deepest love was reserved for the team that he cheered for in the American or National League. Major league baseball recovered quickly from the scandal of the "fixed" World Series in 1919, helped by a livelier ball that increased hitting and by the spectator appeal of homerun champion Babe Ruth and the less charismatic sluggers who imitated him. By the mid-twenties baseball's World Series had become Canada's greatest "national" sporting event, with crowds packed in front of newspaper offices to watch the games charted out on a scale-model diamond, while an announcer with a megaphone recreated the action from a running description provided by the wire services. Before the Cardinal-Yankee series of 1926, the Calgary *Herald* devoted ten column inches of its editorial page to an analysis of "this greatest of all features in the season's baseball program"; an adjacent editorial on the appointment of Lord Willingdon as Canada's new governor general received exactly one inch.[55]

Unlike baseball, Canada's favourite winter sport was more distinctively her own. The annual series of games for the Stanley Cup, symbolic of the championship of Canadian hockey, was the only sporting event that approached baseball's World Series in the excitement it generated among fans. After 1921 the cup was competed for by teams from three Canadian professional leagues: the Pacific Coast Hockey Association, the Western Canada Hockey League, and the National Hockey League. Although the exact format of the playoff varied from year to year, the matching of teams from Central Canada against teams from Prairie and British Columbia cities made Stanley Cup finals a socially acceptable athletic means of releasing regional hostility. In 1923 the NHL Ottawa Senators travelled to Vancouver to eliminate the PCHA Millionaires before defeating the WCHL Edmonton Eskimoes as the last stage of their conquest of the cup. A year later the Vancouver team and the Calgary Tigers journeyed east to take on the Montreal Canadiens. Arthur Meighen dropped the puck in a ceremonial face-off before the decisive game in which rookie Howie Morenz led the Canadiens to the championship with a 3–0 victory over the Tigers.[56]

Wounded Western pride took some comfort in the merger of the PCHA and WCHL to form a single Western Hockey League for the 1924-25 season. The new "major loop," predicted a prairie sportswriter, would "overshadow the present NHL" and become "the predominant hockey league in the world.'' When Lester Patrick's Victoria Cougars easily defeated the Canadiens to bring the Stanley Cup to the West, Western editorialists crowed their satisfaction. The days when ''the effete East looked down upon the plainsman and the far westerner'' seemed to be over, and ''the Easterners are learning how hockey should be played from Western teams.'' But Western arrogance was to melt faster than the natural ice did in most WHL arenas in an unseasonable thaw. The Montreal Maroons took Lord Stanley's silverware back to Central Canada in 1926, and it was not to return for fifty-eight years.[57]

Canadian hockey was revolutionized by American money. In 1924 Boston millionaire Charles Adams was awarded the NHL's first American franchise. Dressed in the brown and gold colours of Adams's grocery chain, the Bruins won only six of thirty games on the ice but were champions at the box office. Before the next season began, bootlegging baron William V. ''Big Bill'' Dwyer had bought the Hamilton Tigers and moved them into the new Madison Square Garden as the New York Americans. Dwyer's publicity ignored hockey's grace, speed, and finesse to emphasize its violence. The game was played, wrote Paul Gallico in the *Daily News*, by ''men with clubs in their hands and knives lashed to their feet''; it was ''almost a certainty that someone will be hurt and fleck the ice with a generous contribution of gore.'' Despite a poor record the Americans attracted 195,579 paying customers to their seventeen home games. In its first season, reported the Edmonton *Journal*, ''New York pro hockey outdrew the combined attendance of any four cities of the Western Hockey League.'' It was painfully obvious that the Regina Capitals or the Saskatoon Sheiks would find the new hockey era too rich for their blood.[58]

Wealthy Americans lined up for a chance at the publicity, prestige, and profit of owning a hockey team. ''Will U.S. cash cripple hockey?'' asked a Toronto sportswriter. ''How long will Canada be able to hold its teams? Our neighbours to the South possess more of that useful commodity, variously known as 'jack' or 'dough' or 'mazuma' than we do [and] the longest purse is bound to win. . . . Star puck chasers will gravitate to the place where they can fatten their exchequers.'' When the NHL awarded franchises to Chicago financier Frederick McLaughlin, New York coffee tycoon John S. Hammond, and a Detroit syndicate that included a Ford and a Kresge among its members, the less affluent Canadian entrepreneurs who owned the six teams of the Western Hockey League came to the same conclusion. They empowered Frank and Lester Patrick, operators of the Vancouver Millionaires and the Victoria Cougars, to peddle the WHL's most valuable athletic chattels to the NHL before such stars as Eddie Shore, Dick Irvin, and Frank Fredrickson could "jump" of their own accord. The WHL owners divided the $258,000 the Patricks received from the NHL for their players and quietly hung up their skates. In 1927 the Stanley Cup became the permanent possession of the NHL and so it has remained; first-class professional hockey was not to venture west again for half a century.[59]

When the "National" Hockey League opened its 1926-27 season, Canada's game had been transformed into a continental commercial spectacle. "Hockey," wrote F.B. Edwards in *Maclean's,*

> which began its career as a rough and ready game played by small boys on home-made skating rinks . . . and grew up to be Canada's national pastime, is Big Business now. . . . Plain, ordinary hockey became Organized Hockey, an air-tight, leakproof, copper rivetted, asbestos packed machine which now controls the professional skate and stick pastime. . . . Millionaires back the organization, fine ladies applaud the efforts of the skating roughnecks with polite patting of gloved palms, ticket speculators buy out the seating accommodations for crucial games and Wall Street commission houses handle bets on the results. Hockey has put on a high hat.[60]

Only four of the ten teams – Montreal's Maroons and Canadiens, Toronto, and Ottawa – were based in Canada, and the NHL's "Canadian" division was brought up to full strength by adding the New York Americans! Ottawa, like the WHL cities, found itself unable to compete with the bankrolls of the new American clubs or to pay for magnificent artificial ice arenas like Montreal's new Forum. Despite laments that it was "a national calamity," Ottawa vanished from the NHL. Only the chutzpah of Conn Smythe saved the Toronto franchise from a similar fate. In 1927 when the St. Patricks were about to be sold to a Philadelphia group for $200,000, Smythe persuaded their owners to accept his smaller offer and kept the team in Canada as the Maple Leafs. Smythe's Leafs, the Maroons, and the Canadiens found it harder to keep the Stanley Cup in Canada. In 1928 the New York Rangers became the first of the American NHL teams to win the cup, and for the remainder of the inter-war period the trophy Lord Stanley had donated to honour "the leading hockey club in Canada" spent most of its time in the United States.[61]

Did the continentalization of professional hockey provide further proof that Canada was being turned into a cultural as well as an economic colony of the United States? Virtually all the players on the NHL's American teams were Canadians, and it made little difference to the Canadian identity of a small boy in the Prairies or the Maritimes if his hockey idol played in Boston or Chicago instead of Montreal or Toronto. Canadians still played the best hockey in the world, as the University of Toronto Grads proved at the 1928 Olympics in St. Moritz, overwhelming their opponents by scores of 11–0, 13–0, and 14–0. Amateur hockey thrived in the cities the pros deserted, and local teams from all regions competed fiercely for the Memorial and Allan Cups emblematic of the junior and senior championships.

In many respects sport in Canada was a more effective national unifying influence during the 1920s than it had ever been. National championships were inaugurated in curling, skiing, golf, badminton, and basketball. Canadian rugby football evolved under rules that were unique and distinct from those used in the American game. Canadians were also quick to boast of native sportspeople who won in international competition. Victory was particularly sweet when a Canadian underdog finished ahead of an American favourite, as when Toronto distance swimmer George Young won the Catalina Island race in 1927, or when John Myles of Sydney Mines showed his heels to America's finest distance runners in setting a new record in the Boston Marathon of 1926. The 1928 Olympic team became a similar object of national pride, and every fan knew that Vancouver sprinter Percy Williams, "the World's Fastest Human," had spurned American colleges to train in Canada for his double gold medal performance. Every fan also knew of basketball's Edmonton Grads, the team that won seventeen consecutive North American women's championships, all against the finest the United States could send on to the court, or of the *Bluenose*, the Nova Scotia schooner with a similar record of confounding her Yankee challengers for the International Cup.[62]

X

Sport illustrates the Canadian cultural conundrum of the inter-war period. American peaceful penetration of Canada seemed to be proceeding at an unprecedented rate, as Canadian children "bowed down to Babe Ruth" and professional hockey became continentalized; yet another set of examples could be used to portray the period as the cradle of Canadian cultural consciousness. Contemporary observers sometimes reached contradictory conclusions. "There is an increasing number," wrote McGill professor P.E. Corbett, "who calmly accept the realization that the distinction [between Canadians and Americans] has for most purposes become imperceptible." Americanization, concluded an article in the *Canadian Forum*, was "like baldness; once caught there is no escape from it." But William Phillips, the first American minister to Canada, soon discovered that the "much-talked-of 'invisible border' was in fact a very real barrier." The Ottawa correspondent of *The Times* of London reached a similar conclusion. "The people of Canada are imbued with . . . a passion to maintain their own separate identity. They cherish the rooted belief that they enjoy in their existing political and social order certain manifest advantages over their neighbours."[63]

Despite all the rhetoric about Canadian-American kinship, and as alike as the two North American societies seemed to Europeans, Canadians continued to cling to a series of negative stereotypes about the United States that had existed since the nineteenth century and used them to buttress a sense of Canada's national moral superiority. The American political and judicial systems were generally believed inferior to Canada's British-derived institutions, and as a result American society was widely held to be immoral, violent, and materialistic. These impressions were not confined to a cultural élite but were held by both English and French Canadians of all walks of life. Sociologist S.D. Clark found them among the businessmen who belonged to the Canadian Manufacturers' Association and the trade unionists of the All-Canadian Congress of Labour, whose paper, *Canadian Unionist*, denounced America as a land "where murderers go unhanged . . . where prohibition is the rule and bootlegging has been the practice . . . where child labour laws will not hold water and where negroes may not vote."[64]

When American mass culture was viewed through eyes narrowed by such *a priori* reasoning, it did not produce in Canadian movie goers, radio listeners, and magazine readers a desire to pledge allegiance to the Stars and Stripes. What they saw and heard provided further evidence to support their longstanding unfavourable interpretation of the United States. This was the conclusion of *Canada and Her Great Neighbor*, the study by H.F. Angus and others of Canadian attitudes toward the United States carried out in the 1930s. The researchers found that Canadian papers were full of United States news, but since a disproportionate amount of coverage was of vice and crime regular readers were left "convinced of the depravity of Americans." Hollywood movies, in addition to entertainment, "gave comfort to the sense of moral or even cultural superiority" of Canadian audiences. "Nearly all" of a group of Nova Scotia school children told the interviewer that when listening to American radio programs, "the impression they get is a very bad one." The Angus study also found English Canadians to be extremely sensitive to any criticism of the British Empire in American media, particularly of war movies implying that U.S. intervention had saved the Allied cause in the Great War. This attitude was confirmed by H.E. Stephenson of the McKim Advertising Agency, who warned his American clients to design special campaigns for Canada, since the Canadian consumer was "sensitive about peculiar British institutions . . . and is apt to be critical of United States political forms, judicial procedure and folkways." This was not confined to English Canadians; French Canadians too had a "distaste for 'Yankee' ways," claimed Stephenson.[65]

"The Americanization of Canada," Douglas Mackay told the readers of the *Century Magazine*, heralded neither the end of Canada's British connection nor the absorption of the Dominion into the United States. If Canada had become "socially American" in some ways, she remained "politically British" in others, so that "when the last diehard Anglophile cancels his subscription to the London *Times* . . . he will still cheer for his empire and his King on appropriate occasions." This judgement must have been difficult for readers in Britain and the United States to understand. English Canadians had become more North American but still felt an attachment to their British heritage; they were less British, yet were resolutely determined that they were not Americans. "It would seem," suggested one of the contributors to *Canada and Her Great Neighbor*, "that Canadians are determined to be both a North American and a British nation, but above all a nation with a distinctive Canadian personality."[66]

CHAPTER 9

The Crisis of Capitalism

I

The Great Depression took Canadians by surprise. The real leaders of their country, its captains of industry and finance, had assured them that their "prosperity [was] so broad, so sound, and so hopeful for the future" that they could have "a new confidence in their country." In their annual reports to shareholders in January, 1929, bank presidents searched for superlatives to describe the economy. "The volume of our international trade will soon rise to new and unprecedented levels," said Sir Herbert Holt of the Royal. "The barometer of our prosperity is rising steadily," contributed Sir John Aird of the Commerce. "Looking farther and into the long future," predicted S.J. Moore of the Bank of Nova Scotia, "it is not too much to expect that an unprecedented period of prosperity lies ahead." Similar expressions of faith were repeated by managers, small manufacturers, merchants, and professional men as they puffed cigars and sipped their coffee after the dinners of their service clubs. Nothing was impossible in Canada for "a go-getter who would go out and make business," said the speaker at the Regina Gyro Club as his listeners nodded in agreement. "We on this continent have solved the problem of eternal prosperity," he concluded, shamelessly plagiarizing the nomination speech of Herbert Hoover, the new American president.[1]

Few of the important indicators of the health of the Canadian economy justified such optimism by the summer of 1929. Wheat prices had declined from their highs of 1927, and the price and demand for newsprint had begun to slip as well. This was a storm signal from the United States, where retail sales, manufacturing output, and residential construction had slumped sharply. The growth of the 1920s had hinged on American consumption of Canadian resources; the reverberations of a downturn in the American economy would soon be felt by Canadian exporters of lumber and base metals. The single encouraging sign was the continued upward movement of the indexes of North American stock markets.[2]

The common stock issue was the financial hallmark of the new economic era. Mining companies had begun the pattern of selling no-par-value common shares to the public, and by the mid-twenties established companies like Simpsons, Massey-Harris, and Canada Cement were using them as an inexpensive means of raising development capital. The decade also saw the extensive use of "margin" buying, the buyer putting up a third to a half of the price of a stock with the remainder provided as a call loan by the broker who had sold the shares. New investors were attracted to the market by newspaper and magazine tales of the fortunes made by Canadians like Arthur W. Cutten, Henry Pellatt, or Harry Oakes. The "Great Bull Market" began on the New York Stock Exchange and there was immediately a "puppet" response on exchanges in Montreal and Toronto; with minor interruptions for what came to be known as "corrections," the upward trend of stock prices continued into August 1929, in defiance of the overall condition of the economy. Older, more conservative businessmen complained that sound investment strategies had been supplanted by speculative fever. Sir Joseph Flavelle was disturbed by the "almost irrational faith" investors showed in Canada's future. "Bears" like Flavelle were rare animals, but not even the gloomiest of the handful of doomsayers was prepared for the autumn of 1929. Canadian markets followed the Big Board in New York into a September slide that became an October panic. International Nickel, Noranda Mines, Canada Power and Paper, Ford Motor Company – the cornerstones of the new economic era – fell the farthest in the general collapse of stock prices. On "Black Tuesday," October 29, over 850,000 shares were dumped on the Montreal and Toronto exchanges. The Toronto *Star*'s index of sixteen key Canadian stocks fell $300,000,000 – a million dollars for every minute that the markets were open for trading. Industrialist Cyrus Eaton was rumoured to have lost a million; former prime minister Arthur Meighen took severe losses; young bandleader Guy Lombardo watched $60,000 disappear.[3]

The Great Crash quickly came to be viewed as the dividing line between the "roaring" twenties and the "dirty" thirties and has remained a watershed in the popular historical consciousness. It was not the collapse of the stock market that flattened the Canadian economy for the subsequent decade, however. The devastation wrought to investor morale was undeniable, and the unquestioning faith in Canada's potential so universal in the late twenties has never revived. But despite the increased participation of small investors, only a tiny percentage of Canadians had "played the market" to the degree that the events of October could have meant their personal ruin. The Great Depression was an international disease that afflicted the entire capitalist world. The crash was its most spectacular symptom, but it was just that, "a symptom rather than a cause of the instability of the world economy."[4]

The roots of that instability, as Cambridge economist John Maynard Keynes had warned in his disturbingly brilliant analysis, *The Economic Consequences of the Peace* (1920), lay in the rickety international economic structure that emerged after the Great War. The costs of four years of fighting left Great Britain no longer capable of her accustomed role as world creditor, and America was unable or unwilling to serve in Britain's stead. Germany was saddled with ruinous reparations payments she could not sustain but upon which Britain and France depended to meet their own obligations. Protectionism impeded trade – the U.S. Fordney-McCumber tariff of 1922 is a good example – and exacerbated the weaknesses of this awkward edifice. The tightening of credit in 1929-30 to check speculation was a shock it could not withstand, and it came tumbling down.[5]

With 80 per cent of the production of her farms, forests, and mines sold abroad, Canada's dependent resource economy was especially vulnerable to international instability and to a decline in foreign demand for her staples. The drop in Canadian exports between the peaks of the twenties and the bottom of the Depression in 1932-33 was stunning, and commodity prices plummeted along with volumes traded. The Prairie wheat farmer was most seriously affected. The drought that struck the plains of southern Alberta and Saskatchewan is the best-remembered horror of the Great Depression, but the most serious problem of the wheat economy in the 1930s was that there was too much wheat, not too little. Increased productivity because of mechanization and huge crops from Argentina and Australia glutted world markets. A bushel of No. 1 Northern that had earned a farmer $1.03 in 1928 was worth 47¢ in 1930, 37¢ in 1931, and 29¢ in 1932. The U.S. Congress spread the misery of the Western grain grower to cattle raisers and to dairy and poultry farmers in other parts of Canada by enacting the Smoot-Hawley tariff, which erected barriers against importation of their products. The Atlantic fishery was crippled when Spain, Portugal, and Italy restricted imports of dried cod, and fresh fish sales were hurt by the sudden cheapness of meat and eggs. As a result, fresh fish prices were cut in half while the price of dried fish fell by 70 per cent.[6]

Producers of the new staples suffered along with the old. The gross value of pulp and paper and base metal production shrank from

$248.5 million in 1929 to $117.5 million in 1932 (see Tables V and VI). Reduced earnings in these industries came at a time when investment in infrastructure and equipment was slowing down. In newsprint, for example, Canadian capacity had tripled during the twenties, so that by 1929 Canadian mills were among the most modern and efficient in existence. Given ideal conditions in American markets there would have been little incentive for continued investment; with the poor profit prospects of the thirties and the large fixed debt remaining from the years of expansion, continued investment was out of the question. Measured in constant dollars, business expenditure for new machinery and equipment in 1933 was only a fifth of what it had been in 1929.[7]

Not all of this, of course, was the result of reduced spending by resource industries. The railways, which had provided a major part of business investment since the 1850s, were forced to cut back planned purchases of rolling stock and to cancel construction projects because of reduced traffic from the decimated resource sector and a sudden decline in American tourism. In downtown Vancouver the skeleton of an unfinished railway hotel stood out starkly against the skyline, and in Montreal the abandoned CNR station-hotel complex left a gaping crater that was derisively dubbed "Sir Henry's hole" in mockery of the railway's president.[8]

Secondary manufacturing was relatively less exposed to world forces because of Canada's high protective tariff, but manufacturing production fell nonetheless by a third between 1929 and 1932. Three key industries were hardest hit. The disappearance of the purchasing power of the farm community deprived the farm implement and auto factories of their best customers. Canadian farmers had purchased 17,000 tractors in 1928; in 1932 they bought 892. Almost a quarter-million vehicles had rolled off the assembly lines in 1929; only sixty-four thousand were assembled in Oshawa and Windsor three years later (see Table VIII). Combined with the virtual standstill in railway construction, this so reduced demand for steel that the four Canadian steelmakers' 1932 output was just a fourth of that of an average year of the late twenties. The consequent declines in profit meant that investment by manufacturers ended as it had in the resource and transportation sectors. The total business investment of 1932, 1933, and 1934 *combined* was less than that of any *one* of the boom years 1927-29. It was this decrease in spending by business in response to the decline in foreign demand for wheat, forest products, and base metals that turned a severe recession into the catastrophic depression that haunted the Canadian economy until the Second World War.[9]

Since nothing like the Great Depression had ever occurred before, and since the downswing took place over a four-year period, awareness of the seriousness of what was taking place came slowly. Canada's business and political leadership parroted the calming words of President Hoover that "the fundamental business" of North America was "on a sound and prosperous basis," despite the crash and the many other signs to the contrary. "The situation is on the whole sounder than in the United States," said one banker. "General conditions in the country are fundamentally sound," added another. In February 1932, the Throne Speech read to parliament by Governor General the Earl of Bessborough continued the refrain that "the Canadian situation is fundamentally sound," but by that time the phrase had become the punch line of a sardonic joke. Jack Dempsey, it was said, was "fundamentally sound" after his savage beating at the hands of Gene Tunney: bleeding, dazed, and semi-conscious to be sure, but "fundamentally sound."[10]

II

For tens of thousands of ordinary Canadians the Great Depression began the day they lost their jobs. Seasonal fluctuations in employment had always been the norm in Canada, but the conventional wisdom was that unemployment was "due in large measure to the will or option of the individual." Saskatchewan Premier Jimmy Gardiner liked to boast that an immigrant to his province could find a job on the day he arrived, yet it was in the West that unemployment in the winter of 1929-30 was most disturbing. Winnipeg mayor Ralph Webb reported that his city had three times the usual number of families asking for public assistance. Along with other municipal officials, he asked the Manitoba government for financial aid. After the province had put him off with a resolution that "unemployment is essentially a national problem," Webb led a delegation of Western mayors to Ottawa in February 1930. Prime Minister King was not impressed. The Westerners had no more than fragmentary local information on which to make their case; the informed guesses of such Canadian experts as there were on the subject held that it was normal for a tenth of the labour force to be out of work at that time of year. Although the delegates represented every band in the political spectrum, Webb was an active Conservative. King rapidly concluded that the delegation "was clearly a Tory device to stir up propaganda against the government . . . an effort to place the government in an embarrassing position" in a probable election year. He "met the delegation in a very unfriendly fashion" and the words exchanged were "rather heated." King reminded the mayors that relief for the unemployed was first a municipal, then a provincial, responsibility and sent them home with the advice that they lobby their provincial governments to introduce an unemployment insurance scheme.[11]

King persisted in this attitude when the question was brought up in the Commons. He argued alternately that there was no unemployment problem – "the Dominion is already recovering from the seasonal slackness at the end of the year" – and that unemployment was a provincial matter. Against the government's wish, the issue became the subject of a week-long debate when A.A. Heaps, Labour member for Winnipeg North, moved an amendment to a supply motion to the effect that "the Government should take immediate action to deal with the question of unemployment." To Heaps and to seconder J.S. Woodsworth, "action" meant a federally sponsored system of unemployment insurance to give "the working man . . . the right to security in life exactly the same way we give security to capital." The Conservatives who cynically supported the Heaps amendment had no desire for unemployment insurance, but they seized the opportunity to lambaste the Liberals for allowing "greater suffering and privation than we have known during the last quarter of a century." It was the government's duty, Conservative speakers insisted, to aid the provinces financially to deal with this national emergency.[12]

As the debate continued, King's annoyance turned to outright fury. Heaps and Woodsworth humiliated him by quoting passages from *Industry and Humanity* and the Liberal platform of 1919, in which King had called for just such a program as they advocated. The Tories implied that he was heartless toward the jobless because he refused to write out a blank cheque to the provincial governments, five of which were Conservative, to pay for unemployment relief. Rising to defend his policies, King was heckled and repeatedly interrupted. He might, he said, be persuaded to give some support to the Progressive governments of Manitoba and Alberta, but he "would not give a single cent to any Tory government." When howls of "Shame!" rose from the opposition benches, King uncharacteristically lost his temper. Goaded beyond endurance, he repeated himself in the most direct of the hundreds of thousands of his words that litter the pages of Hansard. "With respect to giving moneys out of the Federal Treasury to any Tory Government in this country for these alleged unemployment purposes," he snarled, "I would not give them a five-cent piece."[13]

The Heaps amendment was easily defeated by the Liberal majority, but the explosion was a remarkable lapse in Mackenzie King's habitually calm, non-committal manner of dealing with controversy. It demonstrated his lack of recognition of the deepening depression and was all the more extraordinary because he had already informed his cabinet that an election would follow the session. Apart from the Prime

Minister's emotional outburst, Liberal pre-election plans went smoothly. The long-promised transfer of natural resources to the Prairie Provinces was accomplished, and the budget surplus of $47 million dollars announced by new Finance Minister C.A. Dunning was an excellent example of the government's thrifty stewardship of the public purse. The highlight of the budget was a page torn from the Conservative copybook: to counter the barriers to Canadian exports raised by the United States, there were tariff increases on steel and fruits and vegetables. These were combined with cosmetic reductions on British goods, which the government claimed would replace lost American trade with trade within the Empire.

King was brimming with confidence as Lord Willingdon dissolved parliament for an election on July 28. Mrs. Bleaney, his Kingston clairvoyant, was certain that he would win, and a vivid dream had provided an omen of good fortune. King had imagined himself confronted by the new Conservative leader, R.B. Bennett, and frontbencher R.J. Manion, both stark naked, who moaned that he had "stolen their clothes." To King this was a reference to the Dunning budget's tariff changes and confirmation of his "belief that God is on my side." The government's record was "a marvellous one," and he would no longer have to face the relentless Arthur Meighen. King had come to detest R.B. Bennett, but he did not fear him. After listening to a radio broadcast of the opening of the Tory campaign, he recorded in his diary the conviction that "Bennett is one of our greatest assets."[14]

People had underestimated Richard Bedford Bennett all his life. Born in 1870 as the first child of a New Brunswick family of modest but comfortable circumstances, Dick was one of the least popular lads in Albert County. Tall, skinny, and quick-tempered, he was regarded as a mother's boy and an arrogant snob. The year of his fourteenth birthday was the celebration of the Loyalist Centennial, and thereafter Bennett liked to claim that he was of Loyalist descent; in fact, his Yankee ancestors had arrived before the American Revolution to usurp the farms of the deported Acadians. Bennett lived up to his Loyalist myth, however. He was intensely devoted to the British Empire, which had "given to the subject races of the world the only kind of decent government they have ever known," and proud to call himself a "true imperialist . . . who accepts gladly and bears proudly the responsibilities of his race and breed." Like his attachment to things Imperial, his Toryism was an atavism, an inherited reflex rather than a considered belief. An active Methodist who taught Sunday School and neither smoked nor drank alcohol, danced nor played cards, Bennett qualified to enter the provincial teacher-training program at thirteen. The poem beside his name in the yearbook of the Fredericton Normal

School summed up his fellow students' impressions of him: "First there came Bennett/Conceited and young/Who never knew quite when/To hold his quick tongue." With the reference to his youth removed, it might have been written a half-century later by one of his cabinet ministers. [15]

Like many other ambitious young men of his generation, Richard Bennett saw teaching as a road, not as his destination. He put aside most of his salary to pay for a legal education at Dalhousie in Halifax. After graduation he spent four years with a firm in Chatham until his law school connections landed him a place in the Calgary law office of Conservative senator James A. Lougheed. Through a combination of opportunity, talent, and determination, the hard-driving workaholic soon turned the firm into Lougheed and Bennett, equal partners. When he was not in court representing their principal client, the CPR, Bennett found time to amass a small fortune in real estate speculation. He had the business acumen to turn this into a medium-sized fortune by investing in more stable endeavours – Canada Cement, Calgary Power, the Alberta Pacific Grain Company – and the luck to inherit a large fortune from a childhood friend who left him controlling interest in E.B. Eddy Limited, a maker of matches, newsprint, and money. Wealth gave R.B. Bennett the independence to pursue his true goal – the prime ministership. He began his political career in the territorial and provincial legislatures, displaying his Imperial patriotism by denouncing the Mormon settlers of Southern Alberta for their alleged Boer sympathies during the South African War. In 1911 he won the Calgary seat in parliament, where his rapidly delivered speeches won notice for their pyrotechnics rather than their profundity. Piqued when passed over for a cabinet post in the Union government, Bennett chose not to run in the election of 1917. This left him free of the twin albatrosses that hung round the neck of Arthur Meighen – conscription and the War-time Elections Act – and facilitated his political comeback. Defeated on a recount in 1921, he was successful in 1925; in the disaster of 1926 he increased his majority despite a Liberal-Labour alliance against him. [16]

Bennett's ability to get himself elected in a region where the party was in disarray was an important factor in his decisive victory at the first-ever Conservative leadership convention in Winnipeg in October 1927. Had the parliamentary caucus chosen the leader as in the past, it might have turned to H.H. Stevens or Hugh Guthrie, men of greater parliamentary experience. But to the 2,500 delegates, 375 of them the first women to vote in a Canadian political convention, the booming confidence of the tall, immaculately dressed bachelor was irresistible. As a young lawyer, Bennett had worried that his thinness made him seem ineffectual; he had developed the habit of eating five or six meals a day to give himself a more imposing figure. His eating habits thereafter never changed, so that by age fifty-seven he was very imposing indeed. Larger than his girth was his vast personal wealth, which the impecunious Conservative party hoped would be put at its disposal. National organizer A.D. McRae was blunt when an undecided delegate asked which candidate could best lead the party back to office. "Put in Bennett," McRae told him. "He's got money and he can get money." The Central Canadian Tory establishment at first preferred Howard Ferguson to the unpredictable Calgary millionaire, but when the Ontario premier refused to enter the race and threw his support behind Bennett, the Westerner became their candidate as well. The outcome was never in doubt: Bennett headed the first ballot by a wide margin and received the majority he needed to win on the second. [17]

III

Despite their new leader, the Tories were not given much chance by the commentators of winning the election of 1930. It was conceded that they would make gains but that these would be insufficient to surmount the large lead given the Liberals by their stranglehold on the province of Quebec. Most observers predicted a "repetition of the ugly conditions in parliament following the 1925 election," with no party able to command a clear majority. Because the two parties were close in public favour, the campaign took on unusual importance and became a "duel between the Liberal and Conservative leaders," more characteristic of the American presidential system than of British parliamentary politics. The importance of the leaders was further magnified by the first widespread use of radio; many of their local meetings were broadcast, and both King and Bennett made nationwide radio addresses. The 1930 election was also the first to be held in July since 1872. To rouse an electorate made "indifferent or lethargic" by the midsummer heat, predicted one journalist, would "require some lusty tub-thumping on the part of the campaigners." [18]

This was a skill at which Mackenzie King could not hope to equal his opponent. R.B. Bennett flung himself into electioneering with the total dedication that he had given everything he had attempted in his life. He travelled 14,000 miles, crossing the country twice and visiting every province in the fifty-eight days of campaigning. The 107 major speeches he delivered were scarcely comprehensible torrents of run-on sentences. At a Vancouver rally, without pausing for breath, he described the Liberals as a group of mercenaries holding office by shame and subterfuge, look upon them, treacherous to you, self-confessed, deserving of your passionate condemnation. Surely, surely, in this new world you are at least entitled to expect above all else constancy and singleness of purpose. So join with us, the opponents of the faith forsworn by its leaders, and then determine for yourself, forget your allegiance to those leaders, whether the government of today is a government to which you can safely trust the destinies of this country.

The crowd stood and cheered. Bennett's evangelical fervour, powerful delivery, and ear-catching phrases had overcome the deficiencies of logic, syntax, and structure. [19]

Bennett's oratory helped him to establish unemployment and the protective tariff, his solution to it, as the central themes of the campaign. On both issues the Liberals got the worst of it. They were not against the tariff; Dunning's budget had proved that. But they could not match Bennett's strident economic nationalism. Liberal tariff increases, he scoffed, were an impotent gesture against the Smoot-Hawley tariff of the United States. "How many tens of thousands of American workmen are living on Canadian money today?" Bennett asked laid-off steelworkers in Sydney. "They've got the jobs and we've got the soup kitchens. . . . I will not beg of any country to buy our goods," he pledged. "I will make [tariffs] fight for you. I will use them to blast a way into markets that have been closed." When the Liberals argued that Bennett's proposed tariffs would discriminate against Great Britain and endanger the imperial connection, he countered that he was "for the British Empire next to Canada," while "some gentlemen are for the United States before Canada." A Tory candidate in Montreal carried this anti-American chauvinism to its lowest point, calling Mackenzie King the "right-hand man of the American government" and urging voters to send King "back where he belongs – back to work in New York City for the Rockefeller foundation." [20]

The Liberals were badly hurt by unemployment. Instead of decreasing in the spring as in normal years, it continued to climb; the Department of Labour estimated that on June first, 391,000 Canadians were unable to find work. Despite warnings from Minister of Labour Peter Heenan, King felt it was "wiser to leave [the] matter alone." King looked at the issue in political rather than economic terms. "The men who are working," he persuaded himself, "are not going to worry particularly over some of those who are not." Bennett, on the other hand, promised the jobless that "the right to work is the right of every man and woman in Canada." Although he had no answer to unemployment other than to increase the tariff, the Conservative leader accepted the fact that since it had "assumed national proportions," it was "the duty of [his] party to see that employment is provided for those of our people who are able to work." Bennett made it clear that his promise was jobs, not relief, "an opportunity [for the unemployed] to toil with their muscles that their families may live. . . . I will not permit this country," he emphasized on many occasions, "to ever become committed to the dole system." Bennett would renege on this bold pledge, but in the summer of 1930 it caught the public imagination and forced Mackenzie King onto the defensive. King began to talk of co-operation with the municipalities and provinces and a conference to discuss federal aid for unemployment. It was too little, too late. Demonstrations of unemployed workers met his train in Calgary, Regina, and Edmonton; when he tried to address them he was drowned out by shouts of "Five-cent piece! Five-cent piece!"[21]

The suddenly famous outburst that had provided the hecklers with their ammunition was used by the five Tory premiers as an excuse for jumping into the federal fray. Howard Ferguson, E.N. Rhodes, and J.B.M. Baxter were joined by the two new Conservative premiers, Simon Fraser Tolmie of British Columbia and J.T.M. Anderson of Saskatchewan. Their impact on the campaign is difficult to measure, but their support meant that Bennett was able to count on the foot soldiers of the provincial parties to reinforce the federal Conservative organization that A.D. McRae had spent a half-million of the leader's dollars to build. The Tory machine purred smoothly into gear, stealing a march on the Liberals by renting the best halls and booking the most desirable radio time.[22]

The Liberal organization was apathetic and inefficient. It did not want for money; the Beauharnois Power Corporation, grateful recipient of a federal hydroelectric development licence, had protected its privilege with a $700,000 donation to the coffers of its political benefactors. But Senator Andrew Haydon, chief Liberal bagman and campaign magician, was too old and too sick to pull any rabbits from this six-figure silk hat. King's tour meandered from city to city playing to hostile or unenthusiastic audiences. In Halifax things degenerated into farce. A horse pulling a garbage cart broke away from its driver and joined the parade escorting the Liberal leader to the arena; when King arrived, the platform was unsteady, the loudspeakers crackled, and one section of the grandstand collapsed. These disasters so upset the timing of the rally that when King at last got up to speak at ten o'clock, half the crowd had left and the other half was asleep. Mackenzie King expected to win in spite of these fiascos. He concluded his campaign with a nationwide broadcast from Laurier House, his Ottawa residence, "kissed the lips of dear mother's marble statue," and predicted to his diary "a good majority," perhaps even "a real liberal sweep."[23]

The popular vote was divided closely between the two major parties (see Table Id). A quarter-million more Canadians voted Liberal than in 1926, but because of a larger electorate and a higher turnout at the polls, their percentage share slipped marginally from 46.1 to 45.2. At the same time the Conservatives' share increased from 45.3 to 48.8 per cent, but the vagaries of the single-member constituency system rewarded this modest improvement with forty-six seats, while the small Liberal decline was punished with the loss of thirty-seven. Although this gave the Conservatives a majority of twenty-nine, the result can hardly be described as a Tory landslide. In British Columbia and Ontario the Liberals made significant gains in their popular vote, although only in British Columbia were these turned into seats. In the Maritimes the Liberals held their own; New Brunswick's pride in a native son was offset by erosion of the Maritime Rights Conservatives in Nova Scotia.

The election was determined by stunning Tory invasions of Liberal fortresses in the Prairie West and Quebec. Manitoba, Saskatchewan, and Alberta gave R.B. Bennett a retinue of twenty-two colleagues. Thirteen of the Prairie ridings lost by the Liberals were in urban areas, where mounting relief rolls made unemployment the decisive issue. In both the cities and the countryside, the influx of Catholic immigrants from central and eastern Europe was blamed for unemployment, and the Liberal government's agreement with the railway companies was held at fault for the "Bohunk invasion." Conservative candidates tapped this reservoir of nativism, in some constituencies with the help of the "Knights of the Invisible Empire," the Ku Klux Klan. In Regina the Klansmen paraded through the streets on election night to celebrate the defeat of C.A. Dunning.[24]

The Tory showing in Quebec was astonishing to Bennett, whose wildest dream had been ten seats. His party captured twenty-four and increased its popular vote from 34.3 to 44.7 per cent. The paradox of the Conservative majority of 1930 was that it was based on two completely dissimilar groups of voters: urban, English-speaking Protestants in the West and rural, French-speaking Catholics in Quebec. As in the Prairies, an economic question was the paramount issue in Quebec. "Serious economic depression [had] been gnawing at the heart of rural Quebec" throughout the twenties, and preferences granted to New Zealand butter by the King government had made things worse. Bennett's promise of higher protective tariffs for agriculture convinced the Union catholique des cultivateurs to endorse the Conservatives, and its organizers carried the message of economic nationalism to the farm community. In desperation the Liberals countered by playing the conscription card. Three days before the election, *La Presse* ran the banner headline "Threat of Conscription" over a phoney dispatch that claimed the British government was cheering for a Tory victory, which would mean that Canadians would be drafted to fight in imperial wars. To their dismay the Liberals found that portraying Bennett as an "Imperialist snake" did not frighten French Canadians. Old *bleus* who had stayed home or voted *rouge* while Arthur Meighen led their party returned to the ancestral fold as the Conservatives made their best Quebec showing since 1911.[25]

Support for the two major parties, wrote political economist Escott Reid, was once again "very much the same . . . as in the heyday of the two-party system from 1900 to 1910." Nineteen out of every twenty voters had marked their cross beside the name of a Liberal or a Conservative candidate. Only eleven Progressives, all but two from the United Farmers of Alberta Ginger Group, survived. Most owed their re-election to the fortuitous rural-urban distribution of seats, for they had won nine of sixteen Alberta constituencies with less than a third of the total provincial vote. Labour had spun its wheels: Heaps and Woodsworth won handily in north end Winnipeg, but the election of Angus MacInnis in south Vancouver was offset by the defeat of H.B. Adshead in east side Calgary. The election of 1930, concluded Reid, "represents the culmination of that process . . . by which normal pre-War political alignments were gradually restored."[26]

IV

There were few well-known names among the cabinet announced to the press by Prime Minister Bennett on August 9, 1930, a cabinet that represented the usual regional, religious, and ethnic realities of Canadian politics. Ontario, the largest province and traditional Tory bulwark, was given seven ministries – more than a third of those available. Hugh Guthrie, in the Justice portfolio, and Senator Gideon Robertson, in charge of Labour, had both been members of the Union government. R.J. Manion, a genial Fort William physician who had served briefly with Meighen in 1921 and 1926, was assigned Railways and Canals, and Toronto tire manufacturer E.B. Ryckman, another member of the short-lived cabinet of 1926, became Minister of National Revenue. The other three Ontarians were getting their first taste of ministerial responsibility: H.A. Stewart, Public Works, was a Brockville lawyer and a director of a small trust company; Dr. Donald M. Sutherland, National Defence, had won the Distinguished Service

Order as a battalion commander in Belgium; parliamentary freshmen W.A. Gordon, Immigration and Colonization, was a lawyer from Northern Ontario.

Although five places were assigned to Quebec, there was some grumbling because not one was a senior portfolio. Sir George Perley, the oldest member of the cabinet at seventy-one, was not assigned a portfolio at all. The other English-speaking Quebecker, C.H. Cahan, was a wealthy corporation lawyer reputed to speak for the business and financial community of Montreal. Cahan had fancied himself a Justice Minister; when Bennett curtly informed him that his choice was between the Secretary of State's office or the back benches, Cahan decided he would lower his sights. Because the Conservatives had not elected a French Canadian from Quebec for twenty years, the three French-speaking ministers were all newcomers. Postmaster General Arthur Sauvé had spent two lonely decades as a Tory in the Quebec assembly and was an obvious cabinet selection; the reasoning behind the appointment of Montreal lawyer Alfred Duranleau as Minister of Marine was less apparent. Bennett created a minor furor when he passed over Armand Lavergne, a founder of la Ligue nationaliste canadienne, to make Maurice Dupré his Solicitor General. The law partner of Arthur Meighen's son Teddy and the youngest cabinet member at forty-two, Dupré had never before held elective office. His qualifications were nonetheless impressive, for he was perfectly bilingual and had been a Rhodes Scholar; adding to Dupré's appeal was his intense and frequently expressed admiration for R.B. Bennett, whom he invariably addressed as "The Chief."[27]

Each of the other seven provinces was allotted one member of the inner circle. The Prime Minister himself spoke for Alberta. H.H. Stevens, a Vancouver small businessman who had entered the House in 1911, represented British Columbia, while John A. Macdonald (the sixth of that name to sit in the Canadian parliament) became Minister without Portfolio solely by virtue of the fact that he was from Prince Edward Island. The credentials of Dr. Murray MacLaren, Minister of Pensions and National Health, were much stronger; a New Brunswick surgeon with a public health background, he had served overseas and was an expert on the problems of disabled veterans. Manitoba and Saskatchewan presented the most difficult cabinet decisions. Because the party had been shut out there in 1926, all of the potential privy councillors were unproven. Thomas Murphy, a pharmacist from Neepawa, was judged capable of the Interior ministry, a traditionally Western portfolio that had diminished considerably in importance because of the transfer of natural resources to the Prairie Provinces. Robert Weir, a Saskatchewan school inspector who owned a stock-breeding farm, became Minister of Agriculture. With only three ministers with serious cabinet experience (Perley, Guthrie, and Robertson), five House of Commons rookies in the lineup (Gordon, Duranleau, Dupré, Sauvé, and Weir), and two others (Murphy and Sutherland) with less than a year in the Commons, the Bennett team was badly in need of a veteran. Before becoming premier of Nova Scotia, E.N. Rhodes had spent thirteen years as an M.P., six of them as Speaker of the House. The Fisheries ministry Bennett offered him did not reflect the prestige his reputation lent to the government, but the assurance that greater responsibility would soon follow persuaded Rhodes to desert Halifax to fry bigger fish in Ottawa.[28]

For all its collective lack of political skills, the Conservative cabinet was made up of individuals whose private careers gave every indication that they would make effective ministers. It could, R.J. Manion wrote with only slight self-justificatory exaggeration, "compare favourably with any Government in the last half-dozen. Like all cabinets in Canada, where geography race and religion must come into the choosing, it contained some deadwood, but it also had . . . outstandingly able men." It probably equalled in talent the cabinets cobbled together in 1921 and 1925 by Mackenzie King, and because the Conservatives had substantial support in all provinces to draw upon, it was more representative of the diversity of Canada. Yet the King cabinets produced such men as J.L. Ralston, Ernest Lapointe, and C.A. Dunning, while the names of Bennett's ministers have vanished into historians' footnotes. The difference lies in the two prime ministers. Mackenzie King allowed his strongest ministers to develop into genuine spokesmen for their regions, and the stature they acquired added to that of his government; R.B. Bennett ran a one-man show. He liked to describe his cabinet as "the board of directors . . . administering the affairs of this country," but he delegated no authority to the "directors" and left no doubt about who was the chairman of the board. He often introduced legislation into the Commons that should have been handled by one of his ministers and acted as his own Finance Minister until 1932. A meeting of the cabinet, according to Ottawa humorists, was the Prime Minister talking to himself![29]

R.B. Bennett assumed office in a blur of motion. Orders in Council cancelled the immigration agreement with the railways and began the anticipated tariff hikes. The special session of parliament that began barely five weeks after the election was completely dominated by the new prime minister, who introduced two bills that were to set the pattern for his attempts to solve the economic crisis. The Unemployment Relief Act of 1930 provided $20 million to aid those out of work – ten times the amount the federal government had spent on the unemployed during the preceding decade. The money was to go to provide work rather than handouts. Only $4 million were to be spent on direct relief, universally referred to as "the dole." The remainder was directed through the provinces to the municipalities, which were required first to supplement it with their own money and a provincial contribution and then to spend the lot on job-creating public works. Fifty cents of each dollar spent was to come from the municipality, and twenty-five cents from each of the senior levels of government. After all his bold talk about unemployment being a national emergency, Bennett made it plain that he considered the federal expenditure a temporary grant to bridge the gap to the better times he expected in 1931. The preamble to the act could not have been more explicit: relief, it stated, "is primarily a provincial and municipal responsibility."[30]

The Relief Act, Bennett admitted, was "a palliative" rather than an attempt to stimulate recovery. That would be done by the extensive series of tariff increases that were the second item of business. Almost every Canadian manufacturing industry received additional protection, and such agricultural products as fruits and vegetables, which faced import competition, were also sheltered behind the tariff walls. The overall *ad valorem* increase for manufactured goods was almost a third. No specific explanation was provided for any individual item in the five-page list of changes, but Bennett promised, without providing details of the calculations, that they would mean twenty-five thousand new jobs in the industries affected.[31]

The Liberals protested the tariff increases but said nothing against the Relief Act and made no attempt to obstruct either measure. Administrations as diverse in ideology as American Republicans and Australian Labourites were dosing their economies with protectionism, and the Liberals knew of no better medicine to prescribe. King took two and a half hours to read into Hansard a long series of Bennett's campaign speeches in order "to hold him to his promises or to the consequences of his failure," but the only substantive comments he made were directed not at Bennett's legislation but at the whirlwind manner in which it had been "steam-rolled" through parliament. The new prime minister, said King, had "the Mussolini touch. . . . It reminds one of the *Mikado*, where the great Pooh-Bah held all the offices of state." Bennett offered no apologies. "As long as I occupy this position," he replied, ". . . there will be a very earnest endeavour to transact business as though it were business and not make-believe." The Labour members and the UFA Progressives were unanimous in criticizing the accomplishments of the session as inadequate. Bennett's programs would provide jobs for only a fraction of those who needed them. "Do not lose sight of the men and women who are suffering," pleaded J.S. Woodsworth. "A few weeks ago, I stood in my own city of Winnipeg watching a long line of men register so that they might obtain food. . . . This was not a long line of manufacturers approaching the finance minister for favours, but a queue of men four deep stretching for half a block around the corner to the next lane. . . . They were not 'bums,' they were not tramps down and out; most of them were self-respecting men anxious only for work."[32]

V

Ten days after the special session adjourned, R.B. Bennett left for the Imperial Conference in London, which put the finishing touches to the Statute of Westminster. The statute solidified in law the *de facto* transition from Empire to Commonwealth, and despite his effusions of sentimental imperialism, Bennett proved as effective an advocate of Canadian autonomy as King had been. The trip to England forced him to miss "Canadian Prosperity Week," a morale-building exercise in which businessmen went on stage between features in Famous Players Cinemas and gave inspirational speeches that were supposed to "re-establish confidence in the business stability of the country." The Prime Minister endorsed the idea heartily, and filmed a "talkie" calling for optimism that was shown as part of the program. Bennett meant what he said in his film; he was certain that the economic situation would improve rapidly. The new tariff structure would persuade manufacturers to increase production, and to do that they would have to invest and to take on more hands. The tariff alterations would also provide him with the leverage he needed in London to negotiate intra-imperial trade agreements that would reserve the British market for Canadian exporters of natural resources. With a normal surge in agricultural and construction employment, the hard times would be over by the time the Relief Act expired at the end of March, 1931.[33]

But there was nothing "normal" about the 1930s. The British Labour government was hostile to the idea of trade agreements, which seemed to be designed to benefit only Canada. Dominions Secretary J.H. Thomas described Bennett's proposal in public as "humbug" and in private is alleged to have said, "These 'ere Dominions don't only want to milk the old cow dry, they want to bite off her teats as well." Behind their public expressions of confidence, manufacturers privately saw no respite from recession. They used their tariff windfall not to expand but to reduce debt to weather the worst they feared was still ahead. The customary post-harvest buying spree could not take place when farm income was cut in half in most of the country and by four fifths in Manitoba, Saskatchewan, and Alberta. Pulp and paper companies that had teetered on the brink of receivership fell over; the most efficient mills ran at reduced capacity, and the others were shut down. Bankers abandoned their oldest customers in their scramble to consolidate. Businesses that had struggled through the first eighteen months of depression were unable to survive the winter of 1930-31, and their distress was immediately translated into increased unemployment. In March 1931 the number of jobless passed 400,000, almost 20 per cent of the non-agricultural labour force (see Tables XIIIa and XIIIb).[34]

The Relief Act of 1930 had done very little to ease their plight. The $16 million for public works had been divided among the provinces on the basis of population rather than need. After withholding sums for their own projects, the provinces divided what remained among their municipalities not according to the number of unemployed but in relation to what each municipality was prepared to spend on public works. Councils rushed through plans for streets, sewers, and water mains so as not to miss a share of the federal and provincial money; Montreal mayor Camillien Houde proposed to build thirty-two cutstone comfort stations, joking that he would provide the unemployed with "two kinds of relief."

The absurdity of the situation is illustrated by what happened in two Vancouver suburbs: working-class Burnaby, which had eight hundred residents out of work, received $54,000 – $67.50 for each of its unemployed; better-off West Vancouver, with only thirty-five registrants for relief, collected $15,000 – $428.57 for every out-of-work citizen. Since most municipalities simply divided the work available among the unemployed men who applied to do it, there were enormous differences in the total earnings of recipients among municipalities within the same province. In Windsor, the average was $157 for the season, in Hamilton, $103; in Toronto, with one of the largest percentages of unemployed in Ontario, it was only $54. Municipal administration of the projects was haphazard, so that it was impossible to direct the jobs to the neediest families in a community. Married men were given preference over the single, British subjects over immigrants, and there was a residence qualification that was enforced. Apart from crude means tests imposed informally by overbearing supervisors (workers in Toronto were laid off when they were seen in a liquor store), anyone who was unemployed was provided with the same amount of relief work regardless of the number of his children or the length of time he had been out of a job.[35]

Thus most of the federal money never found its way to those who needed it most. Once again municipalities had to provide tens of thousands of families with direct relief, as they had the previous winter. Two thirds of this was supposed to be paid by senior governments, but the federal grants took months to reach provincial capitals and as long again to reach city halls. Hungry residents couldn't wait, so that councils were forced to borrow in the interim. When interest charges were combined with the cost of administration, all of which was paid for by the municipality, the municipal share was much closer to a half than a third. A vicious cycle had been created that was perpetuated throughout the 1930s. The municipalities having the largest numbers of unemployed and the heaviest relief burdens were the very ones that had their revenues eroded most severely as unemployed householders were unable to pay their local taxes. The level of government armed with the smallest and most regressive tax base was forced to hold the front line in the war to survive the Great Depression.[36]

The ultimate casualties of the Depression were the reliefers themselves. Even most large cities had no welfare departments or trained social workers on their staffs to organize and dispense relief; moreover, there was no money to hire such people had they been available. As a result "direct relief under Bennett's 1930 Relief Act was distributed by a ramshackle collection of private charities and hastily organized emergency relief committees." In Quebec, for example, la Société St-Vincent de Paul, the St. George's Society, the Hebrew Society, and other voluntary associations set up parallel relief structures for each religious and ethnic group and received public funds to carry out their work.[37]

The systems of direct relief thrown together by hundreds of municipalities, rural and urban, were myriad, but the framework of each was essentially the same. While public works jobs were provided on simple evidence of unemployment, the dole was available only to those who could prove that they were destitute. The unemployed were required to exhaust every personal resource and those of close relatives, and no one with a car, a radio, or a telephone could expect the public to provide for himself or his wife and children. Relief was charity, as the jobless were deliberately reminded by the humiliations they were forced to endure to obtain it. An applicant waited in line for hours in a church basement or firehall until he reached the counter; there he was forced to answer a list of embarrassing questions and swear that he was destitute within hearing of everyone else in the room. "I've seen tears in a man's eyes," said one relief administrator, "as though they were signing away their manhood, their right to be a husband and sit at the head of the table."[38]

The disgrace did not end there, for reliefers were almost always provided with food vouchers to be used at local stores rather than money. This was done not to take advantage of the bulk purchasing power of the municipality but because, in the words of the London, Ontario, city clerk, "it is felt that relief in cash would only encourage the undeserving, who would probably use the cash for some unnecessary purpose." Fuel, provided only during the coldest months of winter, was often wood that the reliefers themselves cut as a "work test" for their food vouchers. Clothing was available only through private charities. Most municipalities refused at first to pay rent; the reliefer was expected to persuade the landlord to carry him until he found work. No provision was made for medical care, for soap or toiletries, or for anything beyond requirements for bare survival. "No one will starve," promised Saskatchewan Premier J.T.M. Anderson, but significantly he promised nothing more. "Unemployed workers, destitute farmers, and their families," protested the Social Service Council of Canada, were being "forced to exist on a plane below lunatics and criminals" in the asylums and prisons.[39]

R.B. Bennett received thousands of letters from ordinary Canadians telling him of their misery and of the hardships of relief and sometimes asking deferentially for his personal assistance. "Am willing to go anywhere to get work," wrote a butcher from Sarnia. "We have six children and I don't beleive [sic] it right to see them suffer for the want of food." "I ask you Sir how do you think we live on $3 a week," wrote a painter from Sherbrooke. "I dont [sic] want help: I want work I'll do anything to keep my family." A Calgary mechanic complained that "the Civic Relief refused us food tickets as they consider we got too much in March" and reported that his seven children suffered from "Malnuttrician [sic]." Bennett often replied to these letters himself, expressing his sympathy and advising his correspondents to apply to local authorities for help with their problems; sometimes he sent two, five, or even ten dollars out of his own pocket. But if he had compassion for the individual unemployed, he did not comprehend the magnitude of their collective crisis. When H.H. Stevens suggested the creation of a council with representatives from the trade unions, business, and the universities to study unemployment, Bennett dismissed the idea as "nonsense." "Do you think I want a lot of long-haired professors telling me what to do?" he asked his Minister of Trade and Commerce.[40]

When parliament reconvened in March 1931, the throne speech did not mention unemployment. To meet an unanticipated revenue shortfall, Finance Minister Bennett's first budget increased the federal sales tax from 1 per cent to 4 per cent and reduced personal income tax deductions. The tax rate on higher incomes was reduced, however, and dividends from Canadian stocks were made non-taxable; corporate income tax rates went up only from 8 per cent to 10 per cent. These regressive tax increases were combined with a new round of tariff elevation in what the *Canadian Forum* called "not only a Canada-First Budget but a Capitalist-First Budget" made up of "presents to the wealthy [and] greater burdens on the poor." A.A. Heaps made his annual plea for unemployment insurance, and Bennett repeated his annual objections. He was more polite than usual, however, and promised to put the civil service to work on a long-range investigation of the possibility of such a plan. It would not be needed to meet the existing situation, however, for Bennett was certain that "an era of true prosperity, fore-ordained," would arrive in the months just ahead.[41]

Disturbing news from the West forced a reconsideration. Minister of Labour Gideon Robertson had journeyed to view things first hand and sent back alarming reports. The price collapse of 1930 had beggared many wheat farmers, and a spring drought meant that there would be no 1931 crop at all in some areas. "One could never believe the desolation existing in southern Saskatchewan did he not see it himself," wrote Robertson. "The whole country for more than one hundred miles in extent . . . is a barren drifting desert." Thousands of seasonal workers who had in the past found jobs in agriculture or in railway construction could not satisfy municipal relief requirements because they were unmarried and transient; they were "riding the rods" across the prairies to British Columbia and represented a "menace to peace and safety." Railways Minister Manion was alarmed by the information he received from the Canadian National and the Canadian Pacific, and urged federal action at once. "We may hesitate too long and have serious riots verging on revolution," he warned Bennett, "as hungry men can hardly be blamed for refusing to starve quietly."[42]

The Relief Act of 1930 had been drafted in haste; the Unemployment and Farm Relief Act of 1931 was prepared in near panic. Over opposition protests that parliament's right to scrutinize expenditure had been subverted, the government made an unspecified amount of money available to aid the municipalities and the provinces with public works relief projects. The terms were somewhat more generous than those of 1930. The dominion government would pay fifty cents of each dollar spent, the remainder to be divided equally between the municipality and the province. The dole was still discouraged: only one third of the cost of direct relief could be paid with federal grants. To move unemployed transients away from cities, "where they are subject to agitation," provincial highway construction camps would receive federal financial support; the act gave the RCMP broad powers to imprison those who refused to co-operate with relief authorities. Bennett answered shouts of "dictatorship" with reference to the federal power to preserve the "peace, order and good government" of Canada. He argued that while "this is a land of freedom . . . it is not right or just that now or at any other time we should permit such action by words or deeds as may tend to unsettle confidence in the institutions and customs under which we live." Bennett was keen to assume constitutional responsibility for law and order but unwilling to make any commitment to ensure unemployed Canadians a decent standard of living; like the 1930 legislation the Unemployment and Farm Relief Act disclaimed any permanent federal concern in the matter. Dominion aid to relief was once more defined as temporary, and the flow of federal funds was to be turned off on March 1, 1932.[43]

VI

No one could accuse R.B. Bennett of inactivity in the face of the emergency. He worked like a man possessed, rising early to review documents over breakfast in his suite in the Chateau Laurier, then rushing to the East Block at 8:30 to dictate letters at a furious pace as two secretaries struggled to keep up with him. His afternoons and evenings were spent in the House, where he spoke on every government measure and sprang to his feet to rebut each opposition challenge. After the Commons adjourned he would return to his office to labour on past midnight. He took Sunday off, not because he needed a rest, but to keep his boyhood promise to his mother to respect the sabbath. Even on Sunday the telephone kept the task constantly before him. It was as if he felt his own feverish efforts could exorcise the devil of Depression from the soul of Canadian capitalism.

In the last two weeks of August 1931, Bennett travelled west to preach the gospels of hard work and optimism. Prosperity in 1932 was a certainty, he said in his public addresses, and in the meantime the new Relief Act would create "work for all who desire it." His private conversations with the four Western premiers, however, left him disheartened. The severity of the Depression had differed from region to region. For most parts of the Maritimes, the 1930s were less difficult than the long recession that had followed the war. But the Prairie Provinces and British Columbia, with specialized, undiversified, resource-exporting economies, were devastated. The four Western provinces experienced the sharpest declines in per capita personal income in the nation (see Table XIV) and suffered the heaviest relief costs. Bracken, Anderson, Brownlee, and Tolmie told Bennett that they could not afford to undertake the public works projects necessary to qualify for federal funds. Their governments were broke and had used up all possible sources of credit. Rather than give up his relief program, Bennett agreed to lend the four provinces the money to pay their share, yet he continued to cling to the constitutional fiction that unemployment relief could remain a provincial matter. The situation had become ludicrous: the federal government was paying the piper but refusing still another opportunity to call the tune by imposing some order on the crazy quadrille of four separate provincial relief structures.[44]

For all his repeated disavowals of responsibility, Bennett was deeply concerned about the implications for the federal treasury of what he had done. Shortly after his return to Ottawa he received a second shock, this one of seismic proportions. An international financial crisis had loomed since the April failure of the Kredit Anstalt, Austria's largest bank. Great Britain had battled a run on sterling all summer, but even the formation of a coalition National government had failed to halt foreign withdrawals of gold from the Bank of England. On September 21, 1931, Britain detached the pound from gold. Twenty-five other countries followed Britain off the gold standard, but Bennett refused to consider a similar course for Canada. Convinced that to give up gold completely was an immoral act that would ruin the national credit, he instead imposed a half-way measure, strengthening restrictions on gold exports but pledging to international creditors that "the country will continue to meet its obligations . . . to pay in gold where it has promised so to pay." As a consequence, the Canadian dollar was whipsawed between the weak and the strong currencies. It increased in value against the Australian dollar, the Argentinian peso, and the Scandinavian krone, so that Canadian exports lost ground in world markets for wheat, pulp, and newsprint. Against the American dollar, however, it fell to eighty cents. Overnight, corporations and governments with debts in the United States found that their payments had shot up 20 per cent.[45]

The aftermath of the British devaluation pushed Canada still deeper into the pit of depression. Stock prices and values and volumes of natural resource exports dropped sharply as they had in 1929-30, but this time the disaster percolated more rapidly through the rest of the economy. Unemployment climbed past 500,000 in December and continued upward to a peak of 713,000 in February 1933 – 33 per cent of the non-agricultural labour force (see Table XIIIb).

The immediate effect of the gold standard trauma was to force the

Bennett government to a drastic re-evaluation of its financial situation. "We must now talk in thousands where we previously spoke in millions," Bennett cautioned a Saskatchewan back-bencher, "or we will be bankrupt." The Canadian National Railways' debt had grown because of the depression-induced reduction of traffic, and British Columbia and the Prairie Provinces now needed another $11.6 million to avert default on their loans coming due in New York. There had never been a formal ceiling for spending under the 1931 Relief Act, but Bennett and his colleagues had talked of spending $50 million during the winter; despite the soaring unemployment rate, this was cut back to $28.2 million. An already inadequate program was turned into a shambles. The Farm and Unemployment Relief Act of 1931 was even less effective than its predecessor. Without any federal direction, without even an audit, works programs in some provinces were adapted to serve the political needs of their governments rather than the economic needs of their unemployed. Complaints about political discrimination in hiring and in purchasing materials streamed steadily to Bennett, the largest numbers from New Brunswick, Quebec, and British Columbia. Many municipalities found it impossible to finance their share, so that ambitious projects started in the autumn were cancelled as funds ran out, forcing the unemployed back into the morass of direct relief. [46]

Ineffective as it had been, the Relief Act could not be allowed to lapse as planned at the end of February with nothing to take its place. Parliament was recalled a month early to renew the act until May and to approve the first budget of the new finance minister, E.N. Rhodes. Faced with a $100-million deficit, Rhodes exacted a series of draconian tax increases: the sales tax went from 4 per cent to 6 per cent, a special excise duty was added on top of the tariff, and personal income tax exemptions were savaged to enable the government to reach into the pockets of thousands of new taxpayers. Again corporations got off more lightly, as the rate levied against their profits rose only to 11 per cent from 10. All civil servants, with the significant exception of judges, the RCMP, and the armed forces, were to have their salaries cut by 10 per cent. "This course may result in hardship [and] may entail sacrifice," said the Finance Minister, but "the preservation of our national credit is an indispensable prerequisite to the return of prosperity." [47]

The load of hardship and sacrifice, countered the Labour and UFA members, had been disproportionately placed on those with the least ability to bear it; their protests persuaded the government to reduce public service pay by only 5 per cent for those who earned less than $1,200, but the Conservatives refused to change anything else in the budget. United Farmers of Alberta M.P. Robert Gardiner expressed doubt that it was really the politicians who were in charge of things. "No doubt this so-called economy," he said, "has emanated from those who are the real rulers of the country . . . the banking and financial institutions."[48]

The fiscal and monetary policies of the Bennett government, like its tariff policy, were faithful reflections of policies imposed upon other governments by the need to please other bankers. As John Maynard Keynes complained in an article in the *Atlantic Monthly* in May 1932, "competitive wage reductions, competitive tariffs . . . competitive economy campaigns" were everywhere the order of the day. "The modern capitalist," he continued, "is a fair-weather sailor. As soon as a storm arises, he abandons the duties of navigation. . . ." Retrenchment was not the way out of the Depression, Keynes warned, and "the voices which tell us that the path of escape is to be found in strict economy . . . are the voices of fools and madmen." Instead, Keynes advocated *increasing* public investment, regardless of budgetary deficits: ". . . the only way out is for us to discover some object which is admitted even by the deadheads to be a legitimate excuse for largely increasing the expenditure of someone on something!" Otherwise, he concluded sadly, the world would have "to wait for a war to terminate a major depression."[49]

Bennett and his colleagues could not claim ignorance of Keynes and his heretical theories of how to bring about a recovery. His work had been mentioned in the House for the first time in 1923, and during the debate on the 1932 budget, J.S. Woodsworth had quoted directly from the *Atlantic* article. For the first two years of their mandate, although they were certainly unaware of it, the Conservatives had taken a hesitant half-step down the road that Keynes was pointing out through their sponsorship of job-creating public works programs and the deficits that they had incurred to do so. Their motivations and their philosophy, of course, were not Keynesian; they were not trying to "spend their way out of depression." The Bennett government had emphasized public works rather than direct relief because it feared the moral character of the unemployed would be undermined if they were given money through a dole. The budget deficits were accidents and had come about in spite of heavy tax increases, which no Keynesian would have countenanced. The amounts the Conservatives had spent had been only a trickle compared to the torrent of public investment that would have been necessary to fill the gap left by the decline in investment by the private sector.[50]

In the spring of 1932, however, at the precise moment that increased government spending would have done the most good, Bennett decided on his campaign of cutbacks and formally ended his tentative assault on unemployment by means of public works. To economize, all levels of government would thereafter rely on direct relief. Like most of Bennett's decisions, this one was reached unilaterally, but it was ratified unanimously by the federal-provincial conference that he called to announce it in April. Premier Brownlee of Alberta expressed the consensus when he said, "I do not see how we can go on piling up capital expenditure. . . . These conditions may last for three years. . . . More direct relief would only cost 40% of the present schemes. People cannot expect the state to supply work for everyone." Mayors and reeves seconded this conviction. "The old system of soup kitchens," wrote one, "is better from an economical point of view." This did not mean that Canada's leaders no longer were concerned that the dole would "kill the initiative and enterprise of young Canadians," but simply that they feared unbalanced budgets more than they feared direct relief. The unemployed would have to be kept on the straight and narrow by making direct relief as demeaning as possible, and the RCMP could take care of any agitators who tried to make them dissatisfied with their lot.[51]

VII

The new principle was embodied in a third Relief Act later in April. No further public works would be supported; the federal government would pay one third of all direct relief and would lend the provinces enough money to cover the municipalities' third when necessary. The remainder of the act's provisions were an attempt to turn back the clock to a peaceful, pre-industrial Canada, when the peasantry had starved quietly on the farms during lean years. Single men who did not qualify for municipal relief were to be placed with Western farmers as labourers, and for the married unemployed and their families there was a "back to the land" relief settlement scheme. An urban family on relief was to be provided with $600, spread over three years, to establish itself in agriculture, costs to be divided equally among the three levels of government. Some thought the plan too generous: "10 chances to one it will be spent in beer parlours and chippie chasing," grumbled a disgruntled Alberta old-timer. Others who understood the desperate condition of rural Canada condemned the idea as madness: "We can no longer say to a man, go out into the wild [and] stay with it till the bones shine through your skin," wrote a farmer from British Columbia. Businessmen, however, praised the scheme as "a return to fundamentals . . . the sort of thing which strengthens the social structure at its base and which must, ultimately, make for better times." All provinces save Prince Edward Island signed agreements to participate, and Immigration and Colonization Minister W.A. Gordon predicted that 200,000 of the "unemployed and surplus city population" would eventually be relocated. Fewer than seven thousand families actually moved, however, and many of them were simply transferred from an urban to a rural relief roll.[52]

Relief settlement was "a confession of despair" by R.B. Bennett. Every one of his initiatives had ended in disaster, but Bennett had one more card to play, a card he was certain could trump the economic crisis. He had toyed throughout his life with the notion of an economic union of the British Empire; even as he preached autarky in the 1930 election campaign, he would lapse into the rhetoric of Imperial federation and envisage the Empire "as an economic unit [that] can face foursquare every storm that blows." At the Imperial Conference of 1930 he had put forward a plan for increased intra-Empire trade; this was not a contradiction of his tariff increases, for his idea was that goods traded within the Empire would still be subjected to existing duties, while tariff walls were raised higher against trade from outside the Imperial bloc. Ignoring the many British reservations about his scheme, Bennett had won agreement for an Imperial Economic Conference to be held in Ottawa. He vowed on his return from London that the conference would lay "the foundation of a new economic Empire in which Canada is destined to play a part of ever-increasing importance."[53]

Elections in Australia and New Zealand forced postponement until the summer of 1932. The current coalition National government in the United Kingdom was more receptive to the creation of a British trade area, for although Labour's Ramsay MacDonald remained as prime minister, the real power in the coalition rested with the Conservatives, who were less wedded than Labour and the Liberals to Britain's traditional principle of free trade. The delegation that Conservative leader Stanley Baldwin led to Canada contained six cabinet ministers, among them Chancellor of the Exchequer Neville Chamberlain, a sympathizer with the notion of imperial preference. The British were prepared to talk turkey – or rather to talk wheat, fish, lumber, and pulp. If Canada and the other dominions would offer "reciprocal concessions of outstanding importance" on manufactured items, the United Kingdom would give natural products from the Empire an advantage in British markets by enacting tariffs against their non-Empire competitors.[54]

Canadians were encouraged to believe that out of the conference would come the long-promised recovery, and Sunday, July 17, was declared a "National Day of Prayer" for the success of the negotiations. Residents of the capital watched in fascination as their city played host to its first international gathering; heads turned as the sari-clad wives of the Indian representatives descended gracefully from the Buick limousines that transported the dignitaries around Ottawa. The pomp and glitter, muttered civil servants still smarting from their salary reduction, had cost $300,000. The conference was a social triumph and an economic failure. Professions of Imperial brotherhood were cheap over cocktails but dearly bought at the bargaining table. After the first three weeks of discussions proved fruitless, the goodwill expressed in banquet speeches began to evaporate and the "one big family" atmosphere curdled into sour, mean-spirited haggling that, said Lord Beaverbrook, "would have been discreditable . . . between none-too-friendly foreign powers."[55]

The bilateral talks between Canada and the United Kingdom went particularly badly, and rumours circulated that they were at the point of breaking down. Lack of preparation by the Canadians, internal divisions among the British, and the personality of R.B. Bennett were variously blamed for the impasse. Bennett was vague about concessions but precise about demands, and the British delegates were offended by his "very aggressive tone" in the discussions. The patronizing attitude the British adopted with the "colonials" undoubtedly contributed to Bennett's temper tantrums. The most serious obstacles to agreement, however, were the men whose profits would have been hurt by it: British importers of Argentinian grain, Japanese salmon, and Russian lumber; Canadian manufacturers of textiles, iron, and steel. Warned by C.H. Cahan that Bennett intended to reduce the duty on steel plate and cottons to obtain a preference for Canadian wheat and lumber, the presidents of Dominion Foundries and Dominion Textiles rushed to Ottawa to remind Bennett of domestic political realities. He then reneged on commitments that the British negotiators had thought were firm, so that they almost gave up in frustration.[56]

The damage that failure of the Imperial Economic Conference would have done to public morale made it impossible to admit openly to defeat. Literally at the last minute a series of accords were initialled between the United Kingdom and individual dominions; Canada signed at 1:30 in the morning on the final day of the conference. Wheat from Canada was to be helped in British markets by a small duty on foreign wheat, and steps were to be taken to stop the USSR from "dumping" lumber in the United Kingdom. Canada agreed to make more than two hundred changes in her tariffs against British goods and to establish an independent tariff board to study further reductions. Statements were issued to the press about the wonderful work that had been done in Ottawa, and editorials praised the agreement as "an example to the whole world of what can be achieved by mutual confidence and conciliation." In truth, the negotiations had produced little more than bitter hostility. Britain reserved the right to cancel the wheat duty any time dominion wheat was above the world price and evaded her promise about Russian lumber. The Canadian tariff board became a dead letter, and the items on which the tariff was actually reduced were peripheral to the British economy; few British steelworkers could have been called back to the mill because of increased Canadian demand for noisemakers in the shape of Mickey Mouse. The value of the increased trade, concludes Ian Drummond, was "infinitesimal – even at the depth of the Depression," and the boost given to the Canadian economy was "pathetically small."[57]

VIII

The failure of the Imperial Economic Conference left Bennett's last stratagem shattered. He had promised to "blast a way" into world markets; in the autumn of 1932 it was the Canadian resource-exporting economy that had been blasted. He had guaranteed every Canadian the right to a job; in September 1932, one in four of them was not working. He had sworn that there would be no dole; a quarter of a million families celebrated Christmas on direct relief. Bennett had broken every covenant, and the unemployed held him personally responsible. People spoke of "Bennett buggies," autos drawn by horses because the owners could not afford gas; of "Bennett boroughs," the shacktowns of cardboard and corrugated iron crowded with homeless men; of "Bennett blankets," the newspapers under which transients slept on park benches.

At the time of Bennett's election, Richard de Brisay had quipped that the new prime minister's "confidence was as boundless as his imagination was limited." His vain attempts to conquer the Great Depression had not expanded his imagination but had shrunk his confidence. He had worked sixteen-hour days without putting a dent in the problems that faced the country and without being able to prevent things from continually getting worse. Piles of unanswered letters and unread memos began to accumulate on his desk, and the occasional admission crept out that "conditions are now operating in this country . . . which we are not able to control." An Alberta editor who had known Bennett since his days in territorial politics was startled to watch this corrosion of "his old pugnacious and domineering spirit" but had no difficulty in explaining the change: "The chastening hand of the Depression is beginning to tell on him."[58]

CHAPTER 10

Orthodoxy on Trial

I

Among the visitors to Ottawa in the summer of 1932 were six hundred uninvited guests, delegates to the Workers' Economic Conference which convened on August 1 and deliberated on fiscal and foreign policy for three days in an abandoned garage in the capital. The *Canadian Forum* felt the conclave worthy of special mention. "Most of the delegates were unemployed," the *Forum* reported; "their clothes were shabby, faded, and worn out. . . . One feature which distinguished the Workers' Conference from the Imperial Conference was the absence of pot bellies at the former." This "lean and hungry lot" had ridden into Ottawa from points west on freight trains, running the gauntlet of railroad "bulls" and Mounted Police thrown up at key divisional points in anticipation of the event. The conference had been designed as the centrepiece of Canada's "first country-wide Hunger March," a tactic that actually worked better in Britain or in cities like New York with large, concentrated populations. Nonetheless the efforts of conference organizers like J.B. McLachlan, who led a deputation into the Prime Minister's office for a brief interview, made their point with the government.

Following Bennett's histrionic rejection of their policy alternatives, which included non-contributory unemployment insurance for Canadians and self-government for India, the delegates held an open-air meeting on Wellington Street. "In every window of the building which houses the Department of National Revenue, there were half a dozen or more people craning their necks in order not to miss a detail of the activities going on in the market square below," wrote the *Forum* correspondent. The civil servants booed and jeered the police, who intervened to end the speeches, arrest a dozen ringleaders, and forcibly disperse the remaining delegates with blows from their truncheons and the occasional "well-directed punch in the face." The Workers' Conference had served its purpose: to put orthodoxy on trial in the shadow of the Peace Tower. Acting as the prosecution in the case were members of and sympathizers with the Communist Party of Canada.[1]

Thus came to Ottawa a movement of popular resistance that had been evident in a number of important industrial centres as early as the winter of 1929-30. This political theatre had already been acted out in similarly violent street confrontations in Vancouver, Edmonton, Calgary, Winnipeg, Sudbury, Hamilton, Toronto, Sydney Mines – wherever Communists or "red" trade unionists could mobilize Canadians with the party slogan "Fight or Starve." In 1930, the CPC had organized a National Unemployed Workers' Association; attracting the interest of non-Communist workers and activists, the Toronto head office sold 22,000 memberships across the country between January and July, 1931. Because of their leadership, the term "red" was indiscriminately applied to the NUWA and the rest of the unemployed movement, but grass-roots organizations of the out-of-work such as the Verdun Workingmen's Association, the East York Workers' Association, or the Burnaby Workingmen's Protective Association cannot be truly so described. Their educational and political activities crossed party lines and engaged Communists, social democrats, and those who were neither. Their experience of "working against not working," as Bryan Palmer has demonstrated, comprises a rich though largely unrecorded history.[2]

In some cities communist control over the civic-level electioneering of the organized unemployed was more direct. As a general rule, the more cosmopolitan a community, the greater the degree of genuine communist influence. The communist movement in Canada had always been cemented together by ethnic ties within the radical immigrant communities, ties that extended outwards into the international milieu in which Ukrainian, Hungarian, Czech, Jewish, and other "ethnic radicals" functioned. A good example was north end Winnipeg, already represented on city council by Communist William Kolisnyk in 1930. Another was Blairmore, Alberta, where in 1933 the ratepayers elected a "red" town council that included three antifascist Italian Canadians. Among the Communist party's most dedicated supporters were the victims of the Railway Agreement of 1925-30, immigrants from all the newly independent nations of Central Europe. The desperate circumstances in which they were abandoned in the thirties could make communists out of such traditionally conservative groups as the Slovaks. There were about seven thousand Slovaks in Toronto, wrote Father John Pachiliy to Archbishop McNeil in 1932, and "most of them have not had a job in more than 20-22 months. The Railroad that brought them here refuses to repatriate them . . . so the result is that they roam the streets, begging, stealing, eating out of refuse cans. . . . Many in this horrible destitution have bartered their [Catholic] faith for a membership in some radical organization: communism, socialism, protestantism." At the 1931 May Day celebration in Vancouver, greetings were exchanged on the platform among "Scandinavian, Finnish, Finnish women, Jugo-Slav and German workers," and the festivities ended with five thousand voices filling Stanley Park with the choruses of "the rallying call of the Red Front Fighters" – Communist sailors in the German merchant marine.[3]

"Red" trade unionists of the 1930s were a diverse constituency thinly spread from Nanaimo to Glace Bay. Few were card-carrying members of the Communist party, but the Workers' Unity League – the central core of their movement – was communist-led and controlled. The WUL was born at a meeting of the "Politburo" of the CPC in late 1929, in response to a directive of the Communist International to dissolve the ideologically dangerous alliance that had developed between communist and socialist trade unionists in the All-Canadian Congress of Labour. The byzantine politics of post-revolutionary Russia and the momentous conflict between Stalin and Trotsky thus came to have a direct influence on Canadian trade union affairs, for out of the Sixth Congress of the Communist International in Moscow in 1928 had emerged the "left turn" of the worldwide communist movement. Workers were exhorted to separate from "reformist" organizations like the ACCL and to join truly "revolutionary" unions in order to prepare for the coming revolution, which, Tim Buck predicted, "will make the late War look like a chicken fight." No trade unions corresponding to this revolutionary ideal existed in Canada. There were, however, three national unions of miners, loggers, and garment workers that were sufficiently communist in complexion to be persuaded to join the Workers' Unity League to give the red union central its first skeletal form in 1930-31.[4]

The incidence of strikes and lockouts touched record lows in 1930 (see Table XII). Amid the general malaise of the labour movement, the Workers' Unity League swiftly gained a reputation as the "one fighting organization" on the industrial relations scene. Red-led miners in the Crow's Nest Pass fought and won a heroic struggle to preserve a work-sharing agreement negotiated with the coal operators. In British Columbia, shingle and sawmill workers in a WUL union, Chinese, Japanese, and Sikh immigrants among them, stood shoulder to shoulder against wage reductions. French-Canadian workers, supposedly culturally immune to the "red disease," took an active role in both Communist party and union affairs in the British Columbia mill town of Maillardville.[5]

The most notorious strike directed by the WUL involved six hundred lignite colliers at Estevan and Bienfait, Saskatchewan, in 1931. Their demand was straightforward: recognition of their union in the open-shop coal towns. The mine owners, however, turned the strike into a struggle against communism, ensuring themselves the support of politicians and the RCMP in their effort to break the union. It set the pattern of industrial relations in previously non-union settings which repeated itself in Anyox, British Columbia, Flin Flon, and Rouyn-Noranda. Miners and smelter workers would join the WUL-affiliated Mine Workers Union of Canada and ask for a contract; management would refuse to deal with a "red" union and call for Mounties or militia; demonstrations would be banned, and when they took place anyway they would be broken up by force and the "outside agitators" who led them arrested. Strike-breakers recruited among the desperate unemployed would be trucked in to resume operations under police protection, and a police-supervised ballot among the scabs would decide to dispense with the union.[6]

Estevan is remembered best because the police drew their pistols and opened fire on a strikers' parade. The Estevan *Mercury* described what followed on September 29, 1931: "The staccato bark of revolvers, the whine of death-dealing bullets, the dull thud of flying missiles . . . the piercing screams of wildly-excited women and the hoarse shouts of men locked in bitter battle – these shattered the peace and quiet of a beautiful autumn afternoon . . . as tranquil Fourth Street was suddenly transformed into a maelstrom of blood and destruction." Three strikers died: Nick Nargan, Julian Gryshko, and Peter Markunas; though unarmed, they died fighting, not on their knees. Their brothers in the Ukrainian Farmer Labour Temple, a communist-affiliated fraternal organization, carved "Murdered by RCMP" on their common tombstone. Communist intellectual Leslie Morris compared the massacre to the suppression of the Rebellion of 1837, led by William Lyon Mackenzie, Opposition Leader King's grandfather. "Estevan," Morris wrote, "is the Montgomery's Tavern of today."[7]

It was not King but his former labour minister, Peter Heenan, who raised the issue in the Commons. Like most trade unionists, Heenan saw the killings as an act of "cowardness" on the part of the police, and he bluntly accused the government of having "ordered the soldiers [*sic*] . . . to shoot down the strikers in Estevan, who had a legitimate grievance." For saying the same thing without benefit of parliamentary immunity, two Communists who had supported the miners' cause, Sam Scarlett and Annie Buller, served jail sentences of one and two years respectively. A miner from Alberta pointed out the flaw in this strategy of repression in a letter of protest to R.B. Bennett. He and his comrades were "not infidels but God fearing men. . . . Really there are very few communists in Canada but there are hosts of workingmen abounding who are suffering real hunger. . . . To trifle with their grievances," he warned, was "a deadly error," one that only strengthened the hand of the communist faction in the labour movement. The Prime Minister spurned this loyal worker's advice and summarized his anti-communist creed in a Toronto speech in which he urged Canadians "to put the iron heel ruthlessly on propaganda of that kind." Bennett's "iron heel," like King's famous "five-cent piece," would haunt him for the rest of his prime ministership. The unfortunate metaphor was gleaned from Jack London's novel *The Iron Heel*, which Bennett had apparently never read; that epic of revolution in North America concludes with a proletarian triumph, not at the ballot box, but with the sword.[8]

II

The Communists' chances of rallying the Canadian left and the larger body of the discontented around their program of non-parliamentary revolutionary action were remote. Despite its Leninist pretensions, the Communist Party of Canada was highly decentralized, even anarchic. Its leadership was rife with factional intrigue arising out of the debate that split all Communist parties outside the Soviet Union in the post-revolutionary era: were they to be distinct national entities or merely subordinate sections of the Stalinist Comintern? The CPC's founding chairman, Jack MacDonald, and Maurice Spector, Canadian member of the Executive Committee of the Communist International in Moscow, were both advocates of an independent line; they were ruthlessly purged by loyal politburo bosses in 1929. Thereafter knowledgeable members of the non-communist left were wary of the CPC. Had it not been for the opportunities presented by the Great Depression, the party might have sunk into oblivion in the 1930s.[9]

Instead, the Communists went from weakness to strength. The very ferocity of official attacks upon them created a corps of radical martyrs around whom a powerful civil liberties lobby was built under the guidance of one of Canada's most astute Communists, Rev. A.E. Smith, a former Methodist minister. The Conservative government's policy of summarily deporting immigrants who engaged in radical activities or those who became public charges assured that Smith's Canadian Labour Defence League became a mass movement between 1931 and 1934, when over ten thousand immigrants were turned out of the country. New Canadians, naturalized or unnaturalized, signed Smith's petitions of protest by the tens of thousands. "I have had hundreds and hundreds of [petitions]," Justice Minister Guthrie stated in the Commons in 1933. "I have now ceased to acknowledge receipt of them. I merely hand them over to the mounted police in order that a record may be kept of the names and addresses. I can assure the House that . . . there does not appear a single Anglo-Saxon or French-Canadian name – nothing but the names of foreigners, unpronounceable names for the most part."[10]

Guthrie was lying when he dismissed all the signers as "foreign," but even had he been correct, by 1931 these "foreigners" comprised one fifth of the labour force in manufacturing, one third of that in lumbering and mining, and a wide swath of the rural population of the Prairie Provinces. Had the Communists been able to mobilize even one in ten of this group, they would have made themselves a formidable political force. Like all good politicians, the Reverend Mr. Smith watered down the CPC doctrine to suit the exigencies of recruiting; so did the Workers' Unity League and its agrarian counterpart, the Farmers' Unity League. In 1933-34 they broadened out, leading hundreds of strikes and protests under the banner of the United Front. Overlapping memberships in the Canadian Labour Defence League, the WUL, and the FUL exceeded fifty thousand. The "mass" organizations, wrote an unsympathetic labour journalist, "are but symbols to distinguish the groupings of their dupes. The alphabetical combinations . . . fit together in a Russian anagram for the Communist Party of Canada."[11]

Until 1936, the Communist Party of Canada itself was an "unlawful association" as defined by Section 98 of the Criminal Code, an extraordinary statute added to the law books by the Union government in 1919. Genuine revolutionary activity such as stockpiling arms was of course illegal under the normal provisions of the code. Section 98 made it illegal to *advocate* "governmental, industrial or economic change within Canada by the use of force, violence or physical injury to person or property, or by threats of such injury," even if the accused did nothing to bring about such changes. The controversial section placed the burden of "proof to the contrary" on the accused, not the Crown; the accused, in other words, was presumed guilty unless he could prove himself innocent. The drafters of Section 98 were uncomfortable with it, and when the post-war red scare was over, the Commons attempted repeatedly to modify or repeal it; it remained in force because of opposition to repeal from the Conservative majority in the Senate.[12]

By invoking Section 98 against the Communist party in 1931, Hugh Guthrie and the provincial attorneys general, notably William Price of

Ontario, felt that they could kill two birds with one legal stone. First, the annoying opposition in the streets would be eliminated. Second, the sagging prestige of the Conservative party would be enhanced in a wider ideological arena. Anti-communism intersected with the thinly veiled nativism of the Tory campaign of 1930 and was popular with the Catholic Church. The Conservatives won approval from Catholic leaders for their pledge to embargo the Soviet Union, and Catholic, imperialist, and continentalist opinion was unanimous in applauding the Bennett government's dispatch of the destroyers *Skeena* and *Vancouver* to help in the Anglo-American suppression of a communist-led insurrection in El Salvador. A little domestic red-baiting, it was felt, would be a good supplement to these attacks on the "red enemy" overseas.[13]

This was the context in which the well-publicized arrests of eight Communist leaders took place on the night of August 11, 1931. The "Toronto Eight" were a cross-section of the party in the early thirties. Jack MacDonald's successor, an English-born machinist named Tim Buck, rapidly emerged as the spokesman for the group. Scottish blacksmith Tom McEwen was the principal figure in the Workers' Unity League, and Malcolm Bruce, editor of the *Worker*, was old-stock Canadian, Prince Edward Island-born. The presence of these three testified that Canadian communism was more than an obscure sect of Russian-born Bolsheviks. The other five defendants represented fragments of the CPC's ethnic support: Sam Carr the left-wing Jewish community; Matthew Popovich and John Boychuk the Ukrainian associations; Amos T. Hill the party's Finnish connection. Last to be scooped up was Tomo Cacic, a Croatian immigrant who had the misfortune to be reading a propaganda pamphlet in the Toronto CPC headquarters when Attorney General Price's provincial policemen descended. The police did not search hard enough for a French Canadian to balance the ticket; according to the records they seized, a grand total of five French-speaking Quebeckers belonged to the party.[14]

RCMP intelligence on the CPC proved to be dated and inaccurate. The prosecution's star witness was a labour spy named Jack Leopold, who had been discovered and expelled from the party in 1928; in his testimony he confused Tim Buck with Malcolm Bruce. To prove that the CPC was a violent revolutionary conspiracy, Crown attorneys introduced such "evidence" as the *Communist Manifesto* (1848), an approach that gave Buck and his colleagues a golden opportunity to use their time on the stand to expound on the general theory of Marxism. With the Crown cast as the lions, the Communists became the martyrs. "The parallel between the position of the Communist in Canada and the early Christians in the Roman Empire becomes more striking every day," commented the *Canadian Forum*. "Some day there may be a monument in Toronto to the memory of Tim Buck and his fellow-accused," concluded Frank Scott in *Queen's Quarterly*. But however weak the Crown's case, it was impossible for the defence to get around Section 98. All the defendants were convicted and sentenced to terms of three to five years; all but Malcolm Bruce were ordered deported at the end of their sentences.[15]

A.E. Smith immediately mounted a campaign to free them, aided immeasurably by an attempt on Buck's life in Kingston Penitentiary in October 1932. Under circumstances that remain unclear, guards fired repeatedly into his cell during a prison riot. Wire service photos of the frail Communist, led shackled with a ball and chain into a Toronto courtroom to testify regarding the attempted murder, confirmed his role as the embattled underdog. The Toronto Progressive Arts Club dramatized the affair as an "agitprop" play entitled *Eight Men Speak*, which police departments across the country tried unsuccessfully to suppress. Instead of stopping the extra-parliamentary opposition, the show trial of the Eight had encouraged it. The failure of anti-communism was demonstrated in a near-general strike in Stratford in the autumn of 1933, when Workers' Unity League poultry processors and furniture workers fought back against wage reductions. The Ontario government, which had colluded with the federal Department of Justice in the affair of the Eight, ordered out soldiers and armoured cars of the Royal Canadian Regiment. The strikers demonstrated their lack of fear of the troops by parading with wash basins on their heads, towing papier mâché cannon.[16]

The government quietly gave up. In June 1934 the prisoners were released one by one. Tim Buck was greeted in Toronto with a "mass welcome rally" at Maple Leaf Gardens, which moved even the hardened scribes of the daily press to tears. Seventeen thousand attended, and organizers claimed to have turned another eight thousand away at the door. Behind Buck in the arena that night hung a gigantic portrait of the awesome Joseph Stalin. R.B. Bennett's iron heel had worked no better than his relief acts; Buck and his colleagues had become a nightmare. The cover illustration of the Communist party literary magazine *Masses* was apt. It depicted "Canadian Capitalism" as a ship adrift in a hurricane; bolts of lightning stabbed down from a dark, foreboding sky, each labelled with the name of a recent strike led by the Workers' Unity League.[17]

III

By fighting the battle for the streets, the Communists had affirmed the traditional freedoms of speech and assembly at the heart of Canadian democracy – a democracy that they themselves had dismissed as a "hollow thing." Skilled at labour agitation, the Communists lacked a coherent political program, for they were hobbled by the line of the Comintern and by the plain and simple fact that the CPC was not serious about electoral politics. A handful of candidates proclaiming that "a vote for the Communist Party is a vote for revolution" hardly constituted a political movement, and however desperate they became, the Canadian people continued to have faith in the parliamentary system as a vehicle for the redress of their grievances.[18]

As a result, the momentum of popular protest passed into other hands. The *Canadian Forum* sensed the "growing political consciousness" with excitement:

> Conventions, congresses, conferences; United Front, UFA, Socialist Party of Ontario, League for Social Reconstruction; these and other watchwords pass from mouth to mouth in windswept homesteads on the prairies, in smoking compartments on trains, where down-at-the-heel drummers have taken to talking about nationalization of the banks, and the equal wage, instead of the price of mining stocks. Toronto furnishes an interesting example of a process which is going on simultaneously in every city, town, and hamlet in the Dominion. Half a dozen left wing movements have got underway there. . . . Even the students at the University have founded an enthusiastic radical group. . . . When the Canadian student begins to think about politics instead of merely learning to be a good Babbitt like his dad, it is surely a sign and a portent. . . . Of course a lot of this unaccustomed thinking is immature and woolly . . . but the point is that thinking has begun. And that thinking is revolutionary thinking. . . . In Ottawa several hundred well-meaning persons sit and legislate. . . . They no more represent the new, thinking Canadians than they do the hypothetical inhabitants of the planet Mars.[19]

Out of this ferment arose a new coalition to eclipse the Communist party as the cutting edge of the Canadian left, the Co-operative Commonwealth Federation. Socialist-led, the CCF was saturated with "reds" of varying stripes and hues, including Canadian disciples of exiled Russian revolutionist Leon Trotsky. Unlike the Communists, however, the CCF posed its alternative unambiguously within the tradition of parliamentary democracy. The CCF was a third party, which set out with uncommon zeal to capture by election the municipal, provincial, and federal reins of power.

The CCF began as a Depression-induced alliance of the loose fish still swimming in the political mainstream after the Tory victory in the federal election of 1930. Eleven Progressive and Labour M.P.s from Ontario, Manitoba, Alberta, and British Columbia, behind the leadership of J.S. Woodsworth, announced in May 1932 that they would henceforward be the Canadian Commonwealth Party. Most of them were political veterans first elected in 1921, but time had not dulled the commitment that had landed them in Ottawa in the first place. Said Agnes Macphail, lone woman among them, "I am going to put everything I have into this venture." A convention two months later in Calgary was attended by about fifty farmer and labour militants, the great majority from Western Canada. In deference to strongly socialist opinion expressed on the floor, the party was renamed the Co-operative Commonwealth *Federation* to better describe the coalition that had been forged by bloc affiliations of pre-existing provincial organizations such as the Independent Labour Party of Manitoba or the Saskatchewan Farmer-Labour Party. Delegates adopted a short, eight-point program of principles, among them demands for "suitable work or adequate maintenance" for the unemployed, "equal economic and social opportunity without distinction of sex, nationality or religion," and an economy based on the ideal of "supplying human needs instead of the making of profits." In the months after the Calgary meeting, speakers fanned out across the country; the first CCF rally in Toronto, in November 1932, attracted thirty-five hundred people and signed up a thousand new members on the spot.[20]

More than 150 delegates attended the Regina convention in July 1933, where the election platform of the CCF was hammered together. The Regina Manifesto proceeds methodically – as if its implementation were imminent – to lay out a plan for social ownership and public management of the Canadian economy. "All financial machinery . . . transportation, communications, electric power and all other industries and services essential to social planning" were to be nationalized and operated "not by a small group of capitalist magnates in their own interests, but by public servants acting in the public interest and responsible to the people as a whole." To provide for "a stable and equitable transition to the Co-operative Commonwealth," compensation was to be paid to the former owners, but nationalizations to rescue "bankrupt private concerns for the benefit of promoters and of stock and bond holders" were specifically renounced. Although the CCF was not an overt free-trade party, the Manifesto condemned "the strangling of our export trade by insane protectionist policies," and called for "a national plan of external trade through import and export boards." The farmer was promised domestic price supports and "security of tenure . . . on his farm," but the details of land policy were left to provincial affiliates. This was not a concession to the doctrine of provincial rights – which most CCFers regarded as a capitalist canard – but a sign of the unresolved debate within the federation about the nationalization of farm land.[21]

For workers of hand and brain the Manifesto foresaw a "system of genuine industrial democracy," guaranteed by a national labour code to assist the formation of trade unions which would not simply bargain with management but would "share in control of industry and profession." Universal systems of health care, hospitalization, unemployment insurance, and pensions would also be enacted by a CCF government, after appropriate amendments to the BNA Act – amendments that would not infringe upon minority rights or "legitimate provincial claims to autonomy . . . with the control of local matters." The Manifesto upheld Canada's inherited British traditions of civil liberties, and in a forthright passage that lamented the "alarming growth of Fascist tendencies among all governmental authorities," vowed that the CCF would abolish Section 98. The Manifesto concluded with the oft-cited clarion call that "no CCF government will rest content until it has eradicated capitalism and put into operation the full system of socialized planning which will lead to the establishment in Canada of the Co-operative Commonwealth."[22]

Who were the CCF? Unquestioned choice as the federation's chairman was the bearded, ethereal idealist J.S. Woodsworth, descendant of an old Ontario Methodist family, who had given up the ministry to become dean of the Labour M.P.s. The eclectic character of the movement (as the CCF rightly has been described) can be captured in three of his followers who led the CCF forces in the legislatures of Ontario, Saskatchewan, and British Columbia, where the CCF won 320,000 votes in provincial elections in 1933-34. Sam Lawrence, the one-man CCF caucus at Queen's Park, represented the labourite traditions of the skilled craftsmen of Hamilton, the "Pittsburgh of Canada." Rev. Robert Connell, a heretical Anglican from Victoria, seemed an unlikely leader for the primarily working-class British Columbia CCF, but he yielded nothing to his more proletarian colleagues in his knowledge of Marxist doctrine. George Williams, M.L.A. for Wadena, Saskatchewan, was a farmer long active on the left wing of the agrarian movement who had visited Russia and been branded an "agent of Moscow" for his curiosity. Williams summarized the basic conviction that united a diverse group of men and women into the new federation. "I tell you frankly," he said at a United Farmers' convention, "I have less fear of the radical than I have of the conservative. The visionary may get you into trouble but the ultra-conservative will get you into the graveyard. Today it is more dangerous to drift than it is to try new paths."[23]

The radicalizing effect of the Great Depression and its catalytic effect on the formation of the CCF is best seen in the League for Social Reconstruction, founded in the winter of 1931-32. The LSR began when sixty-eight University of Toronto professors signed an open letter on behalf of the persecuted Communists in their city. The leading spirit of the principled protest was not a Communist or a sympathizer; Frank H. Underhill was a liberal-nationalist historian who had supported the Progressives. The league, guided by Underhill and by F.R. Scott of McGill University, avoided socialism and all other "isms" in its first broadsheets. It grew rapidly in its first year, forming some twenty branches from Montreal west to Victoria. The league was proudly middle class in membership – the CCF's most "dangerously bourgeois element," Frank Scott liked to call it – and public spirited enough to offer its talents to any government that would embrace the LSR aim of social reconstruction through state intervention. A broadly similar group of people moved into Washington in 1933 to become the brain trust of Franklin D. Roosevelt's New Deal administrations, but R.B. Bennett rebuffed LSR overtures in the lexicon of Tory anti-communism, describing it in the Commons as "parlour socialism." Nor had the King Liberals any use for it. It was the fate of the LSR to become the "Brain Trust" of the CCF, an alliance sealed at Regina, where the bulk of the Manifesto was written by Underhill and his LSR colleagues. The CCF had begun its "attempt to fuse the proletariat, the agrariat, and the salariat into a cohesive group on a class-conscious basis," wrote Frank Scott.[24]

The attempt was no more than that, however. The CCF was officially an alliance of the non-communist labour parties in all provinces west of Quebec, the British Columbia-based Socialist Party of Canada, and three farm organizations: the United Farmers of Alberta, the United Farmers of Canada, Saskatchewan Section (there were no other sections), and the United Farmers of Ontario. The UFA was to prove a weak reed, and there is little evidence to suggest that the leadership or the rank and file of the UFO supported the program outlined at Regina. The sad experience of Ontarian Progressivism in the 1920s seems to have erased most of their enthusiasm for third-party experimentation. The CCF had no connection whatsoever with the large farm movement in Quebec represented by the Union catholique des cultivateurs.[25]

Almost all the nation's trade unions made sure that they were not present at the Regina convention. The Trades and Labour Congress, oldest of the four labour centrals, had long since been reduced to a handmaiden to the anti-socialist American Federation of Labor. The Workers' Unity League saw the CCF through the prism of the Comintern; members of the Communist party's politburo denounced social democratic movements as "social fascist," and cartoons in communist newspapers showed "Doctor" Woodsworth giving first aid to capitalism. At meetings of WUL locals, members debated the resolution "That the CCF is unworthy of working class support," a resolution invariably posed by a party member. The Confédération des travailleurs catholiques was reminded by the church that the CCF fell within the papal proscription against socialism. The All-Canadian Congress of Labour did endorse the CCF in the sense that its president, Aaron Mosher, was a member of the national council of the federation, but ACCL member-unions did not rally as a bloc behind it.[26]

Despite this lack of official support, many individual trade unionists or locals of the ACCL and the TLC worked hard for the new party. Jimmy Simpson, one of the elder statesmen of the TLC, was elected mayor of Toronto on the CCF ticket. In the Drumheller Valley of Alberta, TLC-affiliated miners' locals simply held meetings at which they declared themselves to be CCF, in defiance of the formal position of their international. In Manitoba, TLC-affiliated trade unions continued to support the Independent Labour Party after its five-member legislative caucus became the Manitoba CCF.[27]

Labour party, agrarian party, Marxist socialist, Christian socialist: the CCF continues to baffle theorists because it fits no single model. Among the coal miners of Vancouver Island, the CCF was a proletarian party in the tradition of the Socialist Party of Canada. The Vancouver CCF was dominated by Ernest Winch and W.A. Pritchard, the former cadre of the One Big Union on the Pacific Coast. M.J. Coldwell, the school principal who originally led the Saskatchewan CCF, patterned his socialism after the British Fabians, and some CCFers had a British Labour Party blueprint in mind. Yet nowhere was the CCF an ideological import from the United Kingdom. The first batches of the Regina Manifesto were printed free of charge by an ethnic press in Toronto operated by anti-Comintern Finns. Jewish social democrats were prominently represented by federal M.P. Abe Heaps and future national secretary David Lewis. The fifteen rural legislators elected between 1934 and 1938 from Manitoba and Saskatchewan are sometimes used to portray the CCF as a protest party from the immiserated dustbowl, but twelve of the fifteen sat for constituencies outside the drought areas. Five were immigrants born in the American Midwest, brought up on the Populist tradition of raising "less corn and more hell." The one characteristic that all fifteen shared was that they were not only "dirt farmers" but also "leaders of the farm communities . . . the co-op organizers, and the Wheat Pool organizers, and the church workers," people who "practised self-help and democratic association as a way of life." This was the common denominator of the CCF.[28]

The influence of the Social Gospel on many members of the CCF is clearly evident, but the Social Gospel was a way-station for the CCF rather than the intellectual end-of-the-line it had been for an earlier generation of reformers. No Protestant church endorsed the CCF, and the Roman Catholic Church attacked it. A Catholic journal in Saskatchewan described the Regina Manifesto as "inspired by the old Jew

Karl Marx, the father of collectivism and author of the Communist Manifesto.'' Students at Notre Dame College in Wilcox, Saskatchewan, were threatened with expulsion for CCF activity. Such opposition had a telling effect on the fledgling CCF movement, especially in Quebec, where the church brought out its heaviest artillery. When the editor of the *Beacon*, a Catholic paper published in Montreal, noted the similarity between the CCF program and the social teachings of the papacy, the episcopate forced him to publish a Jesuit anti-socialist polemic as a corrective. Even in the face of this hostility the Montreal civic elections of 1933 returned a CCF councillor, and a candidate who professed CCF sympathies was chosen mayor of the working-class suburb of Verdun by an electorate that included many French- and Irish-Canadian Catholics.[29]

The Co-operative Commonwealth Federation is best described, in the words Woodsworth used, as ''a distinctly Canadian type of socialism.'' The movement in its formative years crossed boundaries of race, religion, region, and occupation to receive support from a substantial segment of the Canadian population. Its program, mixed together in the militant mulligan stew of the Regina Manifesto, was indigenous as well. ''I refuse to follow slavishly the British model, or the American model, or the Russian model,'' declared federation chairman J.S. Woodsworth. ''We in Canada will solve our problems along our own lines.''[30]

Not only the CCFers themselves were sanguine about their movement's likelihood of becoming a political force to be reckoned with. Capital was frightened; thus the viciousness of its attacks. And in an article in the *American Political Science Review*, a political economist predicted that ''the CCF could probably within the decade force the Liberals and Conservatives into a permanent union.'' A movement with so many farmers should have known better than to measure the crop until the grain was in the bin. In the Maritimes the seeds were refusing to take root, even in the fertile soil of Cape Breton. In Quebec the anti-socialist spade of the Catholic Church was digging up the tender shoots before they could become established. And in Alberta, home to more than half of the Commonwealthers' federal members, the United Farmers were being crowded out by an exotic ideological weed that was growing wild in the burned-out countryside.[31]

IV

The election of a Social Credit government in Alberta on August 22, 1935, was the most sensational Canadian political event of the 1930s. Only the birth of the Dionne quintuplets won Canada more international attention during the Great Depression. The *New York Times* called the election "incredible and impossible," and the correspondent the *Times* rushed to Edmonton reported that "bankers and businessmen . . . are scared." Several firms transferred their liquid assets outside the province. Behind Social Credit was a ground swell of anger at "the capitalist system" which, as newly elected M.L.A. Joe Unwin said, "put your sons into graves in France, [but] swears allegiance to no flag." "Thinking men everywhere agree that our economic system is decadent," affirmed his colleague E.O. Duke. "We must either destroy the machine or let the machine provide for those displaced by it."[32]

The Social Credit victory was the result of an extraordinary conjunction of circumstances. The Depression alone cannot explain it, for neighbouring Saskatchewan went through greater hardship. The dilemma of the UFA went beyond the failure of the provincial government to cope with the crisis, for the farmers' organization had been weakened and undermined long before the appearance of the Social Credit League. From its inception in 1909, the UFA had always represented an agricultural élite; only for a fleeting moment at the end of the war was it a mass-based popular organization. The 17,486 paid-up members in 1930 were only a sixth of the province's farmers, and a quarter of the membership was in the Women's Auxiliary. Less than a tenth of Alberta farm families were actively partaking of the grass-roots culture of the UFA when, freed from the dominance of Henry Wise Wood, it joined in the formation of the CCF. This decision caused division within the UFA and separated the provincial government still further from the farmers' movement that had given it birth. Far from being an embryonic CCF government, Brownlee and his cabinet ran the province "in direct contradition to many of the principles of the Federation," social democrats in the UFA complained. The Premier himself was not a farmer but a wheat pool attorney who had articled with the firm of Lougheed and Bennett; with the onset of hard times he became increasingly cautious and conservative. No longer an agrarian class movement, the UFA government was a political unit corrupted by fifteen years in power.[33]

A more lurid form of "corruption" appeared to be at work as well, for in the autumn of 1933, John Brownlee was sued for seduction by Vivian MacMillan, a junior clerk in the Alberta attorney general's office. A seven-year court battle, which ended in the Imperial Privy Council, failed to establish the precise relationship between the Premier and his "pal," as the newspapers called MacMillan. The two had a mutually acknowledged friendship begun in the summer of 1930, when the twenty-two-year-old high school graduate enjoyed lunch, a drive, and a dance with the forty-seven-year-old politician in her home town of Edson, a meeting arranged by convivial socialist M.L.A. Chris Pattinson. Brownlee helped Vivian get a government job the following year. Otherwise, the defence and plaintiff's stories were completely at variance. Vivian was supported in her case by her father, a foreman in the CNR's Edson shops, and by a boyfriend, a medical student named John Caldwell. The triumvirate were abetted by the Premier's personal and political enemies, who arranged for them to be represented in court by Neil D. MacLean, a prominent and expensive Liberal barrister.³⁴

MacLean unfolded a shocking tale – or fairy tale – calling Vivian and her prompters to the stand to tell of how the "loathsome lothario" had carnally exploited her. No detail was spared. Vivian claimed to have slept with Brownlee in the Premier's own bed and to have been raped in the back seats of government autos. Pregnancy had not taken place, she alleged, only because she had been forced to take potentially lethal abortion-inducing pills. It was a thirties melodrama par excellence, as MacMillan sobbed that she had endured the pain, the pills, and the humiliation to save her ill-paid probationary civil service position. Brownlee's lawyer had little difficulty in demonstrating dozens of inconsistencies in Vivian's testimony and in that of Caldwell. The jury's decision that Brownlee was guilty was reversed on appeal, but the Premier became a political eunuch the day the Edmonton *Bulletin*, the Liberal daily, splashed "Vivian's Ordeal" around the province in red-lettered headlines, distributing the paper free in some communities. Justice Ives eventually silenced *Bulletin* reporters by finding them in contempt of court, but for several weeks parents stood guard on their porches to keep the offending editions from the prurient eyes of their youngsters. Liberal expectations of electoral profit from Brownlee's disgrace were to be unfulfilled, however, for the political vacuum they had manoeuvred to create was exploited instead by Social Credit.³⁵

Social Credit was the brainchild of a Scottish mining engineer, Major C.H. Douglas. Frightened by the Bolshevik revolution and the deep recession of 1920-22, Douglas became convinced that without reform, capitalism was doomed to give way to collectivism. To save it Douglas presented a new economic theory in a long series of books and pamphlets, the central argument of all of which was a formula he called the "A Plus B Theorem." In the formula, "all payments made to individuals (wages, salaries and dividends)" were represented by A, while "all payments made to other organizations (raw materials, bank charges and other costs)" were symbolized by B. The sum of "A plus B" was then held to equal the total value of all goods produced. Since the producers of the goods received only A as income, they would never have enough money to consume everything they had made. The outcome was "a permanent deficiency of purchasing power," which caused depression and unemployment and which, left uncorrected, would destroy capitalism. The solution was simple: to provide "social credit," which would bridge the gap left by B and keep the economy rolling. The first step was the election of a government, committed to Social Credit, that would wrest control of the financial system from an "irresponsible oligarchy" of bankers and place it in public hands. But Social Credit was not socialism; property would remain in private hands. As a second step, the government would issue a "national dividend" to every citizen, a dividend that he would be required to spend to maintain consumption. To insure that this did not cause ruinous inflation, the government would also establish a "just price" for all goods.[36]

The theorem was deceptively simple and sufficiently vague that it was difficult to refute. As C.B. Macpherson has observed, "it had an almost hypnotic quality," and after several popularizers wrote more readable versions of Douglas's work, Social Credit attracted an international following. Originally conceived for the urban industrial economy of Britain, the theory found a ready audience in the Canadian West. The father of Social Credit in Canada was William Irvine, who "added the Douglas system of credit reform to the armoury of weapons in the western agrarian campaign against eastern capital" by inviting the Major to address the Commons banking committee in 1923. Henry Spencer, a UFA M.P., shared Irvine's enthusiasm and promoted Douglas's ideas within the United Farmers.[37]

But the medicine man who bottled the snake oil of Social Credit, added his own label, and peddled it to the people of Alberta was not a Progressive but a portly evangelist named William Aberhart. Born in Ontario in 1878, Aberhart was an arithmetic teacher who migrated to Calgary in 1910 to advance his career and wound up as the principal of one of the city's best secondary schools. He also migrated from the Presbyterianism of his boyhood, through the Methodist and Baptist churches, to the outer fundamentalist fringes of Protestantism. Aberhart's dominant personality, dynamism, and organizational skills turned the Westbourne Baptist Church into the Calgary Prophetic Bible Institute, of which he was president, dean, and radio personality. The Sunday broadcasts he began in 1925 became the most popular radio program in Alberta, with a higher Hooper rating (the Nielson of the day) than comedian Jack Benny; in the early thirties an estimated 300,000 listened in, spread over the wide range of CFCN's powerful signal. Aberhart preached a theology called dispensationalism, in which he maintained that Christians had no need to consider worldly things and was critical of the Social Gospel emphasis on social concern. "God never intended us to reform the world," he said in a sermon that urged other ministers to "eliminate some of the Socialistic, Political and Economic arguments and give us more of *God's Own Word*."[38]

Various explanations of his sudden interest in Social Credit have been put forward: that he was disturbed by the hopelessness of his students, one of whom had committed suicide; that the new doctrine was intended to improve sagging ratings for his program; that he was passing through a "mid-life crisis" and looked on a political career as a new horizon. The moment of his conversion can be precisely dated. In July of 1932 Aberhart the principal was in Edmonton grading departmental exams when a colleague gave him *Unemployment or War* (1928), a Social-Credit-made-even-simpler book by English actor Maurice Colbourne. He stayed up until dawn absorbing its contents and told the other examiners the next morning that he had discovered a cure for the Great Depression.

Aberhart began at once to inject the "economic movement from God Himself" into his radio sermons. He did not bother to read Douglas in detail, but seized on phrases like "poverty in the midst of plenty," the "just price," and especially the "social dividend." His deviation from dispensational theology cost him fundamentalist support, but his bowdlerized version of Social Credit won him a larger congregation of the airwaves. It was the organizational structure of his evangelical network, not the fundamentalist content, that helped sell Social Credit, for the new listeners were Catholics, Anglicans, members of the United Church. Just as they had earlier set up Bible study groups, Aberhart's disciples Edith Rogers and Ernest Manning established circles for the study of Aberhart's interpretation of the scriptures of Major Douglas; a Social Credit web was woven around the province, with the Prophetic Bible Institute at its centre.[39]

Aberhart disavowed political ambitions. His stated aim was to persuade the Liberals, the Conservatives, or the UFA to adopt Social Credit as their economic philosophy. Many among the UFA rank and file were willing. "Why in the name of common sense can't you fellows make some kind of working arrangement with this man on the subject of Social Credit?" asked an activist from the Airdrie local who cut to the heart of Aberhart's appeal to rural Alberta. "As a boy I was taught that the little Red School house and the little Church on the hill was the only hope of the common people in this world and I believe it yet." To rid itself of the "mixture of fakir religion and fakir economics emanating from Abe's distorted brain," the UFA in 1934 invited Major Douglas himself to Alberta to point out Aberhart's errors. The error was theirs, for the public preferred Aberhart Social Credit to the genuine article. Asked about the "social dividend," Douglas would respond with a theoretical digression; Aberhart would announce that every adult would receive twenty-five dollars a month, with larger amounts to the handicapped. Instead of the "slackening of support of Brudder Abe" that the politicians had anticipated, his ideas became more widely known. "I should think it would begin to percolate through the editorial ivory," wrote a farmer to the editor of the UFA magazine, that "every knock in your slimy paper is a boost for S.C."[40]

Stung by UFA criticism, Aberhart conducted a straw poll among his followers. Ninety-three per cent favoured turning their social movement into a political party. Social Credit's enormous election rallies had the flavour of revival meetings. After a picnic, a martial hymn would summon Aberhart to the platform to inveigh against the "Fifty Big Shots" who were strangling Alberta through their control of the banking system. Liberal and Conservative newspapers tried to tar him with the brush of anti-Semitism because of the overtones of racism the movement had taken on in Britain. Aberhart's attacks on financiers, however, were based on the Western populist anti-monopoly tradition, not the *Protocols of the Elders of Zion*, an absurd Judophobic forgery which Aberhart specifically rejected as untrue. The platform on which his candidates contested the election was more than a reiteration of Social Credit. It called for a "new social order," with a reformed educational system, expanded access to university, aid to co-ops for agricultural marketing, state medicine, and occupational health and safety legislation. In an oblique reference to the Brownlee-MacMillan case, Aberhart promised that in Social Credit Alberta, no woman would be forced into "white slavery" because of her need for a "meal ticket"; instead, women would be "uplifted and made more independent." On the strength of such statements, Social Credit mobilized more women than any other political group of the inter-war period. The final plank of the platform on "planning" faintly echoed the CCF's Regina Manifesto. "I have no brief for our present capitalist system," Aberhart wrote. "There is no hope for recovery until it is abolished. . . . [But] compared with the platform of the CCF and other socialistic groups, the Douglas system embodies all the advantages of Socialism, but eliminates its drawbacks."[41]

Alberta CCFers were trapped. Aberhart had corralled their constituency. They had little influence with the UFA government, which had refused to follow their social democratic blueprint, but they believed that Brownlee had been smeared and framed by reactionaries. William Irvine avoided libel suits by expressing this viewpoint in an allegorical play entitled *The Brains We Trust*, in which a socialist holds the balance of power in a minority parliament until his secretary is "bribed and coerced into lying that the socialist leader had willfully seduced her." The CCF decided to run no candidates (one was eventually nominated) and to endorse instead the UFA. The leadership of the challenge to orthodoxy in Alberta had been lost irretrievably to Social Credit, which had done something the CCF had not yet accomplished: built a "people's party which was based neither on an occupational principle nor on class," which drew the support of farmers, ranchers, workers, and small-town business and professional people.[42]

In a record turnout at the polls, Social Credit brought out voters from the coulees, the hollows, and the most "godforsaken slums" in the cities and the mining towns – thousands of people who had never before cast a ballot for anything or anybody. It was a Social Credit avalanche, fifty-six of the sixty-three seats, set in motion by 54 per cent of the electorate. The United Farmers and their uneasy allies, the Alberta Labour party, were banished from the legislature. The Conservatives joined the Communists as a minor party. The Liberals, who had confidently billed their leader, W.R. Howson, as "the next premier of Alberta," hung on to five seats to remain as the opposition. The handful of CCFers in the UFA ranks were dragged down in the general débâcle. As Chris Pattinson, defeated miner M.L.A. from Edson, reflected sadly, "mass movements do not always go in the right direction."[43]

V

Clinging to office in the face of the Great Depression was a near impossibility for provincial politicians. The only government of 1931 to survive until 1939 was the Progressive regime in Manitoba, and John Bracken scraped through only by coalition with the Liberals and because the opposition Conservatives were crucified for the sins of R.B. Bennett. The defeat of the United Farmers in Alberta was simply part of a pattern; the real anomaly was the victory of Social Credit, the only truly new party to capture a provincial capital during the 1930s. Third parties with radical critiques of Canadian capitalism won public attention and popular votes, but the Liberal party was the principal beneficiary of the distemper of depression. Voters dismissed six Tory provincial governments between August 1933 and July 1935, and each time Liberal governments took their places (see Table III). In Nova Scotia, New Brunswick, and Prince Edward Island the Liberals found it unnecessary to make any ideological changes to regain power. They chose new leaders – Angus L. Macdonald in Nova Scotia, A. Alison

Dysart in New Brunswick, and Walter M. Lea in Prince Edward Island – and issued mildly reformist platforms promising the old age pension and free school textbooks while denouncing the Conservatives for "prodigal expenditure" and for "doubling the provincial debt." Then, with no third parties to disturb them, the Maritime Liberals waited for the Depression and the unpopularity of the Bennett government to do their work for them.[44]

In British Columbia and Saskatchewan the leftward current of the CCF made the political waters more turbulent; in those provinces Liberals had to put their party in drydock to scour off the reactionary barnacles before putting it to sea in an election. The new Liberal captain in British Columbia was the first to hoist the flag of reform. An ebullient, self-assured, elegant little man, T.D. "Duff" Pattullo imported his suits from New York, loved lavish parties at the Empress Hotel, and on occasion sent political opponents roses on their birthdays. He had won and lost fortunes in a business career in the Yukon and Northern British Columbia, but his entrepreneurial background had not taught him the rugged individualist ethic associated with frontier capitalism; instead, it had imbued him with a healthy respect for the power of the state "to encourage the greater development of the country." While the Tolmie Conservatives insisted that "government should conduct itself like a private business firm," Pattullo countered that "government is not an ordinary business, but carries responsibility to meet every problem arising from our complex social and economic conditions in order that not merely a few, but all of our people may live in reasonable comfort." He liked to speak of the reformed economy he envisaged as "socialized capitalism," but Pattullo was not a socialist. His ostensible aim, which he characteristically expressed in the idiom of the poker table, "was not so much to change the game as to redistribute the chips."[45]

The Liberal program drafted in September 1932 vowed to restore Conservative cuts in social services and to introduce a state health insurance plan, to reduce taxes on lower incomes, and to form an economic council on which labour would be represented to study the problem of unemployment. The Liberals promised constitutional co-operation with the federal government to introduce unemployment insurance and urged the establishment of a central bank to make possible an expansionary monetary policy. Pattullo called for massive public investment to put Canadians back to work. In wartime, he argued, "they would use the last dollar and the last man. . . . That's what we propose to do . . . use the national credit for a war on poverty." Obscuring the fact that they would have access only to the crippled credit rating of British Columbia, Pattullo and his candidates campaigned for the election of November 2, 1933, under the banner of "Work and Wages" for every provincial resident. He also ignored the accusation that his promise of a "new deal" run by a "brains trust" of talented advisers from outside politics was copied from American president Franklin D. Roosevelt; the president, he maintained, "had been reading our Liberal platform, and some of our speeches." In any case, the origins or exact details of the program were unimportant. What mattered, wrote Vancouver M.P. Ian Mackenzie to Mackenzie King, was that the party had been forged into an "effective fighting force against the menace of socialism."[46]

The Conservative government literally fell apart, dividing into two hostile camps; the best reason Premier Tolmie could offer voters for re-electing him was that he led "the only group with depression experience." Terrified by the socialist wolf baying at the door of the legislature, prominent Tories urged Tolmie to give up to avoid dividing the capitalist vote. "With the CCF message as serious as I have set forth," wrote a federal M.P., "it might be the best part of wisdom to vote the Liberal party in." Liberal candidates were careful to distinguish their own pragmatic excursion down the road to the welfare state from the totalitarian horrors that would follow the election of the CCF; under CCF dictatorship, warned Gerry McGeer, British Columbia's sons would be forced to attend "a school that propagates Socialism and Atheism" while her daughters would be compelled to live "under the heinous system of companionate marriage." Conservatives deserted their party in droves to forestall a CCF victory: the Liberals took 42 per cent of the popular vote and thirty-four seats while the new party's 31 per cent made it the official opposition but elected only seven CCF M.L.A.s. Only one official Conservative candidate was returned.[47]

The Anderson government in Saskatchewan had tried harder than its British Columbia counterpart to moderate the effects of the economic crisis, but its good intentions could neither raise wheat prices nor cause it to rain. Saskatchewan Liberal leader Jimmy Gardiner was a pugnacious bantam who lacked the geniality of a T.D. Pattullo but who made up for this with ruthless partisan intensity. Under his direction, the party exploited the situation adroitly. Premier Anderson was depicted as the helpless creature of R.B. Bennett and the "bloated plutocrats" from the East, insensitive to Saskatchewan's misery; the members of the Saskatchewan Farmer-Labour party (affiliated with the CCF, but not yet officially renamed) were impractical idealists whose experimentation would only make things worse. The Liberals portrayed themselves as the true keepers of the progressive tradition, and Farmer-Labour as a perversion of it. Everything good in

the program of the socialists – unemployment insurance, medical insurance, protection against farm foreclosures – was available from the
Liberals without the need "that everything must be state-owned and
controlled." Liberal orators equated the Farmer-Labour proposal for
"use-lease" of farm land with the collectivization of agriculture under
way in the Soviet Union. "You will have your land only so long as you
are a good socialist," they cautioned the 70 per cent of the population
who were farmers. "Once in power the CCF will nationalize everything
and not wait for votes."[48]

The outcome of the provincial election of June 1934 echoed the
British Columbia result seven months earlier. Without a majority of
the popular vote, the Liberals took fifty of the fifty-five seats, while a
quarter of the vote and the other five seats went to Farmer-Labour.
The Conservatives were annihilated, cabinet minister and back-
bencher alike. There was one important distinction between the two
elections: support for the CCF in British Columbia had come primarily
in the cities and industrial towns; in Saskatchewan, where the wheat
farmer had been taught by depression that his membership in the
capitalist class could be revoked by a bank or an implement company,
CCF strongholds were in the countryside. In each province, however,
the election was the first stage in the creation of an ideological political
dichotomy in which a party that professed socialism would struggle
for power (with very different degrees of success) with a party that
defined its mission as defending capitalism.

VI

The implications of the Western elections were not immediately ap-
preciated, for the CCF proved to be an insignificant factor in Ontario,
where the Liberals won their most astonishing victory in June 1934.
Howard Ferguson had departed to become High Commissioner to the
United Kingdom, but he had bequeathed a seemingly impregnable
legislative majority to his successor, George Henry. The Liberals had
been out of office since 1905 and had degenerated into a leaderless
agrarian Protestant rump, resolutely re-fighting the battles of the nineteenth century as punch-drunk sparring partners for the perennial
Conservative champions. Their accustomed crushing defeat in the
provincial election of 1929 led them in desperation to draw on the
federal caucus for a transfusion of new blood. Mitchell F. Hepburn had
been only twenty-nine when he snatched Elgin West away from the
Conservatives in the 1926 election, but his flamboyant personality and
impulsive oratory had quickly established the baby-faced onion

farmer as the boy wonder of Ontario Liberalism. Mitch Hepburn combined the bucolic back-concession charm indispensable to Ontario politicians with a street-smart sense of the political jugular that would have done credit to a Chicago ward boss. He remade the party in short order, reaching out to the working class, naturalized immigrants, and Roman Catholics while holding firm to his rural base.[49]

Hepburn claimed to set his course "well to the left where even some Liberals will not follow" and expressed the "hope to see a complete realignment of political thought in this country." He attracted men like Windsor mayor David Croll, a respected leader in the Jewish community, to his camp, and gained credibility with the trade union movement by denouncing the Henry government's use of armoured cars and militia at Stratford. "My sympathy lies with those people who are the victims of circumstances beyond their control," he said with calculated outrage, "not with the manufacturers who are increasing prices and cutting wages at the same time." Hepburn was careful to distinguish his position from CCF socialism. "I condemn in no uncertain terms the abuses of the capitalistic system as it has been practised under the Tory administration," he told an interviewer from the *Farmer's Sun*. But he continued, "I am not out to destroy capitalism." The abuses of Conservative capitalism were catalogued at length, but the Liberal alternatives were never specified. The only policies to which Hepburn committed the party firmly were a "wet" answer to the liquor question and reductions in taxation to be financed by ending Tory extravagance and patronage. Otherwise the Liberal party was fuelled only with the high octane of his demagogy, and the electorate had to take on faith his pledge that "there is going to be a new deal in this province." Asked the inevitable question about Franklin Roosevelt's influence, Hepburn replied that the President had not gone far enough; he advised FDR to jail "the financial brigands."[50]

Premier George Henry frantically tried to brand Hepburn as "the Lenin, the Stalin and the Trotsky of Ontario," and the Conservatives ran a full-page newspaper ad with the caption "Do You Want to Be a Kulak?" under a cartoon depicting Hepburn driving farmers onto a collective farm with a bull-whip. Mitch laughed this off, and it probably only legitimized his attempts to portray himself as a reformer. The real "reds" were the thirty-seven CCF candidates; every rural Ontarian knew that the Liberal leader, a farmer himself, was one of their own. At one country rally the only available stage was a manure spreader. Mitch jumped up and pitched into the Henry government. It was the first time, he said to the crowd, that he had given an address on a "Conservative platform." Alluding to charges that the Premier had profited from the Ontario Hydro takeover of a bankrupt private power company, he continued the rural imagery. "If any of you farmers water your milk you go to jail. But if you water your stock you get to be Premier of Ontario." The United Farmers of Ontario repudiated the endorsement a few of their leaders had given the CCF and lined up behind the Liberals. The election was a landslide in favour of the Hepburn forces. There has "seldom been so decisive a reversal in Canadian political history," was the conclusion of the *Canadian Annual Review*. Attracted by Hepburn's disrespect for sacred cattle and his facility for turning complex issues into pithy platform sloganry, Ontarians had massively chosen him as their youngest-ever premier, giving him control of Queen's Park with seventy of the ninety seats.[51]

VII

The crumbling of the Tory ramparts in Ontario was of small comfort to Quebec's long-entrenched Liberal administration. Premier Louis-Alexandre Taschereau, Chairman of the Board, Province of Quebec (in 1935, he actually held seven corporate directorships), symbolized right-wing Liberalism. But his customary paeans of praise to free enterprise, astringent fiscal policies, and exhortations to "work harder" held no more appeal to Quebeckers than they did to other Canadians. Between 1930 and 1935 Taschereau faced an ever louder, if often discordant, chorus of opposition. The working class, notwithstanding its lack of an independent political voice, was clearly stirring. Most salient, however, were the discontents of a broader spectrum of the petty bourgeoisie, crushed, it seemed, under the double weight of the Depression and the "trusts," large-scale English-Canadian and American-owned enterprises. Badly informed critics in English Canada predicted that "nothing short of a revolution" could dislodge the Quebec Liberals from office. There would be no revolution in Quebec in the 1930s. It took three tumultuous elections (in 1931, 1935, and 1936) to produce even a change in government. The unique social, intellectual, and political fermentation that occurred in the course of French Canada's challenge to orthodoxy during the Great Depression did, however, foreshadow profound changes in Quebec society which became known in the 1960s as the Quiet Revolution.[52]

Quebec, along with British Columbia, was the most gerrymandered jurisdiction in the country, with its urban majority sadly underrepresented in the assembly. Liberal power rested ultimately on the manipulation of a well-financed patronage system and an electoral machine whose apparent omnipotence bred alienation and apathy in the body politic. Quebec's women did not have the right to vote in provincial elections, and over 40 per cent of the male electors did not bother to do so in 1919, 1923, and 1927. The catalyst for change was a phenomenon known not by its party stripe, which was Conservative, but in the personalized idiom of Quebec politics as "Houdism." Camillien Houde, born in 1889 in a garret on a Montreal street so poor it had no name, was a fiery nationalist politician first elected to the assembly as deputy for Montréal Sainte-Marie in 1923; in 1929, he captured the leadership of the moribund Quebec Conservative party. His personal recipe for success in provincial politics was simplicity itself: to find a way of inducing large numbers of traditional non-voters, proletarian or petty bourgeois, to come forward on election day and cast a ballot against "the clique."[53]

"Houdism" briefly crystallized the currents of critical nationalist thought of the 1920s that intersected with the new imperatives of the economic crisis. At the zenith of his influence, *"le p'tit gars de Ste-Marie,"* who served nine terms as mayor of Montreal, acquired another nickname: "the Canadian Mussolini." An idealized, Catholic view of Italian "corporatism" popularized in the twenties by nationalist historian Abbé Lionel Groulx, and in the thirties by a legion of French-Canadian (and Italo-Canadian) ideologists, was one of the most important intellectual cross-currents of the era. Houde did treasure his personally autographed portrait of Il Duce, although legend has it that he also kept an unsigned copy of Marx's *Kapital*, just in case the mood of either the masses or the intellectuals should shift decisively leftward. Quebec's genuine fascists, led by the anti-semitic polemicist Adrien Arcand, denounced Houdism as a species of political "gangrene," for Houde was above all an opportunist who combined an ethnically based nationalism that recalled the *Patriotes* of 1837 with populist demands for economic reform and social justice. "They accuse me of being a demagogue," he told Quebec radio audiences, "because I ask for a pension of ten dollars a month for the widows, the orphans, and the elderly." His litany continued, "They accuse me of being a denigrator of reputations because I denounce the [men who] sell out our natural resources to the Americans and force our own people to emigrate across the line . . . and because I denounced those responsible for the loss of Labrador."[54]

Houde's visceral message transcended barriers of language and race; as one of his English-speaking followers wrote to Premier Taschereau in 1931, "*Your* life is finish . . . we are going to shoot you. . . . You have over 1000 famileys in Quebec [City] starving . . . mayor Houde of Montreal said you should of been killed long ago." Houde led his troops into electoral combat with the Liberals in August of that year. Liberal organizer Chubby Power described the campaign as "an almost classic instance of the opposing of the masses to the classes," a re-enactment of "the French Revolution with Taschereau in the role of the aristocrat on the way to the guillotine, and Houde, his head crowned with the red cap of liberty, driving his cart to its lethal destination." The provincial Conservatives captured just over 44 per cent of the vote, and the intensity of the campaign had galvanized three-quarters of the electorate into casting a ballot. Yet only eleven Conservative members were returned to the ninety-member assembly. Ominously, Houde refused to concede these results. In an unprecedented departure from Canadian parliamentary tradition, he mounted judicial challenges to the Liberal victors in sixty-three ridings.[55]

According to *Houdiste* tradition, there had been blatant electoral fraud and intimidation of voters, even by members of the American-controlled underworld in Montreal. It is clear that the Liberal machine had thrown every available ballot, valid or not, into the struggle to defeat Houde in his own constituency. Taschereau dismissed Houde's charges as an "insult to our Province and to our race," and convened the new assembly in special session. The key item on the order paper was the so-called Dillon Act, framed so as to make Houde's recourse to the courts a practical impossibility. Taschereau skillfully exploited post-election schisms within the Tory opposition, between *Houdistes* and the traditional *bleu* forces led by Maurice Duplessis, forty-two-year-old deputy for Trois-Rivières. Taschereau regarded "My Dear Mr. Duplessis" as a more gentlemanly – and weaker – opponent than the "scoundrel" Houde; on the Premier's instructions the Liberal machine had pulled its punches against Duplessis in a narrow race. Taschereau won Duplessis's tacit support for the controversial post-electoral law, thereby precipitating an open bloodletting in the shattered opposition. Supported by the Tory old guard, Duplessis snatched the prize of leadership for himself at the party's 1933 Sherbrooke convention. With Duplessis cast in the role of Brutus, the Premier thankfully proclaimed the "death of Houdism" in Quebec.[56]

Once the Conservative threat to Liberal hegemony had seemingly evaporated, the focus of political debate shifted to within the ruling *bloc* itself. The margin of the Liberals' paper victory in 1931 encouraged factionalism in their own ranks. In early 1932, five Liberal M.L.A.s refused to heed the party whip during the vote on an important piece of legislation while a sixth, Oscar Drouin, was outside the legislature organizing a demonstration against it among his Quebec City constituents! At issue was the government's long-standing policy of granting concessions to Quebec's privately owned electrical companies, bitterly opposed by advocates, like Drouin, of the "Ontario system" – public ownership of utilities. Taschereau wisely withdrew the offending bill, but the struggle proved to be the opening shot in a full-scale political revolt. Dissident spokesman Jean Martineau, a well-known Montreal lawyer and Liberal activist, articulated the broader aims of the anti-Taschereau movement, lashing out at all governments in Canada "for adopting policies dictated by the twenty-five bankers and financiers in control of the Canadian economy." The solution, he urged, lay in "Liberalism which tends to the left, towards socialism."[57]

Abetted by at least one prominent federal Liberal, Ernest Lapointe, the dissidents organized themselves into a reform caucus called Action Libérale, ostensibly dedicated to the advocacy of progressive legislation within the context of the existing leadership. They were younger Liberals for the most part, already "too emancipated," in the words of one Taschereau loyalist, from a healthy spirit of "discipline and deference" toward their elders. If not, as the Premier's men charged, disappointed office-seekers, some were active spirits driven to political agitation by the absence of meaningful jobs for themselves or for others. Unlike Houde, they were not children of the dispossessed. Paul Gouin, who would – with Martineau as a key lieutenant – become the leader of the dissident forces, was the thirty-five-year-old son of Sir Lomer Gouin. He had begged the Premier in 1931 for "a chance to do honour to my name and something, within my own sphere, for our people"; he received no satisfactory reply.[58]

An amateur historian and economist, Gouin was an intellectual with no real political experience. He rose to the front rank of the Action Libérale Nationale, the new title adopted by the rebel Liberal movement, in June 1934, after Taschereau made it painfully clear that the dissidents had to choose between support for the government and open opposition. Fainter hearts, including all but one of the elected Liberal members (Drouin), abandoned the effort. Lapointe made a separate peace with the Premier, removing the main personality to whom the dissidents had looked for leadership. Gouin's credentials rested largely on the fact that his "political heritage and impeccably orthodox nationalist views" forestalled attacks on the ALN as a radical, leftist movement. Nonetheless, he acquired a zest for militant politics. Lacking corporate backing, Gouin appealed to the working population for funds: "A dollar for the ALN is a dollar against the trusts!" In one year, the ALN sponsored eighty rallies, held as far afield from its Montreal-Quebec City base as Lac St. Jean, and forty radio broadcasts. But the ALN enjoyed neither the charismatic leadership of Alberta Social Credit nor the modicum of ideological cohesion of the CCF. As the third-party movement expanded beyond its original constituencies it attracted a motley collection of supporters whose commitment to

Gouin's objective of the reliberalization of Quebec Liberalism was secondary to other goals. Some were disgruntled Tory partisans; others were ideological crusaders offended by Premier Taschereau's cordial relations with Quebec's Jewish community or because "Liberalism prepares the way for the Freemasons' seizure of power," as the parish newspaper *La Bonne Nouvelle* put it. Paradoxically, there *was* an arcane conspiracy close to the ALN in its formative period. The Order of Jacques Cartier, an anti-masonic secret society with a goal of Catholic and French supremacy, appears to have made a serious bid to infiltrate and control the new movement.[59]

The ALN made public its *programme* in the pages of *Le Devoir* in July 1934, citing the need, "in Canada and in the Province of Quebec," for a "dual transformation" in both economic and political spheres and praising the example set in the United States by a "regenerated" Democratic party. For a movement with supposed separatist and indubitable nationalist elements in its mainstream, the ALN's statement was surprisingly silent on basic constitutional questions. It made repeated reference, instead, to avenues of federal-provincial collaboration on specific policy matters and denounced the use of jurisdictional conflicts as a "pretext" for governmental inaction. The ALN document began with a detailed section entitled "Agrarian Reform," calling for improved agricultural credit, rural electrification, and the encouragement of co-operative marketing, but the first plank in the platform, "the planning and execution of a vast programme of colonization," was a hoary conservative panacea for Quebec's industrial and urban woes. Labour reform came second. The ALN manifesto eschewed any reference to socialism but emphasized the "priority of wages over dividends," a concept antithetical to the functioning of a capitalist economy. It proposed a new labour code but, unlike the 1933 Regina Manifesto, did not spell out any actual goals of such a code, such as the encouragement of unionization or worker co-management of industry. Proposed electoral reforms were much more concrete, and spoke directly to the furor over the Dillon law. The ALN proposed identity cards for voters in towns of over 10,000, strict regulation of party financing and campaign spending, and obligatory voting, yet refused to endorse the elementary democratic reform of women's suffrage. Its most ringing language was reserved for its most important economic reform, "the destruction, by all possible means, of the strangle-hold which large financial institutions, the electricity trust and the paper industry have over the Province and the municipalities." The ALN manifesto has been praised as a "refreshingly practical" departure in the history of French-Canadian nationalist politics, but it remains in many ways a curiously flawed and incomplete statement.

At the very least it failed to reflect the wide range of political viewpoints encompassed in the ALN. This may have stemmed from the fact that no free-wheeling policy convention hammered out the ALN platform; instead, its origins lay outside Quebec's political milieu.[60]

To attract powerful supporters and ideological legitimacy, the young reformers had adapted their manifesto from a document published in November 1933, the *Programme de restauration sociale*. The *Programme* had been written by Catholic laymen active in the confessional unions and the farm organizations during the course of a series of study sessions under the direction of Father Joseph-Papin Archambault. A Jesuit and head of the Ecole sociale populaire, Archambault wielded extraordinary influence among Catholic intellectuals in Quebec. Gouin himself had been active in Catholic youth organizations, which gathered behind the ALN. The philosophical thrust of the *Programme*, and thus of the ALN manifesto, derived from Pope Pius XI's 1931 encyclical, *Quadragesimo Anno*. The encyclical attacked the "abuses of capitalism," rejecting – as the church had always done – the practice of economic liberalism. The document served as a reminder that Christianity was a far older institution than capitalism, in no logical way synonymous with it. In the same breath, however, the encyclical excoriated the evils of communism and of socialism which, according to the Pope's world-view, would inevitably lead to communism. In this sense neither the encyclical nor the reform ideas of the Ecole were profound, for they chose to ignore one possible and logical alternative that *was* spoken of in Catholic Quebec in the 1930s: a *Christian* form of socialism. Henri Bourassa, the idea's most prominent advocate, warned in 1933 against the dangers of *anti*-socialism, which might indeed lead to communism. His old comrade Olivar Asselin read the ALN statement and dismissed it as a *"bleu"* document because of its timidity. Blinkered by the need to oppose both capitalism and socialism simultaneously, the men of the Ecole sociale populaire had put forward an agenda which, in the words of Abbé Groulx, was aimed "against the trusts" but also "against the CCF." When the problematic position of the church was translated into the program of Action Libérale Nationale, it meshed with the structured ambiguity of the élite-led third-party movement with ultimately disastrous results for the cause of reform in Quebec.[61]

In 1935, however, the movement appeared very radical indeed, and Premier Taschereau viewed the political landscape without enthusiasm. "I cannot comprehend the attitude of the Reverend Jesuit Fathers," he confessed to a sympathetic cleric. "At the request of the highest religious authorities we have fought the communists and the disturbers of order. . . . And yet these people [go] as far as many communists." Nor was Cardinal Villeneuve, Quebec's highest religious authority, altogether pleased; such clerical musings as "in ordinary times, superfluous riches should be shared with the poor as a matter of charity, in times of crisis, as a matter of justice" attracted the critical attention of His Eminence. Neither the Premier nor the Cardinal could silence the din. Pushed now by an instinct for political survival, Taschereau himself took up the cudgels against the men of the trusts; he denounced the coal combine, "the source of a great deal of dissatisfaction in our Province, especially in Montreal." Unfortunately, combines-investigation lay in the federal domain, and the refusal of the Bennett government to co-operate resulted in a complete lack of action to buttress these words. It was revealing to witness the proud Taschereau begging *Ottawa* for a prosecution.[62]

CHAPTER 11

The Bennett Débâcle

I

The political upheavals in the provinces only complicated a federal-provincial relationship severely strained by the Great Depression. The Vancouver *Sun* compared the battles over relief costs between the Bennett and Tolmie governments, both of them Conservative, to "an Eskimo and a Hottentot endeavouring to discuss Einstein's relativity," and the description could be extended to the acrimony between Ottawa and every other provincial capital. While R.B. Bennett and E.N. Rhodes stood guard over the federal money that the provinces needed to meet ever-increasing relief bills, the easy accord that followed the Dominion-Provincial Conference of 1927 was impossible to maintain; during the 1930s meetings between premiers and prime ministers were rancorous. Little real discussion took place, for Bennett called the premiers together to announce his policies, not to invite provincial guidance in shaping them. In January 1933 he demanded their assent to a constitutional amendment to permit a federal unemployment insurance program and provincial contributions toward paying for it. When the incredulous premiers asked for details, Bennett had none; what he wanted was carte blanche approval in advance of any scheme upon which his government might decide. Ontario, Quebec, and the Maritime Provinces not surprisingly refused their consent. Without any action or a cent in expenditure, the conference had been made to serve an important ceremonial purpose, "to create the illusion of action in the fight against unemployment."[1]

In order to justify reduction, not expansion, of federal expenditure for the unemployed, the relief systems of the four Western provinces had been investigated at Bennett's instance by Charlotte Whitton, director of the Canadian Council on Child Welfare. Eager to discredit amateur relief administrators, Whitton reported a tangle of inefficiency that could only be unwound by the appointment of professional social workers like herself. To the chagrin of its author and the misery of relief recipients, the federal cabinet interpreted the Whitton report as confirmation that the provinces were wilfully mismanaging federal funds. At the Dominion-Provincial Conference of January 1934, the Prime Minister exploded in "an extraordinary diatribe," hectoring the premiers for extravagance and suggesting that the Prairie Provinces give up old age pensions, telephones, and electrical service to "maintain the financial integrity of the nation." After threatening to cease federal aid to unemployment relief altogether, Bennett launched the main attack: as of August 1, 1934, federal grants would no longer be one third of the total expenditure but a lesser figure based on the "proven need" of each province as determined unilaterally by the federal cabinet. When the "negotiations" were finished, federal support had been reduced by 20 per cent overall, although Quebec and the three newly Liberal provinces, Ontario, Saskatchewan, and British Columbia, were cut back most heavily. The Conservatives had no intention of aiding their political opponents as a national general election drew near. The partisan dimension exacerbated the feeling that the provinces had been "put off like poor relations . . . in a niggardly, ungenerous way." In more than a decade in Ottawa, wrote Winnipeg *Free Press* correspondent Grant Dexter, "this writer has never known a Dominion-Provincial Conference which went so deep in stirring up resentment."[2]

Yet the provincial governments treated their mayors and reeves exactly as they had been treated by the federal government, passing the increased burden on to the municipalities. Further municipal tax increases were impossible. Ratepayers were simply turning their buildings over to the city, which was no more able to sell them than the former owners had been. "At the rate we're going now," claimed an Edmonton mayoral candidate, "it won't be long before the entire city is owned by the city." In Greater Toronto every municipality except Forest Hill and Swansea was bankrupt and under trusteeship by July 1934. The trustees adopted the policy of the elected councils of the still solvent municipalities; they passed the buck to the unemployed by squeezing the relief budget and tightening regulations for eligibility. It was the "strict letter of the Constitution" that was the problem, complained George Weir, the university professor whom T.D. Pattullo had persuaded to become Provincial Secretary of British Columbia. "In some respects the British North America Act is quite antiquated," he told Pattullo. "It may afford a legal but not a scientific, or human, justification for inaction. . . . The Fathers of Confederation, in the [eighteen] sixties, were quite unable to foresee conditions such as obtain in Canada at the present time."[3]

The constitutional question was academic to the million Canadians still on the dole; their pressing problem was the source of the next meal. Unemployment declined to 497,000 in September 1934, but the number on direct relief stubbornly refused to show a corresponding decrease. There were several reasons for this. As a Prince Edward Island farmer noted of his neighbours, after four years of depression "many formerly well to do people are at the end of their resources" and were forced at last to apply for public assistance. Henri Bourassa attested gravely to the destruction of the "small bourgeoisie" of his city: "There are today on the paupers' list of Montreal men who for twenty, thirty or forty years worked earnestly and honestly." With a third of the nation out of work, the acceptance of relief had become slightly less a disgrace. A "jobless white collar woman" who had "starved in her room rather than accept charity" after losing her job, could now write of her plight in *Maclean's*. "Heretofore [she explained] when one was out of a job, nobody understood. One was branded a failure. Nobody believed you could make good. Now the whole country is aroused." These new applicants were only part of a worsening relief dilemma. "The longer families are on relief the greater their needs," replied a Manitoba deputy minister asked about his overspent budget. "Clothing needs are greater, and consequently the costs of clothing are mounting. As a family continues on relief it comes to rely to a greater extent for their intimate needs. . . . The net result is that costs per individual are increasing, and even though in some cases the number of individuals shows a slight decrease, the cost is greater."[4]

Once accepted on the relief rolls, a breadwinner was reluctant to take temporary work or seasonal jobs like harvesting for fear he would be unable to get back on when the job came to an end. Nor would relievers travel to seek work, for stories abounded about families that had done so only to become lost in a no man's land, unable to satisfy the residence requirements of any municipality. The tale that most touched the nation was that of Edward and Rose Bates and their young son, Jack. When their butcher shop in Saskatchewan failed, the Bates family sold everything they owned to make a fresh start in the grocery business in Vancouver. When the second store went under, Vancouver refused them relief. The Salvation Army paid their way back to Saskatoon, where they were also rejected as non-residents. An attempted family suicide was as unsuccessful as their relief applications; Jack was the only one to die, and his anguished parents were held for murder by the RCMP. The Saskatchewan jury, however, refused to convict Edward and Rose Bates. Instead it blamed the Depression as the boy's killer and named as an accomplice "R.B. Bennett's unemployment policy with its insistence on local responsibility for the jobless."[5]

II

In contradiction to the constitutional rigidity displayed in its relief policy, the Conservative government's broadcasting policy asserted federal leadership. An unusually wide consensus among business, farm, labour, and religious groups supported the Aird Report's recommendation of a national broadcasting system, and their case was forcefully presented by the Canadian Radio League, organized by three young nationalists: Alan Plaunt, Graham Spry, and Brooke Claxton. By posing the question "Britannia rules the waves – shall Columbia rule the wavelengths?" the league persuaded Bennett that for radio the alternatives were "the state or the United States." After a 1932 decision of the Judicial Committee of the Privy Council established Ottawa's jurisdiction over broadcasting, the Bennett government created the Canadian Radio Broadcasting Commission to ensure "complete Canadian control of broadcasting . . . so that national consciousness may be fostered . . . and national unity strengthened." Empowered to regulate licensing, content, and advertising, the CRBC could also purchase or appropriate private radio stations. Its small budget, however, precluded large-scale nationalization and set the pattern for the development of Canadian broadcasting as a mixed public and private enterprise, borrowing from both the American and British solutions to the radio question.[6]

Encouraged by the popularity of their broadcasting legislation, the Prime Minister and some of his colleagues seemed at last to stumble to the conclusion that their folk-remedies of high tariffs and individual responsibility would neither cure the country of the Depression nor ensure them of re-election. "We cannot float much longer," concluded R.J. Manion, "unless we are anxious to hand over the country to the gentle communistic ideas of Mr Woodsworth and his gang." The Bank of Canada Act was a sudden reversal of the government's long-standing opposition to a central bank. A former director of the Royal Bank, R.B. Bennett had echoed the Canadian Bankers' Association line that it would be dangerous to "disturb the existing system with its proven efficiency and stability." The ruthlessly deflationary policies of the chartered banks, however, guaranteed that this faith in the perfection of the system would be shared by an ever-diminishing number of Canadians. "After four years of producers' depression and bankers' prosperity," commented CCF M.P. Angus MacInnis, "abusing bankers has become a pastime as popular as bridge."[7]

Even Bennett's faith was undermined. Although there was nothing in his public pronouncements to suggest that he disagreed with the banks' tight money policy, he wrote privately to the Bankers' Association to protest their "forcing to the wall customers who are unable to meet liabilities." This disapproval was demonstrated in the appointment of the MacMillan Royal Commission on Banking and Currency. On the commission's recommendation, legislation passed in June 1934 established a central bank to "mitigate fluctuations in the general level of production, trade prices and unemployment . . . and generally to promote the economic and financial welfare of the Dominion."[8]

Farmers had been the most numerous victims of the credit contraction. To them, bankruptcy was more painful than to other small businessmen, for it meant the loss of a home as well as a livelihood. The Farmers' Creditors Arrangements Act was designed to allow families to "remain upon their farms, rather than lose them through foreclosure," by imposing a government-appointed board between a debt-burdened farmer and the lenders hounding him for payment. Through voluntary agreement if possible, compulsory arbitration if it were not, the board was to "write down" debt to manageable proportions and draw up repayment terms which would give the farmer a new start. The FCAA compromised the Conservative government's adamance about the sanctity of private contracts, but the sharpest ideological about-turn was the Natural Products Marketing Act. After four years of stout government denials that free market mechanisms could be improved upon, the NPMA established a federal marketing board with authority over all "natural products of agriculture and of the forest, sea, lake or river" that were exported or sold across interprovincial boundaries. The national board was to set up local or provincial boards at its own initiative or at the request of producers' groups. If the board was supported by a majority vote, all producers of a commodity were compelled to obey its marketing regulations under penalty of a fine and/or imprisonment. This "industrial self-government," promised Minister of Agriculture Robert Weir, would enable farmers, fishermen, and lumbermen to plan production rationally and to obtain better prices through "orderly marketing" as opposed to cutthroat competition.[9]

Debate on the marketing act was protracted and contentious. The bill, said one Liberal, had been "drafted under the searching eye of the dictator." Another spoke of "communism in our marketing" that would have to be forced upon primary producers at bayonet-point. To Mackenzie King the boards would be "self-appointed soviets"; by delegating parliament's authority to non-elected boards, the Conservatives were abandoning the British tradition for "what they have in Russia." This amused the CCF supporters of the legislation. "It is a decidedly interesting experience for me," said J.S. Woodsworth, "to hear [Liberals] denounce the Conservatives for having copied the Russian plan."[10]

Liberal hyperbole aside, neither the NPMA, the Bank of Canada Act, nor the FCAA was a sign that R.B. Bennett was aping Joseph Stalin. In each case the legislation was radical only when measured against previous Tory bombast about economic individualism. Many of Canada's export competitors had marketing boards of the type proposed by the NPMA, and the act did not impose boards on groups of producers who did not request them. Some who did – wheat growers, for example – were not covered by a board despite their requests. Most other capitalist countries had had central banks for some time, and the Bank of Canada was to be privately owned and virtually independent of government. The only government director on the bank's board, Deputy Finance Minister Clifford Clark, would not have a vote. Asked what would happen in the event that the Bank of Canada and the cabinet disagreed over monetary policy, Finance Minister Rhodes was unequivocal: ". . . unquestionably . . . the board of directors of the bank would prevail." The Farmers' Creditors Arrangements Act, wrote one economist, was no more than "a belated piece of compensatory adjustment" for the damage done to the primary industries by the tariff increases. More moderate than the debt adjustment acts of some provinces, the FCAA was supported by banks and other creditors as an alternative to more radical legislation.[11]

Joining the CCF in their complaint that the Bennett government had not gone far enough was W.R. Motherwell, former Liberal agriculture minister. He urged that the FCAA be extended to all debtors as the first stage of "a truly reformed capitalism . . . adjusted to suit the requirements of today." This, he pleaded, "would stop the mouths of these men who are talking socialism and nihilism and communism and all those other isms. . . ." Were Bennett to take this step, Motherwell continued, he "would be looked upon as the great emancipator of the white slaves of Canada . . . just as Abraham Lincoln was the emancipator of the dark slaves of the South." The Prime Minister demurred. "Unfortunately," he explained with condescension to his septuagenarian colleague, "there is a constitution in this country that imposes even upon me limitations and restrictions."[12]

III

Another Tory was more eager to don the mantle of reform and be hailed as the saviour of Canada's petite bourgeoisie. H.H. Stevens was one of them, a self-taught accountant who had had an indifferent career as a grocer, insurance agent, and real estate broker. Stevens's success as a politician stood in contrast to his lack of it as a businessman; perhaps because of this he disliked the wealthy and powerful almost as much as he disliked radicals of the left. Although steadfastly loyal to the Conservative party during his quarter-century as M.P. for Vancouver, Harry Stevens resented the influence that big businessmen enjoyed within it. Little of this resentment showed in public during his four years as Bennett's Minister of Trade and Commerce, as he unfailingly defended government policies, from the tariff to Section 98, in parliament and on the rubber-chicken circuit. Thus Stevens was routinely chosen to substitute for the Prime Minister as speaker at a shoe retailers' convention in Toronto in January 1934.[13]

His performance was anything but routine. Harry Stevens used the stage at the Royal York Hotel to denounce "unfair or unethical trading practices" that had "developed like a canker" until they threatened to "destroy the system" itself. The Depression had made these practices worse, but the cause was economic concentration; Stevens chose Canada Packers as one of his illustrations, but the blackest villains of his melodrama were the major department stores. They used their mass buying power to blackmail manufacturers into selling to them at unrealistically low prices; small merchants, unable to obtain their merchandise on the same terms, were forced out of business. In the frantic scramble for survival, small manufacturers and retailers cut wages and imposed sweat-shop conditions on their workers. Stevens made it plain that he was not a socialist coming out of hiding. The "independent citizen-businessman," he concluded to his cheering audience, was "the finest expression of democratic life to be found anywhere." The capitalist system had not failed; a few big capitalists had failed the system. "Decent businessmen" were urged to help him correct the abuses and to "save the civilization we are proud to call Canadian."[14]

Stevens's speech was an outpouring of the hostility that had long simmered within him brought to the boiling point by complaints from workers, entrepreneurs, and farmers received by his department. Stevens was also prompted by fears about the future of his party; as he later told a Conservative study group, "real conservatism does not consist of being allied with or dictated to by large financial influences, but . . . must find its influence in the home and on the farm where real opinions are formed." To survive, he went on, "this Conservative party must readjust itself"; Harry Stevens regarded himself as the most likely leader for a "readjusted" party. R.B. Bennett showed no sign that he feared this. He reprimanded his minister for the unilateral policy statement but did not consider dismissing him. The government could ill afford a public blood-letting, and if Stevens had offended Eaton's, his speech also attracted favourable letters at the rate of one hundred a day. Instead of the sack, Stevens was given the chairmanship of a parliamentary special committee to "investigate the causes of the large spread between the prices received for com-

modities by the producers thereof, and the price paid by the consumers therefore."[15]

Staffed by members who shared Stevens's small-business bias, the
Price Spreads Committee met sixty times during the session of 1934,
uncovering an iceberg of evidence to support its chairman's allega-
tions. When one of his big business targets was giving testimony
Stevens made no pretence of impartiality and acted as "accuser, pros-
ecuting attorney, judge and executioner." J.S. McLean of Canada
Packers was reminded that since 1929 his company had averaged an
annual profit of $900,000 while the farmers who toiled to raise the cat-
tle and hogs had been paid "ruinous prices" for their animals. Gray
Miller of Imperial Tobacco heard his salary of $25,000 a year plus
bonuses compared with that of a clerk in one of Imperial's United
Cigar Stores, who earned $25.45 for a fifty-four-hour week. Other
witnesses received more sympathetic treatment. Professor Harry
Cassidy of the University of Toronto reported on the men's clothing
industry, in which workers put in sixty hours for a weekly wage that
left them "close to or below the borderline of abject poverty." The
most dramatic price spread uncovered was revealed in the testimony
of seamstresses who did piece-work for department stores. For sewing
together a dozen dresses, Annie Wells told shocked M.P.s, she was
paid 9½¢; each dress sold in Eaton's Toronto store for $1.59. The
committee's hearings made front-page news in a hundred dailies and
were followed by the public like a radio soap opera. Canadians were
fascinated at the exposure of the inner workings of the corporations
that ran their lives, and Stevens was hailed as the champion of the little
man, oppressed by the "arrogant and heartless profiteer." When the
Commons adjourned in July, the Prime Minister elevated the committee to the status of a royal commission so that its public theatre could
continue.[16]

Stevens was never to preside over the royal commission. The inquiry had made "Mr. Price Spreads" a national figure, but it had
undermined his position within the cabinet. Several of his fellow
ministers had the most intimate connections with the same "Captains
of industry" whom Stevens was revealing as "economic dictators."
Stevens overplayed his hand with a supposedly private speech in
which he accused the directors of Robert Simpson Limited of "milk-
ing" $10 million from the company and selling unsuspecting em-
ployees stock that was "not worth a snap of the fingers." Somehow
the speech was printed as a pamphlet by the Dominion Bureau of
Statistics, and despite government attempts to suppress it, portions appeared in the Winnipeg *Free Press* and the *New York Times*.
Simpson's president, C.L. Burton, threatened legal action. When an

angry cabinet demanded that Stevens apologize, he resigned his portfolio and the chairmanship of the Price Spreads Commission, although he continued to sit as an ordinary commissioner and a Conservative back-bencher. [17]

Coming after crushing provincial defeats in Ontario and Saskatchewan in June and four federal by-election losses in September, Stevens's October departure seemed to ring the final peal in the Conservative death knell. His letter of resignation claimed that he had been "thwarted in his efforts to remedy economic abuses by reactionary members of the cabinet" and was taken as evidence of the triumph of the "right" over the "left" within the Conservative caucus. The "right," led by C.H. Cahan (nicknamed by some colleagues "Dino," short for dinosaur), stubbornly insisted that the Depression would "go like a mist before the summer sun" if economic *laissez-faire* and budgetary restraint were continued. The "left," with Stevens as its martyr and R.J. Manion its surviving cabinet spokesman, called for increased public works spending and such regulation of the economy as might be suggested by the Price Spreads Commission. The once dominant Bennett had become strangely marginal to the debate; a disgruntled Conservative complained that he was "sulking in his tent." He had not given a public address in months, and at the height of the Stevens affair and in the midst of the by-election campaigns vanished for six weeks to lead the League of Nations delegation at Geneva. The Prime Minister's silence appeared to confirm that he had sided with the reactionaries. Bennett, wrote United Church minister Francis Stevens to his famous father, "has shown himself for what he is – a man keenly in time with the thoughts of ice-cold financiers and steely-hearted big business men but utterly removed from the thoughts and feelings of the common people." [18]

IV

Tall, stout, dressed in striped trousers and tails, double-breasted waistcoat and silk hat, R.B. Bennett was the robber baron of a cartoon in *Masses* or the *Worker* come to life. Then in a national radio address broadcast live on January 2, 1935, this caricature capitalist revealed to astounded Canadians, "I am for reform. I nail the flag of progress to the mast. I summon the power of the state to its support." Expecting some scepticism, he explained that between 1930 and 1933 "it would have been the height of folly to attempt to introduce reform until the first fury of the depression had been brought under some sort of control . . . a false step might have led us to disaster." In 1934 the

Farmers' Creditors Arrangements Act, the marketing act, and the Bank of Canada had been "the initial measures in the Government's reform program." In the four half-hour talks that followed his New Year's revolution, the Prime Minister outlined the rest of what came to be known – although he never used the phrase on the air – as the Bennett New Deal. In ten days that shook Canada, he spoke of legislation to regulate hours, wages, and working conditions; insurance against sickness, industrial accidents, and unemployment; an extended NPMA and a "far-reaching agricultural credit program." An Economic Council of Canada, composed of the nation's best minds, was to be created to advise the government. As for the "avaricious industrialists, unscrupulous big business wizards and financial promoters who exploited the people," their activities would continue to be investigated; when the Price Spreads Commission's report was ready, parliament would act "to put a stop to these iniquities." Nor would this be all. "I will not pretend to give you a full and detailed statement," said Bennett in his fourth address, "for my program is not yet complete. . . . Earnest men and women who put their country first" would not cavil over details but would unite in support of the "broad principle and practice of reform." The exceptions would be "selfish men . . . whose mounting bankrolls loom larger than your happiness, corporations without souls and without virtue – these, fearful that this government will impinge upon . . . their immemorial right of exploitation, will whisper against us."

The Liberal party would support such men, Bennett charged in his fifth and final broadcast on January 11. "Liberalism . . . has no intention of interfering with Big Business. For Liberalism stands for laissez-faire and the unrestricted operation of the profit system and the complete freedom of capitalism." Reducing the issue to partisan terms, the Conservative leader gave his listeners a choice: "If you are against reform, back Liberalism with all your might . . . if you believe in reform, then support my party."[19]

The content of the broadcasts was a surprise, but the rest was pure Bennett. After stumbling over his text in the first address, he quickly adapted his platform style to his new medium, speaking with the "intensity of a preacher extolling temperance or threatening hell-fire." For the first time, wrote a reviewer, a politician had spoken "almost literally to the whole people," or at least to all of them who understood English. Families without radios gathered around neighbours' sets for "Bennett parties," listening intently to the renegade millionaire's indictment of unrestrained capitalism. In a renewal of his one-man approach to party leadership, Bennett paid for the air time from his personal bank account; his cabinet learned of his plans just as the public did – via the airwaves. "I haven't any idea what he will cover," wrote Robert Manion to his son midway through the series; "he has done all this off his own bat entirely, at least as far as we are concerned."[20]

Where had it all come from? Immediate comparisons were made to the New Deal of American President Franklin Roosevelt, then approaching its second birthday. The sudden announcement of a vast legislative agenda seemed to replicate the President's "hundred days" of 1933 and was an imitation of his frequent "fireside chats" on U.S. networks. Bennett's American connection was William D. Herridge, Canada's minister to the United States. An Ottawa lawyer married to Bennett's sister Mildred, Herridge was the closest thing the solitary prime minister had to a confidant. "The speeches," speculated Chester Bloom, the Winnipeg *Free Press* Washington correspondent, to J.W. Dafoe, "bear plenty of internal evidence that Herridge, not Bennett, is the author of their major portions. . . . The Canadian legation has at all times been open house to the New Deal Crowd." The speculation was correct. Herridge, in collaboration with Bennett's executive assistant, Rod Finlayson, had done most of the speech writing. What had impressed Herridge about the American New Deal, however, was not the Roosevelt programs – which he considered to have failed to achieve their object of recovery – but its positive effect on national morale and on the political fortunes of Roosevelt's Democratic party. As Herridge explained in a memo to his brother-in-law, ordinary Americans didn't understand the legislation of the New Deal "any more than they understood the signs of the zodiac." What Bennett was meant to emulate was Roosevelt's public relations success, to persuade Canadians that his own program would "do everything for them *in fact* that the New Deal here has done *in fancy*." The direct influence of the American example on the Bennett New Deal as it later unfolded was minimal.[21]

Bennett and Roosevelt had a larger objective in common, nonetheless. Both pledged their governments to interventionism in order to save capitalism in North America, not to end it. For all the strong language of his broadcasts, R.B. Bennett underlined that the "keystone of the capitalist arch was the profit system" and that the Conservative party still stood for the "freedom of the individual and private initiative and sound business." When unhappy Tories suggested that his radio rhetoric had earned him a cell in Kingston alongside Tim Buck, Bennett justified it in terms of the need to contain the rising tide of radicalism. "Tim Buck has today a very strong position," he wrote to a New Brunswicker unwilling to follow his new direction. "He openly demands the abolition of the capitalist system. A good deal of pruning is sometimes necessary to save a tree, and it would be well for us in Canada to remember that there is considerable pruning to be done if we are to preserve the fabric of the capitalist system."[22]

The New Deal was also intended to be a political preservative for the Conservative party. The radio addresses were the opening of the campaign for the election that had to come in 1935, and their immediate effect was exactly what the authors had hoped for, as they were well received by the press, the public, and within the party itself. The New Deal, said Toronto Tory Tommy Church, was *"the best news that our Proletarian population have had since the depression started"*; Harry Stevens told reporters that he would stay in the Conservative caucus. C.H. Cahan and E.N. Rhodes were furious, but neither resigned and the façade of cabinet solidarity was maintained. Important sections of the business community were alienated – given their portrayal in the speeches, it could hardly have been otherwise – but their criticism, expressed editorially in the *Financial Post* and the Montreal *Gazette*, added lustre to Bennett's image as a reformer unafraid to challenge Bay and St. James streets.[23]

But whatever momentum the government had gathered dissipated rapidly when parliament opened a week after the final radio address. The Speech from the Throne rephrased the radio talks in much milder language, promising "to remedy the social and economic injustices now prevailing" and to ensure "a greater degree of equality in the distribution of the benefits of the capitalist system." Conservative strategy depended upon the Liberals, goaded by the partisan diatribe of the fifth address, to use the debate on the Throne Speech to attack the New Deal. The Conservatives would then ask for a dissolution and go to the people as outraged reformers obstructed by a reactionary opposition. The Liberals refused to do as expected. Instead, Mackenzie King's tactic for "dealing with the New Deal" was to demand that the government put up or shut up. King read from *Industry and Humanity* to prove that he had been the "first" to propose the social reforms now offered by the Conservatives, implied that Bennett's reformism was a "death-bed repentance," and sat down. J.S. Woodsworth expressed pleasure that both major parties had accepted parts of the CCF platform: ". . . it would seem that we are all pledged, and the reforms should be passed in the present session."[24]

Instead of the usual three weeks, the debate had lasted three days, forcing the Conservatives to reveal the embarrassingly meagre portion of the heady concoction on Bennett's radio menu that was actually ready to be served up on the order paper. Three acts providing for an eight-hour day, a six-day work week, and a federal minimum wage were passed almost without discussion. The centrepiece of the new

Conservatism, the Employment and Social Insurance Act, was delayed because the bill was still at the printers. When the details were disclosed, the promised health insurance was missing, and the unemployment insurance scheme, which was the core of the bill, was very limited in scope. Although the government claimed that it put Canada "on a fair level with Great Britain," the plan fell far short of its British counterpart. A long list of exemptions – farm workers, unskilled seasonal workers, longshoremen, teachers, nurses, civil servants – left more than 40 per cent of wage earners unprotected. The government contribution was to be one sixth of the cost as compared to one third in Britain, and the waiting period for eligibility was longer while the benefit period was shorter – thirteen instead of twenty-six weeks. The regressive flat-rate premium fell more heavily on lower-paid workers, yet the maximum weekly payments, $6.00 for men and $5.10 for women, provided for only the barest subsistence. The amounts were, critics noted, lower than those paid under the Unemployment Relief Act of 1930. CCFers drew attention to these deficiencies and Liberals worried about the constitutionality of the measure, but neither group attempted to block the bill. It passed second reading 101 to 0 and third reading 123 to 3, unheard-of unanimity for important legislation.[25]

Unopposed, said J.L. Ralston, the New Deal had been exposed as a "series of measures which prove to be only a hollow echo of the flow of fulsome rhetoric with which they were announced." Tiring of his experiment, Bennett sank back into his pre-broadcast malaise. In late February he left the Commons complaining of a cold and did not return until mid-May. The official medical explanation was a "cardiac arrhythmia," translated for the reporters as a "mild heart attack." The Prime Minister was not hospitalized but instead remained incommunicado in his suite at the Chateau Laurier. On April 18 a sudden improvement in his health permitted him to depart for England to celebrate the Silver Jubilee of King George V, and for the next month newspaper columns were filled with his weekend at Windsor Castle, his state dinner at Buckingham Palace, and his prominent role in every ceremonial function. With Bennett's absence it became painfully obvious that there had never been a New Deal beyond the words put into his mouth by Herridge and Finlayson. As Robert Manion confessed, "his reform program (whatever it is) has been kept largely in his own hands," and the legislation already drafted, "while all to the good from a reform and progressive standpoint, could not quite fulfill his suggested plan." His strategy in ruins, W.D. Herridge concurred: "The colour has faded from the reform picture. . . . Our big, beautiful reform child is almost dead."[26]

Attempts to resuscitate the New Deal after its parent's return from

Britain were unsuccessful. The Dominion Trade and Industry Commission Act fell far short of the recommendation of the Price Spreads Report for a fair trade commission with broad powers to deal with the abuses catalogued by the inquiry. The new trade commission was to exist only on paper, for no new federal agency was actually created; instead, the already overburdened Dominion Tariff Board was asked to wear two hats. Although given authority to investigate unfair trade practices, the commissioners were provided with no means to enforce fair ones. This was "deliberate sabotage" of the Price Spreads recommendations, suggested economist V.W. Bladen. Asked to compare the Dominion Trade and Industry Commission with New Deal regulatory agencies in the United States, economist C.A. Curtis responded that it was weaker than the U.S. Federal Trade Commission set up by President Woodrow Wilson a quarter-century earlier![27]

In its original form the Canada Grain Board Act, last of the New Deal legislation, came closest to fulfilling the radio promise. As a former merchant of grain himself, R.B. Bennett had brought to office an antipathy to government intervention in the marketing of wheat. The unprecedented catastrophe that struck the wheat economy, however, drew him inexorably toward such a step. In 1930 he had assumed federal responsibility for the liabilities of the Prairie co-operative wheat pools to avoid heavy losses to the banks that had loaned them money. John I. McFarland, manager of Bennett's Alberta Pacific Grain Company, was engaged to dispose of the bankrupt pools' stocks of wheat. As the price continued to plunge McFarland, with Bennett's blessing, used federal money to buy instead of sell, hoping to prevent an even steeper price decline. By 1935 the government owned 235 million bushels of wheat – the equivalent of two thirds of the total crop in a normal year – while the price still hovered at half of pre-Depression averages. "Why kid ourselves," wrote Harry Stevens to McFarland, "that there is going to be a restoration of normal trade?" The grain board proposed in June 1935 was to have a monopoly of the marketing of coarse grains as well as wheat, to take control of all elevators used in interprovincial transport, and to control all wheat exports. This was too much for the Liberals and for the private grain trade, which fought the bill with every means possible. When a segment of the Conservative caucus rebelled against the "step in the direction of state socialism," Bennett backed down. Amendments emasculated the act so that in its final version it covered only wheat and was stripped of its monopoly powers. By failing to fight for the one measure that had truly offended a powerful vested interest, R.B. Bennett had himself driven the final nails into the coffin of his New Deal.[28]

V

A more eloquent epitaph for Bennett and his government was being written across Western Canada by the Depression's most tragic victims, unemployed single men. After 1929 the transient army of workers that had cleared the bush, built the branch lines, and stooked the grain as the country moved westward found that the unemployment that had once been their temporary winter's tale had become permanent. Instead of work, each spring brought a new graduating class of the dispossessed to join them, boys facing manhood without the remotest prospect of a job, let alone a career. Municipal relief denied to them, they were left to the capricious mercy of private charity: the hostel and the soup kitchen. "I estimate," wrote one of them, "that this scheme breaks the spirit of the average man within a year; hence I chose the road." Some seventy thousand other young Canadians did the same, learning the ways of the hobo as they beat their way across the country in empty boxcars, looking for work that didn't exist. "Canada's untouchables" was what a United Church minister who ran a mission for homeless men called them; "the municipalities steer them off, because if they are arrested as vagrants . . . it costs a dollar a day to keep them. So the word is 'keep them moving.' The CPR police advise the men that it is better travelling CNR and the CNR police return the compliment." At the end of a week, a month, or a year, a man was "perched somewhere else like an owl on a limb and is not any farther advanced, except perhaps that he might be just so many miles further from nowhere."[29]

The hungry, hollow-eyed faces beneath the peaked caps aroused near panic in some respectable citizens, but the "crime wave" predicted from the drifters never happened; like the rest of the economy, crime went into a slump in the 1930s. The single unemployed were a greater menace to public health than to public safety; with four thousand of them living in Vancouver's hobo "jungles" amid piles of decaying garbage, the city's medical officer of health warned of "the grave danger of an epidemic of typhoid or other disease." The contagion that frightened governments to action was political, not medical, and its carriers were the cadres of the Communist party of Canada. To prevent the ragged platoons of the single unemployed from being forged into the "storm troopers of revolution," Chief of the Army General Staff General Andrew McNaughton proposed the creation of a system of work camps. "By taking the men out of the conditions of misery in the cities and giving them a reasonable standard of living and comfort," McNaughton explained persuasively, the government would be "removing the active elements on which 'Red' agitators could play." The Department of National Defence was authorized to carry out McNaughton's plan in October 1932, absorbing the camps already operated by some provincial governments. By June 1933, camps for the single unemployed were functioning in every province save Prince Edward Island. At its peak in 1935 there were more than two hundred camps in the system, and 170,000 men passed through them during their three-and-a-half-year existence.[30]

Other than transients pulled off trains, in a strictly legal sense no one was compelled to enter a DND camp. The only coercion applied was the threat of starvation. Nor was anyone forced to remain, although the camps were located as far as possible from cities, and no return transportation was provided. The camps were scattered geographically and ranged in size from those with fifty inmates to a half-dozen capable of accommodating two thousand, so that it is difficult to generalize about physical conditions. Men grumbled about meat "doped with salt petre" and "bedbugs too fresh and eggs not fresh enough," but they were fed, sheltered, clothed, and provided with rudimentary medical care. There were strict codes of behaviour, but military discipline was not enforced; army personnel who acted as foremen and administrators wore civilian clothes. Inmates worked a forty-four-hour week on military construction projects or building roads, clearing land, and cutting railway ties. The twenty cents earned for each day worked violated minimum wage laws but was described as an allowance rather than a wage for work performed. When first set up the camps received praise from all quarters, including the Trades and Labour Congress. Although "not an economic paradise," they were felt to provide the single unemployed with a life "a good distance removed from destitution."[31]

Yet from their inception the camps were detested by the men consigned to them, for they perverted the values that they had been supposed to sustain. Inmates lost their most fundamental democratic right, the vote, for the camps were not considered "domiciles" under franchise legislation. Their work was without dignity, heavy labour done without machinery and designed primarily to keep them busy. Efficiency and the quality of the finished product were of little consequence. "We are playing at highway building," recorded a striker in his diary. "What a joke we are . . . We make a ditch one day and then change the plans and find that it is in the wrong place." After work there was nothing to fill the hours. "Not one cent of public money has been spent . . . on reading material and recreational equipment," bragged a bureaucrat blind to the implications of his boast. Although their minimal physical needs were provided for, relief camp inmates had "no laughter in [their] hours, no hope in [their] young lives." "It is not the condition of these camps that makes us get up and howl for something to be done about our state,'' wrote one of them. "It is really the fact that we are getting nowhere in the plan of life – we are truly a lost legion of youth – rotting away for want of being offered a sane outlet for our energies.''[32]

During their first nine months of operation there were fifty-seven serious disturbances in the camps. In one of these RCMP Inspector L.J. Sampson fell from his horse and was dragged to death as he led a mounted charge against a demonstration in a Saskatchewan camp; in another, the Long Branch camp in Ontario had to be closed when the seven hundred inmates refused to work, despite their supervisors' blandishments. The official explanation in all cases was that a "communistic element" had caused the problems. The Workers' Unity League had chartered a Relief Camp Workers' Union to organize the camps, providing Prime Minister Bennett with evidence that the disturbances were "directly traceable to subversive elements." This claim, however, was as exaggerated as the rest of his fears of revolutionary conspiracy. The communists themselves, never modest about their achievements, admitted that "we would be incorrect to assume credit for everything in the way of struggle that has been waged," and that many of the relief camp protests were "spontaneous in their growth and outbreak." The Relief Camp Workers' Union only co-ordinated these spontaneous outbreaks into a concerted campaign against the work camp system.[33]

In April 1935 the RCWU led half the seven thousand inmates of the "slave camps" in British Columbia in a mass exodus; 1,800 of them converged on Vancouver, refusing to return until promised "work and wages," workers' control of the camps through elected committees, and their federal franchise. Public sympathy for the strikers was demonstrated by the success of their "tin canning" on street corners, which raised $22,000 from local citizens to buy food and rent halls for sleeping quarters. To publicize their demands, strikers snake-danced through department stores and briefly occupied the Art Gallery. They quickly became part of the city's active working-class movement, helping to swell to 25,000 the crowd that celebrated May Day in Stanley Park. Red-baiting Mayor Gerry McGeer claimed that Vancouver was "up against a Communist revolution" and ordered four hundred city police and RCMP to parade through the streets to thwart "Communism, hoodlumism and mob rule." The central strike committee provided him with few excuses to move against them. Demonstrations were orderly and demonstrators well behaved; the RCWU was so well organized, remembered striker Steve Brodie, that "you couldn't slice a loaf of bread into five bologna sandwiches without appointing a committee." After two months in Vancouver, however, the union was no closer to obtaining its demands. With strikers beginning to melt away, the leaders decided on a new tactic. On June 3 and 4, twelve hundred strikers, cheered by "a large crowd composed of all classes of Vancouver citizenry," clambered abroad freights heading east. "Few of the mass contingent," reported the Vancouver *Province*, "were more than 30. . . . Canadian youth was sending its delegation to Ottawa to demand a place in the country's society."[34]

The "On-to-Ottawa" trek gave the relief camp strike back its momentum, and the strikers their morale. "Tanned and smoke-grimed, white teeth gleaming in faces black as coal heavers," they waved from the tops of the boxcars to every "man, woman, child or dog" that watched at trackside, alerted by radio news broadcasts as to the progress of the trek. The discipline that had been developed in Vancouver was maintained on the road, and recruits who flocked to join were rejected if deemed unlikely to adapt to it. Their exemplary demeanour won the trekkers the support of towns and cities along their route. In Golden, British Columbia, they were met at their camp-ground by local women with "various kinds of make-shift cooking vessels," one a full-sized bathtub, "full to the brim with simmering, bubbling, thick, heavenly-smelling beef stew." In Moose Jaw city policemen stripped off guns and tunics to join the Junior Board of Trade serving meals to the trekkers. "I expected them to swarm across the tracks like a mob," wrote a reporter of the trekkers' arrival in a prairie town. "Instead they formed fours immediately on descending from the cars . . . then marched townwards in real army style." This discipline, which won the hearts of citizens, struck fear into those of governments; but municipalities co-operated in hope of a speedy departure, and provincial governments made no attempt to stop the trek. They displayed, in the words of a trek leader, "a marked reluctance . . . to pull the federal chestnuts from an extremely hot fire."[35]

Most of the eighteen hundred trekkers who rode one hundred box-cars into Saskatchewan were "a very fine bunch of young men . . . not showing any connections of a communist sort," but leaders Arthur "Slim" Evans, George Black, John Cosgrove, and James "Red" Walsh made no secret of their communism. Twelve hundred men were waiting in Winnipeg to join the trek, and the prospect of three thousand of the unemployed "under the direction of certain Communist elements" moved the federal government to action. Over Premier Gardiner's protest that they "had no right to stage the affair in Saskatchewan," the RCMP was ordered to halt the trek at Regina. The men were billeted at the stadium and fed at dominion expense, while Mounties guarded the railyards and roads to block their departure from the city. R.J. Manion and Robert Weir, sent west to evaluate the situation, reported public sympathy was "largely with the strikers" and that "strong measures will have to be taken to curb this movement." To buy time to prepare these measures, a delegation of trekkers was invited to Ottawa to present their demands in person.[36]

Slim Evans, spokesman for the delegation, was a hawk-nosed man in his mid-forties whose deep-set eyes had good reason to burn with resentment. His attempts to rouse the working class had cost him three terms in prison, one a conviction under Section 98. Bennett listened to Evans's description of the "hopelessness of the relief camps" without hearing it, interrupting frequently. The inmates of the camps had "been used better than most people in this country," he maintained; work was "the one thing [they] do not want." This lecture was too much for Evans, who pronounced Bennett "not fit to be the premier of a Hottentot village." The interview lost all semblance of decorum. "You could have told us all this by wire," shouted one of the delegates as they were escorted out of the Prime Minister's office.[37]

After the confrontation with the cabinet, the meal tickets that had been provided to the trekkers were cut off. The RCMP threatened to prosecute under Section 98 any citizen who gave them aid, and the illegal but effective blockade of provincial highways continued, so that the trekkers were bottled up in Regina, unable to leave and unable to support themselves if they stayed. On July 1 trek leaders addressed a rally for donations to pay train fares for a retreat to British Columbia. Fewer than a third of the 1,700 listeners that evening in Market Square were relief camp strikers; tired of speeches, most of the boys had stayed at the Exhibition Grounds to watch a ball game. The meeting was quiet and orderly until police whistles shrilled at the fringes of the crowd. Mounted Police Deputy Commissioner S.T. Wood had chosen the moment to make a mass arrest of Evans and the other speakers. Plainclothesmen stormed the platform, while from a nearby garage and from four furniture vans, steel-helmeted constables rushed into the square, "waving baseball bat batons overhead." For three months the strikers had refused to be provoked into a conflict. They hesitated, while the police lines closed upon them, and then exploded, fighting back with sticks, rocks, bottles, and their bare hands. From eight until midnight they battled five hundred Mounties and city police in the side streets; when it was over, "downtown Regina was a shambles. Not a store with a window left in it, the streets piled up with rocks and broken glass, dozens of cars piled up in the streets with no glass in them and twisted fenders and bodies." One plainclothes policeman was dead – killed in error by the police during their first charge, alleged the strikers – and thirty-nine were in hospital. Thirty-nine strikers and Regina citizens were also treated for injuries, half of them gunshot wounds inflicted by police revolvers. Other injuries went unreported for fear of arrest.[38]

The On-to-Ottawa trek had been violently broken up two thousand miles from its goal. One hundred and twenty people were arrested, but only twenty-four came to trial and only eight were convicted. Most of the rest accepted the Saskatchewan government's offer of passage home; some returned to the relief camps. For Bennett and his government, however, the Dominion Day bloodbath was a Pyrrhic victory. Bennett had made his New Deal speeches to "pick up some of Roosevelt's appeal"; the RCMP suppression of the trek instead roused recollections of Herbert Hoover's order to General Douglas MacArthur to disperse the Bonus Marchers of 1932. Editorials condemned his actions as "those of a dictator rather than the head of a great and free people." His explanation that the trekkers had intended to imprison his cabinet and establish a Canadian Soviet was derided as ludicrous. "[Bennett] has done more to create communism than any ten men in Canada," countered the Vancouver *Sun*.[39]

VI

There were no monthly Gallup polls to chart the government's terminal condition, but its symptoms were manifest. In provincial elections in June and July the last two Tory governments fell by astonishing margins: only eight Conservatives were returned in New Brunswick's forty-eight constituencies, and on Prince Edward Island the Liberals carried every seat. On July 6, the day after the seventeenth parliament prorogued for the last time, Harry Stevens announced that he would lead a new party into the autumn federal election, a Reconstruction party dedicated "to the plight of youth" with a program of non-socialist reform. He claimed to be responding to twenty thousand requests. "It may sound mushy to say this to a bunch of hard-boiled newspapermen," he said at his press conference, "but I simply felt I could not desert those 20,000 people." Stevens's schism won many rank-and-file Conservatives, most notably in Ontario, Quebec, and Nova Scotia. No M.P.s bolted to the heretic, but many incumbents refused to seek renomination. Led by E.N. Rhodes and a half-dozen other ministers, nervous Tories sought shelter from the gathering electoral storm in the Senate, on the bench, or on a government-appointed board. In the sort of cabinet shuffle that a later generation of journalists would describe as "rearranging the deck chairs on the *Titanic*," the Prime Minister plugged the holes with the limited resources available. "Mr Bennett," gloated the *Canadian Forum*, "promised in 1930 . . . that he would end unemployment or perish in the attempt. The opportunity has now arrived for the electorate to invite him to perform the second half of his promise."[40]

Conservative defeat no longer had Liberal victory as its corollary. Besides the candidates put forward by the old-line parties, there were 174 Stevens Reconstructionists, 118 CCFers, and 45 Social Creditors, emboldened by their success in Alberta. Eighty-one other candidates joined the field, including eleven Communists, a Technocrat, and a detective suspended from the Ottawa police who ran on an Anti-Communist ticket pledged to "struggle against Communism and the Jews." The bewildering array of aspirants for the October 14 balloting totalled 894 – 363 more than in 1930 – and reflected the ideological turbulence of the mid-thirties. Voters in Verdun, Quebec, had a choice among eleven candidates. Because of the "fantastic extra groups bedevilling our electoral machinery," despaired *Saturday Night*, "the likelihood of . . . a good working majority is fading. People want a change but it is doubtful if enough of them are willing to change over to Mr King to make possible the formation of a Liberal government."[41]

Despite pressure from within his own party to do so, Mackenzie King refused to allow the presence of the new parties to budge him from the strategy of cautious non-commitment he had pursued since 1930. He had brusquely rebuffed proposals of National Liberal Federation president Vincent Massey for a national policy convention, and when T.D. Pattullo called for "definite and concrete" party positions on "finance, social welfare and public works," King pointed to the series of by-election and provincial victories as proof that "we have not suffered by failing to be more specific." A new program that could compete with the CCF and Social Credit, begged for by Western Liberals, was rejected as dangerous and unnecessary; "there is nothing which can prevent victory to the Liberal cause," he warned Alberta leader W.R. Howson, "but possible cleavages or divisions within our own party." The Liberal election statement provided no cause for disunity, speaking of a "just distribution of wealth with increasing regard to human needs," but other than the abolition of Section 98 offering no hint as to how this might be accomplished. It would certainly not be done by the state, for the document was an affirmation of classical economic liberalism, and King in his speeches described the halting interventionism of the Bennett New Deal – most of which he had supported in parliament – as a step "in the direction of Hitlerism, Fascism or Communism." The Liberal leader, commented a journalist after an interview, had been "influenced in a rather interesting and unique way by the depression. While most statesmen and politicians have swung sharply to the left . . . King has come back much more to the middle of the road, almost to the right."[42]

King "really occupies the Conservative seat," concluded former prime minister Robert Borden, "while Mr Bennett has conducted the Conservative party into extreme, even radical paths." Other formerly Conservative businessmen apparently agreed. A last-minute flurry of corporate generosity enabled the Liberals to finance a campaign to make the double point that their party was the only way to restore national harmony and the only safe route to political change. A widely distributed billboard captioned "A United Canada Will Solve Your Problems" featured a map of the country with portraits of the eight Liberal premiers superimposed in a group around Mackenzie King to symbolize the contrast to Bennett's war with the provinces. But the master-stroke of the Liberal campaign came from two Toronto ad men who came up with a catchier way to put the message across. Their slogan "It's King or Chaos" brought political marketing up to date with that used to sell breakfast cereal, toothpaste, and deodorant soap.[43]

The Liberal "policy of having no policy" produced a parliamentary majority that flabbergasted prognosticators – 173 of the 245 seats. Liberals carried every Maritime constituency except one in southern New Brunswick and won fifty-five in Quebec. With fifty-six of Ontario's eighty-two, the Liberal caucus from that province was the largest since 1874. In Manitoba and Saskatchewan Liberals won thirty of thirty-eight ridings and even in that Liberal graveyard, British Columbia, managed six of sixteen. Only Alberta, where the siren song of Social Credit seduced the voters, ran against the tide; just one Liberal, James MacKinnon, in well-to-do Edmonton West, was able to eke out a plurality.[44]

The hundred-seat majority made the election of 1935 the most one-sided since Confederation, but the popular vote suggested otherwise. In Saskatchewan, Alberta, British Columbia, and Ontario and on the island of Montreal, the Liberal vote had actually declined in comparison with that of 1930. Overall, wrote Escott Reid, "in their hour of smashing victory in 1935" the Liberals had received a smaller share of the popular vote than they had "in the hour of their crushing defeat in 1930." As Blair Neatby has put it, "if the choice was between King and chaos, more than half the voters preferred chaos" (see Table Ie).[45]

The most obvious trend was a "Dominion-wide landslide away from the Conservatives." With only forty M.P.s elected and less than 30 per cent of the popular vote, Bennett had led his party to a greater disaster than that of 1921. Once again the Tories were driven back to a narrow regional base: twenty-five of the survivors were from high-tariff industrial Ontario. All five Conservatives from Quebec were anglophones who sat for largely English-speaking areas. More than the Depression was at work here, for Bennett had been unable to consolidate the beach-head of 1930 by integrating French Canadians into the party and the party into French Canada. In the midst of the campaign Canada's apparent support for League of Nations sanctions against Italy because of the invasion of Ethiopia enabled the Liberals to revive the bogies of imperialism and conscription; one pamphlet warned that "if the Conservatives won, the blood of young French Canadians would stain the waters of the Mediterranean." Against this a Conservative campaign based on the need for Section 98 to repel the "Bolshevik menace" did little more than earn Bennett the support of Adrien Arcand, leader of the fascist Parti national social chrétien. "Mr Bennett claims to combat Communism," wrote the editors of *Le Devoir*, "but it is against Italy, the worst enemy of Communism, that he proposes sanctions."[46]

The pattern in the Prairies, for different reasons, matched that of Quebec: all the headway made in 1930 was lost, as only one Conservative was returned from each province. The inequitable rural-urban distribution of seats saved five Tories in British Columbia, but from Manitoba westward the party polled only 24 per cent of the vote, a figure identical with that gained by the CCF in its first federal venture.[47]

Matching the Conservatives in the West was little consolation to the crestfallen Co-operative Commonwealth Federation. The CCF had gone into the election with fifteen M.P.s and emerged with only seven – three in British Columbia and two each in Manitoba and Saskatchewan – or eight if Agnes Macphail, elected as a United Farmer of Ontario/Labour candidate, is included. The entire Albertan CCF contingent was wiped out by Social Credit, which was successful in a third of the constituencies it contested, fifteen in Alberta and two in Saskatchewan. The unfairness of the single-member constituency system in a multi-party contest was one reason for the CCF's poor showing. With twice the national popular vote of Social Credit, it elected fewer than half as many Members of Parliament. In British Columbia the CCF's plurality of 97,000 votes won two seats fewer than the Conservative party's minority of 71,000. But the dilemma of Canadian social democracy cannot be explained that simply. With only 118 candidates nationally, of whom just 50 were in Ontario, 3 in Quebec, and none at all in the Maritimes, the CCF revealed that it was as much a party of Western regional protest as a party of socialism and confirmed the Liberals' claim that they were the only alternative government.[48]

For Harry Stevens and his Reconstruction party the election was an unqualified disaster. They attracted the support of the Canadian Retail

Merchants Association and of other small business groups, but only in Nova Scotia were they able to broaden their base to include working-class elements. As CCF candidate Graham Spry sneered, "a nation of shop-keepers may defeat a Napoleon, but a party of shop-keepers will hardly even fool itself." Reconstructionists received 8.7 per cent of the national popular vote, but it was spread so thinly across the country that only Stevens was able to win a seat. The pattern was the reverse of that of the CCF, with the greatest Reconstruction strength in the Maritimes and Central Canada; an attempt to coalesce with Social Credit failed, and the party was no more than a negligible factor in the West. The votes the Stevens candidates captured were blamed by the Conservatives for the loss of as many as forty seats, but only a half-dozen could realistically have been saved had the renegade stayed a Tory. In 1937, his party long since dead, the prodigal returned to the Conservative caucus.[49]

The two-party system so recently restored had proven too brittle to accommodate Canadian diversity exacerbated by the strain of depression. As in 1921 it had broken down, but unlike 1921 the fragmented opposition lacked even the illusion of cohesion that the Progressives had projected. Regional and national divisions ran as deep as ever, class divisions deeper, but national disunity was masked behind the bland visage of Mackenzie King; if not first in the hearts of his countrymen, he was the undisputed leader of their political nation. The overwhelming parliamentary majority was, to be sure, part good luck and part the result of an electoral game whose rules produced wildly inequitable results when there were more than two players. It was also, however, a tribute to his skill as a tactician, and would be laid alongside the King-Byng thing as one of the foundation stones of the Mackenzie King legend of political infallibility. The victory of 1935 demonstrated the suitability of his unheroic concept of leadership to the Canadian context; in Canada, as King repeatedly proved, "out of ambiguity can come political longevity."[50]

CHAPTER 12

King and Chaos

I

The William Lyon Mackenzie King reborn as prime minister in October 1935 was just two months short of his sixty-first birthday and a
long way removed from the political neophyte who had painfully
pieced together his first administration in 1921. In the intervening
years he had struggled with an expanding waistline and conceded
defeat to a retreating hairline, but politically he yielded to no one. His
Liberal party was in a position of unparalleled strength, and his paramountcy within it was equally secure. During his exile in opposition
King had found time to indulge more deeply his long-standing curiosity about spiritualism and had taken part in seances, but he summoned
no spirits from the beyond to help him with the cold calculations of
cabinet making. Among the flesh-and-blood advisers consulted, only
Ernest Lapointe played a decisive role. At his insistence two former
ministers from Quebec whom King had intended to exclude, P.J.A.
Cardin and Fernand Rinfret, became Public Works Minister and
Secretary of State respectively, and Chubby Power was made Minister
of Pensions and National Health despite King's "not wanting in the
cabinet men who drank." For all his influence, however, the senior
colleague from Quebec was not, as has been suggested, a "co-prime
minister." Lapointe had no similar authority in the choice of ministers
from other provinces, nor was he able to dictate the distribution of
departments to Quebeckers. Even his own Justice portfolio was a compromise, for King retained Lapointe's initial choice of External Affairs
for himself. [1]

King pointedly ignored Mitch Hepburn's advice and ignored the city
of Toronto also, choosing his Ontario group from "the four corners of
the province." Minister of Trade and Commerce W.D. Euler and Postmaster General J.C. Elliott had been members of his government in the

twenties, but the other two were newcomers. Norman Rogers, a Queen's University political economist who had served as a speech-writer for King, was symbolically placed in the Ministry of Labour, which had been the stepping-stone for another young intellectual. Clarence Decatur Howe, a civil engineer from Fort William whose company was the country's largest builder of grain elevators, became Minister of Transport, a combination of the departments of Railways and Canals and Marine. This was one of several amalgamations King made to reduce the size of the cabinet; the reduction also meant that he broke the tradition of a minister from every province. Alberta's lone Liberal was left on the back benches "to teach that province a lesson." Prince Edward Island was also left out in the original selec-tion, but when Charles Dunning left his Montreal business career to return to the Finance Ministry, a seat was found for him on the Island. Because J.L. Ralston refused to return to politics, J.L. Ilsley rep-resented Nova Scotia as Minister of Revenue. Ian Mackenzie, a Van-couver lawyer and a war veteran, was pleased to accept National Defence.

Some appointments did not go smoothly. Saskatchewan premier Jimmy Gardiner was eager to accept King's invitation to enter national politics, but threatened to remain in Regina rather than serve as Minister of Agriculture while his old rival, Dunning, held the prestigious portfolio of Finance. Manitoba's Thomas Crerar, filled with delusions that he was a regional power-broker, felt Mines and Natural Resources beneath him. King reassured both that they were important in his plans but made none of the concessions that they demanded; he eventually obtained the services of Gardiner and Crerar on his own terms. King further demonstrated his toughness when he turned a deaf ear to the pleas of former New Brunswick premier Peter Veniot that he would be "ruined" without a cabinet post and offered the Fisheries ministry to J.E. Michaud. By resisting "all kinds of pressure, lobbying, etc," King had made his ministerial appointments in only nine days. The *Canadian Forum*, no sycophant of the Liberals, described them as "the ablest group . . . who have made up any cabinet since Laurier's great administration of 1896." In the absence of a governor general – the new appointee, Scottish novelist John Buchan (Lord Tweedsmuir), had not yet arrived – King and the chosen were sworn in by Chief Justice Sir Lyman Duff on October 23.[2]

Cabinet-making artistry aside, Mackenzie King treated the situation as the duplicate of that he had inherited from Arthur Meighen fourteen years earlier: Canada was again in the midst of depression, and again he succeeded a government that had got its fingers burned meddling in the economy. His solution was the same governmental retreat that he believed had been so effective in the 1920s. "The aim," he wrote in his diary, "should be to get away from unnecessary regulation as much and as soon as possible." The appointment of C.A. Dunning as Finance Minister was a message to business that there would be no experiments. Dunning's dogma was "the old immutable laws of economics," and he vowed to bring Canada "back more and more closely into harmony" with them. The Bennett government had increased the deficit in 1935 in the hope that the public works pork barrel would aid it electorally. Dunning's budgets of 1936-37 and 1937-38 were a return to fiscal orthodoxy – and to regressive tax increases, as the federal sales tax jumped 25 per cent (see Table II). An expansionary fiscal policy such as advocated by John Maynard Keynes was not explicitly rejected; it simply was not considered. Nor was there any thought that monetary policy might be an appropriate stimulant to recovery. Although the government, as it had promised, bought out the private shareholders of the Bank of Canada, there was no attempt to steer Governor Graham Towers and his board in an expansionary direction.[3]

The Liberals hinged their hopes upon trade policy. In 1933 R.B. Bennett had begun negotiations with the United States about reciprocal tariff reductions, but discussions had dawdled, held up by American domestic politics and by Washington's reluctance to hand the Conservatives a pre-election coup that might help defeat the Liberals, with whom the U.S. State Department correctly estimated it would be easier to deal. Two weeks after winning office, Mackenzie King went south with a softened bargaining position which American negotiators assessed as "a far more favorable set-up than with the Bennett government." A rapidly concluded agreement was announced as "an act cementing our historic friendship" during President Roosevelt's Armistice Day address at Arlington National Cemetery. In addition to granting most-favoured-nation treatment (Canada's British preferences excepted), the United States agreed to admit limited amounts of cream, cattle, lumber, and seed potatoes at reduced rates in return for concessions on manufactures. The accord slightly favoured the United States and because it began an increased north-south trade it has been described as a turning-point on the road to greater continental economic integration; it should not, however, be interpreted as evidence that King and his party had "sold out" Canadian interests. Both the Conservative policy of higher tariffs and the Liberal alternative of freer trade deepened economic dependence on the United States. Between 1929 and 1935, the period at which the tariff was highest, the number of American branch plants operating in Canada increased from 524 to 816. As Stephen Scheinberg has graphically phrased it, Canadians "could only choose the grave digger" of their economic independence, "to be buried by American exports or by American branch plants." Public opinion embraced reciprocity enthusiastically. Even the Montreal *Gazette*, which had once denounced King as "the right-hand man of the American government," gave its editorial blessing to the agreement.[4]

Mackenzie King made no attempt to borrow from Franklin Roosevelt's legislative agenda during his visit to Washington for the ceremonial signature of the agreement. Roosevelt's Works Progress Administration was reducing America's relief rolls with a massive public works program, but the Liberal government had something very different in mind for the 1.3 million Canadians surviving the winter of 1935-36 on the dole. The National Employment Commission was intended to investigate their problem rather than to act on it. The commission was charged with uncovering waste and inefficiency in relief distribution as a step toward "lessening the burden of taxation." Only secondarily was it to look for ways to put the half-million unemployed back to work.[5]

The seven commissioners proved less compliant than expected. The four political appointees were dominated by chairman Arthur Purvis, a Montreal industrialist, Trades and Labour Congress past-president Tom Moore, and W.A. Mackintosh, one of Norman Rogers's colleagues from Queen's. Instead of serving as a watch-dog on the provinces and elaborating a "scientific" justification for relief cuts, the NEC prepared an interim report that advocated an enlarged federal role: a national employment service, extensive aid to residential construction, training programs for the youthful unemployed, and a national Volunteer Conservation Service for single men modelled on the Civilian Conservation Corps, Roosevelt's greatest New Deal success. Mackenzie King was incensed. His investigative commission was "really turning out to be a spending body instead of one to effect economy," and Norman Rogers, the minister responsible, was castigated before cabinet for failing to bring the commissioners to heel. Most of the NEC proposals were rejected, and those adopted were watered down; only $1 million of the $20 million Purvis had insisted were necessary was actually allotted for them.[6]

Just one NEC recommendation was adopted without adulteration. The King government had honoured its pledge to close the relief camps but had provided no substitute for most of the 22,000 inmates. They were forced back on the bum, joining the thousands of single unemployed still roaming the country. To dispel the "ugly spectre of the transient problem," the NEC suggested re-introduction of the 1932 farm placement plan on a national scale. This would cost only one third as much as the relief camps, and "it would take Arthur Evans a long time to organize another On-To-Ottawa Trek from men scattered on farms the length and breadth of Canada." All provinces except Ontario and Nova Scotia agreed to share the cost of paying $5 a month to the unemployed and to the farmers who took them on for the winter, and by January 1937, 37,000 men and 5,000 women had been placed in what government press releases described as "healthful home surroundings." For the young victims of the Depression, however, one thing was unchanged: the certainty of a "dreary future . . . without the chance to save or marry." "I cannot say that you have done any better than our despised R.B. Bennett," wrote one of them to Prime Minister King. "Your farm scheme is still based on R.B.'s policy . . . but it has turned out to be permanent. . . . It is ruining us both mentally and physically, saying nothing of losing our morals [*sic* – morale?] and self-respect."[7]

The farm placement program was all King borrowed from Bennett; the New Deal legislation was immediately referred by Ernest Lapointe for judicial review. After a year-long legal odyssey, in January 1937 the Natural Products Marketing Act, the wages and hours legislation, and the Employment and Social Insurance Act were ruled *ultra vires* by the Judicial Committee of the Privy Council. Legal experts were dumbfounded. The Canadian Supreme Court had quashed the NPMA, but the others had been found within federal powers. It was "a non-Canadian judiciary," complained F.R. Scott in the *Canadian Bar Review*, that had left "this country even more helpless than she was in 1929 to deal with the problems created by a changing economic system." Comparisons were made to the invalidation of parts of Roosevelt's New Deal by the American Supreme Court, but there was a critical difference. The American decisions followed suits brought by businessmen challenging the right of the government to regulate their activities; the legal process that frustrated the Canadian New Deal was initiated by the King government itself, "implicitly asserting that the legislation was not wanted." The American newsmagazine *Time* put this conclusion in its unsubtle style: "Mackenzie King has beat about a good many New Deal bushes, doing little and talking loudly . . . [but] it did not break his heart that in London nearly the whole New Deal was voided."[8]

The Privy Council's vindication of provincial rights did little to smooth federal-provincial relations. The thirties crisis in Canadian federalism was about cash, not about the constitution, and on the question of providing for the unemployed, "it was Ottawa which jealously defended provincial rights while the premiers were centralists." At the Dominion-Provincial Conference of December 1935, the premiers were soothed with temporary increases in grants-in-aid for relief, first in the hope that they would agree to a loan council that would allow Dunning to supervise provincial borrowing, and second, to persuade them to agree to discuss a process for amending the BNA Act. Both proposals came to nothing. Not even the most financially desperate provinces would consider the loan council, and although the complicated amendment formula was given tentative approval by eight provinces, New Brunswick's opposition denied the unanimity necessary for implementation. In March 1936 the federal relief increases were withdrawn, and a steady reduction of the federal contribution began. The premiers, especially the eight who were Liberals, got the message quickly. They were getting the same treatment they had received from the Conservatives, and "King's much vaunted federal co-operation [was] indistinguishable from Bennett's authoritarian approach." King himself concluded that "we would have been better off with Tory Govt's in the provinces." It could be, he speculated, "easier to govern at Ottawa with the provinces *contra*."[9]

II

Events soon tested his hypothesis. On August 17, 1936, the forty-year-old Liberal regime in Quebec was toppled by an unlikely coalition headed by Quebec Tory leader Maurice Duplessis. The previous eighteen months in Quebec political life, wrote Andrew Savage in *Saturday Night*, had been "as exciting as an Oppenheim adventure story. . . . Plots and counterplots, double-crossings, threats of disclosures of incredible corruptions . . . secret and unholy alliances." When Premier Taschereau dissolved the assembly in October 1935, he had faced a divided opposition. To his left was the dissident Action Libérale Nationale, with strong and growing support as a reform alternative but with an electoral war-chest of $29.81. To the right stood the Duplessis Conservatives, who possessed the rudiments of a party machine and a pledge of $150,000 in campaign funds, presumably donated by the province's big business community, hedging its bets against a Liberal defeat. Tory bagman J.-H. Rainville invited ALN leader Paul Gouin to a secret conclave where Gouin accepted the Conservative proposal of an alliance. The Union Nationale was born. But having chosen to sup with the devil, Gouin insisted on a long spoon. Maurice Duplessis could be the premier of any new coalition government, but Gouin would choose the majority of the cabinet. The ALN would bear the brunt of the battle on the hustings, while the Tories were to nominate in no more than thirty of the ninety constituencies.[10]

For the masses the alliance had a simple slogan: "Free Yourself From the Trusts and Vote for the Candidates of the Union Nationale Duplessis-Gouin." *Le Devoir* and a host of smaller papers supported the united front, and Paul Gouin reminded French Quebeckers that "in 1837 there were no Liberals or Conservatives, only on the one side the patriots and on the other the bureaucrats." Duplessis compared the coalition to "the folds of the tricolour flag . . . the blue representing the Conservatives, the white the independents, the red, the Liberals . . . joined together to defend our nationality." This reference to revolutionary France would have shocked the clerical supporters of the anti-Taschereau forces, but Cardinal Villeneuve had discreetly left the province for the duration of the campaign.[11]

The election on November 25, 1935, was almost a draw. The Liberals' vote fell from 56 per cent in 1931 to a bare majority, and their representation was slashed to forty-eight seats. The coalition elected forty-two deputies, sixteen under the Conservative and twenty-six under the ALN label. When the assembly convened, "the Liberal administration was like a prize-fighter who is still on his feet, but so dazed that only the *coup de grâce* is needed to put him down and out." Inexperienced in handling an opposition any larger than a corporal's guard, the Liberals lost control of the day-to-day affairs of the assembly. Duplessis exhumed the long-dormant Public Accounts Committee and electrified the province with a relentless barrage of sensational attacks on Liberal financial mismanagement, nepotism, and corruption. For the first time in a generation, Quebeckers perceived themselves no longer at the mercy of old-style politicians. Now, they reasoned, something would be accomplished in the assembly. One issue ingrained upon public consciousness was the old age pension, denied Quebeckers on various pretexts since 1927, and a highlight of the ALN manifesto. An avalanche of letters addressed to "M. le premier ministre" asked in the "humblest manner" for the pension, and the Liberals acted promptly to provide it. They also jettisoned L.-A. Taschereau for his reform-minded agriculture minister, Adélard Godbout. But the Liberals were besieged by an opposition filibuster, a log jam that could only be broken by dissolution and a second election. "With a government so dissolute," quipped Duplessis, "dissolution was imperative."[12]

Adding to Liberal hopes was a public split within the coalition ranks, as Paul Gouin accused Duplessis of trying to "reconstitute the old Tory Conservative party in the guise of the Union Nationale." But only four ALN deputies followed Gouin. Others felt that the U.N. still offered the best vehicle for implementing the ALN program, while the prospect of the spoils of office rallied the rest around Duplessis. The brooding Gouin was all but forgotten as Duplessis swore that he embraced the ALN's ideals "from A to Z." On August 17, 1936, the Liberal vote plummeted another eight percentage points, and although the U.N. won fewer urban votes than in 1935, it made the rural breakthrough essential to victory; Quebec's small-town and farm population voted *bleu* for the first time since 1892. The Duplessis forces now possessed the crushing majority, with seventy-six seats in the assembly. [13]

The Union Nationale government made minor concessions to the reforming zeal of the ALN. There was some modest social legislation – pensions for the blind and mothers' allowances – although unwed mothers and common-law couples were stricken from relief rolls for "impeccable religious motives." Conscious of which side of the electoral bread was buttered, Duplessis offered low-cost loans to farmers and spent large sums on rural roads. The trusts, villains of the U.N. campaigns, soon discovered they had little to fear. A much-touted law compelling resource companies to register themselves in Quebec simply added a few hundred dollars in legal fees to company expenses; there was no hint of regulation of their activities, much less expropriation. Duplessis had included only one prominent ALN figure in his cabinet, Minister of Lands and Forests Oscar Drouin. During his six months in the cabinet, Drouin fought without success for "competition by the state against the electricity trust, in a word, a provincial hydro." In February 1937 he resigned to join the fragmented leadership of the ALN in carrying on its struggle over the airwaves and in the streets. At a rally outside the assembly in March 1937, demonstrators wore toothpicks with a single strand of wool tied to the tip; these, they told reporters, were the "whips" with which Mr. Duplessis was scourging the trusts! [14]

Instead of confronting "les trustards" Duplessis declared war on the weakest of their opponents – socialists, communists, working men – with the sinister *loi des cadenas*. The so-called Padlock Law came in reaction to the King government's repeal of the controversial anti-communist statute, Section 98 of the Criminal Code. This liberalization was icily received by Quebec's élite, and especially by the Catholic hierarchy, which entertained a morbid fear of communism. The Conservatives had used Section 98 as their Quebec platform in 1935. One of their ads had showed a dirty, bearded Bolshevist accompanied by a wizened crone and chaperoned by the grim reaper, all gazing covetously across the sea to a fair country labelled Canada; the text urged voters to "conserve in our statutes Section 98 which protects us." More vaguely worded than Section 98, the Padlock Law made it illegal to use a house or a hall "to propagate communism or bolshevism" or to publish or distribute literature "tending to propagate communism." Communism was nowhere defined; to Duplessis no definition was necessary. "Communism," he explained, "can be felt." Publications seized under the law included the *Canadian Forum*, the *Labour World*, and copies of the Liberal organ *Le Canada*. Unemployed worker F.X. Lessard was padlocked out of his Quebec City home and received a two-year sentence when he tried to re-enter it. Among the minor comedies of Duplessis's war on communism was the banning of the movie *The Life of Emile Zola*, rated A1 by the Catholic Legion of Decency in the United States.[15]

The Padlock Law evoked a much better organized opposition than had Section 98, led by the newly formed Canadian Civil Liberties Union, but critics of the law within Quebec were in an impossible situation; opposition to the law was a violation of the law. Montreal CCLU spokesman Hubert Desaulniers prefaced his remarks to a protest meeting in Toronto with the comment that "a gathering such as this could not have been held in Montreal at the present time." *Time* magazine, beyond the reach of the Duplessis government, quoted the words that had led to the suppression of a radical newspaper. "The Province of Quebec," the editors of *Clarté* had written, "was a paradise for capitalists and a hell for workers."[16]

III

The Minister of Labour's New Year's address for 1937 contained a warning for Canadians of all classes. "In many countries today, peoples are divided into antagonistic groups. Our success in avoiding tendencies towards Communism and Fascism," emphasized Norman Rogers, "will depend on our willingness to practise forbearance and tolerance [in] industrial relations." Rogers's appeal was well timed, for 1937 would witness the most widespread class conflict since the end of the Great War. A partial recovery in 1936 had restored business profits almost to pre-Depression levels, but as the League for Social Reconstruction observed, "recovery means different things to different classes. Profits have recovered handsomely; employment and working class incomes have not." As workers determined to gain their share through higher wages, a strike wave rolled across every province save Prince Edward Island and on to the Yukon, where silver miners struck to reduce their bosses' deductions for room and board from an astronomical $2.85 a day. The *Labour Gazette* reported

72,000 Canadians on strike or locked out during 1937, an official statistic that errs on the conservative side; 278 disputes affected over 600 enterprises in 135 different communities. The unrest cut deeply into the industrial heartland of the country. Two thirds of the strikers were in manufacturing, a sixth in mining and the rest scattered across the economy (see Table XII).[17]

Characteristic of the new temper of traditionally conservative elements of the working class were the adamant demands the management of the CPR and CNR faced from their 117,000 employees. Their unions, even the aristocratic "running trades," had accepted a 10-percent wage reduction in 1931. Now they demanded the restoration of the pre-Depression wage scale, and as the membership voted a resounding yes in a strike referendum, the biggest event in Canadian labour history loomed: the first general railway strike. The railway presidents, echoed by the business community, insisted that restoring the workers' wages would mean financial ruin, but Winnipeg Liberal M.P. Ralph Maybank, who understood the anger of the men, explained the consequences of a strike or even a slowdown. "Has anyone stopped to think," he asked in the Commons, "how much of a loss there would be on a railway if a 3 per cent slowing up of trains were to be effected?" Rogers averted the crisis at the eleventh hour with an emergency conference held in Ottawa on Good Friday, at which he persuaded management to phase in a return to the 1931 wage schedules over a twelve-month period. His mediation earned him praise from senior cabinet colleagues and the confidence of some labour leaders, but among businessmen he won a reputation as a "radical" who could not be trusted.[18]

Organized labour remained divided as always, yet there had been important shifts in the constellation of forces that comprised the Canadian labour movement, and impressive quantitative growth. Union membership reached 384,619 at the end of 1937, an increase of a third over 1932; "the momentum labour organization has gathered since then," enthused a speaker at the convention of the independent Workers' Educational Association, "has placed within our reach a vast field for cultivation." The internal question for labour was, who would reap the harvest from this field? A schism in the All-Canadian Congress of Labour in 1935 had produced a new "Canadian Federation of Labour" which had some 25,000 members by 1937. The ACCL's attempt to Canadianize the trade union movement, already weakened by the splitting off of the communist faction into the Workers' Unity League, was mortally wounded by this latest round of politically motivated infighting. The leadership of the breakaway federation, following president Zénon Davide, opposed the orientation of the All-Canadian Congress toward the CCF – but only because the CFL itself was intimately tied to the Liberal party. The faces of Ernest Lapointe, Paul Martin, C.A. Dunning, and Mitchell Hepburn graced the covers of the CFL's elegant monthly magazine, graphically illustrating this political connection. Liberal affiliation, however, did not mean that the members were any less militant than those of other federations, as when Huntsville, Ontario, tannery workers struck in 1937 for a closed shop for their CFL industrial union. But neither the CFL nor the All-Canadian Congress stood at centre stage in the events of 1937.[19]

The most important decisions for Canadian labour were taken outside the country, "one in Moscow, the other in Washington." In Moscow the Seventh Congress of the Communist International, awakened by the annihilation of the German party at the hands of Adolf Hitler, made official communist policy the pursuit of a "peoples' front" against Nazism and fascism. In Western Europe and North America the preferred slogan was the "Popular Front," a term stolen from non-communist French radicals. "Revolutionary" organizations such as the Workers' Unity League were henceforward to dissolve and merge their forces with those of the non-communist trade unions. Even before Stalin gave his imprimatur to the Popular Front, WUL president J.B. McLachlan had attempted to put the new line into practice by issuing calls to the Trades and Labour Congress, the ACCL, and the Confédération des travailleurs catholiques du Canada for discussion about the creation of an "all-inclusive" Canadian labour federation. The overture evoked no official response. Although it had accounted for 50 per cent of all strikes and strikers as recently as 1934, the WUL had a hard core membership that year of only 24,086. The non-communist unions were usually perfectly willing to absorb WUL members, even if they were reluctant to negotiate with the red leaders; when the WUL voluntarily disbanded in 1936, most of its affiliates brokered themselves into the welcoming arms of the international labour movement.[20]

At the Washington headquarters of the American Federation of Labor, parent of the internationals operating in Canada, the Committee for Industrial Organization had been formed in 1935 to begin a crusade to "organize the unorganized." Its chairman, John L. Lewis of the United Mine Workers, had a history of anti-communism, but he accepted the communists and their undoubted organizational talents into his movement to form industrial unions. Aided by the Wagner Act – the most radical departure of the American New Deal – which legally guaranteed the right of American workers to unionize, the CIO made rapid progress. But if workers embraced the idea of mass unionization on the industrial principle, the hidebound craft union majority of the American Federation of Labor did not. In 1937 AFL President William Green expelled the CIO, which immediately reconstituted itself as the full-fledged *Congress* of Industrial Organizations.[21]

By this time the CIO in Canada had a membership of 65,000, grouped in old unions like the United Mine Workers or in new ones such as the United Electrical Workers, the Steel Workers' Organizing Committee, and the International Woodworkers of America – which actually had a Canadian, British Columbia shingle weaver Harold Pritchett, as its founding president. The "new industrial unionism" of the CIO marked the revival of unionism as a social movement on a scale that had not been seen since the nineteenth-century days of the Knights of Labor or the One Big Union of 1919. The split in the United States threatened a similar disruption in Canada, but Trades and Labour Congress president Paddy Draper welcomed CIO delegates to his 1937 convention and vowed to use his "good offices" to heal the breach in the ranks of American labour. Draper had a powerful imagination; in 1939 the American Federation of Labor forced him to expel the CIO, threatening to withdraw all AFL affiliates from the Trades and Labour Congress if he did not. For two critical years, however, the CIO was able to organize in Canada under the aegis of the country's senior labour federation, and the CIO-TLC unions were the cutting edge of the militancy of 1937.[22]

As night follows day, the CIO's best-known tactic of factory occupations, which came to be known as "sit-down strikes," crossed the Detroit River during the winter of 1936-37, with sit-down protests at the Kelsey Wheel plant in Windsor and the Holmes Foundry near Sarnia. The Windsor sit-downers won concessions; the Sarnia men were forcibly evicted and brutally beaten by goons while local police watched. Ernest Lapointe voiced the unanimous opinion of jurists that sit-down strikes were "absolutely illegal"; nevertheless the *Labour Gazette* recorded thirteen such strikes over a twelve-month period, the largest at the Kitchener rubber works and at Edmonton meat-packing plants. The last of the series was staged by waitresses in a New Westminster, British Columbia, diner. No sit-downs seem to have occurred in the Maritimes or Quebec, but the broad pattern of industrial unrest they symbolized was not focused in the "radical" West but in Eastern and Central Canada. In these regions labour and the CIO were at the top of the public consciousness in 1937 in ways that quickly overshadowed the conciliatory initiatives of Norman Rogers.[23]

Strikes and Lockouts by Region, 1937

Region	Strikes	Workers Involved	Communities Affected
Maritimes	51	17,941	21
Quebec	46	24,419	22
Ontario	130	24,513	57
Prairies	32	3,271	18
B.C./Yukon	19	1,733	7

The CIO became a household word during the Ontario organizing campaign of the United Auto Workers, which culminated in an eventful sixteen-day strike at the giant General Motors factory at Oshawa. In Northern Ontario organizers of the Mine, Mill and Smelter Workers' Union skirmished with the mining kings over the allegiance of an industrial army of 30,000 with a background of militancy and a long list of social and economic grievances. The Toronto *Globe and Mail*, whose publisher, George McCullagh, had made a fortune in mine speculation, waged a relentless propaganda war against the "lawless," "American," "Red" CIO, reprinting cartoons from right-wing American papers that showed John L. Lewis as a comrade of Hitler and Stalin. Premier Mitch Hepburn, who had wooed the working class in 1934, now found his friends among the industrialists. Hepburn vowed to defeat the CIO at Oshawa, lest Lewis get his "grubby paws on the mines of Ontario." His polemics did not shake the resolve of the seven thousand auto workers, who employed conventional trade union tactics rather than the controversial sit-down strike. Hepburn tried to block every attempt at a settlement with the UAW, a policy that caused the resignation of two of his ministers, Arthur Roebuck and David Croll, the latter explaining that "my place is marching with the workers rather than riding with General Motors." When the federal government wisely declined to send the RCMP or the army to Oshawa, Hepburn provocatively organized his own constabulary, dubbed "Hepburn's Hussars" or "the Sons of Mitches." Confrontation was headed off by General Motors, which instructed its Canadian managers to negotiate a compromise collective agreement with "Mr. CIO" Charlie Millard, Canadian head of the UAW. Far from being the alien labour agitator portrayed in the *Globe and Mail*, Millard came from exactly the same rural Ontario Protestant stock as Hepburn, and they had been born within a few miles of each other in Elgin County![24]

The Premier lost nothing in the short run. He seized the CIO "threat" to seduce several prominent Conservatives, including future premier George Drew, into a coalition against the left. In October he decimated what was left of the opposition in an election that became a sort of referendum on the CIO in true-blue British Ontario. The CCF lost its only seat, and the single labour member left in the legislature was Communist J.B. Salsberg; the new unionism had as yet no electoral muscle. "Where do I stand on the CIO?" crowed Mitch Hepburn. "I'm standing right on top of them and I'll keep on standing there."[25]

In part because of Hepburn's implacable hostility, Nova Scotia became the centre of CIO strength in Canada. The Nova Scotia experience showed that a more constructive approach to the new industrial unionism was possible. The province's heavy industry – coal, basic steel, and steel fabrication – were monopolized by the Dominion Steel and Coal consortium, successor to Besco. Dosco had cut wages by 12.5 per cent in 1932; in 1937 it reported a surplus of $1.3 million. Slowdowns and pithead strikes by the United Mine Workers and the Steel Workers' Organizing Committee forced the company to restore half the cut, and to defuse what remained a potentially explosive situation, the Angus L. Macdonald government made a second concession: a Trade Union Act based on the American Wagner Act. "Responsible" collective bargaining would be encouraged by the establishment of a labour relations board that would supervise union certification votes. If the union won a majority, the employer would be compelled to recognize it and to collect dues by check-off, a giant step away from the Canadian tradition of violent employer resistance to union recognition. The most modern labour legislation in any province belied the homespun image of "Angus L.," but Nova Scotians evidently approved of it. He crushed the Conservatives twenty-five seats to five in the June 1937 election, and "almost every seat that could be considered 'labour' went to the Liberals."[26]

New Brunswick's Liberal government was of two minds on the labour question, as it faced in 1937 a complete shutdown of the Miramichi valley lumber industry by the provincially based Farmer-Labour Union and a bitter fight for recognition by the United Mine Workers in the Minto coalfield. With the support of left-leaning clergymen and student activists, these bodies had organized and united New Brunswick workers – Protestant and Catholic, Loyalist and Acadien, "Polack and Hungarian" – as never before. Premier A. Alison Dysart pledged to the provincial Federation of Labour that his government would seriously consider "a measure to give legal right to workers to join unions of their choice," legislation that he personally supported. Attorney General J.B. McNair, a professed admirer of Mitch Hepburn, had other ideas. Who was running New Brunswick, he publicly demanded, "the politicians – or the CIO?" When the Minto miners faced defeat through actual starvation by the coal operators in the winter of 1937-38, the cabinet vetoed any proposal to intervene on the side of the strikers. Two years later, McNair had replaced Dysart in the premier's chair. [27]

Maurice Duplessis met the CIO with an unhesitatingly hostile reflex that soon dashed the hopes of the movement, organized into the newly formed Fédération des travailleurs du Québec, in French Canada. The Padlock Law was invoked to seize union records and even to disband the thousand-member Steel Workers' local in Montreal. The only Quebeckers to defy Duplessis successfully under the banner of the CIO were six thousand Montreal garment workers who struck for better conditions and recognition of the International Ladies Garment Workers Union in April 1937. The unions in the needle trades had broadened out from their Jewish base to include French Canadian and other workers; the CIO slogan, "Down With Slavery in the Workplace," was broadcast in French, Yiddish, and English. Two weeks into the strike the Premier announced that because of "intolerable disorders" in the streets, he would have union leaders Bernard Shane and Raoul Trépanier arrested and tried on trumped up charges of conspiracy against public order. The intimidation failed: no arrests were ever made. The strike soon ended in a compromise favourable to the ILGWU because the clothing manufacturers, like General Motors in Ontario, saw a negotiated settlement was in their own best interests. [28]

Premier Duplessis always tempered his attacks on communists and "lawless" labour leaders with cynical professions of undying sympathy for "the working class of this province." In practice, he sought to employ in the field of industrial relations the same tactic that had thus far served him well in politics: divide and conquer. In the summer of 1937 the strategy backfired, and Duplessis faced the prospect of a general strike. The U.N. government wanted to use the 53,000-member Confédération des travailleurs catholiques du Canada – part of its original constituency – as a cat's-paw in the struggle against the CIO, encouraging the anti-communist and nationalist Catholic union movement to deploy its organizers in the field and compete with the CIO for the allegiance of the working class. But Duplessis's labour allies suddenly became dangerous agitators when the CTCC turned its guns on one of Quebec's largest "trusts," the Montreal Cottons–Dominion Textiles combine. On August 2, 1937, the largest strike of that year of labour troubles in Canada began when 10,000 textile workers, led by the CTCC, struck nine major plants in Quebec. The Catholic unions threatened, moreover, to strike as a *bloc*, if necessary, in support of the textile workers and against the legislative guillotine with which the U.N. now threatened them, the so-called Fair Wages Act, which allowed the provincial government to decree wages in this sector. This legislation, Duplessis claimed, would solve the problems of textile workers like Ovide Lemay, who supported fourteen children on his weaver's wage of ten dollars a week. Just how the act's proposed schedule of wages of ten, fifteen, and twenty cents an hour would do this was unclear. CTCC president Alfred Charpentier denounced it as a sham, while defiant strikers paraded through the streets of Valleyfield, Drummondville, and Saint-Grégoire de Montmorency shouting, "The Church is with us!!" His Eminence Cardinal Villeneuve alone had the prestige to negotiate an armistice in the textile strike, which he did on August 25.[29]

What was most remarkable as Duplessis, McNair, Macdonald, and Hepburn each answered the labour question in his own way, was the complete absence of any effective federal response. Norman Rogers was stung by humiliating rebuffs from the premiers when he tried to help settle the Oshawa, Minto, and Quebec disputes. The federal government failed to pass the comprehensive collective bargaining legislation demanded by every faction of the Canadian labour movement save the CTCC. J.S. Woodsworth begged the government to act "before there is violence . . . before the workers are crushed by the combination arrayed against them," but the Liberals cited the constitution as an insuperable obstacle to a Canadian Wagner Act. Young labour lawyer Bora Laskin tried to move Mackenzie King to action by appealing to the Prime Minister's obsession with national unity; "not the least of the problems which threaten the unity of the Canadian people," he wrote, "is the one which appears on the surface as 'labour unrest.' "[30]

IV

Mackenzie King could hardly plead ignorance of industrial relations, but it was regional rather than class conflict that preoccupied him. Within the House of Commons he governed almost unopposed. With its forty-member rump, the Conservative party was at the lowest point in its history, and R.B. Bennett fought "an almost single-handed battle" as leader of the official opposition until succeeded by Robert Manion in July 1938. With the exception of J.H. Blackmore, the seventeen Social Creditors were beyond their depth, and the effectiveness of the CCF was limited by the tiny size of its caucus. The *real* opposition came from the provincial capitals, for in 1937-38 King faced a "provincial challenge to national unity" from British Columbia, Alberta, Ontario, and Quebec. King hoped to resolve some of the problems with the Royal Commission on Dominion-Provincial Relations, but its work met constant delays. Although the Chief Justice of Ontario, N.W. Rowell, Winnipeg *Free Press* editor J.W. Dafoe, and Thibaudeau Rinfret of the Supreme Court were eventually chosen as commissioners, complaints from both coasts forced the addition of R.A. Mackay of Dalhousie University and Henry Angus of UBC. An illness forced Rinfret to step down, and there was more time lost while Joseph Sirois, a Laval professor of law, was chosen to replace him. It seemed possible, worried political scientist Herbert Quinn, that before the commissioners could report Canada might dissolve into "a number of smaller, semi-autonomous, self-governing units, with conflicting aims and divergent interests."[31]

Premier T.D. Pattullo had looked forward to King's defeat of R.B. Bennett, for his pledge of "work and wages" for British Columbians depended on a sympathetic and generous federal government. When no easy credit came from Ottawa, his ambitious public works program was impossible, and the province was hard pressed to avoid defaulting on its past debts. The parlous state of provincial finances forced Pattullo to renege on his health insurance plan, over the protest of Provincial Secretary George Weir that such a breach of faith "would make the Pattullo administration a laughing-stock of the public and an object of contempt to future historians of social legislation in Canada." Pattullo pleaded in vain with King for an end to fiscal conservatism. "In Canada," he maintained, "we cannot possibly balance our budget and at the same time carry out essential measures. . . . The old stereotyped [answers] will not meet our problems." The failure of the federal government to defend the Natural Products Marketing Act incensed Pattullo, who warned King that its invalidation was "a very serious matter" for his province's fruit and vegetable growers.[32]

After his re-election with a diminished majority in June 1937, Pattullo fell back to more traditional provincial rights positions. Open conflict came over the never-ending quandary of the single unemployed. The federal farm placement plan was unworkable in British Columbia because of the small number of farms and the large number of transients. Instead, the two governments divided the much greater costs of operating forestry camps, which proved so much more attractive than farm life that migrants flocked to the coast to get into them. Convinced that it was being taken advantage of, the province shut down the camps in April 1938 and told the inmates to "get out and rustle."

The men refused to be pawns in a federal-provincial game. Twelve hundred members of the Relief Project Workers' Union assembled in Vancouver, where they applied the CIO's sit-down tactic in the Post Office and the Art Gallery, the former a federal and the latter a provincial responsibility. Pattullo rejected their demand for work or relief with the comment that "there is a time when you have to suffer, just as Christ suffered on the cross." King maintained that the men were a provincial problem and refused to increase federal aid to transient relief. After a month of bluff and counter-bluff, both governments acted early on the morning of Sunday, June 19. To preserve constitutional propriety, the Vancouver police cleared the Art Gallery while the RCMP emptied the Post Office. The first eviction went reasonably smoothly. At the Post Office, however, sit-downers choking on tear gas were run through a gauntlet of Mountie billy-clubs as they left the building; their leader, Steve Brodie, was beaten senseless despite repeatedly attempting to surrender.[33]

To avenge him his followers surged down Hastings and Granville streets, leaving a wake of shattered store windows. Although it had been federal police who touched off the rampage, the public blamed Pattullo and saw the riot as proof that he had "carried his quarrel with Ottawa too far." After "Bloody Sunday" his reform image was indelibly tarnished, while Mackenzie King emerged almost unblemished. When the sit-downers re-assembled for a march of protest, their destination was Victoria rather than Parliament Hill. As a desperate Pattullo appealed for help against this "insurrection," King was able to defuse the situation with an offer of transportation home at federal expense to all the single unemployed who requested it. The federal-provincial roles of an earlier Depression summer had been exactly reversed, and all at the cost of a few railway tickets.[34]

Alberta's challenge to Ottawa was less easily dismissed. During his first eighteen months in power William Aberhart had caused King little trouble, for he had done nothing to establish the Social Credit millennium. "Seventy-five percent of those who voted for me don't expect any dividend," he told a *New York Times* correspondent, "but hope for a just and honest government." That was what he provided: an increased minimum wage, educational reform, more generous relief, aid to the co-op movement. As one Albertan wrote to the Premier, "You and the government have done more for the poor classes than any government of the past." The *Financial Post* suggested that Alberta was in "the early stages of the Russian revolution" when the government legislated to reduce the interest on private debts and defaulted on a provincial loan, but these measures were not true Social Credit theory. The only concession to purists was the issuing of $250,000 in "prosperity certificates" to civil servants as part of their wages, but when merchants refused to accept the "funny money," the certificates were withdrawn. Insurgents among the Social Credit M.L.A.s grumbled that Aberhart had betrayed the movement, and from England Major Douglas charged that "the failure to progress towards Social Credit rests squarely on the shoulders of Mr. Aberhart."[35]

Faced with a back-bench revolt, Aberhart began in 1937 to implement Douglas doctrines. A Social Credit board was formed; then the Credit of Alberta Regulation Act placed the banks under directorates appointed by the board so that their credit policies would be shaped to suit Alberta producers rather than bank shareholders. The Bank Employees Civil Rights Act made it illegal for bankers to take civil action against the province, and an amendment to the Judicature Act made it illegal to challenge the validity of provincial laws in court. The federal government had left the Social Credit regime alone until this reaffirmation of its radical purpose. In the 1935 election campaign King had promised "non-interference with provincial affairs," and in March 1937 Justice Minister Lapointe had dismissed as virtually obsolete the federal power to disallow provincial legislation. Yet to the consternation of Aberhart and his cabinet, the Credit of Alberta Regulation Act and its companion statutes were swiftly disallowed as "an unmistakable invasion" of federal jurisdiction. Aberhart castigated the federal government for listening to "plutocratic bankers" instead of to "democratic Albertans . . . seeking their economic freedom." With a few cosmetic changes he re-introduced the legislation along with the Accurate News and Information Act, which required newspapers to reveal sources of leaks of confidential material and to publish official refutations of stories critical of Social Credit policies. Lieutenant-Governor J.C. Bowen refused to sign the bills, reserving them for federal scrutiny, and after reference to the Supreme Court they were ruled *ultra vires*.[36]

On the broader question of the validity of the power of the federal government to disallow and reserve provincial laws, the Justices unanimously affirmed that it was as much alive as it had been when Sir John A. Macdonald had used it regularly to curb the provinces. Between 1937 and 1941 eight more Alberta statutes intended to restrict foreclosures and to reduce the interest rate on debts were disallowed. The swift federal action to crush these threats to financial institutions stood in sharp contrast to federal unwillingness to deal with the economic crisis that had given birth to Social Credit in the first place. At a public meeting shortly after the first disallowance an angry crowd had shouted "give us a gun," but William Aberhart sternly warned that he would have "none of that – no secession. We have no desire to leave the home of our forefathers." Instead, he carried on his struggle with Ottawa with such petty gestures as taking away Lieutenant-Governor Bowen's automobile, chauffeur, and secretary. This evidence of his impotence undermined the ambition of Social Credit's leaders to expand to the other western provinces, easing Liberal fears of "a Social Credit empire . . . from the Great Lakes to the Pacific." Within Alberta, however, the disallowance added another bead to the rosary of regional grievance and helped elect Social Credit governments long after the party's early radicalism had become vestigial.[37]

With only one Albertan in the Liberal caucus, King had little to lose by taking a firm hand with the hinterland. He was much more circumspect with the populous central provinces, which provided his party's back-benchers and its bankroll. An Ontario repudiation of contracts to purchase electricity paralleled Alberta's debt adjustment laws, but the Ontario act was not disallowed. Nor was a subsequent act that denied the affected power companies the right to sue for damages. Quebec's Padlock Law was as great an affront to free speech and freedom of the press as the Accurate News and Information Act; "twenty times a month [police in Quebec] have trampled on liberties as old as Magna Carta," argued J.S. Woodsworth in an unsuccessful attempt to convince Ernest Lapointe to refer the law to the Supreme Court. The reason it was neither disallowed nor referred was frankly political; "disallowance would be pretty certain to bring on an election in Quebec, with a certain win for Duplessis," King reasoned. He and his English-speaking ministers were unhappy with the Padlock Law, which, he confessed to his diary, "should not, in the name of Liberalism, be tolerated for one moment." King justified inaction with a twist of the logic he used to explain the draconian treatment of Alberta: ". . . the unity of Canada was the test by which we would meet all these things."[38]

Kid-glove treatment for Ontario and Quebec did not stem the flood of vitriol poured on Ottawa by Maurice Duplessis and Mitch Hepburn. A King-Hepburn feud began in 1935 with the selection of Norman Rogers and C.D. Howe as ministers over Hepburn's personal choice, Toronto lawyer Arthur Slaght. The fact that both governments were Liberal exacerbated the acrimony instead of dispelling it, since competition for control of the party in Ontario was a constant irritant, but the conflict between Premier and Prime Minister had deeper roots. Charles Dunning's refusal to repeal Bennett's gold bullion tax upset the mining promoters who were Hepburn's campaign contributors and drinking companions, and the Oshawa strike revealed a fundamental strategic disagreement. King's policy throughout his career was to co-opt the trade union movement; Hepburn took his line on trade unions from the industrialists: violent repression. King feared that Hepburn would push working-class voters leftward to the CCF or to communism; Hepburn resented King and his "pink socialite" Labour Minister for leaving him "fighting single-handed against [John L.]

Lewis and his Yankee racketeers" during the "CIO invasion of Ontario." King did his best to avoid a public laundering of the party dirty linen, but Mitch Hepburn was never one to hide his feelings. In the summer of 1937 he pronounced himself "sick and disgusted with King and his whole outfit."[39]

Hepburn found an ally in Maurice Duplessis. The two had co-operated to aid the newsprint industry, and the Quebec premier had loudly applauded Hepburn's CIO-bashing. Mackenzie King provided them with a mutual grievance by refusing to permit export of Ontario and Quebec power to New York State without a special act of parliament. When Franklin Roosevelt shortly thereafter banned American importation of electricity, the two premiers suspected collusion between Ottawa and Washington to bully them into an expensive binational project to develop the hydro and transportation potential of the St. Lawrence. Their mutual tastes for philandering, liquor, and late nights helped along their revival of the old Ontario-Quebec axis; after a party at Montreal's Ritz-Carlton in December 1937, Hepburn and Duplessis proclaimed a formal "alliance against the Dominion government." Mackenzie King refused to comment, although he described it as "an outrage" in his diary. His private opinion was that it was "just as well to have these two incipient dictators out in the open linked together" so that "the public will soon discover who is protecting their interests and freedom." The two provincial upstarts, one marinated in Scotch and the other in gin, were handing him the issue he could exploit better than any other. "We will win," he exulted, "on a 'United Canada' cry."[40]

The first months of the intergovernmental cold war seemed to go to the premiers. The St. Lawrence Seaway got no closer to realization, although for reasons that had little to do with provincial obstinacy. Both provinces refused to participate in federal programs for loans to municipalities and for job training. They also blocked a constitutional amendment that would have cleared the way for unemployment insurance. Although expressed in terms of provincial autonomy, the premiers' objection was based on economic self-interest. As Hepburn wrote to Duplessis, "with the western provinces hopelessly bankrupt, [the cost of] any scheme of unemployment insurance will have to be borne by the two central provinces." When the Royal Commission on Dominion-Provincial Relations reached Toronto, Hepburn "ran up the colours of provincial rights," refusing to consider the surrender of the slightest provincial prerogative. He assailed the briefs from poorer provinces proposing that the federal government be given expanded tax revenues to take over the old age pension and the mother's allowance, and was especially hostile to Manitoba's notion that all Canadians had a right to "a common standard of public and social services." Provinces would have those services they could pay for themselves; Ontario was not the "milch cow" of Confederation whose tax dollars could be pumped east and west through the federal treasury. Because Maurice Duplessis refused to appear before the commission, Quebec's terse ten-page submission was read by a government lawyer. It quoted Hepburn with approval, and denied the federal government's power to investigate provincial finances without obtaining provincial permission to do so. "To preserve the French reputation for *politesse*," Duplessis held a party for the commissioners at the Chateau Frontenac. After "considerable welkin-ringing," he began to humiliate his guests with "a good deal of vulgar banter"; the evening concluded with Duplessis hurling champagne glasses at the chandeliers "with such accuracy that the restaurant was soon in semi-darkness and the floor and tables littered with broken glass."[41]

But strident provincialism had worn thin with the public. Although no one looked for miracles from it, Canadians, as *Le Devoir* observed, "had great expectations of the Rowell Commission." Most of them wished the "Fathers of Reconfederation" Godspeed in their work. There were many submissions to the Quebec hearings from non-governmental groups, demonstrating that if the official attitude was "narrowly provincial . . . there are private citizens of Quebec who can see past the Ottawa river." Hepburn's harangue of the commissioners was received coldly, its sarcasm falling "like pancakes in a puddle." He was lampooned as "the Great Hepburn, defender of hard-pressed Ontario against the idle rich of Saskatchewan and Manitoba"; Toronto *Saturday Night* denied that the Premier represented "even the majority, to say nothing of the totality, of the population of Ontario." Undeterred by these bad reviews, Hepburn pressed on with his most ambitious scheme: to take control, with Duplessis's help, of the sources of Liberal campaign funds in Montreal and Toronto. The ultimate goal was to replace Mackenzie King with someone more to the Premier's taste – purportedly Jimmy Gardiner.[42]

Hepburn refused to aid the Liberal candidate in a federal by-election in Ontario in November 1938, and after Gardiner reported that he had been approached by Hepburn, King began to take the bizarre conspiracy very seriously. It was one thing "that this young upstart should seek to array central provinces against the West and East, as he is in attacking representations before Rowell-Commission." It was quite another to join the Union Nationale in a perfidious plot against the Liberal party itself. Norman Rogers and C.D. Howe were chosen to make the counter-attack. At a Liberal nominating meeting in Port Arthur, they publicly accused Hepburn and Duplessis of attempting to set up a government in Ottawa "dependent on and largely controlled by the provincial governments at Toronto and Quebec." When Hepburn shot back a threat to support a third party or to "vote for [newly chosen Conservative leader] Bob Manion – at least he's human," Ontario Liberals were shocked. They were not prepared to be "pawns to be suddenly shuffled across the board to work for the traditional enemies, the Tories." Ontario's senators and M.P.s assembled at once to resolve their complete and unconditional support of Mackenzie King. A humiliated Hepburn suddenly decided on a lengthy trip to Australia to investigate antipodean federalism. The rebuke did not stop his verbal abuse, but it blunted his intrigues into national politics. The "reckless swashbuckler," says Richard Alway, had been beaten by the "wily and experienced fencing master." King's political manoeuvring had done nothing to resolve the regional tensions on which Hepburn had fed, any more than disallowance had solved the problems of the people of Alberta; it had, however, reaffirmed his mastery of the federal Liberal party. [43]

V

The firmer tone evident in relations with the provinces was part of what Blair Neatby describes as a more general "reluctant assertion of federal leadership." There was no guiding philosophy or master plan behind it; an expanded role for the central government evolved as a piecemeal response to a series of political pressures. The transformation of the Canadian Radio Broadcasting Commission into the Canadian Broadcasting Corporation with a national network of powerful stations was the final fruit of the determined lobbying of the Canadian Radio League. The modest beginnings of Trans-Canada Airlines were primarily the work of dynamic Transport Minister C.D. Howe, who referred to TCA as "my airline." These Crown corporations did not represent any enthusiasm for public enterprise; they were created less from socialist than from nationalist demands, as a means of keeping the new forms of transportation and communication firmly in Canadian hands. [44]

TCA and the CBC did nothing to relieve the Great Depression, which renewed its fury in 1937. A searing summer left prairie farmers with only a sixth of a normal crop, making 1937 the worst year in the history of the Western wheat economy. An abrupt reversal of the short-lived American recovery began in the autumn, reducing exports of lumber and newsprint to the United States. Manufacturing and retailing went into a sharper decline than they had in 1929-30. Pessimism was as ingrained as optimism had been a decade earlier; at the first sign of renewed depression, business investment and consumer spending slackened. Stock prices nosedived. Unemployment, which had fallen below a quarter-million in September 1937, ballooned to 437,000 by the following April. Finance Minister Dunning blamed the "secondary depression" on "political tension abroad," but his own policies were also guilty. By reducing the federal deficit and forcing the provinces to do the same with theirs, he had brought about a drop in public investment that helped abort the embryonic recovery. [45]

Neither Dunning nor King understood this, and both argued that "recession made it more imperative that we should economize as much as possible." The final report of the National Employment Commission, revealed to cabinet in December 1937, recommended just the opposite: federal assumption of the financing and administration of unemployment relief and "a policy under which public expenditures might be expanded . . . to offset fluctuations in private expenditures." The report's cautious advocacy of the ideas of John Maynard Keynes came largely from Queen's economist W.A. Mackintosh and suggested the growing academic presence in Ottawa. During the 1930s twenty-four economists or political scientists worked on various government investigations, and within the civil service "mandarins" like O.D. Skelton and Deputy Finance Minister Clifford Clark recruited bright young university graduates. A more active federal state held no terrors for Skelton or Clark, both of whom endorsed the NEC report, and the bureaucracy of which they had laid the foundations meant that there were people in the capital capable of running it. [46]

The NEC report has been called "a watershed in the Canadian welfare state," but Mackenzie King's first reaction to the "academic treatise" was to demand that its authors recant. When they refused, he delayed its publication for five months. The recommendation that Ottawa take over relief was referred to the Rowell Commission for further study. "It sounds very much like a double play in a baseball game," joked Conservative Denton Massey, "Rogers to Purvis to Rowell." The NEC's notions, however, were vigorously taken up by Norman Rogers. C.D. Howe, Chubby Power, J.L. Ilsley, and Jimmy Gardiner supported him, fearful of the political consequences of continued inaction. In the cabinet civil war that ensued, both Rogers and C.A. Dunning, leaders of the two factions, made threats to resign. To avoid an open breach, King engineered a compromise. [47]

The "long-range nationwide program of conservation and development designed to stimulate employment" announced by Rogers on May 20, 1938, combined the usual federal public works with ideas drawn from the NEC report: highway construction to open the middle

North to mining and tourism, forest and fisheries conservation projects, the development of historic sites. The Prairie Farm Rehabilitation Administration, born in the dying moments of the Conservative government, had its budget for reviving the burned-out sections of the West more than tripled. The most significant new departure was a federal program for youth job training. The recovery package came to much less than the $75 million Rogers had requested. He claimed that the new initiatives were worth $40 million, but only $28.8 million was new expenditure; the remainder was the agreed-upon federal contribution to provincial relief. Two attempts to stimulate the construction industry made the recovery program more credible. The Municipal Improvements Assistance Act authorized $30 million in federal loans at 2 per cent interest for "non-ordinary" municipal public works. The National Housing Act made federally backed mortgages easier to obtain than they had been under Bennett's Dominion Housing Act and – at the suggestion of Clifford Clark – offered another $30 million at 2 per cent for municipal housing for low-income tenants.[48]

The total cost was no more than that of one of Bennett's relief acts, but there were to be no new taxes to pay for it. In keeping with the theme of stimulating construction, the 8 per cent federal sales tax was removed from building materials. Although the modest recovery program was not the triumph for cabinet expansionists that Rogers pretended, it did reverse the direction of Liberal fiscal policy. The projected deficit was only $23 million, but a planned deficit was traumatic for the Finance Minister. A week after he presented the 1938 budget, C.A. Dunning slumped over at his Commons desk, stricken by a heart attack. Mackenzie King accepted the change of direction more philosophically:

> The world situation has headed the countries more and more in the direction of the extension of state authority and enterprise, and I am afraid Canada will not be able to resist the pressure of the tide. The most we can do is hope to go only sufficiently far with it as to prevent the power of government passing to those who would go much farther, and holding the situation where it can be remedied most quickly in the future, should conditions improve.[49]

Conditions did not improve. The recovery program of 1938 was ineffective in stimulating investment. Duplessis and Hepburn refused to let their municipalities borrow under the Municipal Improvements Assistance Act, and cities in other provinces were too poor to do so. Not a single low-rental housing project was begun. Unemployment hovered near the half-million mark through the winter of 1938-39, and with the Liberal mandate nearing expiry, electoral imperatives dictated that the experiment be continued. King and Gardiner tried repeatedly to rid themselves of the Wheat Board, symbol of First World War interventionism and sole survivor of the Bennett New Deal, but adamant support for the board from farm organizations made the political price of terminating it higher than they were prepared to pay. In 1939 Clifford Clark, aided by his new assistant, R.B. Bryce, fresh from Keynes's seminar at Cambridge, devised a Central Mortgage Bank which could write down debt for urban mortgage holders as the Farmers' Creditors Arrangements Act did. [50]

The 1939 budget increased federal grants-in-aid for relief and doubled public works spending, again without tax increases; instead, an innovation called the capital cost allowance permitted corporations to deduct one tenth of the cost of new capital investment from their corporate income tax. There was another planned deficit, this time of $60 million, and Finance Minister Dunning, back at his post after his convalescence, admitted that Wheat Board losses could force it still higher. Even Dunning had learned to describe things in the new language of active government. "In these days," he said in his budget speech, "if the people as a whole, and business in particular, will not spend, government must. It is not a matter of choice but of sheer social necessity. . . . The old days of complete laissez-faire, of devil-take-the-hindmost, have gone forever." Glacially, unwillingly, the federal government was back on the road from which it had detoured in the twenties, the road to a more interventionist state. [51]

CHAPTER 13

Canada on the Road to War

I

The King government's planned deficits of 1938 and 1939 cannot be understood in domestic terms only. The cost of rebuilding the armed forces was as important as fighting the Depression in unbalancing the federal budget. Enormous in comparison to anything that had ever been spent on the military in peacetime, the $60 million voted in April 1939 was but a tiny fraction of what eventually proved necessary to defeat the Axis. That it was so little and came so late demonstrated the lack of concern with which Canadians and their leaders had watched the deteriorating international situation and the extraordinary tenacity of their conviction that "Generals Atlantic and Pacific" would defend them. Two groups for the study of foreign policy tried to raise the national consciousness, the League of Nations Society and the Canadian Institute of International Affairs, but despite an articulate and even prestigious membership, they had little influence with the politicians or the public. Sir Maurice Hankey, secretary to the British cabinet, described their members as "highbrows [who] talk a lot of dreadful slop. . . . The mass of Canadians," he concluded after a visit to Canada in 1934, "do not think very much of these matters." Despite the repeated warnings of Winnipeg *Free Press* editor J.W. Dafoe that "the world proceeds hellwards at an accelerated pace," to most people the crises they read about in their newspapers were someone else's problems; someone should do something about them, but the someone was never Canada, whether through the League or through the Empire-Commonwealth.[1]

II

R.B. Bennett's Imperial bombast and the anti-Americanism of the Conservative election campaign of 1930 suggested that Canadian external policies were about to be abruptly altered in 1930. With insignificant exceptions, however, the directions of the King years – "to keep external commitments to a minimum and to steer a course between the two poles of Canada's external relationships: Britain and the United States" – were left unchanged. Bennett followed the tradition of serving as his own Minister of External Affairs, but made no attempt to dismantle the department that King's under-secretary, O.D. Skelton, had built. Skelton was retained in his post and, after a brief period of coolness with his new political master, regained his place as "Ottawa's indispensable man." The lack of departmental growth – there were eighteen officers in 1930 and twenty-one in 1935 – resulted from the financial restraint of the Depression and the lack of alarm over the world situation, not any hostility on Bennett's part. The three legations that the Tories had threatened to close remained in place, and in Tokyo and Paris, Bennett left Herbert Marler and Philippe Roy, the Liberal appointees, undisturbed. The only victim of the transition was the Minister to the United States, Vincent Massey, who had been designated to become High Commissioner to Britain. Bennett deemed Massey unsuitably Liberal for either post and demanded his resignation. He was replaced in Washington with W.D. Herridge, Bennett's future brother-in-law, and in London by Ontario premier G. Howard Ferguson, who rivalled Bennett for the title of Canada's most perfervid imperialist.[2]

   Whatever hopes the British government may have had that the rhetoric of Conservatives like Bennett and Ferguson heralded a reunited Empire were immediately dashed at the Imperial Conference of 1930. Despite Mackenzie King's fear that his successor would "undo one's work," Bennett made no attempt to turn back the constitutional clock but guarded the autonomist ground gained at the conferences of 1923 and 1926 and made a modest contribution to the shaping of the Statute of Westminster. As C.P. Stacey has pointed out, "it was by no means unsuitable that . . . a Conservative prime minister presided over the final stage," for the Statute was the culmination of a lengthy process in which the contributions of Macdonald and Borden had been at least as important as those of Laurier and King. The vestiges of imperial control that remained – amendment of the British North America Act and appeals to the Privy Council – had nothing to do with Bennett but were left with London because the provinces and the dominion had been unable to agree on a way to do these things in Canada. Bennett was less categorical than King in resisting proposals to co-ordinate imperial defence, but his resistance was equally effective. At the 1930 conference he attended a meeting of the Committee of Imperial Defence but requested that his participation be left out of the minutes, lest Canadians jump to the conclusion that Canada had become a member of the committee. After this first session as an observer, he followed King's practice of sending no representative to the CID, and throughout his administration ignored all British attempts to prod Canada to greater military effort. Apart from the relief camps and the construction of barracks in his home constituency, Bennett, says James Eayrs, "remained indifferent to the dilapidated condition of the country's defence forces." As his performance at the 1932 Imperial Economic Conference demonstrated, Bennett's imperialism had greater emotional than practical significance. His proposal for a "new economic empire" foundered on his own unwillingness to reduce Canadian tariffs, for Bennett generally confined his expressions of affection for the Empire to gestures that could be made at no real cost to Canadian manufacturing interests: thus his request in 1933 to His Majesty King George V to resume the practice, abandoned in the heady egalitarianism of the Great War, of granting titles to his subjects resident in Canada. The Prime Minister, Mackenzie King speculated correctly, longed for a title of his own.[3]

Nor was Bennett's attitude to the United States as different from King's as it at first seemed. Although the early thirties were the interwar nadir of the Canadian-American relationship, most of the difficulties were not of Bennett's making. Prohibition, in force until December 1933, continued to provide incidents that wounded Canadian national pride. To the sinking of the *I'm Alone* was added the case of the Nova Scotia rum-runner *Josephine K*, whose skipper was killed as the ship attempted to flee from the U.S. Coast Guard. And the American Congress cast the first stone in the trade war with the Smoot-Hawley Act. As Bennett reminded Americans, even with the large retaliatory increases in the Canadian tariff, "though you have been a good customer of ours, we in Canada have been a still better customer of yours." The American Department of State understood that Bennett was not anti-American. A briefing paper prepared for President Hoover explained that "for political reasons . . . Mr Bennett frequently finds it advisable to criticize us despite the fact that he personally is friendly to this country." Herbert Hoover himself made the largest contribution to the freeze on the forty-ninth parallel. He vigorously pushed the Smoot-Hawley Act, out of either ignorance or indifference to Canada's constant trade deficit with the United States, and Canadians were offended that he lavished attention on banana republics but could never find time to acknowledge them with an official visit. "Look North Mr. Hoover," advised the Ottawa *Citizen*. "If the goodwill of South America is worth cultivating, surely the goodwill of Canada is worth keeping."[4]

Hoover wanted only one thing from Canada, an agreement to build a St. Lawrence seaway that would improve grain transportation and keep the farmers of the midwest voting Republican. He seemed about to get it. A treaty was amicably negotiated and duly signed in July 1932 by W.D. Herridge and American Secretary of State Stimson, but the seaway was not to be constructed for another quarter-century. The fate of the treaty illustrates how Canadian-American relations can move beyond the control of presidents and prime ministers; the United States Senate rejected it, and Mitchell Hepburn repudiated the promise of his predecessor, George Henry, that Ontario would pay part of the Canadian share of construction costs. After Franklin Roosevelt replaced Hoover in the White House in 1933, Canadian-American relations warmed noticeably, and Bennett went to Washington to begin the discussions that led to the Reciprocity Treaty two years later. Because it was initiated by Conservatives but not concluded until the Liberals came to power in 1935, the treaty was, in the words of Ian Drummond, "sired by Bennett, but midwived by Mackenzie King." This instance more than anything else illustrates the continuity of Canada's relations with the United States between 1919 and 1939, whether they were conducted by a Liberal or a Conservative government.[5]

Nor was there much to distinguish Conservative and Liberal approaches to the League of Nations. Both parties viewed the League as a forum in which co-operation and conciliation would help to preserve peace, not as an agency to impose peace through the use of economic or military sanctions. Unlike Mackenzie King, R.B. Bennett was prepared in theory to support sanctions against an aggressor should the League decide to impose them; he recognized, however, that there was no consensus among League members on collective security, and he made no attempt to play a leading role in shaping one. "Canada is not an important member of the League," he explained to a Toronto clergyman; "what can one man do who represents only ten and a half millions of people?" O.D. Skelton had little use for the League, but the permanent officer of the Department of External Affairs in Geneva, Dr. W.A. Riddell, was a devoted believer. Riddell was subordinate, however, to the political delegates who arrived each autumn as their reward for service to the party in power and who regarded their trip as a holiday junket. In 1933 First Delegate R.J. Manion wrote more about the "beautiful little city on a lovely lake" in his reports to Bennett than he did about the alarming portents of a European war. "I had not intended saying a word at all [during the opening debate]," he informed the Prime Minister, "but may do so as Dr. Riddell [is] very strongly of the opinion that Canada should be among those speaking. Should I do so, it will be largely platitudes."[6]

Canada's reticence about collective security was demonstrated most clearly during the League's unsuccessful attempts to resolve the Sino-Japanese dispute over Manchuria. On September 18, 1931, the Japanese army touched off an incident at Mukden that was used as a pretext to invade the northern Chinese province. The forces of the weak and unstable Chinese government were easily routed, Manchuria was conquered, and the Japanese puppet-state of Manchukuo was established in February 1932. Dispatches from the Canadian legation in Tokyo, despite Herbert Marler's pro-Japanese attitude, left no doubt that Japan had violated the League Covenant, the Kellogg-Briand Pact, and the Nine-Power Washington Treaty, to all of which Canada was a signatory. But when the League Assembly met in special session in March, Canadian delegates assiduously avoided this fact, lest it strengthen the case of those nations calling for sanctions against Japan. First Delegate Sir George Perley was instructed "not to assess responsibility or propose punitive measures against Japan" but to insist that "the mediatory and preventative functions of the League" be used to resolve the crisis. To Canada's satisfaction, the Assembly deferred the problem by appointing a commission headed by Lord Lytton to investigate Chinese complaints of Japanese aggression.[7]

The Lytton report rejected Japanese justifications, recommended that Chinese sovereignty be restored in Manchuria, and proposed that League members refuse recognition to Japan's client, Manchukuo. Although the report was mild – no economic sanctions were suggested – Bennett cautioned Canadian delegate C.H. Cahan to speak against any "precipitate action" by the League Assembly that might cause Japan to "take up irrevocably a position of isolation and hostility to the League." Cahan interpreted his instructions very broadly (much *too* broadly, several historians have concluded), delivering a speech so sympathetic to Japan that the Japanese minister personally thanked an embarrassed O.D. Skelton for Canada's support. The Cahan speech brought down a torrent of criticism from those who wanted firm action against Japan, but it was in general agreement with British policy and was never repudiated by R.B. Bennett. It helped persuade the Assembly to refer the Lytton report to a committee for further study, but despite this conciliatory gesture, Japan continued her war in China. When the proposals of the report were at last adopted by the Assembly in February 1933, Canadian delegate Riddell, much to his satisfaction, voted in favour. The only effect on Japan, however, was to persuade her to withdraw from the League, and in October Nazi Germany goose-stepped after her, the first steps in a return to the naked power politics that the League had been created to curtail. The behaviour of Canada in the Far East fiasco made some tiny contribution to that outcome, but Cahan's apologia for Japanese aggression made the Bennett government seem more important than it had really been. Canadian policy in the Manchurian crisis was based on the realistic understanding that Canada could do nothing to enforce sanctions against Japan, and the equally realistic recognition that neither Britain, France, nor the United States, in Norman Hillmer's words, "had the belief that they had the current capability to bell the Japanese cat."[8]

The government's policy reflected opinion in parliament and among the public. Although J.W. Dafoe called editorially in the Winnipeg *Free Press* for "unified action as specified in the Covenant for aggressor nations," and J.S. Woodsworth warned that "through our inactivity we are laying the foundation for a war in the future," theirs was distinctly a minority position. The League's failure to deter Japanese imperialism was interpreted to mean that the League had failed; there was no thought that Canada might have failed the League. From those who had always been hostile to it came a chorus of I-told-you-sos. "The League is a toothless infant," sneered Dafoe's Winnipeg rival, the *Tribune*. Among those who had been undecided, complained the Toronto branch of the League of Nations Society, the "backing and filling . . . on the Sino-Japanese question" had made it "more and more difficult for us to arouse enthusiasm . . . for a body which at Geneva showed so little strength of purpose." In the Senate, Conservative A.D. McRae – a First World War brigadier-general – moved that Canada withdraw from the League altogether. It had been "the greatest effort for peace the world had ever known," but since Japan and Germany had flouted it and withdrawn, the League had been proved useless. To make it work would require military sanctions that Canadians could never accept; it was "unthinkable that Canadian sons should be sent to Europe to war with . . . sons of a decaying civilization." McRae's motion was defeated after a lengthy debate, but it had further illustrated that, as Ramsay Cook has put it, "as gangsterism revived in world affairs, so isolationist sentiment grew in Canada."[9]

III

This growing isolationist sentiment had no impact on the external policy of R.B. Bennett. He disavowed McRae and his motion and categorically denied that his government would abandon the League of Nations. During the second great test of collective security caused by the Italian invasion of Ethiopia in October 1935, Bennett's actions were much more resolute than they had been in the Manchurian episode, providing the one sharp contrast between his and Mackenzie King's conduct of foreign affairs. Italy began trying to provoke a war in East Africa in 1933, and in December 1934 fabricated the border incident between Italian Somaliland and Ethiopia that served as an excuse for invasion. During the next ten months Mussolini ostentatiously assembled his Fascist legions, while the League exhausted all possibilities of conciliation and began to study the application of economic sanctions.[10]

Despite the overwhelming evidence that Italy was bent on a war of aggression, Bennett had no firm policy when the League Assembly convened in September 1935. Preoccupied with the federal election called for October 15, he left external affairs to Under-Secretary O.D. Skelton, who made the case against sanctions: they had little public support, might provoke a general war, and could lead to conflict with the United States, which as a non-member of the League would continue to trade with Italy. Howard Ferguson, assigned to Geneva because every cabinet minister was campaigning, was accordingly instructed to remain silent. On September 4, however, Britain's Sir Samuel Hoare and Pierre Laval of France pledged to enforce the League Covenant, whatever the consequences. British approval of sanctions touched Bennett's imperial patriotism, and he understood that the combined power of Britain and France made effective action against Italy feasible. Over the objections of Skelton, whom he accused of "welshing" on Canada's pledge to support the Covenant, Bennett authorized Ferguson to promise that "Canada would join with other members of the League in considering how, by unanimous action, peace can be maintained." This was hardly a ringing declaration for collective security, but it was a sharp departure from fifteen years of Canadian attempts to define the concept out of existence. Sharper departures were to follow.[11]

Once Mussolini gave his marching orders, the League acted quickly to schedule an Assembly vote to condemn the Italian aggression. With Bennett busy electioneering, Skelton reasserted himself; Ferguson was ordered to "refrain from voting at the present juncture." At this juncture the extremely personal nature of Canadian foreign policy making became evident. Howard Ferguson, excited by the British Empire cooperation he had long talked about and which was actually occurring at Geneva, called Bennett by transatlantic telephone to protest that abstention would humiliate him and make Canada seem to be in the company of the handful of states that sympathized with Fascist Italy. "Fergy" was able to persuade Bennett to allow him to act at his own discretion. When a furious O.D. Skelton evoked Canada's "repeatedly and publicly declared opposition to sanctions," Bennett explained his reasoning with passion: ". . . every part of the Empire sees it clearly. We went into the League [and] must assume responsibilities or get out, not try to hornswoggle ourselves out. We will vote guilty. . . ."[12]

Five days later his government was obliterated at the polls. The Bennett interlude of Canadian foreign policy had ended characteristically with an impetuous decision, taken alone. Unleashed by Bennett, Ferguson thrust Canada into an unaccustomed position on centre stage by accepting a membership on the Committee of Eighteen to determine the details of the boycott against Italy. He proposed an immediate embargo on shipments of munitions, urging the committee to "show the world that the League is no longer to be scoffed or laughed at."

When Ferguson left Geneva after the defeat of the Bennett government, Canadian Advisory Officer W.A. Riddell stepped into his place. Deeply committed to collective security by economic sanctions, Riddell continued the new international activism. Exploiting the hiatus between Bennett's departure and King's arrival, Riddell acted without specific instructions and in defiance of his general directives, taking a leading role in defining the items to be placed under embargo and insisting that "any scheme of economic sanctions be comprehensive." When King issued an ambiguous statement "approving sanctions in this instance [without] necessarily establishing a precedent for future action," Riddell interpreted it as an endorsement. It was nothing of the kind, for Ottawa sent orders four days later that "no position should be taken on any question of importance . . . without definite instructions." King, with the approval of Skelton, had returned to the old course of avoiding initiatives and offering no encouragement to sanctions that had characterized Canadian policy until the two-month aberration at the end of Bennett's regime. But they had underestimated the speed and determination of W.A. Riddell. Before his new instructions arrived, he moved in the Committee of Eighteen to add oil to the list of products to be embargoed; if fuel were denied to Mussolini's mechanized army the war might actually be stopped. It was the boldest proposal yet put forward and was rapidly approved by the committee and submitted to the Assembly, but it was also plain disobedience to blunt directives from Ottawa to remain silent. [13]

For the second time in his career as prime minister, Mackenzie King learned of a critical event in Canadian external relations from the newspaper. Despite his discomfiture, he reacted as he had during the Chanak affair, avoiding public comment in the hope that the oil sanction would soon be obscured by the unfolding drama in Africa and Geneva. Riddell was sternly rebuked and at last gagged, but although he now sat mute in Switzerland, headlines around the world tagged the oil embargo the "Canadian Proposal." With the notable exception of the Winnipeg *Free Press*, editorial supporters of the oil sanction were lukewarm while opponents, including every French-language paper in the country, were outspoken. There is no evidence, however, that King was responding to any direct political pressure when he decided to end the false impression that he supported Riddell. Ernest Lapointe and O.D. Skelton, his only important counsellors on foreign policy, both wanted him to do so; Skelton argued that Anthony Eden, representing Britain on the Committee of Eighteen, had used Riddell as a cat's-paw to help Britain block Italian expansionism. With his help King drafted a statement that Lapointe released to the press December 2. The impression that "the Canadian government has taken the initiative in the extension of the embargo [was] due to a misunderstanding"; Riddell "represented only his own personal opinion . . . and not the views of the Canadian government." Questioned later by journalists, King tried to persuade them that repudiating Riddell did not mean a repudiation of the proposal and that his policy was as expressed a month earlier: sanctions if necessary, but not necessarily sanctions. The argument was specious; in Europe the statement was interpreted as abandonment of collective security, and the Italian government issued a request that the embargo "now be discarded." The British Foreign Office described it as "dirty work at the cross roads" and concluded that "the Canadian government have very easily – and without much dignity – lost their nerve."[14]

The British analysts were too generous; Canada, or at least Canada as personified by Mackenzie King, had never had any nerve to begin with. King was simply re-establishing his control of Canadian policy at the League of Nations and turning it back in the direction in which he had guided it in the 1920s. His renunciation of Riddell was a very personal decision, just as Bennett's decision to support Ferguson and Riddell had been. King was probably closer to the public temper, although there was no national consensus on the matter. The League of Nations Society itself had been unable to come to any decision about sanctions, being divided into one group that supported them and another that supported continued conciliation. At the moment of the repudiation there was a brief furor from dedicated internationalists like J.W. Dafoe and N.W. Rowell and from the imperially minded, who accepted the Toronto *Telegram*'s accusation, "Britain Stands Firm for Sanctions, but Canada Lies Down." Subsequent events left the imperialists with egg on their faces. A week after the Riddell repudiation, a startled world discovered that Hoare and Laval had concocted a secret pact to appease Mussolini by dismembering Ethiopia. The plan was never adopted, but the shocking news that Britain and France had considered allowing the aggressor to enjoy the spoils of his aggression undermined the support for collective security. Oil sanctions were never introduced, and the other sanctions were insufficient to end the invasion: on May 9, 1936, Mussolini annexed Ethiopia and declared the King of Italy to be its emperor. The first and only attempt of the

League of Nations to use serious measures of collective security to contain an aggressor had come to an ignominious conclusion, to which Canada had again made its own modest and distinctive contribution.[15]

Canada played no role in the later stages of the Ethiopian crisis. King refused to discuss the government's policy toward the continuation of sanctions, retreating into silence with the tacit co-operation of Opposition Leader R.B. Bennett. Pressed by J.S. Woodsworth for a statement of policy, King echoed his summation of the Chanak crisis. "When the whole story comes to be told," Canadians would understand that "but for the action of the government in this particular matter at that particular time, the whole of Europe might have been aflame today." King's fear was not the flames in Europe but the sparks that might fly to Canada as a consequence. Although English Canada was far from unanimous in its support of sanctions, French Canada was solidly in opposition. If sanctions led to a war between Britain and Italy, "we shall have the old war situation all over again, with the [Liberal] party divided as it was at the time of conscription." The foundation of King's foreign policy was that "our own domestic situation must be considered first, and what will serve to keep Canada united." Hitler's re-occupation of the demilitarized zone of the Rhineland in March 1936, in defiance of the League and in violation of the Locarno agreements, was a further sign that "Europe is becoming a maelstrom of strife, and that we are being drawn into a situation that is none of our creation by our membership in the League of Nations."[16]

King's preferred technique for ensuring domestic peace was to do nothing. "It is sometimes well to allow sleeping dogs to lie," he advised a back-bencher; "this is especially true when they happen to be the dogs of war." Canada's connection with the League required action, however, and after the smoke from Ethiopia cleared in June, he made a statement in the Commons. "Collective bluffing cannot bring collective security," he declared. Canadian governments, Liberal as well as Conservative, had always rejected military sanctions, and after the Italian experience there could be "no blinking the fact that economic sanctions may lead to war." In the future the League would have Canadian support only so far as it functioned as "a world-wide organization . . . for conference and conciliation." To get his message across, King personally led the delegation to Geneva in 1936. There he was immediately struck by "the absurdity of entrusting the affairs of one's country . . . to an aggregation of the kind which one sees in the Assembly Hall. Countries named by the dozens of which one has seldom or never heard, and none of which . . . would be of the slightest use in the crisis." His speech on September 29 was direct and unequivocal by anyone's standards, let alone Mackenzie King's: ". . . emphasis should be placed upon conciliation rather than coercion . . . automatic commitments to the application of force is not a practical policy." Collective security, even in theory, was out of the question for Canada.[17]

His words were well received at home. All three opposition parties, Conservative, CCF, and Social Credit, had accepted the substance of his June statement to parliament and could hardly object when he repeated it in Geneva. The weight of editorial opinion was massively favourable. It was normal for papers like *La Liberté*, a French-language Catholic journal in Manitoba, to describe the sentiments expressed as "a faithful reflection of moderate opinion in our country," but even Conservative papers like the Ottawa *Journal* conceded ungrudgingly that "Mr. King . . . spoke for the vast majority of Canadians." Disgruntled imperialists like the editor of the Toronto *Mail and Empire*, confused by the similarity between King's views and those of British Foreign Secretary Anthony Eden, criticized the speech as "academic and pacifist" but had no alternative to advocate. J.W. Dafoe, virtually the only dissenter, found this "last in a long series of acts by successive Canadian governments intended to circumscribe the League's power . . . the most discreditable of them all because it amounts to the rejection by Canada of the League." Significantly, however, Dafoe did not pretend it to be unrepresentative of his readers' opinions.[18]

IV

There had been only three possible directions for Canadian external policy, concluded R.A. Mackay and E.B. Rogers in a study prepared for the Canadian Institute of International Affairs: collective security through the League, a "British front policy," or isolation as practised by the United States. With the first emphatically rejected, it remained to choose between the other two, and the weight of opinion seemed to lie with isolationism. "The spirit of isolation is spreading in Canada like a prairie fire," wrote a worried J.W. Dafoe, who was hearing such thoughts from within the cabinet itself. Minister of Resources T.A. Crerar confided that "the more I see of the whole thing, the more certain I am that our destiny is on the North American continent and that if Europe is going to insist on destroying itself, it is no part of our mission to destroy ourselves in attempting to preserve it." The CCF national convention of 1936 resolved that "Canada should remain strictly neutral in cases of wars regardless of who the belligerents may be," and CCF intellectual F.H. Underhill urged that "we must make it *no /*

clear to the world, and especially to Great Britain, that poppies bloom-
ing in Flanders fields have no further interest for us. . . . European
troubles are not worth the bones of a Toronto grenadier."[19]

The strongest voices of isolation came from Quebec, where a North
American perspective had been inculcated by three centuries of existence on the western side of the Atlantic and a distaste for British
wars was universal. To French-Canadian natonalists, war implied conscription, federal incursions into provincial autonomy, and attendant
social crises caused by war-induced economic development: industrialization, urbanization, and an increase in the number of women
working in munitions factories instead of in the home. Like Quebec,
the Department of External Affairs was "a hive of isolationism," with
O.D. Skelton's congenital suspicion of Britain supplemented by that of
confirmed isolationist Loring Christie, who rejoined the department as
a legal adviser in 1935. "Is Canada to regard it as the normal thing that
every generation (or less) she is to invade the Continent of Europe and
join the European battle campaigns of the 20th century?" wrote
Skelton in a 1937 position paper on imperial defence, in a tone that left
no doubt of his own answer to the question.[20]

But the apparent strength of isolationism was illusory. In the United
States isolationism had a broad popular base and the political clout to
force Neutrality Acts that forbade sales of munitions to countries at
war. "The United States are acting wisely in this regard," applauded
Agnes Macphail, but attempts by Macphail and her colleagues to do the
same thing in parliament were repeatedly frustrated. Canada lacked
the long tradition of "no entangling alliances" that dated back to
George Washington, and English- and French-Canadian isolationists
found co-operation difficult. When the CCF's Grant MacNeil, a war
veteran, moved an amendment to the 1937 defence estimates that
called for the money to be spent on social programs, it received the
support of only his own party and some Social Creditors. Despite the
amendment's isolationist intent, not one French Canadian voted for it.
Liguori Lacombe, a 1917 conscript and a fiery apostle of isolation,
raised two objections. He disagreed with federal social security programs, and he felt the increased defence spending was needed to control the domestic left! Nothing could better illustrate the ideological
chasm that made even a temporary isolationist coalition impossible.[21]

The Achilles heel of Canadian isolationism, however, was the emotional bond that the English-Canadian majority felt with Britain, a
bond that transcended region and class. The East York Workers' Association, for example, when demonstrating against a sheriff's eviction
would drape a Union Jack over the door of a threatened household
and concluded their meetings by singing "God Save the King." This

sort of attachment to the Monarchy was intensified between 1935 and 1937, when the Royal Family overshadowed international crises as headline fodder. Within one year came the Silver Jubilee of George V, his death and the pomp of his state funeral, and the ascension to the throne of Edward VIII. Edward was considered Canada's own, for he had served in Flanders with the Canadian Corps and owned a ranch in Alberta; the Canadian Press reported that there would be a special coronation in Ottawa and that he would soon make a Canadian his queen. The second rumour was particularly wide of the mark, but Edward's abdication to marry an American divorcée damaged the Monarchy not at all. The next day Canadian newspapers were praising George VI, his beautiful wife, and the "little Princesses," Elizabeth and Margaret Rose. Millions of Canadians arose before dawn on May 12, 1937, to listen to the CBC's broadcast of George VI's coronation, and local ceremonies were held later that day, an official holiday. The ceremonies illustrated the wide popularity of royalty. In Winnipeg the Polish Falcon Society and the Ukrainian dancers joined the Orange Lodge and the Sons of England to take part in the program, and the highlight of the concert was the Ukrainian National Choir singing Kipling's "Land of Our Birth"![22]

The American legation in Ottawa tried to understand this apparent contradiction of a reverence for things British and an isolationism that appeared as profound as that of the United States. What most Canadians wanted, a report to the State Department concluded, was "continued membership in the British Commonwealth . . . with avoidance of entanglements that might lead Canada into another overseas war." The question was how both desires could be achieved simultaneously, and Mackenzie King epitomized within himself the national dilemma. He shared J.S. Woodsworth's repugnance for war, and could present the geographical case for neutrality better than Agnes Macphail; King believed he understood the deepest concerns of French Canada, and he felt O.D. Skelton's instinctive distrust of the British Foreign Office. Yet he could be as romantic about the imperial heritage as any other Canadian whose roots were in the British Isles. This last factor, emotional rather than logical, was the decisive determinant in King's mind and thus in Canadian foreign policy between 1937 and 1939. Mackenzie King would not risk war for the League of Nations, but as J.L. Granatstein and Robert Bothwell have established, there was never any doubt in his mind that Canada would be at Britain's side in a major European war brought about by fascist aggression. This, he wrote in September 1938, "was a self-evident national duty," but it was a conviction that delicate domestic political realities persuaded him to divulge only to his diary. Pressed by isolationists for a declaration of neutrality, or, less often, from imperialists for a promise to back up a British initiative, King fell back on his time-tested formula. "Over and over again," he responded to J.S. Woodsworth in January 1937, "we have laid down the principle that so far as participation by Canada in war is concerned, it will be for parliament to decide." This, notes C.P. Stacey, obscured the fact that "it would be up to the prime minister and the cabinet (as leaders of the majority party) to tell parliament *how* to decide."[23]

King knew what he would do if war came, but he never lost hope that war could be avoided. To this end at the Imperial Conference held in London after George VI's coronation, he joined with the other dominion leaders in endorsing a united British Commonwealth position on international affairs. There was no little irony in this perpetual opponent of a common imperial foreign policy falling into step with precisely that, but the irony is lessened when the basis of the policy is considered: "the ill-fated policy of appeasement." As James Eayrs points out, in 1937 the word was a synonym for conciliation; only as the policy evolved into feeding small democracies to dictators in a delusory search for "peace in our time" did the term "acquire its present pejorative connotation and become not so much a description as an epithet." British prime minister Neville Chamberlain was appeasement's parent, and some historians credit King with an indirect role in its conception. His unwillingness to commit Canada to bolder imperial foreign and defence policies, however, was just one of many influences that confirmed Chamberlain on his course of appeasement. "No sacrifice can be too great which can save a war," King recorded in his diary, and he did not waver from this conviction.[24]

His faith in appeasement rested on his personal confidence in the two men on whom it depended, Neville Chamberlain and Adolf Hitler. After the conference he told Chamberlain something he would not tell the Canadian people: that if appeasement failed and Britain went to war against a European aggressor, "Canada would assert herself in a strong way." He left London for Berlin, and although he conveyed the same message to Hitler (or claimed to have), his visit with the Führer persuaded him that his promise to Chamberlain would never have to be honoured. Hitler made "a very favourable" impression on King as "a man of deep sincerity," and King was convinced of "the determination of [Hitler] and his colleagues not to permit any resort to war." Thus reassured, for the first and only time in his career Mackenzie King cut his external policies to the pattern printed in London.[25]

The Spanish Civil War illustrates why King found it convenient to have Canadian and British foreign policies intersect between 1937 and 1939. The war began in July, 1936, with an attempt by the military to overthrow Spain's democratically elected government and dragged on until the last government stronghold of Madrid fell to the rebels in March 1939. General Francisco Franco's triumphant right-wing coalition included the regular army, the landed gentry, the Catholic Church, and the fascist *Falange*; from the outset it received troops, tanks, guns, and planes from Mussolini and Hitler. The legitimate government, supported by a mélange of anarchists, Trotskyists, communists, socialists, and liberals, received desultory aid from the Soviet Union. Both sides committed atrocities: German dive-bombers massacred the population of the Basque town of Guernica, while anarchists took it upon themselves to execute priests and nuns as enemies of the people.

Nowhere did the bloody fratricide in Spain arouse greater passion than in Canada. Catholics, whatever their ethnic background, rallied to Franco. "His victory will be that of Christian civilization against Marxist savagery," said *l'Action catholique* in one of fifty pro-fascist editorials it published during the conflict; the rebels, argued the *Catholic Register*, were saving "Europe and the World from the menace of a Red Spain." The left was no less categorical in support of the Republic. "Every man of decent feeling can only hope that the government will prevail," pronounced the *Canadian Forum*. The Trades and Labour Congress resolved for the Republicans; the Confédération des travailleurs catholiques declared for Franco. Students from Loyola College and the Université de Montréal attempted to drive Republican speakers out of halls defended by students from McGill.[26]

There was an important difference between those Canadians who supported Franco and those who supported the Republic. The former confined their role to propaganda and money; the latter were prepared to invest their lives. "It is in Spain that the real issues of our time are going to be fought out," Montreal surgeon Norman Bethune told a colleague; "it is there that democracy will survive or die." With the backing of the Committee to Aid Spanish Democracy, a group that rallied liberals, socialists, and communists to the cause, he went to Spain to organize a mobile blood transfusion service for wounded Loyalist soldiers and civilians. By Christmas 1936, Bethune had been joined by six hundred Canadians who had come to fight for the Spanish Republic. Some, like him, were communists, others simply "premature anti-Fascists." They formed the nucleus of the Mackenzie-Papineau Battalion of the International Brigade, formed in 1937 and named for the leaders of the Canadian rebellions a century before. The "Mac-Paps" eventually had a strength of 1,239; only 649 of them came home. "Excepting France," claims the battalion historian, "no other

country provided so great a number of volunteer soldiers in proportion to its population as did Canada."[27]

Mackenzie King at once recognized that Spain, far more than
Ethiopia, provided a cause for the potential domestic conflict he so
dreaded. The British scheme of non-intervention seemed to offer a
way out. Ignoring the presence of German and Italian troops in
Franco's forces, Britain had made it illegal for her citizens to volunteer
for or to provide aid to either side, in the hope that this would appease
Italy and prevent a formal alliance between Mussolini and Hitler. King
and Lapointe acted without thought for imperial strategy in the Mediterranean; the body of water that obsessed them was the Ottawa River.
Emulating British non-intervention would offer something to all but
the most active friends of Spanish democracy, and the international
crisis of the 1930s that stirred the most profound emotions was solved
with the shortest parliamentary debate. The Foreign Enlistment Act of
1937, described by Justice Minister Lapointe as the British act with "a
very few changes adapting it to Canada," provided two years' imprisonment for those who volunteered to fight in Spain, and the
Customs Act was amended to forbid the sale of equipment or munitions. The legislation seemed even handed, for it applied to both sides;
but all the volunteers had been destined for the Republicans, and the
Republic also bore the full weight of the embargo, for Franco was able
to buy from Canada indirectly because of his control of Spanish
Morocco.[28]

Non-intervention was a political success. Those who viewed the
civil war as – in the words of the London *Free Press* – "Red despotism
on the one hand and Fascist dictatorship on the other" were satisfied
Canada's hands were clean; admirers of Franco had blocked aid to his
opponents. Isolationists had the consolation that King had avoided
European complications; voices of imperial unity like the Toronto
Globe and Mail praised him for copying "Great Britain's decisive action." Only the Mac-Paps, locked in the struggle with Franco and his
fascist allies, were left with nothing to be grateful for. The Prime Minister was puzzled when an American friend expressed disappointment
in his policy. "I am at a loss to understand," he wrote back, "how you
or anyone else could be of the opinion that my sympathies in the
Spanish Civil War have been with Franco and the rebels."[29]

V

In his *Survey of International Affairs* for 1937, Arnold Toynbee
noted that Canada had belatedly joined the rest of the world in a pro-

gram of rearmament. Alluding to Senator Dandurand's oft-quoted description of Canada as "a fire-proof house," Toynbee observed wryly that her government had nonetheless concluded "that it was necessary to increase the premium on her insurance policy." It was not, however (to continue Toynbee's metaphor), to be a British Empire mutual policy. Mackenzie King's willingness to co-operate in the common foreign policy of appeasement was based on an appreciation of its political utility at home; for the same reason he continued his adamant opposition to all schemes for co-operation in imperial defence. Before, during, and after the Imperial Conference of 1937, King rejected proposals for co-operative air training programs, for joint production of weapons, ships, and planes. To be fair to him, the proposals were often presented with monumental insensitivity by the British military. One air training program was leaked to the press in a vain attempt to force his hand; "like the Chanak incident," he muttered, not without justification. He would explain at length to British representatives "how careful we had to be . . . if we were to keep Canada and the Empire united," and that there would be a "drift more strongly towards complete isolation were it to be thought that pressure was being placed upon the Government [of Canada] by the British Government to make anything in the nature of commitments for war purposes." Any "project of co-operation" could not carry "any seeming commitment to participation in war in advance of a decision by Parliament." Not surprisingly, no program sufficiently innocuous to avoid violating these two concepts – "no commitments" and "parliament will decide" – could ever be devised. When the war began, not a single co-ordinated plan for defence existed.[30]

After fifteen years in a budgetary grave, the Canadian armed forces were in desperate condition. The navy, air force, and militia were scarcely armed at all, and their weapons were as dangerous to themselves as to any enemy. Only two of the RCN's four destroyers were seaworthy, and, said Conservative defence specialist George Drew, "the fighting aircraft with which the RCAF are equipped are hopelessly out of date and there are many private aircraft in Canada that could fly rings around them." The militia, he added, was "a bow and arrow army." To meet these problems, expenditures were increased from their low point of $13 million in 1935-36 to $33 million in 1937-38, $35 million in 1938-39, and $60 million in 1939-40. The figures were described to the Liberal caucus – where the real defence debates took place – as "only for the defence of Canada against those who might wantonly assail us or violate our neutrality." King always added carefully that "there is nothing here for an expeditionary force," even though, as his biographer demonstrates, "he saw [privately] a need for going further and actually preparing for the possibility of supporting Britain in a European war." Ignoring the fact that the Conservatives had made not a single official statement on defence between 1935 and 1939, King cajoled reluctant isolationist back-benchers with the bait that the Liberal party was on "the middle course" between the Tories "who would do so much more . . . and Woodsworth [who] would do nothing at all. . . . Let us be united on a sane policy of defence – let us explain that policy to our people and let us above all strive at all times to keep Canada *united*."[31]

By and large the political side of rearmament was a success. Several French-Canadian Liberals voted against the defence estimates on occasion, but the intra-party crisis about which King never-endingly fretted did not take place. In two Quebec by-elections, the first in Lotbinière in December, 1937, and the second in St-Henri the next month, opposition candidates (one of them Camillien Houde) tried to make Liberal "imperialism" the issue, and both were badly defeated. With the assistance of Adolf Hitler, it actually became easier to pass the large budgets of 1938 and 1939 than it had been to pass that of 1937.[32]

The course of rearmament was not as smooth from the military point of view, however, because every nation in the world was scrambling to do the same thing. Canada had no arms industry to supply her own needs, and when the admirals and air vice-marshals went to buy ships and aircraft, the American and British manufacturers did not always have what they wanted and sometimes had nothing at all. The generals, to their chagrin, were given very little to spend. The RCN and the RCAF fitted neatly into the plans for home defence; any increase in the army and militia estimates, warned Senator Dandurand, might be misinterpreted in Quebec as preparation for an expeditionary force for overseas. By September 1939 the navy and the air force, though still incapable of the role assigned to them, had been greatly improved. The army, as its official historian has written, was "utterly inadequate by comparison with the scale of the coming emergency."[33]

The foundation of any Canadian policy of home defence was of course a good relationship with the United States, and with Franklin Roosevelt in the White House the relationship became warmer than it had ever been. Roosevelt seemed to have a genuine interest in Canada, and in July 1936 he found the time that Coolidge and Hoover never had available to make a state visit to Governor General Lord Tweedsmuir at his residence in the Citadel at Quebec. Canadians were thrilled. "It is impossible," effused *Saturday Night*, "to think of one another as foreigners. The common quality of 'North Americanness' . . . overrides international frontiers."[34]

One Canadian caught up in the emotion of the moment was Mackenzie King. It was the second time he had met the president, and the beginning of the personal friendship between "Franklin and Mackenzie" that he came to feel so important to understanding between the two countries. It was a friendship less intimate than King might have liked to admit – he never screwed up his courage to tell Roosevelt that his few close friends called him "Rex" – but there was something there that had never existed before and probably never has since between a president and a prime minister. "To promote enduring friendship between English speaking peoples" was an international mission that King saw as part of the strategy of appeasement. He clung tenaciously to the dream of Ottawa's special role as a "linchpin" between Washington and London and hoped to make the United States part of a scheme of "economic appeasement" of Germany and Italy. This was his exaggerated hope for the trilateral trade negotiations of 1938: "an alliance of three great democratic groups in the interest of world peace." The Canada–United States and United States–United Kingdom agreements that emerged lowered trade barriers in the North Atlantic triangle, but their contribution to projecting an image of Anglo-American solidarity that could prevent war was nil.[35]

On August 18 of that year Franklin Roosevelt was presented with an honorary degree by Queen's University. He used the occasion to make explicit something that had been understood since the Laurier era. "Canada is part of the sisterhood of the British Empire," he told the special convocation assembled in the Golden Gaels' football stadium. "I give to you the assurance that the people of the United States will not stand idly by if domination of Canadian soil is threatened by any other Empire." In the world situation of 1938 this took on a new implication, that Canada and the United States might become active allies, not simply passive friends. In Canada, only the highest of Tory imperialists disapproved of the idea, and in Britain there was cautious enthusiasm for it. King responded that Canada understood her reciprocal responsibility to be sufficiently well armed to see that "should the occasion ever arise, enemy forces should not be able to pursue their way, either by land, sea or air to the United States, across Canadian territory."[36]

To King, the exchange of pledges with the President signified that "we have at last got our defence programme in good shape. Good neighbour on one side; partners within the Empire on the other. Obligations to both in return for their assistance. Readiness to meet all joint emergencies." More dispassionate assessments were less optimistic. No strategic planning had gone on with either the United States or Britain. The enemy was in Europe, and as an External Affairs memorandum warned, Roosevelt had said exactly nothing about "military support for other democracies outside the Americas." The declaration, the memo concluded, "affords no reason for shirking our responsibility for our own defence."[37]

VI

It took Canadians a very long time to come to the understanding that Italy and especially Germany were on an unalterable collision course with the international interests and the domestic values of Britain, many of which Canada shared. Successive diplomatic crises provoked by the dictators could all be rationalized. "Hitler has no doubt violated the Locarno pact by moving his troops into the proscribed area," Nellie McClung told a Victoria Current Events Club after the occupation of the Rhineland, but "after all [it] is German territory." The Winnipeg *Tribune* was one of the many newspapers that argued that "a Germany with her self-respect restored . . . may be the means of dispelling the war clouds hanging so ominously over Europe." The repression of "non-Aryans" in Germany was accurately reported in Canada, but the stories were greeted with indifference. When the Communist party's Workers' Sports Association tried to mobilize a boycott of the 1936 Berlin Olympic Games, it met with utter failure. Sportswriters criticized the protesters, not the Nazis, in language that suggested why repression of minorities in Germany was so easily accepted in Canada. "Roman Catholics or Jews may be given the worst of it [in] Berlin," wrote Ted Reeve, "but . . . it should not be enough to keep away any valiant Irishman or Hebrew from the contests, if a good Mick or Abe is enough athlete to bid for the world's championship." When they marched past Hitler's box in the opening ceremonies, the hundred members of the Canadian team gave the Führer the extended-arm Nazi salute – "as a gesture of friendship," they claimed, although they were the only Commonwealth team to do so.[38]

One explanation of Canadian lack of concern about fascist outrages is the pervasive anti-Semitism of Canadian society itself. Canada's response to the flood of 800,000 Jews who poured out of Europe to escape the concentration camps was to raise the dam of immigration restrictions still higher. Only four thousand were accepted between 1933 and 1939, by far the smallest number in proportion to population among those countries that took the refugees in. Fascism was also excused as an overzealous form of anti-communism. The Toronto *Mail and Empire*'s editorial comment that it "might prefer Fascism to the Moscow-bred program of the CCF" was in no way unusual. Since the Communist party's was the first voice to be raised against Hitler and Mussolini, anti-fascism was handicapped by its red tinge; "they would fasten the opprobrious epithet Fascism on every healthy reaction against Red intrigues," protested the *Catholic Register*. In French Canada, anti-communism and anti-Semitism intersected. Hitler had made mistakes, an article in *l'Action catholique* agreed, but "one has to give him credit for having snatched his country from the hands of the Communists by laying his iron hand on the disorderly elements, very many of whom, in Germany as in Russia, were Jews." Unpleasant as they are to read, such comments did not confirm their authors as fascists. Emboldened by these attitudes, however, and by the totalitarian tide in Europe, Canada's real fascists began to crawl out of the woodwork in 1937 and 1938.[39]

It is a chicken-and-egg argument whether the sudden discovery of an active fascist movement at home sensitized Canadians to international fascism or the cause and effect were the reverse. Although almost unknown until a wave of magazine and newspaper exposés in the first half of 1938, fascists had long been present in Canada. In the 1920s Mussolini had used the Italian consulates to plant *fasci* in the Italian communities of Montreal and Toronto, and after 1933 the German consular service sponsored the Deutscher Bund Canada to spread the doctrines of the National Socialist German Workers' Party to German immigrants and persons of German descent. Both efforts succeeded only to the extent that these communities were *in* Canada but not *of* it, and the *fasci* in particular were as much social as ideological. Neither group made or sought to make contact with the most important native fascist parties: the Winnipeg-based Canadian Nationalist Party; the Canadian Union of Fascists, a purportedly nationwide federation with headquarters in Toronto; and the Parti national social chrétien, which had its strength in Quebec. Members of each of these parties wore solid-coloured shirts with swastika emblems modified to appear "Canadian" – the CNP's was surrounded by maple leaves and topped with a beaver. Each party had a program inspired by Hitler, Mussolini, or Oswald Mosley that called for some version of the corporate state. Each published a scurrilous newspaper with the crudest anti-Semitism as its editorial staple. The PNSC attracted the most attention, probably because its leader, Adrien Arcand, looked more like a führer than the dumpy middle-aged men who led the other parties, and because the virulent anti-Semitism of the right wing of French-Canadian nationalism made Arcand's claim to have 80,000 followers seem less implausible than it should have to English-speaking journalists unfamiliar with Quebec.[40]

Arcand became a celebrity when the Toronto *Globe and Mail* introduced him to its readers in a series on Nazi propaganda in Canada. There followed stories in American magazines and – the ultimate attention-getter – a spread in the new photo journal, *Life*. The fascists read their press clippings and divined that their time had come; on March 3, 1938, the leaders announced that they were combining to form the National Unity Party/Parti unité nationale, with Arcand at its head. "To call Arcand a windbag and his movement a chimera is not quite good enough," warned Frederick Edwards of *Maclean's*, with ominous references to Hitler and Mussolini; "recent history warns of the unwisdom of so casual a rejection." Nine days after the National Unity Party press conference in Toronto came the *Anschluss*, Germany's absorption of Austria into the Third Reich, and in the next issue of *Maclean's* Edwards reversed his ground: "Fascism in Canada is not growing any more. . . . The antics of Adolf Hitler have blasted it, at least temporarily, perhaps for all time."[41]

Hitler's "antics" had barely begun. In May came the shocking revelation that the Reich was using a dummy company based in Holland to buy the St. Lawrence island of Anticosti from the Consolidated Paper Corporation. An embarrassed King government immediately blocked the sale, and the RCMP, which in September 1937 had claimed there were "no Nazi activities nor any Nazi movement in Canada," was ordered to watch the far right with the same energy that it had hounded the left. Reaction to Anticosti, reported the American legation in Ottawa to the State Department, had been greater than that to the *Anschluss*. In conversation with Secretary of State Cordell Hull, Canada's minister to Washington, Herbert Marler, ventured that however nasty and brutal Adolf Hitler and his regime might be, no more than 10 per cent of Canadians would go to war to defend a nation in Central Europe.[42]

People soon learned more about Central Europe than they cared to know. With Austria in his hands, Hitler reached out for the *Sudetendeutsche* areas of Czechoslovakia, and throughout the summer of 1938 Canadians watched in horrified fascination the desperate British attempts to find a way out short of war. Mackenzie King knew that English Canada shared his belief that Canada should be at Britain's side if the war were unavoidable and the cause were just, and Hitler's truculence left no doubt on either score. On August 31 King privately informed Ian Mackenzie and Chubby Power that he "would not consider being neutral in this situation for a minute." The cabinet, he was certain, would unite behind him, but the country would probably be divided. He so dreaded making a public announcement that he literally became ill and spent the first two weeks of September in bed under a nurse's care. Neville Chamberlain's shuttle diplomacy to Munich brought him great relief. King cabled to the British prime minister "profound admiration for the vision and courage shown in your decision to have a personal interview with Herr Hitler" but informed neither Chamberlain nor Canada of his cabinet's decision to fight with Britain if the negotiations went wrong. "We do not consider in the light of all the circumstances known to us that public controversy as to action in hypothetical contingencies would serve the interest of peace or of Canadian or Commonwealth unity," read the official statement issued to obscure the situation. To King's, Canada's, and the world's immense applause, Chamberlain produced a solution. The Czechs would lose a third of their territory, but Hitler promised to take it from them in a gentlemanly fashion and to take no more. The settlement was enormously popular in Canada. *Le Devoir* gave Chamberlain its ultimate accolade, comparing him to Pope Pius XI as an "artisan of harmony among men, races, nations." In later years Munich became a synonym for cowardice, but as Arthur Lower reminds us in his memoirs, "who was there that could not say that he was glad of the respite?"[43]

VII

Munich was the turning point on Canada's road to war. Mackenzie King never ceased to hope for peace, and continued to press appeasement on Chamberlain, but during the dress rehearsal over Czechoslovakia he had faced the cabinet with his intentions and from then on could prepare the public to accept the idea of a European war. There was never a forthright declaration of support for Britain, but King now spoke regularly of it as a possibility. After Hitler seized what was left of Czechoslovakia in March 1939, King did so with uncharacteristic passion: "If there were a prospect of an aggressor launching an attack on Britain, with bombers raining death on London [a remarkably accurate prediction], I have no doubt what the decision of the Canadian people and parliament would be. We would regard it as an act of aggression, menacing freedom in all parts of the British Commonwealth." French-Canadian press reaction to this rejection of isolationism brought a qualification from King: ". . . the days of great expeditionary forces of infantry crossing the oceans are not likely to recur [a remarkably inaccurate prediction]. . . . Conscription of men for overseas service would not be a necessary or effective step. Let me say that so long as this government may be in power, no such measure will be enacted." In a long address the next day, Ernest Lapointe reiterated the two principles presented by his leader: if Britain went to war, there could be no neutrality, but there would be no conscription. Both Lapointe and King added their usual caveats about parliament deciding, but there in essence was the compromise on which they would lead Canada to war in September.[44]

It was a compromise that won broad support. Conservative leader Robert Manion could say nothing but "me too," for he had already established the same two principles as the cornerstones of Tory foreign policy. The spokesmen of English-Canadian isolationism still talked articulately of neutrality, but increasingly they spoke for no one but themselves. The rank and file of the CCF rebelled against the "Intelligentsia group" and "their continuous attempt to force upon the CCF an isolationist policy," and within the party's National Council, Grace and Angus MacInnis, Woodsworth's daughter and son-in-law, argued that "only collective military action by the rest of the world could stop the aggression." Since the League of Nations was unavailable to provide such action, who else but Britain could lead the democracies? Lester Pearson, who had flirted with the isolationism so fashionable at the Department of External Affairs, explained this feeling to his superior, O.D. Skelton:

> . . . would our complete isolation from European events (if such a thing were possible) save us from the effects of a British defeat, and . . . even if it did, could we stand by and watch the triumph of Nazidom, with all that it stands for, over a Great Britain which, with all her defects, is about the last abode of decency, reason and liberty . . .? If I am tempted to become completely cynical and isolationist, I think of Hitler screeching into the microphone, Jewish women and children in ditches on the Polish border, Goering, the ape-man and Goebels, the evil imp, and then, whatever the British side may represent, the other does indeed stand for savagery and barbarism.[45]

The cornerstone of isolationism in French Canada was opposition to conscription. French Canadians were not pacifists; as Maxime Raymond, leader of the isolationist bloc in the federal Liberal caucus, frequently asserted: ". . . every Canadian citizen has the military obligation of defending the soil of his motherland . . . but no one is entitled to ask them to go and shed their blood in Europe, or in Africa, or in Asia for the greater power and glory of another country, even if that country should be England or France." The universal no-conscription pledge, where it was believed, completely disarmed this argument. Maurice Duplessis, at war with King over domestic issues, chose not to exploit isolationist feeling for political purposes – at least not until after the war had begun. He refused to allow René Chaloult's non-participation motion to be debated in the legislature, and when five hundred angry Laval students marched to the legislature to protest King's speech of March 20, he warned them against "unruly conduct" and refused to commit himself on the issue.[46]

Hitler's treatment of the Catholic Church in Germany and in Austria knocked away another isolationist prop by destroying whatever small sympathy the Führer had enjoyed as a corporatist, and his non-aggression treaty with the Soviet Union in August 1939 contradicted his anti-communism and produced an outburst of anger in the French-language press. "The union of these two anti-God forces," wrote a Catholic editor, "is a menace to western civilization." After the Nazi-Soviet Pact, Germans were once more described as "les Boches" in French-language journals.[47]

None of these things was going to make French Canadians enthusiastic about going to war, or help them to understand why their English-Canadian counterparts persisted in acting as if the Statute of Westminster had never been passed. But the cautious policies from Ottawa coupled with the "political banditry" from Berlin made them less apprehensive about the "call of the blood" that had begun to course through the veins of English Canada.[48]

The Commonwealth connection was cemented by the Royal Tour of May and June, 1939. From the moment King George VI and Queen Elizabeth set foot on Canadian soil at Quebec – the first of the seventeen English and French sovereigns who had ruled Canada to do so – until they departed from Halifax a month later, the tour was an imperial public relations masterpiece. In the nine provinces Their Majesties were hailed by two and a half million adoring Canadian subjects. Hundreds of thousands watched their motorcades through cities and towns, but most touching were the families who waited beside the railway tracks, scrubbed and dressed in what little finery they possessed, to glimpse the blue-and-gold painted Royal Special as it flashed past.

Mackenzie King wrung every drop of national unity from the visit and was at his Monarch's side every time a flashbulb popped to make it plain that George VI was Canada's King, not simply England's. His Majesty's addresses were replete with praise for the way "English and French have shown in Canada that they can keep pride and distinctive culture"; and to the astonishment of French Canadians, accustomed to anglophone public men to whom *"bonjour"* was a mystery, the King spoke commendable French. The Queen was fluent. She graciously thanked every prepubescent Canadienne who presented her with flowers and chatted in French for a quarter hour with the Dionne quintuplets and their parents. "By the smile of a Queen and the French words of a King the English have conquered once more the cradle of New France," muttered an unconverted Omer Héroux in *Le Devoir*, for the political point of the pagentry was never far away. The crowd awaiting the royal couple in Montreal was entertained by two men wearing masks of Hitler and Mussolini. "Ach, Benito, ve haf been fooled," read the Führer's placard. "Yes," replied Il Duce's sign, " – and to think we believed that the Empire was crumbling."[49]

Whether the Empire would solidly support him or not, Neville Chamberlain was determined that Poland would not be another Czechoslovakia. When Germany demanded territorial concessions from the Poles, Chamberlain abandoned appeasement and extended guarantees to the Polish government without consulting or informing the dominions in advance. Mackenzie King was angry, but after a dozen years of refusing all consultation he had a very weak case. The Prime Minister of Canada listened to the final prelude to war on the radio, like other Canadians. O.D. Skelton, now an isolated isolationist, issued a memorandum of despair: "The first casualty of war has been Canada's control of her own destinies. In spite of a quarter century of proclamation and achievement of equal and independent status . . . if war comes in Poland and we take part, that war comes as the consequence of commitments made by the Government of Great Britain, about which we were not in one iota consulted." On September 1, 1939, the Panzers rolled into Poland. A British ultimatum to withdraw was ignored. On September 3, King George VI read his British government's declaration of war against Germany, and called on his "peoples across the Seas, who will make our cause their own . . . to stand firm and united in this time of trial."[50]

In the collective psyche of English Canada their country was at war from that moment. It was for imperial solidarity that they went to war, not to fight fascism. "Counterfactual hypotheses" are for social scientists more sanguine about their work than are historians, but J.L. Granatstein's contention that "if Britain had stayed out when Hitler attacked Poland, Canada would have stayed neutral as well" is correct. It must be remembered, however, that for many English Canadians defending the Empire and defending democracy had been welded into one objective, just as they were twenty years earlier during the Great War.[51]

There was little left for parliament to decide – the armed forces had already been put on a war footing – but Mackenzie King acted out the last gesture of his charade. When the House assembled on September 7, only J.S. Woodsworth, Maxime Raymond, Liguori Lacombe, and Wilfrid Lacroix spoke against participation. With fewer than five opposed, the isolationists could not call for a recorded vote. The Commons would have been officially unanimous had not the Speaker agreed as a courtesy to Woodsworth to add the words "on division" to the account in Hansard. On September 9 His Majesty, at the request of his Canadian government, declared a state of war between Canada and the German Reich. He did so on behalf of a country that had none of the giddy enthusiasm of 1914. English Canada looked ahead with quiet determination; French Canada acquiesced because of the pledge of no conscription. The country was not united, but it was thankful not to be irreparably divided.

Canada's entry into the Second World War, without a resumption of the searing debate that had clouded the last phase of the First, has been described by a historian who otherwise conceals his admiration as "the greatest achievement of Mackenzie King's career." It remains one of the few significant achievements of Canadian political leadership in the decades between the wars, and in 1939 it was premature to judge King's manoeuvres successful. The phoney war of 1939-40, as Donald Creighton has emphasized in *Canada 1939-1957*, was only an "ambiguous prelude" to the conflict that followed. In September, 1939, neither King nor country had been tested under fire.[52]

CHAPTER 14

Decades of Discord

The years 1922 to 1939 have an unusual cohesion. In December 1921, the electoral repudiation of the Union government signalled Canada's emergence from the cauldron of the Great War and its turbulent aftermath. In September 1939, when parliament all but unanimously declared war on Germany, the country was immersed in another world war. The decades between have an essential unity, despite the dissimilarity of the labels we borrow from the United States to describe them: the "roaring" twenties and the "dirty" thirties. Both were decades of failure, tragedies of missed opportunities. The previous quarter-century had seen the "nation transformed" by industrialization, urbanization, immigration, and westward expansion. These social and economic changes created regional, ethnic, and class divisions that political structures were unable to bridge. The election of 1921 left Canada with its first minority government and revealed the width of the cracks within Confederation.

The Progressive challenge to political orthodoxy seemed to hold out a bright, democratic promise. "We could work wonders if we would," enthused Manitoba Progressive Janet Wood. "Let us be up and doing, with a heart for any fate." But a national Progressive movement wrecked on the same rocks of region, ethnicity, and class that divided the nation, and the party that won sixty-four seats in its first election was a negligible force five years later. The reforming impulse that had stimulated Progressivism soured into disillusion, as the panaceas of prohibition and women's suffrage fell short of their unrealistic goals. In the churches the Social Gospel, religion's seal of approval for reform, retreated before mysticism and materialism. To Social Gospellers, Jesus had been the world's greatest social reformer; in the 1924 best-seller *The Man Nobody Knows*, he became "an A-1 salesman . . . the founder of modern business."[1]

The two-party pattern was quickly re-established in federal politics, although electoral hegemony went to the Liberal party and to William Lyon Mackenzie King. Rather than honour their reformist platform of 1919, with its ringing calls for health and unemployment insurance, old age pensions, and "equal remuneration for work of equal value" for Canadian women, King and his party fell back to the politics of the lowest common denominator. Ignoring the ominous warnings of the severe recession of 1921-24, they dismantled or emasculated the modest initiatives taken by their predecessors to respond to the needs of a more complex urban and industrial society. The Conservative party offered no alternative vision. "The dominant mood . . . of the two parties," commented an American observer in 1927, "appears to be a timid, more or less helpless, acceptance of the status quo." The powerful central government that had characterized the first fifty years of Confederation was no more. What authority the federal government didn't abdicate the courts took away, as the provinces became co-ordinate with, rather than subordinate to, the dominion.[2]

The real leaders of Canada were not federal or provincial politicians but bankers and businessmen. *These Be Your Gods*, proclaimed the title of a collection of business biographies, and the unprecedented prosperity of the later twenties was taken as proof of the omnipotence of the deities of commerce, finance, and industry. But the wealth of the "new economic era" remained inequitably distributed among regions and classes, and the new staples, minerals and newsprint, proved as vulnerable as the old to the vagaries of international demand. The worldwide depression of the 1930s struck Canada more severely than every other capitalist country except the United States.[3]

To confront the crisis, Canadians chose R.B. Bennett, a blustering millionaire who pledged to defeat the depression but in the end was defeated by it. When his atavistic attempts at recovery failed, Bennett turned to repression and relief camps, leaving a legacy of alienation best symbolized by the bloody confrontation in Regina on Dominion Day, 1935. Provincial regimes did no better. The decentralized federalism of the twenties proved utterly inadequate to meet the needs of the families of the one worker in three without a job. "In this country we do not die of starvation," wrote poet Dorothy Livesay, "we live it."[4]

A cacophony of dissentient voices – communist, fascist, CCF, Social Credit, Union Nationale, Reconstructionist – shouted other answers into the void. Only the Co-operative Commonwealth Federation had a comprehensive program and a national perspective, yet it, like the rest of these movements, failed to make a national mark. Instead all were suppressed, marginalized, co-opted, or confined within a single province. The political beneficiary of the Depression was the Liberal party, which at decade's end ruled in Ottawa and every provincial capital save Edmonton. As even the Bennett Conservatives belatedly called for a "New Deal," King and his party clung to their *laissez-faire*, non-interventionist ideology, investigating the economic crisis while they waited for it to go away. Although the "Ottawa Men," bureaucrats capable of managing a modern, interventionist state, had arrived in the national capital, the political will to take their advice had not. The only challenges the Liberals met with alacrity were those to their own political survival, as they built the coalition that made them Canada's "Government Party."[5]

Achievements on the international stage would seem to offset this unremitting recital of domestic failure. Canada became an international presence during the inter-war years, with her own seat at the League of Nations, a clear definition of her autonomous status within the Empire-Commonwealth, and the launching of legations in Tokyo, Paris, and, most important, Washington. But there was more form to these gestures than substance. Although a more positive attitude on Canada's part would not have saved the League or maintained world peace, Canadians played a disproportionately important role in extinguishing whatever embers of Wilsonian idealism still smouldered by leading the attempts to undermine the collective security provisions of the covenant. As the world swept toward war, Canadians brought nothing to imperial councils except another voice to support the policy of appeasing the dictators. Despite the nationalists' loud protestations of autonomy and the many claims that Canada had become a North American nation, it was English Canada's sentimental attachment to the mother country that placed the country at Britain's side in 1939, not a revulsion against international fascism.

The domestic wounds of two decades of discord were all too evident as Canadians prepared to go to war. A third of a million were still officially unemployed; military service provided thousands of young Canadians with their first job, first new boots, first decent suit of clothes. On a West Coast parade square that September, one recruit "marched out of the ranks and demanded in curt tones, 'When do we eat?'" This soldier knew the truth of what the radicals had long preached: that the federal government would spend money to make war at a rate that King and Bennett had thought immoral to spend for relief of the unemployed. This paradox underlined the narrow vision that was the hallmark of Canada's political leaders during these years of frustration. Canada, wrote Arthur Lower after a lifetime of reflection, "is a country whose major problems are never solved." This could perhaps be said to be true of any country. During the decades between the two World Wars, however, Canada's political leaders did their best to see that those problems were never addressed.[6]

TABLES

Note: For abbreviations used in sources, see NOTES.

Table Ia
1921 Federal Election Results

Province	Seats Won				Popular Vote				Per Cent Popular Vote			
	Cons.	Lib.	Prog.	Other	Cons.	Lib.	Prog.	Other	Cons.	Lib.	Prog.	Other
Nova Scotia	16				83,928	136,064	31,897	7,904	32.3	52.4	12.3	3.0
New Brunswick	5	5		1	61,172	76,733	16,223	1,224	39.4	49.4	10.4	0.8
Prince Edward Island		4			19,504	23,950	6,453	2,537	37.2	45.7	12.3	4.8
Quebec		65			146,236	558,056	29,197	61,487	18.4	70.2	3.7	7.7
Ontario	37	21	24		445,175	338,282	314,092	37,875	39.2	29.8	27.7	3.3
Manitoba		1	12	2	42,218	18,816	75,578	36,151	24.4	10.9	43.7	20.9
Saskatchewan		1	15		37,335	46,448	136,472	3,610	16.7	20.7	61.0	1.6
Alberta			10	2	35,181	27,404	90,791	19,528	20.3	15.8	52.5	11.3
British Columbia	7	3	2	1	74,225	46,249	13,917	20,608	47.9	29.8	9.0	13.3
Yukon		1			707	658		18	51.1	47.6		1.3
TOTAL	50	116	64	5	945,681	1,272,660	714,620	190,942	30.3	40.7	22.9	6.1

Others elected: Man. (2): Independent Liberal (1); Labour (1)
Alta. (2): Labour (1); Independent (1)
B.C. (1): Independent (1)

Table Ib
1925 Federal Election Results

Province	Seats Won				Popular Vote				Per Cent Popular Vote			
	Cons.	Lib.	Prog.	Other	Cons.	Lib.	Prog.	Other	Cons.	Lib.	Prog.	Other
Nova Scotia	11	3			125,283	93,110		3,617	56.4	41.9		1.6
New Brunswick	10	1			90,489	61,087		84	59.7	40.3		0.1
Prince Edward Island	2	2			23,749	25,681			48.0	52.0		
Quebec	4	59		2	269,548	474,192		56,246	33.7	59.3		7.0
Ontario	68	11	2	1	694,240	377,758	112,022	34,357	57.0	31.0	9.2	2.8
Manitoba	7	1	7	2	70,341	34,554	46,067	19,325	41.3	20.3	27.1	11.3
Saskatchewan		15	6		49,821	82,283	62,411	1,904	25.4	41.9	31.8	1.0
Alberta	3	4	9		51,102	44,277	50,574	14,524	31.8	27.6	31.5	9.1
British Columbia	10	3		1	90,016	63,374	11,078	18,161	49.3	34.7	6.1	9.9
Yukon	1				742	508			59.4	40.6		
TOTAL	116	99	24	6	1,465,331	1,256,824	282,152	148,218	46.5	39.9	8.9	4.7

Others elected: Que. (2): Independent Liberal (1); Independent (1)
Ont. (1): Independent Liberal (1)
Man. (2): Labour (2)
B.C. (1): Independent (1)

Table Ic
1926 Federal Election Results

Province	Seats Won				Popular Vote				Per Cent Popular Vote			
	Cons.	Lib.	Prog.	Other	Cons.	Lib.	Prog.	Other	Cons.	Lib.	Prog.	Other
Nova Scotia	12	2			122,965	99,581		6,412	53.7	43.5		2.8
New Brunswick	7	4			87,080	74,465			53.9	46.1		
Prince Edward Island	1	3			26,217	29,222			47.3	52.7		
Quebec	4	60		1	275,280	500,850		27,256	34.3	62.3		3.4
Ontario	53	26	2	1	661,714	474,885	50,360	35,147	54.1	38.9	4.1	2.9
Manitoba		11	4	2	83,100	74,621	22,092	17,194	42.2	37.9	11.2	8.7
Saskatchewan		18	3		67,524	139,262	38,324		27.5	56.8	15.6	
Alberta	1	3	11	1	49,514	38,451	60,740	8,311	31.5	24.5	38.7	5.3
British Columbia	12	1		1	100,066	68,317		16,087	54.2	37.0		8.7
Yukon		1			823	648			55.9	44.1		
TOTAL	91	128	20	6	1,474,283	1,500,302	171,516	100,407	45.3	46.1	5.3	3.4

Others elected: Que. (1): Independent (1)
Ont. (1): Independent Liberal (1)
Man. (2): Labour (2)
Alta. (1): Labour (1)
B.C. (1): Independent (1)

CANADA 1922-1939

Table Id
1930 Federal Election Results

Province	Seats Won				Popular Vote				Per Cent Popular Vote			
	Cons.	Lib.	Prog.	Other	Cons.	Lib.	Prog.	Other	Cons.	Lib.	Prog.	Other
Nova Scotia	10	4			140,503	127,179			52.5	47.5		
New Brunswick	10	1			109,716	75,342			59.3	40.7		
Prince Edward Island	3	1			29,692	29,698			50.0	50.0		
Quebec	24	40		1	455,452	542,357		22,109	44.7	53.2		2.2
Ontario	59	22	1		745,406	590,079	12,815	11,274	54.8	43.4	0.9	0.8
Manitoba	11	4		2	111,294	86,840	9,228	26,027	47.7	37.2	4.0	11.2
Saskatchewan	8	11	2		124,000	150,241	26,854	29,083	37.6	45.5	8.1	8.8
Alberta	4	3	9		67,832	60,126	60,848	11,496	33.9	30.0	30.4	5.7
British Columbia	7	5		2	119,074	98,933		23,626	49.3	40.9		9.8
Yukon and N.W.T.	1				846	557			60.3	39.7		
TOTAL	137	91	12	5	1,903,815	1,761,352	109,745	123,615	48.8	45.2	2.8	3.2

Others elected: Que. (1): Independent (1)
Man. (2): Labour (2)
B.C. (2): Independent (1); Labour (1)

Table Ie
1935 Federal Election Results

Province	Seats Won						Popular Vote						Per Cent Popular Vote					
	Cons.	Lib.	Reconstruction	C.C.F.	Social Credit	Other	Cons.	Lib.	Reconstruction	C.C.F.	Social Credit	Other	Cons.	Lib.	Reconstruction	C.C.F.	Social Credit	Other
Nova Scotia		12					87,893	142,334	38,175			5,365	32.1	52.0	13.9			2.0
New Brunswick		9					56,145	100,537	18,408			672	31.9	57.2	10.5			0.4
Prince Edward Island		4					23,602	35,757	2,089				38.4	58.2	3.4			
Quebec	5	55				5	322,794	623,579	100,119	7,326		92,703	28.2	54.4	8.7	0.6		8.1
Ontario	25	56				1	562,513	675,803	183,511	127,927		44,493	35.3	42.4	11.5	8.0		2.8
Manitoba	1	14		2			75,574	113,887	16,439	54,491	5,751	14,850	26.9	40.5	5.9	19.4	2.0	5.3
Saskatchewan	1	16		2	2		65,078	141,121	4,361	69,376	61,505	4,129	18.8	40.8	1.3	20.1	17.8	1.2
Alberta	1	1			15		40,236	50,539	1,785	30,921	111,249	3,783	16.9	21.2	0.7	13.0	46.6	1.6
British Columbia	5	6	1	3		1	71,034	91,729	19,208	97,015	1,796	8,001	24.6	31.8	6.7	33.6	0.6	2.8
Yukon	1						696	555					55.6	44.4				
TOTAL	40	173	1	7	17	7	1,305,565	1,975,841	384,095	387,056	180,301	173,996	29.6	44.8	8.7	8.8	4.1	3.9

Others elected: Que. (5): Independent Liberal (5)
Ont. (1): United Farmers of Ontario-Labour (1)
B.C. (1): Independent (1)

Table II
Federal Finance, 1919-39

	Total Revenue*	Total Expenditure*	Surplus/Deficit	
1919	349.7	740.1		390.4
1920	436.9	528.9		92.0
1921	395.0	476.3		81.3
1922	409.6	441.2		31.6
1923	407.8	371.8	36.0	
1924	352.5	352.2	0.3	
1925	383.3	355.6	27.7	
1926	401.1	359.2	41.9	
1927	430.8	379.8	51.0	
1928	461.6	394.1	67.5	
1929	453.0	405.3	47.7	
1930	357.7	441.6		83.9
1931	334.5	448.7		114.2
1932	311.7	532.4		220.7
1933	324.6	458.2		133.6
1934	361.9	478.1		116.2
1935	372.6	532.6		160.0
1936	454.1	532.0		77.9
1937	516.7	534.4		17.7
1938	502.1	553.1		51.0
1939	562.1	680.8		118.7

* Millions of dollars

Source: HSC, Series G 21, G 42.

Table III
Provincial Ministries, 1920-40

Date	Premier	Party
Quebec		
23 March 1905-9 July 1920	Sir Lomer Gouin	Liberal
9 July 1920-11 June 1936	L.-A. Taschereau	Liberal
11 June 1936-24 August 1936	Adélard Godbout	Liberal
24 August 1936-8 November 1939	Maurice Duplessis	Union nationale
8 November 1939-30 August 1944	Adélard Godbout	Liberal
Ontario		
14 November 1919-16 July 1923	Edward C. Drury	Farmer-Labour
16 July 1923-15 December 1930	G. Howard Ferguson	Conservative
15 December 1930-10 July 1934	George S. Henry	Conservative
10 July 1934-21 October 1942	Mitchell Hepburn	Liberal
Nova Scotia		
20 July 1896-24 January 1923	George H. Murray	Liberal
24 January 1923-16 July 1925	E.H. Armstrong	Liberal
16 July 1925-11 August 1930	Edgar N. Rhodes	Conservative
11 August 1930-5 September 1933	Col. G.S. Harrington	Conservative
5 September 1933-10 July 1940	Angus L. Macdonald	Liberal
10 July 1940-8 September 1945	A.S. MacMillan	Liberal
New Brunswick		
4 April 1917-28 February 1923	Walter E. Foster	Liberal
28 February 1923-14 September 1925	Peter Veniot	Liberal
14 September 1925-19 May 1931	J.B.M. Baxter	Conservative
19 May 1931-1 June 1933	Charles B. Richards	Conservative
1 June 1933-16 July 1935	L.P.D. Tilley	Conservative
16 July 1935-13 March 1940	A.A. Dysart	Liberal
13 March 1940-8 October 1952	J.B. McNair	Liberal
Manitoba		
15 May 1915-8 August 1922	T.C. Norris	Liberal
8 August 1922-8 January 1943	John Bracken	United Farmers/ Liberal-Progressive
British Columbia		
6 March 1918-20 August 1927	John Oliver	Liberal
20 August 1927-21 August 1928	John D. MacLean	Liberal
21 August 1928-15 November 1933	Simon Fraser Tolmie	Conservative
15 November 1933-9 December 1941	T. Dufferin Pattullo	Liberal

Table III continued

Date	Premier	Party
Prince Edward Island		
9 September 1919-5 September 1923	J.H. Bell	Liberal
5 September 1923-12 August 1927	James D. Stewart	Conservative
12 August 1927-20 May 1930	Albert C. Saunders	Liberal
20 May 1930-29 August 1931	Walter M. Lea	Liberal
29 August 1931-14 October 1933	James D. Stewart	Conservative
14 October 1933-15 August 1935	W.J.P. MacMillan	Conservative
15 August 1935-14 January 1936	Walter M. Lea	Liberal
14 January 1936-11 May 1943	Thane Campbell	Liberal
Saskatchewan		
20 October 1916-5 April 1922	William Martin	Liberal
5 April 1922-26 February 1926	Charles A. Dunning	Liberal
26 February 1926-9 September 1929	James G. Gardiner	Liberal
9 September 1929-19 July 1934	J.T.M. Anderson	"Co-operative"*
19 July 1934-1 November 1935	James G. Gardiner	Liberal
1 November 1935-10 July 1944	William Patterson	Liberal
Alberta		
30 October 1917-13 August 1921	Charles Stewart	Liberal
13 August 1921-23 November 1925	Herbert Greenfield	United Farmers
23 November 1925-10 July 1934	John E. Brownlee	United Farmers
10 July 1934-3 September 1935	Richard G. Reid	United Farmers
3 September 1935-31 May 1943	William Aberhart	Social Credit

* Conservative-Progressive

Table IV
Provincial Finance, 1913, 1921, 1925-37

	Total Revenue*	Total Expenditure*	Provincial Spending As Percentage of Federal Spending
1913	46.4	48.9	26.4
1921	91.1	91.4	19.2
1925	122.8	120.9	34.0
1926	136.2	127.0	35.4
1927	152.5	142.2	37.4
1928	164.2	150.1	38.1
1929	180.3	163.2	40.3
1930	178.3	187.9	42.5
1931	162.0	210.5	46.9
1932	158.4	207.0	38.9
1933	154.3	202.9	44.3
1934	164.9	235.4	49.2
1935	194.7	243.3	45.7
1936	221.6	237.5	44.6
1937	247.0	261.1	48.9

* Millions of dollars

Source: HSC, Series G 310, G 318, from the Royal Commission on Dominion-Provincial Relations, *Comparative Statistics of Public Finance* (Ottawa, 1941).

Table V
The Canadian Newsprint Industry, 1919-39

	Production		Exports to U.S.		New Capacity
	Volume*	Value†	Volume*	Value†	Installed‡
1919	795	54.4	—	—	150
1920	876	80.8	—	—	150
1921	805	78.7	655	63.5	435
1922	1,081	75.9	888	62.8	240
1923	1,252	93.2	1,115	83.8	415
1924	1,388	100.2	1,193	88.9	615
1925	1,537	106.2	1,321	93.1	577
1926	1,889	121.0	1,628	106.7	1,575
1927	2,083	132.2	1,748	114.0	1,600
1928	2,414	144.1	1,935	123.5	1,331
1929	2,725	150.8	2,173	129.0	895
1930	2,498	136.1	2,008	115.2	840
1931	2,227	111.2	1,753	94.3	—
1932	1,919	85.5	1,520	70.0	—
1933	2,022	66.9	1,520	58.3	—
1934	2,605	86.8	1,960	68.0	—
1935	2,765	88.4	2,052	70.9	—
1936	3,225	105.2	2,399	83.5	—
1937	3,674	126.4	2,899	105.6	—
1938	2,669	107.0	1,938	85.1	—
1939	2,927	120.8	2,206	97.0	—

* Volume: thousands of tons per year
† Value: millions of dollars
‡ New capacity: tons per day

Sources: Volume and Value, *HSC*, Series K 157-8, K 165-6.
Production Capacity: J.A. Guthrie, *The Newsprint Paper Industry* (Cambridge, 1941), 59.

Table VI
Canadian Non-ferrous Metallic Mineral Production, 1919-39

	Precious Metals*		Base Metals†	
	Volume‡	Value¶	Volume§	Value¶
1919	16,788	33.6	195,622	37.2
1920	14,095	29.3	218,755	45.0
1921	14,469	22.2	186,683	19.0
1922	19,889	38.7	210,074	20.9
1923	19,835	37.6	320,989	42.8
1924	21,261	44.7	448,387	53.5
1925	21,965	49.9	548,168	63.0
1926	24,126	50.1	632,548	62.2
1927	24,590	51.2	683,865	59.1
1928	23,827	51.8	822,046	76.6
1929	23,071	52.1	882,187	97.7
1930	28,546	43.5	1,007,785	85.1
1931	23,256	64.2	862,557	52.7
1932	21,392	77.3	706,238	32.0
1933	18,137	90.0	848,854	54.5
1934	19,387	110.3	1,138,305	76.3
1935	19,904	126.4	1,217,267	88.2
1936	22,082	139.6	1,307,131	109.4
1937	27,074	153.6	1,537,271	167.3
1938	26,944	175.9	1,582,258	136.2
1939	28,258	193.5	1,618,056	136.2

* Gold and silver
† Copper, lead, nickel, and zinc
‡ Thousands of Troy ounces
§ Thousands of pounds
¶ Millions of dollars

Source: Author's calculations from *HSC*, Series N 3-6, N 9-10, N 13-14, N 19-20, N 25-26.

Table VII
The Canadian Hydroelectric Power Industry, 1919-39

	Hydro Generating Capacity*	Electricity Generated†	Capital Invested‡
1919	1,737	5,353	416
1920	1,754	5,730	448
1921	1,826	5,448	484
1922	2,112	6,570	568
1923	2,282	7,936	581
1924	2,708	9,159	628
1925	3,416	9,942	726
1926	3,609	11,911	756
1927	3,975	14,346	866
1928	4,445	16,106	956
1929	4,718	17,604	1,055
1930	5,144	17,749	1,138
1931	5,422	16,025	1,230
1932	6,036	15,724	1,335
1933	6,306	17,006	1,386
1934	6,560	20,817	1,430
1935	6,808	22,884	1,459
1936	6,810	24,933	1,483
1937	7,023	27,176	1,497
1938	7,155	25,668	1,545
1939	7,241	27,829	1,564

* Thousands of horsepower
† Millions of kilowatt hours
‡ Millions of dollars; includes thermal generators, 14.2 per cent of capacity in
  1919 and 7.1 per cent in 1939

Source: HSC, Series P 2, P 7, P 46.

Table VIII
The Impact of the Automobile, 1919-39

	Automobiles Built*	Motor Vehicle Registration†	Automotive Retail Sales‡
1919	68,408	342.4	—
1920	79,369	408.8	—
1921	57,401	464.8	—
1922	79,094	509.4	—
1923	106,226	576.0	222
1924	98,365	645.3	205
1925	120,205	724.0	241
1926	154,061	832.3	333
1927	137,290	939.7	366
1928	176,096	1,069.3	420
1929	188,721	1,187.3	488
1930	115,535	1,232.5	382
1931	64,629	1,200.7	298
1932	48,332	1,113.5	235
1933	47,510	1,083.2	218
1934	80,118	1,129.5	260
1935	111,782	1,176.1	318
1936	108,340	1,240.1	384
1937	132,835	1,319.7	496
1938	105,392	1,394.9	455
1939	90,148	1,439.2	454

* Passenger cars only
† Thousands of vehicles
‡ Millions of dollars; including car dealers, garages, and filling stations
Source: HSC, Series Q 289, S 222, T 9-10, T 29.

Table IX
Foreign Investment in Canada, 1919-39*

	Britain	United States	Other Countries
1919	2,645.2	1,818.1	173.5
1920	2,577.3	2,128.2	164.6
1921	2,493.5	2,260.3	152.2
1922	2,463.8	2,593.0	150.2
1923	2,470.7	2,794.4	149.2
1924	2,371.6	3,094.0	150.0
1925	2,345.7	3,219.2	149.2
1926	2,591.5	3,108.8	63.3
1927	2,637.8	3,338.5	63.9
1928	2,698.7	3,551.7	71.8
1929	2,773.9	3,794.4	77.3
1930	2,792.3	4,098.5	88.2
1931	2,729.4	4,056.4	84.4
1932	2,687.2	4,045.2	83.5
1933	2,682.8	4,491.7	190.0
1934	2,792.5	4,112.1	123.5
1935	2,729.3	4,044.6	123.6
1936	2,718.9	3,974.0	129.7
1937	2,684.8	3,932.4	147.8
1938	—	—	—
1939	2,475.9	4,151.4	286.0

* Millions of dollars

Sources: 1919-33, Herbert Marshall *et al.*, *Canadian-American Industry: A Study in International Investment* (Toronto, 1936), 229-300.
1934-37, 1939, *HD*, 228.
1938, not available.

Table Xa
Population Growth of Metropolitan Areas, 1901-31

	Within City Limits			"Greater Cities"	
	1921	1931	1941	1931	1941
Montreal	618,506	818,577	903,007	1,023,158	1,139,921
Toronto	521,893	631,207	667,457	810,467	900,491
Vancouver	163,220	246,593	275,353	308,340	351,491
Winnipeg	179,087	218,785	221,960	284,295	290,540
Hamilton	114,151	155,547	166,337	—	—
Ottawa	107,843	126,872	154,951	—	—
Quebec	95,193	130,594	150,757	—	—

Sources: Dominion Bureau of Statistics, *Rural and Urban Composition of the Canadian Population*, Census Monograph 6, 1931.
Census of Canada, 1941, Vol. II, *Population by Local Subdivisions*.

Table Xb
Percentage of Urban Population by Province, 1911-41

	1911	1921	1931	1941
Prince Edward Island	16.0	18.8	19.5	22.1
Nova Scotia	36.7	44.8	46.6	52.0
New Brunswick	26.7	35.2	35.4	38.7
Quebec	44.5	51.8	59.5	61.2
Ontario	49.5	58.8	63.1	67.5
Manitoba	39.3	41.5	45.2	45.7
Saskatchewan	16.1	16.8	20.3	21.3
Alberta	29.4	30.7	31.8	31.9
British Columbia	50.9	50.9	62.3	64.0
Canada	41.8	47.4	52.5	55.7

Source: Leroy O. Stone, *Urban Development in Canada* (Ottawa, 1967), 29, based on 1956 Census definition.

Table XIa
Distribution of the Male Labour Force, 1921-41

	1921		1931		1941	
	Number*	Per Cent	Number*	Per Cent	Number*	Per Cent
All Occupations	2,675	100.0	3,256	100.0	3,363	100.0
Agriculture	1,017	38.0	1,103	33.9	1,064	31.7
Fishing/Trapping	29	1.1	47	1.5	51	1.5
Logging	38	1.4	43	1.4	80	2.4
Mining	48	1.8	58	1.8	71	2.1
Manufacturing	317	11.9	394	12.1	561	16.7
Construction	162	6.1	202	6.2	212	6.3
Transportation	184	6.9	271	8.3	294	8.8
Trade/Finance	245	9.2	295	9.1	296	8.8
Professional	78	2.9	103	3.2	120	3.6
Personal Service	73	2.7	128	3.9	144	4.3
Clerical	127	4.8	141	4.3	159	4.8
Labourers	305	11.4	425	13.1	251	7.5

* Thousands of workers
Source: Census of Canada, 1951.

Table XIb
Distribution of the Female Labour Force, 1921-41

	1921		1931		1941	
	Number*	Per Cent	Number*	Per Cent	Number*	Per Cent
All Occupations	489	100.0	665	100.0	832	100.0
Agriculture	17	3.7	24	3.6	18	2.3
Manufacturing	89	18.3	101	15.2	148	17.8
Transportation	14	3.0	17	2.7	16	2.0
Trade/Finance	47	9.8	56	8.5	74	8.9
Professional	92	19.0	118	17.6	127	15.3
Personal Service	132	27.1	227	34.3	288	34.7
Clerical	90	18.5	117	17.7	154	18.6

* Thousands of workers
Source: Census of Canada, 1951.

Table XII
Labour Organization and Industrial Conflict, 1919-39

	Union Membership	Strikes and Lockouts	Workers Involved	Workdays Lost
1919	378,000	336	148,915	3,401,000
1920	374,000	322	60,327	800,000
1921	313,000	168	28,257	1,049,000
1922	277,000	104	43,775	1,529,000*
1923	278,000	86	34,261	672,000
1924	261,000	70	34,310	1,295,000*
1925	271,000	87	28,049	1,193,000*
1926	275,000	77	23,834	267,000
1927	290,000	74	22,299	153,000
1928	301,000	98	17,581	224,000
1929	319,000	90	12,946	152,000
1930	322,000	67	13,768	92,000
1931	311,000	88	10,738	204,000
1932	283,000	116	23,390	255,000
1933	286,000	125	26,558	318,000
1934	281,000	191	45,800	575,000
1935	281,000	120	33,269	289,000
1936	323,000	156	34,812	277,000
1937	383,000	278	71,905	886,000
1938	382,000	147	20,395	149,000
1939	359,000	122	41,038	225,000

* Years of coal-mining confrontations, Districts 18 and 26, UMWA

Sources: HSC, Series D 426-33; J.K. Eaton, "The Growth of the Canadian Labour Movement," Labour Gazette, Special 75th Anniversary Issue, 1975, 643-49.

Table XIIIa
Estimated Annual Unemployment Rate, 1919-39*

Year	Per Cent	Year	Per Cent
1919	3.4		
1920	4.6	1930	12.9
1921	8.9	1931	17.4
1922	7.1	1932	26.0
1923	4.9	1933	26.6
1924	7.1	1934	20.6
1925	7.0	1935	19.1
1926	4.7	1936	16.7
1927	2.9	1937	12.5
1928	2.6	1938	15.1
1929	4.2	1939	14.1

* Does not include agricultural workers

Source: National Bureau of Economic Research, *The Measurement and Behavior of Unemployment* (Princeton, 1957), 455. Pages 496-503 contain an explanation of the calculation of this rate.

Table XIIIb
Quarterly Estimates of the Unemployed, 1929-39*

Year	March	June	September	December
1929	200	47	48	272
1930	288	391	300	413
1931	402	437	445	543
1932	571	594	606	675
1933	708	659	606	623
1934	598	487	497	571
1935	589	526	455	546
1936	568	480	409	502
1937	519	308	223	381
1938	—	387	346	472
1939	494	369	300	364

* Thousands of workers; does not include agricultural workers

Source: Dominion Bureau of Statistics.
I wish to thank James Struthers for his help in making sense of the several series of statistics on unemployment. See also Udo Sautter, "Measuring Unemployment: Federal Efforts before World War II," *Hs/SH*, 30, 1983, 475-87.

Table XIV
Decline in Per-Capita Incomes by Province, 1928-29 to 1933

	1928-29 Average $ Per Capita	1933 Average $ Per Capita	Percentage Decrease
Saskatchewan	478	135	72
Alberta	548	212	61
Manitoba	466	240	49
British Columbia	594	314	47
Prince Edward Island	278	154	45
Ontario	549	310	44
Quebec	391	220	44
New Brunswick	292	180	39
Nova Scotia	322	207	36
Canada	471	247	48

Source: Rowell-Sirois Report, Book I: *Canada: 1867-1939*, 150.

NOTES

When the Centenary Series was planned in the 1950s, the editors intended each volume to include an annotated bibliography of primary and secondary sources. The length of this volume and the explosion of historical writing about the inter-war period has made this impossible. The notes have been designed to fulfil in part the function of a bibliography; readers will be able to use them in conjunction with the index to find bibliographical suggestions. To make this easier, there is a complete citation of each book, article, thesis, or manuscript collection the first time it is noted in each chapter, even if it has been cited in a previous chapter.

There are now available bibliographies on modern Canada and on many specialized topics. The best reference guide to these, and to all aspects of the history of post-Confederation Canada, is J.L. Granatstein and Paul Stevens, eds., *A Reader's Guide to Canadian History*, 2: *Confederation to the Present* (Toronto, 1982).

ABBREVIATIONS

ANQ: Archives Nationales du Québec
AS: Archives of Saskatchewan
CAR: Canadian Annual Review of Public Affairs
CF: Canadian Forum
CHAAR: Canadian Historical Association, *Annual Report*
CHAHP: Canadian Historical Association, *Historical Papers*
CHCD: Canada, House of Commons, *Debates*
CHR: Canadian Historical Review
CJEPS: Canadian Journal of Economics and Political Science
DCER: Documents on Canadian External Relations
DR: Dalhousie Review
GAI: Archives of the Glenbow-Alberta Institute
HD: C.P. Stacey, *Historical Documents of Canada*, V, *The Arts of War and Peace, 1914-1945* (Toronto, 1972)
HSC: M.C. Urquhart and K.A.H. Buckley, eds., *Historical Statistics of Canada* (Toronto, 1971)

Hs/SH: Histoire sociale/Social History
JCBA: Journal of the Canadian Bankers' Association
JCS: Journal of Canadian Studies
KD: The Mackenzie King Diaries (Toronto, 1973)
L/le t: Labour/le travailleur [now *Labour/le travail*]
MM: Maclean's Magazine
PABC: Provincial Archives of British Columbia
PAC: Public Archives of Canada
PAM: Provincial Archives of Manitoba
PAO: Provincial Archives of Ontario
QQ: Queen's Quarterly
QUA: Queen's University Archives
RhAf: Revue d'histoire de l'Amérique française

All translations are by the author unless otherwise specified in the notes.

NOTES TO CHAPTER ONE

1. Unless otherwise cited, all statistics quoted in this chapter are from Canada, *Sixth Census of Population and Agriculture*, five vols. (Ottawa, 1922-24); Nicholas North, "Canada Counts Noses," *MM*, 15 May 1921.

2. *CF*, March, 1922, 550-52; "Census Padding," Montreal *Gazette*, 27 February 1922; *CAR*, 1922, 701; *Le Canada*, 20 October 1921; Calgary *Herald*, 25 February 1922.

3. E.C. Drury, *Farmer Premier: The Memoirs of E.C. Drury* (Toronto, 1966), 30.

4. W.E. Kalbach and W.W. McVey, *The Demographic Bases of Canadian Society* (Toronto, 1971), Ch. 11.

5. J.A. Stevenson, "The Latest Canadian Census," *Edinburgh Review*, April, 1923, 347-48; *Canada Year Book, 1922-23* (Ottawa, 1923), 185.

6. Toronto *Globe*, 15 February 1922; *Sixth Census*, I, xv; *Le Devoir*, 24 February 1922; *L'Action Française* cited in Susan Mann Trofimenkoff, *Action Française: French Canadian Nationalism in the Twenties* (Toronto, 1975), 136.

7. *Sixth Census*, II, xvii.

8. *Canada Year Book*, 1922-23, 896.

9. *Sixth Census*, IV, viii.

10. Ramsay Cook and Wendy Mitchinson, eds., *The Proper Sphere: Woman's Place in Canadian Society* (Toronto, 1976), introduction.

11. Terry Copp, *The Anatomy of Poverty: The Condition of the Working Class in Montreal, 1897-1929* (Toronto, 1974), 44-56; *Sixth Census*, III, xix-xxi; *HSC*, Series J 139-52.

12. *Canada Year Book,* 1922-23, 700.

NOTES TO CHAPTER TWO

1. Roger Graham, *Arthur Meighen*, II, *And Fortune Fled* (Toronto, 1963), 120-21; *HD*, 75; W.L. Morton, *The Progressive Party in Canada* (Toronto, 1950), 114-16, 302-4.

2. Margaret Prang, "Mackenzie King Woos Ontario," *Ontario History*, LVIII:1, 1966, 15-18; L.J. Edwards, "W.R. Motherwell and the Crisis of Federal Liberalism in Saskatchewan, 1917-26" (M.A. thesis, University of Saskatchewan, 1969), 87-134; R. MacGregor Dawson, *William Lyon Mackenzie King: A Political Biography, 1874-1923* (Toronto, 1958), 351-53; Montreal *Gazette*, 3 December 1921; Toronto *Globe*, 7 December 1921.

·3. Morton, *Progressive Party*, 126.

4. Jean MacLeod, "The United Farmer Movement in Ontario, 1914-1943" (M.A. thesis, Queen's University, 1958), 111; J. Murray Beck, *Pendulum of Power: Canada's Federal Elections* (Scarborough, Ont., 1968), 157-58.

5. A. Ross McCormack, *Reformers, Rebels and Revolutionaries: The Western Canadian Radical Movement, 1899-1919* (Toronto, 1977), 169-71; Martin Robin, *Radical Politics and Canadian Labour, 1880-1930* (Kingston, 1968), 199-218, 241-44; David Frank, "Company Town/Labour Town: Local Government in the Cape Breton Coal Towns, 1917-1926," *Hs/SH*, 27, 1981, 196; Canada, House of Commons, *Sessional Paper* no. 13, (Ottawa, 1922), 520-28.

6. *CAR*, 1921, 518; W.A. Mackintosh, "The General Election of 1921," *QQ*, XXIX: 2, 1922, 314; "The General Election of 1921," *CF*, December 1921, 453-54.

7. C.P. Stacey, *A Very Double Life: The Private World of Mackenzie King* (Toronto, 1976), 157-58; *KD*, 17 June 1895, cited in Dawson, *King*, 47.

8. C.P. Stacey, *Mackenzie King and the Atlantic Triangle* (Toronto, 1976), xv-xvi; H.S. Ferns and Bernard Ostry, *The Age of Mackenzie King: The Rise of the Leader* (London, 1955), *passim*; F.A. McGregor, *The Fall and Rise of Mackenzie King* (Toronto, 1962), *passim*.

9. Paul Craven, *An Impartial Umpire: Industrial Relations and the Canadian State, 1900-1911* (Toronto, 1980), *passim*; Reginald Whitaker, "The Liberal Corporatist Ideas of Mackenzie King," *L/le t*, 2, 1977, 137-69; W.L. Mackenzie King, *Industry and Humanity*, edited and with an introduction by David J. Bercuson (Toronto, 1973), *passim*.

10. Grattan O'Leary, *Grattan O'Leary: Recollections of People, Press and Politics* (Toronto, 1977), 34; Bruce Hutchison, *The Incredible Canadian: A Candid Portrait of Mackenzie King* (Toronto, 1952), 39-40.

11. Grattan O'Leary, "The Decline of Oratory in Parliament," *DR*, II: 2, 1922, 161-64; H. Reginald Hardy, *Mackenzie King of Canada: A Biography* (Toronto, 1949), 289; interviews with J.W. Pickersgill and James Gibson, *Canadian Issues*, I:2, 1977, 16, 39.

12. Frederick W. Gibson, "The Cabinet of 1921," in F.W. Gibson, ed., *Cabinet Formation and*

Bicultural Relations: Seven Case Studies (Ottawa, 1970), 63-104; QUA, T.A. Crerar Papers, Morrison to Crerar, 14 December 1921; E.C. Drury, *Farmer Premier: The Memoirs of E.C. Drury* (Toronto, 1966), 140-42; Ramsay Cook, ed., *The Dafoe-Sifton Correspondence, 1919-1927* (Altona, Man., 1966), 107-9; F.L. Foster, "John Edward Brownlee: A Biography" (Ph.D. thesis, Queen's University, 1981), 165-66.

13. Montreal *Star*, 7 December 1921, quoted in Roger Graham, "Meighen and the Montreal Tycoons: Railway Policy in the Election of 1921," *CHAAR*, 1957, 71-85; "Domino" [Augustus Bridle], "A Bourgeois Master of Quebec," in *The Masques of Ottawa* (Toronto, 1921), 204-14; Paul-André Linteau, René Durocher, and Jean-Claude Robert, *Histoire du Québec contemporain: de la Confédération à la crise, 1867-1929* (Ville St. Laurent, Que., 1979), 461-62.

14. Gibson, "Cabinet of 1921," 73-77.

15. McCormack, *Reformers, Rebels and Revolutionaries*, 39-41, 47-48.

16. *KD*, 29 December 1921, quoted in Allan M. Trueman, "New Brunswick and the 1921 Federal Election" (M.A. thesis, University of New Brunswick, 1975), 391-94.

17. Dawson, *King*, 373.

18. *HD*, 37-43; "Domino," *Masques of Ottawa*, 59.

19. Robert Craig Brown and Ramsay Cook, *Canada 1896-1921: A Nation Transformed* (Toronto, 1974), 228-49, 325-26; David E. Smith, "Emergency Government in Canada," *CHR*, L:4, 1969, 247-75; Robert M. Stamp, "Technical Education, the National Policy and Fed-eral-provincial Relations in Canadian Education, 1899-1919," *CHR*, LII:4, 1971, 421-23; Thomas D. Traves, "The Board of Commerce and the Canadian Sugar Refining Industry: A Speculation on the Role of the State in Canada," *CHR*, LV:2, 1974, 159-75.

20. The analysis of the 1920-22 budgets was made available to me by Dr. Alec Lane; *CAR*, 1922, 252-57.

21. Charles F. Wilson, *A Century of Canadian Grain: Government Policy to 1951* (Saskatoon, 1978), 173-82; H.S. Patton, *Grain Growers' Co-operation in Western Canada* (Cambridge, 1928), 202-5.

22. G.R. Stevens, *History of the Canadian National Railways* (New York, 1973), 306-21; James Struthers, "Prelude to Depression: The Federal Government and Unemployment, 1918-29," *CHR*, LVIII:3, 1977, 278-84.

23. PAC, King Papers, King to Mrs. Ralph Smith, 21 March 1922, quoted in Christopher Armstrong, "The Politics of Federalism: Ontario's Relations with the Federal Government, 1896-1941" (Ph.D. thesis, University of Toronto, 1972), 477; PAM, John Bracken Papers, file 450, F.J. Dixon and R.W. Murchie, "Seasonal Unemployment in Manitoba"; Struthers, "Prelude to Depression," 291.

24. *CF*, July, 1922, 675; *CAR*, 1922, 216; Dawson, *King*, 388-98; H. Blair Neatby, *William Lyon Mackenzie King*, II, *1924-1932: The Lonely Heights* (Toronto, 1963), 59.

25. Morton, *Progressive Party*, 180; Graham, *And Fortune Fled*, 196-99.

26. QUA, Crerar Papers, Crerar to Fred Davis, 19 January 1922 (I am indebted to Professor Foster Greizic

for this quotation); William Irvine, *The Farmers in Politics*, edited and with an introduction by Reginald Whitaker (Toronto, 1976), 238-40.

27. *CHCD*, 1922, II, 1626-27.

28. Irvine, *Farmers in Politics*, 226; GAI, Henry Spencer Papers, "Parliament and the Parliamentary System," 1923.

29. *CAR*, 1920, 543; AS, Saskatchewan Grain Growers' Association Papers, J.B. Musselman to W.R. Motherwell, 17 June 1921; J.W. Brennan, "A Political History of Saskatchewan, 1905-1929" (Ph.D. thesis, University of Alberta, 1977), 507-9; John David Hoffman, "Farmer-Labour Government in Ontario" (M.A. thesis, University of Toronto, 1959), 13-15; Leonard D. Nesbitt, *Tides in the West: A Wheat Pool Story* (Saskatoon, 1961), 394; QUA, Crerar Papers, Crerar to A.B. Hudson, 19 December 1921.

30. *UFA*, 2 July 1924, quoted in Morton, *Progressive Party,* 194-97; William Kirby Rolph, *Henry Wise Wood of Alberta* (Toronto, 1950), 90, 104-5; Wayne C. Brown, "The United Farmers of Ontario: The 'Broadening Out' Controversy" (M.A. thesis, University of Guelph, 1980), 213; Foster Greizic, "The Honourable Thomas Alexander Crerar: The Political Career of a Western Liberal Progressive in the 1920s," in S.M. Trofimenkoff, ed., *The Twenties in Western Canada* (Ottawa, 1972), 125-26.

31. GAI, W. Norman Smith Papers, Arthur Darby to Smith, 12 July 1924; PAC, King Papers, J.F. Johnston to King, 27 November 1925, quoted in Neatby, *Lonely Heights*, 95.

32. Margaret Ormsby, "The United Farmers of British Columbia: An Abortive Third Party Movement," *BC Historical Quarterly*, XVII:2, 1953, 53-73; Martin Robin, *The Company Province*, I, *The Rush for Spoils, 1871-1933* (Toronto, 1972), 173-74, 196-98.

33. Anthony Mackenzie, "The Rise and Fall of the Farmer-Labour Party of Nova Scotia" (M.A. thesis, Dalhousie University, 1969), 1-102.

34. Trueman, "New Brunswick and the 1921 Election," 242-45; Ernest R. Forbes, "Never the Twain Did Meet: Prairie-Maritime Relations, 1910-27," *CHR*, LIX:1, 1978, 28.

35. Robert Migner, "Le Monde agricole québécois et les premières années de l'Union catholique des cultivateurs" (Ph.D. thesis, Université de Montréal, 1975), 91-134; Claude Beauchamp, "Les Débuts de la coopération et du syndicalisme agricoles, 1900-1930," *Recherches sociographiques*, XX:3, 1979, 375-81; Montreal *Gazette*, 19 January 1923, quoted in J.A. Lovink, "The Politics of Quebec: Provincial Political Parties, 1897-1936" (Ph.D. thesis, Duke University, 1967), 329.

36. Peter Oliver, *G. Howard Ferguson: Ontario Tory* (Toronto, 1977), 142; R.S. Pennefather, "The Orange Order and the UFO, 1919-1923," *Ontario History*, LXIX:3, 1977, 169-84.

37. *CHCD*, 1925, II, 1963; George Rawlyk, "The Farmer-Labour Movement and the Failure of Socialism in Nova Scotia," in L.L. LaPierre, ed., *Essays on the Left: Essays in Honour of T.C. Douglas* (Toronto, 1971), 32; Halifax *Chronicle*, 13 July 1920, quoted in Mackenzie, "Farmer-Labour Party of Nova Scotia," 81.

38. Reginald Whitaker, "Images of the State in Canada," in Leo Panitch, ed., *The Canadian State: Political*

Economy and Political Power (Toronto, 1977), 51; Brown, "United Farmers of Ontario," Ch. 5; W.R. Young, "Conscription, Rural Depopulation and the Farmers of Ontario, 1917-19," *CHR*, LIII:3, 1972, 293.

39. Morton, *Progressive Party*, 107-9.

40. James N. McCrorie, "The Saskatchewan Farmers' Movement: A Case Study" (Ph.D. thesis, University of Illinois, 1972), 115; *CAR*, 1923, 737; Foster, "Brownlee," 141-42, 179-80; John Kendle, *John Bracken: A Political Biography* (Toronto, 1979), 37-39.

41. GAI, C.W. Petersen Papers, "Drafts of Addresses," file 2; AS, SGGA Papers, W.A.S. Tegart to A.J. MacPhail, April 1923.

42. Carl Betke, "Farm Politics in an Urban Age: The Decline of the UFA after 1921," in L.H. Thomas, ed.,

Essays on Western History (Edmonton, 1976), 175-79; John H. Archer, *Saskatchewan: A History* (Saskatoon, 1980), 41-42; D.S. Spafford, "The Origin of the Farmers' Union," *Saskatchewan History*, XVIII:3, 1965, 89-98; Leo Courville, "The Saskatchewan Progressives" (M.A. thesis, University of Saskatchewan/Regina, 1971), 170-72.

43. Ian MacPherson, *Each for All: A History of the Co-operative Movement in English Canada, 1900-1945* (Toronto, 1979), 86-101; Migner, "Monde agricole," 127; Rawlyk, "Farmer-Labour Movement," 36.

44. *CHCD*, 1925, II, 1963; on the Crow rate issue, see Alec W.A. Lane, "Freight Rate Issues in Canada, 1922-25: Their Economic and Political Implications" (Ph.D. thesis, McGill University, 1983), Chs. 2-4.

NOTES TO CHAPTER THREE

1. "Platform of the Farmers' Party, 1918," *HD*, 32: Mason Wade, *The French Canadians, 1760-1967*, rev. ed. (Toronto, 1968), II, 781-91; *CHCD*, 1921, III, 2661.

2. Robert Craig Brown, *Robert Laird Borden: A Biography*, II, *1914-1937* (Toronto, 1980), 70-82, 145-61; *HD*, 362-74; Roger Graham, *Arthur Meighen*, II, *And Fortune Fled* (Toronto, 1963), 84-106; Gwendolyn M. Carter, *The British Commonwealth and International Security* (Toronto, 1947), 64; John S. Galbraith, "The Imperial Conference of 1921 and the Washington Conference," *CHR*, XXIX:2, 1948, 145-47.

3. Michael Fry, *Illusions of Security: North Atlantic Diplomacy, 1918-22* (Toronto, 1972), 92-95; *CAR*, 1921, 81; C.P. Stacey, *Canada and the Age of Conflict*, II, *1921-1948: The Mackenzie King Era* (Toronto, 1981), 71.

4. Manitoba *Free Press*, 22 April 1922; *CAR*, 1922, 214-15; H. Blair Neatby, "Mackenzie King and National Unity," in H.L. Dyck and H.P. Krosby, eds., *Empire and Nations: Essays in Honour of F.H. Soward* (Toronto, 1969), 59-70.

5. C.P. Stacey, "Laurier, King and External Affairs," in John S. Moir, ed., *Character and Circumstance: Essays in Honour of D.G. Creighton*

(Toronto, 1970), 90-95; James Eayrs, *In Defence of Canada*, I, *From the Great War to the Great Depression* (Toronto, 1964), 21.

6. *KD*, 18 January 1922; C.P. Stacey, *Mackenzie King and the Atlantic Triangle* (Toronto, 1976), Ch. 1; Douglas Cole, "The Better Patriot: John S. Ewart and the Canadian Nation" (Ph.D. thesis, University of Washington, 1968), 312-13.

7. *KD*, 21 January, 1 April 1922; Robert Bothwell, "Loring Christie: The Failure of Bureaucratic Imperialism" (Ph.D. thesis, Harvard University, 1972), 322-32; Norman Hillmer, "The Anglo-Canadian Neurosis: The Case of O.D. Skelton," in Peter Lyon, ed., *Britain and Canada* (London, 1976), 74.

8. Vincent Massey, "Canada and External Affairs," *JCBA*, XXXIII:3, 1925, 381.

9. *CHCD*, 1922, II, 5, 9; *KD*, 9 March 1922.

10. Quoted in Desmond Morton, *Canada and War* (Toronto, 1981), 93; Eayrs, *In Defence of Canada* I, 168-72.

11. Graham, *And Fortune Fled*, 208; Stacey, *Age of Conflict* II, 17-31.

12. Philip G. Wigley, *Canada and the Transition to Commonwealth: British-Canadian Relations 1917-1926* (Cambridge, 1977), 163; *KD*, 17 September 1922.

13. *KD*, 17, 19 September 1922.

14. Graham, *And Fortune Fled*, 209-12; R. MacGregor Dawson, *William Lyon Mackenzie King: A Political Biography, 1874-1923* (Toronto, 1958), 413-14.

15. *CHCD*, 1924, III, 2976; *KD*, 28 October, 31 December 1922.

16. Shelburne *Gazette*, 16 August 1923, quoted in John Alfred Schultz, "Canadian Attitudes To-

ward the Empire, 1919-1939" (Ph.D. thesis, Dalhousie University, 1975), 34; Murray Donnelly, *Dafoe of the Free Press* (Toronto, 1968), 116-22; Skelton quoted in Ramsay Cook, "J.W. Dafoe at the Imperial Conference of 1923," *CHR*, XLI:1, 1960, 36-37.

17. "Statement by King to the Imperial Conference," 17 October 1923, in Eayrs, *In Defence of Canada* I, 329-31; "King's Statement on Foreign Policy," 8 October 1923, *HD*, 442, 435-43.

18. D.W. Harkness, *The Restless Dominion: The Irish Free State and the British Commonwealth of Nations, 1921-31* (London, 1969), 45-55; G.P. de T. Glazebrook, "Canadian Opinion and Foreign Policy," in Moir, ed., *Character and Circumstance*, 134-35; Curzon quoted in Dawson, *King*, 477; Wigley, *Transition to Commonwealth*, 199; "Proceedings of the Conference," *HD*, 445-51.

19. J.W. Dafoe, "Did the Imperial Conference Fail?" *MM*, 15 January 1924, 45; John Holmes, "Nationalism in Canadian Foreign Policy," in Peter Russell, ed., *Nationalism in Canada* (Toronto, 1966), 206; John Holmes in Claude LeGris, *L'Entrée du Canada sur la scène internationale, 1919-1927* (Paris, 1966), Préface, xi; Dawson, *King*, 479; Ramsay Cook, *The Maple Leaf Forever: Essays on Nationalism and Politics in Canada* (Toronto, 1977), 128.

20. Paul Kennedy, *The Realities Behind Diplomacy: Background Influences on British External Policy, 1865-1980* (Glasgow, 1981), 268-69; Stacey, *Age of Conflict* II, 77-83.

21. Kevin O'Higgins quoted in Ramsay Cook, "A Canadian Account of

the 1926 Imperial Conference," *Journal of Commonwealth Political Studies*, 3:1 & 2, 1965, 51; Norman Hillmer, "Anglo-Canadian Relations, 1926-1937" (Ph.D. thesis, Cambridge University, 1974), 18-65; Vincent Massey, *What's Past Is Prologue: The Memoirs of Vincent Massey* (Toronto, 1963), 111-13; H. Blair Neatby, *William Lyon Mackenzie King*, II, *1924-1932: The Lonely Heights* (Toronto, 1963), 176-91.

22. R. MacGregor Dawson, *The Development of Dominion Status, 1900-1936* (Hamden, Conn., 1965), 103-32.

23. R.A. Preston, *The Defence of the Undefended Border: Planning for War in North America, 1867-1939* (Montreal and London, 1977), 213-33, and Brereton Greenhous, review of Preston, *Defence, CHR*, LX:1, 1979, 77-78; Robert Bothwell, "Canadian Representation at Washington: A Study in Colonial Responsibility," *CHR*, LIII:2, 1972, 125-48.

24. *CHCD*, 1920, II, 2456-60; Stacey, *Age of Conflict* II, 32; *New York Times*, 13 July 1922; Roger Frank Swanson, *Canadian-American Summit Diplomacy, 1923-1973, Selected Speeches and Documents* (Toronto, 1975), 7-10.

25. Wigley, *Transition to Commonwealth*, 175; *KD*, 2 March 1923; W.K. Hancock, *Survey of British Commonwealth Affairs*, I, *Problems of Nationality* (London, 1937), 252-53; Dawson, *King*, 434; Schultz, "Canadian Attitudes," 82-84.

26. Massey, *What's Past Is Prologue*, 109-11, 121-32; LeGris, *Entrée du Canada*, 79-82.

27. Massey, *What's Past Is Prologue*, 123, 144-47; Peter C. Kasurak,

"American 'Dollar Diplomats' in Canada, 1927-41: A Study in Bureaucratic Politics," *American Review of Canadian Studies*, IX:2, 1979, 57; Richard N. Kottman, "Hoover and Canada Diplomatic Appointments," *CHR*, LI:3, 1970, 296; William Phillips, *Ventures in Diplomacy* (London, 1955), 64-70.

28. H.G. Skilling, *Canadian Representation Abroad* (Toronto, 1945), 212-18; Stacey, *Age of Conflict* II, 97-103; *KD*, 22 May 1928.

29. W.L. Morton, review of Neatby, *Lonely Heights, CHR*, XLV:3, 1964, 320-21; Donald Creighton, *Canada's First Century* (Toronto, 1970) and *Canada 1939-1957: The Forked Road* (Toronto, 1976); Schultz, "Canadian Attitudes," 128-29.

30. Christie quoted in Bothwell, "Canadian Representation at Washington," 129; John Weaver, "Imperilled Dreams: Canadian Opposition to American Empire, 1918-1930" (Ph.D. thesis, Duke University, 1973), 73-77; Ramsay Cook, *The Politics of J.W. Dafoe and the Free Press* (Toronto, 1963), 184-86; Agnes Laut, *Canada at the Crossroads* (Toronto, 1921), 276-79; Donald Page, "Canada As the Exponent of North American Idealism," *American Review of Canadian Studies*, III:2, 1973, 31-39.

31. John C. Anderson, "Mackenzie King and Collective Security: The League of Nations and the U.N." (M.A. thesis, University of Alberta, 1977), 56-57; *CAR*, 1920, 84.

32. Ramsay Cook, ed., *The Dafoe-Sifton Correspondence, 1919-1927* (Altona, Man., 1966), 71.

33. Richard Veatch, *Canada and the League of Nations* (Toronto, 1975), 72-90; A. Gordon Dewey,

The Dominions and Diplomacy (London, 1929), II, 220-24.

34. Marcel Hamelin, ed., *Les Mémoires du Sénateur Raoul Dandurand* (Quebec, 1967), 269-76; Griesbach quoted in Veatch, *Canada and the League of Nations*, 90; G.P. de T. Glazebrook, *A History of Canadian External Relations*, II, *The Empire and the World, 1914-1939* (Toronto, 1966), 80.

35. Stacey, *Age of Conflict* II, 63-66; S. Mack Eastman, *Canada at Geneva: An Historical Survey and Its Lessons* (Toronto, 1946), 14-43.

36. ANQ, fonds Gouin, Borden to Gouin, 25 October 1923, quoted in Donald Page, "Canadians and the League of Nations Before the Manchurian Crisis" (Ph.D. thesis, University of Toronto, 1972), 186; Cole, "J.S. Ewart," 271-73; Maclean and Willison quoted in Page, "Canadians and the League," 38-39, 430-31; *Financial Post*, 19 December 1924, 28 September 1923, quoted in Page, "Canadians and the League," 208-9.

37. *KD*, 29 May 1928; Gwenn Ronyk, "The United States in the Twenties As Seen by the Western Canadian Press" (M.A. thesis, University of Regina, 1979), 128-63; R. Douglas Francis, "Frank Underhill – Canadian Intellectual" (Ph.D. thesis, York University, 1977), 52-53.

NOTES TO CHAPTER FOUR

1. *CF*, November 1924, 38; Richard Allen, "The Social Gospel and the Reform Tradition in Canada, 1890-1928," *CHR*, XLIX:4, 1968, 381-89.

2. Hymn cited in Donald L. Kirkey, " 'Building the City of God': The Founding of the Student Christian Movement of Canada" (M.A. thesis, McMaster University, 1983), introduction; Joseph Levitt, "Henri Bourassa: The Catholic Social Order and Canada's Mission," in Fernand Dumont *et al.*, eds., *Idéologies au Canada français, 1900-1929* (Quebec, 1978), 193-222; Susan Mann Trofimenkoff, *Action Française: French-Canadian Nationalism in the Twenties* (Toronto, 1975), 13-15; P.M. Senese, "*Catholique d'abord*: Catholicism and Nationalism in the Thought of Lionel Groulx," *CHR*, LX:2, 1979, 160; Richard Allen, *The Social Passion: Religion and Social Reform in Canada, 1914-1928* (Toronto, 1971), xxiii.

3. E.R. Forbes and A.A. Mackenzie, "Introduction" in Clifford Rose, *Four Years with the Demon Rum* (Fredericton, 1980), v; C.W. Gordon, "The State and the New Church," in *The Social Service Congress of Canada, 1914* (Toronto, 1914), 195; Lionel Orlikow, "The Reform Movement in Manitoba, 1910-1915," in Donald Swainson, ed., *Historical Essays on the Prairie Provinces* (Toronto, 1970), 228; Paul Rutherford, "Tomorrow's Metropolis: The Urban Reform Movement in Canada, 1880-1920," *CHAHP*, 1971, 203-24.

4. R. MacGregor Dawson, *William Lyon Mackenzie King: A Political Biography, 1874-1923* (Toronto, 1958), 249; Winnipeg *Tribune*, 15 May 1923; Richard Allen, "The

Social Gospel as the Religion of the Agrarian Revolt," in Carl Berger and Ramsay Cook, eds., *The West and the Nation: Essays in Honour of W.L. Morton* (Toronto, 1976), 174-86; Allen, *Social Passion*, 197-218.

5. Richard Allen, "Introduction" in Salem Bland, *The New Christianity* (reprint, Toronto, 1973), xxi; D.B. Harkness, "Report of the Social Service Council," quoted in Manitoba *Free Press*, 1 July 1922; *CAR*, 1923, 617; David Thomas, "The Making of a Saint," *Quest*, December, 1982, 21-29.

6. Kirkey, " 'Building the City of God,' " 84; W.W. Judd, "The Council for Social Service," *Journal of the Canadian Church Historical Society*, December, 1965, 76-88; Edward A. Pulker, "The Role of Anglicans in the Reform of the Economic Order in Canada, 1914-1945" (Ph.D. thesis, University of Ottawa, 1974), 111-51; John Cragg Farthing, *Recollections of the Right Rev. J.C. Farthing* (Montreal, n.d.), 170-74.

7. Charles M. Johnston, *McMaster University*, I, *The Toronto Years* (Toronto, 1976), 174-229; Ethel Parker, "Presbyterian Settlement Houses," in Richard Allen, ed., *The Social Gospel in Canada* (Ottawa, 1975), 109-10; Michael Bliss, *A Canadian Millionaire: The Life and Business Times of Sir Joseph Flavelle, Bart., 1858-1939* (Toronto, 1978), 398-99; Ralph W. Barker, "The United Church of Canada and the Social Question" (Ph.D. thesis, University of Toronto, 1961), 186.

8. Gerald Friesen, "Studies in the Development of Western Canadian Regional Consciousness, 1870-1925" (Ph.D. thesis, University of Toronto, 1974), Ch. 5; G.M. Morrison,

"The United Church of Canada: Ecumenical or Economic Necessity?" (B.D. thesis, University of Toronto, 1956), 110-15; Gordon L. Barnhart, "E.H. Oliver: A Study of Protestant Progressivism in Saskatchewan, 1909-1935" (M.A. thesis, University of Regina, 1977), 156-78.

9. Edgar F. File, "A Sociological Analysis of Church Union in Canada" (Ph.D. thesis, Boston University, 1961), 191-99; Marilyn J. Harrison, "The Social Influence of the United Church in British Columbia, 1930-1948" (M.A. thesis, University of British Columbia, 1975), 37-38; C.B. Silcox, *Church Union in Canada* (New York, 1933), 197-208; Allan L. Farris, "The Fathers of 1925," in John S. Moir, ed., *The Tide of Time* (Toronto, 1978), 95-124.

10. J.W. Grant, *George Pidgeon* (Toronto, 1962), 124-26; Stewart Crysdale, *The Industrial Struggle and the Protestant Ethic in Canada* (Toronto, 1961), 76-77; Allen, *Social Passion*, 240-63.

11. Allen, *Social Passion*, 284-301; James Pitsula, "The Emergence of Social Work in Toronto," *JCS*, XIV:1, 1979, 40-41; Andrew Jones and Leonard Rutman, *In the Children's Aid: J.J. Kelso and Child Welfare in Ontario* (Toronto, 1981), 165-66, 175.

12. Victoria *Colonist*, 21 January 1919, quoted in Albert John Heibert, "Prohibition in British Columbia" (M.A. thesis, Simon Fraser University, 1969), 105.

13. The Pas, Man., *Herald and Mining News,* 29 October 1920; Winnipeg *Tribune*, 20 October 1920; J.A. Stevenson, *Before the Bar* (Toronto, 1919), iii; D.K. Stretch, "Prohibition and the United Farm-

ers of Alberta" (M.A. thesis, University of Alberta, 1979), 9-12.

14. Calgary *Herald*, 27 February 1920; Rose, *Four Years with the Demon Rum,* ix-x, 19.

15. Gerald A. Hallowell, *Prohibition in Ontario, 1919-1923* (Ottawa, 1972), 119-22; Charles C. Jenkins, "In the Smugglers' Den," *MM*, 1 December 1920, 33-34, 46, 50; Frank W. Anderson, *The Rum Runners* (Calgary, 1968), 47-51; *Ladies Home Journal* quoted in Claude Mark Davis, "Prohibition in New Brunswick, 1917-1927" (M.A. thesis, University of New Brunswick, 1978), 80-82; Allan S. Everest, *Rum Across the Border: The Prohibition Era in Northern New York* (Syracuse, 1978), *passim*; Richard Kottman, "Volstead Violated: Prohibition as a Factor in Canadian-American Relations," *CHR*, XLIII:2, 1962, 106-26; Winnipeg *Tribune*, 2 June 1923.

16. James H. Gray, *Booze: The Impact of Whisky on the Prairie West* (Toronto, 1972), 151, 201; E.R. Forbes, "Prohibition and the Social Gospel in Nova Scotia," *Acadiensis*, I:1, 1971, 30.

17. Erhard Pinno, "Temperance and Prohibition in Saskatchewan" (M.A. thesis, University of Saskatchewan-Regina, 1969), 242; John H. Thompson, "The Prohibition Question in Manitoba" (M.A. thesis, University of Manitoba, 1969), 84-86; Stretch, "Prohibition and the UFA, " Ch. 3.

18. "Un-British" quoted in John H. Thompson, "The Voice of Moderation: The Defeat of Prohibition in Manitoba," in S.M. Trofimenkoff, ed., *The Twenties in Western Canada* (Ottawa, 1973), 176, 182-83; St. Peter's, Sask. *Messenger*, quoted in Pinno, "Prohibition in Saskat-

chewan," 21; Downes quoted in Thompson, "Prohibition in Manitoba," 182-83.

19. PABC, Pattullo Papers, "Quebec's Temperate Law Solving the Liquor Question," vol. 14, file 9; John H. Thompson, "The Political Career of Ralph H. Webb," *Red River Valley Historian*, Summer 1976, 2.

20. Peter Oliver, *G. Howard Ferguson: Ontario Tory* (Toronto, 1977), 159-69, 269-76.

21. Davis, "Prohibition in New Brunswick," 208-22; Margaret Strople-Campbell, "Prohibition in Nova Scotia" (M.A. thesis, Dalhousie University, 1977), 169-74; *CAR*, 1929-30, 451.

22. *HD*, 187-89; MacGregor, *Edmonton: A History* (Edmonton, 1967), 233; "Entrenching the Liquor Traffic," Winnipeg *Tribune*, 8 March 1930.

23. Linda Kealey, *A Not Unreasonable Claim: Women and Reform in Canada, 1880s-1920s* (Toronto, 1979), 8; Ramsay Cook and Wendy Mitchinson, eds., *The Proper Sphere: Woman's Place in Canadian Society* (Toronto, 1976), 291; Nellie McClung, *In Times Like These*, reprinted with an introduction by Veronica Strong-Boag (Toronto, 1972).

24. PABC, McClung Papers, McWilliams to McClung, 26 July 1921; *CHCD*, 1918, I, 643; S.M. Trofimenkoff, "Henri Bourassa and the Woman Question," in S.M. Trofimenkoff and Alison Prentice, eds., *The Neglected Majority: Essays in Canadian Women's History* (Toronto, 1977), 109.

25. Veronica Strong-Boag, "Wages for Housework: Mothers' Allowances and the Beginnings of Social

Security in Canada," *JCS*, XIV:1, 1979, 31.

26. Montreal *Gazette*, 3 December 1921; Manitoba *Free Press*, 3 and 5 December 1921.

27. Veronica Strong-Boag, "Canada's Women Doctors: Feminism Constrained," in Linda Kealey, ed., *Not Unreasonable Claim*, 127.

28. Doris French, "Agnes Macphail," in Mary Quayle Innis, ed., *The Clear Spirit: Twenty Canadian Women and Their Times* (Toronto, 1966), 184-85, 195; Martha Black, updated by Flo Whyard, *My Ninety Years* (Anchorage, Ak., 1976), 136-47.

29. Catherine Lyle Cleverdon, with an introduction by Ramsay Cook, *The Woman Suffrage Movement in Canada* (Toronto, 1974), 141-45, 267-83; Rudy G. Marchildon, "The Persons Controversy: The Legal Aspects of the Fight for Women Senators," *Atlantis*, VI:2, 1981, 99-113; "The Status of Women," *HD*, 200-202.

30. *KD*, 26 October 1922, 11 February 1930; Bryne Hope Saunders, *Emily Murphy, Crusader* (Toronto, 1945), 256-57; PABC, McClung Papers, Murphy to McClung, 4 March 1930.

31. Anne Anderson Perry, "Is Woman Suffrage a Fizzle?" *MM*, 1 February 1928, 6-7; PAM, WCTU Collection,

"A Call to Young Women," May, 1925: Veronica Strong-Boag, "Canadian Feminism in the 1920s: The Case of Nellie L. McClung," *JCS*, 12:4, 1977, 66.

32. NCW characterized in Deborah Gorham, review of Veronica Strong-Boag, *The Parliament of Women* (Ottawa, 1976), in *Atlantis*, III:1, 1977, 243-46: PABC, McClung Papers, Murphy to McClung, 2 December 1927; Perry, "Is Woman Suffrage a Fizzle?" 58-59.

33. Marie Lavigne, Yolande Pinard, and Jennifer Stoddart, "The Fédération Nationale Saint-Jean-Baptiste and the Women's Movement in Quebec," in Linda Kealey, ed., *Not Unreasonable Claim*, 71-87; Marta Danylewycz, "Changing Relationships: Nuns and Feminists in Montreal, 1890-1925," *Hs/SH*, 28, 1981, 413-34; Luigi Trifiro, "Une Intervention à Rome dans la lutte pour le suffrage féminin au Québec," *RhAf*, 32:1, 1978, 3-18.

34. Ramsay Cook, "Introduction" in Cleverdon, *Woman Suffrage*, xix; "Uplifters," *DR*, IV:2, 1924-25, 237-39; Peter Oliver, "W.E. Raney and the Politics of Uplift," *JCS*, VI:1, 1971, 7.

35. PABC, McClung Papers, McClung to Della Jones, 27 July 1935.

NOTES TO CHAPTER FIVE

1. Robert E. Ankli, "A Note on Canadian GNP Estimates, 1900-25," *CHR*, LXII:1, 1981, 61; *HSC*, Series E 143-55, F 360-79, L 114-18, and Y 215; Stephen Watson, "The Wheat Economy and the Demand for Manufactured Goods, 1910-30: A Quantitative Study" (M.A. thesis,

McGill University, 1980), 38; *CAR*, 1925-26, 314-15; Ronald Rudin, "A Bank Merger Unlike the Others: The Establishment of the Banque Canadienne Nationale," *CHR*, LXI:2, 1980, 191-93; Patricia E. Roy, "Vancouver: Mecca of the Unemployed," in A.F.J. Artibise, ed., *Town and*

City: Aspects of Western Canadian Urban Development (Regina, 1981), 404.

2. *JCBA*, XXVII:3, 1920, 367; *ibid.*, XXVIII:2, 1921, 164-65; Flavelle to David Carnegie, 10 December 1920, cited in Michael Bliss, *A Canadian Millionaire: The Life and Business Times of Sir Joseph Flavelle, Bart., 1858-1939* (Toronto, 1978), 396.

3. Archibald Blue, "A Brighter Financial Outlook," *The Canadian Magazine*, September, 1924.

4. "Facing North," *JCBA*, XXX:3, 1923, 284; Kevin H. Burley, ed., *The Development of Canada's Staples, 1867-1939* (Toronto, 1972), 346-50, 359; J.A. Guthrie, *The Newsprint Paper Industry* (Cambridge, 1941), 59; *HSC*, Series K 156-75.

5. Carl Weigman, *Trees to News* (Toronto, 1953), 101-12; *Pulp and Paper Magazine of Canada*, 19 August 1920, 10 July 1930, reproduced in Burley, *Canada's Staples*, 361-70.

6. V.W. Bladen, *An Introduction to Political Economy* (Toronto, 1946), 152-58; Trevor J.O. Dick, "Canadian Newsprint, 1913-1930: National Policies and the North American Economy," *Journal of Economic History*, XLII:3, 1982, 659-87.

7. Direct quotations from A.R.M. Lower, *Settlement and the Forest Frontier in Eastern Canada* (Toronto, 1936), 115, 123, 130-46; Guthrie, *Newsprint Paper Industry*, 30-37.

8. *Pulp and Paper Magazine of Canada*, 15 July 1920, quoted in Jorge Niosi, "La Laurentide: pionnière du papier journal au Canada," *RhAf*, 29:3, 1975, 403-4; Ferguson to F.J. Sensenbrenner, 10 January 1931, quoted in Peter Oliver, *G.*

Howard Ferguson: Ontario Tory (Toronto, 1977), 208; John Kendle, *John Bracken: A Political Biography* (Toronto, 1979), 54; H.V. Nelles, *The Politics of Development: Forests, Mines, and Hydro-Electric Power in Ontario, 1849-1941* (Toronto, 1974), 384, 391-94; Steven Gray, "Forest Policy and Administration in B.C., 1912-1928" (M.A. thesis, Simon Fraser University, 1977), abstract; J. Murray Beck, *The Government of Nova Scotia* (Toronto, 1957), 167; Lower, *Settlement and the Forest Frontier*, 103.

9. Gilles Piédalue, "Les Groupes financiers et la guerre du papier au Canada, 1920-1930," *RhAf*, 30:2, 1976, 229-31, 248-53; Guthrie, *Newsprint Paper Industry*, 59-63; Herbert Marshall *et al.*, *Canadian-American Industry: A Study in International Investment* (Toronto, 1936), 35-38; James A. Cowan, "Prosperity's Leap from the Bush," *MM*, 15 October 1928, 14-15.

10. H.A. Innis, *Settlement and the Mining Frontier* (Toronto, 1936), 385; W.L. MacTavish, "Manitoba Marches North," *MM*, 15 May 1928, 10-11; "Why Canada Needs a Clear Understanding of the Mining Industry," *MM*, 1 June 1927, 103.

11. O.W. Main, *The Canadian Nickel Industry* (Toronto, 1955), 91; prospector quoted in Innis, *Mining Frontier*, 394; Margaret S. Mattson, "The Growth and Protection of Canadian Civil and Commercial Aviation, 1918-1930" (Ph.D. thesis, University of Western Ontario, 1979), 278-81; G.B. Langford, *Out of the Earth: The Mineral Industry in Canada* (Toronto, 1954), 51-53, 59-68.

12. "Solitary prospector" from Nelles, *Politics of Development*,

436-37; "geophysical prospecting" from E.S. Moore, *American Influence in Canadian Mining* (Toronto, 1941), 104; Allan Swinton, "The Trail of Twenty-six," *MM*, 1 August 1926, 8-9, 38-41; James A. Cowan, "Burrowing for a Billion," *MM*, 15 June 1927, 3-5, 38-40.

13. Leslie Roberts, *Noranda* (Toronto, 1956), 35-52; Marshall *et al., Canadian-American Industry*, 87-102; William A. Buik, "Noranda Mines Limited: A Study in Business and Economic History" (M.A. thesis, University of Toronto, 1958), 17-56.

14. Perrault quoted in Roberts, *Noranda*, 66-67; PAM, Bracken Papers, Address of 6 March 1929, file 338; Robert E. Groves, "Business Government: Party Politics and the B.C. Business Community, 1928-33" (M.A. thesis, University of British Columbia, 1976), 61.

15. John H. Dales, *Hydroelectricity and Industrial Development* (Cambridge, 1957), 182; Albert Faucher, "Le Caractère continental de l'industrialisation au Québec," in A. Faucher, *Histoire économique et unité canadienne* (Montreal, 1970), 168-71; Richard Lowitt, "Ontario Hydro: A 1925 Tempest in an American Teapot," *CHR*, XLIX:2, 1968, 269, 273; Grattan O'Leary, "Power," *MM*, 15 August 1928, 3-5.

16. H.V. Nelles, "Public Ownership of Electrical Utilities in Manitoba and Ontario, 1906-30," *CHR*, LVII:4, 1976, 461-84; Paul-Emile McIntyre, "The Development of Hydro-electric Power at Grand Falls, New Brunswick" (M.A. report, University of New Brunswick, 1972), *passim*; Nelles, *Politics of Development*, 399-421, 493; W.R. Plewman, *Adam Beck and Ontario Hydro* (Toronto, 1947), 352-73; Merrill Denison, *The People's Power: The History of Ontario Hydro* (Toronto, 1960), 168-69; B.L. Vigod, "Responses to Economic and Social Change in Quebec: The Provincial Administration of Louis-Alexandre Taschereau" (Ph.D. thesis, Queen's University, 1975), 94-101.

17. Kendle, *Bracken*, 52-84; J.R. Mallory, *Social Credit and the Federal Power in Canada* (Toronto, 1976), 23-24, 170-71; Christopher Armstrong, "The Politics of Federalism: Ontario's Relations with the Federal Government, 1896-1941" (Ph.D. thesis, University of Toronto, 1972), Ch. 6; Vigod, "Taschereau," 117-19; H. Blair Neatby, *William Lyon Mackenzie King*, II, *1924-1932: The Lonely Heights* (Toronto, 1963), 225-28; A.E. Dal Grauer, "The Export of Electricity from Canada," in R.M. Clark, ed., *Canadian Issues* (Toronto, 1961), 248-85.

18. G.W. Bertram, "Historical Statistics on Growth and Structure of Manufacturing in Canada, 1870-1957," in Canadian Political Science Association, *Papers of the Conference on Statistics* (Toronto, 1962-63), 94-95; A.J.E. Child, "The Predecessor Companies of Canada Packers: A Study of Entrepreneurial Achievement and Entrepreneurial Failure" (M.S. thesis, University of Toronto, 1960), 2-3, 172; author's calculations from *HSC*, Series Q 2, 8, 30-137, 373-75.

19. W.F. Prendergast, "The Automotive Industry of Canada," *JCBA*, XXIX:3, 1922, 319; *HSC*, Series S 222; T.R. Vout, "Canadian Manufacturing Industry, 1900-1957," in Canadian Political Science Association, *Conference on Statistics* (Toronto, 1960), 308.

20. Tom Traves, *The State and Enterprise: Canadian Manufacturers and the Federal Government, 1917-1931* (Toronto, 1979), 103; Stephen Scheinberg, "Invitation to Empire: Tariffs and American Economic Expansion in Canada," in Glenn Porter and Robert Cuff, eds., *Enterprise and National Development: Essays in Canadian Business and Economic History* (Toronto, 1973), 93-98; C.H. Aikman, *The Automobile Industry of Canada,* McGill Economic Series 8 (Montreal, 1926), 31-36; O.J. McDiarmid, "Some Aspects of the Canadian Automobile Industry," *CJEPS,* VI:2, 1940, 259.

21. Robert E. Ankli and Fred Frederikson, "The Influence of American Manufacturers on the Canadian Automobile Industry," *Business and Economic History,* 10, 1981, 101-13; Aikman, *Automobile Industry,* 14-15, 19-20; John De Bondt, *Canada on Wheels: A Portfolio of Early Canadian Cars* (Toronto, 1970), *passim;* Hugh Durnford and Glenn Baechler, *Cars of Canada* (Toronto, 1973), 68-189.

22. PAO, William Gray Papers, undated clipping. (Professor Robert Ankli kindly provided this quotation.)

23. J.L. Stewart, "Canada's Motor Car Industry," *Canadian Geographical Journal,* XIV, 1937, 203.

24. Squire quoted in *CAR,* 1920, 376-77; *ibid.,* 1921, 439; Percy Gomery, *A Motor Scamper Across Canada* (Toronto, 1922), *passim;* D.V. Smiley, ed., *The Rowell-Sirois Report, Book I* (Toronto, 1963), 144-45; *HSC,* Series G 328, S 49, S 216-18; E.C. Guillet, *The Story of Canadian Roads* (Toronto, 1966), 155-62.

25. PAM, Sanford Evans Papers, A.S. Eyolfsson to Dawson Richardson, 25 May 1927; Calgary *Herald,* 1 October 1926; The Pas, Man., *Herald and Mining News,* 29 October 1920; Brantford *Expositor,* 27 January 1933, clipping in PAM, Bracken Papers, file 753; W.A. Mackintosh, *The Economic Background of Dominion-Provincial Relations,* Carleton Library Ed. (Toronto, 1964), 81-82.

26. Mira Wilkins, *The Maturing of Multinational Enterprise: American Business Abroad, 1914-1970* (Cambridge, Mass., 1974), 60-63.

27. Definitions from Kari Levitt, *Silent Surrender: The Multinational Corporation in Canada* (Toronto, 1970), 58-59; *JCBA,* XXVIII:3, 1921, 367; author's calculations from Marshall *et al., Canadian-American Industry,* 21; Donald G. Paterson, *British Direct Investment in Canada, 1890-1914* (Toronto, 1976), *passim;* David Breen, "Anglo-American Rivalry and the Evolution of Canadian Petroleum Policy to 1930," *CHR,* LXII:3, 1981, 284-303; Irving Brecher and S.S. Reisman, *Canada–United States Economic Relations* (Ottawa, 1957), 100-101.

28. William L. Marr and Donald G. Paterson, *Canada: An Economic History* (Toronto, 1980), 297; C.W. Gonick, "Foreign Ownership and Political Decay," in Ian Lumsden, ed., *Close the 49th Parallel Etc.* (Toronto, 1970), 43-73; Levitt, *Silent Surrender,* 116-56; Leslie Roberts, "Wonder Rock," *MM,* 15 September 1928, 66-69; Robert Armstrong, "Nationalizing Asbestos," *CF,* August, 1979, 20-21; D.M. LeBourdais, *Metals and Men: The Story of Canadian Mining* (Toronto, 1957), 334-44.

29. Halifax *Citizen* quoted in E.R.

Forbes, "The Rise and Fall of the Conservative Party in the Provincial Politics of Nova Scotia, 1922-33" (M.A. thesis, Dalhousie University, 1967), 7; W.A. Irwin, "Can We Stem the Exodus?" *MM*, 15 May, 1 June 1927; A.R.M. Lower, "The Case Against Immigration," *QQ*, XXXVII: 4, 1930, 571; Taschereau quoted in Yves Roby, *Les Québécois et les investissements américains, 1918-1929* (Quebec, 1976), 141-43.

30. Bliss, *Sir Joseph Flavelle*, 431-32; *CHCD*, 1928, I, 637; Peter Kresl, "Before the Deluge: Canadians on Foreign Ownership, 1920-1955," *American Review of Canadian Studies*, VI:1, 1976, 93-96; Susan Mann Trofimenkoff, *Action Française: French Canadian Nationalism in the 1920s* (Toronto, 1975), 61-70; Roby, *Investissements américains*, 81-118.

31. Regina *Leader*, 17 December 1924, quoted in Gwenn Ronyk, "The United States in the Twenties As Seen by the Western Canadian Press" (M.A. thesis, University of Regina, 1979), 188-90; Harding speech in *CAR*, 1923, 83-84; C.P. Stacey, *Canada and the Age of Conflict*, II, *1921-1948: The Mackenzie King Era* (Toronto, 1981), 16.

32. Leslie T. Fournier, *Railway Nationalization in Canada* (Toronto, 1935), 52; G.R. Stevens, *History of the Canadian National Railways* (New York, 1973), 310-11; *HSC*, Series S 132.

33. D.H. Miller-Barstow, *Beatty of the C.P.R.: A Biography* (Toronto, 1951), 45-46, 67-87; D'Arcy Marsh, *The Tragedy of Henry Thornton* (Toronto, 1935), 106-10; G.P. de T. Glazebrook, *A History of Transportation in Canada* (Toronto, 1938), 377-94.

34. Glazebrook, *Transportation*, 110-23; Miller-Barstow, *Beatty*, 47-87; Stevens, *Canadian National Railways*, 339-42; Neatby, *Lonely Heights*, 267-70; Fournier, *Railway Nationalization*, 204-9.

35. A.E. Safarian, *The Canadian Economy in the Great Depression* (Toronto, 1970), 50-52, 212; J. Lorne McDougall, *Canadian Pacific: A Brief History* (Montreal, 1968), 101-7.

36. Kenneth Buckley, *Capital Formation in Canada, 1896-1930* (Toronto, 1955), 10; "The Age of Oil," *JCBA*, XXVII:4, 1920, 377; *HSC*, Series N 170, 176.

37. William Kilbourn, *The Elements Combined: A History of the Steel Company of Canada* (Toronto, 1960), 113-40; Duncan McDowall, "Steel at the Sault: Sir James Dunn and Algoma Steel, 1906-1956" (Ph.D. thesis, Carleton University, 1979), 104-35; Traves, *State and Enterprise*, 121-54; L.D. McCann, "The Mercantile-Industrial Transition in the Metal Towns of Pictou County, 1857-1931," *Acadiensis*, X:2, 1981, 57-64; *HSC*, Series F 388-89, N 62-63.

38. C.R. Fay, "Diminishing Returns in Agriculture," *JCBA*, XXXII:1, 1924, 22; Charles Gagné, "Notre Problème Agricole," *l'Action française*, 2 February 1924; Roby, *Investissements américains*, 55-58; Mackintosh, *Economic Background*, 72-96; André Raynauld, *Croissance et structures économiques de la province de Québec* (Quebec, 1960), 46, 590-91; *HSC*, Series L 2-6, 89, 114-18.

39. C.W. Petersen, "How're You Gonna Keep 'Em Down on the Farm?" *MM*, 15 January 1928; John H. Thompson, "The Political Career

of Ralph H. Webb," *Red River Valley Historian*, Summer, 1976, 5-7; S.A. Cudmore and H.G. Caldwell, *Rural and Urban Composition of the Canadian Population*, Census Monograph 6 (Ottawa, 1931), 29.

40. Gilbert A. Stelter and Alan F.J. Artibise, eds., *The Canadian City: Essays in Urban History* (Toronto, 1977), 52; George A. Nader, *Cities of Canada*, I, *Theoretical, Historical and Planning Perspectives* (Toronto, 1975), 211-12; Cudmore and Caldwell, *Rural and Urban Composition*, 29, 35; Leroy O. Stone, *Urban Development in Canada* (Ottawa, 1967), 27-28, 36-40.

41. Stelter and Artibise, *Canadian City*, 52: Buckley, *Capital Formation*, 10-11; Nader, *Cities of Canada* I, 214-24; Jacob Spelt, *Urban Development in South-Central Ontario* (Toronto, 1972), 198-211.

42. George A. Nader, *Cities of Canada*, II, *Profiles of Fifteen Metropolitan Centres* (Toronto, 1976), 272; "slow growth" from Paul Phillips, "The Prairie Urban System, 1911-1961," in Artibise, ed., *Town and City*, 19-22; A.F.J. Artibise, *Winnipeg: An Illustrated History* (Toronto, 1977), 109-22; Patricia E. Roy, *Vancouver: An Illustrated History* (Toronto, 1980), 88-92.

43. Author's calculations from *Canada Year Book*, 1932, 103-8; Paul Voisey, "Boosting the Small Prairie Town," in Artibise, ed., *Town and City*, 161-62, 169-70; Fredelle Bruser Maynard, *Raisins and Almonds* (Toronto, 1972), 39-51; James Forbes Newman, "The Impact of Technology upon Rural Southwestern Manitoba, 1920-1930" (M.A. thesis, Queen's Univer-

sity, 1971), 51-68; Gilbert A. Stelter, "The Industrial Towns of the Nickel Belt," *Laurentian University Review*, VI:3, 1974, 7, 43.

44. P.W. Rutherford, ed., *Saving the Canadian City: The First Phase, 1880-1920* (Toronto, 1974), *passim*; John C. Weaver, "Tomorrow's Metropolis Revisited: A Critical Assessment of Urban Reform in Canada, 1880-1920," in Stelter and Artibise, eds., *The Canadian City*, 393-417; James D. Anderson, "The Municipal Government Reform Movement in Western Canada, 1880-1920," in A.F.J. Artibise and Gilbert A. Stelter, *The Usable Urban Past* (Toronto, 1979), 73-111; Harold F. Greenway, *Housing in Canada*, Census Monograph 8 (Ottawa, 1931), 11; Terry Copp, *The Anatomy of Poverty: The Condition of the Working Class in Montreal, 1897-1929* (Toronto, 1974), 140; Walter Van Nus, "The Fate of City Beautiful Thought in Canada, 1893-1930," *CHAHP*, 1975, 191-206; J.G. Bacher, "The Evolution of a Non-Policy: The Role of the Canadian Federal Government in Housing, 1919-1968" (Ph.D. thesis, McMaster University, 1982), 131-32; planner quoted in Walter Van Nus, "The Plan-Makers and the City: Architects, Engineers, Surveyors and Urban Planning in Canada, 1890-1939" (Ph.D. thesis, University of Toronto, 1975), 320-26.

45. Author's calculations from *Canada Year Book*, 1932, 103-5; Van Nus, "Plan-Makers and the City," 224.

46. Cudmore and Caldwell, *Rural and Urban Composition*, 38; John C. Weaver, "From Land Assembly to Social Maturity: The Suburban Life of Westdale (Hamilton) Ontario,

1911-1951," *Hs/SH*, 22, 1978, 410-11.

47. Deryck W. Holdsworth, "House and Home in Vancouver: Images of West Coast Urbanism, 1886-1929," in Stelter and Artibise, *The Canadian City*, 192-94, 205-6; Greenway, *Housing in Canada*, 44-50, 90-115.

48. John H. Taylor, "Mayors à la Mancha: An Aspect of Depression Leadership in Canadian Cities," *Urban Historical Review*, IX:3, 1981, 3-14; Guy Bourassa, "Les élites politiques de Montréal: de l'aristocratie à la démocratie," *CJEPS*, XXXI:1, 1965, 45-49; John I. Cooper, *Montreal: A Brief History* (Montreal, 1969), 136-44; Robert-Maurice Migner, "Camilien Houde remplace Médéric Martin," *Urban History Review*, 1, 1974, 2-9; Thompson, "Ralph H. Webb," 3-7; Alan Morley, *Vancouver: From Milltown to Metropolis* (Vancouver, 1969), 163-71; Roy, *Vancouver*, 121-23.

49. *Canada Year Book*, 1932, 103-4; Ira M. Robinson, *New Industrial Towns on Canada's Resource Frontier* (Chicago, 1962), 168-72; Rouyn described in Rouyn *Copper-Gold Era*, 15 September 1926, quoted in Arnold Hoffmann, *Free Gold: The Story of Canadian Mining* (Toronto, 1947), 253; Roberts, *Noranda*, 124-26, 131-36; Stelter, "Industrial Towns of the Nickel Belt," 9-10, 14.

50. *CHCD*, 1928, I, 637; Eileen Goltz, "Espanola: The History of a Pulp and Paper Town," *Laurentian University Review*, VI:3, 1974, 86-87; Robert S. Robson, "Flin Flon: A Single Enterprise Community, 1927-1946" (M.A. thesis, University of Winnipeg, 1978), 70-111; Gilbert A. Stelter and Alan F.J. Artibise, "Canadian Resource Towns in Historical Perspective," *Plan Canada*, 18, 1978, 7-16; Rex Lucas, *Minetown, Milltown, Railtown: Life in Canadian Communities of Single Industry* (Toronto, 1971), *passim*.

51. T.D. Tait, "Haileybury: The Early Years," *Ontario History*, LV:3, 1963, 204.

52. Safarian, *Great Depression*, 68; *On the Tide of Prosperity* was the title of a pamphlet published by the Ontario government quoted in Oliver, *Ferguson*, 190.

53. J.M.S. Careless, "Limited Identities in Canada," *CHR*, L:1, 1969, 6-7.

NOTES TO CHAPTER SIX

1. Ernest R. Forbes, "Misguided Symmetry: The Destruction of Regional Transportation Policy for the Maritimes," in David Jay Bercuson, ed., *Canada and the Burden of Unity* (Toronto, 1977), 64-65; S.A. Saunders, *The Economic History of the Maritime Provinces* (Ottawa, 1939), 27-29; T.W. Acheson, "The National Policy and the Industrialization of the Maritimes," *Acadiensis*, I:2, 1972, 3-28.

2. T.W. Acheson, "The Maritimes and 'Empire Canada,' " in Bercuson, *Burden of Unity*, 97; G.W. Bertram, "Historical Statistics on Growth and Structure of Manufacturing in Canada, 1870-1957," in Canadian Political Science Association, *Papers of the Conference on Statistics*

(Toronto, 1962-63), table 8; *Canada Year Book*, 1932, 103-4; J.L. Rutledge, "A Big Job for Small Rivers," *MM*, 15 July 1922, 15, 46.

3. Forbes, "Misguided Symmetry," 62-65; L.D. McCann, "The Mercantile-Industrial Transition in the Metal Towns of Pictou County, 1857-1931," *Acadiensis*, X:2, 1981, 64.

4. Ernest R. Forbes, *The Maritime Rights Movement, 1919-1927: A Study in Canadian Regionalism* (Montreal, 1979), 67-71.

5. Wolvin described in Don Mcgillivray, "Industrial Unrest in Cape Breton 1919-1925" (M.A. thesis, University of New Brunswick, 1971), 11; David Frank, "The Cape Breton Coal Industry and the Rise and Fall of the British Empire Steel Corporation," *Acadiensis*, VII: 1, 1977, 3-34.

6. S.A. Saunders, *The Economic Welfare of the Maritime Provinces* (Wolfville, N.S., 1932), 123; D.M. LeBourdais, *Metals and Men: The Story of Canadian Mining* (Toronto, 1957), 313-33; town described in C.R. Fay, "Problems of the Maritime Provinces," *DR*, IV:4, 1925, 443; David Alexander, "Economic Growth in the Atlantic Region, 1880-1940," *Acadiensis*, VIII:1, 1978, 63-67; fishermen's problems described in Public Archives of Nova Scotia, E.N. Rhodes Papers, vol. 607, M.H. Nickerson to Rhodes, 20 July 1927, cited in Kenneth G. Jones, "Response to Regional Disparity in the Maritime Provinces, 1926-1942" (M.A. thesis, University of New Brunswick, 1980), 30.

7. Hugh G. Thorburn, *Politics in New Brunswick* (Toronto, 1961), 45, 48-50; *Busy East of Canada* quoted in Forbes, *Maritime Rights Movement*, 1-37.

8. Forbes, *Maritime Rights Movement,* viii-ix, 27-30; direct quotation from K.A. McKirdy, "Regionalism: Canada and Australia" (Ph.D. thesis, University of Toronto, 1959), 162, 310-11; J. Murray Beck, *The Government of Nova Scotia* (Toronto, 1957), 170.

9. *KD*, 1 February 1922; PAC, King Papers, R.E. Finn to King, 25 January 1923; H. Blair Neatby, *William Lyon Mackenzie King*, II, *1924-1932: The Lonely Heights* (Toronto, 1963), 67.

10. Halifax *Herald*, 27 July 1922, quoted in G.A. Rawlyk, "Nova Scotia Regional Protest, 1867-1967," *QQ*, LXXV:1, 1968, 121; Corning resolution in *CAR*, 1923, 638; Colin D. Howell, "Nova Scotia's Protest Tradition," in Bercuson, *Burden of Unity*, 184; Forbes, *Maritime Rights Movement*, 141-43.

11. PAC, Meighen Papers, A.R. Landry to Meighen, 21 December 1923, cited in Forbes, *Maritime Rights Movement*, 127-28.

12. Ernest R. Forbes, "The Rise and Fall of the Conservative Party in the Provincial Politics of Nova Scotia, 1922-33" (M.A. thesis, Dalhousie University, 1967), Chs. 1 and 2; Margaret S. Conrad, "George Nowlan and the Conservative Party in the Annapolis Valley, 1925-1965" (Ph.D. thesis, University of Toronto, 1979), 114-18; Paul MacEwan, *Miners and Steelworkers: Labour in Cape Breton* (Toronto, 1976), 144-45.

13. *CAR*, 1924-25, 357; direct quotations from "Provincial Elections," *JCBA*, XXXII:4, 1925, 405; Arthur T. Doyle, *Front Benches and Back Rooms: A Story of Corruption, Muckraking, Raw Partisanship and*

Political Intrigue in New Brunswick (Toronto, 1976), 242, 254-58; Calvin A. Woodward, *The History of New Brunswick Provincial Election Campaigns and Platforms* (Canada, 1976), 49-51; Jean Daigle, review of Forbes, *Maritime Rights Movement, RbAf,* 33:4, 1980, 592-94.

14. Calgary *Herald,* 11 August 1925; *KD,* 27, 28 July and 10 August, 1925.

15. J. Murray Beck, *Pendulum of Power: Canada's Federal Elections* (Toronto, 1968), 163-64; Neatby, *Lonely Heights,* 59; "tariff butchering" from Toronto *Mail and Empire,* quoted in *CAR,* 1924-25, 213; *HSC,* series W, 177-213; *CAR,* 1923, 173-78.

16. Irvine in *CHCD,* 1925, II, 1960; PAC, Borden Papers, Borden to Beaverbrook, 15 December 1923, quoted in Robert Craig Brown, *Robert Laird Borden: A Biography,* II, *1914-1937* (Toronto, 1980), 193; *QQ,* XXXIII:2, 1925, 219.

17. *CAR,* 1924-25, 200-202; Neatby, *Lonely Heights,* 92, 174; Joy Esbery, *Knight of the Holy Spirit: A Study of William Lyon Mackenzie King* (Toronto, 1980), 184-90; Peter Regenstrief, "A Threat to Leadership: C.A. Dunning and Mackenzie King," *DR,* XLIV:3, 1964, 272-89.

18. George C. Perlin, *The Tory Syndrome: Leadership Politics in the Progressive Conservative Party* (Montreal, 1980), 40-42; Bruce Hutchison, *The Incredible Canadian: A Candid Portrait of Mackenzie King* (Toronto, 1952), 20, 38-40, 99-101; R. MacGregor Dawson, *William Lyon Mackenzie King: A Political Biography, 1874-1923* (Toronto, 1958), 340-43, 417-18; Neatby, *Lonely Heights,* 104-7.

19. Meighen quoted in Roger Graham, *Arthur Meighen,* II, *And Fortune Fled* (Toronto, 1963), 143; Norman Ward, ed., *A Party Politician: The Memoirs of Chubby Power* (Toronto, 1966), 71-76; Roger Graham, "Arthur Meighen and the Conservative Party in Quebec," *CHR,* XXVI:1, 1955, 26-27; Borden quoted in Brown, *Borden* II, 193; Flavelle quoted in Michael Bliss, *A Canadian Millionaire: The Life and Business Times of Sir Joseph Flavelle, Bart., 1858-1939* (Toronto, 1978), 426.

20. *KD,* 28 July, 9, 28 September 1925; Graham, *Meighen* II, 328-31; *CAR,* 1925-26, 25.

21. David E. Smith, *Prairie Liberalism: The Liberal Party in Saskatchewan, 1905-71* (Toronto, 1975), 181; Margaret A. Ormsby, *British Columbia: A History* (Toronto, 1958), 423-24.

22. Ward, *A Party Politician,* 377; H. Blair Neatby, "Mackenzie King and French Canada," *JCS,* XI:1, 1976, 3-13.

23. Patenaude quoted in *CAR,* 1925-26; Graham, *Meighen* II, 316-24; Graham, "Meighen and Conservative Party in Quebec," 22.

24. Graham, "Meighen and Conservative Party in Quebec," 30-32; Graham, *Meighen* II, 339-44; Grattan O'Leary, *Recollections of People, Press and Politics* (Toronto, 1977), 46-53; *KD,* 12, 24 September 1925.

25. *KD,* 20, 25, 29 October 1925; C.P. Stacey, *A Very Double Life: The Private World of Mackenzie King* (Toronto, 1976), 163-64.

26. *Globe* quoted in *CAR,* 1925-26, 41-42.

27. King advised to resign in *Willison's Monthly,* quoted in *CAR,*

1925-26, 43; *KD*, 29 October 1925; Esbery, *Knight of the Holy Spirit*, 158.

28. Dafoe to Sifton, 5 December 1925, in Ramsay Cook, ed., *The Dafoe-Sifton Correspondence, 1919-1927* (Altona, Man., 1966), 231; Ramsay Cook, *The Politics of John W. Dafoe and the Free Press* (Toronto, 1963), 153-60; Winnipeg *Tribune*, 26 November 1925; Graham, *Meighen* II, 355-70.

29. Progressive opinion of King from GAI, W. Norman Smith Papers, William Irvine to Smith, 17 November 1925, file 22; W.L. Morton, *The Progressive Party in Canada* (Toronto, 1950), 247-50; Leo Heaps, *The Rebel in the House: The Life and Times of A.A. Heaps M.P.* (London, 1970), 60-62; Kenneth McNaught, *A Prophet in Politics: A Biography of J.S. Woodsworth* (Toronto, 1959), 216-20.

30. Joke from "The Canadian Situation," *QQ*, XXXIII:3, 1926, 367; "The Government Takes the Offensive," *CF*, May, 1926, 235.

31. *Financial Post* quoted in *CAR*, 1924-25, 86-89; "protectionist by day" from Ralph Allen, *Ordeal by Fire, Canada, 1910-1945* (New York, 1961), 256-65; *KD*, 17, 19 August 1925; Neatby, *Lonely Heights*, 114-16.

32. Report quoted in *CAR*, 1925-26, 79-80; *CF*, May, 1926, 236; Allen, *Ordeal by Fire*, 270; Aziz letter printed in *CHCD*, 1926, V, 4865.

33. W.T. Lucas quoted in Morton, *Progressive Party*, 253; J.R.H. Wilbur, *H.H. Stevens, 1878-1973* (Toronto, 1977), 52-60; Heaps, *Rebel in the House*, 67-68.

34. PAC, King Papers, handwritten note, 1 July 1926, cited in Neatby,

Lonely Heights, 145; Byng quoted in *CAR*, 1921, 249; J.R. Mallory, "The Appointment of the Governor General: Responsible Government, Autonomy and the Royal Prerogative," *CJEPS*, XXVI:1, 1960, 98-99; John Cowan, *Canada's Governors-General, 1867-1952* (Toronto, 1952), 111-21; PAC, King Papers, King to Baldwin, 16 April 1926, cited in Neatby, *Lonely Heights*, 146; PAC, Byng to L.S. Amery, 30 June 1926, printed in Roger Graham, ed., *The King-Byng Affair, 1926: A Question of Responsible Government* (Toronto, 1967), 23-24.

35. Arthur R.M. Lower, *Colony to Nation: A History of Canada*, rev. ed. (Toronto, 1977), 508; Eugene Forsey, *The Royal Power of Dissolution of Parliament in the British Commonwealth* (Toronto, 1943), 166; J.R. Mallory, *The Structure of Canadian Government* (Toronto, 1971), 17-18, 49-53; Neatby, *Lonely Heights*, 148-50; Eugene Forsey, "Mr. King and Parliamentary Government," *CJEPS*, XVII:4, 1951, reprinted in Forsey, *Freedom and Order* (Toronto, 1974), 101-2.

36. *CAR*, 1926-27, 65-67. Despite the success of the Robb motion, Meighen's "temporary government" was neither unconstitutional nor unprecedented in Canada or the Commonwealth. Forsey, *Royal Power of Dissolution*, Ch. 6.

37. J. Lambert Payne, "Kilkenny Campaigns," *MM*, 15 December 1927, 17; Ward, *A Party Politician*, 311-27; Robert Rumilly, *Histoire de la province de Québec*, XXVIII (Montreal, 1955), 251-52; Meighen described in Manitoba *Free Press*, cited in Graham, *Meighen* II, 460; Ottawa *Journal*, cited in Beck, *Pendulum of Power*, 187-88.

38. *KD*, 2, 25 August 1926, cited in Neatby, *Lonely Heights*, 159-60; King's speeches, printed in Graham, *King-Byng Affair*, 61-66; Toronto *Star*, 15 July 1926; Ewart cited in Douglas Cole, "The Better Patriot: John S. Ewart and the Canadian Nation" (Ph.D. thesis, University of Washington, 1968), 321; Bourassa in *Le Devoir*, 16 September 1926; Ian Angus, *Canadian Bolsheviks: The Early Years of the Communist Party of Canada* (Montreal, 1981), 166-72.

39. John Diefenbaker, *One Canada: Memoirs of the Rt. Hon. John G. Diefenbaker*, I (Toronto, 1975), 147-48; PABC, T.D. Pattullo Papers, J.H. King to John Oliver, 7 July 1926, vol. 22, file 13; "Let's Hear of Bigger Things," Calgary *Herald*, 13 August 1926; R.J. Manion, *Life Is an Adventure* (Toronto, 1936), 269-70; Rumilly, *Histoire de la province de Québec*, XXVIII, 237-39; Beck, *Pendulum of Power*, 186.

40. Rumilly, *Histoire de la province de Québec*, XXVIII, 252-53.

41. PABC, Pattullo Papers, J.A. Campbell to John Oliver, 7 October 1926, vol. 22, file 13.

42. Anthony Mardiros, *William Irvine: The Life of a Prairie Radical* (Toronto, 1979), 170-71; Morton, *Progressive Party*, 263.

43. Graham, *Meighen* II, 478-89.

44. Guthrie quoted in Montreal *Star*, 20 October 1926; Payne, "Kilkenny Campaigns," 17.

45. *CF*, November, 1924, 35.

46. Aird and Holt quoted in *CAR*, 1926-27, 512, 718-19, 727, 731; business approval of Coolidge in Alex Brady, "The Press in Ontario, 1921-34," in H.F. Angus, ed., *Canada and Her Great Neighbor* (New York, 1938), 277.

47. Janice P. Dicken McGinnis, "From Health to Welfare: Federal Government Policies Regarding Standards of Public Health for Canadians, 1919-1945" (Ph.D. thesis, University of Alberta, 1981), 3, 37-39; Dennis Guest, *The Emergence of Social Security in Canada* (Vancouver, 1980), 74-79; Leonard Marsh, *Report on Social Security for Canada, 1943* (Toronto, 1975), 161-69; Kenneth Bryden, *Old Age Pensions and Policy Making in Canada* (Montreal, 1974), 61-68, 80-91.

48. Jones, "Regional Disparity in the Maritime Provinces," 14-28; direct quotations from Forbes, *Maritime Rights Movement*, 158-81.

49. Donald Avery, *Dangerous Foreigners: European Immigrant Workers and Labour Radicalism in Canada, 1896-1932* (Toronto, 1979), 101-12; Heenan quoted in Neatby, *Lonely Heights*, 237-42.

50. "Lamps on bicycles" from Mallory, *Structure of Canadian Government*, 331-48; D.G. Creighton, "Federal Relations in Canada Since 1914," in Chester Martin, ed., *Canada in Peace and War* (Toronto, 1941), 30-34.

51. Peter H. Russell, ed., *Leading Constitutional Decisions* (Toronto, 1976), 23-45.

52. J.R. Mallory, *Social Credit and the Federal Power in Canada* (Toronto, 1976), 53-56; Christopher Armstrong, *The Politics of Federalism: Ontario's Relations with the Federal Government, 1867-1942* (Toronto, 1981), 107-13, 233-34; F.R. Scott, "The Privy Council and Mr. Bennett's New Deal Legislation," *CJEPS*, III:2, 1937, 240; Alan C. Cairns, "The Judicial Committee and Its Critics," *Canadian Journal*

of *Political Science*, IV:3, 1971, 301-45.

53. Donald V. Smiley, ed., *The Rowell-Sirois Report, Book I* (Toronto, 1963), 138-50.

54. Bernard L. Vigod, *Louis-Alexandre Taschereau: A Political Biography* (forthcoming), *passim* (I must thank Professor Vigod for making the manuscript available to me before publication); Peter Oliver, *G. Howard Ferguson: Ontario Tory* (Toronto, 1977), *passim*.

55. Armstrong, *Politics of Federalism*, 160-77; ANQ, fonds Louis-Alexandre Taschereau, Discours, vol. 23, cited in Vigod, *Taschereau*.

56. Ramsay Cook, *Canada and the French-Canadian Question* (Toronto, 1966), 43-61; Ramsay Cook, *Provincial Autonomy, Minority Rights and the Compact Theory, 1867-1921* (Ottawa, 1969), *passim*; David Kwavnick, ed., *The Tremblay Report: Report of the Royal Commission of Inquiry on Constitutional Problems* (Toronto, 1973), 106-18; Oliver, *Ferguson*, 171-72; Kenneth McRoberts and Dale Posgate, *Quebec: Social Change and Political Crisis* (Toronto, 1980), 87-89.

57. Dominion-Provincial Conference, *Précis of Discussions*, Sessional Paper No. 69 (Ottawa, 1928), 3-5, 9.

58. G.V. LaForest, *Disallowance and Reservation of Provincial Legislation* (Ottawa, 1955), 69-76; Eugene Forsey, "Disallowance of Provincial Acts, Reservation of Provincial Bills, and Refusal of Assent by Lieutenant-Governors Since 1867," *CJEPS*, IV:1, 1938, 47-59; Dominion-Provincial Conference, *Précis*, 25; A.W. Boos, *The Financial Arrangements Between the Provinces and the Dominion* (Toronto, 1930), 57-69; J.A. Maxwell, *Federal Subsidies to the Provincial Governments in Canada* (Cambridge, 1937), 145-47.

59. Taschereau quoted in PAC, Ernest Lapointe Papers, subject file 24, "Minutes of Friday morning, November 4, 1927."

60. King's comment from Dominion-Provincial Conference, *Précis*, 38; Neatby, *Lonely Heights*, 242-43; Armstrong, *Politics of Federalism*, 108-11, 171; Christopher Armstrong, "The Mowat Heritage in Federal-Provincial Relations," in Donald Swainson, ed., *Oliver Mowat's Ontario* (Toronto, 1972), 111-12.

NOTES TO CHAPTER SEVEN

1. Observations on income distribution quoted from F.R. Scott *et al.*, *Social Planning for Canada* (Toronto, 1935), 17; Desmond Morton with Terry Copp, *Working People: An Illustrated History of Canadian Labour* (Toronto, 1980), 125; *Canadian Magazine*, October, 1930, 49-50.

2. *HSC*, Series J 128-31, 303; Gordon Bertram and Michael Percy, "Real Wage Trends in Canada, 1900-1926: Some Provisional Estimates," *Canadian Journal of Economics*, 12:2, 1979, 229-312; Catherine Waite, "The Longshoremen of Halifax, 1900-1930: Their Living and Working Conditions" (M.A. thesis, Dal-

housie University, 1979), 50-60; Terry Copp, *The Anatomy of Poverty: The Condition of the Working Class in Montreal, 1897-1929* (Toronto, 1974), 330-43; David Hall, "Times of Trouble: Labour Quiescence in Winnipeg, 1920-29" (M.A. thesis, University of Manitoba, 1982), 84-90, 154-55; Eleanor A. Bartlett, "Real Wages and the Standard of Living in Vancouver, 1901-1929," *BC Studies*, 51, 1981, 3-62.

3. Norman Reilly Raine, "Tom Moore: Safety Valve of Labor," *MM*, 1 April 1925, 15, 70-72.

4. Robert H. Babcock, *Gompers in Canada: A Study in American Continentalism Before the First World War* (Toronto, 1974), *passim*; Sally F. Zerker, *The Rise and Fall of the Toronto Typographical Union, 1932-1972: A Case Study in Foreign Domination* (Toronto, 1982), 178-204; Irving Abella, *The Canadian Labour Movement, 1902-1960*, Canadian Historical Association Booklet No. 38 (Ottawa, 1975), 4-15.

5. Gregory S. Kealey, "1919: The Canadian Labour Revolt," *L/ le t*,13, 1984, 11-44; David Jay Bercuson, *Confrontation at Winnipeg: Labour, Industrial Relations and the General Strike* (Montreal, 1974) and *Fools and Wise Men: The Rise and Fall of the One Big Union* (Toronto, 1978); politicians' fears voiced in PAC, Robert Borden Papers, vol. 113, 6131, C.H. Cahan to Prime Minister, 28 May 1919; Heenan's apology quoted in Norman Penner, ed., *Winnipeg 1919 – The Strikers' Own History*, 2nd ed. (Toronto, 1975), 229-41; Raine, "Tom Moore," 70-72.

6. *Saturday Night*, 7 January 1922, cited in Margaret A. Prang, "Some Opinions of Political Radicalism in Canada Between the Two World Wars" (M.A. thesis, University of Toronto, 1953), 126-27; Marx criticized in Agnes Laut, *Canada at the Cross Roads* (Toronto, 1921), 42-43; "Industrial Council Suggested," Nanaimo *Free Press*, 30 April 1919; Bruce Scott, " 'A Place in the Sun': The Industrial Council at Massey-Harris, 1919-1929," *L/ le t*, 1, 1976, 158-92.

7. Patricia E. Roy, "The British Columbia Electric Railway and Its Street Railway Employees: Paternalism in Labour Relations," *BC Studies*, 16, 1972-3, 22-24; "Bell Telephone Union Smashers," *Young Worker* (Toronto), May 1926, 1; Susan Mann Trofimenkoff, *Stanley Knowles: The Man from Winnipeg North Centre* (Saskatoon, 1982), 96-104; quotation from J.L. Rutledge, "Satisfied Labor Will Stick," *MM*, 1 May 1922, 28, 49.

8. Edmonton *Journal*, 13 April 1925; Stuart Jamieson, *Times of Trouble: Labour Unrest and Industrial Conflict in Canada, 1900-1966* (Ottawa, 1971), 192-213; Ian Angus, *Canadian Bolsheviks: The Early Years of the Communist Party of Canada* (Montreal, 1981), 133-36; Paul Phillips, *No Power Greater: A Century of Labour in B.C.* (Vancouver, 1967), 85-100; Jacques Rouillard, "Le militantisme des travailleurs au Québec et en Ontario, 1900-1980," *RhAf*, 37, 2, 1983, 206-7; PAC, Department of Labour Records, Strikes and Lockouts Files, Box 322, file 95, clippings and correspondence *re* West Coast longshore, strike, 1923, and some 500 other dossiers, 1921-29; eulogy cited in Satu Repo, "Rosvall and Voutilainen: Two Union Men Who

Never Died," *L/ le t*, 8/9, 1981, 97.

9. McLachlan quoted in *The People's History of Cape Breton* (Halifax, 1971), 13; Christophers in *Alberta Labor News*, 29 March, 1924.

10. David Frank, "Class Conflict in the Coal Industry: The Cape Breton Strike of 1922," in G.S. Kealey and Peter Warrian, eds., *Essays in Canadian Working Class History* (Toronto, 1976), 161-84; Donald A. Macgillivray, "Military Aid to the Civil Power: The Cape Breton Experience in the 1920s," *Acadiensis,* III:2, 1974, 45-65; Morrison's reply quoted in David Frank and Donald A. Macgillivray, *Echoes from Labour's War: Industrial Cape Breton in the 1920s* (Toronto, 1974), 17; GAI, Western Canada Coal Operators Association Papers, file 37, R.M. Young, Secretary, to James Murdock, 15 August, 1922; GAI, West Canadian Collieries Papers, files 83, 120, correspondence *re* 1922 coal strike, District 18.

11. Paul MacEwan, *Miners and Steelworkers: Labour in Cape Breton* (Toronto, 1976), 91-122; David Frank, "The Trial of J.B. McLachlan," *CHAHP*, 1983, 208-25; *Report on Labour Organizations in Canada for 1923* (Ottawa, 1924), 192; McLachlan quoted in Tom McEwen, *The Forge Glows Red: From Blacksmith to Revolutionary* (Toronto, 1974), 146-47; McLachlan was released on 5 March 1924 after nation-wide protests – Beaton Institute, College of Cape Breton, J.B. McLachlan Papers, Livingston to McLachlan, 3 March 1924.

12. Charles A. MacMillan, "Trade Unionism in District 18, 1900-1925" (M.A. thesis, University of Alberta, 1969), *passim*; Sherman quoted in Provincial Archives of Alberta,

Legislative Papers, 64.11, documents of the Alberta Coal Commission, 1925, reply from L.U. 4687 to questionnaire on solutions to the coal problem; J.B. McLachlan, "Strikers Starve while UMWA Officials Loll in Luxury," *Worker* (Toronto), 13 September 1924; PAC, King Papers, vol. 89, C68682-89, F.E. Harrison correspondence, 1924 coal strike; William A. Sloan, "The Crow's Nest Pass During the Depression: A Socio-economic History of Southeastern British Columbia, 1918-1936" (M.A. thesis, University of Victoria, 1968), Ch. 2; Frank P. Karas, "Labour and Coal in the Crow's Nest Pass, 1925-1935" (M.A. thesis, University of Calgary, 1972), 39-57.

13. John Mellor, *The Company Store: James Bryson McLachlan and the Cape Breton Coal Miners, 1900-1925* (Toronto, 1983), 259-318; H.M.E. Evans, R.G. Drinnan, and Frank Wheatley, *The Report of the Alberta Coal Commission* (Edmonton, 1926); Frank Wheatley, "Mining Conditions in Alberta," *Canadian Unionist*, February, 1930, 113-14.

14. Harold A. Logan, *Trade Unions in Canada* (Toronto, 1948), 368-85; Norman J. Ware, "The History of Labor Interaction," in Harold A. Innis, ed., *Labor in Canadian-American Relations* (Toronto, 1937), 37-41; "independence" cited in Charles Lipton, *The Trade Union Movement in Canada, 1827-1959* (Montreal, 1967), 229-36.

15. A.R. Mosher, "The Aims of the Congress," *Canadian Unionist*, June 1927, 1; F. Wheatley, "Nationalize the Coal Mines!" *ibid.*, 5; William Rodney, *Soldiers of the In-*

ternational: A History of the Communist Party of Canada, 1919-1929 (Toronto, 1968), 107-17; Angus, Canadian Bolsheviks, 174-77, 274-77; TLC-ACCL mud slinging quoted in Stuart Jamieson, Industrial Relations in Canada, 2nd ed. (Toronto, 1973), 22, and in Martin Robin, Radical Politics and Canadian Labour, 1880-1930 (Kingston, 1968), 260-61; James Macpherson to the editor, Worker, n.d., PAO, Communist Party of Canada Papers 6B0984.

16. "A Well Fought Fight," Canadian Unionist, February, 1929, 134; Mosher quoted in "Proceedings of the Third Annual Convention, ACCL," Labour Gazette, XXIX, 1929, 1359-60; Craig Heron, "Hamilton Steel Workers and the Rise of Mass Production," CHAHP, 1982, 103-27; Robert Storey, "Unionization versus Corporate Welfare: The 'Dofasco Way,'" L/ le t, 12, 1983, 7-15; William Kilbourn, The Elements Combined: A History of the Steel Company of Canada (Toronto, 1960), 119-24; "Hamilton Strike Forces Company to Stop Wage Cut – Strikers Still being Blacklisted," Young Worker, November 1929, 5.

17. J.K. Galbraith, The Scotch (Toronto, 1964), 143-44; James A. Pendergast, "The Attempt at Unionization in the Automobile Industry, 1928," Ontario History, LXX: 4, 1978, 245-62; John Manley, "The Struggle for Industrial Unionism in the Canadian Automobile Industry, 1922-1936," paper read at the Canadian Historical Association Annual Meetings, Halifax, 1981.

18. Fraser Isbester, "A History of the National Catholic Unions in Canada, 1901-1965" (Ph.D. thesis, Cornell University, 1968), 66-121; Jacques Rouillard, Les Syndicats nationaux au Québec, de 1900 à 1930 (Quebec, 1979), 232-34.

19. Goal of confessional unions quoted in Robert Parisé, La Fondateur du syndicalisme catholique au Québec: Mgr Eugène Lapointe (Quebec, 1978); Desranleau cited in Jean-Claude St-Amant, "La Propagande de l'Ecole Sociale Populaire en faveur du syndicalisme catholique, 1911-1949," RhAf, 32:2, 1978, 216; "born enemies" quoted in Michel Pelletier and Yves Vaillancourt, Les Politiques sociales et les travailleurs: les années 1900 à 1929 (Montreal, 1974), 77-78; Alfred Charpentier, Ma conversion au syndicalisme catholique (Montreal, 1946), passim.

20. Programme-Souvenir du premier congrès de la CTCC (Montreal, 1922), 71; Brian Williams, "Canadian-American Trade Union Relations: A Study in the Development of Bi-National Unions" (Ph.D. thesis, Cornell University, 1964), 321-42; ANQ, Labour Ministry Papers, vol. 118, G23, file "Sorel Strikes," Pierre Gosselin to Gérard Tremblay, 11 May 1937.

21. Jean-Pierre Charland, "Le Syndicalisme chez les cordonniers de Québec, 1900-1930" (M.A. thesis, Université Laval, 1979), 74-88; Nicole Thivièrge-Cloutier, "La Condition sociale des ouvriers de l'industrie de la chaussure à Québec" (M.A. thesis, Université Laval, 1979), 39-44; Labour Gazette, XXIX, 1929, 894-95; Rouillard, Les Syndicats nationaux, passim.

22. Le Droit articles on the Hull strike published in Irving Abella and David Millar, The Canadian Worker in the Twentieth Century (Toronto,

1978), 232-40; chaplain quoted in Michelle Lapointe, "Le Syndicat catholique des allumettières de Hull, 1919-1924," *RhAf*, 32, 4, 1979, 615-24; Veronica Strong-Boag, "The Girl of the New Day: Canadian Working Women in the 1920s," *L/le t*, 4, 1979, 156.

23. Strong-Boag, "Girl of the New Day," 157; Susan Walsh, "Equality, Emancipation and a More Just World: Leading Women in the British Columbia CCF" (M.A. thesis, Simon Fraser University, 1984), Ch. 3; Marie Campbell, "Sexism in British Columbia Trade Unions," in Barbara Latham and Kathy Kess, eds., *In Her Own Right: Selected Essays on Women's History in B.C.* (Vancouver, 1982), 167-86; see the essays by Catherine MacLeod, Dorothy Kidd, Alice Klein, and Wayne Roberts and Genevieve Leslie, in Janice Acton, Penny Goldsmith, and Bonnie Sheppard, eds., *Women at Work: Ontario, 1850-1930* (Toronto, 1974), and also Le Collective Clio, *L'Histoire des femmes au Québec depuis quatre siècles* (Montreal, 1981), 295-300; Joan Sangster, "The Communist Party of Canada and the Woman Question in the 1920s," paper read at the Canadian Historical Association Annual Meetings, Vancouver, 1983.

24. *MM*, 15 March 1922, 56-57; Elaine Bernard, *The Long Distance Feeling: A History of the Telecommunications Workers' Union* (Vancouver, 1982), 50-80; Graham Lowe, "Class, Job, and Gender in the Canadian Office," *L/le t*, 10, 1982, 11-38; Coats's observations in *Sixth Census*, I, xxii.

25. Marie Lavigne and Jennifer Stoddart, "Les Travailleuses montréalaises entre les deux guerres," *L/le t*,

2, 1977, 170-84; Maude Pettit Hill, "What's the Matter with Housework?" *Chatelaine*, March, 1928, 13, 56-57; Helen Lenskyi, "Social Change Affecting Women in Canada, 1890-1930, and Its Impact on Immigrant Women in the Labour Force" (M.A. thesis, Ontario Institute for Studies in Education, 1980), 105-15; Marilyn Barber, "The Women Ontario Welcomed: Immigrant Domestics for Ontario Homes, 1870-1930," *Ontario History*, LXXII:3, 1980, 148-73; H.L. Walkin, "The Honey Dew Shops," *Canadian Restaurant*, January, 1929, 41-44.

26. Veronica Strong-Boag, "Feminism Constrained: The Graduates of Canada's Medical Schools for Women," in Linda Kealey, ed., *A Not Unreasonable Claim: Women and Reform in Canada, 1880s-1920s* (Toronto, 1979), 109-29; Elise Elliot Corbet, "Alberta Women in the 1920s: An Inquiry into Four Aspects of Their Lives" (M.A. thesis, University of Calgary, 1979), 61-71; Stanley Frost and Sheila Rosenberg, "The McGill Student Body," *McGill Journal of Education*, XV:1, 1980, 41-42; Mary E. Hallett, "Nellie McClung and the Fight for the Ordination of Women in the United Church of Canada," *Atlantis*, IV, 2, 1979, 8-15; prejudice cited by J.B. Brebner, "Presidential Address," *CHAAR*, 1940, 13.

27. E.G. MacGill, *My Mother the Judge: A Biography of Judge Helen Gregory MacGill* (Toronto, 1960), 150; Marjorie MacMurchy, *The Canadian Girl at Work* (Toronto, 1920), cited in Strong-Boag, "Girl of the New Day," 160; *Seventh Census*, VII, 584.

28. Leonard Marsh, *Canadians In*

and Out of Work: A Survey of Economic Classes and Their Relation to the Labour Market (Montreal, 1940), 95-99, 273-77; Gail Cuthbert Brandt, " 'Weaving It Together': Life Cycle and the Industrial Experience of Female Cotton Workers in Quebec, 1910-1950," *L/ le t,* 7, 1981, 113-26; H.E. Stephenson and Carlton McNaught, *The Story of Advertising in Canada* (Toronto, 1940), 53, 218-33, 240; "The Roaring Twenties," *Chatelaine,* March, 1978, 44; *HSC,* Series B 75, 79.

29. GAI, Calgary Women's Canadian Club Papers, Business Girls' Club to Canadian Club, 1923; S.J.F. Wilson, "The Relationship Between Mass Media Content and Social Change in Canada" (Ph.D. thesis, University of Toronto, 1977), 102-7; Meg Luxton, *More Than a Labour of Love: Three Generations of Working in the Home* (Toronto, 1980), 29-32; Veronica Strong-Boag, "Discovering the Home: The Last 150 Years of Work in Canada," paper read at the Ontario Museums Association Annual Meeting, Toronto 1983, 1.

30. "The Housewife as Manager," *Saturday Night,* 17 January 1920, cited in Mary Vipond, "The Image of Women in Mass Circulation Magazines in the 1920s," in S.M. Trofimenkoff and Alison Prentice, eds., *The Neglected Majority: Essays in Canadian Women's History* (Toronto, 1977), 120; Dominion Bureau of Statistics, *Household Facilities and Equipment* (Ottawa, 1948); Harold F. Greenway, *Housing in Canada,* Census Monograph 8 (Ottawa, 1941), 126-27; *HSC,* Series L 336.

31. W.B. Hurd, "The Decline of the Canadian Birthrate," *CJEPS,* III:1, 1937, 40-57; Angus McLaren, "Birth Control and Abortion in Canada, 1870-1920," *CHR,* LIX:3, 1978, 323; Angus McLaren, "What Has This to Do with Working Class Women?: Birth Control and the Canadian Left, 1900-39," *Hs/SH,* 28, 1981, 435-54; criticism of Bagshaw quoted in Judy Stoffmann, "The First Lady of Birth Control," *Weekend,* 1 October, 1977; Dianne Dodd, "The Canadian Birth Control Movement on Trial, 1936-1937," *Hs/SH,* 32, 1983, 411-28; Max Braithwaite, *The Hungry Thirties* (Toronto, 1977), 49-51.

32. Enid Charles, *The Changing Size of the Canadian Family* (Ottawa, 1948), 16-17, 34-48; Veronica Strong-Boag, "Intruders in the Nursery: Child-Care Professionals Reshape the Years One to Five," in Joy Parr, ed., *Childhood and Family in Canadian History* (Toronto, 1982), 161-64; Janice P.D. McGinnis, "From Health to Welfare: Federal Government Policies Regarding Standards of Public Health for Canadians, 1919-1945" (Ph.D. thesis, University of Alberta, 1981), 123-26; H. Benge Atlee, "The Menace of Maternity," *Canadian Home Journal,* May, 1933, cited in Suzann Buckley, "Efforts to Reduce Infant Mortality in Canada Between the Two World Wars," *Atlantis,* II, 1974, 81-82; Nora Lewis, "Creating the Little Machine: Child Rearing in British Columbia, 1919-1939," paper read at the B.C. Studies Conference, Vancouver, 1981.

33. "Caddies Bitterly Exploited," *Young Worker,* 6 June 1932; *Labour Gazette,* XXXIV, 1934, 625; "School Board in Session . Tuesday – Children Refusing to Salute

Flag," Drumheller *Mail*, 25 January 1925; Neil Sutherland, *Children in English Canadian Society: Framing the Twentieth Century Consensus* (Toronto, 1976), Conclusion; "Girl Shingle Packers Paid Meagre Wages," Vancouver *Sun*, 12 December 1929; PAM, W. Sanford Evans Papers, Manitoba Employers' Association to Evans, 12 April 1929.

34. Patricia T. Rooke and R.L. Schnell, *Studies in Childhood History: A Canadian Perspective* (Toronto, 1982); Rebecca Coulter, "The Working Young of Edmonton," in Parr, *Childhood and Family*; Jean Barman, "Youth, Class, and Opportunity in Vancouver," paper read at the Canadian Historical Association Annual Meetings, Vancouver, 1983; *Seventh Census*, XII, 584, 646.

35. William Irvine, *The Farmers in Politics*, edited and with an introduction by Reginald Whitaker (Toronto, 1976), 40; George Novack, *Pragmatism versus Marxism: An Appraisal of John Dewey's Philosophy* (New York, 1975), 225; brief quoted in Robert S. Patterson, "Progressive Education," in J. Donald Wilson, Robert Stamp, and L.-P. Audet, *Canadian Education: A History* (Toronto, 1970), 373-78; Jean Mann, "G.M. Weir and H.B. King: Progressive Education or Education for the Progressive State," in J.D. Wilson and David C. Jones, eds., *Schooling and Society in Twentieth Century British Columbia* (Calgary, 1980), 106.

36. John R. Gillis, *Youth and History* (London, 1974), 98-175; Ottawa Collegiate discussed in Robert Stamp, "Canadian High Schools in the 1920s and 30s," *CHAHP*, 1978, 76-77; Fay M. Gonick, "Social Values in Manitoba Education, 1900-1930" (M.A. thesis, University of Manitoba, 1974), 70-76; Copp, *Anatomy of Poverty*, 67-69.

37. James W.H. Rule, "Innovation and Experimentation in Ontario's Public and Secondary School System, 1919-1940" (M.A. thesis, University of Western Ontario, 1977), 28; F.L. Foster, "John Edward Brownlee: A Biography" (Ph.D. thesis, Queen's University, 1981), 359-62; F.H. Johnson, *A History of Public Education in British Columbia* (Vancouver, 1964), 241-42; John W. Chalmers, *Schools of the Foothills Province* (Toronto, 1976), 440-41.

38. B.C. educator quoted in Timothy A. Dunn, "The Rise of Mass Public Schooling in British Columbia," in Wilson and Jones, *Schooling and Society*, 23; W.A. Pritchard, "Address to the Jury," quoted in Peter Warrian, "The Challenge of the One Big Union Movement in Canada, 1919-1922" (M.A. thesis, University of Waterloo, 1971), 28; "rats and scabs" from Lawrence Cremin, *The Transformation of the School: Progressivism in American Education, 1876-1957* (New York, 1961), 32-37; Mary V. Jordan, *Survival: Labour's Trials and Tribulations in Canada* (Toronto, 1975), 262-68; Wheatley quoted in David Jay Bercuson, ed., *The Alberta Coal Industry: 1919* (Calgary, 1978), 87.

39. Timothy A. Dunn, "Teaching the Meaning of Work," in David C. Jones, Nancy Sheehan, and Robert Stamp, eds., *Shaping the Schools of the Canadian West* (Calgary, 1979), 242-52; Scott *et al., Social Planning for Canada*, 36.

NOTES TO CHAPTER EIGHT

1. Lismer quoted in Alexander Munro Beattie, "The Advent of Modernism in Canadian Poetry in English, 1912-1940" (Ph.D. thesis, Columbia University, 1957), 49; Hugh Eayrs, "Renaissance in Canadian Life," *Canadian Bookman*, October, 1922.

2. Robin S. Harris, *A History of Higher Education in Canada: 1663-1960* (Toronto, 1976), 212-52; *HSC*, Series V 184, 196; Mario Creet, "H.M. Tory and the Secularization of Canadian Universities," *QQ*, LXXXVIII:4, 1981, 718-36; R.D. Francis, "Frank H. Underhill at the University of Saskatchewan," *Saskatchewan History*, XXXIV:2, 1981, 48; W.S. Wallace, *A History of the University of Toronto, 1827-1927* (Toronto, 1927), 203; Claude Bissell, "Opinion," in W.S. Wallace, ed., *University College: A Portrait, 1853-1953* (Toronto, 1953), 104-9; Mary Vipond, "The Nationalist Network: English Canada's Intellectuals and Artists in the 1920s," *Canadian Review of Studies in Nationalism*, VII:1, 1980, 32-52.

3. Canadian Clubs described in Mary Vipond, "National Consciousness in English-Speaking Canada in the 1920s" (Ph.D. thesis, University of Toronto, 1974), 224-63; Native Sons' tour in Desmond Pacey, "The Writer and His Public, 1920-1960," in Carl F. Klinck, ed., *Literary History of Canada*, II (Toronto, 1976), 5-7; Barbara Ruth Marshall, "Sir Edmund Walker, Servant of Canada" (M.A. thesis, University of British Columbia, 1971), *passim*; Claude T. Bissell, *The Young Vincent Massey* (Toronto, 1981), 74-91.

4. *Maclean's* and *Canadian Magazine* described in John C. Weaver, "Imperilled Dreams: Canadian Opposition to American Empire, 1918-1930" (Ph.D. thesis, Duke University, 1973), 149-54; *Canadian Bookman* described in Kathryn Chittick, "Making Literature Hum: Canadian Literary Journalism in the Twenties," *Studies in Canadian Literature*, VI:2, 1981, 274-85; Sandra Djwa, "The *Canadian Forum*: Literary Catalyst," *Studies in Canadian Literature*, I:1, 1976, 7-25.

5. *Canadian Historical Review* described in Carl Berger, *The Writing of Canadian History: Aspects of English-Canadian Historical Writing, 1900 to 1970* (Toronto, 1976), 13-14, 42-43, and J.M.S. Careless, "The *Review* Reviewed or Fifty Years with the Beaver Patrol," *CHR*, LI:1, 1970, 48-71; W.S. Wallace, "The Growth of Canadian National Feeling," *CHR*, I:2, 1920, 136-65.

6. George Lawrence Parker, "A History of a Canadian Publishing House: A Study of the Relation Between Publishing and the Profession of Writing, 1890-1940" (Ph.D. thesis, University of Toronto, 1969), vi-xi, 196-211; H. Pearson Gundy, "The Development of Trade Publishing in Canada," Ontario, *Royal Commission on Book Publishing* (Toronto, 1972), 26-29; University of New Brunswick Library, Sir Charles G.D. Roberts Papers, A.M. Stephen to Roberts, 5 October 1927.

7. On the absence of a "lost generation" see W.L. Morton, "The 1920s," in J.M.S. Careless and R. Craig Brown, eds., *The Canadians, 1867-1967* (Toronto, 1967), 226; Sandra Djwa, " 'A New Soil and a

Sharp Sun': The Landscape of a Modern Canadian Poetry," *Modernist Studies*, 2:2, 1977, 3, 16, and Crawford Kilian, "The Great War and the Canadian Novel, 1915-1926" (M.A. thesis, Simon Fraser University, 1972), iii, 2; Deacon quoted in Clara Thomas and John Lennox, *William Arthur Deacon: A Canadian Literary Life* (Toronto, 1982), 87; J.D. Logan and Donald French, *Highways of Canadian Literature* (Toronto, 1924), 7-8; Carl Berger, "The True North Strong and Free," in Peter Russell, ed., *Nationalism in Canada* (Toronto, 1966), 3-26.

8. The text of the catalogue is printed in William Colgate, *Canadian Art: Its Origin and Development* (Toronto, 1943), 82-83, emphasis added; description of technique quoted from Patricia Godsell, *Enjoying Canadian Painting* (Don Mills, Ont., 1976), 127; "cigarette cards" and "bull moose" comments by A.Y. Jackson, quoted in Ann Davis, "An Apprehended Vision: The Philosophy of the Group of Seven" (Ph.D. thesis, York University, 1974), 210-20, 254.

9. Dennis Reid, *A Concise History of Canadian Painting* (Toronto, 1973), 146-50; Arthur Lowe, "Headline Fodder," *MM*, 15 November 1927, 14-15, 59-61; Milne quoted in Ramsay Cook, *The Maple Leaf Forever: Essays on Nationalism and Politics in Canada* (Toronto, 1977), 179.

10. Peter Mellen, *The Group of Seven* (Toronto, 1970), 6-22; Paul Duval, *Group of Seven Drawings* (Toronto, 1965), 2-3; Colgate, *Canadian Art*, 73-76; *London Mercury*, December 1938, quoted in Colgate, *Canadian Art*, 101.

11. Gadsby and Charlesworth quoted in J. Russell Harper, *Painting in Canada: A History* (Toronto, 1977), 263-64, 279; Harris quoted in Davis, "Apprehended Vision," 322-27, 377; Charlesworth quoted in Mellen, *Group of Seven*, 36-37, 99-101.

12. On support for the Group, see Barry Lord, *The History of Painting in Canada: Toward a People's Art* (Toronto, 1974), 121-25, and Margaret F.R. Davidson, "A New Approach to the Group of Seven," *JCS*, IV:4, 1969, 9-16; *Daily Chronicle* quoted in Ann Davis, "The Wembley Controversy in Canadian Art," *CHR*, IV:1, 1973, 72-74; Douglas Cole, "Patrons and Public: An Enquiry into the Success of the Group of Seven," *JCS*, XIII:2, 1978, 76.

13. Patricia Bovey and Ann Davis, *Lionel LeMoine FitzGerald: The Development of an Artist* (Winnipeg, 1978), *passim*; Maria Tippett, *Emily Carr: A Biography* (Toronto, 1979), 144-52; Maria Tippett and Douglas Cole, eds., *Phillips in Print* (Winnipeg, 1982), xxiii-xxv; Lyman quoted in Reid, *Canadian Painting*, 204.

14. Madge Macbeth quoted in Mary Vipond, "The Canadian Authors' Association in the 1920s: A Case Study in Cultural Nationalism," *JCS*, XV:1, 1980, 68-79; GAI, Paul A. Wallace Papers, Wallace to F.H. Wallace, 26 December 1921; "literary kitsch" quoted from Earle Birney, *Spreading Time: Remarks on Canadian Writing and Writers* (Toronto, 1980), 13; AS, A.C. Garner Papers, Garner to Mrs. J.H. Holmes, 4 October, 1928; *Bookseller and Stationer*, April, 1923, 55; GAI, Higinbotham Papers, Charles Mair to Higinbotham, 2 February 1923.

15. Louis Dudek, "Literature in English," in Careless and Brown, *The Canadians*, 647-51; Desmond Pacey, "Fiction, 1920-1940," in Klinck, *Literary History of Canada* II, 168-82; Moore to Canadian Author's Association in AS, CAA Collection, "Report of 1928 Convention"; *Globe* quoted in *Canadian Magazine*, September, 1928, 3; George Morehead to London Literary Society, 25 October 1924, cited in George Paul Fuller, "Aspects of London's Cultural Development from 1900 to World War II" (M.A. thesis, University of Western Ontario, 1966), 100-101.

16. Nancy W. Fraser, "The Development of Realism in Canadian Literature During the 1920s," *DR*, LVII:2, 1977, 295-96; on Sime, see E.L. Bobak, "Seeking 'Direct, Honest Realism': The Canadian Novel of the 1920s," *Canadian Literature*, 89, 1981, 97-98; on Harrison, see Eric Thompson, "Canadian Fiction of the Great War," *Canadian Literature*, 91, 1981, 87-89; on Stead, see Edward McCourt, *The Canadian West in Fiction* (Toronto, 1970), 96-100; on Grove, see Dick Harrison, *Unnamed Country: The Struggle for a Canadian Prairie Fiction* (Edmonton, 1977), 100-23; on Ostenso, see Carlyle King, Introduction to *Wild Geese* (reprint, Toronto, 1971), v-x; B.K. Sandwell, "Only the Rich Should Write Novels," *Saturday Night*, 6 October 1928, 2.

17. S.I. Hayakawa quoted in Peter Stevens, "The Development of Canadian Poetry Between the Wars and Its Reflection of Social Awareness" (Ph.D. thesis, University of Saskatchewan, 1968), 67; Munro Beattie, "Poetry, 1920-1940," in Klinck, *Literary History of Canada* II, 234-35; Jean M. Douglas, "Vacation," Vancouver *Province*, 15 July 1929; Stevens, "Development of Canadian Poetry," 36-39; Lionel Stevenson, *Appraisals of Canadian Literature* (Toronto, 1926), 62.

18. Henry W. Wells and Carl F. Klinck, *Edwin J. Pratt: The Man and his Poetry* (Toronto, 1947), 22-23; Beattie, "Modernism in Canadian Poetry in English," 12-16; Leo Kennedy quoted in Louis Dudek and Michael Gnarowski, *The Making of Modern Poetry in Canada* (Toronto, 1967), 34-37; A.J.M. Smith, "Wanted: A Canadian Criticism," *CF*, April, 1928, 600.

19. *Canadian Mercury* quoted in Sandra Djwa, "The 1920s: E.J. Pratt, Transitional Modern," in Glenn Clever, ed., *The E.J. Pratt Symposium* (Ottawa, 1977), 61, 67; Knister quoted in Carl Ballstadt, ed., *The Search for English Canadian Literature* (Toronto, 1975), 210; Ross quoted in Donald A. Precosky, "Canadian Poetry in English, 1910-1925: The Beginnings of Modernism" (Ph.D. thesis, University of New Brunswick, 1978), 151, 169-71.

20. On socialist realism see Alistair MacLeod, "The Canadian Short Story in the 1930s" (M.A. thesis, University of New Brunswick, 1961), 42-107, and Donna Phillips, ed., *Voices of Discord: Canadian Short Stories from the 1930s* (Toronto, 1979), 11-41; Clyde Gilmour, "The Depression in Good Taste," *CF*, August, 1933, 422; Patricia Morley, *Morley Callaghan* (Toronto, 1978), 27-38; Dick Harrison, "Fiction of the 1930s," in R.D. Francis and Herman Ganzevoort, eds., *The Dirty Thirties in Prairie*

Canada (Vancouver, 1980), 80; Scott cited in J. Lee Thompson, "Emphatically Middling: A Critical Examination of Canadian Literature in the 1930s" (Ph.D. thesis, Queen's University, 1975), 54; Ruth I. McKenzie, "Proletarian Literature in Canada," *DR*, XIX:1, 1939, 63-64.

21. Harry Adaskin, *A Fiddler's World: Memoirs to 1938* (Toronto, 1977), 119-20; Bissell, *Vincent Massey*, 176-78; Peter F. Bishop, "Canadian Music Criticism from 1918 to 1939 As Shown in the Toronto *Star* and *Saturday Night*" (M.A. thesis, University of Victoria, 1979), 35-50; *CAR*, 1924-25, 489-92; *ibid.*, 1925-26, 551-56.

22. Augustus Bridle, "Who Writes Our Music?" *MM*, 15 December 1929, 20, 30-32; George A. Proctor, *Canadian Music of the Twentieth Century: An Introduction* (Toronto, 1980), Ch. 2, 18-31.

23. Patrick B. O'Neill, "The British-Canadian Theatrical Organization Society and the Trans-Canada Theatre Society," *JCS*, 15:1, 1980, 62-64; Michael Tait, "Drama and Theatre," in Klinck, *Literary History of Canada* II, 143-49, 160-62; Calgary *Herald,* 21 March 1924; Robert Barry Scott, "A Study of Amateur Theatre in Toronto, 1900-1930" (M.A. thesis, University of New Brunswick, 1966), 440-41.

24. Tait, "Drama, 1920-1960," in Klinck, *Literary History of Canada* II, 143-50; on Ringwood, see Anton Wagner, *Women Pioneers* (Toronto, 1980), 13-15, 18-19; Betty Lee, *Love and Whiskey: The Story of the Dominion Drama Festival* (Toronto, 1973), 76-129; Jean Béraud, *350 Ans du théatre au Canada français* (Ottawa, 1958), 209-21; George Skillan, "A National Movement," clipping in AS, Regina Little Theatre Collection, George Palmer Scrapbook, 18 May 1939.

25. Elizabeth A. Brown, "Anglo-French Literary Relations in Canada, 1920-1950" (M.A. thesis, University of New Brunswick, 1954), 88-90; Robert Craig Brown and Ramsay Cook, *Canada 1896-1921: A Nation Transformed* (Toronto, 1974), 128; Vipond, "National Consciousness in English-speaking Canada," 68.

26. George Woodcock, "The Servants of Clio: Notes on Creighton and Groulx," *Canadian Literature*, 83, Winter, 1979, 136-38; Guy Sylvestre, *Literature in French Canada* (Quebec, 1967), 20-21; Harvey discussed in Brown, "Anglo-French Literary Relations," 102-26; P.M. Senese, "*Catholique d'Abord:* Catholicism and Nationalism in the Thought of Lionel Groulx," *CHR*, LX:2, 1979, 170-72.

27. Sylvain Simard, "La Production Culturelle" in Paul-André Linteau, René Durocher, and Jean-Claude Robert, *Histoire du Québec contemporain: de la Confédération à la crise, 1867-1929* (Ville St. Laurent, Que., 1979), 618-28; Margaret Atwood, *Survival: A Thematic Guide to Canadian Literature* (Toronto, 1972), 217-31; Ronald Sutherland, *Second Image: Comparative Studies in Quebec/Canadian Literature* (Toronto, 1971), 3, 23.

28. Jean Ethier-Blais and Pierre de Grandpré, "La Poésie de 1900 à 1930," in de Grandpré, *Histoire de la littérature française du Québec*, II (Montreal, 1968), 34-106; Ferland quoted in Gérard Tougas, *The History of French-Canadian Literature* (Toronto, 1967), 76-89.

29. English and French poets com-

pared in Richard Giguère, "Une poésie de dissidence: étude comparative de l'évolution de poésies québécoise et canadienne modernes à Montréal, 1925-1955" (Ph.D. thesis, University of British Columbia, 1978), 49-66.

30. André Renaud and Pierre de Grandpré, "Le Roman de 1900 à 1930," in de Grandpré, *Littérature française du Québec* II, 107-25; Paul Wyczynski, *Le Roman Canadien-français* (Montreal, 1977), 17-19; Sutherland, *Second Image,* 79-85.

31. AS, Gyro, Lions, and Rotary Club Collections; GAI Rotary Club Collection; Provincial Archives of New Brunswick, Rotary Club of Fredericton Collection; Yves Roby, *Les Québécois et les investissements américains, 1918-1929* (Quebec, 1976), 117-18; "harmonious relationship" quoted from PABC, "Dedication of the Harding International Goodwill Memorial of Kiwanis International," pamphlet, 1926.

32. Louis D. Giannetti, *Masters of the American Cinema* (New York, 1981), 66-68; Lary May, *Screening Out the Past: The Birth of Mass Culture and the Motion Picture Industry* (New York, 1980), 163-66; James A. Cowan, "The Battle for Canadian Film Control," *MM,* 1 October 1930, 6-7, 65-66.

33. Peter Morris, *Embattled Shadows: A History of Canadian Cinema, 1895-1939* (Montreal, 1978), 57-93; Hye Bossin, ed., *1951 Yearbook of the Canadian Motion Picture Industry* (Toronto, 1952), 31-37; Alan Dwan, "Canada Has a Movie Future," *MM,* February, 1920, 20.

34. Frederic Beck, "Canadians in Hollywood," *MM,* 15 June 1931,
18-19; Paul Morton, "Starring Canada," *MM,* 15 June 1934, 4-5.

35. Selznick quoted in Morris, *Embattled Shadows,* 57; Charles C. Alexander, *Nationalism in American Thought 1930-1945* (New York, 1969), 7; Giannetti, *Masters of American Cinema,* 7, 10-11.

36. Cowan, "The Battle for Canadian Film Control," 6; PABC, T.D. Pattullo Papers, R.J. Dawson to Pattullo, 29 February 1932, vol. 46, file 4.

37. Morris, *Embattled Shadows,* 72-82.

38. V. Patriarchie, "Thinks Movies No Place for Youth," *MM,* 1 April 1928, 34; E.C. Scott, "Is Canada Going U.S.?" *MM,* 1 March 1930, 8; Doug Bocking, "The Saskatchewan Board of Film Censors, 1910-1935," *Saskatchewan History,* XXIV:2, 1971, 51-62; R. Laird Briscoe, "What the Movie Censor Spares Us From," *MM,* 1 November 1925, 28-29, 49; James Rorty, "Dream Factory," *Forum,* September, 1935, 162-65.

39. Unidentified theatre owner quoted in James A. Cowan, "Is There a Chance for Empire Films?" *MM,* 15 October 1930, 10; George Drew, "Have British Films a Chance?" *MM,* 15 October 1931, 12.

40. Grierson and Vancouver *World* cited in Morris, *Embattled Shadows,* 150, 173; Cowan, "Is There a Chance for Empire Films?" 10.

41. Frank W. Peers, *The Politics of Canadian Broadcasting, 1920-1951* (Toronto, 1969), 3-29.

42. Edmonton *Bulletin,* 8 January 1929; Bernard Montigny, "Les Débuts de la radio à Montréal et le poste CKAC" (M.A. thesis, Université de Montréal, 1979), *passim;* Paul Brand, "The Twentieth Century Bi-

ble: Listening to the Radio in Mont-real, 1924-1939," *The Register,* I:2, 1981, 108-30; Joe McCallum, CKUA *and 40 Wondrous Years of Radio* (Edmonton, 1967), *passim.*

43. RCMP, *Annual Report,* 1928-29, 59-61.

44. Eighty per cent estimate from Margaret Prang, "The Origins of Public Broadcasting in Canada," *CHR,* XLVI:1, 1965, 4; Elton Johnson, "Canada's Radio Consciousness," *MM,* 15 October 1924, 29.

45. John Egli O'Brien, "A History of the Canadian Radio League, 1930-1936" (Ph.D. thesis, University of Southern California, 1964), 43-44; Woodsworth in *CHCD,* 1928, III, 3619-23.

46. Peers, *Politics of Canadian Broadcasting,* 45-55; Roger R. Rickwood, "Canadian Broadcasting Policy and the Private Broadcasters" (Ph.D. thesis, University of Toronto, 1976), 32-41; O'Brien, "Canadian Radio League," 58-69, 159-63.

47. H.F. Angus, ed., *Canada and Her Great Neighbor: Sociological Surveys of Opinion and Attitudes in Canada Concerning the United States* (New York, 1938), 171; Mary Vipond, "Canadian Nationalism and the Plight of Canadian Magazines in the 1920s," *CHR,* LVIII:1, 1977, 43-63.

48. GAI, Calgary Women's Canadian Club Papers, M.J. Hutchinson to G.D. Lamont, 12 April 1921, file 19; Toronto *Globe* cited in Alexander Brady, "The Press in Ontario, 1921-34," in Angus, ed., *Canada and Her Great Neighbor,* 280-81.

49. Vipond, "Plight of Canadian Magazines," 58-62; Isaiah Litvak and Christopher Maule, *Cultural Sovereignty: The Time and Reader's Digest Case in Canada* (New York,

1974), 14-28; *Maclean's* success described in Floyd S. Chalmers, *A Gentleman of the Press* (Toronto, 1969), 321-22; Calgary *Herald,* 13 February 1924.

50. W.H. Kesterton, *A History of Journalism in Canada* (Toronto, 1967), 69-82; H.E. Stephenson and Carlton McNaught, *The Story of Advertising in Canada* (Toronto, 1940), 262-68; Ross Harkness, *J.E. Atkinson of the Star* (Toronto, 1963), 152-53.

51. Stephenson and McNaught, *Story of Advertising,* 14-15; M.E. Nichols, *CP: The Story of Canadian Press* (Toronto, 1948), 194-201; Donald M. Page, "Canadians and the League of Nations Before the Manchurian Crisis" (Ph.D. thesis, University of Toronto, 1972) 400-401.

52. Paul Rutherford, *The Making of the Canadian Media* (Toronto, 1978), 38-76; Carlton McNaught, *Canada Gets the News* (Toronto, 1941), 59-60; Kesterton, *History of Journalism,* 136-41; J.H. Cranston, *Ink on My Fingers* (Toronto, 1953), 74-85; Michael Bliss, *A Canadian Millionaire: The Life and Business Times of Sir Joseph Flavelle, Bart., 1858-1939* (Toronto, 1978), 478; H. Reginald Hardy, *Mackenzie King of Canada: A Biography* (Toronto, 1949), 349.

53. S.F. Wise and Douglas Fisher, *Canada's Sporting Heroes: Their Lives and Times* (Don Mills, Ont., 1974), 28-32; R. Terry Furst, "Mass Media and the Transformation of Spectator Team Sports," *Canadian Journal of the History of Sport and Physical Education,* III:2, 1972, 27-41.

54. William Humber and Eves Raja, "The Baseball Tradition in Western Canada," *Baseball Research Jour-*

nal, II, 1982, 137-41; Nancy Howell and Maxwell L. Howell, *Sports and Games in Canadian Life, 1700 to the Present* (Toronto, 1969), 281-85; George W. Lee, "Baseball in Canada," *MM*, 1 May 1920, 64; Leslie Roberts, "Base Pelotte Comes Back," *MM*, 15 July 1928, 16-17, 59; *CAR*, 1926-27, 653.

55. Alexander J. Young, "The Rejuvenation of Major League Baseball in the Twenties," *Canadian Journal of the History of Sport and Physical Education*, III:1, 1972, 8-27; Calgary *Herald*, 1 October 1926, 2 October 1926.

56. Brian McFarlane, *50 Years of Hockey, 1917-1967: An Intimate History of the NHL* (Toronto, 1967), 30-35; Ronald S. Lappage, "Sport As an Expression of Western and Maritime Discontent in Canada Between the Wars," *Canadian Journal of the History of Sport and Physical Education*, VIII:1, 1977, 50-71.

57. Victoria *Colonist*, 18 March 1924; Calgary *Herald*, 24 March 1925.

58. New York *News* cited in Neil D. Issacs, *Checking Back: A History of the NHL* (New York, 1977), 63-64; Edmonton *Journal*, 27 March 1926.

59. Charles H. Good, "Will U.S. Cash Cripple Hockey?" *MM*, 1 March 1925, 13, 55-56; Eric Whitehead, *The Patricks: Hockey's Royal Family* (Toronto, 1980), 151-60; Henry Roxborough, *The Stanley Cup Story* (Toronto, 1964), 68-69, 138-52; GAI, Calgary Exhibition and Stampede Papers, files 195-97, "Western Canada Hockey League."

60. F.B. Edwards, "High Hat Hockey," *MM*, 15 December 1927, 5-6.

61. McFarlane, *50 Years of Hockey*, 42-54; Conn Smythe, *If You Can't Beat 'Em in the Alley* (Toronto, 1982), 85-88.

62. *CAR*, 1926-27, 652-55; Howell and Howell, *Sports and Games*, 174-75, 180-81, 252-53, 316-17, 321-22; Frank Cosentino, *Canadian Football: The Grey Cup Years* (Toronto, 1969), 59-93; Frank Cosentino and Glynn Leyshon, *Olympic Gold: Canadian Winners of the Summer Games* (Toronto, 1975), 75-77.

63. P.E. Corbett, "The New Canadianism," *Contemporary Review*, October 1931, 479-83; "Babe Ruth" and "baldness" quoted from Robert Ayre, "The American Empire," *CF*, January, 1927, 105-106; William Phillips, *Ventures in Diplomacy* (London, 1955), 70; J.A. Stevenson, "Canadian Sentiment toward the U.S.," *Current History*, XXXIII, October, 1930, 60-64.

64. *Canadian Unionist* quoted in S.D. Clark, "Canadian National Sentiment and Imperial Sentiment," in Angus, ed., *Canada and Her Great Neighbor*, 225-48. For a discussion of the genesis of these attitudes, see S.F. Wise and Robert Craig Brown, *Canada Views the United States* (Seattle and London, 1967), *passim*, and Guildo Rousseau, *L'Image des Etats-Unis dans la littérature québécoise, 1775-1930* (Sherbrooke, 1981), *passim*.

65. Angus, ed., *Canada and Her Great Neighbor*, 126-27, 140, 171, 263-89; Stephenson and McNaught, *Story of Advertising*, 244-59.

66. Douglas Mackay, "The Americanization of Canada," *Century Magazine*, June, 1926, 191-94; G.M. Smith in Angus, ed., *Canada and Her Great Neighbor*, 53.

NOTES TO CHAPTER NINE

1. Robert McKee, President of the Vancouver Board of Trade, quoted in Robert E. Groves, "Business Government: Party Politics and the B.C. Business Community, 1928-33" (M.A. thesis, University of British Columbia, 1976), 11; *CAR*, 1928-29, 673, 687, 692; AS, Regina Gyro Club Collection, file 17.

2. Edward Marcus, *Canada and the International Business Cycle, 1927-1939* (New York, 1954), 47-63; Edward J. Chambers, "Canadian Business Cycles and Merchandise Exports," *CJEPS*, XXIV:3, 1958, 406-10.

3. H.A. Innis, *Settlement and the Mining Frontier* (Toronto, 1936), 383-89; Doug Fetherling, *Gold Diggers of 1929: Canada and the Great Stock Market Crash* (Toronto, 1979), *passim*; James H. Gray, *The Roar of the Twenties* (Toronto, 1975), 337-38; Roger Graham, *Arthur Meighen*, III, *No Surrender* (Toronto, 1965), 8-9; Beverly Fink Cline, *The Lombardo Story* (Don Mills, Ont., 1979), 45.

4. William L. Marr and Donald G. Paterson, *Canada: An Economic History* (Toronto, 1980), 407; Peter Temin, *Did Monetary Forces Cause the Great Depression?* (New York, 1976), 69-83.

5. Charles P. Kindleberger, *The World in Depression, 1929-39* (Berkeley, 1973), *passim*.

6. Robert W. Thompson, *International Trade and Domestic Prosperity: Canada, 1926-38* (Toronto, 1970), 10-19, 54-58; G.E. Britnell, "The Depression in Rural Saskatchewan," in H.A. Innis and A.F.W. Plumptre, eds., *The Canadian Economy and Its Problems* (Toronto, 1934), 98-99; Canada, Royal Commission on Dominion-Provincial Relations, *Report*, Book I, *Canada 1867-1939* (Ottawa, 1941), 143-50.

7. A.E. Safarian, *The Canadian Economy in the Great Depression* (Toronto, 1970), 79-81; Eugene Forsey, "The Pulp and Paper Industry," *CJEPS*, I:4, 1935, 501-9; *HSC*, author's calculations from Series E 34, K 175, N 4, 10, 14, 26.

8. G.P. de T. Glazebrook, *A History of Transportation in Canada* (reprint, Toronto, 1964), 199-210; Peter Stursberg, *Those Were the Days* (Toronto, 1969), 141.

9. Author's calculations from *HSC*, Series Q 138, 233, 289-90, 307, E 32-35.

10. *JCBA*, XXXVI:2, 1930, 125-26, reprinted in Michiel Horn, ed., *The Dirty Thirties: Canadians in the Great Depression* (Toronto, 1972), 32-33; *CAR*, 1932, 38; Fetherling, *Gold Diggers*, 118.

11. G.E. Jackson, "Cycles of Unemployment in Canada," *Contributions to Canadian Economics*, I, 1928, 41-55; Calgary *Herald*, "Unemployment a Complex Problem," 27 March 1925; R.C. Bellan, "Relief in Winnipeg: The Economic Background" (M.A. thesis, University of Toronto, 1941), 177-79; PAM, Bracken Papers, file 343, 451; *KD*, 26 February 1930; Winnipeg *Tribune*, 7 March 1930.

12. *CAR*, 1929-30, 31-33, 53-54.

13. H. Blair Neatby, *William Lyon Mackenzie King*, II, *1924-1932: The Lonely Heights* (Toronto, 1963),

316-19; *CHCD*, 1930, II, 1225-28.

14. *KD*, 1, 9, 14, 17 June 1930.

15. Michael D. Swift, "R.B. Bennett and the Depression, 1930-35" (M.A. thesis, University of New Brunswick, 1964), 13-53; Ernest Watkins, *R.B. Bennett* (Toronto, 1963), 17-33; Carl Berger, *The Sense of Power: Studies in the Ideas of Canadian Imperialism, 1867-1914* (Toronto, 1970), 230-31.

16. Lord Beaverbrook, *Friends: Sixty Years of Intimate Personal Relations with R.B. Bennett* (London, 1959), 11-56; Watkins, *Bennett*, 73-126.

17. Ruth Bell, "Conservative Party National Conventions" (M.A. thesis, Carlton University, 1965), 21-26; John C. Courtney, *The Selection of National Party Leaders in Canada* (Toronto, 1973), 72-81; Alfred E. Morrison, "R.B. Bennett and the Imperial Preferential Trade Agreements, 1932" (M.A. thesis, University of New Brunswick, 1966), 29-30; Peter Oliver, *G. Howard Ferguson: Ontario Tory* (Toronto, 1977), 288-92.

18. Frederick C. Mears, "The Assize of Demos," *QQ*, XXXVI:3, 1930, 397; F.H. Soward, "The Canadian General Election of 1930," *American Political Science Review*, XXIV, 1930, 999; [J.A. Stevenson?] "Canada: The General Election," *Round Table*, XX, 1930, 849.

19. Soward, "Canadian General Election," 997-99: PABC, T.D. Pattullo Papers, "1930 Election," vol. 38, file 15.

20. *CAR*, 1929-30, 97-99; Montreal *Star*, 10 June 1930; *CHCD*, 1930, II, 1826; Montreal *Gazette*, 23 May 1930.

21. PAC, King Papers, Heenan to King, 23 June 1930, and reply, 4 July 1930, cited in James Struthers, *No Fault of Their Own: Unemployment and the Canadian Welfare State* (Toronto, 1983), 45; *KD*, 14 June 1930; H. Reginald Hardy, *Mackenzie King of Canada: A Biography* (London, 1949), 137; *CAR*, 1929-30, 101-3.

22. *CAR*, 1929-30, 104-5; University of New Brunswick, Bennett Papers, Bennett to T.A. McAulay, 7 June 1930, cited in Morrison, "Bennett," 49; J.W. Brennan, "Press and Party in Saskatchewan, 1914-1929," *Saskatchewan History*, XXVII:3, 1974, 89-90.

23. Reginald Whitaker, *The Government Party: Organizing and Financing the Liberal Party of Canada, 1930-58* (Toronto, 1977), 9-15; Patrick John Boyle, "The National Liberal Federation of Canada: Antecedents and Formative Years, 1920-1940" (M.A. thesis, Queen's University, 1975), 34-46; *KD*, 24 June 1930, 26-27 July 1930.

24. GAI, CPR Collection, James Colley to J. MacAllister, 23 April 1929, file 740; J.B.M. Clark, "The Canadian Election," *Nineteenth Century*, CVIII, 1930, 339, 342; William A. Calderwood, "The Rise and Fall of the Ku Klux Klan in Saskatchewan" (M.A. thesis, University of Saskatchewan/Regina, 1968), 213-22; AS, "How Shall I Vote?" *The Klansman*, 2:11, July 1930; J.W. Brennan, "C.A. Dunning, 1916-1930: The Rise and Fall of a Western Agrarian Liberal," in John E. Foster, ed., *The Developing West* (Edmonton, 1983), 264-65.

25. University of New Brunswick, Bennett Papers, Bennett to Harry Allison, 27 July 1930, cited in Morrison, "Bennett," 55; J.A. Stevenson, "The Canadian General Election," *QQ*, XXXVII:4, 1930, 577-78;

Robert Rumilly, *Histoire de la province de Québec*, XXXI (Montreal, 1959), 228-29; *Le Devoir*, "Après le 'roorback' de *La Presse*," 31 July 1930; PAM, W. Sanford Evans Papers, Redmond Code to Evans, 22 July 1930.

26. Escott Reid, "Canadian Political Parties: A Study of the Economic and Racial Bases of Conservatism and Liberalism in 1930," *Contributions to Canadian Economics*, VI, 1933, 7.

27. Richard Wilbur, *The Bennett Administration, 1930-1935* (Ottawa, 1969), 3-4; Marc LaTerreur, *Les Tribulations des Conservateurs au Québec: de Bennett à Diefenbaker* (Quebec, 1974), 26-29.

28. J.K. Johnson, ed., *Canadian Directory of Parliament, 1867-1967* (Ottawa, 1968), *passim*.

29. R.J. Manion, *Life Is an Adventure* (Toronto, 1936), 293-94; H. Blair Neatby, *William Lyon Mackenzie King,* III, *1932-1939, The Prism of Unity* (Toronto, 1976), 124-25.

30. M.F. Smeltzer, "Saskatchewan Opinion on Immigration from 1920-1939" (M.A. thesis, University of Saskatchewan, 1950), 114-15; Donald Avery, *Dangerous Foreigners: European Immigrant Workers and Labour Radicalism in Canada, 1896-1932* (Toronto, 1979), 111-12; Struthers, *No Fault of Their Own*, 46-47.

31. *CAR*, 1930-31, 33-42; O.J. McDiarmid, *Commercial Policy in the Canadian Economy* (Cambridge, 1946), 275-78; W.A. Mackintosh, *The Economic Background of Dominion-Provincial Relations*, Carleton Library ed. (Toronto, 1964), 154-70.

32. *CHCD*, 1930, Special Session, 17, 38, 52, 58-59.

33. Norman Hillmer, "Anglo-Canadian Relations, 1926-1937" (Ph.D. thesis, Cambridge University, 1974), 166-74; *CF*, "Prosperity Rampant," November, 1930, 45.

34. Thomas cited in G.R. Stevens, *A History of the Canadian National Railways* (New York, 1973), 359; Safarian, *Great Depression*, 92-94.

35. Harry M. Cassidy, *Unemployment and Relief in Ontario, 1929-1932* (Toronto, 1932), 129-50; Bettina Bradbury, "The Road to Receivership: Unemployment and Relief in Burnaby, 1929-33" (M.A. thesis, Simon Fraser University, 1976), 47-54; Donald P. Lemon, "Public Relief Policy in Moncton: The Depression Years, 1929-1939" (M.A. thesis, University of New Brunswick, 1977), 15-19.

36. Alma Lawton, "Urban Relief in Saskatchewan During the Years of Depression, 1930-39" (M.A. thesis, University of Saskatchewan, 1969), 46-47; Roger E. Riendeau, "A Clash of Interests: Dependency and the Municipal Problem in the Great Depression," *JCS*, XIV:1, 1979, 50-51; John Taylor, "Relief from Relief: The Cities' Answer to Depression Dependency," *JCS*, XIV:1, 1979, 18-19; D.T. Gallacher, "City in Depression: The Impact of the Years 1929-1939 on Greater Victoria, B.C." (M.A. thesis, University of Victoria, 1969), 23-25, 40-41.

37. Struthers, *No Fault of Their Own*, 48; Yves Légaré, "Crise et chômage dans la ville de Québec, 1929-1939" (M.A. thesis, Laval University, 1980), 30-36.

38. Michael Bliss and L.M. Grayson, eds., *The Wretched of Canada: Letters to R.B. Bennett, 1930-1935* (Toronto, 1971), xii-xiv; Barry Broadfoot, *Ten Lost Years: 1929-*

1939 (Toronto, 1973), 70.

39. PAM, Bracken Papers, "Comparison of Relief Methods, 1930-31," file 547; June Lillian Macpherson, "Brother, can you spare a dime?: The Administration of Unemployment Relief in the City of Montreal, 1931-41" (M.A. thesis, Concordia University, 1975), 16-18; James H. Gray, *The Winter Years* (Toronto, 1966), 14-36; Blair Neatby, "The Saskatchewan Relief Commission, 1931-34," *Saskatchewan History*, III:2, 1950, 41-56; P.A. Russell, "The Co-operative Government's Response to the Depression, 1930-1934," *Saskatchewan History*, XXIV:3, 1971, 81-82; Bracken Papers, "Resolution of the Social Service Council of Canada," file 550.

40. Bliss and Grayson, *Wretched of Canada*, xxi-xxv, 3-5; PAC, Bennett Papers, Bennett to Stevens, 31 January 1931, cited in J.R.H. Wilbur, *H.H. Stevens, 1878-1973* (Toronto, 1977), 93.

41. *CF*, July, 1931, 363-65; Struthers, *No Fault of Their Own*, 54-55.

42. PAC, Bennett Papers, Robertson to Bennett, 1 July 1931, vol. 778; PAC, R.J. Manion Papers, Manion to Bennett, 1 July 1931.

43. *CAR*, 1930-31, 71-74; Swift, "Bennett and the Depression," 160-62; Lawton, "Relief in Saskatchewan," 19-37; PAM, Bracken Papers, "Notes of Calgary Western Interprovincial Conference," file 483.

44. *CAR*, 1932, 25-26; Edmonton *Journal*, 26 August 1931; John Kendle, *John Bracken: A Political Biography* (Toronto, 1979), 114-15; Struthers, *No Fault of Their Own*, 55-56.

45. Kindleberger, *World in Depression*, 148-62, 191-92; *CAR*, 1932, 62-65, 429-32; Irving Brecher, *Monetary and Fiscal Thought and Policy in Canada, 1919-39* (Toronto, 1957), 110-29; R. Craig McIvor, *Canadian Monetary, Banking and Fiscal Development* (Toronto, 1958), 137-40.

46. Struthers, *No Fault of Their Own*, 57-60.

47. *CAR*, 1932, 41-42, 52-54; *CHCD*, 1932, I, 67.

48. *CHCD*, 1932, II, 1768.

49. John Maynard Keynes, "The World's Economic Outlook," *Atlantic Monthly*, 149, May, 1932, 521-26.

50. *CHCD*, 1932, III, 2643-44; Brecher, *Monetary and Fiscal Thought*, 35, 57, 205, 348.

51. Brownlee quoted in PAM, Bracken Papers, "Notes of Unemployment Conference," file 483; *ibid.*, H.A. Arundel to Bracken, 8 December 1931, file 546; PABC, T.D. Pattullo Papers, "F.C. Brown to Committee on Unemployment," vol. 43, file 4.

52. Provincial Archives of Alberta, Premiers' Papers, W.H. Evans to J.E. Brownlee, 14 June 1932, cited in F.L. Foster, "John Edward Brownlee: A Biography" (Ph.D. thesis, Queen's University, 1981), 459-60; PABC, Pattullo Papers, James Moyles to Pattullo, 1932, vol. 46, file 15; GIA, CPR Collection, "Back to the Land Scheme," file 887; T.J.D. Powell, "Northern Settlement, 1929-1935," *Saskatchewan History*, XXX:3, 1977, 89-98; Isabelle George, "Back to the Land Settlement in the Moose Mountains in the 1930s," *Saskatchewan History*, XXXIII:2, 1980, 71-74.

53. Struthers, *No Fault of Their Own*, 69; Morrison, "Bennett,"

37-38; Ian M. Drummond, *Imperial Economic Policy, 1917-1939* (Toronto, 1974), 154-62, 172-73; Watkins, *Bennett*, 149-50.

54. Drummond, *Imperial Economic Policy*, 170-86; J.H. Thomas to the Canadian Government, cited in Robert Bothwell and Norman Hillmer, eds., *The In-Between Time: Canadian External Policy in the 1930s* (Toronto, 1975), 52-53.

55. John Ronald Scratch, "The Editorial Reaction of the Alberta Press to the Bennett Government, 1930-1935" (M.A. thesis, University of Alberta, 1967), 71-81; C.P. Stacey, *Canada and the Age of Conflict*, II, *1921-1948: The Mackenzie King Era* (Toronto, 1981), 135-45; A.R.M. Lower, *Colony to Nation: A History of Canada*, rev. ed. (Toronto, 1977), 512-15; Beaverbrook, *Friends*, 67-79.

56. Keith Feiling, *The Life of Neville Chamberlain* (London, 1946), 212-15; Iain McLeod, *Neville Chamberlain* (New York, 1962), 159-61; Lascelles to Baldwin, 22 November 1932, cited in Bothwell and Hillmer, *In-Between Time*, 86-87; Morrison, "Bennett," 149-53.

57. London *Morning Post*, 22 August 1932, cited in Richard Kottman, *Reciprocity and the North Atlantic Triangle, 1932-1938* (Ithaca, N.Y., 1968), 33; Drummond, *Imperial Economic Policy*, 254-89; Ian M. Drummond, "The British Empire Economies in the Great Depression," in Herman van der Wee, *The Great Depression Revisited* (The Hague, 1972), 221-24.

58. *CF*, November, 1930; *CHCD*, 1932, II, 2447; Lethbridge *Herald*, 1 February 1933.

NOTES TO CHAPTER TEN

1. Ben Borsook, "The Workers Hold a Conference," *CF*, September, 1932, 449-51; *Worker* (Toronto), 6 August 1932; Hugh Garner, *One Damn Thing After Another* (Toronto, 1973), 24; *Canada's Party of Socialism: The Official History of the Communist Party of Canada, 1921-1976* (Toronto, 1982), 93.

2. Lita-Rose Betcherman, *The Little Band: The Clashes Between the Communists and the Political and Legal Establishment in Canada, 1928-1932* (Ottawa, 1982), 86-115; Patricia V. Schultz, *The East York Workers' Association: A Response to the Great Depression* (Toronto, 1975); Bryan D. Palmer, *Working Class Experience: The Rise and Reconstitution of Canadian Labour, 1800-1980* (Toronto, 1983), 206-12.

3. Donald Avery, "Ethnic Loyalties and the Proletarian Revolution: A Case Study of Communist Political Activity in Winnipeg," in Jorgen Dahlie and Tissa Fernando, eds., *Ethnicity, Power, and Politics in Canada* (Toronto, 1981), 68-93; Edward W. Laine, "Finnish Canadian Radicalism and Canadian Politics: The First Forty Years," in Dahlie and Fernando, eds., *Ethnicity, Power, and Politics*, 94-112; Carmela Patrias, "Political Ideology and Ethnic Culture Among Hungarians in Canada, 1920-1940," paper read at the Canadian Historical Associa-

tion Annual Meetings, Guelph, 1984; Dorothy Livesay, "Blairmore" (1936), in *Right Hand, Left Hand: A True Life of the Thirties* (Erin, Ont., 1977), 208-12; Pachiliy quoted in Jeanne R.M. Beck, "Henry Somerville and the Development of Catholic Social Thought in Canada" (Ph.D. thesis, University of Toronto, 1977), 259-65; PAO, CPC Papers, 4A2402, *Worker* report on Vancouver demonstration, 2 May 1931; University of Toronto Library, R. Kenney Collection, Box 2, 8th Dominion Convention, CPC, "Memorandum on the Work of the National Language Organizations" (typescript, 33 pp.), 1937.

4. Attorney General of Ontario, *Agents of Revolution: A History of the Workers' Unity League, Setting Forth Its Aim and Objectives* (Toronto, n.d.); *Plain Facts about the Workers' Unity League* (broadside, WUL, n.d.); PAO, CPC Papers, 3A2310-1, Tom Ewen to Jas. Sloan, Lethbridge WUL, with enclosures, 30 July 1931, and other correspondence; Fernando Claudin, *The Communist Movement, from Comintern to Cominform: Part One* (London/New York, 1975), 103-25; Tim Buck quoted in *Saturday Night*, 2 February 1929, 1.

5. Ian W. Radforth, "The Workers' Unity League in Ontario" (Ph.D. Research Paper, 1978, on file at the Department of History, York University); Allen Seager, "A History of the Mine Workers' Union of Canada, 1925-1936" (M.A. thesis, McGill University, 1977), 81-120; Jeanne Williams, "Ethnicity and Class Conflict at Maillardville/Fraser Mills: The Strike of 1931" (M.A. thesis, Simon Fraser University, 1982), *passim*; Andrée Lévesque, "Le Québec et le

Monde Communiste: Cowansville, 1931," *RhAf*, 34:2, 1980, 171-82.

6. Stanley B. Hanson, "Estevan: 1931," in Irving Abella, ed., *On Strike: Six Key Labour Struggles in Canada* (Toronto, 1974), 33-78; PABC, Pattullo Papers, vol. 53, file 20, Adam Bell, "Report *re* strike of Employees of Granby Consolidated Mining and Smelting Co.," Anyox, 1933; Peter Loudon, *The Town That Got Lost* (Sidney, B.C., 1973), 86-96; Robert Robson, "Strike in a Single Enterprise Community: Flin Flon, Manitoba – 1934," *L/le t*, 12, 1983, 63-86; Evelyn Dumas, *The Bitter Thirties in Quebec* (Montreal, 1975), 28-42.

7. "Death and Destruction Ride Rampant," Estevan *Mercury*, 1 October 1931; Leslie Morris, "Look on Canada Now," in *Selected Writings of Leslie Morris, 1923-1964* (Toronto, 1970), v.

8. *CHCD*, 1932, II, 1482-83; Louise Watson, *She Never Was Afraid: The Biography of Annie Buller* (Toronto, 1976), 45-68; Alberta miner quoted in PAC, Bennett Papers, vol. 421, 267388-9, David Davies, Luscar, to Bennett, 8 October 1931; Bennett's speech reported in Toronto *Globe*, 10 November 1932, as cited in Ivan Avakumovic, *The Communist Party in Canada: A History* (Toronto, 1975), 90; Jack London, *The Iron Heel* (New York, 1908).

9. Ian Angus, *Canadian Bolsheviks: The Early Years of the Communist Party of Canada* (Montreal, 1981), 164-255; William Beeching and Phyllis Clarke, eds., *Yours in the Struggle: Reminiscences of Tim Buck* (Toronto, 1977), 124-40.

10. Suzanne Skebo, "Liberty and Authority: Civil Liberties in Toronto, 1929-1935" (M.A. thesis, Univer-

sity of Toronto, 1968), 74-76; A.E. Smith, *All My Life: An Autobiography* (Toronto, 1949), 98-139; Barbara Roberts, "Purely Administrative Proceedings: A Study in the Management of Deportation, Montreal, 1900-1935" (Ph.D. thesis, University of Ottawa, 1978), 245-71; Henry F. Drystek, " 'The Simplest and Cheapest Mode of Dealing with Them': Deportation from Canada before World War II," *Hs/SH*, 30, 1982, 407-41; Guthrie cited in J. Petryshyn, "Class Conflict and Civil Liberties: The Origins and Activities of the Canadian Labour Defence League, 1925-1940," *L/le t*, 10, 1982, 51.

11. J.H. Thompson and Allen Seager, "Workers, Growers, and Monopolists: The 'Labour Problem' in the Alberta Beet Sugar Industry During the 1930's," *L/le t*, 3, 1978, 153-74; Ivan Avakumovic, "The Communist Party of Canada and the Prairie Farmer: The Interwar Years," in David Bercuson, ed., *Western Perspectives I* (Toronto, 1974), 78-87; David Monod, "Soldiers of the Plough: Popular Protest and Insurgency in Alberta and Saskatchewan" (M.A. thesis, McGill University, 1983), 183-201; *Canadian Unionist*, October 1934, 113, cited in Eric Lyle Dick, "Deportation Under the Immigration Act and the Canadian Criminal Code, 1919-1936" (M.A. thesis, University of Manitoba, 1978), 150.

12. "Section 98," *HD*, 126-28; Arthur R.M. Lower, *Colony to Nation: A History of Canada*, rev. ed., (Toronto, 1977), 504; F.R. Scott, "Communists, Senators, and All That," *CF*, January, 1932, 127-29.

13. Aloysius Balawdyer, *Canadian-Soviet Relations Between the World Wars* (Toronto, 1972), 139-42; Harvey Levenstein, "Canada and the Suppression of the Salvadorean Revolution of 1932," *CHR*, LXXII:4, 1981, 451-69.

14. Ron Adams, "The 1931 Trial of the Leaders of the Communist Party of Canada," paper read at the Canadian Historical Association Annual Meetings, Fredericton, 1977; Tom McEwen [Ewen], *The Forge Glows Red: From Blacksmith to Revolutionary* (Toronto, 1974), 186-90; Anthony Rasporich, "Tomo Cacic: Rebel Without a Country," *Canadian Ethnic Studies*, X:2, 1978, 86-94; Andrée Lévesque Olsen, "The Canadian Left in Quebec During the Great Depression: The Communist Party of Canada and the Co-operative Commonwealth Federation, 1929-1939" (Ph.D. thesis, Duke University, 1973), 82.

15. Lorne and Caroline Brown, *An Unauthorized History of the RCMP* (Toronto, 1973), 52-54; "May Day," *CF*, June, 1932, 325-26; F.R. Scott, "The Trial of the Toronto Communists," *QQ*, XXXIX:4, 1932, 512-27.

16. Betcherman, *The Little Band*, 212-16; Richard Wright and Robin Endres, eds., *Eight Men Speak and Other Plays from the Canadian Workers' Theatre* (Toronto, 1976), xxvi-xxviii, 21-25; Desmond Morton, "Aid to the Civil Power: The Stratford Strike of 1933," in Abella, *On Strike*, 79-91; *Canada's Party of Socialism*, 86; Nancy Stunden, *The Stratford Strikes of 1933* (Ottawa, 1975), *passim*; James D. Leach, "The Workers' Unity League and the Stratford Furniture Workers," *Ontario History*, LX:2, 1968, 39-48.

17. Ralph Allen, *Ordeal By Fire: Canada, 1910-1945* (New York,

1961), 334-35; *Masses* cover illustration, January, 1934, courtesy of Karen Levine.

18. Avakumovic, *Communist Party in Canada*, 54-95; quotations from "Communist Meeting Held Saturday Evening, Harvey Murphy's Statements Freely Challenged by Audience and Atmosphere Warm at Times," Coleman, Alta., *Journal*, 12 June 1930, 1.

19. "The Pot Simmers," *CF*, April, 1932, 243-44; Norman Penner, *The Canadian Left: A Critical Analysis* (Scarborough, Ont., 1977), 171-217.

20. Macphail quoted in the *Farmer's Sun*, 1 December, 1932, as cited in Jean MacLeod, "The United Farmer Movement in Ontario, 1914-1943" (M.A. thesis, Queen's University, 1958), 175; Margaret Stewart, *Ask No Quarter: A Biography of Agnes Macphail* (Toronto, 1959), 157-70; Membership figures from Angus, *Canadian Bolsheviks*, 267.

21. W.A. Godfrey, "The 1933 Regina Convention of the Cooperative Commonwealth Federation" (M.A. thesis, University of Waterloo, 1965), *passim*; Lewis H. Thomas, ed., *The Making of a Socialist: Recollections of T.C. Douglas* (Edmonton, 1982), 76-77.

22. The 1932-33 programs of the CCF are published in Walter Young, *The Anatomy of a Party: The National CCF, 1932-1961* (Toronto, 1969), 303-17.

23. Dorothy Steeves, *The Compassionate Rebel: Ernest Winch and the Growth of Socialism in Western Canada* (Vancouver, 1960), 90-92; Walter Young, "Ideology, Personality, and the Origins of the CCF in British Columbia," *BC Studies*, 32, 1976-77, 139-62; Duff Spafford, "The 'Left Wing,' 1921-1931," in

Spafford and Norman Ward, eds., *Politics in Saskatchewan* (Toronto, 1968), 44-58; Frederick Steininger, "George H. Williams, Agrarian Socialist" (M.A. thesis, University of Regina, 1977), *passim*; George Williams, *Land of the Soviets: A Western Farmer Sees the Russian Bear Change Its Coat* (Saskatoon, 1931); *CHCD*, 1932-33, II, 2109; Williams quoted in James Napier McCrorie, "The Saskatchewan Farmers' Movement: A Case Study" (Ph.D. thesis, University of Illinois, 1972), 192.

24. Bennett quoted in Michiel Horn, *The League for Social Reconstruction: Intellectual Origins of the Democratic Left in Canada, 1930-42* (Toronto, 1980), 30-31; Michiel Horn, "Frank Underhill's Early Drafts of the Regina Manifesto," *CHR*, LIV:4, 1973, 393-418; F.R. Scott, "The CCF Convention," *CF*, September, 1933, 447-49; Sandra Djwa and R. St. J. Macdonald, eds., *On F.R. Scott* (Montreal, 1983), selected essays.

25. Young, *Anatomy of a Party*, 144-45.

26. Patrick George Hill, "A Failure of Unity: Communist Party-C.C.F. Relations in British Columbia, 1935-39" (M.A. thesis, University of Victoria, 1980); cartoon in Vancouver *Unemployed Worker*, 6 August 1932; GAI, G.G. Coote Papers, file 17, Coote to William Irvine, 22 September 1933.

27. Gene Howard Homel, "James Simpson and the Origins of Canadian Social Democracy" (Ph.D. thesis, University of Toronto, 1978); Drumheller *Mail*, 29 March, 24 August 1933; Nelson Wiseman, *Social Democracy in Manitoba* (Winnipeg, 1983), Ch. 2.

28. Ross Alfred Johnson, "No Compromise – No Political Trading: The Marxian Socialist Tradition in British Columbia" (Ph.D. thesis, University of British Columbia, 1975); Varpu Lindstrom-Best, "*Vapaa Sana, 1931-1981*," *Polyphony*, 4:1, 1982, 49-51; Leo Heaps, *The Rebel in the House: The Life and Times of A.A. Heaps, M.P.* (London, 1970); Seymour M. Lipset, *Agrarian Socialism: The Co-operative Commonwealth Federation in Saskatchewan: A Study in Political Sociology* (New York, 1968); Peter R. Sinclair, "The Saskatchewan CCF: Ascent to Power and the Decline of Socialism," *CHR*, LIV:4, 1973, 419-33; John Richards, "Populism and the West," in Larry Pratt and Garth Stevenson, eds., *Western Separatism* (Edmonton, 1981), 65-83; quotation from Doris French Shackleton, *Tommy Douglas* (Toronto, 1975), 62.

29. A.J. Milnor, "Agrarian Protest, 1929-1948: A Study in Ethnic Politics" (Ph.D. thesis, Duke University, 1962), 99-100; *La Patriote*, as cited in Beck, "Somerville," 364-84; Lévesque Olsen, "Canadian Left in Quebec," 95-111.

30. Woodsworth quoted in David Lewis, *The Good Fight: Political Memoirs, 1909-1958* (Toronto, 1981), 81.

31. Escott Reid, "The Effect of the Great Depression on Canadian Politics," *American Political Science Review*, XXVII:3, 1933, 464-65.

32. *New York Times*, 25 August 1935, cited in F. Richard Swann, "Progressive Social Credit in Alberta, 1935-40" (Ph.D. thesis, University of Cincinnati, 1971), 137, 140; GAI, West Canadian Collieries Ltd. Papers, file 102, memorandum, "General Situation in the Country," 24 August 1935; Social Credit M.L.A.s quoted in Calgary *Albertan*, 19 February, 28 August 1936.

33. C.B. Macpherson, *Democracy in Alberta: Social Credit and the Party System* (Toronto, 1953), 10-20; J.F. Conway, "To Seek a Goodly Heritage: The Prairie Populist Response to the National Policy in Canada" (M.A. thesis, Simon Fraser University, 1968), 428-37; Carl F. Betke, "Farm Politics in an Urban Age: The Decline of the UFA after 1921," in L.H. Thomas, ed., *Essays on Western History* (Edmonton, 1976), 175-89; CCF criticism of Brownlee in Archibald Key, "Creating a National Federation," *CF*, September, 1932, 451-53; L.H. Thomas, *William Aberhart and Social Credit in Alberta* (Toronto, 1977), 11-13.

34. John J. Barr, *The Dynasty: The Rise and Fall of Social Credit in Alberta* (Toronto, 1979), 33-37; F.L. Foster, "John Edward Brownlee: A Biography" (Ph.D. thesis, Queen's University, 1981), 539-40. Our account is drawn primarily from the Record of Proceedings, Privy Council, London, "On Appeal from the Supreme Court of Canada Between Hon. John Brownlee and Vivian MacMillan," 1938, containing complete trial records on the case, on microfilm at GAI. We acknowledge, with thanks, interviews with Alan Hustak and Neil McDougall of Calgary.

35. Edmonton *Journal*, 27 June 1934.

36. Macpherson, *Democracy in Alberta*, 93-119; John A. Irving, *The Social Credit Movement in Alberta* (Toronto, 1959), 4-7; John L. Finlay, *Social Credit: The English Origins*

(Montreal, 1972), *passim.*

37. Macpherson, *Democracy in Alberta*, 94, 111.

38. Harold J. Schultz, "Aberhart: The Organization Man," *Alberta Historical Review*, 1959, 20-28; Harold J. Schultz, "Portrait of a Premier," *CHR*, XLV:3, 1964, reprinted in Ramsay Cook, ed., *Politics of Discontent* (Toronto, 1967), 4-7; W.E. Mann, *Sect, Cult and Church in Alberta* (Toronto, 1955), 119-22; David R. Elliott, "Antithetical Elements in William Aberhart's Theology and Political Ideology," *CHR*, LIX:1, 1978, 39-42.

39. Elliott, "Aberhart's Theology," 44-48; David R. Elliott, "William Aberhart: Right or Left?" in R.D. Francis and Herman Ganzevoort, eds., *The Dirty Thirties in Prairie Canada* (Vancouver, 1980), 12-19.

40. GAI, W. Norman Smith Papers, C.W. Nixdorff to Smith, 11 March 1935; J.J. Duggan to Smith, 6 June 1935; C.S. Johnson to Smith, 27 January 1936.

41. Irving, *Social Credit Movement*, 119-44, 318-20, 349-51; Schultz, "Portrait of a Premier," 13-14; GAI, W. Norman Smith Papers, Aberhart to J.H. Caldwell, 29 March 1933; Social Credit Platform in Thomas, *William Aberhart*, 67-69.

42. J.E. Hart, "William Irvine and Radical Politics in Canada" (Ph.D. thesis, University of Guelph, 1972), 214-15; Thomas, *William Aberhart*, 61.

43. Swann, "Progressive Social Credit," 131; Myron Johnson, "The Failure of the CCF in Alberta: An Accident of History," in Carlos Caldarola, ed., *Society and Politics in Alberta* (Toronto, 1979), 87-107; Pattinson quoted in Jasper-Edson *Signal*, 14 March 1940.

44. W.R. Herbert, "Bracken, Butter and Bennett," *CF*, August, 1932, 408-9; John Kendle, *John Bracken: A Political Biography* (Toronto, 1979), 125-26; *CAR*, 1933, 207-8, *ibid.*, 1934, 226-28; and *ibid.*, 1935-36, 446-47, 460-61; Ernest R. Forbes, "The Rise and Fall of the Conservative Party in the Provincial Politics of Nova Scotia, 1922-33" (M.A. thesis, Dalhousie University, 1967), Ch. 6; John Hawkins, *The Life and Times of Angus L.* (Windsor, N.S., 1969), 149-68; Leonard J. Cusak, "The Prince Edward Island People and the Great Depression, 1930-35" (M.A. thesis, University of New Brunswick, 1972), 165-67.

45. J.N. Sutherland, "T.D. Pattullo As Party Leader" (M.A. thesis, University of British Columbia, 1960), 11-14; S.W. Jackman, *Portraits of the Premiers* (Vancouver, 1969), 220-25; Robert E. Groves, "Business Government: Party Politics and the B.C. Business Community, 1928-33" (M.A. thesis, University of British Columbia, 1976), 39, 54; PABC, Pattullo Papers, "Synopsis of Liberal Policy," vol. 53, file 12. I must thank Robin Fisher for his help in interpreting Pattullo.

46. Margaret A. Ormsby, "T. Dufferin Pattullo and the Little New Deal," *CHR*, XLIV:4, 1962, reprinted in Cook, ed., *Politics of Discontent*, 28-37; PAC, King Papers, Mackenzie to King, 8 November 1933, 167628-30.

47. Margaret A. Ormsby, *British Columbia: A History* (Toronto, 1958), 453; University of British Columbia Special Collections, Tolmie Papers, C.H. Dickie to Tolmie, 18 September 1933; F.H. Soward, "B.C. Goes Liberal," *CF*, December, 1933, 88; Ian D. Parker, "Simon Fraser Tolmie: The Last Conservative Premier of BC," *BC*

Studies, 11, 1971, 34-35; Martin Robin, *The Company Province*, I, *The Rush for Spoils, 1871-1933* (Toronto, 1972), 260-65.

48. Peter A. Russell, "The Co-operative Government in Saskatchewan, 1929-34: Response to the Depression" (M.A. thesis, University of Saskatchewan, 1970), 46-86; David E. Smith, *Prairie Liberalism: The Liberal Party in Saskatchewan, 1905-71* (Toronto, 1975), 208-9, 216-20; Norman Ward, "Oppositions and Coalitions: James Gardiner and Saskatchewan Provincial Politics, 1929-34," *CHAHP*, 1979, 158, 161-62; George J. Hoffman, "The Saskatchewan Provincial Election of 1934: Its Political, Economic and Social Background" (M.A. thesis, University of Saskatchewan/Regina, 1973), 89; Sinclair, "Saskatchewan CCF," 422-23; Lipset, *Agrarian Socialism*, 136-38.

49. Peter Oliver, "The Ontario Liberal Party in the 1920s: A Study in Political Collapse," in *Public and Private Persons: the Ontario Political Culture, 1914-34* (Toronto, 1975), 156-78; Richard Alway, "Mitchell F. Hepburn and the Liberal Party in Ontario, 1937-43" (M.A. thesis, University of Toronto, 1965), 15-21.

50. Gerald Caplan, *The Dilemma of Canadian Socialism: The CCF in Ontario* (Toronto, 1973), 49-52; Neil McKenty, *Mitch Hepburn* (Toronto, 1967), 49-52; Neil McKenty, "Hepburn and the Ontario Election of 1934," *CHR*, XLIII:1, 1962, 301; PAO, Hepburn Papers, Hepburn to M.H. Hacker, 31 March 1933, cited in William James McAndrew, "Canada, Roosevelt and the New Deal: Canadian Attitudes to Reform in Relation to the American Reform Experiments of the 1930s" (Ph.D. thesis, University of British Colum-

bia, 1973), 49.

51. Caplan, *Dilemma of Canadian Socialism*, 64; McKenty, *Hepburn*, 55-56; manure spreader story from PABC, Pattullo Papers, George Weir to Pattullo, 22 November 1934, vol. 67, file 6; *CAR*, 1934, 177-78.

52. René Durocher, "Taschereau, Hepburn et les Rélations Québec-Ontario, 1934-36," *RbAf*, 24:3, 1970, 346-51; B.L. Vigod, "The Quebec Government and Social Legislation during the 1930s: A Study in Political Self-destruction," *JCS*, XIV:1, 1979, 59-69; Charles B. Williams, "Canadian-American Trade Union Relations: A Study in the Development of Bi-national Unions" (Ph.D. thesis, Cornell University, 1964), 348-53; Denis Monière, *Ideologies in Quebec: The Historical Development* (Toronto, 1981), 205-23; "nothing short of a revolution" from *CF*, April, 1934, 251, cited in Joseph Levitt, "The C.C.F. and French Canadian 'Radical' Nationalism: A Comparison in Policy" (M.A. thesis, University of Toronto, 1963), 31; Michael K. Oliver, "The Social and Political Ideas of French Canadian Nationalists, 1920-1945" (Ph.D. thesis, McGill University, 1956), 151-224; Fernand Dumont, "Les Années 30: la première Révolution tranquille," in Dumont *et al.*, *Idéologies au Canada français, 1930-1939* (Quebec, 1978), 1-20.

53. Harold Angell, "Quebec Provincial Politics in the 1920s" (M.A. thesis, McGill University, 1960), 152; Paul-André Linteau, René Durocher, and Jean-Claude Robert, *Quebec: A History 1867-1929* (Toronto, 1983), 502; Robert Lévesque and Robert Migner, *Les Boss Politiques à Montréal: Camillien et les années vingt suivi de Camillien au Goulag – Cartographie de Houdisme* (Montreal, 1978), 16-18;

Hertel La Roque, *Camillien Houde: Le P'tit Gars de Ste-Marie* (Montreal, 1961), 49, *passim*.

54. Mason Wade, *The French Canadians, 1760-1967*, rev. ed. (Toronto, 1968), I, 813-14; Robert Rumilly, *Maurice Duplessis et son temps* (Montreal, 1973), I, 75-79; for an excellent discussion of "corporatism" in Quebec see Phyllis M. Sherrin, "The World, the Flesh and the Devil: The Crusade of Lionel Groulx, 1878-1967" (Ph.D. thesis, York University, 1975), 241-302; Houde's speeches quoted in Lévesque and Migner, *Cartographie de Houdisme*, 58, 138.

55. ANQ, Taschereau Papers, vol. 1, file A, death threat, n.d., 1931, filed under anonymous correspondence; Norman Ward, ed., *A Party Politician: The Memoirs of Chubby Power* (Toronto, 1966), 311-27.

56. Conrad Black, *Duplessis* (Toronto, 1977), 48-58; Rumilly, *Duplessis* I, 108, 113; the Premier's remarks cited in B.L. Vigod, *Louis-Alexandre Taschereau: A Political Biography* (forthcoming).

57. Martineau quoted in Patricia Grace Dirks, "The Origins of the *Union Nationale*" (Ph.D. thesis, University of Toronto, 1974), 222-28.

58. ANQ, Taschereau Papers, vol. 2, file D, Honoré Mercier to Athanèse David, 9 November 1933, vol. 3, file G, Paul Gouin to L.-A. Taschereau, 13 July 1931.

59. Gouin described in Dirks, "Origins of the *UN*," 235-80, 326-53; Stanley B. Ryerson, *French Canada* (Toronto, 1943), 186-88; Antonin Dupont, *Les Rélations entre l'Eglise et l'Etat sous Louis-Alexandre Taschereau, 1920-1936* (Montreal, 1972), 254-56; anti-

masonic comments in ANQ, Taschereau Papers, vol. 19, file "La Bonne Nouvelle," clippings, 1932-34; see also Louis Garon, "*La Bonne Nouvelle,*" in Dumont et al., *Idéologies*, 235-56; on the Order of Jacques Cartier see Rumilly, *Duplessis* I, 157-58; Brian McKenna and Susan Purcell, *Drapeau* (Toronto, 1980), 62; Cameron Nish, ed., *Quebec During the Duplessis Era: Democracy or Dictatorship?* (Toronto, 1970), 13-15.

60. Herbert F. Quinn, *The Union Nationale: A Study in Quebec Nationalism* (Toronto, 1963), 58-60, Appendix B: "Programme de l'Action Libérale Nationale," as published in *Le Devoir*, 28 July 1934; J.A. Lovink, "The Politics of Quebec: Provincial Political Parties, 1897-1936" (Ph.D. thesis, Duke University, 1967), 334.

61. Quinn, *Union Nationale*, 54-57; Richard Arès, "Le père Joseph-Papin Archambault et l'Ecole Sociale Populaire," *RhAf*, 35:4, 1980, 563-87; Gregory Baum, *Catholics and Canadian Socialism: Political Thought in the Thirties and Forties* (Toronto, 1980), 20-21, *passim*; Bourassa's address to parliament, *CHCD*, 1934, I, 105-11; Asselin's reaction in Fraser Isbester, "A History of the National Catholic Unions in Canada, 1901-1965" (Ph.D. thesis, Cornell University, 1967), 174; Groulx quoted in Levitt, "C.C.F. and French Canadian 'Radical' Nationalism," 22-27.

62. Taschereau to Père Henri Roy, 17 November, 1933, cited in Vigod, *Taschereau*; ANQ, Taschereau Papers, vol. 1, file A, clippings and correspondence *re* l'Abbé Joseph Raiche's article "Riches and Charity," published in *Le Progrès*

du Golfe (Rimouski), 13 July 1934; vol. 3, file G, correspondence, L.-A. Taschereau and W.A. Gordon, Minister of Labour, 7 January-12 September 1935.

NOTES TO CHAPTER ELEVEN

1. Vancouver *Sun*, 11 February 1932; PAM, John Bracken Papers, "Notes of Dominion-Provincial Conference," file 697; James Struthers, *No Fault of Their Own: Unemployment and the Canadian Welfare State* (Toronto, 1983), 86-94; Christopher Armstrong, *The Politics of Federalism: Ontario's Relations with the Federal Government, 1867-1942* (Toronto, 1981), 479, 499-503.

2. James Struthers, "A Profession in Crisis: Charlotte Whitton and Canadian Social Work in the 1930s," *CHR*, LXII:2, 1981, 174-80; Bennett quoted in *CAR*, 1934, 34-35; Winnipeg *Free Press*, 4 September 1934.

3. Alma Lawton, "Urban Relief in Saskatchewan During the Years of Depression, 1930-39" (M.A. thesis, University of Saskatchewan, 1969), 46-47; Mayoral Candidate J.H. Ogilvie quoted in John Taylor, "Relief from Relief: The Cities' Answer to Depression Dependency," *JCS*, XIV:1, 1979, 18; Roger E. Riendeau, "A Clash of Interests: Dependency and the Municipal Problem in the Great Depression," *JCS*, XIV:1, 1979, 50; PABC, Pattullo Papers, Weir to Pattullo, 21 December, 1933.

4. Judith Roberts-Moore, "Maximum Relief for Minimum Cost: Coping with Unemployment and Relief in Ottawa During the Depression, 1929-1939" (M.A. thesis, University of Ottawa, 1976), 31-35; farmer quoted in L.J. Cusak, "The Prince Edward Island People and the Great Depression, 1930-35" (M.A. thesis, University of New Brunswick, 1972), 68-69; Bourassa in *CHCD*, 1934, I, 107; "The Jobless White-Collar Woman," *MM*, 1 May 1932, 16, 45-46; PAM, Bracken Papers, file 899.

5. PABC, Pattullo Papers, A.M. Manson to George Pearson, 4 September 1934; Bates case described in Struthers, *No Fault of Their Own*, 83-84.

6. Plaunt and Bennett quoted in Margaret Prang, "The Origins of Public Broadcasting in Canada," *CHR*, XLVI:1, 1965, 9-31; Kenneth C. Dewar, "The Origins of Public Broadcasting in Canada in Comparative Perspective," *Canadian Journal of Communication*, VII:2, 1982, 40-43.

7. Michael Swift, "R.B. Bennett and the Depression, 1930-1935" (M.A. thesis, University of New Brunswick, 1964), 240-46; PAC, R.J. Manion Papers, R.J. Manion to James Manion, 15 August 1933, quoted in Harold Naugler, "R.J. Manion and the Conservative Party, 1938-1940" (M.A. thesis, Queen's University, 1966), 22; Bennett quoted in L.M. Grayson and J. Paul Grayson, "Interest Aggregation and Canadian Politics: The Case of the Central Bank," *Canadian Public Administration*, 16:4, 1973, 567; attitudes to

bankers described in George Russell Newell, "The Attitude of Canada's Bankers towards Their Role During the Depression, 1930-1935" (M.A. thesis, University of British Columbia, 1967), 95-101; MacInnis quoted in *CF*, September, 1934, 169.

8. PAC, Bennett Papers, Bennett to J.A. McLeod, 1 June 1933, cited in Linda Grayson, "The Formation of the Bank of Canada, 1913-1938" (Ph.D. thesis, University of Toronto, 1974), 116; role of the new bank described in R. Craig McIvor, *Canadian Monetary, Banking and Fiscal Development* (Toronto, 1958), 135-54.

9. R. McQueen, "The Farmers' Creditors Arrangements Act, 1934," *CJEPS*, I:1, 1935, 104-8; W.T. Easterbrook, *Farm Credit in Canada* (Toronto, 1938), 155-57; J.R.H. Wilbur, "R.B. Bennett As a Reformer," *CHAHP*, 1969, 107-8; J.E. Lattimer, "Natural Products Marketing Act," *CJEPS*, I:1, 1935, 101-4; Weir quoted in "Capitalism Under Fire," *Round Table*, XXV, March 1935, 393-94.

10. W.H. Moore, E. Roberge, and J.S. Woodsworth in *CHCD*, 1934, III, 3098-3117, 3134-37; *KD*, 26 March 1934, 3 April 1934.

11. Rhodes in *CHCD*, 1934, II, 2046; W.C. Hopper, "The NPMA, 1934: Notes on the Administration of the Act," *CJEPS*, 1:3, 1935, 475-81; Alvin Finkel, *Business and Social Reform in the Thirties* (Toronto, 1979), 78, 135, 141.

12. *CHCD*, 1934, IV, 3857-58.

13. J.R.H. Wilbur, *H.H. Stevens, 1878-1973* (Toronto, 1977), 3-110.

14. J.R.H. Wilbur, "H.H. Stevens and R.B. Bennett, 1930-34," *CHR*, XLIII:1, 1962, 7-8; O. Mary Hill, *Canada's Salesman to the World: The Department of Trade and Commerce, 1892-1939* (Montreal, 1977), 456-57.

15. Wilbur, *Stevens*, 133; mandate of committee quoted from *CHCD*, 1934, I, 188.

16. Winnipeg *Free Press*, 7 August 1934; Wilbur, *Stevens*, 114-30; examples of evidence from Canada, House of Commons, Special Committee on Price Spreads and Mass Buying, *Proceedings and Evidence* (Ottawa, 1934), *passim*, and Michiel Horn, ed., *The Dirty Thirties: Canadians in the Great Depression* (Toronto, 1972), 113-28; editorial praising Stevens in *Catholic Register*, 31 May 1934, cited in Margaret Prang, "Some Opinions of Political Radicalism in Canada Between the Two World Wars" (M.A. thesis, University of Toronto, 1953), 180-81.

17. D.F. Forster, "The Politics of Combines Policy: Liberals and the Stevens Commission," *CJEPS*, XXVIII:4, 1962, 512-15; Stevens's accusations quoted in Wilbur, "Stevens and Bennett," 11-16; C.L. Burton, *A Sense of Urgency: Memoirs of a Canadian Merchant* (Toronto, 1952), 306-15.

18. Toronto *Star*, 2 November 1934; Cahan quoted in Ottawa *Journal*, 29 November 1934, cited in Wilbur, *Stevens*, 146; Bennett described in PAC, R.J. Manion Papers, A.A. Allan to Manion, 6 November 1934; PAC, H.H. Stevens Papers, Francis Stevens to Stevens, 29 October 1934.

19. Dominion Conservative Headquarters, *The Premier Speaks to the People* (Ottawa, 1935), *passim*, excerpted in J.R.H. Wilbur, ed., *The Bennett New Deal: Fraud or Portent?* (Toronto, 1968), 80-90.

20. Bennett's speaking style de-

scribed in H. Blair Neatby, *William Lyon Mackenzie King*, III, *1932-1939, The Prism of Unity* (Toronto, 1976), 85-89, and in Donald Forster and Colin Read, "The Politics of Opportunism: The New Deal Broadcasts," *CHR*, LX:3, 1979, 329, 336-37; reception of speeches described in P.E. Corbett, "The Prime Minister on Capitalism," *QQ*, February, 1935, 122; PAC, Manion Papers, Robert Manion to James Manion, 10 January 1935.

21. PAC, J.W. Dafoe Papers, Chester Bloom to Dafoe, 14 January 1935; PAC, Bennett Papers, Herridge to Bennett, 12 April 1934, reprinted in Wilbur, *Bennett New Deal*, 69-70; possible American influences assessed in W.H. McConnell, "The Genesis of the Canadian New Deal," *JCS*, IV:2, 1969, 32-35, and in William James McAndrew, "Canada, Roosevelt and the New Deal: Canadian Attitudes to Reform in Relation to the American Reform Experiments of the 1930s" (Ph.D. thesis, University of British Columbia, 1973), 10-11, 274-78.

22. PAC, Bennett Papers, Bennett to Howard Robinson, 11 June 1935, cited in Alvin Finkel, "Origins of the Welfare State in Canada," in Leo Panitch, ed., *The Canadian State* (Toronto, 1977), 351.

23. Church and Stevens quoted in Forster and Read, "New Deal Broadcasts," *passim;* John Ronald Scratch, "The Editorial Reaction of the Alberta Press to the Bennett Government, 1930-1935" (M.A. thesis, University of Alberta, 1967), 117-22; Montreal *Gazette*, 4 January 1935, 10.

24. Neatby, *Prism of Unity*, 90-97; King and Woodsworth in *CHCD*, 1935, I, 28-89.

25. Finkel, *Business and Social Reform*, 92-93, 99; Struthers, *No Fault of Their Own*, 121-25; L. Richter, "The Employment and Social Insurance Bill," *CJEPS*, I:3, 1935, 436-48; J.L. Cohen, *The Canadian Unemployment Insurance Act: Its Relation to Social Security* (Toronto, 1935), *passim;* W.J. Couper, "The Employment and Social Insurance Bill: A Comment from the Point of View of American Opinion," *CJEPS*, I:3, 1935, 448-56.

26. Ralston in *CHCD*, 1935, II, 2121; Bennett's illness described in *CAR*, 1935-36, 5-6, 26-27; PAC, Manion Papers, Robert Manion to James Manion, 4 March 1935, and Herridge to Robert Manion, 22 March 1935.

27. K.W. Taylor, "Economic Implications of the Report of the Royal Commission on Price Spreads," *CJEPS*, I:3, 1935, 510-17; V.W. Bladen, *Introduction to Political Economy* (Toronto, 1956), 233; C.A. Curtis, "Dominion Legislation of 1935," *CJEPS*, I:4, 1935, 602-5.

28. C.F. Wilson, *A Century of Canadian Grain: Government Policy to 1951* (Saskatoon, 1978), 416-74; PAC, Bennett Papers, Stevens to McFarland, 5 October 1934; V.C. Fowke, *The National Policy and the Wheat Economy* (Toronto, 1957), 256-66.

29. "Experiences of a Depression Hobo," *Saskatchewan History*, XXII:2, 1969, 63; Rev. Andrew Roddan, *Canada's Untouchables: The Story of the Men Without a Home* (Vancouver, 1932), 14; "owl on a limb" quoted from PAM, Bracken Papers, W.J. Hall to Bracken, 4 February 1932, file 660.

30. N.B. Watson, "Calgary: A Study of Crime, Offender and the Police Court, 1929-1934" (M.A. thesis, University of Calgary, 1979), 32, 50, 85;

Marion Lane, "Unemployment During the Depression: The Problems of the Single Unemployed Transient in B.C., 1930-1938" (B.A. essay, University of British Columbia, 1966), 32-33; Vancouver medical officer quoted in Vancouver *Province*, 4 September 1931; James Eayrs, *In Defence of Canada*, I, *From the Great War to the Great Depression* (Toronto, 1964), 124-30; PAC, McNaughton Papers, Memo 3 October 1933, cited in Eayrs, *In Defence of Canada* I, 129; John Swettenham, *McNaughton* (Toronto, 1968), I, 269-75.

31. Descriptions of the camps may be found in G.M. LeFresne, "The Royal Twenty Centers: The Department of National Defence and Federal Unemployment Relief, 1932-1936" (B.A. thesis, Royal Military College, 1962), 49-52; Lorne Brown, "Unemployment Relief Camps in Saskatchewan, 1933-1936," *Saskatchewan History*, XXIII:3, 1970, 90-96; Struthers, *No Fault of Their Own*, 95-103; PABC, Pattullo Papers, T.D. Pattullo to George Perley, 27 April 1935; "not a paradise" from an editorial in the Regina *Leader-Post*, 5 June 1933.

32. Inmates and civil servants both cited in Struthers, *No Fault of Their Own*, 100, 134; "no laughter" quotation from "Strikers' Nights," Vancouver *Sun*, May, 1935, cited in Horn, ed., *Dirty Thirties*, 339-40; "Lost legion" from "Diary of a Relief Camp Worker," *CHCD*, 1935, IV, 4050.

33. Glen Makahonuk, "The Saskatoon Relief Camp Workers' Riot of May 8, 1933: An Expression of Class Conflict," *Saskatchewan History*, XXXVII:2, 1984, 55-72; PABC, Pattullo Papers, Memo by George S.

Pearson, 21 March 1934, vol. 69, file 11; Pattullo Papers, Bennett to Pattullo, 2 January 1935, file 15; *Relief Camp Worker*, 19 August 1934.

34. Ronald Liversedge, *Recollections of the On to Ottawa Trek*, ed. Victor Hoar (Toronto, 1973), 58-84; McGeer quoted in Richard McCandless, "Vancouver's 'Red Menace' of 1935: The Waterfront Situation," *BC Studies*, 22, 1974, 56-63; Brodie quoted in Ben Swankey and Jean Evans Sheils, *Work and Wages: A Semi-Documentary Account of the Life and Times of Arthur H. (Slim) Evans* (Vancouver, 1977), 86-106; Vancouver *Province*, 3 June 1935.

35. "Stew" and "chestnuts" quotations from Liversedge, *On to Ottawa Trek*, 85-103; "coal-heavers" and "real army style" quotation from Swankey and Sheils, *Work and Wages*, 120-21; Victor Howard, "Citizen Support of the On to Ottawa Trek," in R.D. Francis and Herman Ganzevoort, eds., *The Dirty Thirties in Prairie Canada* (Vancouver, 1980), 33-43.

36. "A fine bunch" quotation from PAC, CCF Records, M.J. Coldwell to J.S. Woodsworth, 12 June 1935, vol. 89, cited in Horn, *Dirty Thirties*, 351-52; "Communist elements" quotation from PAM, Bracken Papers, Bracken to Bennett, 10 June 1935, file 962; PAC, Manion Papers, Manion to Bennett, June 17, June 20 1935.

37. Keith A. Parker, "Arthur Evans: Western Radical," *Alberta History*, 26:2, 1978, 21-29; Trek leaders interview with Bennett reprinted in Liversedge, *On to Ottawa Trek*, 195-216.

38. "Strike Supporters Threatened," Regina *Leader-Post*, 28 June 1935; Gladys M. Stone, "The Regina Riot,

1935" (M.A. thesis, University of Saskatchewan, 1967), 69-91, 97, 103, 111; batons described in Regina *Star*, 2 July 1935; "shambles" quotation from Liversedge, *On to Ottawa Trek*, 112-17.

39. "Roosevelt's appeal" quotation from PAC, Dafoe Papers, Dafoe to A.E. Zimmern, 29 May 1935; comparison to Hoover in James H. Gray, "Canada Flirts with Fascism," *The Nation*, 9 September 1935, 406-8; Toronto *Daily Star*, 3 July 1935 and Vancouver *Sun*, 3 July 1935, cited in J. Petryshyn, "R.B. Bennett and the Communists: 1930-1935," *JCS*, IX:4, 1974, 53.

40. J.R.H. Wilbur, "H.H. Stevens and the Reconstruction Party," *CHR*, XLV:1, 1964, reprinted in Ramsay Cook, *Politics of Discontent* (Toronto, 1967), 71; Carman V. Carroll, "The Influence of H.H. Stevens and the Reconstruction Party in Nova Scotia, 1934-35" (M.A. thesis, University of New Brunswick, 1972), 173-75; "Funeral Dirge for Bennett," *CF*, August, 1935, 330.

41. *Le Devoir*, 2 October 1935; *CAR*, 1935-36, 59; *Saturday Night*, 28 September 1935, 1, 4.

42. Patrick John Boyle, "The National Liberal Federation of Canada: Antecedents and Formative Years, 1920-1940" (M.A. thesis, Queen's University, 1975), 110-15; PABC, Pattullo Papers, Pattullo to King, 1 September 1934, vol. 75, file 2; PAC, King Papers, W.R. Howson to King, 30 August 1934 and reply, 7 September 1934, 171050-51, -54; PAO, Floyd Chalmers Papers, Chalmers to Col. J.B. Maclean, 12 February 1934, cited in Struthers, *No Fault of Their Own*, 246; *CAR*, 1935-36, 62-65.

43. Robert Craig Brown, *Robert Laird Borden: A Biography*, II, *1914-1937* (Toronto, 1980), 195-96; Reginald Whitaker, *The Government Party: Organizing and Financing the Liberal Party of Canada, 1930-58* (Toronto, 1977), 69, 77-84; J.L. Granatstein, "Financing the Liberal Party, 1935-45," in Michael Cross and Robert Bothwell, *Policy by Other Means: Essays in Honour of C.P. Stacey* (Toronto, 1972), 184-86; origin of "King or Chaos" explained in Floyd S. Chalmers, *A Gentleman of the Press* (Toronto, 1969), 279-80.

44. J. Murray Beck, *Pendulum of Power: Canada's Federal Elections* (Toronto, 1968), 206.

45. J.W. Pickersgill, ed., "The Flaherty Diary of the 1935 Election," *CHR*, LXII:3, 1981, 365, 369; Escott Reid, "The Canadian Election of 1935 and After," *American Political Science Review*, XXX:1, 1936, 114-15; Neatby, *Prism of Unity*, 123.

46. Reid, "Election of 1935," 115; Marc LaTerreur, "R.B. Bennett et le Québec: un cas d'incompréhension réciproque," *CHAHP*, 1969, 95-102; role of Ethiopia discussed in Robert Rumilly, *Histoire de la province de Québec*, XXXV (Montreal, 1966), 29-33, 37, and in "Canada: the General Election," *Round Table*, XXVI, 1935, 169; Rollande Montsion, "Les grands thèmes du mouvement national social chrétien et d'Adrien Arcand, vus par les principaux journaux fascistes au Canada français, 1929-1938" (M.A. thesis, University of Ottawa, 1975), 104; "La 'Société des Nations' intervient," *Le Devoir*, 11 and 12 October, 1935.

47. Donald K. Alper, "From Rule to Ruin: The Conservative Party of B.C., 1928-54" (Ph.D. thesis, Uni-

versity of British Columbia, 1975), 115-17.

48. John Cripps, "The Canadian Elections," *Political Quarterly*, 6, 1935, 569-70; Beck, *Pendulum of Power*, 216-17; Ken D. Andrews, "The Politics of Reform: Provincial Politics in Saskatchewan, 1935-1938" (M.A. thesis, University of Western Ontario, 1980), 45-47.

49. Carroll, "Reconstruction Party in Nova Scotia," 123-92; Graham Spry, "Politics," *CF*, August, 1935, 324; Wilbur, "Stevens and the Reconstruction Party," 71-76.

50. M. Janine Brodie and Jane Jenson, *Crisis, Challenge and Change: Party and Class in Canada* (Toronto, 1980), 176-81; Whitaker, *Government Party*, 84.

NOTES TO CHAPTER TWELVE

1. C.P. Stacey, *A Very Double Life: The Private World of Mackenzie King* (Toronto, 1976), 166-84; Frederick W. Gibson, "The Cabinet of 1935," in F.W. Gibson, ed., *Cabinet Formation and Bicultural Relations: Seven Case Studies* (Ottawa, 1970), 113-18, 134-37; "men who drank" from *KD*, 21 October 1935; H. Blair Neatby, "Mackenzie King and French Canada," *JCS*, XI:1, 1976, 8-9.

2. *KD*, 17, 19 October 1935; *CF*, February, 1937, 3; H. Blair Neatby, *William Lyon Mackenzie King*, III, *1932-1939, The Prism of Unity* (Toronto, 1976), 126-33.

3. *KD*, 31 October 1935; Queen's University Archives, Dunning Papers, Dunning to J.A. Cross, 27 December 1932; J. Harvey Perry, *Taxes, Tariffs and Subsidies: A History of Canadian Fiscal Development* (Toronto, 1955), 268-69; Irving Brecher, *Monetary and Fiscal Thought and Policy in Canada, 1919-1939* (Toronto, 1957), 94-95.

4. Richard N. Kottman, *Reciprocity and the North Atlantic Triangle, 1932-1938* (Ithaca, N.Y., 1968),

79-116; Roosevelt's speech in Roger Frank Swanson, *Canadian-American Summit Diplomacy, 1923-1973, Selected Speeches and Documents* (Toronto, 1975), 46-48; Mira Wilkins, *The Maturing of Multinational Enterprise: American Business Abroad, 1914-1970* (Cambridge, Mass., 1974), 189-90; Stephen Scheinberg, "Invitation to Empire: Tariffs and American Economic Expansion in Canada," in Glenn Porter and Robert Cuff, eds., *Enterprise and National Development: Essays in Canadian Business and Economic History* (Toronto, 1973), 93-98; Montreal *Gazette*, 18 November 1935, 14.

5. J.R. Rowell, "An Intellectual in Politics: Norman Rogers As Minister of Labour, 1929-1939" (M.A. thesis, Queen's University, 1979), 126-37.

6. James Struthers, *No Fault of Their Own: Unemployment and the Canadian Welfare State* (Toronto, 1983), 142-45, 153-69; *KD*, 4 January 1937.

7. "Length and breadth" quoted from Struthers, *No Fault of Their Own*, 158-61; Stephen Rybak, "A Hasty Patching Up: An Examination of Liberal Unemployment and Relief

Programs As They Affected Canada's Transient and Single Jobless, 1935-1940" (M.A. thesis, Concordia University, 1977), 76-91; "dreary future" from "The Farm Placement Scheme," *CF*, February, 1937, 4; Mr B to King, 25 November 1936, cited in Alma Lawton, "Urban Relief in Saskatchewan During the Years of Depression, 1930-39" (M.A. thesis, University of Saskatchewan, 1969), 21-22.

8. F.R. Scott, "The Consequences of the Privy Council Decisions," *Canadian Bar Review*, 15, 1937, 485-94; W.H. McConnell, "The Judicial Review of Prime Minister Bennett's New Deal," *Osgoode Hall Law Journal*, 6, 1968, 46-86; "New Deal Cancelled," *Time Magazine*, 8 February 1937.

9. Struthers, *No Fault of Their Own*, 209; Paul Gérin-Lajoie, *Constitutional Amendment in Canada* (Toronto, 1950), 244-49; Neatby, *Prism of Unity*, 151-52, 157-61; *KD*, 15 May, 17 August 1936.

10. "No Holds Barred in Quebec Political Fight," *Saturday Night*, 14 January 1939, cited in Cameron Nish, ed., *Quebec During the Duplessis Era: Democracy or Dictatorship?* (Toronto, 1970); Patricia Grace Dirks, "The Origins of the *Union Nationale*" (Ph. D. thesis, University of Toronto, 1974), 343-44.

11. Clipping, *L'Action Catholique*, ANQ, Taschereau Papers, vol. 27, file "Elections – 1935"; *Le Devoir* editorial cited in André-J. Belanger, *L'Apolitisme des idéologies Québécoises: le grand tournant de 1934-1936* (Quebec, 1974), 122-23; Gouin quoted in Dirks, "Origins of the *UN*," 346-7; Duplessis quoted in Joseph Levitt, "The C.C.F. and

French Canadian 'Radical' Nationalism: A Comparison in Policy" (M.A. thesis, University of Toronto, 1963), 40; Bernard L. Vigod, *Louis-Alexander Taschereau: A Political Biography* (forthcoming).

12. *CAR*, 1935-36, 279-83; ANQ, Taschereau Papers, vol. 1, file A, A. Beaudoin, Chevaliers des papas et des fils to Prime Minister, 2 April 1936, and hundreds of other letters on pensions; Jean-Guy Genest, "Vie et Oeuvre d'Adélard Godbout, 1892-1956" (Ph.D. thesis, Université Laval, 1977), 196-212; Herbert F. Quinn, *The Union Nationale: A Study in Quebec Nationalism* (Toronto, 1963), 68; Duplessis quoted in Conrad Black, *Duplessis* (Toronto, 1977), 128.

13. Gouin quoted in Antonio Barette, *Memoires* (Montreal, 1966), 15; Richard Weatherstone, "A Reformist-Nationalist Response to Maurice Duplessis" (M.A. thesis, University of Ottawa, 1982), 16-17; Paul Cliche, "Les Elections provinciales dans le Québec de 1927 à 1956," *Récherches sociographiques*, II:3-4, 1961, 343-65.

14. Richard Jones, *Duplessis and the Union Nationale Administration* (CHA Historical Booklet 35, Ottawa, 1983), 8-9; Black, *Duplessis*, 162-68; Quinn, *Union Nationale*, 78-79; text of Drouin's letter of resignation, 22 February 1937, cited in Dirks, "Origins of the *UN*," 400; "Duplessis Is Pilloried By Quebec Crowd," *Globe and Mail*, 1 March, 1937.

15. "An act to protect the Province from communistic propaganda," R.C. Brown and M.E. Prang, *Canadian Historical Documents*, III (Toronto, 1966), 261; *Le Devoir*, election broadside, October, 1935, "Seul Contre Tous!"; Dirks, "Ori-

gins of the *UN*," 317-18; Duplessis's definition of communism in Eugene Forsey, "Canada and Alberta: The Revival of Dominion Control over the Provinces," in *Freedom and Order* (Toronto, 1974), 201; Stanley B. Ryerson, *French Canada* (Toronto, 1943), 190-91; Michiel Horn, ed., *The Dirty Thirties: Canadians in the Great Depression* (Toronto, 1972), 677-93; *CHCD*, II, 1938, 3374-79; Robert Rumilly, *Maurice Duplessis et son temps* (Montreal, 1973) I, Ch. 16.

16. AS, George Barr Papers, text of address by Hubert Desaulniers, Montreal Civil Liberties Union, 20 November 1937; "Light Locked," *Time Magazine*, 22 November 1937, 46-47.

17. "New Year's Message of the Minister of Labour," *Labour Gazette*, XXXVII, 1937, 23; Eugene Forsey, *Recovery – For Whom?* (Toronto, 1937), cited in Horn, ed., *Dirty Thirties*, 73-76; "Strikes and Lockouts in Canada and Other Countries, 1937," *Labour Gazette*, XXXVIII, 1938, 241-78.

18. *CHCD*, II, 1937, 1736; "Crisis Believed Near in Railway Dispute," *Globe and Mail*, 26 March 1937; "Settlement of Railway Wage Dispute," *Labour Gazette*, XXXVII, 1937, 41.

19. Ian Radforth and Joan Sangster, "A Link Between Labour and Learning: The Workers' Educational Association in Ontario," *L/le t*, 8/9, 1981-82, 59-67; quotation from WEA proceedings, *Labour Gazette*, XXXVII, 1937, 1089-90; see the official organ of the CFL, the *Labour Review*, 1936-39, complete run available in the Library of the University of Saskatchewan, Saskatoon; *Labour Gazette*, XXXVII, 1937, 963-73.

20. Irving Abella, *Nationalism, Communism, and Canadian Labour: The CIO, the Communist Party, and the Canadian Congress of Labour, 1935-1956* (Toronto, 1973), 3-5; "Unite the Canadian Trade Union Movement – An Open Letter and Appeal from the Workers' Unity League," 28 February 1935, found in PAC, Bennett Papers, vol. 420, 266477. We thank Ralph Ellis for sharing his data on the WUL.

21. Harvey Klehr, *The Heydey of American Communism: The Depression Decade* (New York, 1984), 228-29; David Milton, *The Politics of U.S. Labor from the Great Depression to the New Deal* (London/New York, 1982), 69-89.

22. Jerry Lembcke, "The International Woodworkers of America in British Columbia," *L/ le t*, 6, 1980, 113-48; Draper's comment in "Congress Proceedings," *Labour Gazette*, XXXVII, 1937, 1080-86; Abella, *Nationalism, Communism, and Canadian Labour,* 23-40.

23. "Sit Down Strike Declared Illegal," *Labour Gazette*, XXXVII, 1937, 19, 244-45, 391; "Government to Crush Sit Down Strikes," *Globe and Mail*, 25 March 1937; Duart Snow, "The Holmes Foundry Strike of March, 1937: 'We'll give their jobs to white men,' " *Ontario History*, LXIX:1, 1977, 3-31; Henry Blank, "Industrial Relations in Sarnia, Ontario, with Specific Reference to the Holmes Foundry Strike" (M.A. thesis, University of Western Ontario, 1975), 126-64; Terry Copp *et al.*, *Industrial Unionism in Kitchener, 1937-1947* (Elora, Ont., 1976), 1-29; Warren Caragata, *Alberta Labour: A Heritage Untold* (Toronto, 1979), 128-29.

24. Eric A. Havelock, "Forty-Five Years Ago: The Oshawa Strike," *L/*

le t, 11, 1983, 119-24; anti-CIO propaganda in the *Globe and Mail*, 15-17 April 1937 and other numbers; PAO, Hepburn Papers, Box 201, file "Labour Department – 1936"; Hepburn quoted in Brian J. Young, "C. George McCullagh and the Leadership League," *CHR*, XLVII:3, 1966, 206; Croll quoted in Irving Abella, "Oshawa, 1937," in Abella, ed., *On Strike: Six Key Labour Struggles in Canada, 1919-1949* (Toronto, 1975), 113; for the miners and the CIO see Laurel Sefton MacDowell, *Remember Kirkland Lake! The Gold Miners' Strike of 1941-42* (Toronto, 1983), 41, 61-64.

25. Erik Ricker, "George Drew's Letter of Resignation, the 'CIO Menace,' and the Interpretation of Ontario History," *Bulletin of the Committee on Canadian Labour History*, 2, 1976, 9-15; Gerald Caplan, *The Dilemma of Canadian Socialism: The CCF in Ontario* (Toronto, 1973), 82-84; Hepburn quoted in "Mitch," cover story, *Time Magazine*, 20 September 1937.

26. John Hawkins, *The Life and Times of Angus L.* (Windsor, N.S., 1969), 182-83; Moses Coady, *Masters of Their Own Destiny* (New York, 1939), 56-57; George MacEachern, "Organizing Sydney: Steelworkers in the Thirties," in Gloria Montenero, ed., *We Stood Together* (Toronto, 1979), 47-68; Paul MacEwan, *Miners and Steelworkers: Labour in Cape Breton* (Toronto, 1976), 207-23; quotation from *CAR*, 1937-38, 253, 257-58.

27. Patrick Burden, "The New Brunswick Farmer-Labour Union" (M.A. thesis, University of New Brunswick, 1983); Dysart and McNair quoted in Allen Seager, "Minto, New Brunswick: A Study in Canadian Class Relations," *L/ le t*, 5,

1980, 117, 121; Marjorie Taylor-Morrell, *Of Mines and Men* (Minto, N.B., 1982).

28. Black, *Duplessis*, 170-74; Bryan D. Palmer, *Working Class Experience: The Rise and Reconstitution of Canadian Labour, 1800-1980* (Toronto, 1983), 220; Rick Salutin, *Kent Rowley: The Organizer, A Canadian Union Life* (Toronto, 1980), 38, 44; documents on ILGWU strike in ANQ, Labour Ministry Papers, vol. 118, G-21, "Industrie de la robe pour dames," 1937; Evelyn Dumas, *The Bitter Thirties in Quebec* (Montreal, 1975), 53-69.

29. Duplessis quoted in Dumas, *Bitter Thirties*, 66; Fraser Isbester, "A History of the National Catholic Unions in Canada, 1901-1965" (Ph.D. thesis, Cornell University, 1968), 180-82, 186-200; Library of the University of Toronto, R. Kenney Papers, Box 2, file "8th Dominion Convention," Communist Party of Canada, E. Dubé "French Canada Awakes" (typescript, 13 pp.); Alfred Charpentier, *Cinquante Ans d'action ouvrière: les mémoires d'Alfred Charpentier* (Quebec, 1971), 225-33.

30. *CHCD*, III, 1937, 2815-16; Bora Laskin, "Collective Bargaining," in Violet Anderson, ed., *Problems in Canadian Unity: Lectures Given at the Canadian Institute on Economics and Politics* (Toronto, 1938), 79.

31. "Single-handed" from *CAR*, 1937-38, 55-59; J.L. Granatstein, *The Politics of Survival: The Conservative Party of Canada, 1939-1945* (Toronto, 1967), 8-9; on the establishment of the commission see Neatby, *Prism of Unity*, 243-45, Ramsay Cook, *The Politics of John W. Dafoe and the Free Press* (Toronto, 1963), 223-25, and Margaret Prang, *N.W. Rowell: Ontario Na-*

tionalist (Toronto, 1975), 488-91; Herbert F. Quinn, "The Bogey of Fascism in Quebec," *DR*, XVIII:3, 1938, 308.

32. PABC, Pattullo Papers, R.J. Cromie to Pattullo, 23 February 1935, Weir to Pattullo, 6 February 1937, Pattullo to King, 14 February and 6 July 1936, 9 May 1938; Margaret A. Ormsby, "T. Dufferin Pattullo and the Little New Deal," *CHR*, XLIII:4, 1962, reprinted in Ramsay Cook, ed., *Politics of Discontent* (Toronto, 1967), 42-46.

33. PABC, Pattullo Papers, vol. 73, file 5, and Pattullo to King, 6 July 1938; descriptions of "Bloody Sunday" in Pierre Berton, *My Country: The Remarkable Past* (Toronto, 1976), 177-96, and in "Fighting For Labour," *Sound Heritage*, VII:4, 1978, 49-59.

34. Pattullo blamed for riot in "Can Mr Pearson Explain?" Vancouver *Province*, 24 June 1938; Margaret A. Ormsby, *British Columbia: A History* (Toronto, 1958), 467-69.

35. *New York Times* cited in H.J. Schultz, "The Social Credit Backbenchers' Revolt, 1937," *CHR*, XLI:1, 1960, 1; W. Desrosiers to Aberhart, 10 March 1937, cited in L.H. Thomas, *William Aberhart and Social Credit in Alberta* (Toronto, 1977), 141; David R. Elliott, "William Aberhart: Right or Left?" in R.D. Francis and Herman Ganzevoort, eds., *The Dirty Thirties in Prairie Canada* (Vancouver, 1980), 19-20; *Financial Post*, 19 September 1936; GAI, Henry Spencer Papers, Douglas to Spencer, 23 May 1936.

36. C.B. Macpherson, *Democracy in Alberta: Social Credit and the Party System* (Toronto, 1953), 169-79; J.R. Mallory, *Social Credit and the Federal Power in Canada* (Toronto,

1976), 71-90; Aberhart's reaction quoted in *CAR*, 1937-38, 468-73; John T. Saywell, "Reservation Revisited: Alberta, 1937," *CJEPS*, XXVII:3, 1961, 368-72; G.V. LaForest, *Disallowance and Reservation of Provincial Legislation* (Ottawa, 1955), 78-82.

37. Forsey, "Canada and Alberta," 123; Lethbridge *Herald*, 18 August 1937, cited in K.A. McKirdy, "Regionalism: Canada and Australia" (Ph.D. thesis, University of Toronto, 1959), 212; "Social Credit empire" predicted in Toronto *Star*, 16 May 1938, cited in Mallory, *Social Credit*, 104.

38. Christopher Armstrong, *The Politics of Federalism: Ontario's Relations with the Federal Government, 1867-1942* (Toronto, 1981), 181-82; Woodsworth in *CHCD*, 1938, III, 3376; *KD*, 6 July 1938.

39. Reginald Whitaker, *The Government Party: Organizing and Financing the Liberal Party of Canada, 1930-58* (Toronto, 1977), 314-27; Hepburn's comments on the CIO cited in Neil McKenty, *Mitch Hepburn* (Toronto, 1967), 141-53, 169; PABC, Pattullo Papers, Hepburn to Pattullo, 27 July 1937.

40. H.V. Nelles, *The Politics of Development: Forests, Mines and Hydro-Electric Power in Ontario, 1849-1941* (Toronto, 1974), 456-64, 482-83; Black, *Duplessis*, 170, 181-82; "alliance" in *CAR*, 1937-38, 156-57; *KD*, 10 December 1937.

41. PAO, Hepburn Papers, Hepburn to Duplessis, 14 February 1938, cited in R.M.H. Alway, "Hepburn, King and the Rowell-Sirois Commission," *CHR*, XLVIII:2, 1967, 117-21; John Kendle, *John Bracken: A Political Biography* (Toronto, 1979), 158-60; René Durocher, "Maurice Duplessis et sa conception de

l'autonomie provinciale au début de sa carrière politique," *RbAf*, 23:1, 1969, 29-32; description of Chateau Frontenac Party from J.B. McGeachy, "Confederation Clinic," Winnipeg *Free Press*, 13 and 14 May 1938, and D.G. Creighton, *Canada's First Century* (Toronto, 1970), 232.

42. "L'accueil plutot frais à la Commission Rowell," *Le Devoir*, 13 May 1938; Prang, *N.W. Rowell*, 490-96; Winnipeg *Free Press*, 3 May 1938; "The Ontario Brief," *Saturday Night*, 7 May 1938; McKenty, *Hepburn*, 165-70.

43. *KD*, 10 December 1937; Whitaker, *Government Party,* 330-36; Alway, "Hepburn, King," 124-28; Neatby, *Prism of Unity*, 270-72.

44. Neatby, *Prism of Unity,* 249; Frank W. Peers, *The Politics of Canadian Broadcasting, 1920-1951* (Toronto, 1969), 164-221; Roger R. Rickwood, "Canadian Broadcasting Policy and the Private Broadcasters" (Ph.D. thesis, University of Toronto, 1976), 24; Robert Bothwell and William Kilbourn, *C.D. Howe: A Biography* (Toronto, 1979), 104-13; Ramsay Cook, *The Maple Leaf Forever: Essays on Nationalism and Politics in Canada* (Toronto, 1977), 201-2.

45. E.J. Chambers, "The 1937-8 Recession in Canada," *CJEPS*, XXI:3, 1955, 293-308; *CAR*, 1937-38, 62-63.

46. *KD,* 12 January 1938; Leonard Marsh, "Reports of the National Employment Commission," *CJEPS*, V:1, 1939, 80-86; D.B. Marshall,

"The National Employment Commission and the Challenge to Economic and Constitutional Orthodoxy" (M.A. thesis, Queen's University, 1977), 86-95; Barry Ferguson and Doug Owram, "Social Scientists and Public Policy from the 1920s through World War II," *JCS*, XV: 4, 1980-81, 9-13; Michiel Horn, "Academics and Canadian Social and Economic Policy in the Depression and War Years," *JCS*, XIII:4, 1978-79, 8-9; J.L. Granatstein, *The Ottawa Men: The Civil Service Mandarins* (Toronto, 1982), 180-81.

47. Struthers, *No Fault of Their Own*, 175; David McGinnis, "The 'Keynesian Revolution' in Canada, 1929-1945," in Francis and Ganzevoort, eds., *Dirty Thirties,* 54-55; *CHCD*, 1938, II, 2091; Neatby, *Prism of Unity*, 252-58.

48. *CAR*, 1937-38, 62; *CHCD*, 1938, III, 3093; Rowell, "Norman Rogers As Minister of Labour," 196-97.

49. Perry, *Taxes, Tariffs and Subsidies,* 292-96; Rowell, "Norman Rogers As Minister of Labour," 196-201; *KD*, 1 April 1938.

50. Charles F. Wilson, *A Century of Canadian Grain: Government Policy to 1951* (Saskatoon, 1978), 562-63, 582-609; Rowell, "Norman Rogers As Minister of Labour," 248-54; Granatstein, *Ottawa Men*, 257-60.

51. H. Blair Neatby, "The Liberal Way: Fiscal and Monetary Policy in the 1930s," in Victor Hoar, ed., *The Great Depression* (Toronto, 1969), 110-13; *CHCD*, 1939, III, 3146-47.

NOTES TO CHAPTER THIRTEEN

1. "Atlantic and Pacific" cited in R. Douglas Francis, "Frank Underhill – Canadian Intellectual" (Ph.D. thesis, York University, 1977), 174; Han-

key quoted in Desmond Morton, *Canada and War* (Toronto, 1981), 100, and in Robert Bothwell and Norman Hillmer, eds., *The In-Between Time: Canadian External Policy in the 1930s* (Toronto, 1975), 87-91; Dafoe quoted in Ramsay Cook, *The Politics of John W. Dafoe and the Free Press* (Toronto, 1963), 239.

2. Description of Bennett policies quoted from Bothwell and Hillmer, *In-Between Time*, 15; Norman Hillmer, "The Anglo-Canadian Neurosis: The Case of O.D. Skelton," in Peter Lyon, ed., *Britain and Canada* (London, 1976), 74-75; Claude T. Bissell, *The Young Vincent Massey* (Toronto, 1981), 197-202.

3. *KD*, 21 September 1930; C.P. Stacey, *Canada and the Age of Conflict*, II, *1921-1948: The Mackenzie King Era* (Toronto, 1981), 129-35; Norman Hillmer, "Anglo-Canadian Relations, 1927-1937" (Ph.D. thesis, Cambridge University, 1974), 166-74; James Eayrs, *In Defence of Canada*, I, *From the Great War to the Great Depression* (Toronto, 1964), 316-17; *CHCD*, 1932-33, V, 5372.

4. On the *Josephine K* see *DCER*, 5, 117-27, 152-54; Bennett and the American briefing paper printed in Roger Frank Swanson, *Canadian-American Summit Diplomacy, 1923-1973, Selected Speeches and Documents* (Toronto, 1975), 27, 33; Ottawa *Citizen* quoted in Richard N. Kottman, "Hoover and Canada Diplomatic Appointments," *CHR*, LI:3, 1970, 295.

5. William R. Willoughby, *The St. Lawrence Waterway: A Study in Politics and Diplomacy* (Madison, Wisc., 1961), 133-59; Peter C. Kasurak, "American 'Dollar Diplomats' in Canada, 1927-41: A Study in Bureaucratic Politics," *American Review of Canadian Studies*, IX:2, 1979, 62; Drummond cited in Bothwell and Hillmer, *In-Between Time*, 14.

6. PAC, R.B. Bennett Papers, vol. 429, Bennett to R. Roberts, 21 December 1933; Richard Veatch, *Canada and the League of Nations* (Toronto, 1975), 25-26, 127-28; PAC, R.J. Manion Papers, vol. 4, Manion to Bennett, 26 September 1933.

7. Hugh L. Keenleyside, *Memoirs of Hugh L. Keenleyside*, I, *Hammer the Golden Day* (Toronto, 1981), 394-423; Perley's instructions in *DCER*, 5, 306-7.

8. Cahan's instructions in *DCER*, 5, 313-15; the Cahan speech is reprinted in W.A. Riddell, *Documents on Canadian Foreign Policy, 1917-39* (Toronto, 1962), 516-22; on the Cahan speech, F.H. Soward, "The Cahan Blunder Re-examined," *BC Studies*, 32, 1976-77, 126-38, may be contrasted with Donald C. Story, "The Cahan Speech and Bennett's Policy towards the Far Eastern Conflict 1931-3," in Kim Richard Nossal, *An Acceptance of Paradox/Essays on Canadian Diplomacy in Honour of John W. Holmes* (Toronto, 1982), 17-38, and May Anne Keith, "Canadian Foreign Policy and the Manchurian Crisis" (M.A. thesis, University of New Brunswick, 1960), 113-22; Hillmer, "Anglo-Canadian Relations," 223-44.

9. Winnipeg *Free Press*, 7 November 1931; *CHCD*, 1932, II, 3435-40; Winnipeg *Tribune*, 18 July 1932, cited in J.E. Craig, "Public Opinion in Manitoba and the Approach of War, 1931-1939" (M.A. thesis, University of Toronto, 1952), 37-38; PAC, League of Nations Society Papers, W.L. Grant to C.P. Meredith,

6 October 1932, cited in Donald John Herperger, "The League of Nations Society in Canada during the 1930s" (M.A. thesis, University of Regina, 1978), 49; Canada, Senate, *Debates*, 1934, I, 181, 237-44; Cook, *Politics of John W. Dafoe*, 242.

10. Bennett's disavowal in *CHCD*, 1934, II, 1856-57.

11. PAC, Bennett Papers, O.D. Skelton, "Pros and Cons of Canadian Participation," quoted in James Eayrs, *In Defence of Canada, II, Appeasement and Rearmament* (Toronto, 1965), 8-9; "welshing" in "Notes by Loring C. Christie on Discussions with Prime Minister Bennett," appendix B to Veatch, *Canada and the League of Nations*, 191-92; Ferguson's speech in Riddell, *Documents*, 533-35.

12. Ferguson's instructions of 9 October 1935 in *DCER*, 5, 386; Donald C. Story, "Canada's Covenant: The Bennett Government, the League of Nations and Collective Security, 1930-1935" (Ph.D. thesis, University of Toronto, 1976), 308-9; transatlantic call described in Lester B. Pearson, *Mike: The Memoirs of the Right Honourable Lester B. Pearson*, I, *1897-1948* (Toronto, 1972), 87-96; Bennett-Skelton clash in *DCER*, 5, 391-92.

13. Ferguson and Riddell speeches in Riddell, *Documents*, 535-41; King's statement and instructions to Riddell in *DCER*, 5, 403-5; for divergent interpretations of Riddell's insubordination, see John A. Munro, "The Riddell Affair Reconsidered," *External Affairs*, XXI:10, 1969, 366-75, and Robert Bothwell and John English, "Dirty Work at the Crossroads: New Perspectives on the Riddell Incident," *CHAHP*, 1972, 263-85.

14. Press opinion surveyed in Craig, "Public Opinion," 117-19, and in Françoise Caron-Houle, "La presse française du Québec et les crises européenes, 1935-1939" (M.A. thesis, University of Ottawa, 1972), 38-60; King's statement in Riddell, *Documents*, 554-55; Italian government cited in Eayrs, *In Defence of Canada* II, 25; Foreign Office quoted in Bothwell and English, "Dirty Work," 280.

15. Herperger, "League of Nations Society," 93-95; Margaret Prang, *N.W. Rowell: Ontario Nationalist* (Toronto, 1975), 479-85; Toronto *Telegram*, cited in Stacey, *Age of Conflict*, II, 186.

16. *CHCD*, 1936, I, 97-98; *KD*, 29 October 1935 and 7 March 1936.

17. PAC, King Papers, King to Thomas Vien, 11 April 1936, cited in Eayrs, *In Defence of Canada* II, 29-33; King's speech in Riddell, *Documents*, 555-86; *KD*, 29 September 1936; King's Geneva speech in R.A. Mackay and E.B. Rogers, *Canada Looks Abroad* (Toronto, 1938), 363-69.

18. F.H. Soward, *Canada in World Affairs: The Pre-War Years* (Toronto, 1941), 29-32; *La Liberté* cited in Craig, "Public Opinion," 137-39; *Journal* and *Mail and Empire* quoted in Bothwell and Hillmer, *In-Between Time*, 135-38; "Mr King at Geneva," Winnipeg *Free Press*, 1 October 1936.

19. Mackay and Rogers, *Canada Looks Abroad*, 263-324; PAC, Dafoe Papers, Dafoe to Lord Astor, 18 March 1936, and T.A. Crerar to Dafoe, 17 April 1937; CCF resolution in Soward, *Canada in World Affairs*, 42; Underhill quoted in Mackay and Rogers, *Canada Looks Abroad*, 269.

20. Richard Jones, "Politics and Culture: The French Canadians Before the Second World War," *Canadian Defence Quarterly*, XI:1, 1982, 35-41; "hive" in J.L. Granatstein and Robert Bothwell, " 'A Self-Evident National Duty': Canadian Foreign Policy, 1935-1939," *Journal of Imperial and Commonwealth History*, III:2, 1975, 213, 221; Skelton, "Defence Questions," 29 March 1937, *DCER*, 6, 186.

21. *CHCD*, 1937, I, 254 (Macphail), 876-83 (MacNeil), and 937-40 (Lacombe).

22. Patricia Schultz, *The East York Workers' Association: A Response to the Great Depression* (Toronto, 1975), 32-34; coronation rumour in Calgary *Herald*, 15 February 1936; Gordon Beadle, "Canada and the Abdication of Edward VIII," *JCS*, IV:3, 1969, 33-46; PAM, John Bracken Papers, "Coronation," file 1084.

23. American legation's "Canada, Political Estimate," 1 June 1937, and *KD*, 13 September 1938, both quoted in Granatstein and Bothwell, " 'Self-Evident National Duty,' " 219, 222; King's reply to Woodsworth, *CHCD*, 1937, I, 249; Stacey, *Age of Conflict*, II, 196.

24. Eayrs, *In Defence of Canada* II, 48-61; King's comments from *KD*, 27 May 1937, 15 June 1937. There is a considerable debate over the role of the dominions and specifically of Mackenzie King in influencing the decision to appease rather than confront Hitler. British historians anxious to share out the odium like to give King and Canada as much credit as possible; Corelli Barnett, *The Collapse of British Power* (London, 1970), 218-27, and Ritchie Ovendale, *'Appeasement' and the English-Speaking World: Britain, the United States, the Dominions and the Policy of 'Appeasement'* (Cardiff, 1975), 319-20, are but two of many examples. Norman Hillmer's comment, in his review of Ovendale, that this is "speculation" (*CHR*, LXI:3, 1980, 402-3) seems appropriate.

25. "Memorandum by Mackenzie King on his Interview with Hitler," quoted in Eayrs, *In Defence of Canada* II, 226-33; C.P. Stacey, "The Divine Mission: Mackenzie King and Hitler," *CHR*, LXI:4, 1980, 502-12.

26. *L'Action Catholique* cited in Caron-Houle, "La Presse et les crises européenes," 67-99; *Catholic Register*, 24 September 1936, cited in Margaret Prang, "Some Opinions of Political Radicalism in Canada Between the Two World Wars" (M.A. thesis, University of Toronto, 1953), 117-18; *CF*, October, 1936; Richard Martin, "Le Congrès des métiers et du travail et la guerre civile espagnole," *RhAf*, 33, 1980, 575-81; Harvey Levinson, "Montreal's Response to the Spanish Civil War" (M.A. thesis, Concordia University, 1976), 31-55.

27. Bethune quoted in Roderick Stewart, *Bethune* (Don Mills, Ont., 1973), 90; Victor Hoar, *The Mackenzie-Papineau Battalion: Canadian Participation in the Spanish Civil War* (Toronto, 1969), 1.

28. *DCER*, 6, 969-1008; Lapointe in *CHCD*, 1937, II, 1939; effect of embargo discussed in Soward, *Canada in World Affairs*, 62-64.

29. London *Free Press*, 22 July 1936; Toronto *Globe and Mail*, 12 January 1937, quoted in Thor-Eric Frohn Neilson, "Canada's Foreign Enlistment Act: Mackenzie King's Expe-

dient Response to the Spanish Civil War" (M.A. thesis, University of British Columbia, 1982), 78; PAC, King Papers, King to J.L. Counsell, 13 April 1937, cited in Hoar, *Mackenzie-Papineau Battalion*, 105.

30. Toynbee quoted in John Alfred Schultz, "Canadian Attitudes Toward the Empire, 1919-1939" (Ph.D. thesis, Dalhousie University, 1975), 220; Eayrs, *In Defence of Canada* II, 81-133; direct quotations are as cited in Eayrs, 93, 100, 101.

31. PAC, Bennett Papers, Drew to R.K. Finlayson, 4 January 1937, quoted in Eayrs, *In Defence of Canada* II, 141-42; King's comments from a presentation to caucus, 20 January 1937, quoted in C.P. Stacey, *Six Years of War: The Army in Canada, Britain and the Pacific* (Ottawa, 1955), 14; Neatby, *Prism of Unity*, 182.

32. Denis Bertrand, "La Politique extérieure du Canada et la réaction canadienne-française à la veille de la Deuxième Grande Guerre" (Ph.D. thesis, Université de Montréal, 1965), 240-42.

33. Dandurand comment in *KD*, 11 January 1938; Stacey, *Six Years of War*, 75.

34. *Saturday Night*, 8 August 1936.

35. King-Roosevelt relationship discussed in Stacey, *Age of Conflict* II, 230-31; *KD*, 27 May 1937; Granatstein and Bothwell, " 'Self-Evident National Duty,' " 215-16; King's expectation quoted in *CAR*, 1937-38, 49-52; Richard Kottman, *Reciprocity and the North Atlantic Triangle, 1932-1938* (Ithaca, N.Y., 1968), 266-73.

36. FDR's speech in Swanson, *Summit Diplomacy*, 52-54; reaction in Chandler Bragdon, "Canadian Attitudes to the Foreign Policy of the United States, 1935-1939" (Ph.D. thesis, University of Rochester, 1961), 163-69.

37. King's speech in Soward, *Canada in World Affairs*, 107-8; *KD*, 20 August 1938; "Points to be considered re President Roosevelt's Kingston Speech," 19 August 1938, *DCER*, 6, 606-7.

38. Victoria *Times*, 1 April 1936, clipping in PABC, McClung Papers, file 8; Winnipeg *Tribune*, 9 March 1936; Reeve quoted and Olympic team behaviour described in Bruce Kidd, "Canadian Opposition to the 1936 Olympics in Germany," *Canadian Journal of the History of Sport and Physical Education*, IX:2, 1978, 20-40.

39. Irving Abella and Harold Troper, *None Is Too Many: Canada and the Jews of Europe, 1933-1948* (Toronto, 1982), 1-66; Toronto *Mail and Empire*, 11 January 1934; *Catholic Register*, 17 February 1938, cited in Prang, "Opinions of Political Radicalism," 196; *L'Action catholique*, 26 March 1936, quoted in Richard Jones, "Politics and Culture: The French Canadians and the Second World War," in Sidney Aster, ed., *The Second World War As a National Experience* (Ottawa, 1981), 88; Lita-Rose Betcherman, *The Swastika and the Maple Leaf: Fascist Movements in Canada in the Thirties* (Toronto, 1975), is an interesting study that suffers from the author's treatment of anti-Semitism (which was widespread) as a synonym for fascism.

40. John E. Zucchi, "The Emergence of Fascism Among Italian Immigrants in Toronto, 1928-1935," unpublished paper delivered at the

meetings of the Canadian Historical Association, 1984; Jonathan Wagner, "The *Deutscher Bund Canada*, 1934-39," *CHR*, LVIII:2, 1977, 176-200; John Offenbeck, "The Nazi Movement and German Canadians, 1933-39" (M.A. thesis, University of Western Ontario, 1970), 1-95; Rollande M. Montsion, "Les grands thèmes du mouvement national social chrétien et d'Adrien Arcand, vus par les principaux journaux fascistes au Canada français, 1929-1938" (M.A. thesis, University of Ottawa, 1975), *passim*; S, "Embryo Fascism in Quebec," *Foreign Affairs*, 16:3, 1938, 454-66; David Martin, "Adrien Arcand, Fascist – An Interview," *The Nation*, 26 February 1938, 241-44; Herbert F. Quinn, "The Bogey of Fascism in Quebec," *DR*, XVIII:3, 1938, 301-8.

41. Betcherman, *Swastika and Maple Leaf*, 107-8; Frederick Edwards, "Fascism in Canada," *MM*, 15 April 1938, 10, 66-68, and 1 May 1938, 15, 30.

42. RCMP quoted in Offenbeck, "Nazi Movement," 139; Jonathan Wagner, *Brothers Beyond the Sea: National Socialism in Canada* (Waterloo, 1981), 123-28; Robert James Brown, "Emergence from Isolation: United States–Canadian Diplomatic Relations, 1937-1941" (D.S.S. thesis, Syracuse University, 1968), 71-77.

43. *KD*, 31 August 1938; Neatby, *Prism of Unity*, 288-89; King to Chamberlain, 14 September 1938, *DCER*, 6, 1090; Statement by Prime Minister, 17 September 1938, *DCER*, 6, 1093; *Le Devoir* cited in Caron-Houle, "La Presse et les crises européenes," 158; Arthur R.M. Lower, *My First Seventy-Five Years* (Toronto, 1967), 221-25. See also note 24, this chapter.

44. *CHCD*, 1939, II, 2042-43; Granatstein and Bothwell, " 'Self-Evident National Duty,' " 227; *CHCD*, 1939, III, 2426 and 2469.

45. Harold A. Naugler, "R.J. Manion and the Conservative Party, 1938-1940" (M.A. thesis, Queen's University, 1966), 204-9; "intelligentsia" in George Williams to Angus MacInnis, quoted in Walter D. Young, *The Anatomy of a Party: The National CCF, 1932-1961* (Toronto, 1969), 90-95; Grace MacInnis, *J.S. Woodsworth, A Man to Remember* (Toronto, 1953), 246; Pearson to Skelton, 4 November 1938, in Bothwell and Hillmer, *In-Between Time*, 165-66.

46. Raymond quoted in Mason Wade, *The French Canadians, 1760-1967*, rev. ed. (Toronto, 1968), II, 856; Conrad Black, *Duplessis* (Toronto, 1977), 195; Laval incident in Montreal *Gazette*, 29 March 1939.

47. *Northwest Review*, 31 August 1939, quoted in Craig, "Public Opinion," 213-14; P.B. Waite "French-Canadian Isolationism and English Canada: An Elliptical Foreign Policy," *JCS*, 18:2, 1983, 134-35, 139.

48. "Political banditry" was *l'Action catholique*'s description of Hitler's march into Prague, 22 March 1939.

49. Gustave Lanctot, *The Royal Tour of King George VI and Queen Elizabeth, 1939* (Toronto, 1964), *passim*; Victoria Margaret Wilcox, "Prime Minister and Governor-General: Mackenzie King and Lord Tweedsmuir, 1935-1940" (M.A. thesis, Queen's University, 1977), 114-57; George VI's addresses printed in *Their Majesties' Visit to Canada, the United States and Newfoundland* (London, 1939); *Le Devoir*, 19 May 1939; Gordon Young, *Voyage of State* (London, 1939), 95.

50. Skelton, "Canada and the Polish

War," 25 August 1939, *DCER*, 6, 1247-48; the King's declaration quoted in Stacey, *Age of Conflict* II, 253.

51. J.L. Granatstein, "Will this country ever learn the dangers of the politics of hate?" *MM*, 23 January 1978, 10.

52. Stacey, *Age of Conflict* II, 262; Donald Creighton, *Canada 1939-1957: The Forked Road* (Toronto, 1976), Ch. 1.

NOTES TO CHAPTER FOURTEEN

1. Wood quoted in *Grain Growers' Guide*, 2 July 1919; Bruce Barton, *The Man Nobody Knows* (New York, 1925), quoted in William E. Leuchtenburg, *The Perils of Prosperity, 1914-1932* (Chicago, 1958), 188-89.

2. Liberal platform reprinted in *HD*, 36-43; Walter R. Sharp, "The Canadian Election of 1926," *American Political Science Review*, XXI:1, 1927, 113.

3. Leslie Roberts, *These Be Your Gods* (Toronto, 1929).

4. Dorothy Livesay, "Canada to the Soviet Union," in Livesay, *Right Hand, Left Hand: A True Life Of The Thirties* (Erin, Ont., 1977), 72.

5. J.L. Granatstein, *The Ottawa Men: The Civil Service Mandarins* (Toronto, 1982); Reginald Whitaker, *The Government Party: Organizing and Financing the Liberal Party of Canada, 1930-58* (Toronto, 1977).

6. PAC, Naval Service of Canada, RG 24, 1055-2-25, file 1, "Secret: Report on Activities of the Communist Party, BC Section," 12 September 1939; Arthur R.M. Lower, *My First Seventy-five Years* (Toronto, 1967), 213.

INDEX

Aberhart, William, 238-41; and Social Credit legislation, 294-96

Abitibi Power and Paper Co., 80

Accurate News and Information Act (Alta.), 295, 296

Action Libérale, 249

Action Libérale Nationale, 249-51, 282-84

Adams, Charles, 188

Adshead, H.B., 127, 205

Agriculture, 11, 13; in 1920s, 95-96; and Fordney-McCumber tariff, 107; and Great Depression, 195, 209-10, 213, 299

Aird, Sir John, 182; *quoted*, 129, 193

Aird Commission Report, 183, 256

Alberta, 13, 65, 67, 70, 144, 156, 294-96; and election of 1930, 204-205; and CCF, 234, 235; and election of 1935, 274, 275; and 1935 cabinet, 278. *See also* Dominion-Provincial Conferences, Elections, provincial

Alberta Labour Party, 241

Alberta Provincial Police, 64

Alexander, C.C., *quoted,* 177

Algoma Steel, 95

All-Canadian Congress of Labour (ACCL), 144-46, 191, 224, 234; schism in, 286-87

Allen, Ralph, *quoted,* 122

Allen, Richard, *quoted,* 58

Allen Theatres, 177

Aluminum Co. of America, 83

Alway, Richard, *quoted,* 299

Amalgamated Assoc. of Iron, Steel and Tin Workers, 142-43, 145

American Federation of Labor, 139, 143, 233; and CIO, 287-88

American National Conference of Social Work, 62

American Political Science Review, *quoted*, 235

Amery, L.S., 123

Anderson, J.T.M., 203, 215, 243; *quoted*, 212

Anglican Church, 8; and social action, 60

Angus, Henry, 191, 293; *quoted*, 183

Anschluss, 324

Anticosti Island, 324

Anti-masonic feeling, 250

Anti-Semitism, 240, 322, 323

Appeasement, 316, 321; abandoned, 328

Arcand, Adrien, 247, 275, 323-24

Archambault, Father Joseph-Papin, 58, 251

Armstrong, E.H., 111, 142

Arsenault, A.E., 109

Article X (League Covenant), 54-56

Arts Advisory Council, 164

Asbestos, 90

Asselin, Olivar, 58, 251

Associated Press, 185

Association of Canadian Clubs, 159, 175

Atkinson, Joseph, 185

Australia, 39, 47, 49, 299

Automobile industry, 85-87, 146, 196

Auto Workers' Industrial Union, 146

Aziz, Moses, 122

Back to God's Country, 176

Backus-Brooks Paper Co., 80

Bagshaw, Dr. Elizabeth, 153

Bairnsfather, Bruce, 178

Baldwin, Stanley, 123, 219

Klein, A.M., 169
Knister, Raymond, 168
Kolisnyk, William, 223
Kredit Anstalt, 215
Ku Klux Klan, 204

Laberge, Albert, 175
La Bonne Nouvelle, quoted, 250
Labour Gazette, 18; *quoted,* 285, 288
Labour movement, *see* Unions
Labour parties, 32, 34, 127, 239, 244, 260; and election of 1930, 205; and Bennett legislation, 208, 216; British, 234
Labour World, 285
Lacombe, Liguori, 314, 328
Laconics, 169
Lacroix, Wilfrid, 328
l'Action catholique, quoted, 317, 323
l'Action française (journal), 173; *quoted,* 6-7, 96
l'Action française, 174
Ladies Home Journal, 183; *quoted,* 65
La Liberté, 313
Lambeth Conference (1930), 60
Lamontagne, Blanche, 174
Langlois, Mgr. Alfred, 148
Lapointe, Ernest, 23, 41, 44, 49, 51, 120, 121, 128, 136, 207, 249, 281, 287, 288, 295, 296, 311, 318, 325-26; relationship with King, 21, 115, 277
La Presse, 181, 183, 186; *quoted,* 17, 205
Laskin, Bora, 292
Laurentide Paper Co., 79
Laurier, Sir Wilfred, 15, 19, 23, 40, 45
Lausanne Conference (1922), 45
Laval, Pierre, 309, 311
Lavergne, Armand, 206
Lawrence, Sam, 232
Lawson, Cons. Steve, 65
Lea, Walter M., 242
Leacock, Stephen, 166; *quoted,* 63
League for Women's Rights, 75
League for Social Reconstruction (LSR), 232-33, 285
League of Nations, 44, 185, 261, 275,

308, 332; relations with, 54-56; Bennett and, 306-10; King and, 310-13
League of Nations Society, 56, 303, 308, 311
Le Canada, 285
Le Devoir, 17, 250, 283; *quoted,* 126, 275, 298, 325
Le Droit, quoted, 148
Lee, "Knotty," *quoted,* 186
Lemay, Ovide, 292
Lemieux, Alice, 174
Lemieux, Rodolphe, 18, 25
Le Nignog, 174
Leopold, Jack, 228
Lessandro, Florence, 65
Lessard, F.X., 285
Lewis, David, 234
Lewis, John L., 143, 287, 289, 296-97
Liberal party, 14, 24-25, 27, 262, 277, 282, 312, 331-32; election of 1921, 16, 20, 109; election of 1925, 115, 117-18; election of 1926, 124-28; election of 1930, 203-205; election of 1935, 273-74; in opposition, 1930-35, 208, 214, 257, 264-66; in Alberta, 237, 241; in B.C., 242-43; in Manitoba, 241; in New Brunswick, 110, 111, 241-42, 243, 272; and CFL, 286-87, 290; in Nova Scotia, 110, 241-42, 243, 290; in Ontario, 244-45; in P.E.I., 110, 242, 243, 272; in Quebec, 115, 118-19, 246, 248, 282-84; in Saskatchewan, 243-44; King-Hepburn conflict, 296-97, 299
Liberal platform, *1919,* 15, 38, 112, 131, 198, 331; *1925,* 114
Liberal-Progressives, 127, 128; Manitoba, 241
Ligue nationaliste canadienne, 206
Lions Club, 175
Lismer, Arthur, 161; *quoted,* 158
Little Orphan Annie, 186
Little Theatre movement, 171-72
Livesay, Dorothy, 169; *quoted,* 331
Livingston, "Red" Dan, 143, 145
Lloyd George, David, 44
Locarno Treaty (1925), 48, 312, 322
Logan, Hance J., 109

66, 67, 74-75, 228, 284, 317, 327;
and CCF, 234-35
Roosevelt, Franklin D., 243, 245,
263, 279-80, 297, 306; and Cana-
dian-American relations, 320-21
Roquebrune, Robert de, 174
Ross, W.W.E., 168, 169
Rosvall, Viljo, 142
Rotary Club, 175
Rouillard, Jacques, 146
Routier, Simone, 174
Rouyn-Noranda, Que., 81, 102
Rowell, Newton W., 54, 293, 311. See
also Royal Commission on Domin-
ion-Provincial Relations
Roy, Philippe, 304
Royal Bank, 193
Royal Canadian Academy, 164
Royal Canadian Mounted Police
(RCMP), 1, 182, 214, 218, 225, 228,
269, 270-72, 294, 324
Royal Canadian Navy, 42. See also
Canadian armed forces
Royal Commission on Dominion-
Provincial Relations (Rowell Com-
mission), 292-93, 297-98, 300;
Report, 133
Royal Commission on Price Spreads,
259-60, 261, 262, 266
Royal Tour (1939), 327-28
Royalty, 40, 314-15. See also Royal
Tour
Rush-Bagot Agreement, revision of,
50-51
Russell, R.B., 17, 156
Ruth, Babe, 186, 187, 190
Rutledge, Joseph Lister, 159
Ryckman, E.B., 205
Ryerson Press, 160

Safarian, A.E., quoted, 103
St. George's Society, 211
Saint John, N.B., 97
St. Lambert, Que., 99
St. Lawrence Paper, 80
St. Lawrence Seaway, 134, 297, 306
Saint-Martin, Albert, 147
Sales tax, 25, 212, 216, 279, 301

Salsberg, J.B., 290
Sampson, Insp. L.J., 269
Sandwell, B.K., quoted, 167
Saskatchewan, 25, 117, 120, 243-44,
254, 255; prohibition in, 65-66, 67;
election of 1930, 204; drought in,
213, 299; election of 1935, 274,
275. See also Elections, provincial;
Prairie Provinces
Saskatchewan Farmer-Labour party,
231, 243-44
Saskatchewan Wheat Pool, 36-37
Saturday Evening Post, 183
Saturday Night, quoted, 140, 152,
176, 273, 298, 320
Sauvé, Arthur, 206
Savage, Andrew, quoted, 282
Scarlett, Sam, 225
Schaefer, Carl, 164
Scheinberg, Stephen, quoted, 279-80
Scott, Duncan Campbell, 167
Scott, F.R. (Frank), 168, 174, 228-29,
233; quoted, 169, 281
Second World War, 328-29
Selznick, Lewis, quoted, 177
Sénécal, Eve, 174
Service, Robert, 166
Sex Disqualification Removal Act
(Alta. and B.C.), 70
Shane, Bernard, 291
Shaughnessy, Lord, 171
Shawinigan Power, 84
Sherman, William, 143
Shillington, W.P., quoted, 86
Shipman, Ernest G., 176, 177
Shore, Eddie, 189
Siegfried, André, 7
Sifton newspaper chain, 185
Sime, Jessie, 166
Simpson, Jimmy, 234
Sinclair, John E., 22-23
Sino-Japanese dispute, 307-308
Sirois, Joseph, 293
Skelton, O.D., 41, 46, 300, 304, 306-
307, 314; and sanctions against
Italy, 309-11; quoted, 328
Skillan, George, quoted, 172
Slaght, Arthur, 296

THE CANADIAN CENTENARY SERIES

A History of Canada in Nineteen Volumes

The Canadian Centenary Series is a comprehensive history of the peoples and lands which form the Dominion of Canada.

Although the series is designed as a unified whole so that no part of the story is left untold, each volume is complete in itself. Written for the general reader as well as for the scholar, each of the nineteen volumes of *The Canadian Centenary Series* is the work of a leading Canadian historian who is an authority on the period covered in his volume. Their combined efforts have made a new and significant contribution to the understanding of the history of Canada and of Canada today.

W.L. Morton (d. 1980), Vanier Professor of History, Trent University, was the Executive Editor of *The Canadian Centenary Series*. A graduate of the Universities of Manitoba and Oxford, he was the author of *The Kingdom of Canada; Manitoba: A History; The Progressive Party in Canada; The Critical Years: The Union of British North America, 1857-1873;* and other writings. He also edited *The Journal of Alexander Begg and Other Documents Relevant to the Red River Resistance*. Holder of the honorary degrees of LL.D. and D.LITT., he was awarded the Tyrrell Medal of the Royal Society of Canada and the Governor General's Award for Non-Fiction.

D.G. Creighton (d. 1979), former Chairman of the Department of History, University of Toronto, was the Advisory Editor of *The Canadian Centenary Series*. A graduate of the Universities of Toronto and Oxford, he was the author of *John A. Macdonald: The Young Politician; John A. Macdonald: The Old Chieftain; Dominion of the North; The Empire of the St. Lawrence* and many other works. Holder of numerous honorary degrees, LL.D. and D.LITT., he twice won the Governor General's Award for Non-Fiction. He had also been awarded the Tyrrell Medal of the Royal Society of Canada, the University of Alberta National Award in Letters, the University of British Columbia Medal for Popular Biography, and the Molson Prize of the Canada Council.

Ramsay Cook, Professor of History, York University, co-author with R.C. Brown of *Canada 1896-1921*, volume 14 of the series, is the Executive Editor of *The Canadian Centenary Series*, 1983.